THE PLEASANT NIGHTS

Volume 1

THE DA PONTE LIBRARY SERIES

Giovan Francesco Straparola

THE PLEASANT NIGHTS

VOLUME 1

Edited with Introduction and Commentaries by
Donald Beecher

Translated by W.G. Waters
Thoroughly Revised and Corrected by the Editor

UNIVERSITY OF TORONTO PRESS
Toronto Buffalo London

Toronto Buffalo London
www.utppublishing.com

ISBN 978-1-4426-4426-7

The Lorenzo Da Ponte Italian Library

Library and Archives Canada Cataloguing in Publication

Straparola, Giovanni Francesco, ca. 1480–1557?
The pleasant nights / Giovan Francesco Straparola; edited with introduction and commentaries by Donald Beecher; translated by W.G. Waters, thoroughly revised and corrected by the editor.

(Da Ponte library series; v. 1)
Translation of: Le piacevoli notti.
Includes bibliographical references and index.
ISBN 978-1-4426-4426-7 (v. 1)

I. Beecher, Donald II. Waters, W.G. (William George), 1844–1928
III. Title. IV. Series: Lorenzo da Ponte Italian library series; v. 1

PQ4634.S7P513 2012 853'.3 C2012-902024-9

Publication of this book assisted by the Istituto Italiano di cultura, Toronto.

This book has been published under the aegis and with financial assistance of: Fondazione Cassamarca, Treviso; the National Italian-American Foundation; Ministero degli Affari Esteri, Direzione Generale per la Promozione e la Cooperazione Culturale; Ministero per i Beni e le Attività Culturali, Direzione Generale per i Beni Librari e gli Istituti Culturali, Servizio per la promozione del libro e della lettura.

University of Toronto Press acknowledges the financial assistance to its publishing program of the Canada Council for the Arts and the Ontario Arts Council.

Canada Council for the Arts
Conseil des Arts du Canada

ONTARIO ARTS COUNCIL
CONSEIL DES ARTS DE L'ONTARIO

University of Toronto Press acknowledges the financial support for its publishing activities of the Government of Canada through the Book Publishing Industry Development Program (BPIDP).

Contents

Acknowledgments

First to be acclaimed is my research assistant, Emma Peacocke, who for more than two years joined in the enterprise of documenting these stories, keeping track of references, gathering resources, and compiling lists with an infectious enthusiasm. Our meetings and conversations have been a source of great intellectual joy. Next, I extend my warmest gratitude to my colleague and friend, Prof. Maurizio Ascari, for facilitating and hosting my stay at the University of Bologna's Istituto di Studi Avanzati, and for showing me some of the hidden treasures of Bologna and the Lunigiana. I wish to express my heartfelt thanks, as well, to Prof. Barbara Cimati and to the Istituto itself for its generous sponsorship which has enabled me to consult, in the rich holdings of the university's network of libraries, many of the more elusive resources required to complete this edition.

I would also like to thank Prof. Paul Keen, chairman of Carleton's Department of English, for his continuing support, and Prof. John Osborne, Dean of Carleton's Faculty of Arts and Social Sciences, for his unfailing encouragement. I am most grateful to have received the faculty's Marston LaFrance Research Leave Fellowship, which has enabled me to complete this sprawling project in something like a timely fashion. I am likewise indebted to Rosemarie Hoey, long-time colleague in the Department of English, for her careful perusal of substantial numbers of these stories and commentaries. I want to signal here, as well, my great appreciation for all the Herculean efforts made on my behalf by the librarians and staff of Carleton's Inter-Library Loan Services, without whose collaboration a project of this nature would have been nearly impossible. It may prove that Straparola lays dubious claim to the greatest predation upon those services in their entire history for a single project!

As well, it is my pleasure to acknowledge the valued collaboration and support of the general editors of the Da Ponte Library Series, Profs. Massimo Ciavolella and Luigi Ballerini of UCLA's Department of Italian. It has been a satisfaction prolonged to be working with them on a second project for the series. Finally, I am grateful to Ron Schoeffel, Anne Laughlin, and the members of the staff at the University of Toronto Press who have participated in the processing, editing, and production of this heavy pair of tomes, and I extend a very special thanks to Beth McAuley and her assistants Nina Hoeschele and Laura Cok and to John St James whose editorial skills were remarkable and invaluable. It has been a long and challenging round trip of a kind which can never be made alone; my warmest thanks to all who have joined in the venture, including my beloved Marie-Andrée, captive traveller, who has heard far more about Straparola over these past several years than she ever would have imagined.

THE PLEASANT NIGHTS

Volume 1

Introduction

The seventy-three stories compiled by Straparola in his *Pleasant Nights* constitute a miscellany, a Renaissance story book, an anthology of folk and literary *novelle*, fables, wonder tales and jests, a cabinet of literary curiosities, and a dramatized festal entertainment. Straparola was conventional in his use of the framing tale, but enigmatic in referring to all of his stories as *favole*. He was anomalous in his mixture of high and low styles and boldly experimental in presenting such a large component of materials extrapolated from popular culture. His precise sources, in nearly all cases, are elusive, increasing the likelihood that he relied heavily upon oral productions, of which many of the present stories are the earliest 'near' representations. That point is subject to diverse interpretations. His bid for novelty in transcribing these tales into literary form for recirculation through the technologies of print culture was entirely in keeping with the enterprises of the Venetian printers to satisfy the broadening cultural interests and supply the consumption demands of their clientele. That is an important contextual feature of the work in its bid for popularity and frequent republication. But in the process, Straparola hit upon something with far greater cultural and intellectual import than he could have known, insofar as the stories from the 'folk' carried in their narrative genes the themes and motifs of their collective heritages. For this reason they assume membership in a grand continuum of tales often reaching back to ancestral forms in ancient Sanskrit and Persian, and as far forward as the folk tales gathered throughout Italy and other parts of Europe in the nineteenth century. How these resemblances came about in both comparative and filiational terms remains a leading question. Straparola knew them only as popular stories from his own times, but their 'remembered' traits tie them to the streams of stories that form the great ocean of interconnected world folklore, to borrow from an ancient title. For Straparola's purchasing public, the collection constitutes a novel compendium – one of the most delectable of all such Renaissance productions. For subsequent ages with a sense of literary hindsight, it is a seminal display of the remarkable variety of literary genres from *novelle* and *facetiae* to proto-fairy tales and beast fables then current in both the visible and invisible venues of Renaissance story dissemination. Hence, in its infinite variety, it is a work apt for presentation in many lights in relation to its own age. At the same time, a major portion of the commentaries to follow will be concerned with the relationship of each tale to its own narrative 'tradition,' many of which stretch across centuries. That was my calling.

I. The Straparola Dilemma, or the Biography of an Invisible Author

A biographical profile of Straparola is, in all probability, beyond recovery. The name itself, meaning 'garrulous,' looks like a playful pseudonym of a kind routinely adopted by members of academies. Yet it is only natural to seek to know what we can about the author of *Le piacevoli notti* (its two parts published in 1550 and 1553, respectively), because such a designed artifact implies a conscious maker with presumed intentions, after all, and in travelling that hermeneutic loop we feel certain we will know something of value about the stories by knowing what we can about their creator. Paradoxically, however, the intellectual value in knowing the maker depends upon the nature of his cerebral participation in the creative process, and that, in turn, will depend upon a critical profiling of the collection itself – whether it is constituted of literary inventions, of the reworking of novelistic materials by an active 'author,' or of material gathered up from contemporary oral and popular traditions and transcribed more or less as it was found. In brief, the work problematizes what constitutes an author.

Certain claims have been made for the man, one of them being that he is the 'father of the literary fairy tale.' That, in a sense, is true, because several of his seventeen 'wonder tales' were taken over by the French founders of the new genre late in the seventeenth century.[1] Without him,

---

1 The defining features of this 'genre' are the employment of magic and the supernatural, roles for speaking animals and imaginary characters, and fantasy settings, but these are of such a varying nature that estimates of the number of 'fairy tales' among the stories of the *Notti* range from as few as fourteen to as many

they would have had a far more meagre start. But whether Straparola created these tales, and 'fairy tales' per se, comes down to his use of sources as well as to the precise defining of a genre. The work of tracing the origins of the 'fairy tale' to periods as early as the Middle Ages and beyond has preoccupied the writers of several recent monographs, with no signs of consensus on the critical horizon. Hence there is little agreement that the genre's inauguration should all come down to Straparola's creative genius, although there is wide agreement that his collection is a milestone in the assembly and presentation of such tales. In the words of Nancy Canepa, 'the fairy tale reached full literary autonomy only with Straparola's *Notti* and then, of course, with [Basile's] *Lo cunto*.'[2] That fact is difficult to deny to him, even though the level of his cognizance in matters regarding both genre and posterity remains open to discussion.

Further to the debate, in her review of Ruth Bottigheimer's *Fairy Godfather: Straparola, Venice, and the Fairy Tale Tradition*, Gillian Adams sought to qualify any claims regarding his pioneering of a genre or the inventing of original stories by reminding readers that Straparola 'borrowed shamelessly, while protesting his originality, from numerous written sources, ancient, medieval, and contemporary.'[3] Accordingly, none or very few of his stories may prove to have been of his own devising, and worse, in his shameless appropriation he may be considered a plagiarist into the bargain. Here is a variation upon the familiar problem posed by the Renaissance humanist habits of imitation and *riscrittura*, or rewriting, whereby the new is generated out of the works of the ancients, or even the recent masters such as Boccaccio, Petrarch, and Ariosto. This usually entails an assimilation process, a personal interiorizing and regeneration of forms, styles, and contents whereby the imitator once again becomes an author – and an honest one to boot. (To be sure, whether such activity, in all its many levels of expression, is tantamount to larceny is a point for ongoing debate against the moving target of what constitutes

as twenty-one. See Victoria Smith Pozzi, 'Straparola's *Le piacevoli notti*: Narrative Technique and Ideology' (PhD diss., University of California Los Angeles, 1981), p. 78.

2 *From Court to Forest: Giambattista Basile's* Lo cunto de li cunti *and the Birth of the Literary Fairy Tale* (Detroit: Wayne State University Press, 1999), p. 16. This contribution will be described in a subsequent section as a unique 'moment' in cultural history, and one which Straparola actualized.

3 'A Father of the Literary Fairy Tale: Giovanfrancesco Straparola,' *Children's Literature* 32 (2004), pp. 209–15.

inviolable intellectual property as opposed to taking inspiration and building upon the past in the time-honoured manner of humanist scholarship.) But this avenue may prove to be misleading as well insofar as it remains to be determined whether Straparola relied upon literary sources at all, as Adams and others assume.

Our author, at one point, reacts vigorously to accusations of plagiarism, seemingly inculpating himself, but then defends himself by proclaiming that he wrote everything down as he *heard* it, claiming nothing for himself at all – he was merely the messenger. Whether that is a feint or a truth is still subject to investigation. By my own calculation, after an exhaustive search (and in corroboration of his claim), the count of identifiable written sources employed (the twenty-two translations from Morlini aside) seems to be fewer than half a dozen. For the more than forty remaining tales, there are no compellingly evident literary texts by any reasonable criteria constituting plausible and usable sources upon which he clearly relied. That salient point was not clear to W.G. Waters, who tallied up the book's contents as fifteen fables derived from the *novellieri*, twenty-two from Morlini, four from medieval sources, and seven from oriental legends, leaving twenty-two original works.[4] This count assumes not only that Straparola worked from written sources, but that where none are found, he may ipso facto be granted authorship. (Waters accepts that any remote cognate version of a story, even as an oriental tale, is as good as a working source, necessitating the understanding that all the changes constituting the Renaissance renditions of the stories were made by Straparola himself.) Such assumptions now appear to be entirely misleading (although Waters goes on to state that 'a more extended search will very likely find a fresh source for those of the fables in the "Notti" which have heretofore been classed as the original work of Straparola.') This preliminary statement about Straparola's sources (to be taken up in section IV below) brings us once again to the question of authorship and the relevance of literary biography. What is the right answer in the case of a man who, by all appearances, relied neither upon written sources nor invented a single story of his own? Is he an 'author' in the conventional sense of the term, and if his intentionality is minimized by that doubt, is he a man whose biography will help us understand

4 In Giovan Francesco Straparola, *The Nights of Straparola*, trans. W.G. Waters (London: Lawrence & Bullen, 1894), vol. I, p. xxv.

the stories? At this nadir of his fortune as an 'author,' Straparola risks becoming merely the pseudonym of a compiler.

Returning to the defense against plagiarism, one Orfeo dalla Carta, in his greeting 'to all delightful and loveable ladies' prefacing the earliest edition, intriguingly explains that the author's negligent style is no fault of his own because he 'wrote his fables, not as he wished to write them, but as he heard them from the ladies who related them, adding nothing to them and taking nothing away.' Surely no one believes this for a moment – taking it all for a conventional apology on the part of a bookseller (or more likely Straparola himself). But, the ladies aside, Straparola may indeed have heard the tales and copied them faithfully. If by some technologically reliable process he actually did record his stories verbatim from his oral sources, then he is working with all the trustworthiness and fidelity of a proper field worker, providing us with an anthology of early modern Italian (European) folklore containing more than forty tales – work completed some 250 years before the Grimm brothers hit upon a similar idea. In this way, his authorial function becomes rather like one of his own riddles. He wrote more than forty stories, borrowed none from literary sources, and yet invented none. What is he? In his own words he has been downgraded to an anthologist, but in those very words the author as folklorist is born.[5] Straparola as a scribe was not only the founder of the literary fairy tale; he was the founder of literary ethnography. That claim has mighty implications and may be largely true, even though in his heart, in reproducing these tales as faithfully as possible from oral recitations, Straparola may have thought of himself as their author, having taken them over in typical humanist fashion from a new font of narrative sources apt for literary enhancement. The argument goes in circles. Such is the dilemma surrounding his career in relation to a complex debate concerning authorship, what it is, and how it is to be defined.

Meanwhile, not all readers will be reconciled to the idea of Straparola the folklorist *tout court*, that he made no 'contaminating' contribution to these stories in a quasi-authorial capacity, or that he created no new ones of his own. Authorship now returns by the backdoor. His tales, though from time immemorial in their substances, are nevertheless the

5 Michèle Simonsen points out the particular and unique value of the tales assembled by Straparola and Basile: 'These two collections are precious to folklorists because the existence of many of the popular tales is confirmed here for the first time.' *Le conte populaire* (Paris: Presses universitaires de France, 1984), p. 24.

children of Straparola's memory (with its necessary limitations and confabulations), together with his syntax, his vocabulary, and his sense of idiom – unless he had the capacity for instant memorization and perfect recall, or had mastered a method of shorthand. It is counterintuitive to assume that as one of the literati of his era Straparola, in passing the materials of the folk through his own cranium, left no voice, no residue of an active stylist, in his reconstructions. It is in the very nature of the transmission of narratives, orally or in written form, to remember and recompose, to rationalize odd narrative features, combine elements, modernize the diction, heighten motivations, and invent when memory fails. These matters will be taken up in a subsequent discussion of folklore and its transmission. Just how much Straparola might have stylized and modified his originals remains a moot point. And how can we ever know, given the ephemerality of his exact sources?[6] In sum, the authorship question hinges upon these competing perceptions of his work: that he was one of the *novellieri*, a stylist and maker who sometimes turned to popular sources for start-up material, even contributing a few of his own fairy tales along the way; or that he was fundamentally an anthologizer of popular materials, both fantastic as well as realistic, which he set down in a relatively faithful manner for the delectation of his readers. Opinions remain divided.

With these preliminary qualifications in place, we come to the biography of the author-compiler of *Le piacevoli notti* – one of the scantiest there is, despite the efforts of many to fill out the picture, the most notable being that of Ruth Bottigheimer in her seminal study, *Fairy Godfather: Straparola, Venice, and the Fairy Tale Tradition.* Straparola was presumably born in the Lombard town of Caravaggio, simply because that fact is repeated so often by his bookseller. In his first published work, *Opera nova* (1508), a collection of poems published in Venice, he called himself 'Zoan' – the Lombard spelling of the nickname for Giovanni (Orfeo dalla Carta in his Proem calls him 'Gioan'). It is related to the name Zanni. This Zoan was known as the 'straparola' (literally 'chatterbox'), but we have no idea when and where he took on the name, or

6 Those ancient and medieval texts cited by Waters and others will prove to be earlier borrowings from the folk traditions Straparola employed and thus rich in comparative value. Nevertheless, none are like Straparola's tales. To argue that he used them as sources is to argue that he extracted from them versions of some forty narratives with close cognates in the later folk record, a performance not even remotely conceivable.

whether it was also applied to other members of his family. 'Chatterbox' is as good a nickname as any to distinguish one Zoan from another. It was for this reason that 'da Caravaggio' was later added in his publications, in the manner of many another in that age. So he became 'Talkative John from Caravaggio.' That he published both of his books in Venice, separated by forty-two years of silence, that he set his story anthology on the island of Murano, and that he published one of his stories (V.4) in Paduan dialect hint at a career of some kind in either Venice or the Veneto. We know too that an application was made to the Venetian Senate for a licence to publish the *Nights* in the late spring of 1550 in the name of Straparola. His last sign of life is the phrase 'ad instanza dell' autore' (by the author's instigation), which appeared in the edition of 1555 and those post-dated up to 1557. Ruth Bottigheimer conjectures that his death was the 'catastrophe' that led to the estimation of diminished sales on the part of Comin da Trino, the printer, which led in turn to the extended publishing date.[7] But why his death should adversely affect sales is not entirely clear. Of the man himself we know little more, despite the efforts of many since the time of La Monnoie in the preface of his edition of 1725 to add to the scanty stock of facts, to paraphrase W.G. Waters.[8]

The Pleasant Nights was not Straparola's first publication. Forty-two years earlier his *Opera nova* appeared in Venice, published by Georgio de Ruschoni (1508). It contained 115 sonnets, 35 strambotti, 7 epistolae, and 12 capitoli, his next-to-last sonnet (no. 114) celebrating his native town and its ruler, Giacomo Secco. In these poems he proved himself a competent versifier in the favoured forms of the day, to which we may attribute all the usual causes for publishing a book of fashionable poetry. It was good enough, in fact, to merit a second edition in 1515, but there is no evidence that it won for him a patron or employment. On the assumption that Straparola was actually present to negotiate the publication of his early work, we may risk placing him for a time in the Serenissima, and then incorporating into his biography the city's social and political history from 1508 onward. Venice is compact, after all, the lives of many of its famous men well documented, and its many

7 *Fairy Godfather: Straparola, Venice, and the Fairy Tale Tradition* (Philadelphia: University of Pennsylvania Press, 2002), p. 117.

8 *The Facetious Nights of Straparola*, 4 vols. (London: The Society of Bibliophiles, 1901), vol. IV, p. 237.

institutions and festivals well researched. Nevertheless, the records of the city have to date borne no evidence that he was there, that he knew Pietro Bembo, partied in Murano, joined an academy, chatted with Anton Francesco Doni, ran for public office, worked as secretary to a well-born patron, or belonged to a charitable organization. That he visited Venice is plausible; who did not? That he lived there, who can say? Moreover, if memory serves, only four of his tales involve the city: the story of 'Polissena and the Priest' (I.5), 'The Widow's Broken Promise' (VI.3), the passage of Zambù (XI.4), and that of Pietro Rizzato (XIII.13), none of them textured in Venetian detail. Alternatively, Bottigheimer posits – reasonably, I think – that Straparola may have spent his career in the service of a noble merchant or petty nobleman in or around Padua (five of his stories are set in the city or the region), or perhaps Vicenza. The setting of one of the stories translated out of Morlini is moved from Naples to Vicenza and an unidentified member of the Trissino family, a Signor Hector 'of the ancient and noble family of the Dreseni' (XI.4), becomes one of the central characters. There are innuendoes of personal motivation behind these choices, but no more. Pirovano, in his bottom-of-the-page commentaries, faithfully points out the many words in Venetian dialect that dot the stories, including those in the translations out of Morlini. Such regional usage suggests an extended first-hand experience with life in the Veneto, adding credence to his presumed sojourn in the general area. That Straparola applied for and received a licence on 8 March 1550 from the Venetian Senate to publish the *Nights* – a document which also granted to him a ten-year privilege to reap the benefits of authorship – also serves to place him in the vicinity, at least for a time.[9] Pirovano also makes mention of a book that is today in the Biblioteca A. Mai in Bergamo, a copy of Bernardino Corio's *Historia mediolanensis* – in Latin, it may be added, in support of his knowledge of the language – bearing the bookplate of one 'Franc si [the 'si' in small letters over the 'c'] Streparolle,' presumably our author.[10] Yet despite these traces of the maker, we must remain content with a book that is

9 Pirovano cites the wording from the Register of the Archivio di Stato di Venezia, Senato Terra, filza 37, carta 4 in his 'Nota Biografica,' vol. I, p. liii. Straparola's name therein is spelled 'Zuan Francesco.' It is telling that his application was not unanimously approved, for five members had voted against it – a foreshadowing, no doubt, of the censorship to come.

10 Pirovano, 'Nota Biografica,' vol. I, p. lii.

more pertinently a product of a literary age, of commercialized printing and a book-buying public, than it is a work inviting interpretation through the life of a historically documented author. Someone there was with a reliably workmanlike mind, someone who had the brilliant idea of collecting narratives from new quarters, ignoring the humanist antipathy to the 'lower' forms of literature while replicating the Boccaccian conventions, someone with an eye to a commercial opportunity, and with a measure of literary talent. Elaborating further in this vein makes nearly all critical appraisal of the work a form of literary biography, for what a man writes may be a large part of the life of his mind, but the conclusions are merely circular and the anxiety misplaced; the *raison d'être* of *Le piacevoli notti* does not seem to be autobiographical.

II. The Genre, Design, and Conventions of *Le piacevoli notti*

Presumably even years before the publication of the first volume of the *Notti* in 1550, Straparola had been collecting stories – who can say how? There is no indication – the Morlini translations aside – that more than five or six of them were available to him from written sources. His kinds of materials had not been systematically collected before, at least not in the forms then current among the folk narrators upon whom he must have relied (and relatively the same forms in which they would resurface in ethnographic collections three centuries later). Straparola managed to carry out that work by keeping records – mental or written – of what he heard, from undisclosed sources. He may have relied upon villagers, household members, street professionals, courtesans, or storytellers even higher up the social echelons who had already done the work of lifting elements of the oral culture for the amusement of elite circles. In this resides so much of his importance and originality as a writer.

Once the critical mass to make his collection had been reached, Straparola began at his desk by ensconcing his folk *récits* in a Boccaccian-style framing tale with its social setting and band of storytellers. He then embellished each night with one of his polite 'Petrarchist' poems, and each story with an enigma pulled from another pile. (He may have been the first to join enigmas to stories.) These supplementary appurtenances were entirely in keeping with contemporary practices and conventions, but served to baffle earlier critics, who failed to see the folk materials behind the trappings. In the manner of the *novellieri* (the many writers of *novelle* in the tradition of Boccaccio), Straparola went on to equip his characters with historical-sounding names, many from the *Reali di*

Francia.[11] Still at his desk, he composed rubrics in lieu of titles in which each story is given in resume, just as in the *novelle* collections. Finally, he resituated his 'fables' in possible geographical places, more often than not Italian cities and towns, a goodly number of them in Lombardy or the Veneto. Such conventions as these were sufficient to convince many that his book was a stock collection of short stories in the Boccaccian manner. For that reason, the originality of his folk miscellany for a long time remained systematically undervalued or misrepresented.[12]

Nevertheless, the *novella*-like features cannot be discounted, for they remain central to the design and experience of the work – particularly the Boccaccian *cornice* or framing tale, which in turn aligns this production, inevitably, with many of the collections of his near contemporaries in those culminating years of the Italian *novella.* Anton Francesco Grazzini published his *Cene* in 1545, at the same time that Anton Francesco Doni was incorporating *novelle* into his larger works. Meanwhile, Giovanni Brevio's *Rime e prose volgari* came to light in Rome in 1545. Five years later, in the same year that Straparola's first volume appeared, Girolamo Parabosco published his *Diporti,* with the *Varii componimenti* of Ortensio Lando appearing two years later. Then in 1553, the date of Straparola's second volume of the *Notti,* the *Dodici giornate* of Silvan Cattaneo cleared the presses. Pietro Fortini was active in this same decade, as was Matteo Bandello, who published his first volume of *novelle* in 1554. Not long thereafter came the *Ecatommiti* of Giovanni Battista Giraldi (1565) and the *Sei giornate* of Sebastiano Erizzo (1567). *Le piacevoli*

11 As part of Straparola's fitting of his stories with the external trappings of the *novella,* he reassigned his characters with names from a variety of literary sources: Galeotto, Isotta, and Ancillotto from Breton romance; Gabrina, Doralice, and Brunello from chivalric romance; and Salardo, Costanzo, Nerino, Gilfroi, Attarvante, Dambruno, Lucaferro, Guerrino, and Dusolina from the *Reali di Francia,* with its settings in Turkey, the Balkans, and the Near East. Letterio di Francia, *Storia dei generi letterari italiani novellistica,* vol. I, *Dalle origini al Bandello* (Milan: Francesco Vallardi, 1924), pp. 725–6.

12 Among those who considered Straparola as one of the *novellieri,* and the *Notti* as a work in the tradition of Boccaccio, are John Colin Dunlop, *The History of Prose Fiction,* ed. Henry Wilson (New York: Burt Franklin, 1970), vol. II, p. 207; Giuseppe Rua, ed., *Le piacevoli notti di Messer Gian Francesco Straparola* (Rome: Ermanno Loescher, 1898), pp. 1*ff.*; Robert J. Clements and Joseph Gibaldi, *Anatomy of the Novella: The European Tale Collection from Boccaccio and Chaucer to Cervantes* (New York: New York University Press, 1977); Manlio Pastore Stocchi, ed., *Le piacevoli notti* (Bari: Laterza, 1975), p. v; Janet Levarie Smarr, ed., *Italian Renaissance Tales* (Rochester, MI: Solaris, 1983).

notti is of their company, seeking to capture the attention of the same book-purchasing clientele. Moreover, to complicate matters a bit more, certain of these authors appear in the annotations to follow, for in their collections there are stories resembling Straparola's – elaborations upon similar narratives – perplexing the matter of influence in light of the proximity of their publications in time and the geographical distances between them. The comparative prospects are rich, but the logistical barriers and the marked differences in ethos in the stories themselves suggest that such cognate tales came about through means other than direct borrowing. The choices, however, are few: either common written sources now lost; or the circulation of *novelle* as popular tales through the oral culture. The idea that Straparola might have relied upon the latter fund nearly exclusively for his materials gains in credence by the fact that, on a far less frequent basis, his contemporaries relied upon that same repository, as the *novellieri* had done since the inception of the genre.

The social world of Straparola's framing device is curiously conceived, for it consists of a select group of historical men – among them some of the noted literati of the age – and a parallel group of ten idealized, non-historical damsels who, in an order determined by lot, are designated to tell the fifty stories that arguably constituted Straparola's original design.[13] There are some signs of assigning stories to specific narrators, many of the more salacious ones going to the men, conceivably to liberate the girls from telling misogynist or scatological tales otherwise too good to jettison. The upshot, at the cost of the formal design, was that certain of the men – notably Antonio Molino and Benedetto Trivigiano, followed by Antonio Bembo – are prevailed upon to tell 'substitute' stories, which turn out to be five of the most ribald of the lot. The design of the work emerges and becomes diversified.

---

13 The first volume contained twenty-five stories; hence, there were five stories for each of the five evenings. The girls were divided into two groups and the five names for each evening were placed in an urn from which they were drawn out one after the other, thereby establishing the order of presentation. This rather symmetrical design was presumably to have been repeated in the second volume, so that by the end each girl would have recited five tales. Thus the supposition that he initially intended fifty stories – half a *Decameron*, as it were. That he ended up with forty-eight in the second volume is no doubt due to the fact that the average length of the stories in the first volume is twice that of the stories in the second, so that in order to fill out the latter, new material, including the twenty-two translations out of Morlini, made up the shortfall.

Readers are invited to judge for themselves whether there is a categorical falling off in matters of content, inspiration, and aesthetics in passing from the end of the fifth night to the beginning of the sixth – that is to say, from the 1550 volume to the 1553 volume.[14] That impression, I suspect, will depend upon the primacy and excellence assigned to his seventeen 'wonder tales' (to the critical prejudice of the remaining works), those stories associated with the later fairy tale and hence the most critically discussed. If these are the markers of Straparola's originality and genius, with twelve of them in the first volume and only five in the sequel, the later volume may well appear to be inferior. Worth underscoring, however, is that the remaining thirteen tales of the first volume are not 'wonder' (fairy) tales. Straparola, at a time of rich supply, also had an interest in popular trickster tales and *novelle*, ten of the latter having no immediate literary sources and displaying many of the narrative features of oral tales. Thus, while stories involving imaginative royal offspring, fantasy kingdoms, and speaking animals make up nearly half of the first volume, at no time were they Straparola's exclusive concern. The second volume is considerably more diversified, featuring jest tales, beast fables, anecdotal *novelle*, *bon mot* tales and smart replies, pseudo-histories, and two or three of his finest wonder tales. It may be a misplaced bias to say that he ran out of the stories about magic and the miraculous and was compelled to fall back on secondary materials, as some of those 'filler' pieces turn out to have long-standing literary pedigrees among the writers of *facetiae*, *fabliaux*, and jest books, which form an important part of Straparola's miscellany. It is clear that, in terms of composition and assembly, tactics do change in the last two nights if only because the last twenty tales, with one exception, are translations from Morlini. Yet even these fall naturally into place, sustaining the spirit of the popular 'omnium gatherum' which prevails to the end. Returning to the outset, when the entire cache of stories was still available to the author, we find that variety prevailed even then; the first night is comprised of a *novella*-exemplum, two popular tales of cunning or trickery, a wonder tale of incest, and a realist *novella* of adultery and punishment. All appear to

14 Letterio di Francia was exercised in particular by this apparent decline, for despite the work's integrated conception and design 'fu iniziata bene, proseguita male e finite pessimamente, con l'oscenità della material e con un plagio disonesto, inverecondo, sfacciato' (though it began well, it grew worse, and finished badly, with obscene materials and plagiarism which was dishonest, shameless, and impudent). *Storia dei generi letterari italiani: Novellistica* (Milan: Vallardi, 1924), vol. I, p. 731.

have been shaped by the folk imagination, but none is a fairy tale, and only one relies upon supernatural plotting elements. Straparola merits celebration for introducing such wonder tales among his varia and for incorporating them into the *soirées* of the elite, but they were far from his sole preoccupation. Just how much Straparola prioritized his tales of the fabulous will never be known, but he did not group them together; the design of his work, in effect, imitates the random order in which stories of all kinds might have been told at a social gathering by narrators who do not confine their interests by genre, but simply tell the tales they know, reflecting perhaps the frequency of the story types in the popular culture at large. That aesthetic principle, if it is a principle at all, may prove to be the reigning factor in the design of the work.

It had become a tradition among the *novellieri* to situate their individual tales within a framing narrative that constituted the social setting in which the tales were doubly presented – first to the audience described within the book, and secondly to us, the readers, who are essentially eavesdroppers treated to a privileged glimpse into an exclusive coterie of nobles and their entourage, all of them engaged in the structured social recreations that denoted privilege and civility. The stories that they hear as viva voce presentations we must read, suspended imaginatively between the fictional representations of time, place, and persons in Renaissance Venice and the concrete reality of the book as an instrument of storytelling. The conventions of the framing fiction through which the recitations of the stories are given historical particularity and dramatic immediacy were an integral part of the collections of the *novellieri* from the inception of the genre. Giovanni Sercambi (1347–1424) imagined his *novelle* as a performance for the benefit of high society on the island of Murano, one of the fashionable smaller islands in the Venetian lagoon, famous for its glassworks and for its villa retreats owned by many of Venice's finest families. It was here that Straparola situated his own collection over a century later, because it was here that Ottaviano Maria Sforza, bishop-elect of Lodi, rented a villa for his daughter Lucrezia in 1536 after exiling himself from his Sforza domains. The mental tease arising over the historicizing of the *Nights* as a one-time event in the recreational lives of Signora Lucrezia and the members of her literary salon is that the personalities are real, the activities plausible, the circumstances historical, but the actual event impossible, for at no point in the late 1530s were all the *convives* simultaneously in Venice, or out of prison, or alive. We know that the thirteen nights are a fiction retrofitted upon a pseudo-historical situation and that the stories were never recited by ten demoiselles, and yet it is the conventional prerogative of such authors to visit their collections upon the living or the dead in a complimentary fashion, as though the entire event were a nostalgic portrait of bygone days.

Just why Straparola chooses Ottaviano and Lucrezia, retells their political story, describes how they selected their charming palazzo, and shows how they celebrated the carnival season in their own special way is beyond our knowledge. He tells us nothing of great particularity about them. The setting is entirely conventional and more bookish in the Boccaccian tradition than it is real. Their circle of friends and luminaries is as historical or as fantastic as the author wishes. The probable continually graduates into the merely possible, while illusion is ruled by convention. Straparola tells us all we need to know about his little society in his Proem, but for the record, Ottaviano Maria Sforza was born in 1477 and died around 1541; he was the youngest son of Duke Galeazzo, who was murdered before the boy was born. As an illegitimate son, he was never in line for the throne. He had been made bishop of Lodi but was singularly unpopular and was already in retirement when his office fell under the control of the Holy Roman Empire in 1535. That, rather than hostile relatives, was the cause of his flight. Documentation survives confirming his presence in Venice as late as 1538, but strangely he does not participate in his daughter's carnival *veglie.* Lucrezia was not a legitimate daughter, although she managed to become married to one of the non-ruling Gonzagas, Giovanni Francesco, cousin of the marquis of Mantua. She became his widow in 1523. By calling her Lucrezia Gonzaga, rather than by her real name, Sforza, Straparola may be setting up a parallel with the better-known Lucrezia Gonzaga, who ruled over the Mantuan social set and commissioned the stories of Matteo Bandello.[15] But it is unclear what Straparola would have gained by evoking either Mantua or Bandello, whose first published volume of *novelle,* in any case, would not appear for another four years. The greater question is why Straparola favours

15 Ruth Bottigheimer, *Fairy Godfather: Straparola, Venice, and the Fairy Tale Tradition* (Philadelphia: University of Pennsylvania Press, 2002), pp. 93–4. It may be added that the first seventy-eight of his *novelle*, published in Lucca in 1554 in three volumes, originated in Mantua and Milan between 1506 and 1524. The second group was written in Verona between 1526 and 1527, and the last group in France before 1541, published posthumously in Lyons in 1573. Of the first group, sixty-three of the seventy-eight *novelle* were historical. There would seem to be little probability that Straparola and Bandello knew each other's work.

this widow, foregrounds her story, and sings her praises. Was she a patron, an employer, his hostess, or a fancy known only through hearsay? On these matters the record is silent. But such a lady once breathed the air of mortals and her father spent time in Venice in the late 1530s; that much is historical.

The framing tale suggests that the numbers present were considerably greater than those named. But for lack of further information, our sense of the group shrinks to those who are identified and participate in the recitations. Highest in rank and eminence is Giambattista (Gregorio) Casali of Bologna, a bishop and ambassador to Venice from the court of Henry VIII of England. He was in Transylvania in 1535 and died in Bologna in 1536, putting an early terminus upon his possible presence. On the occasions in which the guests were placed according to social rank, he would have led the way. Just beneath him is Pietro Bembo of *Asolani* fame, not yet a cardinal, but already a monsignor and a man of prestige and renown who figures prominently in Castiglione's *Il cortegiano.* Significantly, he is not drawn into the demeaning enterprise of telling folk tales except for a modest offering on the final night. The merchant of Treviso, Ferier Beltramo, was also present – the man who had come to the aid of the newly arrived exiles, giving them asylum and helping them establish their new lives. On the last night he offers his second little story, and we are told then that he had 'a cheerful and happy face.' Beltramo died in 1537, putting a terminus upon his historical participation. Among them, as well, was Bernardo Capello (1498–1565), a poet and friend of Bembo's with a rather serious turn of mind. His *Rime* appeared after the publication of the *Notti.*[16] There was also Benedetto Trivigiano, the Venetian poet, who joined in the musical offerings both as a singer and performer on the viol. His fellow musician, Antonio Molino, both a vocalist and violist, was also an actor and comic poet with a specialty in regional dialects. The author, Antonio Bembo, is also present. Both he and Molino tell tales, whereas Bishop Vangelista de' Cittadini, secretary to Cardinal Triulzi, is named as one of the audience members but takes no part in the activities.[17] Among the women are the two matrons, sober and venerable, who are closest to the Signora; they are Chiara Guidiccione and the widow Veronica Orbat from Crema. Completing this little society are the ten damsels, along with a mysterious

16 Pirovano, *Piacevoli notti* (Rome: Salerno, 2000), vol. I, p. 9n6.
17 Pirovano, *Piacevoli notti,* vol. I, p. 9n4.

eleventh named Diana who appears from nowhere to tell two stories. The final count would appear to be seven or eight men and fourteen women.

The ten demoiselles are surely little more than a necessary fiction for the purposes of telling stories and entertaining the guests. Even as the representations of persons they seem to have no real social counterparts. They are tentatively differentiated: one has nice eyes, another has a pretty carriage, while another is a touch arrogant but really quite kind, while yet another has lovely hair and is devoted to the Signora. Another is a touch disdainful but has languishing glances that captures hearts, while another is particularly witty, another particularly virtuous and prudent, while yet another is grave and sedate for her years. But insofar as these distinctions escape the memory of even the most attentive reader, these women tend to become interchangeable. In the little discussions following the stories there are bits of rivalry, a touch of haughtiness here or of pouting there, but no one can recall whether these moods coincide with the initial profiles. The impression is of a bevy of charmers, their attributes condensed from the language of the love poets, their profiles merely preliminary to their functions as flirtatious, socially sophisticated members of an elite gathering who, at the same time, in their classless and anonymous way, are suited to the telling of tales that do not originate in elite culture.[18] Who they were or could be in relation to Venetian society as it was historically constituted may hence be the wrong question. The diverse statuses, training, and social circulation of young Venetian women might be investigated to see from whence the Signora might have drawn ten such talented young ladies without family connections or class origins. Are they ladies-in-waiting, friends and companions of the Signora, Venetian debutantes, or courtesans? The answer, I suspect, is none of the above; rather, they are narrators embodied according to carefully calibrated conventions – conventions which permit them to be, at the same time, objects of Platonic admiration, partners in banter, models of innocence, yet instruments of the culturally low and the morally marginal in their erotic enigmas, which they primly recall from the gutter to the amusement of all. As carnival entertainers masquerading as demoiselles of the better classes, or vice versa, they appear to have

18 Manlio Pastore Stocchi, in his introduction to *Le piacevoli notti* (Bari: Laterza, 1975), p. v, says the girls are of uncertain ethical and social definition. They are there to carry out four social rituals: singing, dancing, storytelling, and riddles.

little ground in documented social history to claim as their own.[19] To attribute to them a degree of historical probability is also to assume the currency of folklore on the lips of young women of the better classes as early as the 1530s. That may not have been the case.

The work recommends itself as a repository of materials apt for memorization by those in fashionable circles seeking to replicate the activities epitomized by the Signora's salon. In that respect, it raises questions about the uses of art and the book itself as an accessory to social practices. In brief, Straparola appears to have fudged a past 'reality' to encourage a future employment of his stories as part of his purpose in the commercialization of the folk tale. But he had a problem with decorum to resolve, for who among the elite society could recite the tales of the folk and escape the opprobrium of handling the 'low'? That dilemma was later confronted by Girolamo Bargagli who, in his *Dialogo dei giochi* (Dialogue on games, 1572), stated his preference for *novelle* in the context of social gatherings while objecting to the recitation of *favole* by dignified guests. Nevertheless, he allowed for their recitation by 'semplici fanciullette' (simple, ordinary little maidens) – precisely Straparola's solution.[20] But is this confirmation that by 1572 the Straparolan formula had become common social practice and that actual young girls were invited to fill the roles of the ten demoiselles in the recitation of *favole*? That may be more than we can know.

Meanwhile, the entire event in Murano is pointedly carnivalesque; not only are the gatherings held on the thirteen nights preceding Lent but there is a sense of licence, liberty, invention, and delectation in the air, together with a measured touch of mischief, a testing of the margins of decorum, which the Signora, in diminishing outbursts, seeks to maintain according to her own working sense of propriety. These negotiations are part of the spirit of play that reigns throughout the work. Lucrezia does not hesitate to cut short an overheated conversation, quell ribald laughter, or terminate indulgent displays of grief, but there is an ambiance of carnival beneath it all. The stories, meanwhile, are incitements to

19 Basile treated the participation of these ideal beauties with their impeccable talents not only as a convention but a cliché, which he parodied eighty-five years after Straparola with his ten ancient and ugly women participants.

20 *Dialogo dei giochi* (Siena: Accademia Senese degli Intronati, 1982), p. 220. Bargagli does not date the origin of this practice, again leaving open the question of whether Straparola's social representation in the framing tale was taken from life or whether it was an invention that was later imitated.

communal response, at times as bald and as indecorous as the plots demand. There is irrepressible laughter, weeping, sniggering, divisions by gender, banter, and discussion. In the process, the collective emotions of the group constitute a form of critical reaction and commentary. Inevitably, as a choral audience (sometimes antiphonally), their display of feelings contributes to our reception of these stories, for by dint of seeking membership in a virtual community defined by hedonics and neurobiological thresholds we are inclined to match our feelings to theirs.

Examples of these group dynamics follow nearly every story. During the telling of 'Biancabella, or the Damsel and the Snake,' many of the listeners are several times moved to tears (III.3). By contrast, with the happy issue for Adamantina in marrying King Drusiano, there are no tears of joy or sorrow, but 'laughter loud and long as everyone remembered the habits of the doll and the manner with which it clamped its teeth into the king's behind and clawed his nether parts' (V.2). The Trevisan's tale of Tia Rabboso (V.4) creates a gender divide, for it particularly pleases the women, so clever is the heroine's management of her silly husband. But in the end, both sexes in the audience, the men in spite of themselves, nearly split their sides with laughter, thereby making them again of one accord. On the whole, these responses are devoid of subtlety or nuance; by and large they depict merely degrees of empathetic joy or sorrow, or a sense of the ridiculous. But this is quite in accord with the human response system, which has but laughter and tears to express, through its neurophysiological mechanisms, a wide range of emotional colouring along the complex continuum between the improvement of our chances for survival, well-being, and self-advancement, or the inverse. In the end, evolutionary selection has confirmed only these mechanisms for marking increased or decreased adaptiveness: comedy or tragedy. We weep over the diminution of well-being for those about whom we have been brought to care and we laugh on behalf of those who have been delivered from death, oppression, error, or misery. And though we sometimes weep for joy or laugh over the punishment of fools deserving of their adverse fates, all such paradoxes are as familiar to us as our own thoughts. We must interpret our emotions and feelings. These stories are hence exercises in group dynamics, in rising and falling hedonic states of a vital kind, in accordance with the perceived destinies of imaginary persons. In his framing-tale 'commentary' through the language of emotions, Straparola is mindful of these simple but archetypal responses to these often simple but archetypal tales. The meanings of these stories begin here.

Among those group responses is not only the laughter that accompanies deliverance from danger into happiness, but the laughter that responds to situational incongruity, comic or hyperbolical sexuality, or downright barnyard humour. Straparola might have revealed more to us than he did concerning the right and wrong social responses to the graphic, erotic, and scatological elements that are so prevalent in the collection. There are times when the women literally bury their faces in their skirts to hide their forbidden amusement or their display of embarrassment or shame with regard to these salacious and risqué stories. The men, meanwhile, take pleasure in discussing them with a frankness designed to exacerbate the women's show of discomfort. In this way, the stories contribute to the display of sensibilities distinguishing the sexes, amidst laughter that is both aggressive and retiring, with carnival as the justifying context. But just why Straparola took such delight in off-colour tales, and whether he found them in oral circulation in their present forms or amplified their prurient potential, are questions open to discussion, for arguably the *Pleasant Nights* is one of the lewdest collections of stories to appear in the age of Rabelais. In fact, the magnitude of Straparola's indulgence was brought home by the number of passages that had to be restored by the present editor to a translation that is in nearly all other ways a supremely faithful and idiomatic rendition of the original. The Victorian readers, unless they read French or Italian, were deprived of all details concerning the farmer who anointed Castorio's groin, made an incision with his knife, and inserted two fingers into his scrotum, or of the bird that thrust its head right up the donkey's fundament in search of half-digested grain mixed in the manure, or of the priest who took out the thing which men have and, lifting the lady's nightgown, inserted it without hesitation into the furrow. There was no case to be made with Waters that Straparola's bawdy was frank, open, robust, earthy, honest, and innocent.[21] Beyond that, there is perhaps

21 This fact is made particularly ironic by the degree to which Waters comes to the defense of Straparola in just such matters in his 'Introduction': 'In few of the collections of a similar character is there to be found so genuine a vein of comedy, and for the sake of this one may perhaps be permitted to beg indulgence for occasional lapses – lapses which are assuredly fewer in number and probably not more lax in character than those of novelists of greater fame.' In spite of this apology, Waters saw fit to alter them to avoid offending Victorian tastes. *The Nights of Straparola*, 2 vols. (London: Lawrence & Bullen, 1894), vol. I, p. xix.

little more to add concerning a choice of materials that was most apparently as Straparola liked it and as his readers liked it, in defiance of the censors.

The preliminary or paratextual materials in the two volumes are minimal, consisting in the first volume of an address to the women readers by the bookseller, Orfeo dalla Carta, and another address to the same readership by the author himself in the second. (This 'Orpheus from the paper' is very likely Straparola himself, but we will accept the ruse at face value for the time being.) Both statements, hastily read, appear entirely conventional. The bookseller singles out the ladies and chats with them over the nature of their purchase, going on about the author as a well-intentioned man with minor faults who, in a spirit of humility, wished his readers the maximum of pleasure from the best his poor talents could give them. Such a book of entertainments was honest, a gift, a trifle, an act of devotion, a pastime, an idle recreation, while at the same time it was an enormous labour of love, novel in its design, and the result of incalculable obstacles overcome. In courting his female readers in this way, he goes so far as to style himself their personal admirer, one who pays them a perfunctory compliment in offering them a book as a bid for virtual favours. That was all business as usual for authors, but cheeky in the extreme on the part of a man usurping the author's place. Such are the games authors play.

Read more closely, the amiable ladies are given a medley of opinions: that the book is full of 'elegance and learning,' even though other writers may provide them with greater pleasures; that it contains variety, subtle wit, and instruction, yet is poor and negligent in style. How curious. Nevertheless, the failure to achieve stylistic distinction (for inadequacy can only be measured in relation to expectations) is no fault of the author's. The style is intrinsic to the materials he recorded, for the matter was none of his own (in this case, stylistic poverty is not the measure of the man, but the mark of an honest and careful transcriber). Dalla Carta's last disclaimer is that Straparola did not really want to publish his stories at all. Then he changes topic, explaining that the book is now a gift from him, their bookseller, who can give them even better stories another time, and thereafter wishes them all happiness and asks to be remembered: 'Be happy and remember me!' Quite apart from the question of authorship, how bad a stylist does Straparola (or his bookseller) think he is? Can there be any possible truth in the thought that he was disinclined to publish his wares after applying for the privilege and going to such lengths to gather the requisite materials?

No doubt this was the author himself striking a pose of modesty through a kind of apologia. But had the book already been critically demoted for its modest style, in contrast to the flights of artifice that had become part of the idiom of the *novella*? Had the novelty of his folk materials and his refusal to tamper inordinately with them by turning them into 'art tales' already come back to haunt him? One need only look ahead to the *suavitas* of Basile in transforming local folk tales into baroque salon pieces of considerable stylistic fancy.[22] Moreover, style may be extended to include all such matters as psychological motivation, individuation of characters, linear episodic structuring, mimetic consistency, realistic social settings, extended speeches, and dramatized encounters – indeed, all that pertains to the standards and conventions of the writers in the great Boccaccian tradition. These are precisely the measures of authorship denied to Straparola in following his sources, for they are the qualities typically lacking in folk tales. Their absence was particularly felt by the nineteenth-century critics who placed Straparola among the least accomplished of the *novellieri*. Did the folk materials, faithfully recorded, likewise fall below the expected standards in Straparola's day? If, in meeting or anticipating such objections, he forges a preface in the name of a bookseller-publisher, is it conceivable as well that Straparola had no such sponsor and was thus free to invent one? Was Straparola compelled to pitch his own publication and presumably finance it into the bargain? Under such circumstances, he might well have constructed an alter ego through whom he could soften the reception of the book by anticipating criticism of its drab and plain style, while insisting, meanwhile, upon its value as entertainment (*dolce*) and instruction (*utile*).

The even stranger 'apologia' appended to the second volume would appear to be a result of the fulfillment of his worst fears, that by disclaiming authorship to excuse his style he sets himself up for accusation as a literary plagiarist. That is the issue, at any rate, that provokes his postured indignation in the 1553 greeting to the ladies. But was the accusation true, or was this a *trompe-l'oeil* of injured merit by which the author creates yet another framing tale around the work, now in relation to its reception in the world of Venetian criticism and gossip? Perhaps there was no better way to arouse interest than to generate a drama of ad hominem attack.

22 N.M. Penzer, ed., *The Pentamerone of Giambattista Basile*, trans. Benedetto Croce, 2 vols. (1932; reprint, Westport, CT: Greenwood Press, 1979), 'Preface,' p. xlviii.

But the fumbly and unfocused manner in which he shapes his reply gives little confidence that much of substance was at stake. He begins with a vehement denial of the allegations, only to confess again that his material was entirely recycled, taken over verbatim from his several oral sources. Thus he admits to theft, but not from texts. Or is it because he is trapped by his fictional framing tale, which he has put forward as a historical event? If that truth is to be maintained, then sources become circular insofar as he must now credit his stories exclusively to the young ladies whose recitations he has recorded, or ambiguously, to others who tell them in the manner of the young ladies; it is not clear.[23] If it seemed to him a necessary mendacity, it is one that has served to depreciate and devalue his real legacy ever since. The collector of fables had to make a full confession of his hidden practices or else declare himself a maker and creator in some full and conventional sense; Straparola, it seems, could not make up his mind.

The question of plagiarism during the Renaissance pertains, in any case, not only to texts and transcriptions per se, but to training, the authority of the past, and the act of referential creativity. In resuscitating forms, imitating style, committing the touchstones of antiquity to memory, revitalizing speeches, and modernizing plots, the humanist maker works at the edges of plagiarism, driving a thin wedge between inspiration and theft. Shakespeare's incessant borrowing (barely a single plot was his own) and Barnabe Riche's compulsive fusion of sources earned praise for the former and condemnation for the latter, although in substance their procedures were the same. In fact, in his *Farewell to Military Profession* (1580) – the work that introduced *novella*-writing to England – Riche melded as many as three to eight sources (with echoes from many more) into each of his stories. Straparola, in transferring folk tales into print, was working with materials more patently anonymous and in the public domain than the written sources of the *novellieri*, yet he does not allow himself to say so in his own defense. He merely rallies his readers to ignore or do worse to the curs who were snapping at him, without troubling himself to explain precisely where he obtained his materials

23 He says literally that the stories in the two volumes are 'not mine' (*non siano mie*), but 'those from whom I have thievishly stolen them' (*ma da questo, et quello ladronescamente rubbate*). Thus 'I cannot possibly claim them as my own without lying. Nevertheless, I faithfully wrote them down in precisely the manner in which they were recited by the ten young ladies' (*fedelmente scritte secondo il modo che furono da dieci damigelle nel concistorio raccontate*).

and what he did to them. Thereafter, he wishes the ladies happiness in the manner of Orfeo, assures them that their names are written in his heart, and concludes. The irony here is that of all the authors working in the age of humanism, Straparola is the one who most assiduously avoids the employment of literary sources. Or, as W.G. Waters points out, the more his writing is traced to these popular sources through the efforts of the folklorists, the more the 'charge of plagiarism' will be rendered 'almost meaningless.'[24] Indeed.

What holds true for his plots holds equally true for his curious stylistic habits. In the commentaries to follow there appear examples, by no means exhaustive, of Straparola's remarkable proclivity to integrate the words and phrases of his favourite authors into his stories – Boccaccio and Sannazaro in particular. Why or how he managed to do this only raises more questions about his recollective capacities. Is it conceivable that from his recreational reading he retained a substantial cache of quotable quotations suitable for adaptation to his own endeavours, or did he merely read and write at the same time, tipping in the transformed passages from his reading in a random and opportunist fashion? We are invited to think that his remarkable capacity to remember and transcribe folk tales was of a kind with his equally remarkable capacity to remember enigmas, as well as potentially hundreds of often-mundane passages from the extensive works of several writers. The evidence may be pointing towards a man who enjoyed an outstanding capacity to retain information in ways far exceeding the norm, even in the prime age of mnemonics manuals and guides to enhanced recollection.

One example must serve. In the next-to-last story in the collection (XIII.12), Master Gotfreddo, a humble, common-sense doctor, prefaces his advice to the king with a word about himself in relation to the rich and ostensibly learned physicians there present with the following words: 'although, among these honorable fathers, I am the most insignificant, the least learned, and the least eloquent, nevertheless I ... ' Straparola had written '*quantunque tra questi onorandi padri il piú infimo e il men dotto e il men eloquente meritamente dir mi possa.*' Many of these words recur in Book VI of Sannazaro's *Arcadia*. There Serrano, one of the rustics, a man of the mountains, is asked to sing to the noble company. He replies to Opico, '*Quantunque il piú infimo e 'l meno eloquente di tutta questa schiera*

24 *The Nights of Straparola*, 2 vols. (London: Lawrence & Bullen, 1894), 'Introduction,' p. xxvi.

meritamente dir mi possa nondimeno,' which is to say, 'although deservedly one may call me the meanest and the least eloquent of all this band, nevertheless not to play the part of an ingrate ...'[25] Something is there, it would appear, in the word echoes between the two passages. Coincidence is inconceivable, especially with so many similar passages throughout the *Notti.* Rather, the challenge is for us to imagine how Straparola's mind worked to bring about such echoes, and particularly those from the works of Boccaccio, often presented in detached and rearranged fashion, with cognate words placed here and there in passages expressing entirely different concepts. In short, Straparola's vocabulary was extended to include a repository of phrases from which he could take scattered inspiration in matters of diction. That he did so to the end of setting up intertextual resonances for his readers is most unlikely, or at least unrealistic. That he employed the words of others because he could not supply their equivalents on his own appears quite implausible. Was it merely a private pleasure, the compulsive habit of an equally compulsive if not monstrous memory? And was it literary theft? The matter seems morally negligible yet intensely interesting. That whole phrases of others sometimes flew into his mind more readily than his own words is witness to an intellect equipped somewhat differently than the standard-issue brain. As a codicil to the example given above, this practice occurs in one of the late tales translated out of Morlini, suggesting that the same talent responsible for the earlier stories was still at work, that Straparola had not given up in Book XI, leaving the Latin translations to a collaborator – unless that subaltern had cloned his citation habits and dialectal vocabulary in the process. That any of this scattered literary echoing should be deemed an impropriety would altogether seem to miss the point of his achievement in the context of the humanist-trained mind and its referential habits.

A further feature worthy of mention is that each story is provided with a moralizing prelude, dutifully setting up the 'fable' as an exemplum illustrating a point of general wisdom, a principle of human nature, or a directive for intelligent and reasonable conduct. The formula is often repeated by the storytellers themselves, promising that the expressed ethical principle will be patently exemplified in the *récit* to follow. Such preambles are generic to the *novella* formula and ostensibly represent an

25 Sannazaro, *Arcadia & Piscatorial Eclogues,* trans. Ralph Nash (Detroit: Wayne State University Press, 1966), p. 65.

act of critical interpretation on the part of the author, as though stories achieve their ends only in themes or abstract principles – each story an allegory guided by an axiom concerning ethical conduct and the considered life. But often there is something peculiar about these inferences, these axiomatic claims imposed upon polyvocal tales, which causes readers to discount them altogether. Quite apart from a resistance to such moralizing, rarely does the precept take a meaningful measure of the story's range of connotations, ambiguities, and subversive undercurrents. We are promised, for example, that the story of Travaglino (III.5) (about the cowherd who cannot bring himself to lie and is hence rewarded after turning states evidence against himself), will make clear the principle that Truth always prevails, always comes to the surface like oil in water. That ostensible truism is in turn related to the emblem of Truth prevailing over Calumny through the help of her father, Time. But this allegedly universal principle falls palpably short of the story's many narrative paradoxes. Truth prevails only because Travaglino, after several tries, cannot perfect a cogent lie, and his reputation for truth survives as a virtue only because the circumstances of the bet bring rewards to his patron. His ignorance of these contextual matters produces victory by default rather than by providential guidance or moral resolve. Honesty really is the best policy, as it turns out, but irony beggars the relevance of the universalizing precept.

In closing this discussion of the work's genre, conventions, textual parts, and social practices, something might be added about the musical performances within *Le piacevoli notti*. They were an integral part, called for at the outset of each evening, with the guests spontaneously taking part in accordance with their talents. Venetian society, by this time, had demonstrated its desire for secular vocal and instrumental music for precisely these kinds of 'at-home' recreational occasions, and music publishers such as Antonio Gardano were answering the demand. That market would only grow as the century advanced, as musical literacy increased among amateur performers from the elite classes, and as such tastes spread throughout the rest of Europe. Of the lyrics sung at the beginning of each night, only a few can be assigned to particular composers and to music that still survives. But those few give reason to think that others, as well, were more than fictive creations on Straparola's part. On the seventh night, Lauretta performs Giovanni Nasco's 'Ardo tremando,' which survives in a publication by Girolamo Scotto of 1562. Vincenzo Ruffo's 'Questa fera gentile,' performed for the eighth night, can be found in a Gardano publication of 1556. And Nasco's 'Se'l tempo invola' was chosen for the twelfth night, again to be found in a Scotto publication of 1561.[26] That is a beginning.

The evidence provided by Straparola concerning performance practices and musical genres is typically slight and imprecise, but he mentions the many instruments involved, including the flutes employed for the dancing, as well as the lutes, viols, *lironi*, and *lira da braccio* used to accompany the singing. In naming so many, there are hints of considerable versatility in the instrumentation and variety in the sound colours. This is in keeping with the evidence suggesting that five-part madigrals or *canzone* might be sung at times *a cappella*, at others as solos with the lower lines supplied by instruments – such as the *lironi* upon which two of Straparola's young damsels are proficient – and at still other times with the vocal lines instrumentally doubled. That Straparola sometimes calls for instruments and sometimes not is evidence of a kind. Musicologists have been debating the question for decades from just such sketchy hints. The canzonets, likewise, could be performed as lute songs or with fuller instrumentation. We are told that the two men at times lead the dancing and at others accompany themselves on lutes or *lironi* while singing cantilenas or *canzonettas* together. For the music of night thirteen, they perform 'Donna quanta bellezza e leggiadria' to their lutes, whereas they sing a canzona to their *lironi* for night eleven. This instrument was a large, flat-bridged viol with many sympathetic strings designed for just such chordal accompaniments and is surprisingly prominent in the *Notti*, given its relatively elusive history. For the ninth night, the Signora asks five of the young ladies to sing a *canzonetta* specifically accompanied by two such instruments, which they performed in an angelic manner only to be imagined; the instrument produces a wonderfully ethereal sound, and if there were two of them together – and properly tuned – accompanying the ladies' high voices, the effect may well have been divine indeed.

The affections of these songs, dominated as they were by the humours of love, were undoubtedly an invitation for mannerist renditions employing the subtleties of the human voice and the expressivity of the instruments to achieve the potential sought by the ideals of musical humanism. Such performances were outstanding occasions, moreover, for a show of *sprezzatura*, of making demanding skills appear simple and

26 For further details on these compositions, see Cathy Ann Elias, 'Musical performance in 16th-century Italian literature: Straparola's *Le piacevoli notti*,' *Early Music* 17, no. 2 (1989), pp. 161–74.

spontaneous, so that musical expression might contribute to the graces of courtship. Music was likewise part of the progression of genres that made up the aesthetic designs of the various *soirées*, culminating in the stories and their scherzo-like enigmas, each of which provided a little closing denouement.

In sum, *Le piacevoli notti* is a compendium of tales of striking dissimilarity, yet homogenized into a coherent collection by dint of the charming representation of the carnival activities of Signora Lucrezia and her erudite circle. Through a fiction that may or may not have had a basis in fact, the reader's imagination is carried away to a *locus amoenus* where storytelling and the playful recitation of enigmas take place amid banqueting, dancing, singing, and conversation. This adaptation of the Boccaccian framing tale enabled Straparola to introduce an altogether new repertoire of folk materials, including *novelle*, jests, and tales of fancy and magic, into the recreational activities of the elite. His moralizing introits reflecting humanist culture only partially disguise the novelty. There is hence an appearance of orthodoxy, yet it is deceiving; the work is not a complete imitation of the *Decameron*, but a miscellany of new materials not yet completely naturalized within the world of the book. In all of this, Straparola may have been at least partially mindful of the degree to which his collection was innovative in its style and contents, challenging both the standards of literary decorum and those of social morality. Ultimately, his book appears at the crossroads between learned and popular cultures, originality and plagiarism, decency and immorality, the authorial and the anonymous, the high style of the framing tale and the often low styles of the stories, and finally the crossroads between the folk tale and the fairy tale – one of the most debated features of the work. Still to come are discussions of the tales and their sources (chapter four) and enigmas as a unique and popular genre (chapter five).

III. Polite Society and the Gaming Culture of Renaissance Italy

In the framing device that depicts the ways in which Lucrezia Sforza presides over her salon of young ladies, matrons, and guests, Straparola provides a formulaic representation of a series of recreational *soirées* as an actual series of events, thereby socially contextualizing the delivery of his stories while at the same time providing a provisional template for social gatherings in kind. But this was no novelty, for equally to the point the little society in Murano profiles the social gatherings then in vogue among the Venetian high life in general. In effect, bookish conventions and social practices had become synonymous, enabling authors to present their works as transcriptions of lived events. Many have remarked upon the debt of Straparola's framing tale to the Boccaccian model, having in common the ten narrators, the palazzo, the garden retreat, the organized activities, the inclusion of music, dance, and banqueting (see the end of the fifth night), the choice of a moderator for each day or evening, and the formal procedures of recitation. That he might honour such bookish conventions in a framing device depicting contemporary social practice reveals the degree to which a complex interaction had grown between books and readers. More broadly implicit is that the Boccaccian *cornice* served as a template for social imitation. Subsequent *novellieri*, in modifying the conditions and circumstances surrounding the recitation of their stories, diversified the models upon which readers might base the recitations and improvisations within their own social gatherings. Inversely, the activities of gaming circles could also be reflected in the organization of books, as the present work suggests.[27]

This circularity was fostered throughout the sixteenth century by the new fashion for salon 'games,' which had arisen among the *gens du bien* of Florence, Mantua, Siena, Venice and elsewhere. Their *veglie* or evening entertainments included not only singing, debating, posing riddles, charades, impersonations, impromptu speeches, and memory games in an ambience of flirtation, but the recitation of fictional narratives of many kinds, presided over by a games master or mistress who set the rules of play, imposed civility, and settled disagreements. In time (as in the *Notti*), the Boccaccian frame came to resemble an elaborately 'choreographed'

27 What the Boccaccian framing tale had been during three centuries of efflorescence would entail a lengthy enquiry, but it began in what may be referred to as the 'disaster cornice' in which the storytellers are in refuge from some catastrophe – such as the Florentine plague of 1348, in the case of the *Decameron*, down to the twenty *rescapés* from the sack of Rome in 1527 who, aboard a ship, perform the tales that make up the *Héptameron* of Marguerite de Navarre. New formulas, however, appear in Parabosco's *Diporti* (1552), in which several famous men, including Aretino, go hunting and fishing along the lagoon and are forced indoors by three days of inclement weather, where they wile away the time telling the stories that form the collection. This idea for a frame was contemporary with Straparola's. Sabadino degli Arienti's *Porrettane* (1483) purports to be the tales he heard at the baths of Porretta as recited by a gracious company of noble men and women. The practice of framing tales within increasingly diversified contemporary situations was well established by the mid-sixteenth century. Each one appeals to historical possibility, as though the stories told were the products of an actual event. Straparola follows suit.

evening of games, one that demanded of participants a preliminary repertory not only of tales, but of jests, proverbs, devises, characters, love poems, enigmas, mimicries, caricatures, improvisatory speeches, and more. These were among the requisite knowledge attributes of a successful courtier, along with singing, dancing, and the art of conversation. It was perhaps an instance in which life imitated art as gentlemen and ladies equipped themselves to shine in the world of polite society, while authors and musicians, through the emerging book trade, came to their rescue with new materials imaginatively framed within just such social gatherings. These bookish conventions and the play of illusions constitute some of the best that Straparola had to offer, being precisely the kind of projection of novel realities through print culture that the Venetians had come to love.

Just how a literary convention of the *novellieri* became an urban fad is a chapter in social history only partially written. The format is already clear in Castiglione's *Book of the Courtier*, first published in 1528, which, like Straparola's framing-tale society, is set in former times, for in the opening pages Castiglione describes his work as 'a portrait of the Court of Urbino' involving personalities who by then were deceased.[28] Fundamentally, the book is an elaborate colloquium involving some of the finest and wittiest courtiers of the age in conversation over the qualities of the ideal courtier. That discussion, however, emerges in the context of a series of 'evenings' governed by the conventions of an organized game. The duchess of Urbino, to whom all defer, deputized her Lady Emilia to organize the first evening's entertainment. We are given, as in Straparola, the names of all the distinguished male guests, who freely intermix with the ladies of the court, the latter as equal participants. Emilia then calls upon each of the men to propose a game and their suggestions reveal some of the improvisatory favourites then most in vogue. (Straparola's Signora Lucrezia holds a similar opening forum on the organization of their activities.) Many were flirtatious and bantering in nature, involving love, the battle of the sexes, knowing women's minds, or revealing one's own strengths and weaknesses as a lover. At last, the company in Urbino hits upon a self-laudatory game based on the examination of their own social and courtly virtues. The game is never formally

28 *The Book of the Courtier*, trans. Charles S. Singleton (Garden City, NY: Doubleday, 1959), p. 3. This work was originally published in Venice in 1528, frequently printed thereafter, and translated into several European languages, including English, *The Courtyer of Count Baldesssar Castilio*, trans. Sir Thomas Hoby (London, 1561).

adopted, but emerges through their rich conversation over several evenings, presided over by the appointed mistress. Castiglione not only describes the activities, the ordered sequence of dancing, the musical performances, questions, games, and recitations, but he prescribes the ideal ethos, the decorum, and the graces of the players while cautioning against affectation, calling rather for the cultivation of modesty. In so doing, he creates a template for the age. That they are in the celebrated palace of Urbino enjoying food and song is all part of the Boccaccian convention – superimposed upon a pseudo-historical reality, modified by the procedures for organized play.[29]

This conversational formula, originating perhaps in the medieval love courts in which aristocratic ladies (and sometimes gentlemen) gathered to debate the paradoxes and fine points of conduct according to the precepts of *amour courtois*, had spread by the sixteenth century to the polite salons of the mercantile classes as well as to the academies. In Siena, members of the Intronati held *soirées* with their womenfolk, devising and playing games to wile away the time, even when their city was under siege by the Florentines. A retrospective on their activities was written by Scipione Bargagli in his *I trattenimenti dove da vaghe donne, e da giovani huomini rappresentati sono honesti et dilettevoli giuochi, narrate novelle, e cantata alcune amorose canzonette*, published in Venice in 1587. They spent their evenings playing improvisatory games, telling tales, and playing music in variations upon the formula employed by Straparola. After the conquest of the city, Cosimo I, who was fearful of all manner of potentially seditious gatherings, nevertheless for a time permitted such polite gaming, for in those programmed gatherings there were few opportunities for the subversive. Bargagli describes the social life of the city before 1563 with a tone of nostalgia; after that time, the activities of the Academy of the Intronati, which had fostered such gaming, were suspended for forty years. The games for Bargagli were the epitome of a way of life, an era of social refinement, freedom, and invention that may also have been passing as the spirit of the Counter-Reformation invaded private life.

---

29 Castiglione's account of the courtly life of Urbino, however, is merely a convenient point of reference, for the organized activities of polite society did not begin there. Giovanni da Prato, in his *Paradiso degli Alberti*, written in Florence in 1389, contextualized his stories in the garden of a villa amid dancing and music, in full anticipation of all that was to follow. See the edition by Alessandro Wesselofsky, 4 vols. (Bologna: G. Romagnoli, 1867).

From that same academy (the Intronati) emerged the most influential of all the books of the age on the delectable arts and multiple formats of the gaming evening: Girolamo Bargagli's *Dialogo de' giuochi che nelle vegghie sanesi si usano di fare* (1572), a dialogue about the games that they used to play in Siena.[30] It called for the selection of the master or mistress of the games, to be designated by a laurel wreath in the now familiar fashion, and outlined that person's responsibility for setting the rules, appointing the order of players, maintaining the spirit of polite conduct, and administering rewards and forfeits, such as the pawning of some personal item which could be redeemed only through reciting a tale or poem, or making an amorous pledge. But above all, it was a full set of instructions for the playing of more than 130 social games of recitation and improvisation, summarizing the entire social phenomenon in the process.

The chapters of greatest interest for our purposes contain Bargagli's instructions for the recitation of stories.[31] Above all, they should be new, notable, true to life, yet full of extraordinary and hence memorable events. Ideally, there should be topical continuity linking one story to another, or a contrasting view to provoke conversation. (Straparola's organization is notably feeble in this regard, but not entirely deficient.) Moreover, such narratives should always be pleasing in their delivery, whatever the subject, and tailored to the dignity and tastes of the company, especially by avoiding indulgent sorrow or the mockery of religion. (Just such infractions are the subject of commentary or social reaction in Straparola's collection.) Finally, they should contain examples of liberality, constancy, bravery, loyalty, magnanimity, or their opposites in a cautionary way. These are instructions for improvisatory oral delivery, but aspiring *novella* writers might want to take notice. And if the story is a familiar one, it should be given a freshened appearance, although it was acceptable that some might wish to show their brio in reciting stories verbatim from the *Decameron* as a feat of memory. Isabella, in prefacing her story for the twelfth night (XII.5), openly attributes it to Boccaccio, yet introduces changes which make it more suitable to the tastes of the present company, the matter of decorum on that occasion trumping

30 The work was first published in Siena by Luca Bonetti in 1572, but was reprinted in Venice in 1574, 1575, 1581, 1591, and 1598 in witness of its popularity and influence, and of the activities which it fostered.

31 This discussion comes at the very end of the treatise, *Dialogo de' giuochi*, ed. Patrizia D'Incalci Ermini (Siena: Accdemia senese degli Intronati, 1982), pp. 218–30.

fidelity. Bargagli allows too that narrators may enter into the performance, act out the characters' parts, and speak in appropriate dialects (of which there are examples in the *Nights*). Finally, stories are of two kinds: those that ask only for personal reflection and those that invite group responses by raising questions or *dubbi*, such as determining which character has shown the greatest liberality or performed the most remarkable feat. (Straparola includes several stories in which players and readers are asked to judge: which nun has surpassed the others as in VI.4; which rescuer should marry the heroine, VII.5; who has imposed the meanest trick upon her husband, VIII.1; or who has performed the greatest act of laziness, VIII.1.) Implicit in Bargagli's perspective is that the recitation of such works in a suitably accomplished and engaging way was central to the activities of polite society and an art to be cultivated through wit and memory by those who aspired to membership.

There is documentation from earlier decades, originating in Venice itself, that concerns the culture of polite gaming. One of the most ingenious of recreations was devised and printed by Francesco Marcolini, namely his *Le sorti intitulate giardino di pensieri* (1540), comprising 107 games of fortune played with dice on the pages of the book itself – games that touched upon humanist, artistic, and philosophical *topoi.*[32] The book was embellished with woodcuts by Salviati (not the more famous Florentine-Roman Salviati), emblematically representing the themes of the games. The framing device by which the book was placed into play was composed of an assembly of the Venetian literati gathered in Marcolini's own garden. Once again the book was both a conception for play and the implicit record of a historical event, including a real *locus amoenus* for the gathering, a master of the revels, and a set of rules that conducted the company through the book's pages as a kind of memory theatre through which they visited the repertory of great humanist ideas. It was a harbinger of the gaming culture that was to emerge throughout Italy and an early display of the book as a programmed social event.

At the same time that Straparola published his *Nights*, Innocenzo (Innocentio) Ringhieri published his book of 100 liberal and witty games,

32 Further to this work, see Lina Bolzoni, *The Gallery of Memory: Literary and Iconographic Models in the Age of the Printing Press*, trans. Jeremy Parzen (Toronto: University of Toronto Press, 2001), pp. 117–19.

Cento giuochi liberali et ingegno.[33] This is the only work of the era that does not digress into portraits of gaming societies as elaborate fictions, or into philosophical and moral reflections on the social game, yet it was seminal. Ringhieri presents his activities and their rules *tout court* with almost ethnographic precision, as though they were fading national and folkloric traditions collected from the people and preserved for posterity. His intended audience was identified specifically as lettered and cultivated aristocratic women for whom such games were a vital form of expression and self-definition; men became participants only when they were invited according to the rules set out by the society of women. The work is suffused, moreover, with the conventions of Petrarchan love contained within the games and perpetuated by the inventions called up by the terms of play. In that spirit, each of the ten books closes with a poem in deference to the model set out by the *Decameron*. F. Lecercle refers to the entire collection as 'un *Décameron* ludique' (a 'playing' *Decameron*), which at the same time forms a little utopia, a little world withdrawn into its own idealized and microcosmic order, perfect civility, and social hierarchy.[34] To be sure, these games of attention, verbal dexterity, wordplay, micro-recitations, and *dubbi* are particular in their ethos and execution, for they are intent upon putting players out of action when they are led into error, but the appointment of the games master, the structuring of the social order, the Petrarchan overtones, and the Decameronian conventions participate in the same cultural phenomenon that fostered Straparola's *Notti*.

Even closer in spirit and procedures to Straparola's book is Ascanio de Mori's *Giuoco piacevole* (1574), which is dedicated to Vincenzo Gonzaga, duke of Mantua, for the exclusive use of the ladies of the court.[35] This collection is likewise provided with a historical setting: the city of Brescia at the time of Carnival, 1566. There, a group of young aristocrats found themselves stranded when their theatre play had been cancelled. To wile

33 Ringhieri was Bolognese, and the work was published there by the printer-publisher Anselmo Giaccarelli in 1551, before it was taken to Venice for new editions in 1553 and 1558. It was dedicated to Caterina de' Medici (the queen of France). For a further description of this and related works, see Thomas Frederick Crane, *Italian Social Customs of the Sixteenth Century* (1920; reprint, New York: Russell & Russell, 1971), pp. 285–90.

34 'La culture en jeu: Innocenzo Ringhieri et la Pétrarquisme,' *Les jeux à la renaissance*, ed. Philippe Ariès and Jean-Claude Margolin (Paris: J. Vrin, 1982), pp. 185–200.

35 *Giuoco piacevole* (Mantua: Presso Giacomo Ruffinello, 1574).

away their time, they turned to music and social games, one of them the famous 'Game of Fools' in which each player must describe the form of madness towards which another person present is most inclined. Cesare Gonzaga had proposed the same in Castiglione's *Book of the Courtier*, and it is the same as is described by Bargagli in his *Dialogues* (Nos. 71 & 72), Ringhieri in his *Cento giuochi liberali* (fol. 87, game 71), and Sorel in *Les recreations galantes*, which may in turn have given the idea to Tommaso Garzoni for his *Hospidale de' pazzi incurabili* (1581). This game is a test of social judgment and brinkmanship at its most demanding, but was surely the occasion for much invention, banter, and laughter. Once again, gaming practices and the formatting of a book are brought into close alignment.

Closest to Straparola, however, is the Sienese nobleman, Pietro Fortini, writing just after mid-century; his *Le giornate delle novelle de' novizi* and *Le piacevoli et amorose notte de' novizi* appear frequently among the commentaries on the stories to follow. Without any conceivable possibility that either knew the work of the other, they hit upon common narrative materials and devised similar story collections reflecting the gaming *Zeitgeist*. Fortini's books offer models for the playing of 'narratives,' which were often used as 'forfeits' or punitive recitations in the context of other games. His five young women and two young men meet in a garden where, first, they weave a crown for the 'Lord' of the gathering, and then proceed with the recitations, intermixed with singing and dining. Appropriately, the songs are *canzonettas*. On the third day, two of the women sing; on the fourth, Ippolito performs a solo to the *gravicembalo* or harpsichord; and on the seventh day the men sing a dialogue about the palace of Venus and the wiles of fortune. The readings are followed by a grand supper served to the strains of a hidden consort and the performance of a comedy.[36] Here again, a fictive society prompts an anthology of narratives that is designed to serve real future gatherings. It is a theatricalized set of *veglie*, a collection of *novelle*, a Boccaccian nod, and a book of game narratives intended for the training of 'novices' aspiring to perform at such fashionable gatherings.

The intent of this survey is to reveal the specific social practices then in vogue to which Straparola's *Notti* contributes. His stories are stories

36 Each day has a new 'gallant lady' or 'gentleman cavalier' as leader. The company engages in a great deal of banter and love play. Day six is given over to it entirely, while day five had been devoted to the disorderly lives of monks and nuns. There were forty-nine works in all.

and his book a miscellany, but it is conceived as a social event of a specific historical kind. For a more comprehensive account of the entertainments and cultural practices of Italian Renaissance polite society in the 'age of Straparola,' Thomas Frederick Crane's chapter on the 'Parlor Games in Italy in the Sixteenth Century' remains a standard introduction.[37] It serves to corroborate the importance of contextualizing Straparola's literary endeavour within the gaming culture then fashionable in courtly and elite circles. Storytelling had gained a new venue for presentation, further enabling the movement of *favole* from echelon to echelon in a vertical society through the pressures of demand and supply. That the activities within Straparola's book were redolent of practices at large, representing them both descriptively and prescriptively through the framing tale tradition of the *novellieri*, is one of its most salient features. In this regard, the design vacillates between a mere repository of narratives and the employment of stories as 'turns' in an organized sequence of play. At the same time, the thriving Venetian book trade, in search of novelty and an expanded clientele, found that it could exploit the mode by creating anthologies of stories apt for reading or recitation during the 'pleasant evenings' or *veglie* of polite society. In that circularity, authors found new and playful modes of layered social representation.

As a coda, it may be added that the procedures involving folk materials and their integration into the gaming activities of the elite were extended into the composition of madrigals. In light of the demonstrated musical talents of those in Straparola's coterie of performers, it is perhaps not so extraordinary that a demand arose for music books in which activities pertaining to the games were incorporated into madrigal cycles representing, in their aggregate, fictional social occasions into which the singers might project themselves. Such games and social vignettes involving mimicry, tongue twisters, characters, and Petrarchan inventions in social

37 *Italian Social Customs of the Sixteenth Century* (1920; reprint, New York: Russell & Russell, 1971), chap. 6, pp. 263–322, which also contains a brief account of the framing-tale society in Straparola's *Nights*, pp. 292–4. Crane, for example, describes the *Discorsi* of Annibale Romei and the games and recitations performed at the Este court (ca. 1578) with the countess of Scandiano as the Queen of the Games (p. 231), as well as the activities of several of the polite gatherings described in the *novelle* of Bandello; for example, the group of Venetians who convened in the palazzo of Signor Cesare Fregoso in Verona (pt. II, no. 10), where they are treated to a Lucullian banquet followed by dancing, games, a discussion of the *Decameron*, and storytelling of their own (p. 249). All such descriptions extend the portrait of the social world which Straparola recreates as the context for his tales.

settings created through music began to appear in the late 1560s with Alessandro Striggio's *Il cicalamento* about women scrapping with one another while washing clothes before making up and retiring to a bakery for treats. But the most pertinent among them is Orazio Vecchi's *Veglie di Siena* (1604), a collection of forty-six madrigals subdivided into three evenings of games in the Sienese fashion in which the same singers take the turns of all the personalities in the gaming set – including Margherita who, for the life of her, cannot get her *bisticcio* or tongue twister right, despite the fact that the same singers had just shown her how while representing the games master. Here is convention upon convention through several mimetic levels, and it is all quite wonderful. The madrigalists together perform all the requisite parts from choosing the leader to offering social commentary upon the contributions made by each player. Vecchi turned to popular culture for his materials, whether in the imitation of foreign or local dialects, the street cries of the vendors, or the word games of children.[38] Musical settings add one further dimension to the gaming culture such as it was enacted in polite societies in ways that marked and defined an era.

IV. Folk Culture, Wonder Tales, and Fairy Tales

A typical profile of affairs to emerge in the commentaries to follow upon many of the individual stories is that they contain familiar motifs known from medieval *fabliaux* or romances, saints' lives, or jest books, but that in their present forms are the first of their kind to be written down. Arguably, that paradox can only be resolved through a glimpse into the culture of folklore. The data in the commentaries points to a centuries-long pattern of literary borrowing from story traditions of the 'folk' on the part of many medieval and Renaissance writers, stories that otherwise never found 'whole cloth' representation in the literary record before the publication of the *Piacevoli notti.* The implication for Straparola is that he worked with sources, not one of which survives independently,

---

38 Orazio Vecchi, *Le veglie di Siena* (The night games of Siena), ed. Donald Beecher (Ottawa: The Institute of Mediaeval Music, 2004). Other musicians of the era were instrumental in bringing folk music to high culture, such as Luca Marenzio, who introduced both 'Girometta' and 'La bella Franceschina' into his madrigals along with other musical representations based on the *canti carnascialeschi* – carnival songs in which members of the trade classes sing of their wares and occupations, often in a state of inebriation.

thereby precluding any final judgment about his habits as a writer. Nevertheless, we are not without *comparative* versions. When folklorists began their systematic collecting and cataloguing of the European folk tale after the middle of the nineteenth century, nearly all of Straparola's forty or more '*novelle*' and 'wonder' tales reappeared in at least a few cognate versions. Just what that implies is crucial to an appraisal of his work. Complex stories sharing a common nucleus of narrative order and a common vocabulary of literary motifs – sufficient to warrant a single designation in the Aarne-Thompson-Uther type index – arguably must belong to a single story tradition, given the near impossibility for two such creations to have been independently generated.[39] If the 'same' story, by these criteria, is told by Straparola and by a nineteenth-century raconteur in Lorraine or Iceland, then Straparola's story must have given rise to the same story all over Europe, or more plausibly must be a close version of that story as it existed among the popular traditions in the sixteenth century. In brief, I take the representation of the tales in Straparola as the first 'hard evidence' of their existence in the oral culture of the Renaissance, even though the many allusions to folk characters and motifs in the literatures of prior centuries give proof for many of their greater antiquity. At the same time, the folk record assembled in the nineteenth century – as in the case of 'Cesarino the Dragon Slayer' (X.3) or 'Constantino Fortunato and his Wonderful Cat' (XI.1) – offers hundreds of variants from across the whole of the Eurasian continent, revealing how such stories become diversified over time and occur in many geographical regions. Such a process entails a 'theory of evolution' of its own pertaining to the survival and adaptation of transmitted narratives. The implication for Straparola is that many of his stories appear to have been captured from the repertory of oral tales as they were recited in his era and in his region of the continent; his contribution was to fix each of them in a published record. Stated otherwise, Straparola's

39 Joseph Bédier, for example, made an assault on the one-locale theory concerning the origins of complex folk tales and promoted the theory of 'polygenesis.' Slicing between these choices does not greatly affect an appraisal of Straparola in relation to the great labyrinth of implied stemmata representing the spread and interrelationships of these stories. But the argument that the same complex story could originate in several places, as opposed to dissemination through memory and orality from a single source, seems intuitively less logical or possible. Joseph Bédier, *Les fabliaux: Études de literature populaire et d'histoire littéraire du moyen âge* (Paris: Honoré Champion, 1893).

literary productions are typically bookended by fragmentary or variant versions of the tales in former works of literature, as well as by the later renditions collected by folklorists. His participation must hence be calibrated in relation to the cultural practices whereby these stories maintained their identities over centuries independent of their occasional literary adaptations – adaptations from which it is inconceivable for the original folk tales to have been restored.

But these are troubled waters. The nature of folk literature and its genres remains at the centre of intense critical debate on many fronts. Who are the folk? What distinguishes their modes of creativity? How many kinds of popular tales are there? Must they be presented orally? Are they invariably corrupted in the process of committing them to print? More specifically, is Straparola a proto-folklorist or merely another of the *novellieri* basing his stories on popular narratives? After all, many of the preceding writers of *novelle* had found inspiration in folk tales. And what should his stories be called? Straparola employed the word '*favole*,' conveying all the equivocal characteristics of 'fable'; it would appear to be a discerning choice. But is it because the fable's miraculous elements and imaginary setting can never happen in the 'real' world, whereas the *novella*'s setting, characters, and action allow for a basis in actual social events?[40] The problem with Straparola's employment of the term is that it refers to all of the stories in the collection and not merely to the seventeen 'wonder tales'; it is not a synonym for 'fairy tale.' The others, although far-fetched and fanciful, even implausible in the extreme, nevertheless feign to have happened in real places and to realistic people at some possible moment in time. Yet they too remain *favole* to his way of thinking. Is it because of their affiliation with folk culture? Is it thus that he distinguishes himself from the *novellieri*? Is it because *favole* are anonymous in nature, stories with established and persistent histories, because they are passed down from generation to generation by word of mouth and hence belong to oral culture?[41] The connotations of

40 Both are distinguished from *historia*, which, at least in terms of persons, places, and events, professes actually to have happened in real times and locations, despite elements of confabulation.

41 Stefano Calabrese grapples with this issue in defining the word *fiabe*. Tales are stories outside of official culture, less realistic, often employing magic; they are tolerant of distortion, of things that are impossible, serving as toys of the imagination. *Gli arabeschi della fiaba* (Pisa: Pacini, 1984), pp. 39*ff.* A more sustained study of the folk tale is Max Lüthi's *The European Folktale: Form and Nature*, trans. John D.

this term may express as much as we can know about Straparola's awareness of the uniqueness of the materials he selected, or his awareness of himself as a proto-folklorist.

By inference, if Straparola's book is a representative anthology of popular literature under the aegis of the *favole*, then *novelle*, jests, social vignettes, lives of the saints, *fabliaux*, and sermon exempla, in parallel to their representations in print culture, were also in circulation among the 'folk.' That there is so little distinction between the oral and the literary in terms of content and story types may even prove disconcerting. What, then, demarcates the folk *novella* from the literary *novella*? It can only be the legacy or simple fact of oral provenance.

A matter of critical debate is the degree of contamination produced by literary transcription and the fidelity of the tales in relation to their oral recitals. At stake is whether the collection has any validity as a record of popular narrative art. Does not the stylist in the man, especially one with novelistic ambitions, turn transcription to treason, as the old adage has it? N.M. Penzer, in his preface to Giambattista Basile's *Pentamerone*, takes for granted that 'in the pages of all these writers the tales were regularized and often metamorphosed into bourgeois stories shorn as far as possible of the marvelous and nearly always related in the traditional style of the Italian *novellieri*. This was the case even of Straparola, of whom Grimm wrote that "he strove to tell his stories according to the prescribed and customary form and did not know how to strike a new cord [*sic*]," and only on two occasions, almost as if he foresaw the need of a new form, did he resort to dialect.'[42] In short, many critics in the past have been certain that Straparola had but one voice and style – that of the *novella* writer – and that his stories were rewritten and enhanced to meet the stylistic tastes of his elite and mercantile class readerships.

Niles (Bloomington: Indiana University Press, 1986). He seeks to anatomize the genre by its generic characteristics, using such terms as 'one-dimensionality' in the mingling of the natural and supernatural in a single world; 'depthlessness,' or the absence of psychological motivation or life histories of the characters; 'abstract style,' a plain, essential narrative style without embellishment and metaphor; 'isolation and universal interconnection,' or a lack of long relationships that bring about character growth; and 'sublimation and all-inclusiveness,' or an archetypal scope with thematic potential because of the lack of limitations imposed by realism (p. 73). Many of Straparola's tales find apt description in these terms.

42 *The Pentamerone*, trans. Benedetto Croce, 2 vols. (1932; reprint, Westport, CT: Greenwood Press, 1979), p. xlviii; Jacob and Wilhelm Grimm, *Kinder- und Hausmächen* (Göttingen: Dieterich, 1856), vol. III, p. 291.

We have been over this ground before. Penzer assumes that every recorder of fairy tales based on popular models seeks to make them conform, in all essential ways, to the stylistic norms of literary culture. Peter Burke does not go so far, for he honours Straparola as an early collector of popular literature, yet takes for granted that many of the formulas of orality are lost in the transcription: 'In prose there is not the same need for formulae of this kind [the repeated phrases and stock diction still prominent in poetry] to help the performer along; it is also possible that the folktales from the early modern period which have come down to us in collections like those of Straparola or Timoneda lost their formulae in the course of preparation for the printer.'[43] The first temptation to betrayal is the lure of conventional literary forms and styles.

Another challenge, as already mentioned in the discussion of the author versus the compiler, is the compromised capacity to transcribe with precision. One of the early recorders of folk tales was Lucius, who revealed a common dilemma when he overheard, in the form of a donkey, the tale of Cupid and Psyche, which forms the centrepiece of Apuleius's *The Golden Ass*: 'I stood not far off, grieving by Hercules! that I had no tablet and pen to note down so pretty a nonsense.'[44] The option is to fill in from what can be remembered, or simply to recreate the *fabula* in one's own literary image, as when Apuleius imposed the pantheon of gods upon an old wives' tale told to a girl in prison. In retrospect we know that the tale of Psyche is far from the originating folk tale, versions of which persisted long enough to supply the source for 'Beauty and the Beast.' Lucius's lament, however, has to do with memory. We can only imagine how Straparola came by so substantial a repertory of popular narratives and what combination of internal and external 'devices' he employed to retain what he had heard: rote mental retention, repetition, an impromptu mnemonics system, notes, or shorthand. There are not many options, and no one has suggested that Straparola was himself a professional storyteller who merely inscribed his repertory at the end of his career. The alternative is partial reconstruction and literary confabulation.[45]

---

43 *Popular Culture in Early Modern Europe* (1978; reprint, Aldershot: Ashgate, 1999), p. 131.

44 Trans. Jack Lindsay (Bloomington: Indiana University Press, 1965), p. 142.

45 The critic to read on the corruption of folk literature through literary transcription is Albert Wesselski in his *Versuch einer Theorie des Märchen*, Prager Deutsche Studien 45 (Reichenberg: F. Kraus, 1931). He is followed in this stance by Michèle Simonsen

Yet if Straparola was compelled to rely upon his own vocabulary, fall back on his personal habits of syntax, and compensate for his flaws in memory, so was every reciter in the oral tradition. For while it is well to speak of popular culture as the collective creation of 'the folk,' the act of transmission is carried out by individuals, each with his or her own lexicon, sense of style, and habits of memory, along with the characteristic deletions and substitutions concerning peripheral detail or the recombinant parts of the plot whereby the tale might be accommodated to his or her times and auditors.[46] Turning to literary habits, Basile in *Lo cunto de li cunti* (The Pentamerone), despite the look of authenticity in his use of local dialect, reshaped the spontaneous recitations of the popular imagination with his own ingenious and picturesque diction, full of wit, craft, and baroque exuberance. Straparola, by contrast, has been slated for his flat and under-fashioned style as one of the least gifted of the *novellieri*, a writer who produced formulaic plots devoid of descriptive detail, characters short on interiority, and who spoke in simple and unadorned language.[47] Ironically, this may be a smoking gun with regard to his preservation of the folk styles and iterative designs. Stylistic evidence in kind will be taken up towards the end of this chapter. From a different perspective, Straparola's fidelity is implicit in the cases of those

in *Le conte populaire* (Paris: Presses universitaires de France, 1984), p. 19. See also Robert Scholes and Robert Kellogg, *The Nature of Narrative* (Cambridge, MA: Harvard University Press, 1966), p. 23.

46 That oral is distinct from written narrative is not so much a matter of its contents as of its mode of production and the formal particularities that inhere in oral literature because of its techniques of transmission. Many of these features are preserved in the literary transcriptions of oral literature. The matter has been much investigated from the time of Milman Parry, whose theories were brought into full view by Albert B. Lord in *The Singer of Tales* (1960; reprint, Cambridge, MA: Harvard University Press, 2000). Their combined analysis of the singer's attachment to tradition, the use of poetic formulas, the levels of mastery, the schemata for retention, and the shaping of the work through these processes has established the terms of discussion for all subsequent generations of scholars. They were principally concerned with epic traditions and the orality of Homer, but many of the principles pertain to the orality of shorter forms in the popular tradition, including works in prose.

47 Giuseppe Rua, despite his grasp of Straparola's connection to folk culture, viewed him essentially as one of the *novellieri* – and one of the least notable, particularly in his failure to study sentiment and the creation of interiorized characters, separating him from Grazzini, Bandello, and Giraldi. *Tra antiche fiabe e novelle: Le piacevoli notti di Messer Gian Francesco Straparola* (Rome: Ermanno Loescher, 1898), p. 111.

stories that are closely approximated in design and ethos by later tales which arguably preserve in later years the very order of narrative that inspired Straparola. The argument appears weaker than the sheer fact of the striking correspondences themselves, many of which will be profiled in the commentaries to follow. Arguably, those resemblances could not have occurred if he had tampered inordinately with the integrity of the stories as he heard them. Hence Michel Bideaux may have the last word, after all, that 'Straparola was sufficiently inspired by these creations of the popular imagination that he felt no need to spoil them by refined literary elaboration.'[48] Vittorio Rossi concurs that Straparola was 'satisfied to work in the special mode of collecting from the oral tradition the fables of the people and to retell them exactly as he found them without touching and altering anything at all concerning the marvelous and supernatural ... The tales did not shed their original ingenuity or their spirit of sympathy ...'[49] In consequence, with allowances for essential stylizing and the occasional flourish, Straparola's 'creations' remain representative renditions of the versions upon which they are based.

We can never know whether Straparola collected in cottages, mercantile households, or palazzi, whether from professional bards or elderly women, but to understand Straparola's enterprise we must imagine the scope of Renaissance storytelling culture, for every village and town had its raconteurs, both men and women, and stories were told at all echelons of society, from hovel to court. They were told in workshops and households and they were passed down from generation to generation as vehicles of delight and instruction.[50] The point is of singular importance, not only because Straparola is thereby provided with ubiquitous sources, once the idea is conceived of collecting such materials, but because the pervasiveness of that parallel culture intimates not only a contemporary circulation of stories, but a template for a culture that reaches across vast

---

48 Gabriel Chappuys, *Les facetieuses journées*, ed. Michel Bideaux (Paris: Honoré Champion, 2003), p. 129 (my translation).

49 *Storia della letteratura italiana* (Milan: Vallardi, 1906), p. 351 (my translation).

50 Much of far greater specificity than can be offered here on the spread of folk tales in the Renaissance is to be found in Peter Burke's chapter on 'The Transmission of Popular Culture' in his *Popular Culture in Early Modern Europe* (Aldershot: Ashgate, 1999), pp. 91–115, concerning the professional and amateur raconteurs, their ubiquity, their repertories, and their audiences. For the important part played by women, including the proverbial 'old wives,' in the transmission of folk tales, see Marina Warner, *From the Beast to the Blonde: On Fairy Tales and Their Tellers* (London: Vintage, 1995), 'The Old Wives' Tale: Gossips I,' pp. 12–25.

times and spaces back to antiquity and beyond. As Milman Parry projected backwards from contemporary recitations of Yugoslavian epics, we may project similarly from the story cultures of the nineteenth century on the assumption that equivalents of the practices that kept these tales alive existed in former times.

In projecting recent past practices upon more remote past practices, James M. Taggart's book entitled *Enchanted Maidens: Gender Relations in Spanish Folktales of Courtship and Marriage* is most instructive.[51] Working in rural Spain, Taggart documented practices and interviewed storytellers who explained how they had learned their repertory from family members, how new stories emerged from faraway places, and how some were taken over from books, memorized, and circulated in the oral culture. Older and younger generations were involved in the process. They specified how they had heard the same stories many times over the years and how the most talented in these arts achieved reputations and were in demand. They demonstrated reciting techniques and told how the performers asked for nods and answers, played the audience, and recited in dramatized voices. Some trained regularly and had formidable memories. Stories were also constantly on the move, arriving with new marriage partners, by travel and resettlement, or through travelling merchants. Taggart tells more particularly of the paprika seed pickers in groups of ten to twenty women who, like the tobacco workers, would tell stories as they worked.[52] Of particular interest is the manner in which narratives were communally invigilated and how the reciters were sometimes interrupted to be corrected. It was important in all contexts, as a matter of authority, that stories were retold exactly as they were heard and that a conservative sense of the tradition prevailed. At the same time, through a slow process of repetition, rationalization, and accretion, variations emerged and the stories slowly evolved through reconstruction, improvements to logical coherence, contamination from other stories, or conscious accommodation to local settings and concerns. Such stories become patterned and iterative in unique ways, performing their 'work' with narrative efficiency and transparency. These practices and values must, in some critical sense, be imputed to the practitioners of oral culture in all ages, without which there could be no evidential rapport among stories separated by such tracts of time – and of which Straparola's transcriptions bear evidence.

51 (Princeton: Princeton University Press, 1990).
52 James M. Taggart, *Enchanted Maidens*, p. 36.

That Straparola was working with folk sources is further confirmed for Burke by the prominence of triple patterns in the structural layers and iterative actions of his work – patterns which characterize folk narratives to the point of obsession. Characters are often grouped in threes in order to carry out triple quests, as when two brothers search for a third, or when three siblings go on a quest for the dancing water, the singing apple, and the truth-speaking bird. Burke takes Straparola in hand and begins with the three opening stories. 'In the first, a man is told by his dying father to observe three precepts; he breaks them one by one. In the second, an official defies a thief to steal three objects, but the thief succeeds. In the third, a priest is tricked by three rogues, but revenges himself on them in three stages. All of these illustrate what Olrik called "the Law of Three," another of his "laws of folk narrative."'[53] These are the simple repetitions with variations that lead to structured climaxes at an anticipated rate. The triplicity or trinary rule may be calibrated to the limits of audience memory, or to minimal but sufficient narrative density and variety, as well as to simple plot design: a father's interdiction, a son's methodical disobedience, and the felt consequences, as in the first story. The degree of Straparola's stylistic grooming is difficult to assess with precision, but in substance and design the stories carry so many features of the oral tradition that folk provenance becomes nearly self-evident.

The proclivities of human memory, its strengths and weaknesses in the process, can only be mentioned here, but clearly memory is the vital factor in the remarkable stability of the generic plots, while, at the same time, it is the active agent in the gradual evolution of the particulars whereby nearly every substantive element of character, setting, and stylistic register may receive alteration. It is this much-studied yet quasi-mysterious process that accounts for the idiosyncrasies of the 'folk' style, the stratified plot designs, the generic characters, and the gradual transformations that give rise to the major and minor variants that distinguish stories separated by time and geography.[54] Thus a perception of

53 *Popular Culture in Early Modern Europe* (Aldershot: Ashgate, 1999), p. 138.

54 On these matters, see Jocelyn Penny Small, *Wax Tablets of the Mind: Cognitive Studies of Memory and Literacy in Classical Antiquity* (London: Routledge, 1997); and Thomas L. Charlton et al., eds., *Handbook of Oral History* (Lanham, MD: Altamira Press, 2006), esp. Elinor Maz, 'Memory Theory,' and Mary Chamberlain, 'Publishing Oral History: Oral Exchange and Print Culture.'

substitutions and slippages exists alongside a sense of the remarkable staying power of the central narrative fuse, the story 'type,' many of which have persisted over centuries, allowing for the comparative grouping of literally hundreds of variants.

This entire discussion may appear to be drifting away from Straparola's endeavours, but as stated at the outset, nearly all of the annotations to follow are predicated on the reality of this vast network of storytelling, the work of oral traditions reaching back to antiquity and outward to remote regions of the world where traces exist of the same stories told by Straparola, thereby linking his 'fables' to this 'ocean' of stories.[55] The procedures for handling folklore are not universally agreed upon and thus specific critical approaches require their rationales – hence my anxiety. To begin with, the structural associations among stories do not appear to be merely comparative, as though such variants emerged by coincidence, but the result of an underlying kinship created by the centrifugal force inherent in good stories – stories transmitted through hundreds of minds and corrected on a feedback basis to retain the integrity of their respective identities. Thus what holds true for Jan Ziolkowski concerning the cognate relationships between certain tales from the Latin Middle Ages and their reappearances in the Grimms' *Kinder- und Hausmärchen* holds equally true for Straparola's tales, their sources, and their analogues.[56] Where scattered elements of these stories appear in the medieval literary record, they may at times be literary allusions, but in light of the variants, they are far more readily explained as independent borrowings from the folk – borrowings of specific renditions of the respective story types as they were passed along through the

55 The image is made in reference to Somadeva's great tenth- or eleventh-century Sanskrit story anthology, the *Katha sarit sagara* (The ocean of the streams of stories). The overtones of this title are of a collection that represents the cumulative stories of a people, each told as a variant on the preceding story, progressing systemically through all the phases of human nature, human institutions, and memorable social challenges. It is as though for everything there is a story and that when all stories are told, the anatomy of the species is made manifest.

56 His recent yet seminal study, *Fairy Tales from Before Fairy Tales: The Medieval Latin Past of Wonderful Lies* (Ann Arbor: University of Michigan Press, 2007), is a source of valuable perspectives on the antiquity and transmission of popular literature, the Latin (thus learned) heritage, and the challenge of nomenclature and story taxonomy.

vast network of folk raconteurs.[57] This assessment recurs often in the ensuing commentaries as the only plausible explanation of the data that are present.

To posit only this much is to assume a number of critical hypotheses concerning the folk tale which I might otherwise do well not to formulate. My work is not as a folklorist per se, but as an editor of tales with affinities to a world of tales. But those associations led me progressively to a series of hypotheses: that Straparola's tales cannot be contextualized without a context, which in turn depends upon an historical reconstruction of the story types of which his are often the earliest recorded versions. The reconstruction of those histories entails the recognition of

57 Ruth Bottigheimer represents a dissenting view in 'consciously reject[ing] a deeply ingrained and widespread prejudice against the concept of the literary creation of tales that have long been defined as quintessentially "folk" in nature.' She does so 'because no evidence supports that belief, despite the nearly universal assumption that authors like Straparola "appropriated popular lore" (Zipes 1997, 1800), imitated "origini orale" [*sic*] (Mazzacurati 1971, 77–81 *passim*), or wrote down oral tradition (Pozzi 1981, 20).' *Fairy Godfather: Straparola, Venice, and the Fairy Tale Tradition* (Philadelphia: University of Pennsylvania Press, 2002), p. 6. Her principal objective is to assert Straparola's authorship of the several 'rising'-type fairy tales in which paupers become rich and marry princesses, such as XI.1, 'Constantino,' a prototype for 'Puss in Boots.' Bottigheimer's views have been published in a long article entitled '*Fairy Godfather*, Fairy-Tale History, and Fairy-Tale Scholarship: A Response to Dan Ben-Amos, Jan M. Ziolkowski, and Francisco Vaz da Silva,' in the *Journal of American Folklore* 123, no. 490 (2010), pp. 447–96. The larger question is whether the fairy tale, per se, is a literary invention and a product of Renaissance book culture or a genre of the folk with mysterious origins reaching back to antiquity. This debate has served to bring Straparola to the centre among folklorists in recent years. Jack Zipes, in *The Irresistible Fairy Tale: The Cultural and Social History of a Genre*, goes beyond this immediate debate to explore the qualities of the fairy tale in relation to the origins of story as a phylogenetic human characteristic representing our deepest motives for communication, our earliest capacities for imaginative play, the preservation of our cultural 'memes' through their competitive appeal on the basis of their evolutionary adaptation to human nature, and our long-standing practice of inventing imaginative tales of places and beings that never existed, yet which compel our deepest attention. At the end, however, he returns specifically to the discussion concerning the sixteenth-century literary origin of fairy tales proposed by Bottigheimer in his Appendix A, 'Sensationalist Scholarship: A "New" History of Fairy Tales,' *The Irresistible Fairy Tale* (Princeton: Princeton University Press, 2012), pp. 157–73, in which he provides a summary of the accumulating evidence supporting the antiquity of wonder tales with and without fairies and their anonymous shaping through the practices of oral culture reaching back into the Middle Ages and beyond. It has been a bracing polemic.

'types' and a sense of their historico-geographic diffusion. That diffusion, moreover, depends upon a theory of genesis, whether all tales in the group must ensue from a common source (monogenesis) or may also arise coincidentally in more than one location (polygenesis). The 'types' involved must also be anatomized through a morphological reduction to the common denominators that distinguish one tale from another, on the assumption that we are computationally reliable in the identification of signature elements.[58] Comparison is hardly possibly otherwise. These are among the necessary critical prerequisites for imagining the historical place of Straparola's tales within a sprawling subculture of folk narrative. Support is taken from Peter Burke's placement of Straparola at the centre of a discussion of folk motifs as the semi-independent building blocks which recur in folk tales, noting their aptness for cataloguing. Thus, 'if we take the tales which Straparola published in 1550 and look them up in Thompson's motif-index, it soon becomes clear that they contain many well-known themes.'[59] He then follows with several examples illustrating the moveable motifs and their configurations in specific stories. Whether the principles involved in creating these formations constitute a 'grammar' or conform to 'schemata' is work for the folklorists, but the existence of such a repertory of motifs will find demonstration throughout the commentaries to follow. For further perspectives on the nature of memory, and on the formation of narrative units and motifs as well as their systemic modification, see the opening paragraphs of the Commentary on IV.3, 'The Truth-Speaking Bird.'

58 Thus, on occasion, I make use of Carl Wilhelm von Sydow's *oikotype* as a useful term designating the 'home' type. It carries critical baggage of its own, because it assumes that tales begin with a master version from which all the others spread out, fitting themselves into their respective eco-niches. The term was first applied to generic plants which later became diversified through the pressure of new environments. It is a valuable model for thinking about the organic processes of 'meme' survival in human memory – of stories that cheer and find repetition, or that cloy and die, or that in their complexity defy memory and redelivery. But *oikotype* does not here, as it may have for its founder, signify an *Ur-tale*, for there is no certainty that such tales ever existed in full original versions. Even so, it is useful at times to speak of a 'home' type when there are distinct branches splitting off at historical moments from a common source. This will become clear in the history of 'the three brothers' type (VII.5), and the complex relationship the mutants maintain with their common source, including Straparola's variant.

59 *Popular Culture in Early Modern Europe* (Aldershot: Ashgate, 1999), p. 132.

Such an approach, meanwhile, raises concerns among those intent upon escaping the tyranny of source studies as the only test and criterion of the Renaissance fable. The obsession with origins potentially obscures the many other ways in which these stories may be studied, whether thematically, narratologically, culturally, comparatively, stylistically, or in relation to audience reception and book production.[60] For an assessment of Straparola in relation to the great ocean of stories, however, it is nearly impossible to avoid theorizing about the production of the folk tale. Those interconnections are to be established not only on comparative grounds, but on an implicitly filiational basis, even if those stemmata cannot be precisely or specifically reconstructed. Perhaps the problem is in the label itself: 'source studies.' The remarkable irony in the case of Straparola is that we have no sources for his tales, only vast story traditions – which, in the absence of any proof of invention on his part, become the principal contexts of his tales. We know them according to their properties of membership. Nevertheless, I do not see the investigation of structural motifs as incompatible with many other forms of study, whether comparative, thematic, mythological, stylistic, or cultural, all of which are pursued in the commentaries. My interest in all these approaches, in fact, gave me too much to do in the commentaries that follow.

The commission to research Straparola's tales as part of that 'ocean' of international folklore was made by Giovanni Macchia in the introduction to his edition of *Le piacevoli notti* (1943). He accepted the profound connection these stories had to oral culture, acknowledged the interchange of motifs, and recognized the need to situate them in relation to this vast narrative world, even as he cautioned against the pitfalls of undertaking so demanding a task. From his perspective in the early 1940s, the oral tradition and the origins of folk stories posed seemingly insoluble problems – problems of the same order as those concerning Straparola's influence on subsequent authors from Shakespeare to Perrault. 'These matters are dense like a millenarian forest, which, to

60 Giancarlo Mazzacurati in 'La narrativa di Giovan Francesco Straparola e l'ideologia del fiabesco,' *All'ombra di Dioneo: Tipologie e percorsi della novella da Boccaccio a Bandello,* ed. Matteo Palumbo (Florence: La nuova Italia [Scandicci], 1996), pp. 151–2. This is echoed by Ute Heidmann as 'an epistemological problem that arises when tales are systematically treated as folklore according to their types' insofar as this reductionist approach for the sake of classification impoverishes the grounds for comparative study or 'dialogue intertextuel.' *Textualité et intertextualité des contes* (Paris: Garnier classiques, 2010), pp. 20, 37, 40.

penetrate, entails the risk of enchantment, the risk of forgetting the principal work that gave rise to the trip. If in certain ways [*Le piacevoli notti*] resembles a scientific puzzle, in others it is like a romantic charm which approaches a literature without place or time, full of shadows, not spoiled by history.'[61] This was my 'Bluebeard's Castle.' A trek through this forest, following the story leads from record to record, seemed the surest means for taking the measure of Straparola's many narratives – not as trees in a homogenous forest, to tweak the metaphor, but as individual trees along their respective forest paths.[62] Nevertheless, the caveat concerning distraction is well taken, for story traditions are potentially seductive and can easily draw the investigator down many a literary byway. Given the abundance of the undergrowth, even the copious annotations to follow have been terminated at arbitrary points of mere sufficiency. The endless forest, to mix metaphors, had to be contained and selectively managed. Thus when redundancy threatened or potential accounts of cognate tales became incrementally less instructive, the commentaries were rounded off by condensing a great deal of matter into lists accompanied by fat footnotes for the benefit of the curious.

Concerning the precocity of Straparola's ethnographic enterprise, speculation is free as to why folk tales were never collected in former years in the same concentrated and consistent manner. One theory pertains to the rigid separation between high and low cultures, the elite and the folk, the written and the oral. Yet even Latin, the language of the

---

61 G.F. Straparola, *Le piacevoli notti*, ed. Giovanni Macchia (1943; reprint, Milan: Bompiano, 1952), 'Introduction,' p. x (my translation). The spirit of Macchia's commission was anticipated sixty years earlier by W.G. Waters, who stated in his 'Introduction' that 'it is hard to say what new and strange fruits may not be gathered from the wide field now covered by the folk-lorist. Formerly he hunted only in the East; now we find him among the Lapps and the Zulus – in Labrador, and in the South Pacific as well. A still more extended search will very likely find a fresh source for those of the fables in the "Notti" which have heretofore been classed as the original work of Straparola, and will discover for us a new and genuine author of "Puss in Boots."' *The Nights of Straparola* (London: Lawrence & Bullen, 1894), vol. I, p. xxvi.

62 There is concurrence in this view on the part of Graham Anderson. Writers who borrow from the oral tradition take on their motifs and character types, yet 'very little attention has been paid to the depth and extent of their borrowings and the intercultural layers of their tales.' Thus, he deemed the work of locating sources and analogues as 'extremely important' if we want to know how the genre of the fairy tale emerged and stabilized itself. *Fairy Tales and the Ancient World* (London: Routledge, 2000), p. xii.

Church, the schools, and international diplomacy, had been employed now and again in the telling of folk tales, if only for pedagogical reasons, during the more open centuries after AD 1000 – before the remnants of pre-Christian lore came under theological and inquisitorial scrutiny. Elements of folk culture abound in such miscellanies as Egbert of Liège's (b. 972) *Fecunda ratis*, Walter Map's (d. 1209) *De nugis curialium*, and Gervase of Tilbury's (d. 1220) *Otia imperialia*, while the names Boccaccio and Chaucer speak for themselves. The cumulative annotations to follow will bear abundant testimony to the extensive appropriation of folk materials in medieval romance, *fabliaux*, saints' lives, exempla collections, and jest books. Traces of the stories are everywhere, but they are never represented as being of the folk, and the conventions of more formalized genres prevail. Straparola, in that regard, is entirely ambiguous in styling himself as an author while at the same time disclaiming authorship of the stories, and in replicating the folk structures while importing bits of humanist phraseology and adding certain appurtenances of the *novella*. Nevertheless, his production was a first of its kind, a concentrated effort, the product of a 'moment' in the sense of the term developed by Patrick Cruttwell, a configuration of historical circumstances that gave rise to the idea of a folk anthology ensconced in the trappings of Boccaccian high culture.[63] Just as the moment was right for Shakespeare – the culture of the theatre, the actors, the audiences, and the literary models of Marlowe and Kyd – the moment was right for Straparola: the Venetian book culture and its public, the experiments of the *novellieri* and *poligrafi* in popular commercial publishing, the gaming *soirées*, the published collections of enigmas, the book as a metaphor for places and occasions, the quest for novelty in forms and contents, and the appropriation of low cultures by high cultures in matters of dance, music, poetic forms, and improvisatory theatre.[64] His dare was to regale the Signora's salon with popular narratives as presented by his designer damsels. In a sense, he

63 I am referring to his book *The Shakespearean Moment and Its Place in the Poetry of the 17th Century* (London: Chatto & Windus, 1954).

64 Donato Pirovano adds a substantial dimension to the construction of that moment in his account of the Venetian book publishing industry at mid-century in 'Una storia editoriale cinquecentesca: "Le piacevoli notti" di Giovan Francesco Straparola,' *Giornale storico della letteratura italiana*, 177 (2000), pp. 542–9. Venice was the European leader in publishing, catering not only to a wealthy public at home, but to a widespread clientele in a number of specialized areas. The censors became more active beginning in 1543, but traditionally it had been a city free of repres-

made no advances over Boccaccio in bringing folk materials into the circle of the *novella*, but with the difference that he imposed no alternate literary forms, arguably made no reductions to the magic of the wonder tales, maintained many of the vestigial features of 'uncorrected' folk narratives, and kept to the plainer styles presumed to characterize his sources.

Turning now to the meaning and interpretation of folk tales, it is in their social 'usefulness' that we gain insights into the constancy of their basic designs and the gradual transformation of their peripherals across centuries. The compulsive preservation of their essential conceits accounts for the palimpsest factor through which observers have seen the many anthropologically inspired interpretations of past cultures visited upon the hermeneutics of the folk tale. Accordingly, a tale may have served variously as ancient liturgy, a mythological truth, a legend, a trace of traditional wisdom, an amusing anecdote of our ancestors, or a bit of good advice to the denizens of nurseries, having passed through a sea change of purposes and audiences. Yet arguably, at each moment in this vast chronology, the tale had to prove itself to be culturally useful in terms meaningful to each audience; it had to do cultural work, according to the hypothesis that stories settle into their received forms only when they speak to a vital element of the human experience. The argument seems self-evident that a tale's survival depends upon its ability to address relevant truths in relation to specific auditors. But applying that principle to a reading of the tales comprising the *Notti* gives us pause, not because we cannot imagine relevant meanings on their behalf, but because we are hard pressed to describe what Renaissance audiences, both popular and elite, were qualified to understand regarding the emblematic designs and enigmatic allusions of these stories. How far had they progressed in their mentalities along the trajectory from myth to social exemplum to fanciful entertainment? This may be a cul-de-sac.

In alternate terms, it might be ventured that the work conducted in these tales has to do, in all ages, with social relationships, the management of resources, initiation rites, religious observances, the education of children, discipline, justice and fairness, bride selection and marriage, war and combat, the cult of the hero, the management of gender rela-

---

sion. 'In questo clima un oscuro personaggio di Caravaggio' (in this climate [of production] an obscure person from Caravaggio ...) (p. 542) published his collection of '*novelle*.' Pirovano recreates that publishing moment in great detail.

tions, inter-generational conflict, courage, generosity, tenacity, the ages of life, reasonable self-advancement, malignant evil, and leadership. That these negotiations are projected through tales that could never transpire in the real world, involving entities and agents known only to the imagination, is one of the greatest of all literary inventions. Such stories play to the imagination where they assume a reality of their own, while appealing to our inferential capacities to extract insights from their emblematic designs, archetypal conflicts, and generic characters into the psychological and motivational conditions of our own world.[65] 'Magic, charms, disguise and spells are some of the major ingredients of such stories, which are often subtle in their interpretation of human nature and psychology.'[66] In the words of Hans Schumacher, the folk tale is 'a popular form that nevertheless carries intrinsic symbolism, of which it is unaware and makes no effort to explain, and is thus unknown even unto itself.'[67] Understanding begins in this paradox; meanings take shape through instruments unaware of their own inflections.

Pursuing the argument in more abstract terms, the folk tale becomes a potential testing ground for the interface between the evolutionary psychologists in search of the biological inheritances composing the phylogenetic brain to which culture plays and the cultural constructivists concerned with the plasticity of learning, whereby programming fills in the mental 'blank slate' with human understanding and beliefs. (I am smiling with sincerity.) We are what we are as a species because competition and fitness have shaped our faculties and generic perspectives on the world in terms of our genes, our instincts, our emotional readings of experience, and related biological roles at play in our survival strategies. Nevertheless, there is latitude for self-definition according to cus-

65 Much has been written on the 'work' of fairy tales in terms of the issues they take up that are of vital interest to the well-being of groups, regulating norms, seeking equity in the face of illiberal mores, and alleviating fear while inculcating the survival virtues of benefit to the group. Gerhard Kahlo in *Die Wahrheit des Märchens* (Halle: Niemeyer, 1954), pp. 14*ff*, provides a list of his own: the meanings of rituals, customs and laws, family power relations, dynastic and clan pressures, the place of the firstborn, bride selection, magic children, the transformation of people into plants and animals, the intervention of non-human creatures in human society, and the spirit animation of nature.

66 J.A. Cuddon, *Dictionary of Literary Terms and Literary Theory* (London: Penguin Books, 1991), p. 324.

67 *Narziss an der Quelle: Das romantische Kunstmärchen* (Wiesbaden: Athenaion, 1977), p. 12.

toms, mores, selected knowledge, conditioning, and training. Stories change as the world changes, but as the human constitution remains constant and our biological proclivities have evolved too slowly to register change over, say, the last 50,000 years, stories also stay the same. Cro-Magnon laughed, cried, feared, and felt relief according to the identical mechanisms that provoke those responses in modern man. True stories must deal with this double condition of humankind, as folk tales are equipped to do in playing to scenarios of rising and declining fortunes with their attendant emotions while adjusting the social details to accommodate the orientations of immediate audiences, bringing archetypes into alignment with local mores and morals. Straparola's stories often achieve their resonances in these terms. Such considerations will matter when it comes to the readings of the *Notti* according to single ideologies or political agendas. But let us move on.

Of salient interest to all recent students of Straparola is a subset of those popular tales to be found in the *Nights*, referred to above and throughout the commentaries as 'wonder tales.' They are the tales of fanciful characters, supernatural events, and fairy-tale-like plots, of magic horses, speaking cats, and seven-headed dragons. It is a bibliographical given that the *Piacevoli notti* was the first publication in the West in which stories of this kind received substantial representation. Indeed, among them are half a dozen bearing self-evident kinship with some of the world's best-known fairy tales. The collection not only confirms the circulation of these story types as early as the sixteenth century, but provides evidence, in the case of some, of their developmental pasts, thereby pushing the genesis of the Western fairy tale back to the late Middle Ages.

So why should they not be called 'fairy tales' outright? In the first instance, while there are many imaginary creatures, there are very few fairies, and those that appear have perfunctory roles in setting up and resolving the conditions pertaining to the hero or heroine. More pertinently, these creatures lack a home base of their own in a fairy world existing in parallel with the human world.[68] In one story, a fairy in a

68 Further to the definition of the wonder tale, see M.-L. Tenèze, 'Du conte merveilleux comme genre,' *Revue des Arts et traditions populaires* (1970), pp. 11–65. Michele Rak also adopted a similar usage in the case of Basile. See his 'Il sistema dei racconti nel *Cunto de li cunti* di Basile,' in *Giovan Battista Basile e l'invenzione della fiaba*, ed. Michelangelo Picone and Alfred Messerli (Ravenna: Longo Editore, 2004), p. 14.

cameo appearance curses a child to be born a pig (II.1) and in a second, a fairy transforms a wild man (V.1). The list may be this short. In other stories, there are voyages to imaginary lands where exploits must be conducted, but these are treated as points along an initiatory route. In the story of 'Fortunio, the King's Daughter, and the Mermaid' (III.4), the hero is abducted and taken to a kingdom under the sea, but nothing of his life with the mermaid is described. Nevertheless, Straparola's stories are pregnant with precisely the kinds of persons and places out of which the French writers of the *conte de fées* would build their fairy worlds. Even so, Raymonde Robert argues that subtle but essential attitudes and practices distinguish the tales of Galland and Straparola from those by Le Noble and De Murat, with only the latter qualifying as true 'fairy tales.'[69] Her thesis turns upon the auxiliary helpers in the wonder tales with their purely occasional and functional appearances in contradistinction to the fairy guides and their continual presence in the French *conte de fées.* The latter genre entails helpers with histories and personhoods of their own. This came about through the conscious adaptation and overhauling of the narrative sources on the part of the French court and salon writers, in accordance with the tastes and aesthetic ideas of their age. They transformed such folk tales into the *conte galant* through a process that Ute Heidmann describes as a 'nouvelle variation générique' (new generic variation).[70] Only then did the fairy tale proper come into existence.

---

69 Raymonde Robert, *Le conte de fées littéraire en France de la fin du XVIIe à la fin du XVIIIe siècle* (Nancy: Presses universitaires, 1982), p. 39. While honouring Robert's distinction, I remain amenable to the arguments made by Jan Ziolkowski in his perceptive study, *Fairy Tales from Before Fairy Tales: The Medieval Latin Past of Wonderful Lies* (Ann Arbor: University of Michigan Press, 2007), in which he sets out to show that certain tales told by the Grimm Brothers were the same tales, essentially, as were told in twelfth-century Latin manuscripts, referred to as 'The Donkey's Tale,' 'The Turnip Tale,' and 'One-Ox.' To make his point, he allowed that the nomenclature appointed to the later tales may apply equally to the medieval tales. In the generic sense of the term, they are fairy tales. But it is revealing that in the subtitle to his book, he redefines them as *favole.*

70 Ute Heidmann and Jean-Michel Adam, *Textualité et intertextualité des contes: Perrault, Apulée, La Fontaine, Lhéritier* (Paris: Garnier classiques, 2010), p. 37. She is asserting on behalf of the French authors and founders of the *conte de fées* the same degree of originality and independence from their sources as Bottigheimer sought to establish on Straparola's behalf concerning the oral culture. That Raymonde Robert describes de Murat's borrowing from Straparola as larceny is the kind of tarring which Heidmann seeks to dilute in her theory of generic reconfiguration.

Meanwhile, such subtle distinctions have been downplayed by those who accept 'fairy tale' as an appropriate translation of '*Märchen*,' designating the kinds of stories we all know and recognize by their elemental plotting, castles and princesses, tractable villains, speaking animals, sorcerers and magicians, and heroes and heroines who routinely marry and live happily ever after, thereby fulfilling the wishes of a popular audience. By such usage, the term 'fairy tale' as a translation of *conte de fées* has become established to the point of retroactively taking over many related tales of the supernatural, including those with ghosts returning to life to aid their benefactors. Such a definition easily includes those in the *Pleasant Nights*, so why resist progress? But then, if usage historically confines the term to the makers of late seventeenth-century France and their imitators, why spoil its specificity? Eager to please, I have opted for a more neutral term.[71] Jack Zipes creates space for my indecision in his statement that 'we lack an adequate history of the transitional period between the folk and fairy tales.'[72] In consequence, we are uncertain just where to draw the line. In any case – wonder, folk, or fairy – Straparola knew none of these terms. Yet, no other publication from the period rivals his as an ideal workbook for the study of the intersection between these several classifications – from the oral to the written, and from the folk tale to the fairy tale. Meanwhile, those who mock my demur will be comforted by the fact that Straparola figures prominently in two of the most influential anthologies of fairy tales recently published; one by Jack Zipes, entitled *The Great Fairy Tale Tradition: From Straparola and Basile to the Brothers Grimm*, and the other by Maria Tatar, called *The Annotated Classic Fairy Tales*.[73] They make us all closet collaborators.[74]

---

71 For a more formal definition of the 'wonder tale,' see Vladimir Propp, *Theory and History of Folklore*, trans. Adriana and Richard Martin, ed. Anatoly Liberman (Minneapolis: University of Minnesota Press, 1984), pp. 65–123.

72 *Breaking the Magic Spell: Radical Theories of Folk and Fairy Tales* (Austin: University of Texas Press, 1979), p. 20. In support of a middle view, Zipes states that 'just a superficial glance back into history will tell us that fairy tales have been in existence as *oral folk tales* for thousands of years and first became what we call *literary fairy tales* toward the end of the seventeenth century' (p. 2). I can live with that.

73 The former published (New York: Norton, 2001), the latter (New York: Norton, 2002).

74 The adoption of the term 'wonder' carries overtones of a different kind, explored by Suzanne Magnanini in her study entitled *Fairy-Tale Science: Monstrous Generation in the Tales of Straparola and Basile*. The tales are indeed 'wondrous' in their evocations, linking them potentially to the age of *meraviglie*, the *cabinet de curiosité* or

The transformation of a few of Straparola's wonder tales into fairy tales by the French school of the late seventeenth century receives passing investigation in the following commentaries; critics dealing with the rise of the fairy tale genre in general have made note of his influence, now universally acknowledged, although questions remain concerning scope and degree. We are reminded again of De Murat's famous confession that she had taken inspiration from him, along with all the others in her group, leaving the particulars to innuendo.[75] 'Ideas' for stories were his principal contribution, for the degree to which his tales are otherwise altered to accommodate later tastes

---

wunderkabinette, and the world of Pare's monsters and prodigies – the anomalies of nature. While few of the stories discuss natural anomalies per se, such as 'Of Filomena the Hermaphrodite Nun' (XIII.9), 'wonder' remains an open signifier, taking in the supernatural elements of the proto-fairy tales, to be sure, even though they belong to a different order of the imagination. Magnanini states at the outset of her study that 'not all early modern *meraviglie* were created equal'; her work explores that diversity (Toronto: University of Toronto Press, 2007), p. 20. The 'wonder tale,' in all its Manichean confrontations and hyperbolical agents, may provoke a kind of amazement, although differing, arguably, from the emotional shiver of the monstrous, the horrible, or the sublime. Paradoxically, even the conversion of Filomena from female to male, or into a hermaphrodite through a medical procedure performed in public, aroused neither shock nor amazement, but laughter (XIII.9). Straparola's wonder tales are of a new order, eliciting the responses that pertain to realms of the impossible, suffusing the imagination with the novelty and enchantment characteristic of select folk tales. If Straparola's work, in this regard, becomes a 'statement' about the scientific ethos of his age, it must do so largely by offering up folk narratives to audiences culturally inclined to read the stories in just those terms, for otherwise they remain the same old folk tales without overt scientific promptings. Meanwhile, the sixteenth-century readers' response records remain a silent night. They were interested in tales and in monstrosity. Whether the latter interest of a scientific and superstitious kind was brought hermeneutically to bear on the fantastic creatures and anomalies of nature in these tales is a moot point. Certainly it was possible.

75 'I am perfectly willing to inform the reader of two things: the first is that I took the ideas for certain of these tales from an ancient author [his work] entitled *The Comic Nights of Mr. Straparola,* imprinted for the sixteenth time in 1615 [the French edition]. These stories were apparently quite in vogue during the preceding century because there are so many editions. The ladies who have written before now in this genre [her associates d'Aulnoy and Lhéritier] have been mining the same source, at least for the greatest part [of their work].' 'Avertissement,' in *Histoires sublimes et allégoriques, dédiez aux Fées Modernes,* 1699 (my translation). The 'modern fairies' referenced in the title were, again, d'Aulnoy, Lhéritier, and the members of their writing circle.

French author	Title	ATU story type	Straparola	
Chevalier de Mailly	*Fortunio*	316	'Fortunio'	III.4
Le Noble	*L'apprenti magicien*	325	'Lattanzio'	VIII.4
Chevalier de Mailly	*Blanche Belle*	403	'Biancabella'	III.3
Mme d'Aulnoy	*Le prince Marcassin*	433	'The Pig Prince'	II.1
Mme de Murat	*Le Roy Porc*	433	'The Pig Prince'	II.1
Chevalier de Mailly	*Guerini*	502	'Guerrino'	V.1
Mme d'Aulnoy	*Le Dauphin*	675	'Pietro the Fool'	III.1
Mme de Murat	*Le Turbot*	675	'Pietro the Fool'	III.1

For further consideration:

French author	Title	ATU story type	Straparola	
Charles Perrault	*Le chat botté*	545	'Constantino'	XI.1
Mme de Murat	*Le sauvage*	502	'Guerrino'	V.1
Mme d'Aulnoy	*Belle Belle*	513	'Costanza'	IV.1
Gueullette	*Le Centaur bleu*	513	'Costanza'	IV.1
Mme d'Aulnoy	*Princesse Belle-Étoile*	707	'The Truth-Speaking Bird'	IV.3
Mme d'Aulnoy	*L'Oiseau bleu*	432	'Fortunio'	III.4
Mme d'Aulnoy	*La belle aux cheveux d'or*	314	'Livoretto'	III.2

and values is transparently clear. Quite evidently, as De Murat reveals, the translation of the *Notti* by Louveau and Larivey (1560 and 1572) had gained a special status among the inaugurators of the *conte de fées*. In *Le conte populaire français: Un catalogue raisonné des versions de France et des pays de langue française et d'outre-mer*, Paul Delarue and Marie-Louise Tenèze itemize 155 tales by this group of writers, thirty-six of which are in some fashion based on folk narratives – among which, by their count, eight are inspired directly by Straparola. But an arguably more accurate count, according to the investigations made in the commentaries to follow, might go as high as fifteen. The exact number is clearly a matter of interpretation involving sources and their degrees of influence and inspiration. Hence, the following list is not so much a contradiction as it is a set of suggestions for further study and demonstration, while fortifying the claim on Straparola's behalf that he was verily the spiritual father or *éminence grise* of the modern fairy tale.

The remaining discussions in this chapter pertain to the wonder tales in relation to ideology and the chance that the *Notti* might have been conceived with the political and economic conditions of Venice, or of certain of its social classes, in mind. It is true that an economic profile might be put upon the Venice of 1550, and it is equally true that folk tales are invariably apt for symbolic interpretation and subversive construction. They sometimes tell wish-fulfillment stories of remarkable good luck wherein bumpkins are rewarded with princesses, or take the reader's imagination to charmingly faraway places. Indeed, the entire collection, as a literary diversion, might be construed as escapist. In that regard the thoughts of readers are free to indulge in vicarious victories, illusions of self-empowerment, or total evasion on a story-by-story basis. But there are caveats to assuming a high level of intentionality on Straparola's part. There is nothing sufficiently remarkable about the Venetian economy at mid-century to explain *tout court* the foundation of a literary genre destined to bring wish-fulfilment solace to the labouring poor. Moreover, the lucky pauper tales are but few and they are buried among love tragedies, tales of theft, adultery, jests, unsavoury adventures in the night, incest, voluntary mutilation, and ritual beheadings. The diversity of the volume poses real problems to the imposition of ideological uniformity of any kind. Even the most promising tales of fantasy compensation are ambiguous. Adamantina marries her king by pulling her doll off his ass. Constantino gets his princess by bullying the peasants and taking over the castle of a man killed in a road accident. Even the focus of these rags-to-riches tales is ambiguous. Moreover, who was both suffering from the Venetian economy and yet likely to be buying Straparola's expensive tomes?[76] Straparola, after all, seems to be pitching his miscellany to the elite clientele he depicts in his framing tale. Perhaps the final challenge is the degree to which the entire collection can be weighted in contrasting terms. Victoria Smith Pozzi took for the prevailing ethos of the work an incremental portrayal of human depravity as sharpsters, cheaters,

76 The question of readership as determined by class had arisen with regard to *sotties*, *facetiae*, and *fabliaux*. Who were they for? Joseph Bédier in *Les fabliaux* favoured the mercantile classes (the middle class did not yet exist per se), whereas Per Nykrog in *Les fabliaux* believed they were intended for the aristocracy. Both infer that the stories are shaped by authorial intentionality in relation to their audiences. The former was published (Paris: Honoré Champion, 1894), the latter (Copenhagen: E. Munksgaard, 1957).

adulterers, and treacherous friends are profiled in tale after tale.[77] Selective approaches may be made in support of these theses, but the cavalier diversity of the overall collection tends to dilute their effect.

To pursue the matter at greater length entails a reconsideration of the folk tale per se as a vehicle of cultural concerns, and of whether the collective vision of the folk is dispositionally that of the downtrodden and the oppressed. Many have dealt with Mikhail Bakhtin's thesis that fantasy literature fits into an alternate mode of storytelling through which freedom is expressed in opposition to oppression, exercising the power of the subversive by separating discourse from meaning and pushing towards nonsignification by hollowing out the relation of signifiers to signifieds.[78] But this position is not as popular as it once was. Among others, Linda Dégh strikes out in a new direction. As early as the feudal era in Europe, folk tales were recited at banquets as fantasies, while for the 'folk' those same tales may have pertained to the possible or the probable. But tales of assertion against wicked authority do not seem to be made in the name of a class. Even the folk tales of the nineteenth century are pre-industrial in their perspectives and show no signs of class goals against oppressors. Nevertheless, all folk literature in some sense is a 'practical criticism of oppressive conditions,' as when scarcity makes for greed and distribution is inequitable, or when inheritances are mishandled. These are tales generated within basic survival groups (small communities, tribes, or micro-kingdoms) in which humans seek collaborative self-advancement, weighing constantly the levels of individual participation as cheaters and benefactors, and the strategies for realizing personal entitlements within the group.[79] Qualifiers are accumulating to suggest that the folk tale is not always the subversive instrument for racial and class protest that agenda-oriented critics had hoped. Jack Zipes concurs in resisting the ideology factor necessary to convert folk tales into sociocultural movements in the name of groups, races, or classes, although he allows for social complaint.[80] Such stories may, by all means, deal with

77 Victoria Smith Pozzi, 'Straparola's *Le piacevoli notti*: Narrative Technique and Ideology' (PhD diss., University of California Los Angeles, 1981), *passim*.

78 See Rosemary Jackson, *Fantasy: The Literature of Subversion* (London: Methuen, 1981), esp. pp. 39–42.

79 *Folktales and Society* (Bloomington: Indiana University Press, 1969), pp. 27, 65–6.

80 *Breaking the Magic Spell: Radical Theories of Folk and Fairy Tales* (Austin: University of Texas Press, 1979), pp. 22–3. Zipes, in this same work, concurs that such tales may speak for the disenfranchised and marginal. That Bakhtinian stance (he is not

hunger, poverty, exploitation, powerlessness, humiliation, injustice, wrongful expulsion, and the quest for compensation (revenge). These are not tales of subversion so much as tales of justice, destiny, and wish fulfilment. Each is a little equity court, doing the work of distributive justice or psychological compensation. Hence, their remarkable capacity to escape class barriers and hold their appeal for readers up and down the social ladder. But that Straparola's stories represent an economic class or appeal directly to a specific purchasing clientele is open to doubt, given their diversity and the classless nature of 'folk' tales in general. Surely, in commercial terms at least, his audience was anyone who liked stories of all kinds and had the money to purchase books.[81]

That Straparola's publication alone altered the status or prospects of the realist social *novella* or jeopardized the future of the great Boccaccian tradition seems improbable, but perhaps his inauguration of wonder tales with their supernatural characteristics in a Boccaccian frame was symptomatic of a genre on the wane. His gesture of rejection, at the least, places him in an anomalous or equivocal position in relation to the dominant fictional form of the preceding two-and-a-half centuries. If we leave him among the *novellieri*, he is one of those compromising the genre's conventions; if we remove him, he is among those responsible for challenging its pre-eminence. In effect, all through the preceding era, *novelle* writers had been catholic in their borrowing proclivities, but a certain centre had held in terms of social ethos and realism, contemporary plots, modest interiorizing of characters, literary *topoi* – all that pertains specifically to the *novella* as a story-telling genre. Initially, authors were not particular about its designations. Boccaccio in his Proem to the *Decameron* spoke of 'novellas, or fables, or parables, or histories, whatever you wish to call them.' John Florio echoed this open approach in *Queen Anna's New World of Words*: 'a novel, a new discourse, a tale, a fable, a parable. Also a tiding or newes.' The spirit of the form

---

mentioned in the book) is implicit in the statement that 'folk and fairy tales have always spread word through their fantastic images about the feasibility of utopian alternatives, and this is exactly why the dominant social classes have been vexed by them.' (London: Heinemann, 1977), p. 3.

81 Vittore Branca maintained that the *novella* targeted the bourgeois or mercantile spectrum of readers and that this was deliberate on the part of the writers. It was literature by, for, and mostly about this emerging class. *Boccaccio medievale* (Florence: Sansoni, 1964), pp. 71–99. Behind the argument are varying interpretations of the notion of class, a notion which, before the nineteenth century, was quasi-anachronistic.

was its variety, for such *récits* were serious or comic and about all social classes. Pietro Bembo celebrated Boccaccio as the very master of variety.[82] Meanwhile, Masuccio of Salerno spoke of his creations as histories, emphasizing their truth, or at least their possibility, while Matteo Bandello protested that his stories 'non sono favole ma vere istorie' (are not fables but true histories), and Marguerite de Navarre said much the same of hers. But more was at stake than nomenclature; the genre itself was now under assault. The Boccaccian matrix was being undermined. Penzer and others were keen to style Straparola as one of the *novellieri* who, in keeping with past tolerances, had merely turned to the folk for materials, all of which were entirely transformed by his 'elite' authorial interventions. But that was wishful thinking, for, as Paolo Valerio confirms, Straparola was among the earliest to showcase the folk tradition for itself, which in making its gradual appearance was 'one of the distinctive features of European culture from the late fifteenth century up to the end of the sixteenth.'[83] The perceived effect of such departures was the systematic decline of the humanist *novella*. In the words of Nancy Canepa, 'the "bourgeois realism" of Boccaccio's model was on the wane' in the second half of the sixteenth century.[84] Bandello had turned to tales of horror, Straparola to tales of wonder. Thus, just as the literary folk tale threatened to destroy the authentic stories of the folk in the estimation of those writing in defense of popular culture,[85] the literary folk and

82 Pietro Bembo, *Prosa della vulgar lingua* (1525), in *Opere in volgare*, ed. Mario Marti (Florence: Sansoni, 1961), pp. 334–40.

83 'The Language of Madness in the Renaissance,' *Yearbook of Italian Studies* 1 (1971), p. 208.

84 Nancy Canepa, *From Court to Forest* (Detroit: Wayne State University Press, 1999), p. 54.

85 Stephen Greenblatt speaks of the damage done to folk culture by the elite who sap it of its vitality, freeze it into formulae, fix it by conventions, and surround it with words. *Learning to Curse: Essays in Modern Culture* (New York: Routledge, 1990), p. 68. Straparola must plead guilty if such is a sin, although folk culture also feeds on the printed. Moreover, while one may criticize the sterility and rigidity of the literary imitation, the folk culture from which it is derived goes blithely along undiminished, for acts of appropriation alter nothing in the cultures from which they borrow. Folk culture is not a quantity subject to deletion when its stories are borrowed, nor is it dismantled by transcription into print. It is true, however, that folk culture as a universal donor has been displaced in recent decades, not so much by books as by technology, cataclysmic world events, the media, and changing social mores and structures that have destroyed the mentalities, practices, and contexts by which it was fostered. That is a different matter. Jack Zipes concurs with Greenblatt,

fairy tale threatened to destroy the revered forms of bourgeois culture by catering to new tastes. Straparola's invention, in fulfillment of his literary moment, disguised as elite culture and proposed to high society, was simultaneously an attack upon the epitomizing form of that culture; he had crossed a line and the historians of the *novella* have held him to account.

V. The Enigmas

Easily overlooked is the fact that the *Piacevole notti* is also an anthology of enigmas; there are as many of them as there are stories, making up a collection that, on its own, might fill fifty pages. Clearly this literary *forme simple* was in vogue, having its own defining properties of obscured questions and projected answers presented in artificial verse, whether octaves or sonnets, formally if not in fact for the purposes of social recreation. The enigma is thus both a private and a communal form, to be enjoyed as a guessing game for solitary readers or be assembled into a prompt book for persons in groups playing the popular game of 'riddles.' As a 'simple form' in the sense described by André Jolles in his *Einfache Formen* (1930), it takes its place beside other kinds of guessing games, questions-and-answers, proverbs, emblems, epigrams, characters, jokes, and quotable quotations as a minimal but precise literary entity.[86] In the mansion

---

however, in *Breaking the Magic Spell* (London: Heinemann, 1977), *passim*, that the folk tale, once it is commercialized or adapted to the ends of the elite or the masses, becomes an eviscerated instrument of collective truth. This has been much theorized in recent years. Walter Benjamin made much of the 'realm of living speech' and of the damage done to oral narrative by the book as a product of nineteenth-century capitalism. 'The Storyteller: Observations on the Works of Nikolai Leskov,' in *Walter Benjamin: Selected Writings*, ed. Howard Eiland and Michael W. Jennings (Cambridge, MA: Harvard University Press, 2002), vol. III, p. 146. Books contain only dead narratives, whereas orality alone builds stories within living communities. Even Jacques Derrida involved himself in this dichotomy on the side of the lived experience of 'aphoristic energy' as opposed to the 'encyclopedic protection' of lifeless matter in books indifferent to gesture and storytelling, in *Of Grammatology*, trans. G.C. Spivak (Baltimore: Johns Hopkins University Press, 1976), p. 18. Straparola does not have to bear the entire brunt of the matter, although he was decidedly among the earliest to turn popular culture into book culture, and what is worse, to deliver it to the elite for their own social ends.

86 For a contrasting view of the enigma, see Stefano Calabrese, who attempts to bring a kind of unity to the collection by associating the cognitive demands placed upon the reader by the riddle with the demands imposed by the sometimes inconclusive

of Renaissance literature, these miniature forms may be confined to storerooms and walk-in closets, but by adjusting the metaphor the book itself, conceived as just such a space, was the perfect vehicle for them. The riddle was ideal content for the book as a topical storehouse or treasury of wit and wisdom, its entries arranged in short, memorable units. Such a conceptualization of the Renaissance book has been explored in recent years by, among others, Lina Bolzoni in *The Gallery of Memory: Literary and Iconographic Models in the Age of the Printing Press.* For the sixteenth-century Venetian literati, the book was no longer thought of as simply an object with pages containing information, but as a metaphor of its function as a visual encyclopedia, a tree of knowledge, a labyrinth, a memory game, a collection of ciphered codes, a natural museum, a building, gallery, or theatre in which things are stored or displayed, or as an instrument of invention with recombinant parts.[87] Its pages presented the visual codes corresponding to the mental operations they incited. In particular, members of the famous academies and the *poligrafi* were fascinated by the capacities of the book to stir and exercise the memory through its spatial, diagrammatic, and dissonant forms of representation, whether as map, maze, *cabinet de curiosité,* itinerary, gallery of emblematic pictures, or game board. Enigmas pertain to a specific set of problems, generating epistemic shortfalls which orient attention in the search for specific solutions. The book as their instrument of conveyance becomes part of the message.

That Straparola's book should combine enigmas with the telling of *favole* is merely an extension of the compound formula he was seeking to fulfill – one through which the book expresses its literary contents as a social event, making it both passively readable and actively performative. According to the surrounding fictional setting, his songs, stories, and riddles are performed before our eyes as miniature 'programs' at a

---

endings to a very few of the stories, such as VII.5 in which no choice is made of a husband, or VI.4 wherein no choice is made among the contestants seeking to become the next abbess. Whether riddles call upon the same social problem solving computations elicited by the stories is a point for discussion; there is a loose resemblance. More certain is that both fables and enigmas inspired communal guessing, conversation, and amusement among the members of the *cornice* or framing-tale society in an ambience of contained competition. *Gli arabeschi della fiaba* (Pisa: Pacini, 1984), pp. 44*ff.* For yet other ideas, see Elli Köngas Maranda, *Theory and Practice of Riddle Analysis* (Urbino: Università di Urbino, 1972).

87 *The Gallery of Memory,* trans. Jeremy Parzen (Toronto: University of Toronto Press, 2001).

fashionable carnival gathering. The riddle, as a poetic and literary form, is also a feature of the social interchange. An enigma, no matter how prettified as poetry, must ask a question, its answer encoded in the clues embedded in its lines. It is all a matter of language, inferential reasoning, and the reduction of options through a close scrutiny of the verbal prompts; it is an invitation to play. What enigmas require of the computational mind is, in fact, quite complex, even though players grasp intuitively what must be done through a combination of 'best fit' trial-and-error reasoning, troping and metaphorizing of the data, and inspirational luck. Riddles are initially disorienting. 'Georges and Dundes point to the most important technique of confusion in the construction of riddles when they emphasize the importance of establishing internal contradictions or "oppositions" within the riddling description.'[88] Riddles play upon anomalies of language and conceptual dissonances. They are little epistemic jags which may be catalogued and remembered both by makers and by the habitués of social gatherings where such games are played.

Enigmas allow for many proximate guesses, yet promise to have only one best answer (unanswerable riddles are grounds for assassination). They are delivered to the company on a competitive basis and test both the wit of the maker and the acumen of the auditors. Socially, they represent a pitcher and batter confrontation, the strike-out or the home run. Hence, on the few occasions in the present work when the enigmas are actually resolved, the young ladies reciting them take umbrage, pouting and planning revenge, which could only come in the form of answering correctly the enigmas of their adversaries ahead of all the others. Just how to account for this bad sportsmanship in a light-hearted setting can only pertain to the instinctual combativeness of animals programmed to measure their survival fitness in intellectual terms. Enigmas, in that regard, carry a social liability, to the degree that their cognitive opacity constitutes the mental acumen of the maker – which, when guessed, diminishes his intellectual stature – while a correct answer is a mark of the cognitive adaptiveness and social fitness of its solver. We are in the world of Solomon and Hiram, king of Tyre, who allegedly gambled fortunes on their respective powers to make and solve riddles. Behind the salon enigma is ritual combat or the mysteries of initiation in which

88 Roger D. Abrahams and Alan Dundes, 'Riddles,' *Folklore and Folklife*, ed. Richard M. Dorson (Chicago: University of Chicago Press, 1972), p. 131. The allusion is to Robert A. Georges and Alan Dundes, 'Toward a Structural Definition of the Riddle,' *Journal of American Folklore* 76 (1963), pp. 111–18.

the initiate must complete the quest for answers upon peril of life or reputation.

More specifically, riddles play upon a handful of computational plasticities, as when things described as fact embed tropes or symbolic applications. 'The man who walks with you but can never catch up with you' must not be a literal man but the 'man' created by your own shadow. All enigmas rely upon such projections of logic, as in the case of the bookworm as that which devours a great deal of literature but never learns a thing. Here, through the pun on 'devour,' the literal must be imagined in the place of a metaphor so familiar that it passes unnoticed. The same principle pertains with such buried metaphors as 'money is the root of all evil,' which is nothing for our brains to decode, yet requires some reflection to identify the literal behind the metaphoric 'leap': root is to money what X is to evil, or tree is to evil what root is to money, or root is to X what money is to evil, or none of these.

Meanwhile, the possibility for double meanings and misguided associations – a built-in feature of the clues and the manner in which they are expressed – recommended the enigma as a form of social play and flirtation, provoking fake prurience and reconciling laughter. Thus any set of clues evoking an object long and narrow that is brought into proximity with a receptacle of any form, especially accompanied by jiggling, shoving, or twisting, is apt for a scatological (Freudian) reading, while an equally apt but innocuous answer would have to do with, say, handles inserted into brooms (one of many possibilities). Straparola indulged in several of these, each time provoking sniggers and the Signora's disapprobation. Amusingly, in the process, even this monitor of morals demonstrates a ready wit for smut, for she never misses the slightest allusion. This is, of course, the carnivalesque bonus of the double-entendre enigma. As part of the social tension and release, the maker always denies the erotic intent and tosses the guilt back upon the accusing parties.[89] There are hints that the ideal enigma was one that reflected some element of the story it

89 For a contrasting view, see Manlio Pastore Stocchi, who agrees that obscenity was part of the enigma culture, but that the girls who recited them were innocent and reclaimed their propriety in all sincerity. The tittering among the auditors, essentially the men, was provoked by ambiguous signifiers which the Signora seeks to expunge as part of her essential social role. Nevertheless, we, the readers, have had those double signifiers thrust upon us as part of the book's culture, bringing Stocchi to such terms as 'constitutional ambiguity' and 'hypocrisy.' Straparola, *Le piacevoli notti* (Bari: Laterza, 1975), p. xi. There were others like Giuseppe Pitrè who, for the obscenity of these little poems, was against publishing them. *Indovinelli, dubbi, scioglilingua del popolo siciliana* (Turin: C. Clausen, 1898), pp. xxi–xxviii.

followed, and on a few occasions the reciters meet that challenge to the particular delight of the company. But more typically, these enigmas are transitional treats in their own right, little servings of sherbet between courses, generating moments of social interchange.

Riddles were an integral part of medieval culture, most notably as forms of amusement among scholars and clerics. Rua asserts that in Straparola's times and before, they pervaded the popular traditions as well.[90] That fact holds open the prospect that Straparola found many of his enigmas through the same oral traditions that preserved the stories which he collected and that, moreover, enigmas were everywhere. Many of the medieval creations were erudite in nature and were written out in verse. These in turn were polished, elaborated, and preserved for posterity in conjunction with maxims, charms, bestiaries, and instructional poetry. Arguably, these formed the foundation for the Renaissance riddle and were passed from the classroom to the salon. In bookish form they might contain their answer in the title, their wit consisting of the poetic manner in which they pose the questions. Among the earliest publications of such literature is the *Adevineaux amoureux*, printed in Bruges by Colard Mansion in 1479; it contains a gamut of types, including jesting and obscene riddles as well as wisdom and biblical forms. Another fifteenth-century collection was the *Demandes joyeuses en maniere de quolibets* which Wynkyn de Worde translated into English and published in 1511.[91] As Welsh points out, it brings in the new order of Renaissance wit: 'What is the cleanliest of all the leaves?' 'Why, holly to be sure, for with this leaf no man wipes his arse.' Cervantes places riddles in his *Galatea* and composed many of his own. The oldest known from Italy are in Venetian dialect and originated in the eighth century.[92] Ettore Allodoli speaks of a generation of writers creating enigmas in the spirit of Berni, Il Mauro, Il Lasco (Grazzini), and Il Burchiello.[93] De Filippis also lists Il

90 Giuseppe Rua, ed., *Le Piacevoli notti di Messer Gian Francesco Straparola* (Rome: E. Loescher, 1898), p. 130.

91 Andrew Welsh, 'Riddles,' in *Medieval Folklore*, ed. Carl Lindahl et al. (Oxford: Oxford University Press, 2002), p. 343.

92 M. de Filippis, 'Straparola's Riddles,' *Italica* 24, no. 2 (June 1947), p. 136. His impression was that Straparola mitigated the obscene effect by mixing the nice with the nasty and by surrounding his creations with polite conversation. *The Literary Riddle in Italy to the End of the Sixteenth Century* (Berkeley: University of California Press, 1948), pp. 13–17. Moreover, riddles are associated with carnival, as in Straparola, and thus with a period of licence.

93 Introduction to Antonio Malatesti, *La sfinge: enimmi* (Lanciano: Carabba editore, ca. 1910), p. i.

Burchiello, the Florentine Barber, Domenico di Giovanni (1400–48), along with Sannazaro, Pietro Bembo, Pietro Aretino, Antonio Alamanni, and Ariosto. But those who brought the form to perfection were Angelo (Angiolo) Cenni (Il Resoluto), Ascanio dei Mori da Ceno, Giulio Cesare Croce (of *Bertoldo* fame), and Giovan Francesco Straparola.[94] Rua mentions the enigmas of Doni and Parabosco, poetic developments which came to fruition in the thirty-five enigmatic sonnets of Il Resoluto and the poems of Grazzini.[95] With so many luminaries engaged, the popularity of this little genre is hardly to be denied; the circulation of the poems was widespread. For a sampling, *Il libro degli indovinelli italiani* contains some 1,142 riddles, including many by Pietro Fallone, Paolo Giovio, Luigi Grotto, Firenzuola, Bembo, Angiolo Cenni (Il Resoluto of Siena), Antonio Malatesti, Francesco Moneti, and Giulio Cesare Croce.[96] The argument implicit in the listing of so many names is that Straparola's contribution, while particularized by his juxtaposing of fables and enigmas in an elite social context, is yet a commonplace creation among so many contemporaries practicing the same literary form.

In such a climate of recycled motifs, of variation and polishing, the question of intellectual property re-emerges, now involving the witty kernel of the riddle as 'idea,' and the practices of imitation. Regarding Straparola's originality, Rua takes him for a borrower but specifies no sources (although he repertories the several riddles Straparola borrowed from the popular tradition, as well as those found in a fifteenth-century manuscript in the Riccardiana Library in Florence),[97] while De Filippis – the acknowledged authority on the Renaissance riddle and author of the *History of the Literary Riddle in Italy to the End of the Sixteenth Century* – states nothing untoward about Straparola in placing him among those who trafficked in such materials. The truth in this matter depends upon a carefully qualified definition of what constitutes 'borrowing,' for riddles consist of a 'conceit,' a poetic form, diction, and embellishment. General inferences based on a limited sampling would suggest that Straparola's poetic settings are his own, provided he is allowed, on occasion, to take quilt-work inspiration from others in matters of diction. The 'conceits,' the witty ideas (What can a man give to a woman but never have for

94 M. de Filippis, 'Straparola's Riddles,' *Italica* 24, no. 2 (June 1947), p. 136.

95 Giuseppe Rua, ed., *Le piacevoli notti di Messer Gian Francesco Straparola* (Rome: Loescher, 1898), p. 130.

96 Carlo Lapucci, ed., *Il libro degli indovinelli italiani* (Milan: Garzanti Editore, 1994).

97 Giuseppe Rua, 'Di alcune stampe d'indovinelli,' in *Archivio per lo studio delle tradizioni popolari* (Palermo, 1888), vol. VII, pp. 427–65.

himself? A husband; Why is the moon so pale? It doesn't get much sleep at night), by contrast, belonged to a lending library of 'riddle memes,' many of them circulating freely in the popular culture, apt for endless elaboration and refitting. Straparola recirculates one as old as the hills about the chicken who wears a crown but isn't a king; wears spurs, but isn't a cavalier, and so on, concluding story IV.4. Yet, paradoxically, his riddles, reconceived, stylized, and poetically elaborated according to his own talents, become as much his creations as they are the creations of those from whom they are randomly and indifferently derived.

A sampling to follow will indicate that Straparola treated the cupboard of popular enigmas as much his own as he did the trove of tales he reduced to print. That so many of his riddles, most without contemporary written analogues, were collected in the nineteenth century in such publications as the *Archivio per lo studio delle tradizioni popolari* merely underscores the hypothesis that Straparola collected his wares assiduously from the popular culture of his day. Moreover, that Straparola shares several in common in both of his volumes (1550 and 1553) with Madonna Dafne, whose work was published in 1552, entails that she borrowed from him and then he from her, or that, far more likely, both were supplying themselves from a common popular trove in which such riddles were in ubiquitous supply. That relationship to the 'sub-literary' world of oral culture is once again made manifest – a little piece of the *Zeitgeist*.

One of the remarkable features of Straparola's style was his penchant for transferring words and phrases from other poetic contexts to his own in piecemeal fashion. The resonances are not at the level of topic or verse, but at the level of word echo. He does this in his stories as well. The enigma following story XIII.7 is a case in point. In effect, he turns a few lines from a Petrarchan canzona (no. 135) into an enigma by implicitly asking, 'What am I?' It is a remarkable game of literary metamorphosis, of creating anew from the old by altering registers and purposes. Petrarch rambles through his knowledge of the paradoxes of the natural world in search of images to highlight the moods of love. In the process he hits upon the 'catopleba' (Pliny's catoblepa), a basilisk-like animal which lives in the West, with a slim body and huge head, the eyes of which cause death when looked upon.[98] Petrarch's lines read as follows:

98 Pirovano, *Le piacevoli notti*, vol. II, p. 760 describes the beast as an imaginary quadruped similar to a basilisk, able to kill by its glance, localized to western Ethiopia near the source of the Niger River. The name is Greek, meaning 'low-looking,' because of its oversized, heavy-hanging head. The reference in Pliny is in

Far in the distant west
Exists a gentle beast, and one more calm
Than all the rest, but she
Bears woe and plaint and death within her eyes.
Most cautious sight must be
If it in her direction turns; if it
Looks not into her eyes,
The rest of her, then, it can safely see.[99]

By analogy, the heedless lover, already blinded by love, runs to his death by continuously seeking out his lady's murderous eyes. Straparola expresses his riddle in eight lines (the standard octave), which merely describes the animal according to its intrinsically enigmatic traits. Signor Beltramo's auditors take for granted that their task is to identify the creature as a straightforward trivia question about a rarely mentioned mythological beast which had become part of poetic culture, although not by name. Words in Straparola in common with Petrarch's poem are: 'l'estremo Occidente,' 'queta,' 'pianto,' 'la mira,' 'accorta convien,' and 'morte dentro gli occhi porta.' But they are scattered and used in different contexts. Petrarch writes: 'una fera è soave et queta tanto'; Straparola: 'e si dimostra queta, e paziente.' Straparola either had the *Songbook* open before him or had it fresh in his memory, making an enigma out of its poetic conceit, while retaining a few scattered words for good measure perhaps from memory, for to pick them off the page at random as he does makes little sense. The relationship between the two provides a glimpse into the Renaissance mind at work: referential, word oriented, retrospective in its search for materials, intertextual, yet in quest of renewal, novelty, and witty metamorphosis in the presentation of the subject. At least in the transposition of poetic material from the high to the low, Straparola makes something light and amusing from the Petrarchisms that, in their overuse, had made the work of the founder

---

the *Natural History*, trans. H. Rackham (Cambridge, MA: Harvard University Press, 1938–63), vol. VIII, p. 32. This is one of several enigmas in the collection involving animals – a favourite topic. See also I.4, III.4, IV.3, IV.4, V.1, and XIII.1.

99 *Petrarch's Songbook*, trans. James Wyatt Cook (Binghamton, NY: MRTS, 1996), no. 135, ll. 31–8, p. 197.

seem stuffy.[100] In short, his enigmas appear to be his own, but their forms, diction, and ideas have the 'feel' of the referential about them.

As stated earlier, the 'conceits' themselves were in free flow. All five from Straparola's second night bear conceptual resemblances to those in the *Accademia d'enigmi in sonetti di Madonna Dafne di Piazza* (Venice, 1552), and another from the second volume of the *Nights*, that of story VII.2 about the silkworm, has its counterpart in this same work.[101] There were others as well. Rua, moreover, convincingly traces the riddle of the scissors (*forbici*) of XI.4 to the *Sonetti del Risoluto de' Rozzi* (Siena, 1547),[102] while the riddle of VII.4 refers unequivocally to the 'Carità romana,' the story of Cimon's daughter who breastfed her father through the grate of his prison. This theme was remarkably handled by another artist from Caravaggio, the great painter of that name who, during his sojourn in Naples in 1607, depicted the scene among the seven works of mercy. This sampling of correspondences implies that Straparola worked in the manner of his contemporaries in his composition of enigmas, resetting many of the tried and proven chestnuts of wit to verses of his own devising through a second level of *imitatio* of words and phrases fixed in his poetic lexicon through a close perusal of the canonical poets. Such procedures reflect the habits of the times.[103]

---

100 That was Rua's impression of Straparola's more humble enterprise, while Parabosco in his *Diporti* was merely repeating the stale conceits and vocabulary of the love poets. *Tra antiche fiabe e novelle*, vol. I, *Le Piacevoli notti*, ed. Giuseppe Rua (Rome: E. Loescher, 1898), p. 130.

101 This elusive work was also published in Mantua as *Academia di Enimmi di Madonna Dafne di Piazza agli academici fiorentini suoi amante*. It is quoted by Rua in his edition of *Le piacevoli notti* (Rome, 1890), p. 133, and by De Filippis in 'Straparola's Riddles,' *Italica* 24, no. 2 (June 1947), p. 143. The author is Maddalena Sigiuzzi, born in Piazza, Sicily in 1499. That others in the collection hold similar alignments with Madonna Dafne, such as IX.4 (Madonna Dafne, no. 57), XI.4 (Madonna Dafne, no. 14), XIII.2 (Madonna Dafne, no. 63), and XIII.9 (Madonna Dafne, no. 71), would indicate that the authoress draws upon our author, or that for those in Straparola's second volume (1553), that he draws upon her. But a far more plausible suggestion is that both, almost simultaneously, are drawing upon a common repertoire of enigmas in wide circulation in the popular culture.

102 Giuseppe Rua, ed., *Le piacevoli notti di Messer Gian Francesco Straparola* (Rome: E. Loescher, 1890), p. 132. Il Resoluto is Angiolo Cenni, one of the founders of the Rozzi Academy. The *Sonetti del Risoluto* [*sic*] were first published in 1546.

103 The most comprehensive list of Straparola's borrowings in the enigma department may be pieced together from the annotations in Pirovano's edition of the *Notti* (Rome: Salerno, 2000). He cites a number of parallel texts from Madonna Dafne and Resoluto. But XI.4 by Resoluto is also in Madonna Dafne, so that, again, the

Straparola did his part to maintain the popularity of the enigma, in his way adding to the collective repertory of those in circulation – another probable instance of the circulation of materials between written and oral cultures. Louveau, as part of his translation of the first twenty-five tales into French (1560), provided literal versions of the enigmas, but many fell short of their potential. Pierre Larivey, Italian by birth, in completing the translation (1572), reworked Louveau's efforts and went so far as to replace some twenty-four of the original enigmas with new ones which he selected out of such Italian authors as Angiolo Cenni. Thereafter, *The Pleasant Nights* became a supplier of enigmas in its own right. Alexandro Sylvano incorporated several of them into his *Quarenta Aenigmas en lengua Espannola*, published in Paris by La Casa de Giles Beys in 1581, and a year later in French by the same house as *Cinquante Aenigmes françoises.* Gabriel Sculteti Onghero took fifty-one and had them published in Leipzig in 1679 by Hans Colero in a self-contained work entitled *Degli spiriti generosi. Passatempo Toscano ciò è ingegniosi enimmi di M. Giovan Francesco da Caravaggio.* De Filippis concludes his survey by saying that almost all of Straparola's riddles found favour with European collectors and publishers and enjoyed an independent future of their own.[104]

VI. The Publishing History of *Le piacevoli notti*

Surely only bitten specialists could be interested in the publishing history of *The Pleasant Nights.* But, in fact, the vicissitudes encountered by this work at the hands of typesetters and churchmen during its first sixty years is something of an epic in the history of book publishing and reception. Questions arising pertain to the number of printings and editions because books are performances looking for approbation as commercial commodities, while demand for copies is a revealing indicator not only of material success, but of the popularity and appeal of the contents. Other questions pertain to the authority of the *princeps* editions of the two parts and the ongoing participation of the author in the subsequent printings of each. But perhaps the most engaging of them all is the question of ecclesiastical and civic censorship and the textual modifications

currency of such enigmas in the popular culture provides a more plausible explanation than direct literary borrowing on Straparola's part; such cases, for the curious, require closer study.

104 M. de Filippis, 'Straparola's Riddles,' *Italica* 24, no. 2 (June 1947), p. 146.

and excisions introduced in accordance with the increasing rigour of the Counter-Reformation Church concerning fictive representations of the clergy, the devil, the saints, magic, doctrinal issues, and smut. By the end of the century, Straparola's 'folk' anthology will have endured the knife on two major and several minor occasions concerning its anticlerical allusions, irreverence, and blasphemy, to end up a leaner version of its former self by ten stories and many passages. In that respect, its 'editorial' history becomes a mirror to the oppressive tastes of the times and a measure of changing values. In effect, we see the spirit of Renaissance secular humanism shutting down before our eyes.

As stated earlier, Straparola produced a pair of volumes that together constitute the whole of the *Notti*, and while the two parts evince a general homogeneity of style,[105] they nevertheless show signs of tinkering and adjusting during the course of their composition and publication. It would seem that he began with ten nights of five stories each, relative to the Boccaccian model, but by 1553 he had discovered that the second set of twenty-five was considerably shorter than the first. He thus added three nights, which he filled with shorter pieces to be found wherever he might, for by the second story of the eleventh night his stock of folk tales had been entirely depleted. So it came about, presumably, that twenty-two of Morlini's little jests and social anecdotes, full of popular potential but lost to the many who could not read Latin, supplied Straparola with precisely what he needed for translation to balance the books. Initially, with his first compilation of twenty-five stories in hand, accompanied by their rubrics, morals, and enigmas, he had approached the 'censors' (the Venetian Senate), received his 'privilege' despite objections, and enlisted the services of the printer Comin da Trino di Monferrato, no doubt indirectly through his bookseller. Comin was a prolific printer of popular wares whose press was in the heart of the city near San Giovanni Crisostomo, just to the north-west of the Rialto Bridge; he was from Brescia and had been in Venice since 1540.[106] Among his earliest commissions was the re-edition of Pietro Bembo's *Asolani*, one of the defining works of the era – the same Bembo who fictively or in reality attended the *veglie* (evening social gatherings) which form the

105 Giorgio Boscardi made a stylistic analysis of the *Notti* and concluded that it is the same well-balanced, calm, clear, and measured prose throughout. 'Le novelle di G.F. Straparola,' *Rassegna Lucchese* 8 (1952), pp. 2–7.

106 Further information about this printer (Comino Giolito Ferrari) may be gleaned from 'La marca tipografica di Comin da Trino,' *Gutenberg-Jahrbuch* 65 (1990), pp. 162–74.

cornice or framing device of the present collection. Comin had also printed the verse of Antonio Molino. He was inclined to take printing jobs from the dealers who, in fronting some or all of the money, became the actual publishers of the work. In Straparola's case, the title page of the 1550 edition identifies that man as one Orfeo dalla Carta of Sant'Alvise, a local parish church on a small square in the remote Canareggio district of the city. It was there that his first volume of tales was introduced to the world in January 1551, and it was this elusive book-seller who, ostensibly at least, wrote the preliminary address to the ladies. But no one is quite certain who he was.[107] This first collection seems to have done so well that the author was encouraged by the book merchants to make a companion volume, if it had not been planned from the outset (which I believe it was). Meanwhile, sales of the first volume justified a second printing in the same year, entailing the labour-intensive task of resetting the type which had already been disbursed. The book-seller for this second edition had a shop in San Luca at the sign of the Diamond, a far more central location about halfway between the Rialto Bridge and San Stefano, and just off the Grand Canal.

The second volume appeared in 1553, about equal in length to the first but asymmetrical in design, for instead of twenty-five stories there were now forty-eight, spread over eight nights rather than five, with considerably more replacements among the narrators, breaking up the nearly regular design of five young women presenters per evening, their respective 'turns' established by drawing their names from a golden vase. (There are signs here of the breakdown of the Boccaccian model.) This publication first appeared in a shop at the sign of the Little Dove in the parish of San Bartholomeo.

Concerning the particulars of the work's subsequent publication history, the acknowledged specialist is Donato Pirovano, whose scrupulous investigation into the matter will, I should think, exclude a 'bis' performance for a very long time. He has travelled the libraries of the world tracking down copies of all of the early printings and editions on a comparative basis, calling here for a simple resume of his data appropriate

107 Both Pirovano and Bottigheimer offer speculations, following upon those by Giuseppe Rua and Steno Zanandrea. For a summary see Bottigheimer's *Fairy Godfather*, p. 107. One suggestion was that he was a member of the Danza family. Rua calls him 'editore,' while Pirovano calls him 'finanziatore/promotore.' But he may be Straparola's invention, used as a means to write his own apology as though from an independent party. The address to the ladies in the second volume, now in Straparola's own name, uses many of the same rhetorical ploys.

to a critical edition in translation.[108] It is important that he carefully established on sound bibliographical grounds the high priority to be given to the earliest editions of the two parts as the only reliable basis for an edition or translation (which of course includes his own, published in Rome in 2000). He worked backwards by determining that after 1557 there is little of authority to be taken into consideration, for by then the work had already undergone the first round of substitutions on grounds of censorship, after which there appears to have been no further possibility of authorial intervention, reaction, or reparation. It is conceivable that Straparola supplied the two replacement stories inserted in 1555, but he could not have supervised the work's publication very closely, given the discrepancies concerning the names of the storytellers left over from the unrevised edition. By then approaching his mid-seventies, he presumably died shortly thereafter and his portrait was removed from subsequent editions. Pirovano doubts even the authority of those two replacement stories for VIII.3 (VIII.3A and 3B). Moreover, in the edition of 1555 he found many typographical errors not present in the earlier editions, while the few improvements are merely the corrections of former typographical errors well within the competence of the typesetters. There is no evidence of Straparolan input. This takes Pirovano back to the two earliest editions of the two parts, which, carefully reviewed by a modern editor, provide the only acceptable texts upon which to build a critical edition or authoritative translation.

During the period between 1550 and 1608, there were twenty-nine reprintings or editions of one or both parts of the *Nights*, the first part printed in 1550 and reprinted in 1551, 1555, 1556, and 1557, and the second part printed in 1553 and reprinted in 1554, 1555, 1556, and 1557. There were thus five printings each of the separate volumes, marketed independently, before they were brought together in 1558 and published as a single work. That combined collection, during the following half-century, enjoyed nineteen editions. Statistically, then, it may be said that the whole of the *Piacevoli notti* received twenty-four printings in fifty-eight years, the tally of a true bestseller. Straparola had gone through the formal procedures of applying for permission to publish, which, with its reception, meant not only that the book had passed inspection concerning its contents, but that Straparola gained something equivalent to copyright. It had been submitted to the council and approved on 8 March

108 His findings were published in a long article entitled 'Per l'edizione de la *Piacevoli notti* di Giovan Francesco Straparola,' *Filologia e Critica* 26 (2001), pp. 60–93.

1550, with five members voting against it. The first volume was probably printed at the author's expense, which may account for the delays in the printing and the split run while the author calculated his risks and rustled up resources. It is clearly marked 'In Venegia per Comin da Trino ad instanza dell'autore' (at the instigation of the author).[109] The first traces of censorship appear in the reprinting of the second volume in 1555, in which 'The Priest and the Image-Carver's Wife' (VIII.3), with its patently blasphemous overtones and brutal handling of a lecherous priest, not surprisingly found disfavour and was replaced. The subsequent pages of the work were not disturbed, however, for the length of the two replacements; 'The Woes of an Old Gallant' and 'The Merchant's Monkey' occupied the same number of pages. This was the first assault upon the integrity of the collection and the coherence of the framing tale.

That the production of the edition of 1558 passed into the hands of Domenico Giglio is of indifferent importance. Comin da Trino returns to the scene with the edition of 1562 and then dissociates himself from the title. It is with the edition of 1565 that the work arrives at a new critical moment, for the invasion of the censors is now pervasive. Eight stories are revised or rewritten, each one for having represented one or more members of the clergy in a comic or morally unfavourable way. The three nuns in VI.4 no longer perform their outrageous feats but merely deliver their pious homilies, while the amorous priest in I.5 is reduced to a minor clerk. Others among the eight are XI.3, XI.5, XIII.9, XIII.11, and two misnumbered by Pirovano, one of which I can identify as III.1. These changes appear to have become a permanent feature of the text in all subsequent editions. In 1569 the printing was taken over by Domenico Farré and the title was thereafter changed to *Le tredici piacevoli notti del S. Gio. Francesco Straparola da Caravaggio.* When Altobello Salicato took over in 1573, he claimed that the entire work was diligently revised and corrected. Pirovano provides an elaborate chart of the revisions and corrections imposed during that half-century of printings, revealing many more corruptions than improvements.

Thirty-two years after the major alterations of 1565, the *Nights* encountered radical censorship and were thereafter published only 'con licentia de' superiori.' In the edition by Daniel Zanetti printed in 1597, five of the stories were suppressed: II.4, 'The Devil's Marriage to Silvia Ballastro'; VI.4, 'Who Will Become Abbess?' even after the former revisions; XI.5,

109 For technical information on this printer, see P. Veneziani, 'La marca tipografica di Comin da Trino,' *Gutenberg-Jahrbuch* (1990), pp. 162–73.

'Frate Begoccio Takes a Wife and Leaves Her'; XII.4, 'Of the Sons who Disobeyed their Father's Testament'; and XIII.8, 'Midnight Feast and Famine.' This is the result of truly humourless rigour. Three of the five involve members of the religious community, the fourth involves the Devil himself, and the fifth includes arguments concerning the destiny of the soul after death. Other stories are merely mutilated. No more tricks would be practised upon priests, not even the luring of the priest into Cassandrino's sack in I.2, and no more references to conjuring witches in VII.1. Other changes were made to IX.4, X.4, and even VII.3, as well as to nine other tales. Likewise, the enigmas came under scrutiny and the last, following XIII.13, was patently altered, leaving a collection altogether more straight-laced and proper. There are interesting compensations in these later editions in the form of dozens of woodcuts and additional enigmas, beginning in 1597. In 1598, even the songs and madrigals were censored. The 1599 edition appeared 'espurgate nuovamente da molti errori e di bellissime figure adonate'; what could possibly be left? Those figures included illustrations from the work of Sansovino, along with 100 enigmas and seven sonnet enigmas by Giulio Cesare dalla Croce. In 1601, four more stories were deleted entirely: IV.5, 'Flamminio in Seeking Death Discovers Life'; VIII.4, 'Lattanzio and the Secret Arts of Sorcery'; XI.2, 'The Grateful Dead'; and XIII.3, 'On the Liberality of Spaniards and Germans.' Readers may ponder on their own the plausible reasons for taking umbrage to these seemingly innocuous creations. The cumulative and incremental objections to his stories become tantamount to an anatomy of those censorious times as the imaginations of the 'superiori' become increasingly sensitized to the topics and humour of popular culture. What Straparola once thought fit for the carnival recreation of the elite, with the odd polite reprimand, within fifty years found itself considerably reduced. But for some, even this was insufficient. The *Piacevoli notti* was listed on the Index of Forbidden Books first in Parma in 1580, then by Pope Sixtus V in 1590, and Clement VIII in 1596, and again in 1600, which means, in effect, that all publications of the work after 1590 were in defiance of the papal ban, even though these papal interdictions were not rigorously enforced. Nevertheless, Straparola was finished in Italy for nearly three centuries.[110] The Venetian publishers who had retained the rights to this work exclusively for themselves lost

110 Further to the ecclesiastical tribunals, censorship, and the Venetian Press, see Paul Grendler, *The Roman Inquisition and the Venetian Press 1540–1605* (Princeton: Princeton University Press, 1977). Grendler explains how a book was sent first to an inquisitor or his delegate who examined the work for doctrinal or moral errors,

a book in high demand, and while Straparola would enjoy circulation in other nations, he would not see a revival in Italy before the edition by Giuseppe Rua at the turn of the twentieth century.[111]

His nadir was undoubtedly the nineteenth century, for while he was known to specialists and historians, his star had decidedly set – if Rachel Harriette Busk, active in Italy as a folk tale collector in the 1870s, is an acceptable witness: 'Straparola's collection seems, in Rome at least, to have fallen into the oblivion which Mr. Campbell says is its merited lot. At least, not only was it not mentioned to me at any of the dêpots where rare books are a *spécialité*, but my subsequent inquiry for it by name failed to produce a copy.'[112] Adding insult to this injury is the entry for the city of 'Caravaggio' in Franciscus Arisius' *Cremona literata* of 1702, in which Straparola merits a reference merely as the author of a book of 'favole et enimmi' (fables and enigmas) listed on the index of the holy inquisition for its sordid obscenities, its obnoxious and vulgar materials, for which reasons Possivinus S.J. and others laboured to liberate the later editions of their iniquities.[113]

The first twenty-five stories were translated into French quite faithfully by Jean Louveau and published by Guillaume Rouille in Lyons in 1560. The second volume of stories was translated by Jean de Larivey and published in 1572; de Larivey subsequently reworked the entire collection in his own rather freer and more inventive style. Between 1572 and 1589

---

p. 151. Next it was sent to the public reader, looking for political content. Finally, the book was taken to the ducal secretary to assure that prevailing policies of state were not contradicted.

111 Giuseppe Rua's edition of Straparola was published three times, first as *Le 'piacevoli notti' de Messer Gian Francesco Straparola* (Rome: Ermanno Loescher, 1898), with an introduction of 136 pages, then as *Le piacevoli notti di M. Giovanfrancesco Straparola* (Bologna: Romagnoli-dell'Acqua, 1899–1908), and again simply as *Le piacevoli notti*, 2 vols. (Bari: Laterza, 1927), this last edition without the enigmas. To complicate this report, Rua wrote his 'Intorno alle *"Piacevoli notti"* della Straparola' for *Italiana* 15 (1890), pp. 111–51, in anticipation of his full introduction. For the complete reference and the second half, see the bibliography.

112 *Roman Legends: A Collection of the Fables and Folktales of Rome* (Boston: Estes & Lauriat, 1877), p. viinl. Campbell is the editor of the collection of tales from the West Highlands mentioned in several of the subsequent annotations; he thought that copies of the *Piacevoli notti* had been taken to Scotland as early as the David Rizzio period in the 1560s and had launched several of the tales which he collected three centuries later. It is odd that his opinion of Straparola should hence be so low.

113 'Caravaggio,' in *Cremona literata, seu in Cremonensis doctrinis & literariis dignitatibus eminentiores chronologicæ adnotationes* (Parma: Pazzoni & Montius, 1702).

there were twelve reprints or new editions, some of them published in Rouen, others in Paris. This work became well known and supplied materials for many subsequent French authors. Later editions of this translation appeared in 1699 (all copies lost); 1725, with a preface by La Monnoie and notes by Lainez,[114] reissued in 1775; and the editions of the nineteenth century described below. The first German translation appeared in 1575, with subsequent printings in 1582 and 1590, all of which have perished. Johann Fischart refers to this translation in the preface to his *Naupengeheurlichen Geschichtklitterung* (1577). The next translation containing some twenty-four stories appeared in 1791,[115] followed by the partial edition (eighteen stories) translated by Valentin Schmidt for publication in 1817 with his extensive critical annotations. Adalbert von Keller translated twelve for his *Italiänischer Novellenschatz*, published in Leipzig in 1851. The complete text reappeared again only in 1904, in the translation by Alfred Semerau, as *Die ergötzlichen Nächte*.[116] The Grimm brothers spoke well of these stories in some senses, but warned that they were 'not merely dirty, but even shameless and obscene.'[117] In Spain the work made an early debut, the first in Zaragossa in 1578, in the translation by Francisco Truchado, condensed to twelve nights, after purging it of all obscenity and irreverence. The *Honesto y agradable Entretenimiento da Damas y Galanes* was printed in Grenada by René Rabut in 1583, and thereafter in Madrid in 1598 and 1612.[118] I have not made a methodical enquiry into the number of languages into which Straparola has been

114 (Amsterdam: Jean-Frédéric Bernard, 1725).

115 *Die Nächte des Strapparola von Caravaggio* [*sic*], 2 vols. (Vienna: Alberti, 1791), with a wordy but unreliable preface attributed to Mazzuchelli, no doubt because of his edition of Bandello published that same year.

116 *Die ergötzlichen Nächte* reappeared in 1908 in Munich by M. Müller, perhaps the same as that published by him in 1920 as *Die Novellen und Mären der Ergötzlichen Nächte*, trans. by H. Floerike.

117 The original reads: 'nicht bloss unanständig, sondern bis zum schamlosen unzüchtig.' *Kinder- und Hausmärchen* (Göttingen: Dieterich'schen Buchhandlung, 1856), vol. III, p. 285.

118 According to Doris Senn, this work also appeared in several other cities in the intervening years, first appearing in 1578, while in her title she gives the dates as 1569–81. She names seven more, bringing the count up to ten and nearly equal to the number of editions in France. '*Le piacevoli Notti* (1550/53) von Giovan Francesco Straparola, ihre italienischen Editionen und die spanische Übersetzung *Honesto y agradable Entretenimiento de Damas y Galanes* (1569/81) von Francisco Truchado,' *Fabula* 34 (1993), p. 49. For a comparative appraisal, see Marcelino Menéndez y Pelayo, *Orígenes de la novella*, ed. E. Sánchez Reyes, 4 vols. (Santander, 1943), vol. III, pp. 40*ff.*

translated. But in addition to Spanish, Italian, French, and German there is the Chinese *Shi ye tan* and the Russian *Pri i atnye nochi*.[119]

VII. The Translation and Editorial Procedures

The translation of *The Nights of Straparola* made by William George Waters (1844–1928) has received general approbation since its first appearance in 1894. Waters had travelled extensively in Italy, knew the language and its idioms well, and exercised his skills as a translator not only in the present work, but in his translations of Ser Giovanni's *Pecorone*, appearing in 1897, and Masuccio's *Novellino*, published in 1895.[120] In these magisterial endeavours, all three of them sumptuously illustrated by the incomparable E.R. Hughes, ARWS, Waters claimed his place in translation history for having introduced to English readers three of the most important of the Italian *novellieri* after Boccaccio. The Masuccio and Straparola volumes were published by one of London's most distinguished late Victorian publishers, the house of Lawrence and Bullen in Covent Garden. Both were printed in two-volume sets, in large quarto format, each edition enjoying a press run of 210 numbered copies on Japanese vellum, bound in half leather and boards with red stamping. The present edition was produced using copy no. 210. *The Pecorone* was published privately for members of the Society of Bibliophiles in three volumes of 100 numbered copies bound in full leather with gold stamping and gilt-edged pages, the illustrations coloured aquarelles, again by E.R. Hughes.[121] Because of the authority and elegance of these translations, the prospect of retranslating Straparola initially seemed both audacious and unnecessary. Readers would be served best by a fully annotated edition of this classic, for it carries a stylistic cachet of considerable imagination and grace.

But with the passage of time, the tinkering began. In the first instance, Waters left parts of the story of the rival nuns (VI.4) in French, on the

119 *Shi ye tan* [by Shi te la pa luo no], ed. Jian yi Du (Xianggang xiang jiang chu ban gong si, 1986); *Pri i atnye nochi* (Moscow: Voskhozhdenie, 1993). See also *Prii a tnye nochi* (Moscow: Izdatel'stvo 'Nauka,' 1978).

120 W.G. Waters was one of the great Italianists of his age, for in addition to his translations of the *novellieri*, he was the author of *Jerome Cardan: A Biographical Study* (1898); *Piero della Francesca* (1901); *The Journal of Montaigne's Travels in Italy* (1903); and *Italian Sculptors* (1911).

121 The first edition of *The Pecorone* of Ser Giovanni was published in London by Lawrence & Bullen in 1897 in a press run of 110 copies, my own, no. 5, ex libris Glmi:Georg:Waters (his name Italicized on his bookplate).

assumption, one would suppose, that if readers can deal with the language of Racine, they are qualified to know how nuns might remove mustard seeds from the face of a die by farting, or piss through the eye of a needle – otherwise, not. He also resorted to French in VI.2 to avoid explaining how Castorio became reconciled to his emasculation. These little Victorian lacunae were easily enough restored from the original. But upon closer scrutiny, this modesty was more the rule than the exception throughout. We are not told how Adamantina's little doll (V.2) not only bit down hard upon his majesty's arse, but also grabbed his jingle bells and squeezed them as hard as it could. There were several more restorations in kind to follow. But once the sanctity of a 'whole' text had been broken, the mystique exposed, there was no retreat. At first piecemeal, then more systematically, and ultimately rigorously, the translation was revisited and adjustments ensued by the hundreds if not thousands. The intent was by no means to eliminate Waters's voice, for in so many ways he got matters exactly right. But he had his own stylistic quirks which he repeated endlessly, such as parenthetic syntax. He was also given to interpretive elaboration, the reinsertion of names, and at times he made the simplest of speakers worthy of the salon, while at others, for the sake of concision, he left out Straparola's doublings or awkward details. In the original, Adamantina's doll states: 'Mamma, mamma, caca,' on several occasions, but Waters confines this iterative baby talk to: 'The stool, mother, the stool,' and then says that 'the doll replied in the same words as before.' This is no error, but modern readers can handle the domestic realism of the original. This is equally true for Straparola's amusing metaphors for sexual activity. Waters was content to report of the serving man who crept into a lady's bedroom, that he placed himself beside her and without her resistance took his pleasure with her. But the original is clear in the matter; that 'he took his rod in hand, which was quite rusty, and shoved it into her forge' (VIII.1). The collection is a veritable study in these playfully off-colour metaphors, taking their cue from Boccaccio, inter alios, who famously gave us the one about running the devil into Alibec's cave that devolved into sending the Pope to Rome or the Great Turk to Constantinople, inter alia – all of which have their appeal to those of us with arrested adolescent tastes. These too, with apologies, have been restored, with the critical observation that Straparola seemed to go out of his way to find occasions for such constructions, perhaps giving away something of his own compound sense of aesthetics and audiences. Parental supervision advised.

Otherwise, Waters's outright errors of commission are few indeed. In one instance he took 'mendicante' (beggar) for a doctor; a mere slip. In another (VIII.4 at the end), he took a 'trombone' for a trumpet and thus could make little of the sliding up and down motion, which he translated as 'held close and swayed up and down by the player.' But on the whole, he was closely attentive to the logic of the stories and, in certain cases where Straparola makes little sense, he tweaked the words into intelligibility. This raises new problems for the editor. In this same story of Lattanzio and Dionigi (VIII.4), the boy throws himself into the river 'e trasformatosi nel pesce squallo, s'attuffò nell'onde' (and turning himself into a shark fish, plunged beneath the waves), both sharks and waves hardly pertaining to rivers. Waters sensibly translates this passage as 'a little fish that hides in the deepest water' to avoid the anomalies. Moreover, the shark would be pursued by a tuna fish, which, without consulting specialists, doesn't seem to be the natural predator of sharks. One might say that he betrayed the literal sense, but he enhanced the logical coherence of the story and after long debate over these rare instances, I opted to follow him. At stake is the evidence which such apparent lapses may contain concerning confusions in the folk sources that Straparola dutifully preserves. Inversely, Waters slips when he has Violante the princess out collecting pebbles, for her lady-in-waiting is clearly intended, as she later presents the ruby she finds to the princess; and he slips again when he has the 'cattiva risposta' (ill-mannered or unfavourable response) to the physician delivered by the princess rather than by the king, who, in the next line, has her called in ('chiamata la figliuola in presenzia del medico'). These have been adjusted, along with many other critical words and phrases, as when, at the end of XIII.4 where the Signora asks Signor Bernardo Capello to tell a story, the phrase 'che partecipasse con esso noi' (who participated with us) is left out as a mere redundancy. If Capello was there, of course he was participating, except that the telltale 'noi' also suggests that the author was present. It is a rare moment in the confirmation of Straparola's fiction that he had been a part of the *veglie* of which the *Nights* pretends to be a mere transcription. But more justification for these adjustments and emendations seems ungrateful. Waters remains substantially present in a text which is still essentially his, even though, through myriad stabs of the pen, he has been pervasively altered in microscopic ways in the interests of rendering Straparola's 'voices' with greater diversity and accuracy, while recovering many missing little pieces or significant allusions. In short, his translation has been thoroughly checked and revised against the original. The text employed in this rather arduous task was Donato Pirovano's critical edition of *Le piacevoli notti*, published in Rome by Salerno editrice in 2000. His careful rationale for the original texts he employed is set out in the history of the text above.

Herewith, then, is an edition of both parts of the Straparolan original, including the two substitute stories of 1555 as well as all the preliminary materials and enigmas, which are often omitted in popular editions. The titles of the stories are entirely editorial, for there were none in any of the early editions, and by rights they should be in brackets. Richard Burton assigned titles of his own in the two-volume Carrington edition of 1906 that might have been adopted. But the present titles are slightly longer, more descriptive, and more frequently incorporate the protagonists' names. Burton called X.4 'The Strange Testament'; here, it is 'The Diabolical Testament of Andrigetto di Val Sabia.' For XI.1, his reads 'The Fairy as a Cat,' while mine is 'Constantino and his Wonderful Cat.' For XI.3, his 'Pot Calling the Kettle Black' is called here 'Wind, Water, and Shame, or the Gluttony of Dom Pomporio.' Burton's have the virtue of brevity, often touching on a feature of the story that requires elucidation through reading. Those in the present edition are more prosaic, being based on the one- or two-sentence rubrics heading each story in lieu of titles in the original. Nevertheless, one of Burton's decisions in his otherwise strange production nearly prevailed in the title of the present work.[122] His *The Most Delectable Nights* had been my working title since the project's inception. The Italian 'piacevoli' carries a variety of nuances around the concept of pleasing, pleasurable, or delightful. Other synonyms include

---

122 Burton does not seem to have returned to textual ground zero to generate his translation, but rewrites the Waters rendition in a more flamboyant, perhaps orientalized, certainly more aureate style. Why he would do that is not entirely clear, for Waters is already a notch above the more prosaic Straparola and in need of stylistic downsizing. That Burton undertook so enormous a task is, nevertheless, a gesture of commitment to a collection of stories he thought worth the investment. He saw the work as belonging to the same class of literature as the *Decameron*, the *Cent nouvelles nouvelles*, and the queen of Navarre's *Heptameron*, and found it 'in no way unworthy of comparison with any of these. Its contents are eminently varied, diverting and (for a work of this *genre*) original.' *The Most Delectable Nights of Straparola of Caravaggio: The first complete translation into English of* Le tredici piacevolissime notti (Paris: Charles Carrington, 1906), p. xxv. His boast of presenting the first complete translation of the work is either a bibliographical fiddle or an out-and-out lie. It is not my intention here to expose him by citing sizeable chunks of word-for-word transcriptions from Waters. Only in the technical sense of citing the edition entitled *Le tredici piacevolissime notti* is his statement true, and why anyone would want to base an edition on that later and much massacred edition is open to questioning. Anyone interested in these matters can easily follow his trail by having Waters, together with his source, open beside Burton and his proclaimed source, which is any edition appearing after 1569. See the history of the text above.

merry, joyful, pleasant, enchanting, and delectable. Waters could not make up his mind and fell back on 'The Nights.' 'Merry' has also been used in a modern popular edition. The French employed 'facétieuse,' meaning humourous, but with overtones of impish, mischievous. The Germans have preferred 'ergötzlich,' meaning delightful, but with overtones of amusing or funny. Both are impressions as well as translations. Insofar as a choice had to be made of an adjective between 'The' and 'Nights,' after trying out as many as I could think of, it fell on 'pleasant,' which, for me, carries the happiest combination of nuances describing the atmosphere surrounding the Signora's circle in Murano, for the title appears to refer to the occasion itself, rather than to the stories in all their diversity, some of which are by no means mirthful, funny, or pleasant.

The poems and enigmas in the Waters translation remain largely unchanged. These are challenging recreations on his part, effective, and difficult to improve upon in piecemeal fashion. They are very free translations, to be sure, as they were in the case of Larivey's French. Moreover, because they are, in several cases, translations of the lyrics of known madrigals and canzonets of the era with their often heady Petrarchan overtones, Waters's Victorian idiom seemed altogether appropriate. The ordering of the stories in books VIII and IX is confusing in the extreme, or was made so by subsequent editors. Within Straparola's lifetime the first of many deletions took place. Originally, VIII.3 was the tale most likely to offend the clergy: that of the nude priest who simulated Christ on the cross in the image-carver's shop to escape attention. In its place, Straparola (presumably) substituted two stories of equivalent length, which could be inserted without disturbing the pagination. These have been added to Book VIII as numbers 3A and 3B. Brilliant so far. But Straparola assigned these tales to new speakers without changing the assignment of tales in the opening selection of names or at the ends of the preceding stories. Thus, when subsequent editors, such as Waters, left the replacements in situ and moved the original tale of 'The Priest and the Image-Carver's Wife' to Book IX, confusion reigned. Waters made adjustments, changing names and enigmas, all of which have been restored to the order of the earliest edition.

In need of explanation, perhaps, is the absence of a general bibliography for the commentaries. The reading for these annotations was carried out in three Canadian libraries, including Toronto's Robarts Library, and in eight of the many libraries at the University of Bologna, supplemented by some 250 titles sent to my own university through the Inter-library Loan System over a three-year period – thus, books at my disposal for limited periods of time. Hence, many of the same works were consulted in whatever editions were available at different times and places. The upshot was that it became impossible to standardize the references to a goodly number of these works short of retracing many steps, reordering many books, and revisiting many places, all to largely ceremonial ends. In consequence, each reference carries its own full bibliographical documentation – the alternative to citing three or four different editions of the same work in a bibliography and encoding all the footnotes to designate which. But virtue may be made of this reality insofar as I have given, in addition to page references, book and chapter numbers as well as titles to facilitate location in whatever editions readers may have available to them (which, in many instances, will not be the same as those available to me). Hence, insofar as each reference is full and complete in itself, the requisite documentation is immediately visible. Readers may find that beneficial. The only drawback is the redundancy of certain publishing information in the footnotes where the same work is employed on multiple occasions. In the bibliographical references, first dates of publication are often found in brackets before the date of the quoted edition, or, when rare early editions are being cited, references to later editions and reprints may also appear.

Moreover, as a matter of convenience, I did not always consult such diversely published works as Grimms's *Fairy Tales* and *The Thousand Nights and One Night*, or Masuccio or Ser Giovanni, for that matter, in the canonic critical editions. When I was merely looking for confirmation of a plotline, I relied on the translations in my own library. But this pertains only to well-known, widely published authors whom readers will consult in their own particular editions, in any case. Most others I read in the only English, German, French, Italian, Spanish, Latin (I even tried Portuguese) editions available of these works. But the problem became acute when I found myself in Bologna's Casa Carducci Library consulting editions of now rare Italian folklore that were, in their day, also published in parallel editions which I had already consulted elsewhere. I simply cite the editions I used when and where I found them. If this merits an apology, you have it.

APPENDIX I

A Provisional Table of 'Genres' and Provenances

The following chart is an attempt to profile the entire collection in terms of the genres and provenances of the seventy-five stories. It can have but approximate working validity because most of the designations are purely impressionistic or inferential. The 'types' of folk tales are usually determined by their characteristic actions or motifs, while 'genre,' here, can mean nothing more than 'kind' or 'class,' such as jest, trickster tale, social vignette, tale of adultery, beast fable, legend, wonder tale – a quadruped's breakfast of labels. The purpose of the exercise is merely to demonstrate at a glance the variety of the contents, of which we might well ask not 'what is present?' but 'what is missing?' Straparola's stories, in rather balanced proportions, make their way through the popular 'genres' of the age, from the jest of parking a pasty on a lady's posterior as an error in the night (XIII.8) to the hauntingly moving tragedy of Malgherita Spolatina, led out to sea, swimming, by her own brothers in a boat, there to drown of exhaustion (VII.2). Such a chart allows for a quick appraisal of the collection's design, or lack thereof, as a miscellany of popular and erudite tales, the latter recycled through the oral tradition. As for the thorny matter of provenance, there are only educated guesses. This column is the sum of the appraisals made in the course of compiling the commentaries, reflecting my best inferential reasoning about how the stories came to Straparola. The underlying hypothesis is that where cognate versions exist in later oral traditions, often in abundance, of stories lacking any proximate literary versions predating Straparola, probability favours a popular source for the version in the *Notti*. This is not to say that traces of that story tradition are non-existent in the prior literary record; in fact, most of the stories have left such traces of their passage. But the reason they cannot have served Straparola as sources is that, in order to arrive at what he wrote, he would have been compelled to restore those texts, in every instance, to a version often nearly identical to those surviving centuries later in the oral tradition. The chance that he reinvented the folk versions in such a manner, to my way of thinking, is smaller than infinitesimal. The harder call to make is whether the oral tale was once based on a written source and subsequently assumed the traits of orality. That could well have been the case with certain of the *fabliaux*-like or *novella*-like stories, followed by two centuries or more of oral modulation and structural stratification. The parentheses around 'from written' mean 'possibly' or 'conceivably,' nothing more. Speculation remains free. The telling statistic in it all is that of the fifty-three stories in the collection not traceable to Morlini, only five have acknowledged and demonstrable literary sources.

	Short Title	Class of Tale	Presumed Source
I.1	'Salardo's Disobedience'	moralizing novella	oral (from written)
I.2	'Cassandrino'	popular tale of trickery	folk tale
I.3	'Scarpacifico'	popular tale of trickery	folk tale
I.4	'Doralice'	wonder tale	folk tale
I.5	'Polissena and the Priest'	novella of adultery	oral
II.1	'The Pig Prince'	wonder tale	folk tale
II.2	'Filenio's Revenge'	novella	Ser Giovanni
II.3	'Carlo da Rimini'	saint's life / novella	oral (from written)
II.4	'The Devil's Marriage'	fantasy novella	folk tale (from written)
II.5	'Simplicio de' Rossi'	novella	oral (from written)
III.1	'Pietro's Magic Fish'	wonder tale	folk tale
III.2	'Livoretto'	wonder tale	folk tale
III.3	'Biancabella'	wonder tale	folk tale
III.4	'Fortunio and Mermaid'	wonder tale	folk tale
III.5	'Isotta and Travaglino'	novella of adultery	oral / popular
IV.1	'Costanza, Girl-Knight'	wonder tale	folk tale
IV.2	'Erminione and Filenia'	novella	Francesco Bello
IV.3	'Dancing Water'	wonder tale	folk tale
IV.4	'The Physician's Wife'	novella	Ser Giovanni
IV.5	'Flamminio's Quest'	wonder tale	folk tale
V.1	'Guerrino and Wild Man'	wonder tale	folk tale
V.2	'Adamantina's Doll'	wonder tale	folk tale
V.3	'The Three Hunchbacks'	novella-farce	folk tale *(fabliau)*
V.4	'Tia Rabboso'	novella of adultery	oral / popular
V.5	'Modesta's Shoes'	novella / popular tale	new / oral
VI.1	'Wives in Common'	novella	Boccaccio, et al.
VI.2	'Castorio's Castration'	pop. tale / jest	oral / popular
VI.3	'The Widow's Promise'	novella / anecdote	oral / popular
VI.4	'The Three Rival Nuns'	jest / popular tale	oral / popular
VI.5	'The Virtue of Stones'	anecdote / jest	Morlini
VII.1	'The Wife and the Witch'	fantasy novella of adultery	oral / popular
VII.2	'Malgherita Spolatina'	novella	oral / popular
VII.3	'Flogged at Court'	jest	oral / popular
VII.4	'Share and Share Alike'	novella / anecdote	oral / popular
VII.5	'The Three Brothers'	wonder tale	folk tale
VIII.1	'Three Idle Rogues'	jest / popular tale	folk tale
VIII.2	'Handling Wives'	novella	oral / popular
VIII.3	'Image-Carver's Wife'	novella from *fabliau*	oral (from written)
VIII.4	'Lattanzio's Sorcery'	wonder tale	folk tale
VIII.5	'The Donkey's Skin'	jest	Morlini
VIII.3A	'Woes of an Old Gallant'	novella	oral (from written)
VIII.3B	'Merchant's Monkey'	jest	Morlini
IX.1	'King Galafro'	novella	oral (from written)
IX.2	'Rodolino and Violante'	novella	Boccaccio

	Short Title	Class of Tale	Presumed Source
IX.3	'Francesco Sforza'	pseudo-hist. novella	written / oral
IX.4	'Papiro Schizza'	jest	oral / popular
IX.5	'Bergamasques'	jest	oral / popular
X.1	'Veronica's Jewels'	jest / anecdote	no known sources
X.2	'The Lion and the Ass'	beast fable	popular (from written)
X.3	'Cesarino and Dragon'	wonder tale	folk tale
X.4	'Andrigetto's Testament'	jest / anecdote	oral / popular
X.5	'Rosolino's Confession'	novella / anecdote	oral (from written)
XI.1	'Constantino's Cat'	wonder tale	folk tale
XI.2	'The Grateful Dead'	wonder tale	folk tale
XI.3	'Dom Pomporio'	jest based on proverb	oral / popular
XI.4	'The Stolen Veal'	jest	Morlini
XI.5	'Frate Bigoccio'	novella / anecdote	Morlini
XII.1	'Florio's Jealousy'	novella / anecdote	Morlini
XII.2	'The Fool's Blackmail'	novella / jest	Morlini
XII.3	'Pozzuolo's Wife'	novella / cautionary tale	Morlini
XII.4	'The Disobedient Sons'	novella / anecdote	Morlini
XII.5	'Pope Sixtus IV'	pseudo-hist. tale	Morlini
XIII.1	'Madman and Hunter'	jest / tale	Morlini
XIII.2	'Diego and the Friar'	jest	Morlini
XIII.3	'Spaniards and Germans'	jest	Morlini
XIII.4	'The Servant and the Fly'	jest / popular tale	Morlini
XIII.5	'The Fateful Sack'	Apuleian farce	Morlini
XIII.6	'The Good Day'	jest / popular tale	Morlini
XIII.7	'Giorgio and His Master'	jest / popular tale	Morlini
XIII.8	'Midnight Famine'	jest	Morlini
XIII.9	'Hermaphrodite Nun'	novella / anecdote	Morlini
XIII.10	'Doctor of Laws'	popular tale / anecdote	Morlini
XIII.11	'The Novice in the Barn'	novella	written sources including Morlini
XIII.12	'Healing of Guglielmo'	anecdote	no known sources
XIII.13	'Pietro Rizzato'	moral tale	Morlini

Morlini	22
Wonder tales (& beast fable)	17
Oral with possible written affiliations	11
Other popular tales, farces, anecdotes from oral sources	17
No known sources, written or oral	2
From known literary sources other than Morlini	5
From written source, but source unknown	1

APPENDIX II

Folk Tale Types According to the Aarne-Thompson-Uther (ATU) Index

Scattered at random throughout the commentaries to follow are story-type numbers originating in the universally employed Aarne-Thompson *Types of the Folktale.* That work, now called *Types of International Folktales,* as revised by Hans-Jörg Uther, is the source of the corresponding numbers supplied below. Also appearing sporadically throughout the commentaries are motif numbers derived from Stith Thompson's *Motif-Index of Folk-Literature* – numbers which are comprehensively listed by D.P. Rotunda in his *Motif-Index of the Italian Novella in Prose,* and again by Donato Pirovano in his edition of *Le piacevoli notti* at the bottom of the first page of each story. Given this redundant record of the motif numbers, there is far less need to supply them again here. In the course of the commentaries to follow, my intention has been to identify and profile the many works antecedent to the *Piacevoli notti* that contribute to an understanding of his story types, and in the process of doing so I have devised analyses tantamount in some cases to early histories of the relevant types. In the centuries after Straparola, those type traditions often luxuriated into proportions far beyond my purposes, resulting in a selective representation of their afterlives. For those wishing to corroborate my type histories and fill in the later centuries from folklore reference works incorporating the ATU numbers, the following, modified from the list initially compiled by Luisa Rubini for the *Enzyklopädie des Märchens,* should prove useful.[123]

Night	Story	ATU Number	Description of the Type
I.	1	910A	Excellent advice
I.	2	1737	Priest in the sack
I.	2	1525A	The master thief
I.	3	1538	Revenge of the betrayed, or Deceiving the deceivers
I.	3	1551	The cheating contest
I.	3	1539	Trickery and gullibility
I.	3	1535	Unibos or One-ox
I.	4	510B	The princess in the chest
II.	1	433B	König Lindwurm (a wingless dragon)

123 'Straparola,' in *Enzyklopädie des Märchens,* ed. Rolf Wilhelm Brednick (Berlin: Walter de Gruyter, 2007), vol. 12, pp. 1360–9.

Night	Story	ATU Number	Description of the Type
II.	1	441	Hedgehog Hans
II.	1	425A	The beast bridegroom
II.	4	1164B	Belfagor
II.	4	1862B	The sham physician and the devil in league
III.	1	675	The lazy boy
III.	2	531	Ferdinand the Faithful and Ferdinand the Unfaithful
III.	2	554	The grateful animals
III.	2	314	The girl with the golden hair
III.	3	403	The black bride
III.	3	706	The girl without hands
III.	4	316	The nixie in the pond
III.	4	554/159	The quarrel over the stag
III.	4	665	Grateful animals grant powers of metamorphosis to hero
III.	5	889	The faithful servant
IV.	1	884/514	Woman dressed as a man
IV.	1	328	Corvetto
IV.	2	1418	Isolde's trial by ordeal
IV.	3	707	The three golden sons
IV.	4	1364	Wife of the sworn brothers
IV.	5	326	The boy who learned to fear
V.	1	502	The wild man
V.	2	571C	The biting doll
V.	3	1536B	The three hunchbacks
V.	4	1419C	The one-eyed husband
VI.	1	1424	The nose-maker
VI.	2	1133	How to get fat
VI.	3	1565	Agreement not to scratch
VII.	1	891	The man who abandoned his wife
VII.	2	666	Hero and Leander
VII.	3	1610	The sharing of gifts and blows
VII.	5	653	The four skilful brothers
VIII.	1	1950	The laziness contest
VIII.	2	901	The taming of the shrew
VIII.	3	1359C	Tricks of adultery
VIII.	4	325	The magician's apprentice
VIII.	5	1862C	The naïve diagnosis
IX.	3	958	The shepherd's cry for help
IX.	4	1562A	The barn is burning
IX.	4	1940	Extraordinary names
X.	2	103C	The old donkey meets the bear
X.	2	118	The horse that terrifies the lion
X.	2	125B	Contest between the donkey and the lion
X.	3	300	Dragon, battle, and dragon-slayer
XI.	1	545B	The cat in boots
XI.	2	505	The grateful dead

Night	Story	ATU Number	Description of the Type
XII.	2	1355A	Lord of all
XII.	3	670	The man who knew the language of animals
XIII.	2	1526A	One who leaves without paying the bill
XIII.	4	1586	The fly on the judge's nose
XIII.	4	1600	The buried sheep's head
XIII.	5	958C	Robber shroud
XIII.	6	1641	Doctor Know-all
XIII.	7	1562B	The list of duties
XIII.	8	1775	The hungry priest

APPENDIX III

A Table of Burton's Titles, the Narrators, and the Settings

The names of narrators in parentheses are those of the young ladies originally designated to tell the story by the drawing of lots, but who were then replaced. The forward slash between setting locations indicates movement in the story from one place to the other.

	Burton's Titles	Narrator	Setting
I.1	The Disobedience of Salardo	Lauretta	Genoa / Monferrato
I.2	The Stratagems of Cassandrino	Alteria	Perugia
I.3	Outwitting the Robbers	Cateruzza	Near Imola
I.4	Incestuous Designs of a King	Eritrea	Salerno / England
I.5	Surprised with a Priest	Arianna	Venice
II.1	From Swine to Man	Isabella	Anglia (England)
II.2	The Scholar and the Three Ladies	A. Molino (Fiordiana)	Bologna
II.3	Punishment of a Libertine	Lionora	Rimini
II.4	The Devil Worsted by his Wife	Benedetto (Lodovica)	? / Amalfi
II.5	The Lover in the Sack	Vicenza	Santa Eufemia, Padua
III.1	Story of Pietro the Fool	Cateruzza	Capraia Island, Liguria
III.2	Livoretto's Wonderful Horse	Arianna	Tunis / Cairo / Damascus
III.3	The Damsel and the Snake	Lauretta	Monferrato / Naples
III.4	Fortunio and the King's Daughter	Alteria	Lombardy / Polonia
III.5	The Outcome of a Woman's Wiles	Eritrea	Bergamo
IV.1	The Girl Knight	Fiordiana	Thebes / Bithynia
IV.2	The Husband Outwitted	Vicenza	Athens
IV.3	Misadventures of Royal Offspring	Lodovica	Provino (Provence)

	Burton's Titles	Narrator	Setting
IV.4	The Physician's Wife	Isabella	Padua
IV.5	The Finding of Life	Lionora	Ostia / environs
V.1	The Wild Man of the Woods	Eritrea	Sicily / Irlanda
V.2	The Wonder-working Doll	Alteria	Bohemia
V.3	The Three Hunchbacks	A. Molino (Lauretta)	Valsabbia / Venice / Rome
V.4	An Adulterous Wife's Ruse	Benedetto (Arianna)	Salmazza, Padua
V.5	Shoes for Love-service	Lucrezia (Cateruzza)	Pistoia
VI.1	Friends with Wives in Common	Alteria	Genoa
VI.2	Castrated and Content	Arianna	Carignano, near Fano
VI.3	The Widow's Broken Compact	Cateruzza	Venice
VI.4	Three Rival Abbesses	A. Bembo (Lauretta)	Florence
VI.5	The Virtue of Stones	Eritrea	Bergamo
VII.1	Wife, Harlot and Witch	Vicenza	Florence / Flanders
VII.2	Daring Death for Love	Fiordiana	Ragusa, Dalmatia
VII.3	Flogged at the Pope's Court	Lodovica	Brescia / Rome
VII.4	Share and Share Alike	Lionora	Naples
VII.5	The Three Brothers	Isabella	'Our city' / Chios
VIII.1	The Three Idle Rogues	Eritrea	Siena / Rome
VIII.2	The Right Handling of Wives	Cateruzza	Corneto, near Rome
VIII.3	The Sin of Luxury	Arianna	Florence
VIII.4	The Secret Arts of Sorcery	Alteria (Lodovica, 1555)	Messina
VIII.5	The Donkey's Skin	Lauretta (Veronica, 1555)	Antenorea (Padua)
VIII.3A	The Woes of an Old Gallant	Arianna	'Our city'
VIII.3B	The Merchant's Monkey	Alteria	Genoa / Flanders
IX.1	Vain Precautions	Diana	Madrid
IX.2	The Fatal Grief of Love	Lionora	Budapest / Austria
IX.3	Whilst Chasing a Stag	Isabella	Milan / environs
IX.4	The Danger of a Little Learning	Vicenza	Brescia
IX.5	Outwitting the Wise	F. Beltramo (Fiordiana)	Bergamo
X.1	Naked as When Born	Lauretta	Verona
X.2	Ser Brancaleone	Arianna	Morea, Arcadia
X.3	With the Help of Beasts	Alteria	Calabria / Sicily
X.4	The Strange Testament	Eritrea	Como
X.5	For Love of a Son	Cateruzza	Pavia
XI.1	The Fairy as a Cat	Fiordiana	Bohemia
XI.2	The Reward of Goodness	Leonora	Trino, near Monferrato / Novara
XI.3	Pot Calling the Kettle Black	Diana (Lodovica)	'Famous monastery'

	Burton's Titles	Narrator	Setting
XI.4	The Repast of Veal	Isabella	Vicenza
XI.5	The Gloves	Vicenza	Rome / Florence
XII.1	The Garb of Religion	Lionora	Ravenna
XII.2	The Reward of Loquacity	Lodovica	Pisa
XII.3	Conjugal Correction	Fiordiana	Naples / Pozzuolo
XII.4	Good Counsel	Vicenza	Pesaro
XII.5	The Two Vases	Isabella	Rome / Naples
XIII.1	The Wise Madman	Casale of Bol.	England / forest
XIII.2	The Spaniard's Feast	S. Lucrezia	Cordova
XIII.3	Servant's Chatter	Pietro Bembo	A hostel
XIII.4	Post-mortem Cuckoldry	S. Veronica	Ferrara
XIII.5	The Fatal Sack	Bernardo Capillo	Pistoia
XIII.6	The Good-day's Greeting	S. Chiara	Cesena, Romagna
XIII.7	The Letter Killeth	F. Beltramo	Padua
XIII.8	The Peasant's Pasty	Lauretta	Noventa, Padua
XIII.9	The Hermaphrodite Nun	A. Molino	Salerno
XIII.10	The Subtle Ignoramus	Cateruzza	Naples
XIII.11	The Novice	Benedetto of T.	Near Rovigo (Ferrara)
XIII.12	Doctor Common-sense	Isabella	Brittany (Normandy)
XIII.13	The Friends	Vicenza	Padua

APPENDIX IV

Straparola's Illustrators

Straparola's stories were first illustrated at the end of the sixteenth century, beginning with the Zanetti edition of 1597, followed by the editions (by the same publisher) of 1601, 1604, and 1608. Without having inspected copies of each, it cannot be said with certainty that the same set of woodcuts was used (four stories were deleted from the 1608 edition), but early practice and the recycling of such valuable printing-house commodities suggest that they were.[124] (Those I saw were from the edition of 1608.) The work, by that date, was routinely printed in two octavo volumes – the first of which, in the 1608 edition, contains twenty-eight woodcuts illustrating the first thirty-one stories, less the three deleted

124 The odd edition out is that published in Venice in 1599 by Alessandro de' Vecchi, 'con licenza de' superiori,' to which enigmas by Giulio Cesare dalla Croce were added, along with illustrations from an anthology by Sansovino issued previously by the same printer.

by the censors (II.4, IV.5, and VI.4). The illustrator was clearly commissioned to produce one picture for each story. The second volume undoubtedly contains a similar number of woodcuts and arguably more, given that forty-two stories remained, less the seven from this group deleted by the authorities. This represents a substantial endeavour, whatever the final count, and a clear commitment to the book's ongoing commercial success, despite the indexing and censorship. Some of these woodcuts are more accomplished than others in terms of poses, designs, and execution. A few are striking in the detail of their interiors, or for their accomplished perspectives. By contrast, that of Guerrino standing with his bow and arrow beside the prison grate where the wild man is imprisoned (V.1) is rigid and two-dimensional. The depiction of Tia Rabboso performing her incantations and dancing around her husband, his head inside the sifting basket (V.4), is a successful representation of a scene that would attract all the subsequent illustrators. Surprising to see, meanwhile, are the two which depict conjuring circles surrounded by mysterious symbols (VI.1 and VII.1), given the Church's displeasure with anything having to do with black magic, spells, divination, and necromancy. The latter is of the witch Gabrina and the naked Isabella standing within the magic circle as the devil Farfarello enters at the left. Three design plans are employed in relation to the narratives: a single scene taking up the entire foreground; two scenes juxtaposed side by side on a split field; or double and even triple story episodes represented in the foreground, near, and distant backgrounds. These strategies relate to matters of aesthetics and late Renaissance design; representations of these pictorial strategies may be seen, for example, in the woodcuts illustrating Sir Thomas North's *The Fables of Bidpai* (*The Moral Philosophy of Doni*), published in 1570 with blocks cut in Antwerp.[125] The illustrator must choose either one salient scene to represent the entire story – usually a culminating moment – or show relations of cause and effect, or before and after, through the double use of the space. The picture then achieves a kind of kinetic effect as the viewer fills in the peregrinations that lead from one episode to the other. Insofar as these woodcuts are placed before each text, in a sense they also serve as emblems or enigmas that can only be explained through reading. By dint of these preliminary

125 *The Moral Philosophy of Doni*, ed. Donald Beecher et al. (Ottawa: Dovehouse Editions, 2003). This illustrator was partial to foreground-background representations of contrasting episodes, but did not use the side-by-side arrangement with vertical separations.

pictures, the stories become explanatory in the same way that the texts of the emblem books complete the meanings of the images.

Coming to later centuries, Straparola illustrated calls for an introduction to two little-known but accomplished, late nineteenth-century painters and book illustrators: Jules Arsène Garnier (1847–89), who was called upon to supply fourteen images for the 1882, French, four-volume edition of *Les facétieuses nuits*; and Edward Robert Hughes (1849–1914), who was commissioned for twenty images to grace the Waters translation, which first appeared in the luxurious, two-volume edition of 1894 described above. All of these illustrations were subsequently brought together in the privately printed, four-volume edition of the Waters translation for the Society of Bibliophiles, the first printing in 1898, the second in 1901 (together totalling 1,300 numbered copies). Clearly, both the French and English publishers had recognized the great pictorial potential in these stories and, to redeem their ventures, relied upon the love of handsome and exclusive illustrated books among the purchasers of the Victorian and Belle-Époque periods. For lack of particulars, we can only presume that both illustrators were provided with copies of the stories and invited to choose the subjects, plots, and scenes that most readily inspired their artistic predilections. Intriguingly, they hit upon only a few stories in common, seizing upon moments that appealed to their respective creative impulses or that were deemed the most representative moments of the stories themselves. Those two criteria must, in some ways, have been in competition. There is a particular pleasure in examining their pictures to determine, first, the precise moments in the stories which they represent, perhaps even to supply the corresponding sentences or phrases; second, why the exact scenes they chose best epitomize entire stories; and third, how their artistic talents, tastes, and proclivities found expression through the treatment of their subjects.

The matter of their periodicity merits comment, for both artists were men of their times. Garnier, arguably, makes a more concerted effort than Hughes to create interiors appropriate to historical pasts, or at least to keep them relatively spare and neutral, whereas Hughes luxuriates in the rich textures and decorative clutter of his own age. In matters of period costume, however, Hughes may have the better imagination. Garnier's clerics appear particularly unconvincing and his young women at times look like gypsies, but specialists in these matters will be more adequately informed. Garnier has a sense of humour, of drama, and of the erotic, as well. The pose of the naked young woman fleeing the barn as the novice falls down from the loft (XIII.11) is hauntingly familiar from a formerly depicted scene of disaster. Hughes, by contrast, is thoroughly imbued with the aesthetics of the Pre-Raphaelites and has a penchant for beautiful women, nudity, and eroticism with overtones of mysticism, along with a tendency towards expressionist symbolism all his own. Many of his illustrations began as full-scale salon paintings and are circulated today under different titles. 'Bertuccio's Bride' (XI.2) is one of his best known in this regard (it is still widely available as an art print). As the beautiful maiden, the subject of male barter, stands apprehensively in the background, Bertuccio spreads all his wealth on the ground before the rigid and death-like man, hooded and armed with a massive sword. The scene is the psychologically revealing moment of contest and suspense that culminates most renditions of 'The Grateful Dead.' But without that story line, the figures assume enigmatic poses, their respective gestures generating rich symbolic overtones at correspondingly archetypal levels: 'Youth, Death, and the Maiden,' or 'The Vanity of Worldly Goods.' His painting called 'Biancabella and Samaritana' (III.3) – representing the moment at which the snake sister provides the heroine with a beautifying bath of milk – when viewed independently from the narrative depicts a childish Venus, delightfully pretty, innocently naked, and erotically entwined by a serpent. Out of context, the snake might incite a number of interpretations, and perhaps intentionally so, for in 1895 the painting was taken to Venice for the Biennale where it raised a sensation. The most mystical of them all is the portrait of Isabella Simeoni (from 'The Wife, the Courtesan, and the Witch,' VII.1) on the back of the devil Farfarello, here converted into a magnificent black Pegasus flying high above the city of Florence with its Duomo and the River Arno in clear view below. She is seated side-saddle, holding the backs of the wings, her flaxen hair streaming in the wind. Today, the picture is known as 'The Valkyrie,' far from its source of inspiration. But Hughes was not always a symbolist. A naked man leaping from on high to escape the fatal cut in the presence of the two kneeling nuns and the image-carver's bemused wife may be but a naked man ... (VIII.3). This grand 'tutti' scene is the finale of the tale and features the escapee suspended in mid-air; it is the work of a consummate illustrator of stories, revealing meanwhile that Hughes had a reasonable sense of humour. At the same time, the symbolism of the world-upside-down in the nuns' amazement at the miracle of the resurrected Christ appearing in the person of a 'defrocked' priest is not Hughes's symbolism, but originates in the story itself.

Jules Garnier was born in Paris but trained for a time in Toulouse and later at the École des Beaux-Arts, where he was the student of J.-L. Gérôme. He travelled a great deal thereafter, venturing as far as Holland, Spain, and Morocco. The restive and truculent scenes he found in the pages of Rabelais marked his artistry and some of the Straparola illustrations are clearly in this vein. Beginning in 1869, the Salon exhibited his works annually until 1888. In his lifetime he achieved a considerable reputation for his paintings of social drama, many of them concerned with punitive attitudes towards extramarital sexuality and the exploitation of women, as in 'Constat d'Adultère' (1883); 'Supplice des Adultères' (1876), set in Medici Florence; and 'Le Droit du Seigneur' (1872). These themes are not demonstrably visible, however, in the Straparola interpretations. Garnier had been sickly in his youth, followed the tastes of the academy, married twice (his first wife died a year after their marriage), had an influence on Seurat, and was by no means a radical, although he was a man of polemical tendencies in his painting.[126] Tellingly, only shortly after Garnier had completed his illustrations for *Les facétieuses nuits* (1882), he was engaged in the creation of a vast circular panorama of Constantinople. It was a study in geometry and perspective involving architecture and landscape, to be viewed by popular audiences from a platform in the centre of the room.[127]

E.R. Hughes was born in London, an only child who nevertheless spent much of his time with his uncle – Arthur Hughes, the painter – and Arthur's five children. He was of a gentle and docile nature, which continued with him throughout his career; he was retiring and without marked ambition, yet he was widely liked and admired. He entered the Royal Academy Schools after being encouraged by his uncle, became a student of the watercolours of Edward Burne-Jones, and was part of an active circle of young painters and architectural draughtsmen. He started exhibiting at the Royal Academy in 1872 and had his own studio in Chelsea by the time he met Burne-Jones in person. The greatest part of Hughes's early production was devoted to portraiture, but at the fashionable galleries and shows he turned towards symbolist subjects, often painted in rich golds and blues, many of his themes influenced by Italian

126 E.E. Hirshler, 'A French Salon Painting Reconsidered,' *Apollo*, no. 121 (June 1985), pp. 413–14.

127 Ian Russell, *Images, Representations and Heritage* (New York: Springer, 2006), p. 301.

literature. He took particular pride in his fine gift for representing nudes, including the several to be seen in the Straparola illustrations, their snowy textures in stark contrast to the dark backgrounds. He was also among the outstanding illustrators of Shakespeare's plays. Later in his career he became an assistant to Holman Hunt who, with his diminishing eyesight, needed a careful and meticulous collaborator; Hughes actually finished some of his most famous paintings, including 'The Light of the World' in St. Paul's Cathedral and 'The Lady of Shalott.' Among the paintings still in his own studio at the time of his death was his splendid 'Night and her Train of Stars,' which was purchased from Hughes's estate by friends and presented to the Birmingham Art Gallery in 1914.

The effect of these often pictorially imposing images, positively or adversely, is the transposing of Straparola's stories to other ages and airs. With Hughes in particular, the Victorian world is before our eyes, as in the love scene between Galeotto and Feliciana (IX.1). We see them in a Pre-Raphaelite pose in a bourgeois parlour with a period piano, a Wilton-style carpet, a Chinese, multi-drawered chest in the background covered with flowers in vases, and still more potted flowers. These scenes likewise interpret characters in most particular ways through their gestures and expressions, their levels of social energy or lassitude. Ultimately, they may be said to violate the imagination in all the ways for which book illustrators have been blamed, which is essentially by imposing upon and replacing our own text-generated representations. Yet these images are, in themselves, no more tyrannical than the interpretations of theatrical roles by individual actors. They lend particularity, substance, and often a grandeur beyond the capacities of scantier imaginations. In brief, they are readings, an added aesthetic dimension – and, in the instances of Hughes and Garnier, often very fine pictures in their own rights, employing all the most refined workshop methods from a great age of book illustration.

The images by the two hands in the Burton edition of 1906 are of a different order. Presumably both artists were commissioned by Charles Carrington, the publisher, to embellish a semi-pirated translation intent upon displacing the Garnier-Hughes-Waters extravaganza of 1898, published for the Bibliophiles. Certainly in numbers of images, this edition takes the prize. Every story is graced, often with two or three pen and ink drawings of considerable skill scattered throughout, the text forming columns around them. They are signed by a Dombrecht or Gombrecht and appear to have been executed in 1900 – six years before the book was released. News of this artist would have been welcomed, but only at a cost proportional to the level of my curiosity. This holds equally true for the Lebègue who is responsible for the spirited but naïve and sometimes cartoon-like full-page aquarelles. These are printed on thick paper and surrounded with elaborate rose-gray or burnt-sienna borders featuring intertwined figures and stylized knights with lambrequins, or naked caryatids and harpies – all too redolent of illustrated fairy-tale books for children. The colours are nevertheless varied and subtle and the nature scenes, with their ferns, flowers, and tuffets, have a significant charm bespeaking the tastes of an age. These aquarelles, no doubt expensive to produce, are covered with printed paper tissues identifying nights, fables, and the specific texts to which the pictures refer.

The pen and ink illustrations by Inge Jastram of the twenty-five Straparolan stories in *Die ungetreue Polissena* (1989) are of yet a different order, for while they are rather more minimal in their execution they are full of movement, expression, humour, and conceptual imagination. These are not essays in scenic representation or historicism, but in intrapersonal relations, moods, human frivolity, or human vanity, with playful eroticism galore. The contrasting expressions on the faces of the three nuns staring at the priest who is masquerading as the nude Christ on the cross are, to borrow a cliché, precious (VIII.3). These drawings contribute generously to the spirit intended by the publisher in choosing all of Straparola's raciest tales, a collection to which is appended the descriptive title, 'ergötzliche and tolldreiste Novellen aus dem alten Italien' (amusingly absurd, impudent, and wanton tales out of old Italy). Of the nun about to catch an apricot seed, Jastram has her standing on her head, headgear and all, with her robe down around her waist, prepared to seize the falling pit between her nether cheeks (VI.4). No greater graphic fun with Straparola could be imagined. Jastram creates a spirit of Renaissance life of her own, reading the stories in a personal way and taking impressions, which she then drafts into these striking and memorable images.[128] This artist has also illustrated Lucian of Samosata's *Hetärengespräche* (Dialogues of the courtesans, 1983) and *Süsser als Liebe is nichts* (Nothing is sweeter than love, 1988), the sayings and poems of nine Greek women from antiquity.

---

128 Jean-Joseph Keller, 'Die Lust en der Lust,' *Illustration* 29, no. 2 (1992), pp. 54–7.

A Chart of Selected Illustrators of the *Piacevoli notti*

	Title	Early Italian	Garnier	Hughes	Burton	Jastram
	Lucrezia's Circle		X	X		
I.1	'Salardo's Disobedience'	X			X X̲	X
I.2	'Cassandrino'	X			X	X X
I.3	'Scarpacifico'	X	X		X	X
I.4	'Doralice'	X		X	X	X X
I.5	'Polissena and the Priest'	X			X	X
II.1	'The Pig Prince'	X		X	X	
II.2	'Filenio's Revenge'	X	X	X	X	X X X
II.3	'Carlo da Rimini'	X			X X̲ X	
II.4	'The Devil's Marriage'	deleted			X	
II.5	'Simplicio de' Rossi'	X			X̲ X	X X
III.1	'Pietro's Magic Fish'	X			X X̲	
III.2	'Livoretto'	X			X X̲	
III.3	'Biancabella'	X	X	X	X X̲ X	
III.4	'Fortunio and Mermaid'	X		X	X	
III.5	'Isotta and Travaglino'	X		X	X X̲	X
IV.1	'Costanza, Girl-Knight'	X	X		X X̲	
IV.2	'Erminione and Filenia'	X		X	X	X
IV.3	'Dancing Water'	X			X̲ X X	
IV.4	'The Physician's Wife'	X			X	X X
IV.5	'Flamminio's Quest'	deleted			X	
V.1	'Guerrino and Wild Man'	X		X	X̲ X X	
V.2	'Adamantina's Doll'	X			X X	
V.3	'The Three Hunchbacks'	X			X X̲ X	X
V.4	'Tia Rabboso'	X	X	X	X X X	X X
V.5	'Modesta's Shoes'	X			X	X
VI.1	'Wives in Common'	X			X̲ X	X
VI.2	'Castorio's Castration'	X			X	X X
VI.3	'The Widow's Promise'	X			X̲ X	
VI.4	'The Three Rival Nuns'	deleted	X			X
VI.5	'The Virtue of Stones'	X			X	
VII.1	'The Wife and the Witch'	X		X	X	
VII.2	'Malgherita Spolatina'		X	X	X	X X
VII.3	'Flogged at Court'				X X̲	X
VII.4	'Share and Share Alike'				X	
VII.5	'The Three Brothers'				X̲ X	
VIII.1	'Three Idle Rogues'				X X̲	
VIII.2	'Handling Wives'		X		X	X
VIII.3	'Image-Carver's Wife'	deleted	X	X	X X	X
VIII.4	'Lattanzio's Sorcery'	deleted		X	X	
VIII.5	'The Donkey's Skin'					
VIII.3A	'Woes of an Old Gallant'				X X̲	X
VIII.3B	'Merchant's Monkey'				X	

	Title	Early Italian	Garnier	Hughes	Burton	Jastram
IX.1	'King Galafro'			X	X	
IX.2	'Rodolino and Violante'	deleted			X X	
IX.3	'Francesco Sforza'			X	X	X
IX.4	'Papiro Schizza'					
IX.5	'Bergamasques'				X	X X
X.1	'Veronica's Jewels'		X		X X	X
X.2	'The Lion and the Ass'				X?	
X.3	'Cesarino and Dragon'				X X X	
X.4	'Andrigetto's Testament'				X	
X.5	'Rosolino's Confession'				X X	X X
XI.1	'Constantino's Cat'		X		X	
XI.2	'The Grateful Dead'			X	X	
XI.3	'Dom Pomporio'				X	
XI.4	'The Stolen Veal'				X	
XI.5	'Frate Bigoccio'	deleted			X	
XII.1	'Florio's Jealousy'		X		X X	
XII.2	'The Fool's Blackmail'			X	X X	
XII.3	'Pozzuolo's Wife'				X X	
XII.4	'The Disobedient Sons'	deleted			X	
XII.5	'Pope Sixtus IV'					
XIII.1	'Madman and Hunter'					
XIII.2	'Diego and the Friar'					
XIII.3	'Spaniards and Germans'	deleted				
XIII.4	'The Servant and the Fly'				X? X X	
XIII.5	'The Fateful Sack'				X	
XIII.6	'The Good Day'				X	
XIII.7	'Giorgio and His Master'				X X	
XIII.8	'Midnight Famine'	deleted		X		
XIII.9	'Hermaphrodite Nun'				X X	
XIII.10	'Doctor of Laws'				X	
XIII.11	'The Novice in the Barn'		X	X	X	
XIII.12	'Healing of Guglielmo'				X	
XIII.13	'Pietro Rizzato'				X	

NB: In the Burton Edition the many black and white drawings are by G/Dombrecht, while the coloured illustrations are by Lebègue and are designated by the underlined X. The question marks beside the pen and ink drawings indicate a potential error in their placement, for they bear no self-evident relationship to the text.

Illustrations of *The Pleasant Nights* (1894) by E.R. Hughes, ARWS

Proem: E.R. Hughes, 'The Palace at Murano'

Night I, Fable 4: E.R. Hughes, 'Doralice in the King's Chamber'

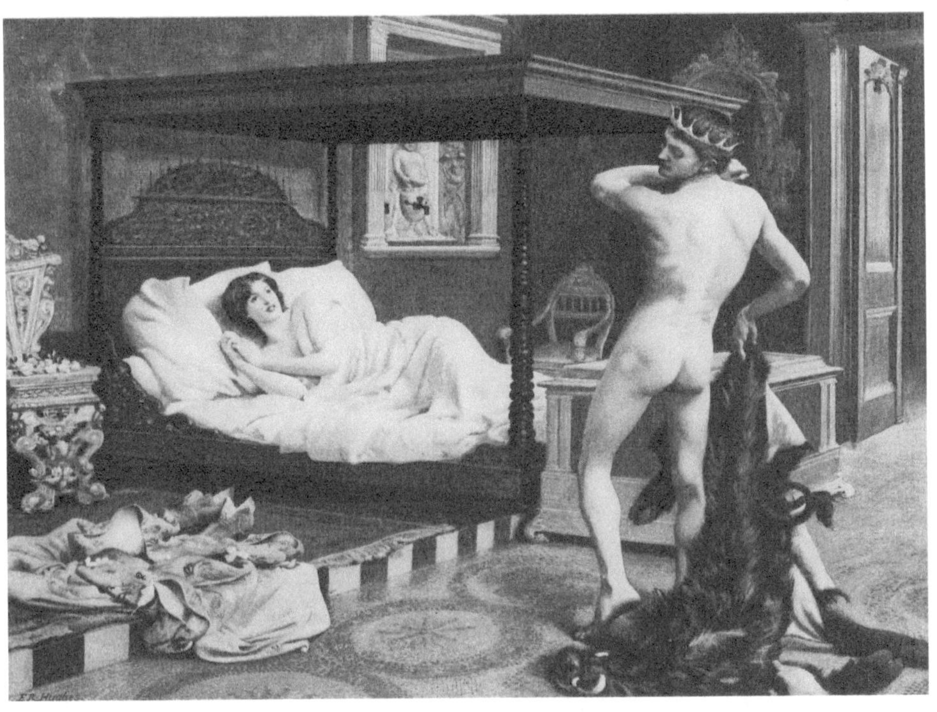

Night II, Fable 1: E.R. Hughes, 'The Pig Prince'

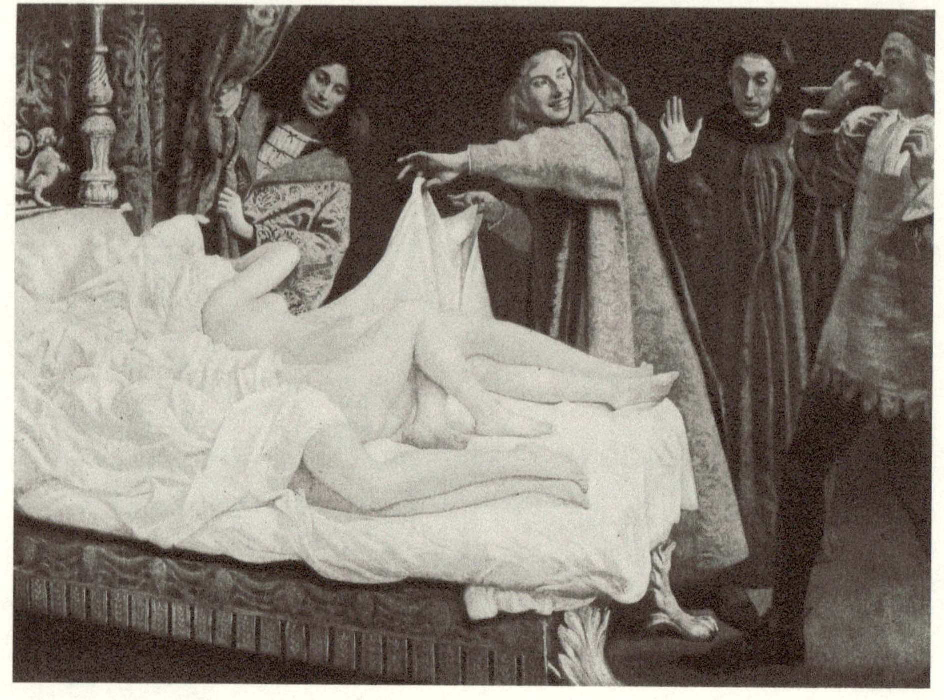

Night II, Fable 2: E.R. Hughes, 'The Scholar's Vengeance'

Night III, Fable 3: E.R. Hughes, 'Biancabella and the Serpent'

Night III, Fable 4: E.R. Hughes, 'The Siren'

Night III, Fable 5: E.R. Hughes, 'Isotta and Travaglino'

Night IV, Fable 2: E.R. Hughes, 'The Trial of the Serpent'

Night V, Fable 1: E.R. Hughes, 'Golden Hair'

Night V, Fable 4: E.R. Hughes, 'The Conjuration of the Kite'

Night VII, Fable 1: E.R. Hughes, 'The Demon Horse'

Night VII, Fable 2: E.R. Hughes, 'On the Hermit's Isle'

Night VIII, Fable 3: E.R. Hughes, 'Quinquino's Miracle'

Night VIII, Fable 4: E.R. Hughes, 'The Ruby Ring'

Night IX, Fable 1: E.R. Hughes, 'In the Queen's Tower'

Night IX, Fable 3: E.R. Hughes, 'Francesco Sforza'

Night XI, Fable 2: E.R. Hughes, 'Bertuccio's Bride'

Night XII, Fable 2: E.R. Hughes, 'More Knave than Fool'

Night XIII, Fable 8: E.R. Hughes, 'The Tart'

Night XIII, Fable 11: E.R. Hughes, 'A Clerical Meeting'

Illustrations of *Les facétieuses nuits* (1882) by Jules Arsène Garnier

Frontispiece: Jules Garnier, 'Storytelling in Murano'

Night I, Fable 3: Jules Garnier, 'Scarpacifico Resuscitates his Housekeeper'

Night II, Fable 2: Jules Garnier, 'The Three Wives Exposed'

Night III, Fable 3: Jules Garnier, 'Biancabella and Samaritana in the Forest'

Night IV, Fable 1: Jules Garnier, 'Costanza and the Laughing Satyr'

Night V, Fable 4: Jules Garnier, ‘Tia Rabboso Sends her Lover Away’

Night VI, Fable 4: Jules Garnier, 'Sister Modestia's Precision Performance'

Night VII, Fable 2: Jules Garnier, 'Malgherita Spolatina Arrives at the Island'

Night VIII, Fable 2: Jules Garnier, 'The Battle for the Breeches'

Night VIII, Fable 3: Jules Garnier, 'The Nuns' Critique of the Crucifix'

Night X, Fable 1: Jules Garnier, 'Veronica and the Wine Barrel'

Night XI, Fable 1: Jules Garnier, 'The Cat with the Country Folk'

Night XII, Fable 1: Jules Garnier, 'The Affectionate Welcome of Brother Felix'

Night XIII, Fable 11: Jules Garnier, 'The Novice Tumbles Down'

Bibliography

Abrahams, Roger D., and Alan Dundes. 'Riddles.' In *Folklore and Folklife*. Edited by Richard M. Dorson. Chicago: Chicago University Press, 1972. pp. 129–43.

Adams, Gillian. 'A Father of the Literary Fairy Tale: Giovanfrancesco Straparola.' *Children's Literature* 32 (2004): 209–15.

Barberi-Squarotti, Giorgio. 'Problemi di tecnica narrative cinquecentesca: Lo Straparola.' *Sigma* 5 (1965): 84–108.

Bonomo, Giuseppe. 'Motivi magico-stregonici in una novella dello Straparola.' *Rassegna della letteratura italiana* 62 (1958): 365–9.

Bottigheimer, Ruth. *Fairy Godfather: Straparola, Venice, and the Fairy Tale Tradition*. Philadelphia: University of Pennsylvania Press, 2002.

– '*Fairy Godfather*, Fairy-Tale History, and Fairy-Tale Scholarship: A Response to Dans Ben-Amos, Jan M. Ziolkowski, and Francisco Vaz da Silva.' *Journal of American Folklore* 123, no. 490 (2010): 447–96.

Brakelmann, F.W.J. *Giovan Francesco Straparola da Caravaggio*. Göttingen: E.A. Huth, 1867.

Bryant, Mark. *Riddles, Ancient and Modern*. New York: Bedrick Books, 1984.

Burke, Peter. *Popular Culture in Early Modern Europe*. Aldershot: Ashgate, 1999.

Calabrese, Stefano. 'L'enigma dal racconto dallo Straparola al Basile.' In *Gli arabeschi della fiaba*. Pisa: Pacini, 1984. pp. 37–70.

Canepa, Nancy, ed. *Out of the Woods: The Origins of the Literary Fairy Tale in Italy and France*. Detroit: Wayne State University Press, 1997.

– *From Court to Forest: Giambattista Basile's 'Lo cunto de li cunti' and the Birth of the Literary Fairy Tale*. Detroit: Wayne State University Press, 1999.

Clements, Robert J., and Joseph Gibaldi. *Anatomy of the Novella: The European Tale Collection from Boccaccio and Chaucer to Cervantes*. New York: New York University Press, 1977.

Cottino-Jones, Marga. 'Princesses, Kings, and the Fantastic: A Re-vision of the Language of Representation in the Renaissance.' *Italian Quarterly* 37 (2000): 173–84.

Crane, Thomas Frederick. *Italian Social Customs of the Sixteenth Century*. New York: Russell & Russell, 1971.

De Filippis, Michele. 'Straparola's Riddles.' *Italica* 24, no. 2 (1947): 134–46.

Demnati, Faouzia, *Le merveilleux et la réalisme et leurs implications sociales et culturelles dans les 'Piacevoli Notti' de Giovan Francesco Straparola*. Manouba, Tunisia: Faculté des Lettres, 1989.

Dunlop, John Colin. *History of Prose Fiction*. Edited by Henry Wilson. 4 vols. New York: Burt Franklin (1896), 1970. Vol. II, pp. 207–14.

Guglielminetti, Marziano. 'Delle "novella" del Morlini alle "favole" dello Straparola.' *Medioevo e rinascimento veneto con altri studi in onore di Lino Lazzarini*. II. Dal cinquecento al novecento. Padua: Editrice Antenore, 1979. pp. 69–81.

– *La cornice e il furto: studi sulla novella del '500.* Bologna: Zanichelli, 1984.

Heidmann, Ute, and Jean-Michel Adam. *Textualité et intertextualité des contes: Perrault, Apulée, La Fontaine, Lhéritier.* Paris: Garnier classiques, 2010.

Keller, Jean-Joseph. 'Die Lust an der Lust: Inge Jastram als Illustratorin.' *Illustration 63: Zeitschrift für die Buchillustration* 2 (1992): 54–7.

Klotz, Volker. 'Giovan Francesco Straparola.' *Das europäische Kunstmärchen.* Stuttgart: J.B. Metzler, 1985. pp. 31–40.

Lüthi, Max. *The European Folktale: Form and Nature.* Translated by John D. Niles. Bloomington: Indiana University Press, 1986.

– *Once upon a Time: On the Nature of Fairy Tales.* Translated by Lee Chadeayne and Paul Gottwald. Bloomington: Indiana University Press, 1976.

Magnanini, Suzanne. *Fairy-Tale Science: Monstrous Generation in the Tales of Straparola and Basile.* Toronto: University of Toronto Press, 2008.

Mazzacurati, Giancarlo. 'La narrativa di Giovan Francesco Straparola e l'ideologia del fiabesco.' In *All'ombra di Dioneo: Tipologie e percorsi della novella da Boccaccio a Bandello.* Florence: La Nuova Italia, 1996. pp. 151–89.

McGlathery, James M. *Fairy Tale Romance: The Grimms, Basile, and Perrault.* Urbana: University of Illinois Press, 1991.

Motte, Anne. 'La theme de la beffa dans les *Piavevoli Notti* de Giovan-francesco Straparola.' In *Formes et significations de la 'Beffa' dans la littérature italienne de la Renaissance.* Edited by André Rochon. 2 vols. Paris: Université de la Sorbonne Nouvelle, 1972. Vol. I, pp. 167–77.

Perocco, Daria. 'Trascrizione del'oralità. Il gioco delle forme in Straparola.' In *Favole, parabole, istorie. Le forme della scrittura novellistica del Medioevo al Rinascimento.* Edited by Gabriella Albanese et al. Rome: Salerno, 2000. pp. 467–82.

Picone, Michelangelo. 'La cornice novellistica dal *Decameron* al *Pentamerone.*' *Giovan Battista Basile e l'invenzione della fiaba.* Edited by Michelangelo Picone and Alfred Messerli. Ravenna: Longo, 2004. pp. 105–21.

Piejus, Marie-Françoise. 'Le couple citadin-paysan dans les "Piacevoli notti" de Straparola.' In *Ville et campagne dans la littérature italienne de la renaissance.* Edited by Anna Fontes-Baratto et al. Paris: Université de la Sorbonne Nouvelle, 1976. pp. 139–77.

Pirovano, Donato. 'The Literary Fairy Tale of Giovan Francesco Straparola.' *Romanic Review* 99, nos. 3/4 (2008): 281–96.

– 'Per l'edizione de *Le piacevoli notti* de Gian Francesco Straparola.' *Filologia e Critica* 26, no. 1 (2001): 60–93.

– 'Una storia editoriale cinquecentesca: "Le Piacevoli notti" di Giovan Francesco Straparola.' *Giornale storico della letteratura italiana* 177 (2000): 540–69.

Rizzardi, Simona. 'Le *Piacevoli notti* di Giovan Francesco Straparola e le "comedie elegiache" latine medievali.' In *Moving in Measure: Essays in*

Honour of Brian Moloney. Edited by Judith Bryce and Doug Thompson. Hull: Hull Univeristy Press, 1989. pp. 63–77.
Robert, Raymonde. *Le conte de fées littéraire en France de la fin du XVIIe à la fin du XVIIIe siècle*. Nancy: Presses universitaires, 1982.
Röhrich, Lutz. *Folktales and Reality*. Translated by Peter Tokofsky. Bloomington: Indiana University Press, 1991.
Rozzo, Ugo. 'Italian Literature on the Index.' In *Church, Censorship and Culture in Early Modern Italy*. Edited by Gigliola Fragnito. Cambridge: Cambridge University Press, 2001. pp. 194–222.
Rua, Giuseppe. 'Intorno alle "Piacevoli Notti" dello Straparola.' *Giornale storico della letteratura italiana* 15 (1890): 111–51.
– 'Intorno alle "Piacevoli Notti" dello Straparola.' *Giornale storico della letteratura italiana* 16 (1890): 218–83.
Rubini, Luisa. 'Fiabe in ottava rima.' In *Il cantare italiano fra folklore e letteratura*. Edited by Michelangelo Picone and Luisa Rubini. Florence: L.S. Olschki, 2007. pp. 413–40.
– 'Straparola.' In *Enzyklopädie des Märchens*. Edited by Rolf Wilhelm Brednick. Berlin: Walter de Gruyter, 2007. Vol. 12, pp. 136–69.
Schmidt, Friedrich Wilhelm, ed. *Die Märchen des Straparola*. Vol. I, *Sammlung alter Märchen*. Berlin: Duncker & Humblot, 1817.
Senn. Doris. '*Le piacevoli notti* (1550–53) von Giovan Francesco Straparola, ihre italienische Editionen und die spanische Übersetzung *Honesto y agradable Entretenimiento de Damas y Galanes* (1569/81) von Francisco Truchado.' *Fabula* 34 (1993): 45–65.
Smarr, Janet Levarie, ed. *Italian Renaissance Tales*. Rochester, MI: Solaris Press, 1983.
– 'Una storia editoriale cinquecentesca: "Le Piacevoli notti" di Giovan Francesco Straparola.' *Giornale storico della letteratura italiana* 177 (2000): 540–69.
– 'The Literary Fairy Tale of Giovan Francesco Straparola.' *Romanic Review* 99, nos. 3/4 (2008): 281–96.
Straparola, Giovan Francesco. *Die ungetreue Polissena: Ergötzliche und tolldreiste Novellen aus dem alten Italien*. Translated by Adelbert von Keller and Hanns Floerke. Edited by Gerda Böttcher. Illustrated by Inge Jastram. Berlin: Eulenspiegel Verlag, 1989.
– *Les facétieuses nuits de Straparole traduites par Jean Louveau et Pierre de Larivey*. Edited by Paul Jannet. Paris: P. Jannet, Bibliothèque Elzévirienne, 1857.
– *Les facétieuses nuits du Seigneur J.-F. Straparole*. Edited by G. Brunet. Translated by Jean Louveau and Pierre de Larivey. Illustrated by J. Garnier. 4 vols. Paris: Librairie des Bibliophiles, 1882.
– *Les nuits facétieuses*. Edited by Joël Gayraud. Paris: Librairie José Corti, 1999.
– *Le piacevoli notti*. Edited by Giuseppe Rua. Rome: E. Loescher, 1898.
– *Le piacevoli notti*. Edited by Giovanni Macchia. Milan: Bompiani, 1943.

– *Le piacevoli notti.* Edited by Bartolomeo Rossetti. Rome: Avanzini & Torraca, 1966.
– *Le piacevoli notti.* Edited by Manlio Pastore Stocchi. 2 vols. Bari: Laterza, 1979.
– *Le piacevoli notti.* Edited by Donato Pirovano. Rome: Salerno Editrice, 2000.
– *The Facetious Nights of Straparola.* Translated by W.G. Waters. Illustrated by E.R. Hughes and Jules Garnier. 4 vols. London: The Society of Bibliophiles, 1898 (1,000 copies) and 1901 (300 copies).
– *The Most Delectable Nights of Straparola of Caravaggio.* Translated by Sir Richard Burton. 2 vols. Paris: Charles Carrington, 1906.
– *The Nights of Straparola.* Translated by W.G. Waters. 2 vols. London: Lawrence & Bullen, 1894.

Taggart, James M. *Enchanted Maidens: Gender Relations in Spanish Folktales of Courtship and Marriage.* Princeton: Princeton University Press, 1990.

Tatar, Maria. *Off with Their Heads: Fairy Tales and the Culture of Childhood.* Princeton: Princeton University Press, 1992.

Taylor, Archer. *The Literary Riddle Before 1600.* Berkeley: University of California Press, 1948.

Tiffin, Jessica. *Marvellous Geometry: Narrative and Metafiction in [the] Modern Fairy Tale.* Detroit: Wayne State University Press, 2009.

Uther, Hans-Jörg. *The Types of International Folktales: A Classification and Bibliography.* 3 vols. F.F. Communications, no 284. Helsinki: Suomalainen Tiediaktemia, 2004.

Villani, Gianni. 'Da Morlini a Straparola: Problemi di traduzione e problemi del testo.' *Giornale storico delle letteratura italiana* 159, no. 505 (1982): 67–73.

Warner, Marina. *From the Beast to the Blonde: On Fairy Tales and Their Tellers.* London: Vintage, 1995.

Ziolkowski, Jan. *Fairy Tales from Before Fairy Tales: The Medieval Latin Past of Wonderful Lies.* Ann Arbor: University of Michigan Press, 2007.

Zipes, Jack. *Breaking the Magic Spell: Radical Theories of Folk and Fairy Tales.* London: Heinemann, 1977.
– *The Great Fairy Tale Tradition: From Straparola and Basile to the Brothers Grimm.* New York: W.W. Norton, 2001.
– *The Irresistible Fairy Tale: The Cultural and Social History of a Genre.* Princeton: Princeton University Press, 2012.
– 'Straparola, Giovan Francesco.' *The Oxford Companion to Fairy Tales.* Oxford: Oxford University Press, 2002.

THE PLEASANT NIGHTS
(Le Piacevoli notti)

VOLUME I

Nights I–V

To all Delightful and Lovable Ladies, Greetings from Orfeo dalla Carta

Dear Ladies, I have been thinking about how many heaven-born and illustrious spirits there have been, how truly excellent, both ancient and modern, who have written those various fables which, in reading them, have given you so much pleasure. You are aware, I am certain, that they were motivated to write for no other reason than to provide you with entertainment, comfort, and consolation. Such is my opinion, or rather my certainty, pleasant and adorable as you all are, that you will not now be angry if I, as your good servant, should publish in your name the fables and enigmas of the ingenious Messer Gioanfrancesco Straparola da Caravaggio, which he presents with so much learning and elegance. Even if the contents of his tales do not bring to your ears the same pleasure and delight to which you're accustomed, please don't condemn him for that reason and thrust him aside in rejection, but accept him with joyful faces as you have accepted the others. As you read him, keep in mind the variety of events and the subtlety of wit, for at the least, you will derive no small instruction from his pages.

Moreover, you must not over-scrutinize our author's poor and negligent style, because, after all, he wrote his fables, not as he wished to write them, but as he heard them from the ladies who told them, neither adding nor taking anything away. So if you find anything amiss or lacking in any respect, accuse him not who laboured to the best of his power and knowledge, but blame me who has published these works against his will. Accept, therefore, with cheerful looks this little gift from your servant, who, if he learns (as he hopes to) that his offering has pleased you all, will do his best in the future to lay before you other things which may prove to be even more to your delectation and contentment. Be happy and remember me!

From Venice on the XIth day of January, MDLI

Here Begins the Book of Fables and Enigmas of Mr. Giovanfrancesco Straparola da Caravaggio entitled The Pleasant Nights

The First Night

Proem

Milan, the principal city and one of the most ancient of Lombardy, is well furnished with fair and gracious ladies, adorned with splendid palaces, and contains all things appropriate to a famous city. Therein dwelled Octaviano Maria Sforza, bishop elect of Lodi, who, by right of succession, was entitled to assume the lordship and sovereignty of the state, now that Francesco Sforza, duke of Milan, was dead. Yet by reason of those dangerous and evil times, cruel hatreds, bloody battles, and the never-ending hazards and changes of state affairs, it was necessary for him to leave the city and take himself to Lodi, along with his daughter Lucrezia, wife to Giovan Francesco Gonzaga, cousin of Federico, marquis of Mantua, where they remained for some while. But in time his kinsmen began to annoy and harass him, doing him considerable harm. Finding himself still subject to their persecution and ill-will, the unhappy prince took with him what poor jewels and treasure he had been able to save and, with his daughter, only recently made a widow, he retired to Venice.

Here they found refuge with Ferier Beltramo, a man of noble lineage and of a kindly, amiable, and gentle nature, who welcomed them to his house with great honour and courtesy. Still, insofar as sharing another man's home for a long time often breeds inhibitions and ill feelings, the duke, with his ripe and deliberate judgment, resolved presently to set out again to find a dwelling place of his own.

Embarking one day with his daughter in a small vessel, he went to Murano, where his eyes fell upon a marvellously beautiful palace at that time standing empty. He entered and found everything there perfectly to his taste: its lovely position, its spacious courtyard, its superb loggias, its pleasant gardens filled with smiling flowers and rich in all sorts of fruit and blooming herbs. Then he mounted the marble staircase and surveyed the magnificent hall, the exquisite bedrooms, and the balcony built over the water, which commanded a view of the whole area. The princess, captivated by the charm of the place, so compellingly begged her father with her soft and tender speeches, that to please her fancy he signed the lease. With that she was greatly delighted. Now both morning and evening she might go upon the balcony where she could see fish of every sort swimming about in great shoals through the clear salt water. In seeing them dart about here and there, she took the greatest pleasure. And because she was now forsaken by the ladies who had formerly made up her court circle, she chose in their places ten others, no less graceful and pretty – their virtues and comely gestures too many to recount.

The first among them was Lodovica, who had lovely eyes that sparkled like the brightest stars, so that everyone who looked upon her was entirely dazzled. The next was Vicenza, who carried herself beautifully, had a fine figure, polished manners, and a lovely and delicate face that shone with refreshing beauty upon all who beheld it. The third was Lionora, who, having as part of her natural beauty a certain air of superiority, was nevertheless as kindly and courteous as any lady to be found in the entire world. The fourth was Alteria with the lovely fair hair, whose devotion to other women was reserved entirely for the Signora. The fifth was Lauretta, handsome to look upon, but disdainful in manner, whose languishing and alluring glances nevertheless enslaved any lover who ventured to charm her eyes. The sixth was Eritrea, small of stature, yet who yielded to none of the others in beauty and grace, seeing that she had two brilliant eyes, sparkling brighter than the rays of the sun, a small mouth, and a rounded bosom. In fact, there was nothing about her that did not merit the highest praise. The seventh was Cateruzza, also known as Brunetta, a girl of sweet grace and amorous words; not only could she entangle men in her snares, but could as easily have drawn down mighty Jove himself from the skies. The eighth was Arianna, still young in years, yet grave and sedate in her manners, gifted with a fluent tongue, as well as divine virtues shining in her like the stars in heaven and deserving the reward of unending praise. The ninth was the clever and spirited Isabella, who won the admiration of the entire company with her wit and skillful repartee. The last was Fiordiana, a prudent damsel with a mind stored up with worthy thoughts and a readiness to do virtuous deeds beyond any lady I have ever known. These ten charming young women both individually and as a group rendered their services to the Lady Lucrezia. In addition to these, the Signora chose two matrons of sober aspect, noble blood, mature age, and sterling worth to be always present to assist her with their wise counsel. One of these was the Signora Chiara, wife of Girolamo Guidiccione, a gentleman of Ferrara, and the other was Signora Veronica, the widow of Santo Orbat, from one of the oldest houses of Crema.

Many nobles and men of learning came to join this gentle and honourable company, among whom were Casal of Bologna, bishop and likewise ambassador of the king of England, and the learned Pietro Bembo, knight of the Grand Masters of Rhodes and preacher to the citizens of Milan, a man of distinguished parts and the one who stood highest in the Signora's favour. After these, there came Bernardo Capello, considered one of the principal poets of the age, the amiable Antonio Bembo, Benedetto of Treviso, a man of jovial and easy manners, as well as Antonio Molino, surnamed Burchiella, with his pretty wit, the ceremonious Ferier Beltramo, and many others whom it would be tedious to name more particularly. It was the custom of these, or at any rate of the greater part of them, to assemble nearly every evening at the palace of Signora Lucrezia, there to entertain her with graceful dances and playful discourse, interspersed with music and song. Thus they beguiled away the fleeting hours to the great delight of the Lady and her talented damsels. Sometimes, too, certain enigmas were proposed, to which the Signora would supply the solutions.

With the final days of Carnival approaching, dedicated as they were by custom to all manner of pleasures, the Signora asked them, under pain of her displeasure, to assemble next evening expressly to decide what manner of pastime they themselves should keep. The next evening at dusk they all duly appeared in obedience to her request, and once they had been seated according to their several ranks, the Signora addressed them: 'Honourable gentlemen and gracious ladies, now that we are come together in our usual manner, it seems good to me that we should organize these pleasant and polite diversions of ours, finding what delightful amusements we may at this time of Carnival, of which only a few days remain. Each one of you is therefore invited to propose what you prefer most. Whichever activity proves to be to the taste of the greatest number will be adopted.'

Both the gentlemen and the ladies, at that, spoke up with a common voice that the choice should be left entirely to the Signora. Seeing their will so united, she replied to this noble company: 'Because it is your pleasure that I settle the order of our entertainment, I, for my part, suggest that every evening, for the duration of Carnival, we start off with a dance, after which five ladies will sing a song of their own choosing. When this is finished, each of these five ladies, in an order to be determined by drawing lots, must tell a story, to be concluded with an enigma that we will all try with the best of our wits to solve. Then, when the storytelling is over, we'll all seek repose in our own homes. But if these propositions of mine aren't pleasing to you all, I'll readily bow to others you find more appealing. Let me hear your thoughts.'

This proposal, as set out by the Signora, won the favour of everyone. She therefore called for a golden vase to be brought, into which sheets of paper were cast bearing the names of five of the ladies present. The first to be drawn was that of the charming Lauretta, who, all blushing and bashful, turned red as a morning rosebud. Next to be chosen was Alteria, then Cateruzza, then Eritrea, and last Arianna. The order established, the Signora called for musical instruments to be brought in, while on Lauretta's head she placed a little wreath of green laurel as a sign of sovereignty and excellence, signifying that hers would be the first of the pleasant tales on the following evening.

It was now the Signora's pleasure that all the company should fall to dancing, and almost before she had made this wish known to Signor Antonio Bembo, this gallant gentleman took the hand of Fiordiana, enamoured as he was of her, and without delay the others in the company followed his example and merrily kept up the dance. So great was their pleasure that no one wanted to stop. Amid the bandying of gentle words, and with great reluctance, the young men and women withdrew to another room where tables had been laid out with delicacies and fine wines, and there they spent a delightful time in conversation over merry matters of every kind. Then, when the time for parting arrived, they took their leave of the Signora, who saluted each one in her graceful way.

As soon as this honourable company had gathered the following evening, and had performed certain dances in the accustomed manner, the Signora signalled to the fair Lauretta to begin her song in expectation of the tale to follow. Making no hesitation in the matter, Lauretta stood up, respectfully greeted the Signora, and stepped onto the raised platform where a beautiful chair had been placed, covered with draperies of rich silk. Then, calling her four chosen companions, they sang in angelic and harmonious voices the following canzonetta in praise of the Signora:

Lady, by your kindly hand,
Which ever waits on love's behest;
By your voice of sweet command,
That bids us in your presence rest;
You hold in fee your servants' love,
And rank with spirits blest above.

You quit the city's din and heat,
And let us in your smile rejoice;
You call us willingly to your feet,
To listen to our lady's voice.
Then let us loudly celebrate
Your dignity and queenly state.

And though upon our charmed sight
Earth's fairest visions soft may fall;
Your grace, your wit, your beauty bright,
Will blur them and outshine them all.
To laud another should we seek,
Our tongues your praise alone would speak.

After the five damsels had fallen into silence, their canzone having come to its elegant conclusion, and the instruments had ceased to play, the graceful Lauretta, upon whom the lot had fallen to tell the first story of the evening, without further word from the Signora began to recite her tale.

I. Fable 1
The Disobedience of Salardo

LAURETTA

Salardo, the son of Rainaldo Scaglia, quits Genoa for Monferrato, where he disobeys certain injunctions imposed upon him by his father's testament. For that reason he is condemned to death, but, being delivered, he returns to his own country.

In every endeavour that we undertake, or think to undertake, whether good or bad, we should first consider the results. Now that we are about to begin our pleasant and playful entertainment, I could have wished that another besides myself had been chosen for the first recitation. In truth, I feel unequal to the task, for I am not experienced in the art of ornate and polite discourse in which my gracious companions are so adept. But if it is your pleasure, insofar as the drawing of lots has decided that I must go first, I will commence in order not to inconvenience this honourable company, vowing to make the best use I can of the scant abilities Providence has granted to me, while leaving an ample and spacious field to my companions to follow to tell their stories in a manner more graceful and fluent than ever I could master.

That son is held for blessed, even more than blessed, who obeys his father with all due reverence, because in so doing he carries out the commandments of God, lives long in the land, and prospers in all his works. Contrarily, he who is disobedient may be held for unhappy, even more than unhappy, when all his undertakings come to a miserable and ill-fated end, as you will easily see from the tale I'm about to tell you.

So to begin, gracious ladies, in Genoa – which is an ancient city, and as pleasing, perhaps, as any in the world – there lived not long ago a gentleman named Rainaldo Scaglia. He was not only a man of great wealth, but equally endowed with knowledge and wit. Salardo, his son, he loved above anything in the world and had trained him up in his youth in every worthy and liberal art, omitting nothing that would lead to success, honour, and personal glory. Now it came about that in his advancing years, Rainaldo fell into a grave sickness and, seeing that his end was near, he called to a notary to make up the will that would give to Salardo all his earthly goods. In exchange, in the manner of a good father, he begged his son to honour his memory by fixing certain precepts firmly in his mind and promising never to go against them. The first was that, no matter how much he loved his wife, he should never trust her with his secrets. The second was that in no wise should he bring up the son of another as his own or make him the heir of his own goods who was not of his own flesh and blood. The third was that he should never subject himself to a prince who ruled over his state entirely according to his own unconstrained will. When these matters were completed and his final blessing bestowed, Rainaldo turned his face to the wall and in less than a quarter of an hour gave up the ghost.

With Rainaldo deceased, Salardo became his universal heir. But now that he was a rich, young, well-born gallant, he showed but moderate grief, and instead of troubling himself with the administration of his estates or of taking his father's precepts to heart, he went in hot pursuit of a wife, searching where he thought most to find one from a good family and with a pleasing personality. Thus it came about that, within a year of his father's death, he had married Theodora, the daughter of Messer Odescalco Doria, a Genoese nobleman of the highest standing. She was very beautiful and of a virtuous mind, although she was somewhat haughty. Salardo was so deeply enamoured of her that, whether night or day, he couldn't let her out of his sight. They remained together as the years went by, but still no child was born to them. Yet Salardo yearned for an heir. Disregarding his father's counsel, he decided to adopt a child, to rear him as his own legitimate and natural son, and in the end to leave him all his earthly wealth. So, with his wife's consent, he lost no time, but carried out his purpose, for he adopted the son of a poor widow, named the boy Postumius, and gave him the very best education.

Some time later, Salardo took it into his head to quit Genoa and seek a home elsewhere, not because he did not find the present city fair and pleasant, but out of a surging desire for change of a kind that often seizes upon those uncontrolled by the will of an elder. So with great store of money and jewels, and with sumptuous equipage, he left Genoa with his beloved wife Theodora and his adopted son Postumius and set out for Piedmont, making a halt at Monferrato. Here by slow degrees he made the acquaintance of many of the citizens, accompanying them on the hunt or attending social gatherings – things in which he took no small delight. So great was the generosity that he displayed towards each one of them that not only friendship but honour was granted to him by all.

Before long, the rumour of Salardo's splendid hospitality came to the ears of the prince, the marquis of Monferrato, who, seeing that this newcomer was a handsome gentleman, well born, rich, courtly of manner, and ready for any gallant enterprise, took him into high favour and would seldom let a day pass without seeing him. His influence over the marquis became so extensive that, at last, it came about that anyone seeking a favour from the ruler would contrive to have his petition pass through the hands of Salardo, without whose intercession nothing would follow. Mindful of the new favour he enjoyed, Salardo studied the arts of ingratiation, ever eager to devise new pleasures for his patron, who, as became a young man, was passionate about the sports of the field. To this end, he kept a great number of falcons and hounds for the chase, together with all the appurtenances of venery worthy of his high estate. And for all such hunting or hawking excursions, Salardo's company was indispensable.

Being alone one day, Salardo began to consider the great fortune that had befallen him through the favour of the marquis. Then his thoughts turned to his son, Postumius, of how discreet and dutiful he was, how upright and graceful. Dwelling upon such matters, he said to himself, 'Ah, how sorely mistaken was my poor old father. Dotage must have overtaken him with age, as it does many of the elderly. I can't imagine what frenzy or folly urged him to command me so particularly against raising a child not of my own blood, or against making myself subject to an absolute prince. I now see the foolishness of his precepts, for what son born to a father could be more sober, courteous, gentle, and obedient than my adopted Postumius? Where could I find greater affection and more honourable treatment than is given to me by the marquis, even though he answers to no superior? In truth, exalted as he is, he pays me so much love and worship that it seems as though I've been placed in charge and that he is my subaltern. I'm so amazed by these things I don't know what to say. But one thing certain is that with old people it's a common trick for them to forget the tastes and inclinations of their youth, for in laying down rules and regulations, they impose burdens on others they wouldn't have touched with the tips of their own fingers. In this, they're not moved by love, but by a craving to keep their offspring in prolonged subjection. Now that two of the injunctions imposed upon me by my father against all expectations have been proven false, I should now put the third to the test of experience, for I feel certain that my sweet and beloved wife will confirm beyond all doubt her warm and grounded affection. She whom I love more than the light of mine eyes will give ample proof of the foolishness and folly of miserable old age that takes such joy, with the hand of the dead, in imposing intolerable restrictions on the living. Truly, my father must have been insane when he made his will, deprived of memory, senseless with age, and acting worse than a child. To whom do I owe my trust if not to the one who has left her home, abandoning her father, mother, brothers, and sisters to become one with me in heart and soul? Surely, I may reveal all my secrets to her, however important they may be. So I will put her fidelity to the test, not on my own account, for I doubt it not, but only as an example to all those simple-minded youths who think it an unpardonable sin to disobey the commandments of their doddering old fathers living in their illusions, their thousand-fold frenzies, and continuous vacillations.'

In these terms, Salardo took exception to his father's wise injunctions and considered how he could best be rid of them altogether. After a time he left his room, descended the stairs without being seen by anyone, and went over to the mews at the palace where the falcons of the marquis were kept. Of these, he took one which was a great favourite of its owner and secretly conveyed it to the house of a friend whose name was Fransoe. To this man he handed over the bird and begged him, for the sake of their friendship, to keep it for him till the time came when he might reveal the reason for his request. Then, upon his return home, he took a falcon of his own, secretly put it to death, and carried it to his wife, saying, 'Theodora, my beloved wife, as you know well, I find it hard to get a moment's rest on account of the many hours I'm constrained to spend in attendance on the marquis in hunting, fowling, jousting, and other sports. Sometimes I barely know whether I'm dead or alive. So to keep him from spending all his time at the hunt, I've played him a trick he will relish but little. But perhaps it may keep him at home and give us and others some repose.'

To this his wife said, 'So what have you done?'

'I have killed his best falcon,' Salardo replied, 'the favourite of them all. When he looks for it in vain, I swear he'll die of rage.' And with that, he lifted his cloak and took out the falcon which he had killed and handed it over to his wife, directing her to have it cooked that they might dine upon it in honour of the marquis.

When Theodora heard this speech and saw the dead creature, she was sorely grieved and thereupon, turning to Salardo, she reproached him severely for his foolish jest. 'Why have you committed such a serious offence,' she said, 'insulting the marquis in this way, who thinks so highly of you and heaps such great favour upon you, and places you above all the others? Alas, Salardo, I'm afraid our ruin approaches. If the marquis should discover what you've done, you'll certainly be in great danger of death.'

Salardo answered, 'But how could this ever come to his ears? The secret is yours and mine alone. So now, by all the love there is between us, I beg you to be careful not to reveal it, for should he find out, our ruin would be complete.'

'Have no fear,' said Theodora, 'I would rather die than disclose such a secret.'

The falcon was cooked and supper was served while Salardo and his wife took their places at the table. But the lady refused to eat any of the bird, even though with gentle words Salardo urged her to do so. Remaining obstinate to the last, however, he gave her such a blow to her face that her cheek turned scarlet red. Then she began to cry and complain bitterly of his abuse until at last she arose from the table muttering under her breath that she would carry that blow in her mind for as long as she lived and that in due time she would repay him. The next morning, she crept out of bed early and hastened to tell the marquis of the falcon's death. The news so fired him with rage that he ordered Salardo to be seized immediately and to be hanged by the neck like a common criminal. Then all his goods were to be divided into three parts, the one part given to his wife as accuser, the second to his son, and the remaining part to the man who would serve as hangman.

Postumius by this time had become a vigorous and well-grown youth. When he heard his father's doom and the disposition of goods according to the orders of the marquis, he ran quickly to Theodora and said to her, 'Mother, would it not be wiser for me to hang my father myself and gain the third of his goods than to let them go to a stranger?'

To which Theodora replied, 'Truly, my son, you speak well, because in doing this your father's wealth will remain intact with us.'

So Postumius went straightway to the marquis to ask for permission to hang his father and thus earn the third part due to the executioner – a request which the Prince graciously allowed.

Salardo now took precautions to confide the entire secret to his faithful friend Fransoe, asking him at the same time, that, when the hangman should be ready to do his work, he beg for him an audience with the marquis so that, by the Prince's grace, he might say what he could in his own defence. Fransoe carried out this request most faithfully. Meanwhile, the wretched Salardo, in prison and bound in shackles, awaited from hour to hour the time when he would be led to a shameful death on the scaffold.

With bitter weeping, he said to himself, 'Now I know and clearly understand that my good old father in his wisdom gave me those precepts for my profit. He gave me sage counsel and I cast it aside, senseless fool that I am. Mindful of my safety, he warned me against the enemies of my own household. But see now how I have delivered myself into their hands and given them my riches to enjoy. He understood well enough the temper of despots who, in the space of an hour, can love and hate, exalt and cast down. These things he warned me of, but I had to thrust my head into the jaws of this marquis and put my faithless wife to the proof, as though I were eager to sacrifice at the same time my substance, my honour, and my life. God forbid that I should have put my wife's treachery to the test. Ah, Salardo, better to have followed in your father's footsteps and to let others seek out the company of princes. Now I see into what straits my foolish confidence in myself, in my wife, in my wicked son, and above all, in this ungrateful marquis have led me. Now I see the value of the love this prince holds for me. How could he deal more cruelly with me than by robbing me of my goods, my life, and my honour at a single blow, showing thus how his love is turned to hatred? Now I recognize the truth of the proverb, "a prince is like wine in a flagon, sweet in the morning and sour at eve." Where now is my nobility and where are my kinsmen? Is this the end of my wealth, loyalty, uprightness, and courtesy? O my father, dead though you may be, I believe that when you gaze into the mirror of the Eternal Goodness and see me about to be hanged for no other reason than disbelieving and disregarding your wise and loving counsel, you will pray to God to have compassion on my youthful errors. Disobedient and ungrateful though I am, I pray to you for pardon.'

While Salardo in his misfortune was thus communing with himself, his son Postumius, with the air of a practised hangman, went with all the court to the prison and, arrogantly presenting himself to Salardo, said, 'My father, insofar as you are condemned to be hanged today by order of the marquis, and given that a third of your goods goes to the one who ties the noose, I know that for the love you have for me, you won't be angry about the role I've chosen to play, because by this means your goods won't fall into the hands of strangers, but will remain in the family. I'm sure you'll be pleased by this.'

Salardo listened attentively to his speech and replied, 'God bless you my son. The course you have chosen pleases me greatly. At first the thought of death terrified me, but now I'm content to die after hearing your words. So do your work as quickly as you can.'

Postumius first implored his father's pardon and then, having kissed him on the mouth, put the halter about his neck and exhorted him to meet his death with patience. When Salardo saw this turn of events, he stood astonished. After a short time, he was led out of the prison with his arms bound and a rope around his neck, accompanied by the hangman and the officers, and was hurried towards the place of execution. Once there, he turned his back towards the ladder standing against the gibbet, and in this position he climbed up, step by step. When he had reached the top, he looked down courageously upon the assembly and told them in detail the cause that had brought him to the gallows, and with gentle words he implored pardon for any offence he might have given. Then he exhorted all young people to be obedient to their fathers. When the crowd heard the cause for which Salardo was condemned, to the last person they lamented his unhappy fate and prayed that he might still be pardoned.

While these events were taking place, Fransoe raced to the palace and made this address to the marquis: 'My most illustrious Lord, if ever you have been prompted to show one drop of pity towards anyone, I now doubly urge you to employ your customary clemency and gentleness in the case of your friend, who has been led out to suffer a shameful death for faults entirely unknown to him. What reason do you have, my Lord, to condemn this wretched Salardo, who loved you so dearly and who never wrought an offence against you in thought or in deed? Most gracious Prince, merely allow your faithful friend to be brought into your presence and I will demonstrate to you his utter innocence.'

Such a petition made the marquis's eyes flame with rage as he sought to thrust Fransoe out of his presence, but the suppliant threw himself down at the Prince's feet and, embracing his knees, he cried out with tears, 'As you are a just Prince, have pity. Don't let this guiltless man die because of your anger. Calm yourself and I will prove his innocence. Hold your hand but one hour for the sake of that justice which you and your father have always revered. Let it not be said that you put your friend to death without cause.'

Still enraged, the marquis replied, 'I see you too wish to go the way of Salardo, and you will if you go on antagonizing me like this, for I'll have you placed beside him.'

'My Lord,' Fransoe replied, 'after making an enquiry, if you don't find Salardo entirely guiltless, I ask for no greater favour than to be hanged next to him in reward for my years of service.'

This last speech somewhat moved the marquis, for he reasoned that Fransoe would never have said as much without being sure of Salardo's innocence, now that he ran the risk of being hanged himself. So he granted the hour's delay, warning Fransoe that he must look to be executed if he failed to prove his friend's innocence. With that, he sent a messenger straightway to the place of justice with an order to stay the execution, and to bring Salardo, bound as he was and with the rope around his neck, along with the hangman and the officers, immediately back to the palace.

Upon appearing before the marquis, Salardo noted that his face was all clouded with anger. Still, he spoke out with a clear voice and a calm manner: 'My Lord, the service I freely gave you, and the love I bear you, hardly deserved such a reward as this shame and indignity you have put upon me in condemning me to a disgraceful death. I confess to a fault that deserved your anger, but I was guilty of no crime wicked enough to warrant, unheard, such hasty condemnation. The falcon for which your wrath has been so enflamed is alive, safe and sound. It was never my intention to kill it or to insult you. It was but an instrument in a test, the details of which I will herewith reveal.'

Salardo now asked Fransoe to fetch the falcon and return it to its master. Then he told the marquis the whole story of his father's precepts and how he had disregarded them all. When he had heard this frank and candid speech and saw the falcon as handsome and well nourished as ever, the marquis was dumfounded. But presently he raised his eyes, by then full of tears in recognizing his grievous error in condemning a guiltless man to death unheard, and said to Salardo: 'If you could see into my heart at this moment, you would know that the suffering which you feel is nothing to mine in seeing the halter around your neck and the cords about your arms. I may never hope to be happy again knowing that I have injured a man so grievously – one who loved and served me so faithfully. If it were possible to undo it all, how glad I would be, but since this is beyond all question, I will do my utmost to wipe out my offence and make to you whatever reparation I can.'

His speech at an end, the marquis unfastened the halter from Salardo's neck with his own hands and loosened his bonds, embracing him with the greatest tenderness at the same time. Then, taking him by the right hand and leading him to a seat next to his own, he ordered the halter to be put around the neck of Postumius for his wicked conduct, and the youth to be led away to execution.

But Salardo would not allow this to happen. 'Postumius,' he said to the wretched youth, 'what shall I now do with you whom I've nurtured from childhood, for the love of God, only to be so cruelly deceived? On the one hand is my past love for you; on the other, the indignation I feel for the wicked deed you had planned. One calls upon my fatherly kindness to forgive you, while the other bids me to harden my heart against you. What shall I do? If I pardon you, men will jeer at my weakness. If I punish you as you deserve, I shall go counter to the divine exhortation to forgiveness. But that men may not tax me with either too great leniency or too great severity, I will not make you suffer in your person, but I will certainly no longer endure the sight of you. Hence, in place of the wealth you so greedily sought, you shall have the halter that you knotted around my neck. Keep it always as a souvenir of your cruel intent. Now go far from here and make certain that news is never heard from you again.'

With these words, he drove out the wretched Postumius, of whom nothing more was ever heard. Now as soon as Theodora was told of Salardo's liberation, she fled to a convent of nuns where, not long after, she died in misery. When he heard the news of her death, he took his leave of the marquis and returned to Genoa, and there he lived in happiness for many years, giving to God the greater part of his riches and keeping for himself only what was necessary for his livelihood.

While Lauretta told her story, many of her listeners were moved to tears. But when they heard that Salardo was delivered from the gibbet, that Postumius was ignominiously banished, and that although Theodora fled she died star-crossed, they were exceedingly glad and gave thanks to God for his justice and mercy. The Signora now gave the word to Lauretta to pose her riddle, in keeping with the order of entertainment they had agreed upon the previous evening. Thus with a smile, the young lady offered the following words:

Pent in a prison all forlorn,
A tiny son to me was born.
Ah, cruel fate! The savage elf,
Hardly bigger than a mite himself,
Devoured me in his ravenous lust,
And changed me into sordid dust.
A fond mother I was of late,
Now worse than a slave's is my own fate.

There was great delight in the reception of this clever enigma which the charming Lauretta delivered with such verve, and the entire company made an effort to interpret it one way or another. But when she saw that no one was likely to solve it, this beautiful girl said with a smile, 'This enigma of mine concerns the dry bean which is imprisoned between two husks, where, in time, she engenders a worm no bigger than a mite. This worm feeds upon her until it finally consumes her, so that not only is she destroyed as a mother, but not even the condition of a servant is possible for her.' Everyone was pleased by her explanation, and Alteria, who sat beside her, having been selected as the next speaker, began her story at once, without awaiting the Signora's command.

I.1 Commentary

Straparola opens his collection with a sample of 'wisdom literature' in the guise of a *novella.* A patriarchal figure offers cautionary precepts or interdictions on his deathbed, a headstrong son disobeys, and experience harshly demonstrates the error of his ways. It is a complete sermon, for the doctrines are illustrated by the corresponding exempla and the whole is duly punctuated by two long soliloquies, the first of which registers the prodigal's defiance, the second his acknowledgment of the wisdom of preceding generations. The father's injunctions cannot be said to constitute a complete guide to living, but in touching upon marriage, the loyalty of children, and the duplicity of rulers, they implicate three relationships of trust by which a man is made vulnerable to betrayal. Taken together, they paint a rather dark picture of human nature in illustrating that the loyalty of wives is conditional, that children not in the bloodline are subject to hypocrisy, and that rulers above the law will be arbitrary and capricious in their administration of justice. Hence, their ramifications are broad enough. Let all readers be edified.

The genius of the story is in the economy with which each act of disobedience meets a correspondingly bitter revelation. The narrative design is patently compound, for while the opening scene unifies the three motifs involving rulers, wives, and adopted children and brings them to a synchronized denouement, they are nevertheless independent ideas which at some point had been assembled from disparate sources. Whether these motifs originated in the tales of ancient Rome or among the fables of the East remains a question open to investigation.[1] But

1 The Sultan of al-Yemen's tale begins with a deathbed scene in which a father divides his earthly goods among his three sons and sends them into the world to prosper and cooperate with one another. To each he bestows special gifts. The third receives a talent relating to animal behaviour, making this story similar to those associated

medieval and early Renaissance collections of exempla and vignettes contain versions of them, at first singly and then increasingly in groups that begin to resemble the design of the present story. Something of that recombinant trajectory can be reconstructed from the scattered literary remains both predating and postdating Straparola's story.

Speculation is free whether these literary traces are borrowings from a vast and diversified oral tradition through which these motifs were transmitted, or the hand-me-down materials passed from writer to writer through *imitatio.* The question holds true for many of the stories to follow, whether they are re-creations from largely dissimilar literary sources, or far more likely, transcriptions from contemporary oral sources. Typically, as in the present case, generic literary cognates are not lacking, but can hardly be imagined as direct sources in light of their differences. Such a paucity of immediate literary sources repeatedly suggests that Straparola drew upon oral versions of these tales, and particularly so when closely cognate tales abound in the collections of the later ethnographers and folklorists. The question lingers in the background of nearly all the commentaries to follow.

A signature feature of this story type is the testament composed of precepts, warnings, or interdictions, themselves differing from version to version, but which invariably organize the plots of their respective stories. Tales of deathbed admonitions ipso facto represent highly charged moments as a member of the experienced generation seeks for the last time to hand down the keys to successful living to the less experienced. But these tales are often characterized by rather bizarre and cryptic expressions of that wisdom, as though spoken by a sage participating in a literary genre with conventions of its own. Cato and Saint Augustine left little lists consisting of three teachings, such as never to tell secrets to women (this one is nearly universal), never to travel by sea if you can go by land, and always to leave a proper will. As will be seen in the analogues to follow, there are injunctions against dining in households where brown bread is served to guests, or riding horses headlong

with 'The Three Brothers' (VII.5), the third of which often learns the language of animals. Thereafter, the story goes in directions tangential to the present story as the boys travel to foreign courts seeking counsel, only to reveal such inductive powers concerning the nature of things that they are sent home as far too clever to need advice from foreigners. *Arabian Nights,* ed. Jonathan Scott, 6 vols. (London: Longman, 1811), Nights 329–34, vol. VI, pp. 1–7.

into valleys.[2] They are almost riddles or else simple prognostications of future accidents. Common to nearly all such narratives is a warning against confiding in wives or marrying women from neighbouring cities, who by definition are beyond the pale of local gossip by which means their misprisions might otherwise have been exposed.[3] As a literary motif, the deathbed scene may have been influenced by Eastern tales. In *The History of the Forty Vezirs or the Story of the Forty Morns and Eves*, the twenty-seventh tale of the Vezir tells of an old merchant dying who cautions his son in financial affairs and leaves him a halter should he end up in bankruptcy. After folly and failure, the son resigns himself to a despondent suicide, but the noose is attached to the rafters of the house which, by design, collapse to reveal a ceiling stuffed with treasure, thereby giving the boy a second chance. This closural episode has been added to several of the cognate tales in the "Salardo" group as a means for re-establishing the destitute hero after his return home from a foreign court.[4] Even more pertinent is the Lady's ninth story in which a great king, on his deathbed, urges his first son to build a house in every city, the second to marry a new virgin every night, and the third to eat only honey and butter. The

2 These motifs have been catalogued by Dominic Peter Rotunda in his *Motif-Index of the Italian Novella in Prose* (Bloomington: Indiana University Press, 1942). These appear under such headings as J21.22, 'Do not tell a secret to a woman,' or J21.27, 'Do not adopt a child.' They have been scrupulously cited by Donato Pirovano at the bottoms of the first pages of each fable in his edition of *Le piacevoli notti* (Rome: Salerno Editrice, 2000). The motifs correspond to those in *Motif-Index of Folk Literature* by Stith Thompson (Bloomington: Indiana University Press, 1955–8); they are cited from time to time, in conjunction with the customized investigations into motivic design, in the commentaries to follow.

3 The formula was widespread, consisting of commands, usually three, often strange, but pronounced with the authority that comes with royal pronouncements or the wishes of the dying, all of which are broken and thereby teach valuable lessons. 'Salomos drei Lehren' constitutes such a set, a work that can be found in the *Compilatio singularis exemplorum* from MS. Tours 468, ed. Alfons Hilka, in *Neue Beiträge zur Erzählungsliteratur des Mittelalters* ([Breslau: Aderholz, 1913]), no. 32, p. 9. The topic is dealt with by Friedrich Seiler in his edition of *Ruodlieb, der älteste Roman des Mittelalters, nebst Epigrammen* (Halle: Buchhandlung des Waisenhauses, 1882), pp. 47–74. See also Felix Liebrecht, *Zur Volkskunde: Alte und neue Aufsätze* (Heilbronn: Henninger, 1879), pp. 36–7, who discusses early versions of this story type in the writings of Walter Map and confirms the motif in the early eleventh-century, fragmentary, anonymous Bavarian romance, *Ruodlieb*. See also Albert Wesselski, *Märchen des Mittelalters* (Berlin: Herbert Stubenrauch, 1925), pp. 219–20.

4 Attributed to Sheykh Zada and edited by E.J.W. Gibb (London: George Redway, 1886), pp. 144–53.

sons live foolishly in interpreting these figurative sayings literally. By the first was meant to build friendships everywhere, the second to be moderate in one's pleasures, and the third never to eat to repletion. So interpreted, they constitute a miniature book of the good life.[5] Such examples support the thesis that "Salardo" began as an Eastern tale, at least in its design, if not in its precise substance. A similar scene in the *Ruodlieb*, dating to the eleventh century, pushes the entry of the story idea back to a very early date (or challenges the Eastern provenance). These early instances clearly feature the global design around cryptic injunctions and their disobedience, but the specific commandments of the present tale are variations of a later date.

Of the three episodes that constitute Straparola's plot – the adopted son who becomes his father's executioner, the king who subjects a loyal follower to harsh and cruel punishment for a trifle, and the wife who betrays a mortal secret in revenge for a slap – the last of these has the longest and most complex history as a story 'meme.' A conventional place to begin is the *Gesta romanorum*, the 126th story of which tells of the boy Papirius who overhears the secrets of the Senate. When his mother browbeats him into revealing them, famously the boy concocts a false report about new legislation allowing for multiple wives. Despite her sworn secrecy (in effect the boy is putting his own mother to the test), she spreads the news by gossip until all the women of the city storm the Senate in protest. When all is revealed, the boy is celebrated for not trusting real state secrets to women.[6] This story, in its own right, is amply

---

5 *History of the Forty Vezirs* (London: George Redway, 1886), pp. 114–19.

6 *Gesta romanorum*, ed. Wynnard Hooper, trans. Charles Swan (London: Bohn, 1876; reprint, New York: Dover, 1959), pp. 227–8. The tale originates with Macrobius in his *Saturnalia*, bk. II, chap. 6, according to Hooper, pp. 398–9. For those further interested in the story, the *Attic Nights* of Aulus Gellius as well as the *Speculum historiale* of Vincent of Beauvais may prove fruitful. It also appears as the story.of 'Papirius and how his father brought him to the Council' in *Le cento nouvelle antiche*, translated as *The Novellino* by Robert Payne, with an introduction by Janet Smarr (New York: Peter Lang, 1995), no. 67, p. 101. It is also included in the *Sermones vulgares* of Jacques de Vitry, ed. Thomas Frederick Crane (London: David Nutt, 1890), no. 235, pp. 230–1. See also Johannes Pauli's *Schimpf und Ernst*, ed. Johannes Bolte (Hildesheim: Olms, 1972), no. 392. It was also known early in England in Brit. Lib. MS. Harleian 463, folio 19, and no. 21 in the *Shakespeare Jest-Books* (from *Mary Tales and Quicke Answeres*, 1535), ed. William Carew Hazlitt (London: Sothoran [1864], 1881), vol. I, p. 31. It is also retold by Hans Sachs in his *Fabeln*, 'Papirius mit den Frauen,' *Sämtliche Fabeln und Schwänke*, ed. Edmund Goetze and Carl Drescher (Halle: Max Niemeyer, 1903), vol. IV, pp. 25–7.

represented in medieval and Renaissance anthologies. Another from the same collection, the 124th story, 'Of Confidence in Women,' approximates the test in Straparola even more closely.[7] It belongs to the riddle tradition. A knight in bad graces with his king was offered clemency if he could demonstrate to satisfaction who makes the best friend, the best jester, and the worst enemy. The knight, upon reflection, provides his solution by going to court with his dog, his child, and his wife. The dog, after being wounded with a sword, returns at his master's call as a true friend would do, the child prattles and amuses like a jester, but the wife, when struck and accused of adultery with the king, reveals a homicide formerly committed by her husband which she had promised to keep secret. In the tradition of Straparola's tale, the homicide had been feigned by burying a calf in the place of a pilgrim reportedly slain for his money.[8] The simulated crime is a piece of Straparola's design, but ensconced here in a different story structure; these were movable and adaptable parts.

A particular representation of this motif appears in *El Conde Lucanor* of Juan Manuel, a work completed in 1335.[9] A father counsels his son to make true friends to accompany him through life, and when the boy mentions them by the dozens, the father urges him to challenge their loyalty in times of hardship by feigning to commit a murder and to ask each to hide the body, which is, in fact, a pig in a sack. All refuse. The father then boasts of having but one-and-a-half true friends. The half friend agrees to hide the body in a cabbage patch and refuses to reveal the truth even when he is dealt a blow to the face. The complete friend, however, forces his own son to confess to the crime in order to save the friend's son from

7 *Gesta romanorum* (New York: Dover, 1959), pp. 223–5.

8 This story is retold by Hans Sachs at about the same time that Straparola was writing the *Notti*. 'Der Hecker mit den dreyen selczamen Stücken' (The peasant with the three strange commands). He is told that he must appear at court half riding and half walking, identify his worst enemy, and demonstrate who his best friend is. He too kills a calf, shows the bloody sack to his wife, and tells her of a murder he has committed. He then goes to court half on, half off, his horse, strikes his wife a blow on the face to make her betray him, and beats his dog, which nevertheless returns to fawn on him. Sachs elaborates upon the evil nature of the wife in the 'böse Weib' tradition of the Germans, attributing to her every imaginable diabolical attitude. *Sämtliche Fabeln und Schwänke*, ed. Edmund Goetze (Halle: Max Niemayer, 1913), vol. I, pp. 547–51.

9 *El Conde Lucanor: A Collection of Mediaeval Spanish Stories*, ed. John England (Warminster: Aris & Phillips, 1987), 'De lo que contesçió a uno que provava sus amigos,' pp. 284–91. There is also a version in August Wünsche, *Midrasch Ruth Rabba* (Leipzig: Otto Schulze, 1880-85), pp. 73*ff.*

execution, with the bizarre coda that the boy is actually hanged and the pig's corpse is never disinterred to prove the innocence of either. Juan Manuel, in effect, abandons the integrity of the anecdote to reveal a greater truth about the sacrifices made in the name of true friendship. Nevertheless, he provides witness to the wide currency of the motif involving feigned crime, the loyalty test, and the physical provocation that leads to betrayal, with the evidence held in abeyance that leads to exoneration.

Further elements of Straparola's design can be seen in a story by Franco Sacchetti which he most probably derived from an oral version collected towards the end of the fourteenth century.[10] This tale represents an important parallel group. It is set in Siena, where a dying citizen gives his son three final instructions: never to overstay your welcome; to spend frugally and share your savings with others; and never to marry a foreign wife. Clearly represented here is Straparola's generic design: three deathbed injunctions, disobedience, and a learning curve pertaining to all three. When a friend, burdened with many children, serves the protagonist a single onion for supper, he realizes his first error and hangs the onion on his wall as a reminder. Overpricing a horse that dies before it is sold leads him to cut off its tail and place it on the wall as a second reminder of his disobedience. He then travels to Pisa and there is contracted in marriage with a woman whose dishonesty in due course becomes manifest. The distance has deprived him of the means for knowing her true condition. Suspecting her lubricity, the protagonist creeps into her room and makes off with her lover's trousers. By the time the bridal party arrives in Siena, the trousers have already been fastened on the wall of 'souvenirs.' Following the supper, the host is entreated to explain their meaning; he tells the entire story, beginning with his father's cautionary precepts. By the end of the explanation the marriage is called off; the bride's party of friends and relations retreats in shame and humiliation. In this tale we have the design, the wisdom pertaining to wives, animals, and friends, but not those specific to the present story. Arguably, all that remains is the substitution of parts, whether by Straparola himself, based on his reading, or by a collective process of oral transmission from which he borrows. There are still a few more surviving literary antecedents to inspect for clues to the evolving story type.

10 *Trecentonovelle*, ed. Emilio Faccioli (Turin: Einaudi, 1970), no. 16, pp. 41–6. Sacchetti died in San Miniato in 1400, in his sixty-eighth year. Of his 300 *novelle*, some 223 survive, more often as anecdotes and vignettes than fully elaborated *novelle*. Many were taken from the oral culture of the time or reworked from books of exempla.

Sacchetti's rendition, with modest variations, is also represented in the collection at one time said to have been assembled by Antoine de la Sale around 1460 under the name *Les cent nouvelles nouvelles.*[11] The title of the fifty-second story is 'The Three Reminders' in reference to the objects placed on the wall. The injunctions are never to stay in the house of one who serves black bread; never to gallop a horse into a valley; and never to marry a foreign wife. Each sets up an episode in the story. The protagonist is served black bread by a jealous neighbour as a hint to leave. Then his horse breaks its neck as he gallops it recklessly in pursuit of a hare. Lastly, he marries a woman who arranges to sleep with her chaplain even on her wedding night. Bread, a horse's hide, and clerical britches end up on the trophy wall, providing an opportunity to recount his father's injunctions and to escape a cheating bride. This story is in turn taken over for publication in Italian by Celio Malespini as no. 14 in his *Duecento novelle*, published in Venice in 1609. Therein, the hero is warned not to impose upon a friend who serves him brown bread (pane di rimondini), not to ride his horse pell-mell into ravines, and not to marry a foreigner. One by one, the trophies of his errors are affixed to the wall, providing him the occasion to explain the presence of the coachman's trousers to the bridal party.

---

11 (Paris: Philippe LeNoir, [ca. 1525]), trans. as *One hundred merrie and delightsome stories* by Robert B. Douglas (Paris: Charles Carrington, 1899). It also appears as 'Les trois monuments,' in *Les cent nouvelles nouvelles,* ed. F.P. Sweetser (Geneva: Droz, 1966), no. 52; *The Hundred Merry Tales,* trans. Rossell Hope Robbins (New York: Crown Publishers, 1960), pp. 216–20; Celio Malespino, 'Tre utilissimi precetti lasciati da un padre à suo figliuolo nelle articolo della morte,' in *Ducento novelle* (Venice: Al Segno dell'Italia, 1609), no. 14, pp. 39v–41v. Malespini fills in many details and adds dialogue in novelistic fashion, together with a great deal of glossing on the morals, but changes few facts and no episodes. The clergyman lover becomes a coachman or carter and the author elaborates on the terracotta wall separating the rooms of the newly-weds, which the unnamed protagonist pushes with his shoulder in order to get a glimpse of his wife in bed with her lover. Also among early writers, the story appears as no. 64 in *Le grand parangon* of Nicolas de Troyes, a MS. of which dating to 1535–7 is in the Bibliothèque Nationale in Paris. But the work itself was largely derivative and was not discovered and circulated before 1622 or known widely to scholars before the late nineteenth century, according to Krystyna Kasprzyk in the introduction to her edition (Paris: Marcel Didier, 1970), p. ix. Émile Mabille published the first edition in 1866 (Paris: A. Franck, 1869), although the WorldCat listing cites an edition (s.l., s.n., 1510). The possibility of influence upon Straparola is slight, in any case, although such analogues speak to the wide circulation of the story type in sixteenth-century Europe.

Doubling back chronologically to late fourteenth-century France, there is a parallel literary tradition even closer to Straparola in substance, one that is derived, arguably, from a popular story type more directly in the ancestral line leading to the present tale. Its earliest trace is a story in *Le livre du Chevalier de La Tour Landry* entitled 'Cy parle des trios enseignemens que Cathon dist à Cathonnet, son filz' (This tells of the three teachings that Cathon gave to his son Cathonnet).[12] The work is clearly in the 'wisdom' tradition, created as a manual of instruction for the author's three daughters. The first injunction is never to take office under a sovereign without knowing him well. The second is never to do favours for malefactors, for the evil they do later will be held to the account of the tender-hearted, an injunction which bears an oblique relation to the trust misplaced in an adopted son. The third is to test your wife to make certain she will keep your secrets. In this version, the object of the loyalty test is neither a slain pilgrim nor a slain falcon, but the king's own son, who is safely stowed in the keep of a Baron.[13] Cathonnet goes so far as to tell his wife that he has sent the child's heart to be eaten by the emperor and empress. Revealingly, the wife commits her breach of confidence through gossip with her confidantes, as in the Roman tale of Papirius. The drama comes to its crisis, as in the present tale, when the ruler, in a pique of tyrannical bluster, nearly refuses to hear the countering evidence that would release the protagonist from the gibbet. In this tale, the disloyalty of wives, the capriciousness of rulers, and the ingratitude of malignant and transgressive personalities are thematically featured. We are at last fully in Straparola's neighbourhood.

Francesco del Tuppo supplies a version of the tale which is perhaps closest of all to Straparola's, even though it cannot be demonstrated to be his source. In this story, the protagonist breaks the rules pronounced by his father one by one, first in taking a house in a prohibited place, then in making gifts to the king. One day, seeing a thief about to be hanged, he negotiates to have him set free. Then he hides the prince's

12 Geoffrey de La Tour Landry, *Le livre*, ed. Anatole de Montaiglon from the MSS. (Paris: P. Jannet, 1854), chap. 128, pp. 277–90. The book dates to 1371–2 and was first translated into English by William Caxton in the second half of the fifteenth century.

13 This motif has an oblique relationship to an episode in the *History of the Forty Vezirs*, the Vezir's eleventh story, in which a king's son is reported slain but hidden away until the wrath of his tyrant father subsides. Attributed to Sheykh Zada, edited by E.J.W. Gibb (London: George Redway, 1886), pp. 133–8.

falcon, hears the royal proclamation of death for the perpetrator, and tells his secret to his wife. Later he strikes her for a frivolous reason, causing her to report his secret abroad. Condemned to death, no person could be found to carry out the execution except the thief for whom he had once begged grace. Then all is revealed to the king, including the precepts of the protagonist's father, how he had defied them to his cost, and ultimately recognized their wisdom.[14]

An anonymous fifteenth-century manuscript in the Ambrosiana Library entitled *Dell' ingratitudine e de molti esempli d'essa* (Concerning ingratitude with many examples thereof) likewise contains an intriguing variant upon the story in full novelistic treatment.[15] This work, like Cynthio de Fabritii's, is an illustration of the proverb, "Do not rescue the man condemned to be hanged, who will have you hanged instead," which, in turn, may have originated in an exemplum. Once there was a realm in Persia with its king and a baron to whom he committed the care of his entire kingdom. This baron one day read and took to heart a book of proverbs in which he found admonitions not to rescue a condemned man lest he hang you later, not to reveal secrets to a spouse, and not to enter into matters that will test a sovereign's love. Nevertheless, on his rounds the baron liberates a noble gentleman condemned to the gibbet. Later he requests and receives from the king a most precious ring, but upon pain of death never to reveal its provenance or to gift it to another. His curious wife persists, however, until the secret is shared. Then, following a simple reprimand, she threatens to blackmail him. When he strikes her, she peremptorily takes the ring as a sign of her guilelessness and goes straight to the king to accuse her husband of treason. Finally, the condemned man offers to execute his benefactor. But in a final audience

14 Del Tuppo, *Aesopus. Vita et fabulae latine et italice*, ed. D. De Frede (Naples: Associazione napoletana per i monumenti e il paesaggio, [1485], 1968), exemplum 8, pp. 156–7. The alleged slaughter of a favourite royal falcon is replicated in the first cantica of 'La va da tristo a cattivo' of Aloyse Cynthio de gli Fabritii, *Libro della origine delli volgari proverbi* (Venice: Bernardino e Matteo dei Vitali, 1526); ed. Francesco Saba Sardi ([Milan]: Spirali, 2007), pp. 136–9.

15 'Della ingratitudine' was published in the journal *Il Propugnatore*, II. 1 (1869) (Bologna: Getano Romagnoli, 1869), pp. 398–441, but esp. 411–14, where it is attributed to Antonio Ceruti. The story was drawn from the *Trattato dell'ingratitudine* which was published without place, publisher, or date, in the second half of the fifteenth century. Further to these references, see *Le piacevoli notti*, ed. Donato Pirovano (Rome: Salerno, 2000), vol. I, p. 14, and Giuseppe Rua, *Di alcune novelle inscrite nell'* Esopo *di Francesco Del Tuppo* (Turin, 1889), pp. 9–10.

begged of the king, a feature developed by Straparola, the baron explains the prescient proverbs, including that which warned against redeeming malefactors such as the one about to execute him. The king then reverses his ruling, has the ungrateful cavalier dragged about the city, and the treacherous wife burned. All such potential sources give proof that Straparola was, in a conventional and unacknowledged way, an imitator, just as each of those sources entails a comparative relationship to the others. The intriguing question is whether these many literary renditions came about through the rewriting of texts (imitation or *riscrittura*) or the transcription of tales refashioned by folk culture. Traditional source studies largely discount the latter, granting to authors the inspirations that differentiate their works from earlier literary versions, but the degree to which these stories are also embedded in the oral tradition suggests an alternative scenario of genesis. That argument is less easily substantiated in the present case than it is for many of the stories to follow. Given the large number of literary antecedents, we can imagine Straparola at his desk building his own rendition from the pieces, particularly from del Tuppo. Alternatively, that assembly may have come about through the methodical integration of parts that characterizes oral transmission during years of repetition over expanding areas. But whether Straparola acquired his materials through oral or literary channels, his story remains part of the history of an emergent narrative type, one already centuries old before it appeared in the *Piacevoli notti.*

Subsequent to its publication in 1550, the story of Salardo would become one of Straparola's most widely disseminated tales. This might indicate something of particular appeal in its sense of the human condition or suspenseful design; thoughts are free on that score. But as early as 1558, it had already appeared in two chapbooks, where it is treated as a contemporary event and circulated as "moralizing" news – a cautionary story of disloyal children and treacherous wives 'useful as well as entertaining to hear.' It bore the title *Copia di un caso notabile intervenuto a un gran gentiluomo Genovese* (A picture of the notable events that happened to a Genoese gentleman) and was reprinted down to the end of the eighteenth century bearing Straparola's name.[16] But his greatest influence

16 *Le piacevoli notti*, ed. Donato Pirovano (Rome: Salerno, 2000), p. 810. This pamphlet was still being printed as late as 1790 in Venice, as a 'novel' by Gian Francesco Straparola.

was in France where the Louveau translation, *Les facetieuses nuits*, enjoyed twelve editions or re-impressions in the sixteenth century alone. No doubt through this channel, Thomas-Simon Gueullette found his inspiration for the 'Story of Sinadab the Son of Sazan the Physician,' included in his *Mille et un quart d'heure*, which is an orientalized rewriting of the tale of Salardo.[17] This is one of five stories in the collection that owes its origins directly to Straparola, making Gueullette a leading exponent of his materials, exceeded only by the Countess d'Aulnoy. Sinadab, the only son of Sazan, was a disappointment to his father; he had failed in his training as a physician and was content merely to live off his inheritance. The father's deathbed preachments are precisely those of Straparola: never attach yourself to a prince of unproven character; never trust your wife with secrets; and never adopt a son. Bankrupted by extravagance and abandoned by friends, the protagonist sets off with a hunting hawk as his only possession. The bird brings him to the attention of a foreign king, eventuating in an offer of marriage to the king's sister, Bouzemghir. When it was determined that she could never bear children, they adopt Rumi, the son of a slave. Only after ten years does Sinadab recall the words of his father, laughing at such foolishness in light of his present fortunes. To prove his father entirely wrong, he likewise feigns the slaughter of the king's hawk, entrusting the real creature to a deaf-mute to keep as proof of his innocence. A dead bird is then shown to his wife who solemnly promises secrecy. But when marriage to a handsome young minister is offered to any woman able to reveal the thief, Bouzemghir becomes her husband's accuser. As a prisoner, Sinadab reminds the king of his promises, but to no avail. When no executioners present themselves, his own son volunteers, in league with his mother to gain further control over the estate. But while Rumi was trussing up his father, the friend arrives with the king's hawk and the truth is made known. The king then begs forgiveness for his part and invites the protagonist to behead both wife and son. Sinadab refuses, but an executioner takes his place. Reticent now to remain at a foreign court, he returns home, only

17 (Paris: J.-B. Mazuel, 1715); 'Histoire de Sinadab,' in *Contes*, ed. Jean-François Perrin (Paris: Champion, 2010), vol. I, pp. 560–73; *A Thousand and One Quarters of Hours; Being Tartarian Tales* (London: Jacob Tonson, 1716), pp. 71–100. See also *Tartarian Tales: The Thousand and One Quarters of Hours*, trans. Thomas Flloyd (London, 1785), pp. 71–99.

to lose his treasure on the way. Proof of Gueullette's knowledge of versions other than Straparola's is seen in the sequel of the summer house (in *The Forty Vezirs*' tradition) where the despondent and indigent protagonist, after returning to his native city, finds an admonitory letter from his father together with a rope for hanging himself. By this means, he is given a second chance when the rope pulls down the ceiling to reveal additional treasures. Only then does he come to a full appreciation of his father's prescience and wisdom. In joining Salardo's tale to the story of 'King Tograï Bey and his Three Sons,' Gueullette's creative tactics are transparent enough, confirming his part in maintaining the legacy of Straparola in later times by "orientalizing" his stories in the spirit of eighteenth-century French parlour fiction.[18]

This tale was also translated into English in 1579 for inclusion as the thirty-ninth and last entry in *The Forrest of Fancy, wherein is conteined very prety Apothegmes and pleasant histories, both in meeter and prose, Songes, Sonets, Epigrams, and Epistles, of diverse matter and in diverse manner.* The title is worth citing nearly in full to reveal the variety within this Tudor miscellany in which all manner of recreational and edifying pieces are assembled ragtag as a commercial offering to general readers. The story in question is entitled, 'One named Salard, departing from Genes, came to Montferat, where he transgressed three commaundementes that his father gave him by his last will and testamente, and being condemned to dye, was delivered, and returned againe into his owne countrey.' It reads like the description of a full-length prose romance, but it is, in fact, Straparola's tale in thirteen pages with the usual moral pronouncements, one of the few to appear in English in the sixteenth century.[19]

That Straparola's tale originated in popular culture is further strengthened by the folk tales carrying its themes and motifs in after years. Either

18 The story 'Du roi Togrul-Béy & de ses enfans' corresponds to the present work in its opening scene with the three sons gathered around their father's deathbed to hear his final words of wisdom. Thereafter, all features change, for the sons are given symbolic commissions which they interpret literally, and are taught by a wise man how to interpret them through a second tale in which the ambiguity of signs is illustrated. *Cabinet des fées, ou, collection choisie des contes des fées et autres contes merveilleux,* assembled by Charles-Joseph Mayer and Clément Pierre Marillier (Geneva: Barde, Manget & Compagnie, 1785–9), vol. 16, pp. 89–96.

19 H.C., *The Forrest of Fancy* (London: Thomas Purfoote, 1579), no. 69. H.C. has been identified by Ritson as Henry Chettle, by Malone as Henry Cheeke, and by Warton as Henry Constable.

Straparola's *Notti* provided the template for these renditions or, far more plausibly, they are descendants from the oral tradition that informed the *Notti* and all its literary antecedants. There would appear to be no other options. One such tale is found among those collected by Giuseppe Pitrè in his *Fiabe, novella e racconti popolari siciliani.*[20] The familiar story has been given a modern setting. It tells of a man with a 'most trustworthy wife,' a house with a trellis, and a policeman for a 'friend.' He decides to test them by professing to have murdered a man whose head he threw into the well. His wife cajoles the secret from him, promising never to tell, but in little time reveals it to the policeman, who immediately tells the judge, who sends officers to arrest the man by going to the house with the trellis.[21] Another folk tale is invoked as the policemen descend the well to find a head which is hairy and has horns, for the protagonist has thrown a goat's head in the well (see 'Post-Mortem Cuckoldry,' XIII.4). Once the explanation is in, the story pronounces the triple moral concerning wives, policemen, and trellises by the house.

That the story circulated widely is demonstrated by a version found in the Caucasus. Chatym is the favourite of the Prince of Abacasia. His good fortune has made other courtiers jealous and he attempts to placate them. Then he tells a life-endangering secret to his wife about killing the king's favourite falcon. The talkative wife tells a friend who tells another until it comes to the ruler's ears. Chatym is condemned to die. In making his final preparations, he leaves a part of his estate to his wife, another to his adopted son, and a third to the executioner. True to the tradition, this adopted son offers to become his father's executioner in order to reap the third portion. When the falcon is proven not to be the

---

20 *Fiabe*, 4 vols. (Palermo: Pedone Lauriel, 1875), no. 252; *The Collected Sicilian Folk and Fairy Tales of Giuseppe Pitrè*, ed. and trans. Jack Zipes and Joseph Russo, 2 vols. (New York: Routledge, 2009), vol. II, pp. 727–9.

21 Pitrè's no. 169, 'Never Trust a Woman!' is a slightly clumsier and more abbreviated version of this tale in which a man boasts of the loving attention and devotion of his wife, which a friend convinces him to challenge by purchasing a goat's head, telling his wife he has committed a murder, and then throwing it down the well. Without provocation she goes directly to the judge and the judge comes to the door. When the well is examined they find a man with horns, redolent of the joke about the master in the well with horns that embarrasses his wife in 'The Servant, the Fly, and the Master' (XIII.4). *The Collected Sicilian Folk and Fairy Tales of Giuseppe Pitrè* (ref. in previous note), vol. I, pp. 617–18.

ruler's, the hero is liberated. This version, by necessity implying many others, is further testimony to an established story tradition that had diversified itself regionally over time. Arguably, then, Straparola's tale enjoys comparative and filiational membership in a popular tradition at least several centuries old.[22]

22 One last variant may be found in Xavier Marmier, *Contes populaires des différents pays* (Paris: Hachette, 1888), pp. 135*ff.*

I. Fable 2
Cassandrino the Master-Thief

ALTERIA

Cassandrino, a noted robber and a friend of the Provost of Perugia, steals the Provost's bed and his bright grey horse, and thereafter puts Father Severino into a sack, before becoming a man of good standing and careful management.

Most honourable ladies, herewith let me propose that the wit of man is so keen and subtle that there is hardly anything in the world that can baffle it, for in time matters of the greatest complexity or difficulty are solved with ease and facility. Indeed, there is a familiar saying of the common folk which goes, 'Where there's a will there's a way,' and this very proverb has suggested to me the tale I'm about to tell. It contains little comic business, I'm afraid, yet it may give you some pleasure and even some practical knowledge by showing you the skill and cunning of the consummate thief.

In Perugia, an ancient and noble city of the Romagna, renowned for its learning and sumptuous living, there dwelt, not so long ago, a handsome young scapegrace more robust than any of his day and known to all as Cassandrino. His reputation with the citizens was so evil, by reason of his many robberies, that men of all stations made frequent and lengthy complaints to the Provost of the city. But this Provost, although he soundly berated Cassandrino for his misdeeds, seemed loath to punish him. Now this Cassandrino, although past all gainsaying a most notorious knave and beyond all hope of reform, had one virtue which gained him credit with the Provost, which was that he did not rob merely for the love of money, but rather to be able to spend magnificently and offer handsome gifts, now and again, to those who favoured him. For this reason, as well as because he was affable, courteous, and witty, the Provost looked upon him so kindly that hardly a day would go by without spending time in his company.

Even so, Cassandrino was so intent not only in his thievish ways that the Provost was forced to listen to the complaints which, with complete justification, were laid against him day after day. Yet, reluctant still to bring the culprit to justice by reason of the kindly feeling in his heart, he summoned Cassandrino, one day, into an inner chamber and began to admonish him with friendly words, exhorting him to consider the perils, to put an end to his evil ways, and follow a virtuous life. Cassandrino listened attentively to the Provost's words and made this reply, 'Sir, I hear and clearly understand the good counsel that you're giving to me, and I know it comes from the goodness of your heart. I'm truly grateful for this. But I'm just the victim of fools who are jealous of the prosperity of others, scandal-mongers with poisonous breaths ready in a moment to steal a man's honour and reputation. All those who are spreading these tales about me would do better to park their venomous tongues between their teeth than to work them to my injury.'

The Provost, whose eyes were dazzled by his esteem for the scoundrel, needed little persuading. He gave full assent to Cassandrino's words and turned a deaf ear to the citizens' complaints regarding his felonies. Soon afterwards it came about that Cassandrino, while a guest at the Provost's table, began telling him of a youth who was so marvellously light-fingered that he could steal anything he had a mind to, no matter how carefully guarded and protected it might be. Hearing this tale, the Provost said, 'Cassandrino, this youth can be no other than you yourself, for there can't be a craftier, more malicious and astute trickster anywhere. [So on pain of death if you refuse], tonight you have to steal the bed from the room where I'm sleeping. If you succeed, it's worth a hundred gold florins to you.'

Cassandrino feigned distress over these words and answered, 'Sir, it would appear that you take me for a thief, but I assure you that I'm not one, nor the son of one. I live by the sweat of my brow and by my own industry, such as it is, and do the best that I can for myself. But if it's your pleasure to see me killed in such a business, I'll do it or anything else you want for the esteem I have for you and die contented in the process.'

After this speech, without waiting for an answer, Cassandrino withdrew, for he was very anxious to humour the Provost's whim, and so he went about all day cudgelling his brains to devise a way to steal the Provost's bed right out from under him without betraying himself. At last he hit on the following scheme. A poor beggar of the city had recently died and was buried on that very day in a vault outside the church of the preaching friars. After midnight, Cassandrino stole to the place of the burial and, once he had opened the vault, pulled the dead body out by the feet. Then, after he had stripped it, he dressed it again in his own clothes, which fitted so well that anyone would have taken him for Cassandrino and not for the beggar. He hoisted the corpse upon his shoulders as best he could, and getting himself safely to the palace, he scaled the roof with the beggar's body on his back using a ladder he had taken with him. Then he began quietly to remove the tiles with an iron crowbar, at last making a large hole in the ceiling of the room in which the Provost was sleeping.

The magistrate, who was wide awake and distinctly heard all that was going on, nevertheless laughed to himself, even though his roof was being pulled to pieces, for he expected every moment to see Cassandrino enter the room and attempt to carry off the bed. 'Do your worst, Cassandrino,' he said to himself, 'because you won't be stealing my bed tonight.' But while he was thus lying there with his eyes wide open and his ears straining, expecting to have his bed snatched from under him, Cassandrino let the dead body of the beggar fall into the Provost's room through the breach in the ceiling. The noise of it made him jump straight out of bed and light a candle, and then he saw – given the familiar clothing – what he took to be the body of Cassandrino lying mangled and crumpled up on the floor. In profound grief he cried out, 'Ah, what a wretched sight is here! To gratify my silly caprice I have killed this man. What will men say if it gets noised abroad that he met his death in my house? One must be careful in these matters.'

Still lamenting, the Provost heard one of his loyal and faithful servants knocking at the door of his chamber. When the fellow was fully awake, he told him of the unhappy event, begging him to go dig a hole in the garden and therein bury the dead body to prevent the scandalous fact from ever coming to light in the future. But while the Provost and his servant were dealing with the deceased in the garden, Cassandrino, who had watched all their movements in silence, seeing and hearing no one else in the room, let himself down by a rope and, having made a bundle of the bed, carried it away with all possible haste. The Provost, after he had buried the cadaver, returned to his room, but when he prepared to get into bed, there was no longer one to get into. Craving sleep, he was now obliged to make alternate arrangements, thinking all the while of the sagacity and cunning of this most accomplished thief.

The next day, according to his custom, Cassandrino went to the palace and appeared before the Provost, who cried out upon seeing him, 'Without any question, Cassandrino, you are the very prince of thieves! Who else could have contrived so cunningly to steal my bed?'

Cassandrino was silent, feigning the utmost astonishment, as if he had taken no part in the matter.

'You have played an excellent trick upon me,' the Provost went on to say, 'but I must get you to play me yet another in order to judge how far your ingenuity can carry you. If you can manage tonight to steal my light grey horse – the finest and most pleasing I ever owned – I'll give you another hundred florins to add to the hundred I've already promised you.'

Cassandrino, on hearing of this fresh task which was put upon him, pretended to be greatly troubled and loudly lamented that the Provost should so discredit him, begging him at the same time not to be his ruin. The Provost, deeming that Cassandrino refused assent to his request, grew angry and said, 'Well, then, if you won't do as I bid you, look for no other fate than to be hanged by a halter from the city wall.'

Cassandrino now saw how dangerous his case had become, no mistake about it, and so he replied, 'I'll do all I can to gratify you in what you ask, but believe me the task you propose is well beyond my powers,' and with those words he departed.

No sooner was he gone than the Provost, more resolved than ever to put Cassandrino's ingenuity to the severest test, called one of his servants and said to him, 'Go to the stable, and when you're there saddle and bridle my fine grey horse, then mount him and keep on his back all night, taking every precaution all the while that he isn't stolen.' Then he gave orders to another to make certain that all the doors of the palace and stables were well secured with bolts.

When the dark of night had come, Cassandrino took all his gear and made his way to the principal gate of the palace, where he found the porter quietly dozing. But because he knew all the secrets of the edifice, he let the porter sleep on. Taking another passageway, he gained the courtyard and from there passed on to the stables, which he found locked fast. With the help of his implements, he easily broke open the door and, once done, there to his amazement he perceived a man sitting on the Provost's favourite horse with the reins in his hand. But upon approaching him, he saw that he was sound asleep. Then the crafty rascal, noting that the sleeping lackey was as senseless as a statue, suddenly hit upon the cleverest plan the world had ever seen. Carefully, he measured the height of the horse and then stole away into the garden. From there he brought back four stout poles – the kind used to support vines on a trellis. Having sharpened them at the ends, he cunningly cut the reins which the sleeping servant held in his hand, and then the martingale, the cinch, and the crupper, and everything else that stood in his way. Then, after fixing one of the poles in the ground with the upper end dexterously inserted under one corner of the saddle, he did exactly the same on the other side, and repeated the operation at the two remaining corners. Next, he raised the saddle off the horse's back – its rider fast asleep all the while – and let it rest entirely on the four poles all firmly fixed in the ground. With no further obstacles in his way, he haltered the horse and led it away.

The Provost was astir early the next morning and went immediately to the stables, where he expected to find his horse all safe. But the sight which met his eyes was that of his servant, still fast asleep on the saddle, propped up by the four poles. Once the Provost had awakened him, he loaded him with abuse, and then, astonished by all he had seen, left the stables and returned to the palace. At the usual hour in the morning, Cassandrino made his way there and gave the Provost a merry salute as soon as he appeared.

'Cassandrino,' said the latter, 'assuredly among robbers, you carry off the palm. I could dub you, "King of Thieves." Yet I would still like to know, once and for all, whether you're as clever and ingenious as you appear to be. I presume you know Father Severino, rector of the church of San Gallo, not far from the city? Well, if you bring him here to me tied up in a sack, on my faith I promise to double the number of gold florins you have already earned. But if you fail in this, be assured I'll hang you up by the neck.'

Now this priest, Severino, was a man of the holy life and of the best repute. Yet he knew nothing of worldly affairs, having devoted his entire life to the service of his church. Cassandrino, seeing that the Provost had set his mind on working him an injury, said to himself, 'This man, I plainly see, is bent upon seeing me dead, but in this he'll find himself deceived, because I swear that if it can be done, I'll bring off this task as well as I did the others.' Once he'd made up his mind to do the Provost's bidding, Cassandrino began casting about how he might play a trick upon the priest that would serve the purpose he had in mind, and ultimately he came up with the following stratagem. He borrowed a priest's alb from one of his friends, one long enough to come down to his heels, along with a white stole all embroidered in gold. These he took home to his lodging. Then he got ready a beautiful pair of wings all painted in different colours which he manufactured out of pasteboard, and also a tinsel diadem that shone radiantly.

At nightfall, he crept out of town with all his trappings and headed for the village where Father Severino lived. There he hid in a thicket of sharp thorns, remaining until daybreak. Then Cassandrino donned the sacerdotal vestment, placed the stole around his neck, set the diadem on his head, and fixed the wings on his shoulders. This done, he hid himself again and wouldn't stir till the time came for the priest to go out and ring the bell for the Ave Maria. But Cassandrino was scarcely dressed before Father Severino, with his altar boy, arrived at the church door, which he left standing open as he went in to do his morning office. Cassandrino was on the watch, and seeing that the church door was wide open while the good priest was ringing the bell, he crept out of his hiding place and made his way softly into the church. Once inside, he went up to the altar and stood there bolt upright, holding open a great sack in his hands. Then he spoke in a soft, low voice, 'Whosoever would enter into the joys of paradise, let him climb into this sack.' These words he said over two or three times. While he was performing this mummery, the altar boy came out of the sacristy. When he saw the snow-white alb, the diadem shining like the sun, and the wings as gorgeous as a peacock's – to say nothing of the words he heard – he was altogether amazed. Once he had recovered himself, he went off to find the priest, saying, 'Sir, sir, I have just seen in the church an angel of heaven holding a sack in his hands and saying, "Whosoever would enter into the joys of paradise, let him climb into this sack," and Father, I want to go with him.'

The priest, who was fairly weak in the gourd, gave full credence to the acolyte's tale, and as soon as he walked through the sacristy door he saw the angel standing there in his celestial garb and heard the words for himself. So anxious he was to arrive safely in paradise, and fearful that the altar boy might forestall him by climbing into the sack first, he pretended to have left his breviary behind him at his lodging and said to the boy, 'Hasten back home and search my chamber diligently and bring back my breviary which I left somewhere on the couch.'

Now while the acolyte was gone to search for the breviary, the priest approached the angel, made him a deep bow, and crept into the sack. Cunning and mischievous as he was, and seeing that the game was going just as he had hoped, Cassandrino at once closed up the mouth of the sack and tied it firmly. Then he removed the alb, the diadem, and the wings, tied them into a bundle which, together with the sack, he hoisted onto his shoulders. Then he set out for Perugia, arriving as soon as it was clear daylight, and at the customary hour he presented himself before the Provost with the sack on his back. Having untied the mouth, he lugged out Severino the priest, who found himself in the presence of the Provost in a state more dead than alive, and fully aware that he was the butt of a knavish trick. Then and there he made a weighty charge against Cassandrino, crying out at the top of his voice that he had been robbed and inveigled into the sack by craft, to his great loss and humiliation. He begged the Provost to make an example of the villain and not to let so great a crime go without severe punishment, at the same time giving a clear warning to all other malefactors. The Provost, who had already fathomed the business from beginning to end, could no longer contain his laughter and, turning to Father Severino, thus addressed him, 'So, my little bumpkin priest, be quiet and don't torment yourself further; you won't lack for favours or for justice, for in this business, as far as I can see, you're the butt of a mean prank.' It took all his best efforts to pacify the priest, after which he took out a little packet in which there were several pieces of gold; these he placed in the priest's hands with instructions to have him escorted out of town. Then, turning to the thief, he said, 'Cassandrino, Cassandrino, it's true as can be that your knavish deeds exceed your knavish reputation, which is known to everyone. Wherefore, take these four hundred gold florins which I promised you, for you have won them fair and square. But take care that you conduct yourself more honestly in the future than you have in the past, for if I hear any more complaints about your rascally tricks, most assuredly you'll be hanged without pity.'

With that, Cassandrino took the four hundred gold florins and, having duly thanked the Provost, went his way. With this money he traded skillfully and successfully so that in time he became a man of wisdom, and in his business dealings was highly respected of all.

The company was greatly pleased with Alteria's story – the ladies above all – and commended her heartily. But Molino, with an admiring look and a merry smile, said, 'Mistress Alteria, the way I see it, you are a little thief yourself, for by the admirable way you see through their roguish slights, I'm convinced you've worked out an understanding with these fellows.'

To this Bembo replied, 'No, not at all. She is no thief of other men's worldly goods, but with her flashing eyes she steals away the hearts of those who look upon her.'

Blushing red at the words, Alteria turned towards Molino and Bembo and said, 'I'm no thief of other folk's goods, nor a robber of hearts; I'm only telling this story of Cassandrino exactly as I heard it from others.'

At this point, the Signora, seeing that the dispute might turn into a lengthy one, intervened and called them to silence, asking Alteria to proceed to her enigma. Her pique and excitement somewhat calmed, she offered the following lines.

While I my nightly vigil kept,
A man I spied, who softly crept
Adown the hall, whereon I said,
'To bed, Sir Bernard, get to bed.
Two shall undress you, four with care
Shut fast the doors, and eight up there
Shall watch, and bid the rest beware.'
While these deceiving words I said,
The thievish man in terror fled.

This ingenious enigma gave no less pleasure to the company than the tale she had previously recited. And though each and every one present hazarded a guess, no one could discover and reveal it. At last, Alteria, seeing that the hour was late and that no one was likely to solve her riddle, rose to her feet and gave this explanation. 'A gentleman had gone into the country with his entire household, as he often did, especially in summer time, and had left an old woman to guard his palace, who prudently made a practice of going about the house at nightfall to see if she might espy any thieves. One evening the good woman, going about the house as if on household business, spied a robber on a balcony who was watching her through a hole. The good old woman refrained from crying out and wisely made believe that her master was in the house, and a throng of servants as well, by saying "Go to bed, Messer Bernardo, and let two servants undress you, and four shut the doors, while eight go upstairs and guard the house." And while the old woman was giving these orders, the thief, fearing to be discovered, stole away.' When Alteria's clever riddle had been solved, Cateruzza, who was seated next to her, remembered that the third story of this first night was to be told by her, so with a smile on her face she began her tale.

I.2 Commentary

This story is set in Perugia in Umbria, a university town belonging to the papacy. San Domenico is south-west of the city. The exploits of 'master-thieves' – the story type to which Cassandrino belongs – like those of tricksters in general, depend upon a special and admirable brand of intelligence. By definition, such practitioners inhabit a social space outside the law and are therefore vulnerable to apprehension and incarceration or worse. Nevertheless, even those who are responsible for upholding law and order may find themselves attracted to the outlaw personality, or at least fascinated by his consummate skills of enactment or evasion, leading to negotiations between them according to the rules of a contest or wager. Straparola's Cassandrino is a man who has not only aggravated the populace in general by his repeated thefts and avoidance of the law, but paradoxically has won for himself the highest reputation for his expertise. By conventions of the story type, we are to imagine that such a robber has been invited by a magistrate to demonstrate the extent of his powers through a gaming structure that entails the performance of seemingly impossible tasks. In short, the magistrate sets the objectives, which, if achieved, bring to the thief exoneration, material rewards, and even marriage to the magistrate's daughter, while failure to meet them entails death. In a sense, this is merely an oriental-style framing tale surrounding an engaging micro-repertory of fanciful performance riddles and their witty solutions. Yet the psychology of the gaming relationship between the amused magistrate and the daring criminal is a feast for the imagination, given the subtle communication between the two of them that lies just below the words. Out of their transactions there emerges both a display of the indomitable trickster's skills and the recovery of a social exile who wagers his life to regain a lawful place within society. In a unique way, this tale hovers between the mythos of the clever and evasive outlaw and the mythos of the riddle-solver who thereby gains a sudden rise in status in quasi-fairy-tale fashion, while, on another level, it represents on the part of the Provost a brilliant scheme for the rehabilitation of a criminal mind by financially investing in his mercantile future, while threatening execution for any trace of recidivism.

It is notable in this regard that Straparola's version is lacking the making-of-the-robber-apprentice prologue that is attached to so many of its analogues. The return to society is rather more prepared for when the extenuating circumstances that initially make the thief are a part of our moral calibrations. A generic version of that preamble might tell of a poor mother's three sons who are compelled to wander out into the world to learn their trades. The first two will find mundane but respectable occupations, while the third meets up with robbers and, in the exchange, sees his advantage in joining the band and learning their profession – something he so entirely masters that he becomes their leader. Then, in due course, according to a prior pact, the three must meet together to return home, each with his new trade. The transition into the skill-testing contest follows when someone in a position of authority – a member of the family or community – calls the third son to account.[23] The story is altered to the extent that the boy is both a victim and a clever survivor, further contextualizing his redemption. Arguably such a combined tale was in circulation in Straparola's time, for they are legion in later centuries. Straparola (and presumably his source) begins *in medias res* with a committed thief, a scourge of the surrounding regions, who is virtually beyond the reach of the law. This rebalancing may have to do with the pragmatic fact that Straparola intended to tell a story elsewhere in the collection so closely resembling the apprenticeship prologue that he did not wish to repeat it here, namely 'The Three Brothers' (VII.5), in which the third son does not become a thief, but a wild man who learns the language of animals. In fact, Straparola's version may actually gain in force and intrigue through the omission of this opening sequence.

The salient feature of Cassandrino's character is that he pretends to honesty and dignity by protesting the Provost's accusations, murmuring against the harshness of the conditions of the game and the impossibility of the tasks, even while, in his hidden thoughts, he embraces the challenges with alacrity and sets to work immediately in planning what will prove to be an incrementally brilliant performance in imaginative problem solving and execution. That is as much as we have of his interiority. Yet in structural terms, their face-off is rich in motivic connotations, for while the demanded goals involve thievery, the issue is no longer crime but the terms of play and the pitting of skills, one player seeking to protect, the other to remove the designated objects.

Tales of thieves and their remarkable exploits have been collected over centuries. Outlawry was sometimes the result of class warfare, or of an unacceptable change of regimes in which civil disobedience to the new order led to exile in the greenwood.[24] In the case of Gamelyn, dispossessed by his brothers, a man of talent is driven into hiding until he can

23 This precise configuration is retained in a tale from the Ligurian coast in which the third son apprentices to thieves, becomes their master, returns home with his booty, asks to move up in society, declares his occupation, and must prove his craft to escape with his life. His fortune allows him to marry a princess and turn honest at a subsequent place and time. 'Le fin voleur,' in James Bruyn Andrews, *Contes Ligures: Traditions de la rivière recueillis entre Menton et Gênes* (Paris: E. Leroux, 1892; reprint, Marseille: Laffitte Reprints, 1979), no. 30, pp. 137–42.

24 See Maurice Keen, *The Outlaws of Medieval Legend* (London: Routledge & Kegan Paul, 1987), pp. 1–8.

successfully challenge the corrupt legal system by which he is deprived of his rightful possessions.[25] Behind the tale of Cassandrino, we may see a much reduced version of the exiled son who engages in dangerous play through which he can regain a rightful place in society. English writers in the last decades of the sixteenth century invented a new form of underworld literature ostensibly based on the roving, low-life practitioners of confidence games, petty theft, rigged gambling and dicing, pickpocketing, and the sale of compromised merchandise. Greene, Chettle, and Dekker, as writers of imaginative fiction and plays, could not resist expanding the descriptions of their manners, canting jargon, and techniques into confidence-game narratives, the better to expose their swindling tactics.[26] Such writing was also highly entertaining and popular. The double rationale that includes the cautionary pertains only marginally to such a fanciful creation as Straparola's, yet his story remains remotely linked to that class of literature that anatomizes the range of criminal activity such as François de Calvi's *Histoire générale des larrons* (1623), which is partly a documentary account of the most outrageous and elaborate swindles on record.[27] The exploits of Cassandrino pass over the line that separates the imaginatively implausible from the protohistorical. Yet therein consists the essence of the fable – the subtle play between flights of invention and the margins of probability.

There are hints of individual motifs from this story tradition borrowed by authors as early as the late fifteenth century, such as Matteo Maria Boiardo's allusion to the horse-stealing trick as practiced by Brunello upon Sacripante.[28] But Straparola's version is the earliest full literary rendition of the folk tale of 'the master-thief,' followed by a tale by Master Skelton, and another by Nicolaus Remigius, all three published between 1550 and 1598. Straparola's predates the Englishman's by a scant seventeen years,

---

25 *Middle English Verse Romances*, ed. Donald Sands (New York: Holt, Rinehart, & Winston, 1966), pp. 154–81.

26 *Cony-Catchers and Bawdy Baskets: An Anthology of Elizabethan Low Life*, ed. Gamini Salgado (London: Penguin, 1972), contains five works by Robert Greene. Henrie Chettle, *Kind-Hart's Dreame*, ed. G.B. Harrison (London: The Bodley Head, 1923). Thomas Dekker, *Lantern and Candlelight*, ed. Viviana Comensoli (Toronto: CRRS Publications, 2008).

27 *Histoires des larrons, or The history of theeves. Written in French, and translated out of the originall by Paul Godwin* (London: Printed by Iohn Raworth, and are to be sold by Thomas Slater, at the signe of the Swan in Duck-lane, 1638).

28 *Orlando innamorato*, ed. Charles Stanley Ross (Berkeley: University of California Press, 1999), bk. II, cantos 39–43, p. 443.

and the German's by forty-eight. Their appearances in regions geographically separated, each story imbued with narrative features characteristic of the oral culture, each different in detail while sharing the same narrative motifs, suggests that by the mid-sixteenth century, 'the master-thief' type (ATU 1525) was sufficiently disseminated throughout European folk culture to allow for the differentiation from a common ancestor represented in these stories. How far back the date must be pushed to allow for such widespread diffusion is complicated by the near certainty that the story type originated in Eastern sources which became known in the West at an unspecified date, but potentially any time from the twelfth to the fifteenth century. It is not an untypical profile. In sum, these three early modern renditions of the 'the master-thief,' Straparola's leading the way, provide the earliest literary records of a tale that must have enjoyed up to eight centuries of unbroken oral recitation in the West after its arrival from the East. Skelton treats the tale as a popular one, widely familiar to his audiences. Moreover, insofar as versions closely resembling these were found in the nineteenth century, not only throughout Europe but in Russia and the Near East, adds further weight to the presumption of a long-standing folk tradition, not to mention the versions from Persia, Bengal, Tibet and Mongolia described below in which many of the familiar motifs are to be found, such as stealing objects from a ruler's bedroom or leaving the guards straddling walls instead of their horses.

The thirteenth of the *Merry Tales Made by Master Skelton* (1567) is entitled 'How Master Skelton's miller deceived him many times by playing the thief, and how he was pardoned by Master Skelton after stealing away of a priest out of his bed at midnight.'[29] The tale opens with a miller pilfering grain in good English fashion using tricks profiled by Chaucer in 'The Reeve's Tale.' This miller, to gain a pardon, is compelled to show himself the master-thief he thinks he is or be hanged. First he must steal the master's cup, then the sheets off his bed, which he does by covering them with yeast. The effect was to make the occupants accuse each other of befouling the bed themselves. The priest is finagled into the sack by the use of snails in the church with candles fastened to their backs to create an unearthly sight. The thief puts on vestments and stands behind the altar with a book, tolling the bell and playing St. Peter. Even after the priest is hung up in Skelton's chimney, Skelton is not satisfied, but

29 In *A Hundred Merry Tales and other English Jest Books*, ed. P.M. Zall (Lincoln: University of Nebraska Press, 1963), pp. 339–46.

demands the horse stealing as well. Already, the features of the tradition have found an English ethos, derived, no doubt, from jest book type materials of uncertain provenance, or directly from a folk raconteur. By implication, given the apparent absence of prior literary models, Straparola, for his template, must have relied upon the same oral tradition from which Skelton's story is drawn.

That tradition was likewise available to Nicolaus Remigius who, less than fifty years after Straparola, preserved yet another version of the magistrate who would test a thief by putting him up to impossible missions, certain of them surviving in later folk tales, such as stealing the bed sheets from under him. This thief likewise creates a dummy which he hoists up to the bedroom window and which falls to the ground when shot, thereby distracting the magistrate while his bed is stolen. The repertory of such tricks was destined to grow throughout the following three centuries, so that by the nineteenth century the story could be found in many diversified forms throughout Europe. Henry Mayhew would offer a version, one of many to appear in the British Isles, in *London Labour and the London Poor.*[30]

The perdurability of 'the master-thief' design can be demonstrated by leaping forward nearly 250 years to the Grimm brothers' tale in the *Kinder- und Hausmärchen*, no. 192, in which the gentleman master-thief is compelled by his noble godfather to steal first his horse, then his bed sheets, and finally the local priest, having for his reward merely a chance to go free without punishment.[31] The points of comparison with Straparola,

---

30 Nicolaus Remigius, 'Der vermeinte zauberische Dieb,' in *Daemonolatria, das is, von unholden und zauber Geisten* (Frankfurt: Palthenius, 1598), bk. III, chap. 39. For Mayhew, see *London Labour and the London Poor* (London: Griffin, Bohn & Co., [1851], 1861), vol. III, p. 388.

31 'The Master-Thief,' *Grimm's Complete Fairy Tales* (New York: Nelson Doubleday, n.d.), no. 178, pp. 565–70. For a comparative version see Sir George Webbe Dasent, *Popular Tales from the Norse* (New York: G.P. Putnam's Sons, 1888; New York, Johnson Reprint Corporation, 1970), 'The Master-thief,' pp. 232–51. A later North German or Scandinavian version appeared some time before 1850 in which the peasant's oxen are stolen by dropping shoes in the road, first one, and then the second, causing the peasant to abandon the animals to go back for the first shoe. A requisite precondition in all of these tales is that the victims of the thefts should endure no bodily harm. In another ruse, the thief stages a feigned hanging of himself in three places, creating a distracting illusion. Soon the apprentice surpasses his fellow professionals. He returns the poor peasant's oxen, but makes off for home with the robbers' own gear, telling his father of his exploits. In the second part, a rich magistrate (Amtmann) with an attractive daughter puts the young thief to the test.

Skelton, and Remigius are already patent. This version of the tale, Jacob and Wilhelm found in the *Zeitschrift für deutsches Alterthum* 3 (1843), from a folk source collected by Friedrich Stertzing. Another had been found in those same years by Christen Asbjørnsen and published in his *Norske Folke-eventyr* in 1841.[32] The inevitable conclusion is that such stories were derived from the same story type, preserved through an oral tradition, the same from which the three Renaissance versions were generated.

One further version from northern Europe merits mention, not only for preserving so many of the features familiar from Straparola, but for having established itself in far-away Iceland by the early nineteenth century. Grey-man is caught stealing the king's sheep and is offered a chance to escape death by performing seemingly impossible feats involving his talent. As the king's men lead the prize royal ox through a forest, the

---

First the hero plays the trick of the three hares to distract the kitchen staff and steal the roast beef. When the priest jeers at the boy, he shams the angel of the annunciation and inveigles him into a sack to be transported to heaven. The clergyman is then bounced over stones to the Amtmann's goose house. Then comes a version of the horse theft featured in Straparola. Ultimately, he tricks the master himself, steals the sheet off his bed along with his wife's nightgown, causes the Amtmann to shoot a dead corpse on a ladder, and finally tricks his way into a profitable marriage. Benjamin Thorpe, *Yule-Tide Stories: A Collection of Scandinavian and North German Popular Tales and Traditions* (London: Henry Bohn, 1853), pp. 265–78, from Peter Christian Asbjørnsen's *Norske Folk-eventyr* (Christiana: J. Dybwad, 1850).

32 This story appears in English in *Blackwood's Edinburgh Magazine* 70, no. 433 (November 1851), pp. 595–604, and represents a remarkable reconfiguration of many of the now familiar elements. One of three sons falls into the hands of thieves and joins the band by way of escape. He engages in a series of ruses mostly with cattle, finally making off with the band's gold and silver before returning home. He now seeks to marry the squire's daughter, but while the marriage is promised, there are delays. He is first challenged to steal the Sunday roast. Then, as the result of mocking the squire's gullibility, the master-thief is commanded to lure the local priest into a sack with all his worldly goods. Still not content, the squire asks to have all twelve of his horses stolen from the stable, which the thief manages by disguising himself as an old woman and drugging the guards with brandy. The final test is the theft of the bed-sheets and his wife's shift as well, which he accomplishes by using a dead body to distract them, as does Cassandrino, but which the squire shoots with his rifle. The story concludes with the promised marriage, largely because the squire comes to fear the thief's prowess and decides to remain on his best side. A similar tale is part of the folk heritage of Bengal in which the thief takes the gold chain from the queen's neck as she sleeps. A camel with gold on its back is driven through the city intentionally to tempt the thief to a further exploit. The thief drugs the driver and makes the heist. 'Adventures of Two Thieves and their Sons,' in *Folk-Tales of Bengal*, trans. Lal Behari Day (London: Macmillan, 1883), pp. 174–81.

hero seeks to distract them by hanging himself first in one place and then farther along by running ahead of them through the trees. When they abandon the beast to confirm the illusion, the thief has his opportunity. As for stealing the king's own sheets, Grey-man gains entry to the palace by stealth and pours warm mush into the royal bed (in the tradition of Skelton some centuries earlier), bringing the couple to cross accusations over who was responsible for fouling the bed. His second opportunity was thus created. The king now orders that he himself, together with his queen, must be stolen. By staging the sack trick in the chapel with a costume covered in candles, this 'angel of good tidings' lures their majesties into the sack, whereupon he drags them about until their fear elicits from them promises of marriage into the royal family and half the realm. Despite the variations, the persistent frame is in clear evidence, again confirming the astonishing stability of such traditions over time and across wide spaces. Together, these many tales of 'the master-thief' type presuppose an early oikotype, or 'forme internationale' to use Propp's term, which may be teased out by computational inference from the many surviving versions, including the cognate tales known in Eastern countries.

There are numerous additional folk analogues available for investigation, which, for our purposes, must be confined to a scant few. 'Jack the Cunning Thief' was an Irish favourite in the nineteenth century. Three sons go into the world to learn trades, although the youngest was only interested in amusement and trickery. He takes lodging in the house of six robbers and the contest begins for becoming the master of the thieves. First he performs the shoes-on-the-road trick, dropping first one and later the other, causing the peasant to tie up his sheep to retrieve the first shoe. The farmer is cheated of another animal when Jack leads the farmer into the forest with his feigned bleating. Then the thieves themselves are lured out of the house and their treasure stolen. Once back home, Jack plays the grandee, demands the neighbour's daughter in marriage, and demonstrates to his prospective father-in-law the sleights of his trade. The burgher challenges the boy to steal meat off the spit, then six horses, then his own horse, then the sheets on his bed, which concluded the contest and won him the wedding. The story has the combined elements of cheating the thieves and cheating the magistrate, epitomizing one major branch of the story type.[33]

33 Patrick Kennedy, *The Fireside Stories of Ireland* (Dublin: McGlashan & Gill, 1870; reprint, Norwood, PA: Norwood Editions, 1975), pp. 38–46.

Calvino, in his *Italian Fables*, no. 117, 'The Art of Franceschiello' (collected originally in the Abruzzi), tells of the boy lured into a gang of thieves who returns home to give an account of his apprenticeship in the 'respectable trade.'[34] The two parts are present, as in the Irish tale. He enters into a contest with a priest who challenges him to steal a lamb from his own flock, then to bring a certain hermit to him in a sack. The priest bets money that he will fail, simply to find out how well he has mastered his calling. By promising paradise to anyone willing to crawl into his sack, Franceschiello captures the holy man and wins his 200 ducats. So the story ends a mere skeleton of what it was in Straparola. Another, collected after the mid-nineteenth century in Lorraine, is more elaborate but less coherent in its retention of fragments and details no longer understood. In 'Le franc voleur,' Pierrot, the thief, also an apprentice in the trade, steals a horse by plying the guards with strong drink before absconding with a herd of steers bound for market.[35] In the closing episode, the kidnapping of the priest, he takes crabs or crayfish with him, which he leaves in a dish on the altar before luring the priest into the sack by promising him entry into heaven. The Grimm tale, among many analogues, explains the original use of the crabs, for the thief, intent upon playing the role of Saint Peter on the Day of Judgment to the fullest, first sets the crabs loose in the cemetery with candles fixed to their backs to imitate the stirring of the resurrected souls.[36] It is an elaborate ruse, but only marginally more imaginative than the disguise assembled by Cassandrino to impersonate an angel. The horse theft sequence, carried out by hoisting up the saddle with the sleeping rider, is nearly universal to this narrative group. Cosquin finds it in tales from Norway, Ireland, Germany, Tuscany, Lorraine, Brittany, Scotland, Flanders, the Basque country, Catalonia, Serbia, and Russia (but not in

34 Trans. George Martin (New York: Pantheon Books, 1980), pp. 414–17.

35 Emmanuel Cosquin, *Contes populaires de Lorraine*, 2 vols. (Paris: F. Vieweg, 1886), vol. II, pp. 271–4.

36 The motif of the crabs and the candles seems to have circulated widely; it has been attributed to actual practice. The English Protestant, Henry More (one of the Cambridge Platonists at mid-seventeenth century) believed that 'medieval priests used to tie candles to the backs of crabs and set them loose in churchyards to simulate the souls of the dead.' Keith Thomas, *Religion and the Decline of Magic* (London: Penguin, 1991), p. 703.

the Icelandic version cited above).[37] Clearly, this story has a history of success that covers many centuries and that spreads out geographically. Straparola's tale assumes value as a snapshot of that tradition at an early point between its medieval origins and the rich gathering of variants in the nineteenth century. These folk analogues include the twenty examples located in Spain by Aurelio M. Espinosa, the tale of 'Ladrón y picaro' telling of three sons who set off from home and part ways, with the third becoming a master-thief. He steals coins from the king, eggs from an eagle, and animals guarded by the king's servants, as well as the bed sheets of the queen, while in another variant he places the sacristan in a sack.[38] This sampling could be extended to include dozens more examples.

---

37 Cosquin (ref. two notes above), vol. II, p. 277. See Jean-François Fleury, 'Jacques le voleur,' in *Littérature orale de la Basse-Normandie* (Paris: Maisonneuve, 1883), pp. 167–79. This boy tells his mother he wants to be a thief. She then enters the church to consult the Blessed Virgin and gets her answer in the affirmative from the boy behind the altar impersonating her voice. This little trickster begins his career with the cow stealing trick on the road by hanging himself in two places to lure the attendants away from the animal. Next, he drugs the horsemen and steals their mounts. For a sequel, he steals bread out of a baking oven by drilling a hole at the back. Now the magistrate who has put him up to all the tests wants the sheets stolen from his own bed while he is sleeping. The boy comes up with another distraction at the window, an effigy, which leads the good man to murder. While attending to the 'body,' the boy does his work in the bedroom. The next day he turns hares loose in the yard to distract dinner guests and so steals the entire banquet. The final trick is to lure the priest into a sack by playing the angel who leads the *curé* to 'paradise.' This story retains many of the elements familiar from Straparola, pointing to a narrative tradition with considerable stability that circulated throughout Europe for half a millennium. Another was collected by Auguste Dozon, *Contes albanais* (Paris: Leroux, 1881), 'Les deux voleurs,' p. 169. In this tale one of the thieves poses as the angel Gabriel to get the priest into the sack. This was one of the popular features of the folk tradition. In 'The Gypsy and the Priest,' from Francis Hindes Groome's *Gypsy Folk Tales*, ed. Walter Starkie (London: Hurst and Blackett, 1899; reprint, London: Herbert Jenkins, 1963), no. 12, pp. 46–53, the Turkish gypsies tell of the candles and angel's clothes used to dupe the clergyman. Once inside, the priest is mercilessly abused by being dragged over rough roads and through thorns. Ultimately he dies and the gypsy makes off with a considerable sum of money. Groome provides five further versions of the tale principally from North and South Wales.

38 *Cuentos populares españoles* (Madrid: S. Aguirre, 1947), vol. I, pp. 502–5. This is ATU type 1525A. Further post-Straparola versions with one or more of the familiar motifs are to be found in Justin Edouard Mathieu Cénac-Moncaut, *Contes populaires de la Gascogne* (Paris: E. Dentu, 1861), pp. 99–101; Carolina Coronedi-Berti, *Novelle*

There are potentially two remote literary sources for the tale of Cassandrino. The first may be called the 'Rhampsinitus' type and the second the 'Bakhtishu' type, although the second is altogether more germane. Bakhtishu is the name of the doctor who takes Caliph Mutawakkil's wager that within three days the master-thief known as Al-Uqab or 'the Eagle' could steal something from him before his very eyes. This tale occurs in the *Muruj al-Dhahab* (Golden Meadows) written before 947 by the Islamic geographer and historian Abu al-Hasan 'Ali al-Mas'udi, who was born in Baghdad in 896.[39] According to the terms of the bet, if al-Uqab succeeds, the doctor would pay 10,000 dinars to the Caliph, but if the thief fails, the Caliph would give the doctor a country estate. The first challenge is to steal sheep, closely guarded, which Al-Uqab manages by fraternizing with the shepherds in order to share with them his drugged wine. Then he disguises himself as an angel, in the manner of Cassandrino, and appears to Doctor Bakhtishu himself

---

popolari bolognesi (Bologna: A. Forni, 1983), no. 39; and Heinrich Pröhle, 'Der gelehrige Dieb,' in *Kinder- und Volksmärchen* (Leipzig: Avenarius & Mendelssohn, 1853; reprint, Hildesheim: Georg Olms, 1975), no. 49, pp. 148–57. This tale is a unique collection of the many familiar tricks. The first is to rob a cattleman of his three oxen by making him think the beasts had sunk into the moor. Achieving this, the thief returns to the band of robbers with the first proof of his skill. The second episode is concerned with a merchant's shop in Hamburg and the fabrics and jewels for the wedding of the king of Morocco to the daughter of the emperor of China. By sundry impersonations and ruses, the thief gets the goods back to the robbers' cave. By the end he becomes the leader of the gang. For others in 'the master-thief' group see Johannes Bolte and Jiří Polívka, *Anmerkungen zu den Kinder- und Hausmärchen der Brüder Grimm* (Leipzig: Dieterich, 1913–37), vol. III, pp. 379–406. Another of this kind was collected by Angelo de Gubernatis, 'Il ladro,' in *Le novelline di Santo Stefano* (Turin: A.F. Negro, 1869), no. 29, pp. 54–5. A clever third son steals a horse, meets up with thieves who attempt to rob him, and ultimately offers to join them to master their trade without the use of violence. His greatest exploit was the robbery of a stagecoach. When he returns home and reports his new skills to his family, he is turned over to the authorities and imprisoned. But he makes his escape and is offered pardon by these same gaming authorities if he can demonstrate his skills. He too steals the peasant's cattle, then a ring by distracting the household with a puppet, so that from one exploit to the next he at last gains his freedom. There is a story by the same name in Giuseppe Pitrè's *Novelline popolari toscane* (Palermo, 1878), no. 41. Laura Gonzenbach collected another as 'Die Geschichte von Caraseddu' in her *Sicilianische Märchen* (Leipzig: Wilhelm Engelmann, 1870), no. 83, vol. II, pp. 142–5.

39 Al-Mas'udi, *Muruj al-Dhahab* (The meadows of gold: The Abassids), ed. Paul Lunde and Caroline Stone (London: Kegan Paul, 1989), pp. 355–7.

as an emissary of the Christ offering him a shortcut to heaven, all of which prevails upon the doctor's compromised judgement. So many of the markers are present in Al-Mas'udi's tale that it warrants consideration as the prototype for the entire thief-and-magistrate-contest group. It was such a tale as this that carried 'the master-thief' design to the West where it left few literary traces before Straparola, Skelton and Remigius, but where it must have circulated widely in the oral cultures in order to have generated the rich harvest of tales of the 'Bakhtishu' type in the nineteenth century.

Altogether more speculative are the means whereby tales from the East possessing common narrative structures and motifs arrived in the West, where, and at what times. The Cassandrino or 'master-thief' group is a prime case in point, insofar as several tales from the Orient of indeterminate age tell of just such heroes who, with incredible bravura, steal objects from the royal palace to prove their consummate skills. These derive from the same early tales that provided the template for the motif of the clever thief in the Occidental stories. W.A. Clouston relates one from Mongolia concerned with a man of great reputation for his cleverness who is challenged to steal the Khán's talisman. He first gets the palace guards drunk and removes their horses, leaving them straddling walls. He then disables the palace staff in various ways, enters the Khán's room, takes the talisman before his eyes, and completes his escape. The guards awake and find themselves ridiculously stranded. The following day the thief, having made his point, offers to return the talisman, but the Khán does not accept it. That was a foolish move, for it contained the secret of his life force. Hence when he orders the death of the thief, the latter breaks the talisman on a stone. With blood pouring from his nose, the ruler sinks into death.[40]

---

40 *Popular Tales and Fictions* (Santa Barbara, CA: ABC Clio, 2002), pp. 349–50. He tells another from Tibet, which combines elements of Herodotus and the robbery of the treasury and the severing of the companion's head with the exploits of the clever thief who first honours and buries by stealth the body of his companion lost in the heist gone wrong, then meets the king's challenge by getting the princess pregnant. The discovery device employs a motif soon to be seen in the story of Pietro the Fool (III.1) in which all men are called to court to determine the paternity of the princess's baby. The thief is identified as the father when the child being carried around the room bestows the wreath upon him. The king now has his culprit, but rather than punish him, in admiration of his skills he honours him. This comes from *The Bible of Tibet: Tibetan Tales from Indian Sources*, trans. by Franz Anton von Schiefner (into German), and by W.R.S. Ralston (into English) (London: Trübner,

In tracing the Oriental stories there are extensive gaps, but enough hints have come to light to posit a running tradition of 'master-thief' tales going back to the end of the first millennium. The *Bahar Danush* (The Garden of Knowledge) of Inayat Allah Kanbu (Einaiat Ooolah), completed in Delhi in 1651, is a collection of tales about faithless wives and the tricks they played on their husbands, all of them taken from earlier Indian sources. Among them is the tale of a master-thief who is intent upon stealing a jewel-studded golden fish kept under the king's pillow.[41] By using ropes he clambers up to the roof after eluding the guards and enters the bedroom of the king. He must wait for a slave girl to fall asleep who had been rubbing the king's feet, a task which the thief takes up until the king turns in his sleep and the precious object can be seized. This he wraps in a veil and decorates with white flowers as though it were his dead child which he then carries past the sentries to bury outside the city. Another thief follows him, however, and watches where he buries the treasure. Certain he has been observed, the first thief looks about and sees the second playing dead on one of the execution stakes. He does all he can to determine whether the other is alive or dead by holding his nose and mouth and running him through the cheek with his sword. But the second thief had perfect discipline and thus remained behind to bury the treasure elsewhere. The daring exploit is announced the next day and a reward is offered for the jewel. The first thief now has the option of going to the palace and negotiating a pardon by revealing the actions of the second thief, all of which he could prove by the inflicted wound. The king then has all the medical practitioners interrogated and thereby finds the wounded culprit who is brought in for execution, while the first escapes with his reward. The profile of the story speaks for itself as a variant somewhat removed from Straparola, for it deals with one trick only, although the perpetrator tricks guards and scales walls as in several of the Western analogues. Moreover, he targets royal residences and attempts the seemingly impossible as an artist more taken with the execution than with the object itself, which is but material proof of his virtuosity and finesse – a spirit common to all these stories.

1882); the modern edition is edited by C.A.F. Rhys Davids (London: Kegan Paul, 2003), pp. 37–43. See the debate on p. 37 by von Schiefner concerning the Eastern vs. Western claims for the origin of the tale. Despite the presumed Eastern origin, it occurs in Pausanias's *Description of Greece*, IX, 37.

41 Inayat Allah, *Bahar Danush, or, Garden of Knowledge* (the *Bahār-i-dānish*), trans. Jonathan Scott, 3 vols. (Shrewsbury: J. & W. Eddowes, 1799), vol. II, pp. 225–48.

Because so many of Straparola's past editors and translators have also mentioned 'The Treasury of King Rhampsinitus' as a probable source (ATU type 950), it merits a moment's consideration, particularly because certain of its features and episodes find their way into the master-thief stories in the Bakhtishu group. The story hails from the second book of Herodotus, Sect. 121, which tells of an ancient architect who knew the design of the king's treasury – information that was passed along to his son, who, with a friend, made use of it to commit the perfect robbery.[42] Missing his goods, however, the king turned sleuth, took counsel, burned green wood inside the building to find the chinks in the structure, then strategically placed a cauldron of hot pitch beneath the hidden entry on the assumption that the thieves would return. When the friend falls into the pitch and cannot get out, the only means for the architect's son to hide his identity is to behead his unfortunate colleague. The king becomes obsessed with catching the felon, not so much to punish the crime or retrieve the goods as to identify the clever fugitive. The cadaver of the beheaded friend becomes the principal means for detection, but the architect's son also manages to steal it for burial. Defeated at last, the king offers complete amnesty and marriage to his own daughter if the thief would only identify himself, at which time the boy comes forward to claim his reward. The beheading of the partner whose body is left in the treasury is a distinct marker of the narrative, together with the canvassing of the city door-to-door in search of the culprit, who must escape by subterfuge. The two story types share common materials in the cheating of the king's guards and related forms of trickery. Herodotus appears to have generated this now famous 'history' out of a somewhat compromised version of an ancient Eastern folk tale.[43] The differences separating his version from Somadeva's in the *Katha sarit sagara* are considerable,

42 *The Histories of Herodotus*, ed. George Rawlinson, 2 vols. (London: J.M. Dent, [1910]), bk. II. sect. 121, vol. II, pp. 191*ff.* W.A. Clouston mentions a parallel tale from antiquity told by Pausanias (IX.37) pertaining to the treasury of Hyrieus in which the thief is swallowed up by the earth. *Popular Tales and Fictions* (Santa Barbara: ABC Clio, 2002), pp. 335–6.

43 Missing in his version is an articulation of the surviving thief's need to mourn over, recover, and bury the body of his beheaded companion, even though just such signs are at the foundation of the king's methods for trapping him. These features are evident in many cognate versions, for it is thought that this story originated in the obligations concerning the burial of the dead such as they are expressed in Sophocles' *Antigone*. See also the commentary to 'The Grateful Dead' (XI.2) in the present collection.

but must be explained in terms of substitutions and alterations to a sprawling common story tradition.

This story circulated widely in medieval and Renaissance Europe, appearing early as one of the stories of *The Seven Sages of Rome*, a collection that appeared in many languages in prose and in verse, one of which is the *Dolopathos*, translated from the Greek *Seven Sages* by Johannes de Alta Silva, a Cistercian monk active between 1184 and 1212.[44] Perhaps the most accomplished literary recension of the Rhampsinitus type appears in the *Pecorone* (IX.1) of Ser Giovanni Fiorentino, a work completed by 1390, and one that Straparola could have consulted. Giovanni transfers the tale to Venice where it is the Doge's treasury that is robbed by a father and his son, Ricciardo – the son now compelled to behead his own father mired in the pitch and begging him to act to save his honour.[45] The Doge has the body displayed throughout the city, causing the boy's mother to expose emotions which he must disguise by cutting off his own thumb. Beggars are sent from door to door looking for clues. After exhausting all other means of detection, the Doge resorts to a sleepover in the palace for the city's most notorious lechers, placing his

44 *Dolopathos or The King and the Seven Wise Men*, trans. Brady B. Gilleland (Binghamton, NY: MRTS, 1981), pp. 43–50. It also appears in *The Seven Sages of Rome (Southern version)*, ed. Karl Brunner (London: Early English Text Society, Humphrey Milford-Oxford University Press, 1933; reprint, Nendeln: Kraus Reprints, 1971), ll. 1219–1350. *Dolopathos* was also versified by Herbert as *Li romans de Dolopathos*, ed. Charles Brunet and Anatole de Montaiglon (Paris: Bibliothèque Elzevirienne, 1856), pp. 215*ff*, for the current story. For a further study of the clever thieves and the Rhampsinitus tradition see N.M. Penzer, *Poison Damsels and other Essays in Folklore and Anthropology* (London: Chas. J. Sawyer, 1952), pp. 75–109. The story also made its way early to England via William Painter as 'The Duke of Venice and Ricciardo,' in *Palace of Pleasure*, ed. Joseph Jacobs (London: David Nutt, 1890; reprint, New York: Dover, 1966), vol. II, pp. 8–17. This is Ser Giovanni's story. A tragedy must have been written on the tale of 'Bindo and Ricciardo,' now lost, to which Philippe Henslowe makes reference in his *Diary*, on March 4 and June 5, 1592. See *Henslowe's Diary*, ed. R.A. Foakes and R.T. Rickert (Cambridge: Cambridge University Press, 1961). Henri Estienne also contributed to its wide circulation through his *Traite preparative a l'Apologie pour Herodote*, ed. Bénédicte Boudou (Geneva: Droz, [1566], 2007). Henry William Weber recovers the story from a metrical version of the *Seven Sages* in his *Metrical Romances of the Thirteenth, Fourteenth, and Fifteenth Centuries*, 3 vols. (Edinburgh: A. Constable, 1810).

45 *The Pecorone of Ser Giovanni*, trans. W.G. Waters, 3 vols. (London: Privately Printed for Members of the Society of Bibliophiles, 1898), vol. II, pp. 3–34. The story receives an elaborate retelling by Matteo Bandello as 'Egito la vicenda,' in *Tutte le opere*, ed. Francesco Flore (Milan: Mondadori, 1934–5), part I, no. 25, pp. 257–66.

daughter in bed in the midst of them on the curious assumption that the thief would also be the first to attempt her virtue. But Ricciardo was equal to this test as well, for in detecting that the girl had marked him with dye, he took the pot and marked all the others in the room, some of them several times. Baffled to the end, the Doge, in nearly fairy tale fashion, calls for a truce and offers his daughter in marriage to the man who could prove himself the master escape artist. The story is retold by Prato in *La leggenda del tesoro di Rampsinite* and it likewise made its way into the oral culture.[46] Calvino, in his *Fiabe italiane* (Italian Fables), no. 17, offers a folk version entitled 'Crack and Crook,' which repeats not only elements of the well-worn Rhampsinitus story, but incorporates the sheet-stealing episode from the Cassandrino group, at last associating the two traditions in a modest way.[47] For those interested in pursuing the Rhampsinitus type in modern folk tale versions, there are several with

46 Stanslao Prato, 'La leggenda del tesoro di Rampsinite,' in *Quattro novelline populari livornesi* (Bologna: A. Forni, [1976]). Other versions of the tale appear in Giovanni Sercambi, *Il novelliere*, ed. L. Rossi (Rome: Salerno, [1374], 1974), no. 88; Matteo Boiardo, *Orlando innamorato*, trans. Charles Stanley Ross (Berkeley: University of California Press, 1989), bk. II, chaps. 5, 39.

47 (New York: Pantheon Books, 1980), pp. 50–2. This story from Sicily was first collected by Pitrè, no. 159 of his *Fiabe*, and appears in the English translation of this work, vol. I, pp. 577–9, for which, see the following note. For further traces of this story tradition, see Max Müller, *Chips from a German Workshop*, 5 vols. (New York: Charles Scribner's Sons, 1889–91; or 4 vols. (London: Longman's Green, 1867–75), vol. II, p. 230. For a comprehensive list of the represention s of the Rhampsinitus type in modern folk and literary tales see Johannes Bolte and Jiří Polívka, *Anmerkungen zu den Kinder- und Hausmärchen der Brüder Grimm* (Leipzig: Dieterich'sche Verlag, 1913–32), vol. III, pp. 395–406. One of the curious facts of the Rhampsinitus tale is that it found its way from Egypt through Herodotus back to the East where it appears in the *Katha sarit sagara* of Somadeva as 'Karpara and Ghata,' in *The Ocean of Streams of Story*, ed. N.M. Penzer, trans. C.H. Tawney, 10 vols. (London: Chas. W. Sawyer, 1927), vol. V, pp. 142–51 (the same page numbers in the edition printed in Delhi by Motilal Banarsidass, 1923, 1984). In this version it is a princess who is the treasure, and while one lover (thief) is taken and hanged, the second digs a passage to her apartment, takes her away, and then takes down the body of his friend which the king was using as a means to catch the thief. He continually tricks the guards and gets the body. Somadeva or his source joins the Rhampsinitus opening to a misogynist Kashmirian tale on the treachery of women, for the princess dissuades the second thief from claiming his half of the kingdom as his reward for turning himself in and prevails upon him to flee, only to give herself to a beggar, then kill Ghata her liberator, and in turn betray the beggar for a merchant. Penzer includes a substantial commentary on the probable origins of this

which to begin, including another located in Sicily by Pitrè, one in Bologna by Coronedi-Berti, and one in Monferrato by Comparetti.[48]

The two story groups share only broad generic features: they deal with thieves and magistrates, involve skill-testing episodes, and conclude with leniency and even rewards for men who are otherwise malefactors. To be sure, both protagonists exercise their genius in ready and creative thinking. But Ricciardo and Cassandrino perform under contrasting circumstances, the one demonstrating his prowess as an escape artist, the other as a break-in artist. Their stories do not share common episodes, initially, and it matters that the former protagonist plays cat-and-mouse with a pursuing magistrate who is the trickster-manqué in trying to catch him, whereas the latter is in constant negotiation with the games-master who drives the action.

Nevertheless, the stories have been associated and occasionally blended into a single narrative, particularly by the folk raconteurs of Eastern Europe. F.H. Groome relates just such a tale in his *Gypsy Folk-Tales* which begins with the master-thieves in contest, the one stealing bird's eggs without disturbing the mother while the other steals the pants of the first thief. But then, instead of following the pattern of the *fabliau* in the pork stealing contest, recounted above, they go to the king's treasury, the one of them falling into the king's molasses trap and the other cutting off his head to hide his identity. Once the beheaded thief's body is recovered, however, the story returns to the Bakhtishu type, now with the king as

---

story and opines that there are some forty versions surviving from the medieval period beginning in 1150 with *The Seven Sages of Rome* and *Dolopathos*. He cites the Middle English version from MS. Cotton Galba E. ix.

48 'The Mason and his Son,' in *The Collected Sicilian Folk and Fairy Tales of Giuseppe Pitrè*, ed. and trans. Jack Zipes and Joseph Russo, 2 vols. (New York: Routledge, 2009), no. 160, vol. I, pp. 580–5. This is a full relation of the Rhampsinitus type in which the builder of the treasury uses his inside knowledge of the architecture to steal from the king, aided in the exploit by his son until, becoming mired in pitch, the father must be beheaded to prevent identification. The story is retold from Pitrè by Thomas Crane in *Italian Popular Tales* (Boston: Houghton Mifflin, 1885), pp. 163–7. Carolina Coronedi-Berti, 'La fola dla bêla Filadora,' in *Favole bolognesi* (Bologna: Arnaldo Forni, 1883; reprint, Bologna: Forni, 1981), no. 14, pp. 54–8. Domenico Comparetti, 'Crich e Croch,' in *Novelline popolari italiane* (Rome: E. Loescher, 1875), no. 13, pp. 52–4. For readers particularly interested in the story type and its European-wide circulation in folk literature, consult W.A. Clouston, *Popular Tales and Fictions* (Santa Barbara, CA: ABC Clio, 2002), pp. 338–49, where versions may be found from Greece, Albania, Brittany, Scotland, Holland, the Tyrol, Denmark, Russia, and Kabaïl in North Africa.

the magistrate testing the clever thief. He sends him out to steal the oxen from the peasant, a feat he manages by cutting off the tail of the one he steals and placing it in the mouth of the other to make the peasant think the one ox had eaten the other. Then he is sent to steal the priest out of the church, which to accomplish is to win the king's daughter for good and all. Tellingly, the story contains the crabs and candles trick coherently remembered, culminating in the sack trick, a sack in which the priest thought he would make his way to heaven but in which he only gets as far as the palace. The story represents a narrative creation conceived by intermingling these long-associated stories.[49]

Both story types appear among those collected by J.F. Campbell in the West Highlands. In 'The Son of the Scottish Yeoman who stole the Bishop's Horse and Daughter, and the Bishop Himself,' a Scots boy takes employment with the chief magistrate of London and preys upon the Bishop of London, first by wagering he can steal his brown horse – which he does by lowering a hanged man down the chimney – then the bishop's daughter and her maid, and finally the bishop himself by impersonating a holy man preaching from the bishop's own pulpit, having dressed himself in the eerie silver of fish scales. The bishop finds himself the subject of the homily, comes to repentance, and follows the light-giving stranger directly into the trap. In the end, the bishop is urged to marry his daughter to such a crafty chap. The second tale, that of 'The Shifty Lad, The Widow's Son,' is less like Straparola's, but is remarkable for having joined into one long story the clever exploits of an apprentice thief who defeats

49 'The Two Thieves,' in Francis Hindes Groome, *Gypsy Folk-Tales* (London: David Nutt, 1899), pp. 41–6. This story derives from Barbu Constantinescu, 'îl diu coir,' in *Probe de Limbu si Literatura Tiganilor din Romania* (Bucherest, 1878), no. 6, pp. 79–87. See also Rudolf von Sowa, 'O rom th-o rasai,' in *Die Mundart den slovakischen Zigeuner* (Göttingen: Vandenhoeck and Ruprecht, 1877), no. 8, pp. 174*ff.* The story of one thief getting away with the trousers of the other is known from as far away as Kashmir. See J. Hinton Knowles, *Folk-tales of Kashmir* (London: Trübner, 1888), p. 111. The story in combined form is also known in Scandinavia, as in the old Swedish fifteenth-century version recorded by G.A. Aberg, *Nyländska Folksagor*, 2 vols. (Helsinki: Nylandska Afdelningen, 1887), in which the student who steals the body from the gibbet manages to dress the twelve drunken guards in priest's cassocks. See Norman Mosley Penzer, *Poison Damsels and Other Essays in Folklore and Anthropology* (London: C.J. Sawyer, 1952), pp. 126–8; new edition (London: Kegan Paul, 2002).

his master and the theft of the king's treasury and the decapitation of the trapped thief in imitation of the story of Rhampsinitus.[50]

In Straparola's story, there appears the first of a number of brief citations lifted directly from Boccaccio's *Decameron.* The full passage in question is that in which Cassandrino goes into a churchyard to disinter a dead body: 'At last he hit on the following scheme. A poor beggar of the city had recently died and was buried on that very day in a vault outside the church of the preaching friars. After midnight, Cassandrino stole to the place of the burial and, once he had opened the vault, pulled

50 J.F. Campbell, 'The Son of the Scottish Yeoman Who Stole the Bishop's Horse and Daughter, and the Bishop Himself,' in *Popular Tales of the West Highlands* (Edinburgh: Birlinn, 1994), no. 40, vol. II, pp. 18–38; Campbell, in his annotations, studies this story in relation to the Norse 'Master-thief' tale translated by Dasent in Peter Christian Asbjörnsen's *Tales from the Fjeld* (London: Chapman & Hall, 1874). See also Campbell, 'The Tale of the Shifty Lad, the Widow's Son,' no. 17d, vol. I, pp. 351–78. This second version has many variants with elements unlike those in Herodotus, but similar to those in 'The Master-thief,' revealing yet again a conflation of the two story types. The mother of the Lad becomes reconciled to his life of thievery and promises to have him trained by the Black Rogue. So the boy is sent on several trial missions in which he succeeds brilliantly. He finds his advantages by outwitting his own teacher and ultimately tricks him into submitting himself to a trial hanging which the Lad turns into a real one. The final episode, that of breaking into the king's storehouse, returns to the Herodotus type. The Shifty Lad puts his master in ahead of himself who then becomes mired in the pitch. The Lad steals his body from the gallows by getting the watch drunk on whiskey. Then he must avoid all the techniques employed by the king to trap him, until a banquet is called, at which the Lad makes use of the princess's ink to mark twenty bystanders so that he could not be singled out. Finally, by confession, he wins the princess, yet makes a final mistake while being suspended over a wall in a 'pocket napkin,' for the princess, being startled, turns loose; he dashes out his brains and leaves her a widow. Yet another version combining the sheep robbing on the road with an attempt on the king's treasury is found in 'Voleur par nature,' in *Contes grecs,* collected by Émile Legrand, *Recueil de contes populaires grecs* (Paris: Leroux, 1881), p. 205. 'Le voleur avisé' (The wise thief) is one of many compound versions of the story in Brittany, this one beginning with 'the master-thief' who issues from a poor household to learn his trade and in the process frightens off a band of thieves who leave behind their 'disappearing' cap and 'levitating' coat, with which implements the protagonist becomes rich. The stories join when he includes his poor father in a second attempt at robbing the king's treasury. The rest of the story deals with the exposure of the headless body and the many ruses he must practice to cover his sister's cries, then steal the body by getting monks drunk to appropriate their habits to dress the soldiers guarding it – all in rather fanciful ways. More episodes follow, including the marking of many more doors than his own with white crosses, until at last he becomes king.

the dead body out by the feet. Then, after he had stripped it, he dressed it again in his own clothes, which fitted so well that anyone would have taken him for Cassandrino and not for the beggar. He hoisted the corpse upon his shoulders as best he could' and headed for the palace. In Boccaccio's story, Madonna Francesca wishes to get rid of two lovers by having one disguise himself as a dead man and the other fetch him out of the tomb. In conceiving her plan, she uses a sequence of words and phrases which Straparola borrows in describing Cassandrino's quite different grave-robbing mission. Boccaccio's 'Era, il giorno che questo pensiero le venne, morto in Pistoia uno il quale ...' who was 'sotterrato in uno avello fuori della chiesa de' frati minori ...' in Straparola becomes, 'Era, il giorno che questa imaginazione li venne, morto in Perugia un mendico, lo quale era stato sotterrato in uno avello fuori della chiesa de' frati predicatori.' Further instances of common diction are scattered through the next few lines: 'e in su le spalle levatoselo verso la casa' becomes 'e levatoselo su le spalle meglio che ei puoté, verso il palagio,' which concludes the passage cited above. The larceny is petty to be sure, but may be a secret homage, or merely a harmless little intertextual game which emerges when a playful mind, imbued with an intimate knowledge of the *novellieri,* simply cannot resist a citation where the words of another can coincidentally supply his own text.

I. Fable 3
How Scarpacifico Swindles the Swindlers

CATERUZZA

Father Scarpacifico, having been duped once by three robbers, dupes them three times in return. Thus he comes out victorious and lives on happily with his Nina.

The end of Alteria's story, which she set forth with such wise skill, supplies me now with a theme for my own, which by chance may please you no less than hers. But there will be a difference on one point. Her story pictured to us Father Severino neatly entrapped by Cassandrino, while here, Father Scarpacifico throws the net just as adroitly over a group of rogues who were trying to get the better of him, as the plot of my fable will fully reveal.

Not far from Imola, a city always plagued by factious quarrels which in our own time nearly reduced it to extinction, there once lived a priest named Scarpacifico, who served the village church of Postema. He was well to do, but miserly and avaricious beyond measure, and he had for a housekeeper a shrewd and clever woman named Nina, who was so alert and pushy that she wouldn't hesitate to tell anyone, whatever their rank, just what came into her mind. Yet she was faithful and prudent in her administration of his affairs, for which he held her in high esteem.

Now when this goodly Father Scarpacifico was young, he was as lusty and lively a priest as could be found in the whole countryside. But now that his advanced age had made walking on foot irksome to him, the attentive Nina was forever coaxing him to buy a horse so that he might not shorten his life with too much fatigue. At last, Scarpacifico, overborne by her persuasive arguments, one day went to the market and there, seeing a mule which appeared to suit his exact needs, bought it for seven golden florins.

Now by chance there were three merry fellows at the market that day of a mind to live off the goods of others rather than on their own earnings – as it happens even in our own times. So as soon as they saw the bargain struck, one said to the others, 'Comrades, I'm of a mind that the mule over there should belong to us.'

'How can we manage that?' said the others.

Then the first replied, 'We have to post ourselves along the road he'll take on his journey home about a half kilometre apart from each other, and as he rides by, each one of us must swear firmly that the mule he's bought isn't a mule at all, but a donkey, and if we're brazen enough in our declarations, the mule will be ours.'

Accordingly, they left the market and stationed themselves separately along the road, just as they had planned, and as Scarpacifico passed by, one of the rogues, feigning to be on his way to market, shouted out, 'God be with you, sir!'

To which Scarpacifico replied, 'Good day to you, brother.'

'Whence come you, sir?' said the thief.

'From the market,' answered Scarpacifico.

'And what good bargains have you picked up there?' the scoundrel asked.

'This mule,' said Scarpacifico.

'What mule?' exclaimed the robber.

'Why, the mule I'm riding,' returned Scarpacifico.

'Are you speaking in sober truth, or do you mock me?' asked the thief.

'Why?' the priest replied.

'Because it seems to me to be a donkey and not a mule.'

'What do you mean, a donkey?' Scarpacifico retorted, and without another word he went on his way. He had not ridden two bowshots before he met the next robber, who likewise greeted him.

'Good morrow, sir, and where may you be coming from?'

'The market,' answered Scarpacifico.

'And was there anything worth having?' asked the robber.

'You bet,' said the priest.

'So did you come up with any good buys?'

'Sure,' answered Scarpacifico, 'I bought this mule which you see.'

'How, my good man, do you mean to say that you bought that for a mule?'

'I certainly did,' replied the priest.

'Well, I hate to tell you, but it's a plain ass,' the robber persisted.

'What do you mean, an ass?' the priest repeated. 'If somebody tells me this one more time, I'll make him a present of the stupid beast.'

Then going along, he soon met the third thief, who said to him, 'Good morrow, sir. I'd guess you're coming from the market?'

'I am,' replied Scarpacifico.

'And what may you have bought there?' asked the robber.

'I bought this mule which I'm riding.'

'Mule?' said the fellow. 'Are you telling me straight or just kidding around?'

'It's the truth and no joke,' replied the priest.

'Poor fellow, can't you see it's an ass, not a mule? O, those dirty traders; they've really bamboozled you.'

When he heard this tale, Scarpacifico said to the fellow, 'Two other men I've met told me the same story and I refused to believe them.' So climbing off the beast, he said, 'Here, take it, I make you a present of it.' The blackguard took charge of it right off, thanked the priest for courtesy, and went off to join his companions, leaving the good Father to make his way home on foot.

As soon as he came to his house, he told Nina how he had bought a nag at the market thinking it to be a mule, but that it had proved to be a donkey, and how, having been told that he had mistaken one for the other by several people he'd met on the road home, he had given the beast to the last of them.

'Ah, you poor simpleton!' cried Nina. 'Can't you see they've played a trick on you? I thought you were cleverer by far. I can tell you, by God, they wouldn't have fooled me like that.'

'Well, there's no use to grieve over it,' said Scarpacifico. 'They may have played me a trick, but see if I don't play two in return on them. You can rest assured that after fooling me once, these fellows won't be satisfied with that. You watch, they'll soon be weaving a new scheme to plunder me.'

Now in the same village not far from the priest's house there lived a peasant who, among his goats, had two that were so much alike that it was impossible to tell them apart. These two goats the priest bought, and the next day he ordered Nina to prepare a good dinner, because he planned to invite in a few of his friends, specifying a repast of boiled veal, some roasted fowls, together with a loin in a savoury sauce, plus the tart she so often served to him. Then he took one of the goats and tied it to a hedge in the garden, and once he had given it some fodder, he put a halter around the neck of the other and led it off to market, where he was at once accosted by the three companion swindlers.

'Well, if it isn't our friend! And what brings you here today? No doubt, you've come to make another good purchase?'

To this Scarpacifico replied, 'I've come to buy various provisions for a supper I'm having for a few of my friends. If you'd care to join in, it would please me greatly.'

The cunning bounders willingly accepted Scarpacifico's invitation, and when he had bought everything he required, he attached all his purchases to the back of the goat, right there in front of these three rogues, and said to the beast, 'Now go home and tell Nina to boil this veal, and to roast the fowls and the loin, and tell her, moreover, to make a savoury sauce with these spices, and a fine dessert pie just the way I like it. Do you understand? Now get along with you.' With these words, he sent the laden goat packing, which, being left to its own devices, wandered away, and what became of it nobody knows. Meanwhile, Scarpacifico and his companions, along with a few other friends, strolled about the marketplace till the hour of dinner, and then they all made their way to the priest's house. There, the first thing they saw on entering the garden was the goat which Scarpacifico had tied to the hedge calmly ruminating after its feed of grass. The three adventurers at once took it for a truth that it was the same goat that Father Scarpacifico had dispatched home with his purchases, at which they were greatly amazed.

When they had all entered the house, the priest said to Nina, 'Have you prepared everything the way the goat told you to?'

She, taking his meaning, replied, 'Yes, sir, and in a few minutes the roast loin, the fowls, and the boiled veal will be ready, and the sauce made with the spices, and the tart as well – just as the goat explained to me.'

'Well done,' said the priest.

Now when they saw the roast, the boiled veal, and the tart placed before them, and heard what Nina said, they were more bewildered than ever and at once began to figure out how they could get this goat into their possession. But when the dinner was over and they were still far from their goal, they said to Scarpacifico, 'That goat of yours, you must agree to sell it to us.'

Scarpacifico replied that he had no desire to part with it, for it was worth more money than there was in the whole world. Then, after a little while, he reconsidered his thoughts and offered to accept in exchange for it fifty golden florins. Then the knaves, thinking they had made a killing, right away paid out the fifty gold pieces.

'But take heed,' Scarpacifico added, 'and don't blame me afterwards if the goat doesn't obey you at the first as it does me. It'll take him a little time to get used to you and your manner.'

Hardly listening and without adding a word, the three adventurers carried off the goat, rejoicing in their bargain. When they came to their house, they said to their wives, 'Don't bother to make any food for tomorrow except what we'll send home to you by this goat.' The next day they went to the marketplace and purchased fowls and other kinds of meats, packed them all on the goat's back, and ordered it to go back home with instructions to the wives concerning the preparations. The goat, all loaded up, once it was set at liberty, ran away into the country and was never seen again.

When dinner time rolled around, the three confederates went straight back home and demanded of their wives whether the goat had come back safely with the provisions, and whether they had cooked them all up according to their directions. The women, amazed at what they heard, yelled at them, 'What a bunch of fools and numbskulls you are to think that a beast like that would do your bidding! Have you ever had the wool pulled over your eyes. What with all your cheating of people every day, it had to happen that you'd be caught in the end.'

As soon as the three robbers realized what fools Scarpacifico had made of them, besides lightening their pockets by fifty golden florins, their anger got the best of them. Seizing their arms, they set forth to find him, swearing they would have his life. But the cunning priest, fully expecting the robbers would seek vengeance upon him as soon as they discovered how he had tricked them, took counsel with his housekeeper.

'Nina, take this bladder which is full of blood and wear it under your dress. When these robbers come, I'll put all the blame on you, and in my rage I'll pretend to stab you, but I'll only thrust the knife into this bladder and you must fall down as if you were dead. Then, leave the rest to me.'

Scarpacifico had scarcely finished speaking when the confederates turned up and at once set upon him to slay him.

'Hold off, brothers,' he shouted, "what you're accusing me of is none of my doing, but the work of this servant wench of mine, and all over some wrong or other I know nothing about.' Turning towards Nina, he stuck his knife into the bladder which he had previously filled with blood, and instantly she feigned to fall down dead while the blood gushed in streams all around where she lay. Then the priest, looking upon his deed, made a great show of repentance and howled out loudly, 'O, what a wretched man I am! In my folly I've killed the woman who was the prop of my old age. How shall I ever live without her?' Then, after a short spell of time, he fetched a bagpipe made according to a fancy of his own. Lifting up her clothes, he stuck it between her buttocks and blew so strong a blast into it that soon after Nina came back to life and got up on her feet again as hale and healthy as before.

Astonished at seeing this, the robbers forgot their anger and, after a little haggling, they bought the bagpipe for two hundred florins and returned home hugely delighted with their bargain. A day or two after, it happened that one of them had a falling out with his wife and in his state of rage he stabbed her in the breast with his knife and killed her. Then immediately he took the bagpipe they had bought from Scarpacifico, slid the tube between her buttocks, and blew away, just as the priest had done, in hopes of reviving her, but he spent his breath in vain, for the poor woman had indeed passed from this world to the next.

When the second thief saw what his comrade had done, he cried out, 'What a fool you are! You have bungled the whole affair. Wait and see how I do it.' With these words, he seized his own wife by the hair and cut her throat with a razor. Then, taking the bagpipe, he stuck it right up her arse and blew with all his might, but for all of that, the wretched woman wouldn't come back to life again. The third fellow, who was standing near, by no means daunted by the failure of the others, served his own wife in the same way, but to no better purpose, so that now all three of them were deprived of their wives. Their rage against Scarpacifico was now at a white heat, so they hurried to his house, this time resolved to pay no attention to his seductive tales. They seized him and thrust him into a sack, planning to drown him in a neighbouring river. But as they bore him along, something alarmed them and they ran to hide themselves, leaving Father Scarpacifico tied up in his sack by the roadside.

They had not been gone many minutes before a shepherd came along, driving his flock to pasture. As he drew close, he heard a plaintive voice saying, 'They want me to take her, but I'll have none of her, for I'm a priest and have no interest in such matters.'

The shepherd stopped short, somewhat afraid, because he couldn't discover where the voice was coming from, which kept repeating the same words over and over. Having looked all around, here and there, his eye at last fell on the sack in which Scarpacifico was tied up. The shepherd opened it and let the priest crawl out, demanding why he had been tied up like that and what he meant by the words he kept repeating. At that, Scarpacifico declared that the Lord of that region had insisted on marrying him to one of his daughters, but that he had no stomach for the match because, not only was he a priest, but he was too old to take a wife.

Like a simpleton, the shepherd believed every word the clever cleric told him and spoke up directly, 'Good father, do you think he would give her to me?'

'I believe he would,' said Scarpacifico, 'provided you get into this sack and let me tie you up.' The silly shepherd at once crept in and Scarpacifico, having fastened the sack, got away from the place as quickly as he could, driving the poor shepherd's flock in front of him.

Before an hour had passed, the three thieves returned to the place where they had left the priest in the sack and, without looking inside, they bore it to the river and threw it in, thus sending the wretched shepherd to the doom they had intended for Father Scarpacifico.

Thinking themselves well avenged, the robbers set out for home, and as they were talking together they perceived a flock of sheep grazing hard by and at once began to scheme up the easiest way to make off with a couple of the lambs. But when they drew closer, imagine their astonishment at seeing Scarpacifico, whom they believed to be lying at the bottom of the river, now tending his flock like a shepherd. Once recovered from their shock, they asked him how he had managed to get out of the river, and he answered them right back, 'Get away with you! You've all got the brains of idiots! If you'd thrown me a little farther out into the stream, I'd have come back with ten times as many sheep as you see here.'

When the robbers heard this, they said in chorus, 'O, Sir, will you do us a good turn? Will you put us into sacks and throw us into the river? Then, you'll see that we'll no longer need to be highwaymen and rogues, but will live as honest shepherds.'

'Well,' answered Scarpacifico, 'I'll do this much for you. In fact, there's no favour in the world I wouldn't do for you, loving you all as I do.' Then, having gotten hold of three good sacks of strong canvas, he tied the three thieves so firmly inside there was no chance of their getting out and threw them into the river. Thus they went to the pitch-black place where eternal sorrow reigns, and Scarpacifico went back to his house rich in money and sheep, and there with his Nina he lived on for a number of years in happiness and prosperity.

Cateruzza's tale gave great pleasure to all the company and won high praise, above all for the great wit and cunning of this ingenious priest who, in exchange for the mule he gave away, gained so much money and a such fine flock of sheep, to say nothing of the revenge he had of his enemies for the wrong they did him, and the merry life he afterwards lived with his Nina. Then, to maintain the established order of events, she set forth her riddle in these words:

A sturdy blacksmith and his wife,
Who lived a simple honest life,
Sat down to dine, and for their fare
A loaf and a half of bread was there.
But ere they finished came the priest,
And with his sister joined the feast.
The loaf in twain the blacksmith cleft,
So three half loaves for the four were left.
Each ate a half, each was content.
Now say what paradox is meant.

Thus ended the ingenious riddle propounded by Cateruzza. But although each and all listened to it with great attention and admiration, no one in all that noble company could extract the true kernel from the hard shell. Seeing this, Cateruzza said, 'Charming ladies, the sense of my enigma is that a blacksmith took for his wife the sister of a priest, so that when the husband and wife had sat down to their meal and the priest came in to join them, it seemed they were four in all, which is to say, the blacksmith and his wife, and the priest and his sister. But in reality there were only three. Thus, as each one had a third of the bread (half a loaf), they were all contented.' After Cateruzza had explained her subtle enigma, the Signora gave the signal to Eritrea to give them her story, and she forthwith began.

I.3 Commentary

This tale is set in Imola, about thirty kilometres south-east of Bologna, a city annexed into the Papal States by the beginning of the sixteenth century. The story of Scarpacifico the trickster priest carries the reader into a vision of reality all its own in which there are only sharp rascals, gulls deserving their losses, and the innocent victims of their contest. It is also a tale of 'turn about is fair play,' because in Straparola's telling, the priest is first victimized and provoked by those upon whom he later plays his tricks in revenge. To achieve this symmetry of action and counter-action, three distinct narrative units or motifs had been conjoined: the robbers who swindle Scarpacifico out of his mule; his retaliatory tricks involving the speaking goat and the life-resuscitating bagpipe; and his final escape from the sack in which he was to have been drowned. The effect is a miniature trickster cycle which has grown up around a set of common antagonists. The tricks are micro-plots conceived in the mind of a perpetrator and tailor-fitted to the susceptibilities of his victims, whether to ridicule their naïveté, to make material gains at their expense, to seek revenge, or in extreme cases to lure the victims into collaborating in their own destruction. This story features an 'end-game' scenario in which all adversaries perish, leaving the trickster hero alone and at peace in his new-found prosperity. Scarpacifico is a trickster made, not born, but once established in his new role he might have continued indefinitely, were there victims available. His spree is short-lived because the robbers grow impatient, refuse to be further gulled, and determine to kill him. To turn the priest into a trickster like Tyl Eulenspiegel, he too would have to travel, seeking out new victims to draw out the cycle.

Because we are led by design to see events from his vantage point, we participate in the light comedy of a successful prankster sufficiently sinned against to annul any sense of unfairness – discounting, of course, the collateral slaughter of three innocent wives and a silly shepherd. The point is that the three robbers 'went to the place they deserved.' Psychological interiority hardly comes into play. The reader is thereby free to revel in the novelty of the pranks themselves and to concentrate on the quid pro quos in this tale of primitive justice and survival. All such trick-oriented narratives are inevitably reminders of the strategies of deception predicated on the weaknesses of others by which humans may pursue their own advantage, whether by gossip, by planting misleading evidence, or acting out false scenarios.

The materials for this four-trick cycle derive from two distinct sources, the one going back twelve to fourteen hundred years, the other at least five hundred. The idea of confusing the victim by placing interlocutors with a common lie at intervals along a route may be found in the third book of the *Panchatantra*, a collection of Hindu tales originating in the earliest centuries of the Christian era.[51] This jest type will be referred to as 'The Brahmin's Goat.' The second part involves selling 'wonder'

51 'The Brahmin and His Goat,' in *The Panchatantra*, trans. Chandra Rajan (London: Penguin Classics, 1993), bk. III, no. 4, p. 298.

implements at high prices to gullible purchasers who, in the third part, retaliate by placing the trickster in a sack or barrel to be cast into the water. This compound configuration we may call 'One-Ox,' because its earliest surviving written version is found in the Latin verse *fabliau* 'Unibos,' an eleventh-century creation that survives in a single manuscript in the Brussels Bibliothèque Royale.[52] These two stories comprising the three parts were destined to be conjoined into a single folk tale by the middle of the sixteenth century in accordance with the explicit evidence in the present story.

In the first, a holy man on his way to sacrifice a goat is met by three rogues spaced out along the way, who, one by one, assure him that his goat is a dog and hence an animal unfit for religious rites. How this story arrived in Europe is open to speculation, but once in circulation it became the prototype for endless variations upon the confusion of object classification that is provoked by having one's convictions contradicted by several ostensibly independent and disinterested observers. In precisely this way, with little variation upon the ancient formula, Scarpacifico loses his mule to those who conspire to convince him it is an ass. One means of entry to the West may have been the eleventh-century Byzantine physician Symeon Sethi's translation of the *Kalila wa Dimna* (known in the West as *The Fables of Bidpai*), or more plausibly the translation of that same work by Johannis de Capua as the *Directorium vitae humanae*, translated circa 1270.[53]

---

52 Marc Wolterbeek, '*Unibos*: The Earliest Full-Length Fabliau (Text and Translation),' *Comitatus: A Journal of Medieval and Renaissance Studies* 16 (1985), pp. 46–76. See also the commentary by Jan M. Ziolkowski in *Fairy Tales from Before Fairy Tales: The Medieval Latin Past of Wonderful Lies* (Ann Arbor: University of Michigan Press, 2007), pp. 128–52, and his translation of the tale, pp. 264–85. Ziolkowski states that this folk tale 'is certainly the oldest expression of a tale type that is attested in hundreds of versions throughout the world, especially in Europe and particularly in Belgium and the Netherlands,' p. 130. It was also undoubtedly collected from the folk for literary elaboration in Latin by a cleric.

53 Symeon Sethi, *Specimen sapientiae indorum veterum* (Berlin: Johann Michael Rüdiger, 1697). The *Directorium vitae humanae, alias parabola antiquorum sapientum*, ed. Joseph Derenbourg was published in Paris by F. Vieweg in 1887, although the work dates to the twelfth century and was first printed in Strasbourg in 1488. The story was not passed on to the Italian edition, trans. Anton Francesco Doni as the *Filosofia morale* (Venice: Marcolini, 1552), or to the English *Moral Philosophy of Doni*, trans. Thomas North (1570), ed. Donald Beecher, John Butler, and Carmine di Biase (Ottawa: Dovehouse Editions, 2003).

The tale of 'One-Ox' provides the template for the second and third parts of Straparola's tripartite structure. The folk protagonist is the only poor farmer among his many rich neighbours. His fortune turns when, after selling the hide of his ox for a pittance, he finds a bag of coins. Harassed by the mayor, the provost, and the priest over his new wealth, he reports that it came from the lucrative sale of the hide and that if they too wished to prosper in the same way, they need only slaughter all their animals and take the hides to the neighbouring market. This goading by his betters is the prompt that makes a trickster out of the lowly farmer. When the three high stakeholders find themselves ridiculed and deprived of their prize animals, they seek their revenge. To distract them, Unibos stages the murder of his wife, having attached to her collar the blood-filled bladder that will leave her 'caked with blood.' Of course, at the proper moment, he brings out the magic willow flute that not only resuscitates but rejuvenates and beautifies his wife. According to formula, the triumvirate purchases the flute at a very high price and each of them slays his wife with the intent of making her young and attractive. The failure of the flute puts them in a rage that can only be diverted by more astonishing prospects. There follows the prank of the coin-excreting horse which Unibos had prepared in advance, again leading to a costly purchase and the anticipated failure. The three men then return to slay the jokester, and like Marcolphus, Unibos asks merely to choose the manner of his death, which is to be placed inside a barrel and thrown into the water.[54] The protagonist's escape and the counter trick by which he lures his oppressors to their deaths are closely imitated by Straparola. All that remains, in a sense, is to substitute the story of the ox hides for the episode of the smart goats, eliminate the tale of the coin-emitting horse, and add on the Hindu preamble to arrive at the present story. But how and when those substitutions were made is open to speculation. Presumably it was brought about through the usual evolutionary processes in the creation of folk tales.

What remains clear is that in the interim five centuries, materials from these sources circulated widely throughout Europe, were borrowed variously for literary purposes, and continued to circulate in both literary and folk forms down to the nineteenth century. Only a few may be

54 Marcolphus famously asks King Solomon to let him choose the tree upon which he is to be hanged and with the king's permission leads his army all over the known world without ever finding one to his satisfaction. *The Dialogue of Solomon and Marcolphus*, ed. Donald Beecher (Ottawa: Dovehouse Editions, 1995), p. 199.

mentioned out of the hundreds possible to illustrate the fortunes of these literary motifs as coherent identifiable structures and simple forms. The tale of the Brahmin and his goat passed in ancient times from the *Panchatantra* to the *Hitopadesa* of Narayana, bk. IV, fable 9, in which a priest is again talked out of his sacrificial goat by three rogues encountered at intervals who ask him repeatedly why he is carrying a dog on his shoulders.[55] The history of this motif then leaps forward to the *Fabula moralis contra cupidos et divites* by the Anglo-Norman monk Nicole Bozon (Borzon), a work written by 1320.[56] It is memorable largely because the three rogues who execute the trick are called Croket, Hoket, and Loket.

---

55 *Hitopadesa of Narayana*, trans. M.R. Kale, 6th ed. (Delhi: Motilal Banarsidass, 1967), chap. 4, fable 9, p. 112. It also appears as 'The Brahmin, The Goat and the Rogues,' in the *Katha sarit sagara* (Ocean of the streams of story) of Somadeva, trans. C.H. Tawney (New Delhi: Munshiram Manoharlal, 1992), vol. II, pp. 68–9; in the ten-volume edition, *The Ocean of Story*, ed. N.M. Penzer, trans. C.H. Tawney (Delhi: M. Banarsidas, [1923], 1984), vol. V, p. 104. For a version drawn from the *Hitopadesa*, see 'The Story of the Brahman and the Goat,' in *The Book of Good Counsels: From the Sanskrit of the Hitopadesa*, ed. Edwin Arnold (Edinburgh: John Grant, 1924), p. 131; and 'The Story of the Camel, the Lion, and his Court,' pp. 132–4. See also the *Hitopadésa ou l'instruction utile*, trans. Édouard Lancereau (Paris: p. Jannet, 1855), p. 192. Lancereau thought the story arrived in Europe through the *Anwari-i Souhaili*, or any of the related versions of the celebrated 'Fables of Bidpai' or 'Pilpay,' but the early medieval references to this work, translated as the *Livre des Lumières*, seem earlier. Husayn Va'iz U'l-Kashifi translated the 'Fables of Pilpay' in Persian as the *Anvar-i Suhaili*. See 'Of the thieves who by persisting in one story persuaded the Devotee that his Sheep was a Dog,' in *The Lights of Canopus*, trans. Edward B. Eastwick (Hertford: Stephen Austin, 1854), chap. 4, no. 7, pp. 331–5.

56 *Les contes moralisés de Nicole Borzon*, ed. Lucy T. Smith (Paris: Librairie de Firmin Didot, 1889; reprint, New York: Johnson Reprints, 1968), no. 132, p. 135. But by all appearances, the motif was in Europe much earlier. Köhler in the journal *Orient und Occident*, a quarterly published in Göttingen from 1860–6, describes a Latin poem dating to the tenth or eleventh century which contains all the essential motifs, vol. 2 (1863), pp. 486*ff.* The bull of a poor peasant dies, forcing him to sell the hide. On the way home, however, he finds a treasure. He borrows a bushel basket to count his money and is accused of theft. He then reports that hides were selling well and with that tempts three of the richest in the village to slay their bulls, only to be disappointed with the returns. They return in anger, but are induced to buy a trumpet that brings back the dead to life and, in a third episode, a mare that makes money. In the end, the hero is enclosed in a barrel and left beside the sea while the dupes go to a tavern. He cries out that he doesn't wish to become 'provost' and a swine-keeper takes his place. This story may be very close to the European oikotype, featuring both the one-ox motif and the escape from drowning, along with the 'miraculous' objects fraudulently sold at high prices.

But the motif was known in the Latin West at least a century earlier in the *Exempla or Illustrative Stories*, no. 20, from the *Sermones Vulgares* of Jacques de Vitry wherein five rogues connive to convince an unsuspecting rustic that his lamb is a dog.[57] Perhaps the motif made its way to the West through de Vitry, who was, during the final years of his life, the cardinal-bishop of Acre (Akko in Northern Israel). The motif also turns up in the *Summa praedicantium* of John de Bromyard (d. 1352),[58] and in the *Anecdotes historiques, legends et apologues tirés du recueil inédit d'Étienne de Bourbon.*[59]

By the time of Bromyard's death, however, the little plot had already received literary elaboration in Boccaccio's tale of Calendrino (IX.3). Three companions agree to deceive this notorious dimwit by meeting him at intervals to read the symptoms of disease into his appearance. With so much insistence, the victim takes to his bed and is finally diagnosed as being pregnant, for which reason he reviles his wife for assuming the superior position during sex, thinking he now inherited the woman's part in everything to follow.[60] One last example nearer to

57 Jacques de Vitry, *The Exempla or Illustrative Stories from the Sermones Vulgares* (London: David Nutt for the Folk-Lore Society, 1890; reprint, n.p.: Kessinger Publications, 2008), no. 20.1, p. 141.

58 A work first published in Basel in 1484 and last published in Antwerp in 1627. See 'De rustico et agno' in Thomas Wright, *A Selection of Latin Stories from Manuscripts of the 13th and 14th Centuries* (London: Percy Society, 1842; reprint, New York: Johnson Reprints, 1965), p. 29. This was taken from the British Library MS. Arundel, no. 506, fol. 46v. In this account a rustic heads to market with his lamb but is brought to confusion by six mercenaries who convince him that it is a dog; it is very similar to the story in de Vitry.

59 Étienne de Bourbon, *Anecdotes historiques*, ed. Albert Lecoy de La Marche (Paris: Société de l'histoire de France, 1877), pp. 287, 339. The story is also retold in the *fabliau*, 'Les trois larrons,' in *Fabliaux ou contes du 12e et 13e siècle*, ed. Pierre Jean Baptiste Le Grand d'Aussy (Paris: n.p., 1781), vol. III, p. 1.

60 *The Decameron*, trans. Edward Hutton (New York: Heritage Press, 1940), pp. 441–4. Others who follow Boccaccio in using this ploy to deceive healthy persons by playing upon their hypochondria include Poggio Bracciolini in no. 268 of his *Facetiarum liber*, dating to 1420, in which the man is not only convinced of his malady, but is induced to climb into his coffin and be carried towards his own burial. 'Le mort qui parle,' in *Les Facéties de Pogge Florentin*, ed. Pierre des Brandes (Paris: Garnier, 1900), vol. II, p. 223. The same anecdote is told in the *Gesta romanorum*, ed. Wynnard Hooper, trans. Charles Swan (London: Bohn Library, 1876; reprint, New York: Dover, 1959), no. 132, pp. 236–7, in which three physicians seek to destroy a younger rival by convincing him that he has leprosy, a potentially diabolical trick in light of the Hippocratic adage that he who fears leprosy may infect himself simply through the powers of the imagination. The story figures, as well, among the *Fabeln* of Hans

Straparola's own time may be cited as perhaps one of several more. When Eulenspiegel was at the fair in Ueltzen he saw a farmer buying green fabric. To get the cloth for himself he picked up a tramp and a 'Scottish priest' and stationed them along the road ahead of the farmer, telling each to greet him and compliment him on the purchase of such fine blue fabric. Eulenspiegel met him first and said he would bet him twenty guilders it was blue, and the farmer was certain enough of his interpretation of colours (a matter of qualia still discussed among cognitive philosophers!) that he took the bet. The priest, the third in the line-up, was the clinching witness, for otherwise the farmer would have called them all rogues. He turned the fabric over to Tyl.[61]

Returning now to the second and third parts derived from 'One-Ox,' we need look back only as far as the anonymous fifteenth-century *Storia di Campriano contadino*, known exclusively from the first printed edition in 1521.[62] This may well have been Straparola's immediate source, although variations separate them that are perhaps best accounted for by oral versions in concurrent circulation. *Campriano* has motifs from the 'One-Ox' group not found in Straparola, such as the gold-excreting donkey and the self-boiling kettle. The instrument that allegedly resurrects the slain wife is a trumpet, and the animal that carries messages

---

Sachs, 'Der schwanger Pauer' (The pregnant farmer), or 'Die Kranckheit Kalandrin, der ein Kind drüeg' (Calendrino's sickness, who was expecting a child), in *Sämtliche Fabeln und Schwänke*, ed. Edmund Goetze (Halle: Max Niemeyer, 1913), vol. I, pp. 234–7, and Claude Du Moulinet (comedian), *Facétieux devis et plaisans contes* (Paris, 1612; reprint, Paris: Techener, 1829), p. 88. The Sachs story is clearly based on Boccaccio's *Decameron*, IX.3. It begins when three jokesters pass in front of the fool's door, tell him he looks ill and in a fever. Thereafter he takes to his bed, a doctor is called in who is willing to play along with the prank, and the fool begins to spend great sums of money for medications. It also appears as an anonymous *Fastnachtsspiel* entitled *Der Karg Kalendrus, 'Bocacius dut uns für halten,'* March 1549. See also Johann Gottlieb Büsching, *Volkssagen, Märchen und Legenden* (Leipzig: C.H. Reclam, 1812; reprint, Hildesheim: Olms, 1969), part I, p. 296.

61 *A Pleasant Vintage of Till Eulenspiegel*, trans. (from the 1515 edition) Paul Oppenheimer (Middleton, CT: Wesleyan University Press, 1972), pp. 169–71. A peasant is cheated of his cloth and sheets in the same manner in Le Sieur Du Moulinet's *Facétieux devis et plaisans contes* (Paris, 1612).

62 Ed. Albino Zenatti (Bologna: Presso Gaetano Romagnoli, 1884), pp. 3–29, and trans. Jan Ziolkowski in *Fairy Tales from Before Fairy Tales* (Ann Arbor: University of Michigan Press, 2007), pp. 285–95. A story closely related to this one is part of the *Nachtbüchlein* of Valentin Schumann (*Eine schöne Historia*, 1559), ed. Johannes Bolte (Hildesheim: Olms, 1976).

is a rabbit (a motif with an independent life of its own). At the end, the herdsman is lured into the sack with promises of marrying a noble maiden. This tale circulated widely, left popular phrases in Tuscany, and influenced Italian folklore down to the nineteenth century when tales of the Peasant Campriano (Capriano) could still be heard in several regions of the country.

The most perplexing pre-Straparolan version occurs in the *Baldus* of Teofilo Folengo – its earliest appearance dating to 1517.[63] Here for the first time the opening trick from the Brahmin tradition is conjoined with materials from the 'One-Ox' group, but the sequence lacks the closing motif of the drowning sack or barrel. Moreover, these materials are incorporated into a more elaborate plot appearing only in Books 8 and 9 of this sprawling work. Nevertheless, the borrowing is entirely apparent. In the manner of the Brahmin with his goat, Zambello, the foolish peasant, is duped of his cow, Chiarina, by being convinced that it is a goat. But then he is induced to go along to a monastery where he joins in with thirty monks in the consumption of his own cow. Cingar, his trickster friend, then arranges to kill Berta by attaching the bladder full of blood to her collar.[64] The implement of resuscitation is now a magic knife which the farmer Zambello purchases at a high price in anticipation of trying it out on his own wife, Lena. There is to be a trial for his crime, but the tale modulates into a new plot to liberate Baldo from prison. That Straparola extracted his far more schematic usage of these materials from the fanciful elaborations of Folengo is inconceivable. Both undoubtedly derived the materials for their respective purposes from popular stories in the oral tradition, but Straparola may claim the credit for having first presented the three parts of the tale in written form, although that invention was likely the work of a folk raconteur.

Following the publication of the *Piacevoli notti*, the materials found many new venues both in jest collections and fairy tales, as well as in the oral traditions of the folk. Giulio Cesare Croce, in *Le sottilissime astutie di*

63 Teofilo Folengo, *Baldus*, ed. E. Faccioli (Turin: Einaudi, 1989); *Baldo*, trans. Anne E. Mullaney (Cambridge, MA: Harvard University Press, 2007), bks. 8–9, vol. I, pp. 247–327.

64 The trick of the blood-filled bladder originates in Achilles Tatius's *Leucippe and Clitophon*, trans. S. Gaselee, *Collected Ancient Greek Novels*, ed. B.P. Reardon (Berkeley: University of California Press, 1989), p. 219. Leucippe is to undergo a mock sacrifice to deceive the robbers by being stabbed with a sword that retreats into the sheaf, the point alone breaking a bladder of blood hidden under her robes.

Bertoldo, first published in 1606, fills out his version of the Solomon and Marcolphus heritage by adding tricks from the repertory of literary jests.[65] In his story of the trickster hero who exasperates a royal court, it is the queen whose impatience propels her to have the protagonist drowned in a sack. He borrows the motif, perhaps directly from Straparola, but alters the episode by allowing the substitute victim to escape. More of these materials turn up in Claude Du Moulinet's *Les facétieux devis et plaisans contes.*[66] In addition, Valentin Schumann, in his *Nachtbüchlein,* Nos. 5 and 6, tells stories of a wife revived with a fiddle and peasants who drowned themselves.[67] But just how widely these motifs circulated can be seen even more clearly through the folk tale gathering efforts of the nineteenth-century ethnographers, not to mention the adaptations of the Unibos tale by the northern fairy-tale writers, including both the Grimm brothers and Hans Christian Andersen.

Emmanuel Cosquin found the tale in Lorraine entitled 'René et son Seigneur,' in which a medley of motifs appear, as though selected at random from the great coffer of interchangeable parts that constitute the generic story, including the sale of hides, the money-pooping donkey sold at a high price, the self-cooking bean pot which must be prodded into action by whipping it, the bladder of blood and the resuscitation of his slain wife with a magic whistle, and the final exchange of places with a passing shepherd. Of note is that René explains to his potential replacement that he is being forced to become a priest, a calling welcomed by the shepherd who knew how to read and write.[68]

---

65 Giulio Cesare Croce, *Le sottilissime astutie de Bertoldo* (Milan: Mursia, 1973), pp. 69–79.

66 (Paris, ca. 1612). In this telling, a peasant is deprived of his linen.

67 In Johannes Bolte and Jiří Polívka, *Anmerkungen zu den Kinder- und Hausmärchen der Brüder Grimm,* 5 vols. (Hildesheim: Olms-Weidmann, 1992–4), vol. II, p. 9

68 Emmanuel Cosquin, *Contes Populaires de Lorraine,* 2 vols. (Paris: F. Vieweg, 1886), vol. I, pp. 108–11. In his 'Remarques' to this story, Cosquin cites several other folk sources from across Europe and as far as Afghanistan, India, and the Antilles. In his own collection there is 'Richedeau,' vol. I, pp. 223–31, in which a poor man leads his seigneur to believe he had become rich by selling his cow at market hair by hair, causing the lord to slaughter his entire flock, only to meet disillusionment. There follows the sequence of fraudulent wonder gadgets, including the one by which Richedeau's wife is ostensibly resuscitated. The funeral of the lord's wife provides the occasion for the hero to escape by trading places with a shepherd whose flock he later claims to have come from under the water. Among the many others is Angelo De Gubernatis's 'I due furbi e lo scemo,' in the *Novelline di Santo Stefano* (Turin: A.F. Negro, 1869), no. 30, pp. 55–7. When two thieves go to visit their

Two more from Italian sources and three from northern sources must complete the survey for our purposes. More apparently in Straparola's debt is the tale of 'Uncle Capriano,' in which the hero is at odds with thirteen robbers and manages to deceive them four times.[69] But a more

brother, he sells them a 'self-cooking' pot. This is the beginning of a series of tricks by which he puts off their rage for the failure of each 'miraculous' object. The second is the blood-bladder and false murder trick involving a magic whistle. After the *furbi* slay their wives they are back for revenge, but fall for the horse primed to defecate gold coins. The final episode is the sack and drowning, which is averted by the victim's lament that he doesn't wish to become pope. A passing shepherd exchanges places with him and the 'new shepherd' lures his brothers into sacks of their own to find sheep at the bottom of the river. The similarity to Straparola is remarkable. Another with correspondences to the Lorraine version was collected by J.-M. Luzel for his *Contes Bretons* (Quimperlé, 1870), p. 85; it reappears in his *Contes populaires de la Basse Bretagne* (Paris: C.P. Maisonneuve and Larose, [1887] 1967), vol. III, pp. 414–26. Paul Sébillot knew of several further versions in France. In a tale from the Auvergne, the boy taken for an idiot shows his cunning in reversing his mother's oath that he would never 'take the wolf by the tail.' This he manages by catching one backing down a tree. They dress the beast in a sheep's hide and sell it to shepherds. When the wolf follows its nature among the flocks, the contest begins when the shepherds come back in anger. First Touéno-Bouéno sells them a whistle after whistling his old mother back to life in a planned trick. The three shepherds then hatchet their wives to death. Enraged, they return with a sack, but the boy makes his escape by trading places with a beggar desirous of becoming a bishop. 'Touéno-Bouéno,' in *Littérature orale de l'Auvergne* (1891) (Paris: G.-P. Maisonneuve and Larouse, n.d.), no. 7, pp. 69–80, in the series *Les littératures populaires de toutes les nations*, vol. 35. Very similar is the tale collected by Justin Cénac-Moncaut, 'Le juste et la raison,' in *Contes populaires de la Gascogne* (Paris: E. Dentu, 1861), p. 175. See also Jean-François Fleury, *Littérature orale de la Basse-Normandie* (Paris: G.-P. Maisonneuve, 1883), pp. 179*ff.* This trickster also gets his start by pulling a wolf by the tail and selling it to shepherds. The resuscitation object is a knife and the man he tricks into the sack is a pig farmer who wants to marry a princess. The story is also told in Norway, collected there by Eugène Beauvois, *Contes de la Norvège, de la Finlande, et de la Bourgogne* (Paris: E. Dentu, 1862), p. 218.

69 This story is derived from Albino Zenatti's *Storia del Campriano contadino* (Bologna, 1884), pp. 3–29, in which a verse version published in 1572 is also cited. *Italian Popular Tales*, trans. Thomas Crane (London: Macmillan, 1885), pp. 303–9; Vittorio Imbriani, 'Le tre fornarine,' in *Novellaja milanese* (Milan: Rizzoli, [1871], 1976), no. 23, pp. 290–7, and no. 47, pp. 587–92 (this is the same story collected by Nerucci, see below, and footnote 73); Giuseppe Pitrè, *Fiabe, novelle e racconti populari siciliani*, 4 vols. (Palermo: Pedone-Lauriel, 1875), vol. III, pp. 194–9, and vol. I, p. 157, included in William A. Clouston, *Popular Tales and Fictions*, vol. II, p. 421, as well as in Isaia Visentini, *Le 50 fiabe manatovane* (Parma: Astrea, [1879], 1993), no. 13. To this may be added 'Los dos compadres' collected in Spain by Aurelio M. Espinosa in *Cuentos populares españoles*, 3 vols. (Madrid: S. Aguirre, 1947), vol. I,

probable source is the legacy of the *Storia di Campriano contadino,* given that the original rabbit remains in the place of Straparola's goat as an intelligent load-bearing animal which is sold at a high price.[70] Dissatisfied,

---

pp. 437–43, and his commentary, vol. III, pp. 151–62. The story has been collected in nearly every region of Europe as well as throughout the world, including those from Italy by Laura Gonzenbach, nos. 70 (in which the resuscitating instrument is a guitar) and 71 (in which there is the gold-pooping donkey, the pot, and a rabbit that does chores like Straparola's goat); Nerucci, 'Manfane, Tanfane e Zufilo,' in *Sessanta novelle,* ed. Roberto Fedi (Milan: Rizzoli, 1977), pp. 218–22 (see below); Gottfried Keller, *Die Märchen* (Jena: Diedrichs, [1931]), pp. 85–95; Karl Müllenhoff, *Sagen, Märchen und Lieder der Herzogthümer Schleswig, Holstein und Lauenberg* (Kiel: Schwerssche Buch, 1845), pp. 457–63; Felix Bobertag, *Geschichte des Romans,* 2 vols. (Breslau, 1876–84), vol. I, pp. 160–4; and Ulrich Jahn, *Schwänke und Schnurren aus Bauern Mund* (Berlin: Mayer & Müller, 1889), pp. 125–39. In the version collected by Campbell in the West Highlands, 'The Three Widows,' each widow has a son, but the two elder boys gang up on the younger and kill his cattle, so he pretends to sell the hides. After catching and selling an ordinary bird for a good price as a divinatory creature, he convinces the brothers that the money came from the hides, inducing them to kill their own cattle and make fools of themselves. In revenge they kill the boy's mother. He uses her body, strategically placed by a well, to extort money from a man who accidentally pushes her in, and so the two elder boys kill their own mothers in expectant imitation. Deceived again, they place the younger one in a barrel to drown him, but a gullible shepherd changes places with him. Now with his new flock of sheep, the younger son convinces the two older ones to try their luck in similar barrels and thus he becomes the lone survivor in possession of all. Campbell made a guess that this tale was based directly on Straparola whose work may have found its way to Scotland shortly after its publication through associates of David Rizzio, who died in 1567. 'The Three Widows,' in *Popular Tales of the West Highlands,* 2 vols. (Edinburgh: Birlinn, 1994), no. 39, vol. II, pp. 1–17; in the four-volume edition: (London: Edmonston & Douglas, 1860), no. 39, vol. II, pp. 218–38. See also *The Royal Hibernian Tales* (Dublin: n.p., n.d.), p. 61.

70 The tale of the rabbit sent on a mission with money in a purse attached to its neck is of ancient standing. It was known at least as far back as the twelfth century in several sources, including 'De simplicitate hominum de Willebege,' from British Library MS. Arundel no. 292, fol. 14, most readily found in Thomas Wright, *A Selection of Latin Stories from Manuscripts of the 13th and 14th Centuries* (London: Percy Society, 1842), no. 93, p. 80; the twelfth-century *The Merry Tales of the Wise Men of Gotham, who attach their rent money to a hare and send it to Newark via Leicester, etc.,* ed. J.O. Halliwell (London: John Russell Smith, 1840), pp. 14–15; and Odo of Chariton (ca. 1185–ca. 1247), 'Direct Simplicity in Paying One's Debts,'in *The Fables,* ed. John C. Jacobs (Syracuse: Syracuse University Press, 1985), no. 62, p. 117–18. Certain foolish men from Wilby, facing their taxation deadline, choose the hare to get the money delivered on time because of its rapidity afoot. Straparola's goat is a variation on the animal that scampers or ambles into the wild and disappears, but now as a prepared trick to dupe the robbers.

the robbers return with revenge on their minds but are distracted by the self-cooking pot (also in *Campriano*), the failure of which Capriano pretends to blame upon his wife whom he then, by prearrangement, proceeds to stab. The instrument of resuscitation is a whistle which the robbers purchase, only to fail in the reanimation of their wives. The escape from the sack is at the expense of a herdsman who climbs inside with the promise that he will marry the king's daughter. The robbers seek their own destruction in trying to imitate Capriano, who claims to have returned with his new flock from the bottom of the river. But as with all the later renditions of this tale, the 'Brahmin' prelude is lacking. This is confirmed in the closely related 'Story of Campriano,' retold by Italo Calvino, in which the protagonist deceives an unknown number of opponents with his gold-coin-defecating donkey and the self-boiling pot.[71] Blamed by his neighbours, he too retaliates by stabbing his wife whom he reanimates by blowing through a magic straw. But in this version the law steps in first to arrest the murderers, thereby cutting short the neighbour's revenge and the entire episode of the sack in which the trickster is normally destined to be drowned.[72]

---

71 Italo Calvino, *Italian Folktales*, trans. George Martin (New York: Pantheon Books, 1980), no. 82, pp. 298–300.

72 There is an amusing variation on the motif in *Folktales of the Jews*, ed. Dan Ben-Amos, entitled 'Froyim Greidinger Revives the Dead' in which all the tricks are played against the Gentiles, luring the last one to replace the hero in a crate, telling him in Ukrainian that he would become the king. *Tales from Eastern Europe* (Philadelphia: The Jewish Publication Society, 2007), no. 65, vol. 2, pp. 459–60. The tale is also known in Scandinavia; see Peter Christen Asbjörnsen, *Tales from the Fjeld*, trans. George Webb Dasent (London: Chapman & Hall, 1874), p. 94, in which there is a resurrecting bagpipe and a self-boiling pot. In the Siberian version, Eshigældi recovers his stolen resources by tricking three brothers repeatedly until they decide to kill him. He then changes places with a rich man who is drowned in his place and the hero returns to lure the brothers to their deaths. Vasilii Vasilevich Radloff, *Proben der Volkslitteratur der türkischen stämme Süd-Sibiriens* (Saint-Petersburg: Akademii nauk, 1866), vol. III, p. 332. Yet another is to be found in S.S. Thorburn, *Bannú, or our Afghan Frontier* (London: Trübner, 1876), p. 115, and still another in *Lo Rondallayre, quentos populars catalans*, ed. Francisco Maspons y Lebros (Barcelona, 1875), vol. II, p. 82, in which the hero cries from inside the sack that he doesn't want to become king. Finally, it was told by the Basques in a story entitled 'Le curé joué' (The tricked priest) which begins with the hare that delivers messages, the priest deceived because there were in fact two. The Basque flute is used to resuscitate the woman rigged up with the bladder of blood. The priest (curé), deceived a second time, returns with a sack to throw Petarillo into the sea. When the boy complains about having to marry a princess, a passing shepherd volunteers to take his place.

A more elaborate version combining two story types was collected by Gherardo Nerucci and published under the name 'Manfane, Tanfane e Zufilo.' It is the last of the three brothers, the runt of the family, scorned by the older two, who makes good through his trickery. In the Unibos tradition, his one wretched cow is slaughtered and the hide is to be sold, but before he gets to market, he wraps himself up in the skin, climbs a tree, and then by accident falls into a band of robbers below (ATU type 1654). Taking him for the devil, they flee and leave him their pelf. Representing this money as profit from the sale of the hide, he is able to induce his brothers to slaughter their cattle in hopes of similar gains. Like Scarpacifico, he is now targeted for revenge and must turn up new get-rich schemes to stall those who want his skin. His next exploit is to cover with honey the tops of barrels filled with excrement and induce his two brothers to take them to market. Disgraced once more, they are now prepared to kill their brother, opting to put him in a sack and leave him on the beach for the fish or the tide to deal with. Zufilo, however, in the manner of Scarpacifico, dupes a passing shepherd, then appears to his brothers with the flock, thereby luring them to their deaths in their vain hope of finding sheep at the bottom of the sea.[73]

Turning now to Hans Christian Andersen's 'Little Klaus and Big Klaus,' the story tradition looks back not only to 'Unibos' but to the tales of 'Peasant Kibitz' and to the 'Little Fairly' group – somewhat more removed from the Straparola's sources, but squarely within the general tradition of the tale. Little Klaus gets into a row with Big Klaus over the ownership of Big Klaus's horses, another tale of the little guy against the powerful big guy.[74] The deceptions work, as they do in Straparola, by inducing the

---

Impressed by Petarillo's new flock, the priest seeks his own at the bottom of the sea. Wentworth Webster, *Basque Legends* (London: Griffith & Farran, 1877), consulted in *Légendes basques*, trans. Nicolas Burguete ([Anglet]: Aubéron, 2005), pp. 214–17.

73 Gherardo Nerucci, *Sessanta novelle popolari montalesi*, ed. Roberto Fedi (Milan: Rizzoli, 1977), no. 21, pp. 205–10.

74 The story may be found in *Fairy Tales*, ed. Jackie Wullschlager, trans. Tina Nunnally (New York: Viking, 2005), but comes originally from *Fairy Tales Told for Children*, 1837, trans. by H.W. Dulcken as *Stories for the Household* (New York: E.P. Dutton, 1888), pp. 24–33. Straparola's story of Scarpacifico was translated into Danish in 1818 by Johann Christian Riise, which may have influenced Andersen through his father; see Jan Ziolkowski, *Fairy Tales from Before Fairy Tales* (Ann Arbor: University of Michigan Press, 2007), p. 159. For the story of 'Little Fairly,' which is quite like Straparola's tale in significant ways, see Samuel Lover, *Legends and Stories of Ireland* (London: Chapman & Hall [185-]), reprinted in Clouston's *Popular Tales and*

gullible Big Klaus to imitate what Little Klaus does, but always to his detriment, namely selling hides at market for high prices and selling his grandmother's corpse, which entails first the senseless slaughter of his herd and then the murder of his own grandmother. The retaliation comes in the form of the sack exchange, but ends in reverse with Big Klaus's ultimate request to be thrown into the river to increase his cattle holdings.

In the Grimm brothers' tale of 'The Little Farmer,' no. 61 of the *Fairy Tales*, it is again the underdog who seeks to increase his store by trickery.[75] With a wooden calf, he deceives a cowherd and wins from him a living animal. This he slays for lack of provender in order to sell the hide. As

---

Fictions, vol. II, p. 402. See also J.F. Campbell, *Popular Tales of the West Highlands*, 4 vols. (Paisley: Alexander Gardner, 1890; reprint, Detroit: Singing Tree Press, 1969), vol. II, p. 229, also in Clouston, *Popular Tales and Fictions*, vol. II, p. 417. Other Germanic versions include those in J.G. Büsching, 'Peasant Kibbitz,' in *Volks-Sagen, Märchen und Legenden* (Leipzig: C.H. Reclam, 1812; reprint, Hildesheim: Olms, 1969), p. 296, trans. in Clouston, *Popular Tales and Fictions*, vol. II, p. 413; Max Müller, 'Master Thief,' in *Chips from a German Workshop*, 4 vols. (London: Longmans, Green, 1867–75), vol. II, p. 232; Heinrich Stahl (pseudonym for Jodocus Temme), in *Mitternachtblatt für gebildete Stände* (Braunschweig: Friedrich Vieweg, 1829), nos. 35, 36, and Heinrich Pröhle, 'Der bunte Bauer,' in *Märchen für die Jugend* (Halle: Buchhandlung des Waisenhauses, 1854), no. 15, pp. 55–61. This story offers its own tricks put upon the villagers and concludes with the sack, the distraction, and the return of the hero. On this group of tales, see Jan Ziolkowski, *Fairy Tales from Before Fairy Tales*, pp. 156–61. Finally, the tale was also known to the gypsies in a form that combines 'the master-thief' type of the previous story (I.2) and 'The Little Peasant' of the Brothers Grimm. See Francis Hindes Groome, 'Jack the Robber' and 'The Fool with the Sheep,' in *Gypsy Folk Tales*, ed. Walter Starkie (London: Herbert Jenkins, [1889], 1963), nos. 68 and 69. These stories are separate treatments of elements already assembled in Straparola. In the first, the gypsy boy and his mother play the blood-bladder trick on 'the master.' He purchases the enchanted stick with which the gypsy mother was returned to life, then kills not only his wife, but the servant girl and his waggoner, whose heads he literally cudgels with the stick to bring them back to life. In the second story, the rogue is put in a sack and remains there until a drover happens along who is willing to leave his herds and exchange places upon the promise of going directly to heaven. Three years go by before the master meets the boy and his herd, hears the tall tale, and asks to be chucked into the same river in search of another herd of cattle.

75 *The Complete Stories of the Brothers Grimm*, no. 61; 'The Little Farmer,' in *Grimm's Complete Fairy Tales* (Garden City, NY: Nelson Doubleday, n.d.), no. 4, pp. 13–17. The Grimm brothers knew the 'Unibos' *fabliau* directly, for they published the *edition princeps* in *Lateinische Gedichte des X. und XI. Jahrhunderts* in collaboration with Andreas Schmeller.

in the Andersen tale, there is the inset story at the hotel where Little Farmer overhears the preparations by the hostess for meeting her priest-lover and sees where the provisions are hastily hidden when the husband arrives early.[76] All this he turns to advantage by pretending that his little raven can reveal secrets, including those of the clergyman hiding in the closet, who is later taken for the devil because of his black clothes. The trickster sequence continues by inducing all the townsfolk to slaughter their herds of cattle to sell the hides at high prices. Their deception leads them to an attempted execution of Little Farmer by placing him in a barrel and rolling him into a lake. But again he escapes when a shepherd agrees to take his place in order to become mayor. In the end, the entire village is wiped out by leaping into the water to find their fortunes in sheep.

As a final example of the fortune of folk motifs emanating from a central tradition, consider 'The Story of Sigurdur, Sack-Knocker,' collected in Iceland in the middle years of the nineteenth century.[77] Sigurdur is a blacksmith so clever that he becomes the envy of the king's sons, who burn down his forge. An honest man is thereby made a trickster in a world order in which deception alone will enable him to regain his losses. His first trick is to turn the ashes of his forge to gold whereby he induces the princes to attempt the same by first burning down the royal forge. The derision following their failure provokes the race for retaliation and the blacksmith's countermanding *fourberie.* To deflect their anger, Sigurdur sells to them a coin-excreting horse, only to blame the purchasers for not following precise instructions. (This routine appears in many other versions of this tale and is the central feature of Straparola's tale of 'Adamantina,' V.2, with its many analogues.) He then convinces them that his cudgel can beat hillocks into butter, once again relieving them of their money in exchange for a hoax. At this point, only the procedures of this tale coincide with Straparola's. But the next episode involving the king himself is more familiar, because the blacksmith dresses his mother in rags, blows her over with a set of bellows, then causes her to rise as the rags fall off making her appear rejuvenated. This episode resonates with the blood-bladder trick and its various instruments of resuscitation leading to the trial slaughter of wives. The princes

76 One of the earliest versions of this inset tale is the old German poem *Der Kündige Knecht,* Viennese MS. 428, no. 62.

77 *Icelandic Legends,* ed. Jón Arnason, trans. George E.J. Powell and Eiríkur Magnússon (London: Longmans, Green & Co., 1866), pp. 606–9.

purchase the equipment and perform similarly upon their foster mother who dies, beaten inside a sack. They then kill Sigurdur's mother in retaliation, which inaugurates a trick with an independent history of tying dead persons to horses and driving them into places where others can be blamed for their deaths. In keeping, the blacksmith ties his mother to a horse, and by frightening the royal oxen with this apparition, he positions himself to accuse the king's employees. In the final episode, the blacksmith is placed in a sack and suspended over the sea from a cliff, but as in the Straparola tale, he lures a passing rustic into the sack with false promises and escapes with his sheep. Seeing this, the king's sons are induced to seek herds of their own from the bottom of the sea and so perish, leaving the realm to their excluded sister and to Sigurdur, whom she marries for having served as her agent in ridding her of these despicable siblings. It is fascinating that a romance dimension has been found even for this configuration of trickster routines and that the inherent narrative structure persists intact after so many borrowings from parallel stories.

Straparola's tale is clearly part of this lengthy tradition, but the contribution it makes to its elaboration is less sure. It would appear that the folk repertory was fully fitted out with motifs from popular sources and did not need to fall back on written versions to revitalize the narrative of the clever thief. Given the absence of the 'Brahmin motif' in all subsequent folk versions, it would appear that Straparola's tripartite design did not find imitators in the oral tradition. It was nevertheless replicated in a literary retelling of the tale by Thomas Simon Gueullette in the 'Adventures of the Young Kalandar' in his *Thousand and One Quarters of Hours* (*Tartarian Tales*), a work first published in French in 1723. At least five of the tales in this collection have direct alignments with stories in the *Piacevoli notti*, further confirming the presumption that this creator of 'oriental' tales had the Louveau translation of the *Notti* frequently before his eyes, making him perhaps second in the magnitude of his dept to Straparola after the Comtesse d'Aulnoy.[78] Gueullette (sometimes Gueulette), under the influence of Galland and Count Hamilton, situates his tales in Eastern settings. Thus the Kalandar buys his mule in Shiraz

78 Trans. Leonard C. Smithers (London: H.S. Nichols, 1893), pp. 238–57. Thomas-Simon Gueullette, *Les mille et un quart-d'heure, contes tartares*, 3 vols. (Paris, 1753), no. 106, vol. III, p. 202. This work was translated shortly thereafter by Thomas Flloyd as *Tartarian Tales, or A Thousand and One Quarters of Hours* (London: J. & R. Tonson, 1759).

before meeting the three rogues along the road. He plays upon them the trick of the goat sent home with provisions and commands. The blood bladder trick is now played upon the cook who had failed to explain to the rogues the precise secret for managing the goat, while a magic hunting horn replaces the scatological bagpipes as the instrument of resuscitation. All along, in fact, Gueullette adds novelistic detail and draws out the episodes. When the three murder their wives, two are taken and executed, while one escapes to carry forward the attempted revenge. The sack episode follows and it is now a jinn (genie) at the bottom of the river who will supply the three robbers with sheep in abundance – Gueullette having forgotten that two of the robbers had already been killed off. It is a lively retelling and a small monument to Straparola's part in the transmission of this popular narrative cluster of folk materials.[79]

79 The story tradition also remained current in the East, perhaps in some places influenced by Western elements. In the Santal folk tale, 'The Story of Bitaram,' the hero employs the trick of the gold coin left in the bottom of the counting basket to induce the king and his sons to kill their cattle in order to sell the hides. This trick was employed in many of the 'puss in boots' analogues in order to convince the court that the cat's ward was a rich nobleman (see the commentary to XI.1). This story ends with the sack episode and the hero's escape when the sons leave the sack unattended to cook their food. The animals herded by the new victim were cows and buffaloes. That this version told by the Santals of India so closely resembles certain of the European stories outlined above testifies further to the complex dissemination of these tales. 'The Story of Bitaram,' in *Santal Folk-tales,* trans. Andrew Campbell (Pokhuna [Pokhara]: Santal Mission Press, 1891), pp. 25–32. Another in this same collection, 'The Greatest Cheat of Seven,' pp. 98–101, combines 'master-thief' elements with 'little peasant' elements as the hero induces his victims to burn down their houses to sell the ashes, to purchase a magic fishing rod and a wonderful dog, and to kill their wives, certain they had the means to resuscitate them.

I. Fable 4
Doralice and Her Incestuous Father, Tebaldo

ERITREA

Tebaldo, prince of Salerno, desires to marry his only daughter Doralice. But because of her father's persecution, she flees to England where she marries Genese and bears him two children. These, having been slain by Tebaldo, are avenged by their father, King Genese.

I believe there is not one among you who has not learned by experience how great the power of Love is, and how sharp the arrows are that he shoots into our corruptible flesh. Like a puissant sovereign, he directs and governs his empire without a sword, but by the sole might of his will, as you will understand from the story I'm about to tell.

My fair ladies, according to the story I've many times heard told by my ancestors, Tebaldo, prince of Salerno, had a modest and prudent lady from a good family for his wife, and by her he had a daughter whose beauty and grace outshone all the other ladies of the city. Yet it had been better for Tebaldo if she had never seen the light of day, for then he would have escaped all that befell him later. His wife, young in years but mature in her wisdom, as she lay dying, begged her husband, whom she loved very dearly, never to take for his wife any woman whose finger would not exactly fit the ring which she wore. The prince, who loved his wife no less than she loved him, swore by his life that he would honour her wish.

After this beautiful lady had breathed her last and had been honourably buried, Tebaldo began to think of remarriage, keeping well in mind the promise he had made to his wife and resolving firmly to keep her counsel. Soon the news was spread throughout the land that Tebaldo, prince of Salerno, was seeking a new spouse – news that came to the ears of many maidens who were equal to him in worth and estate. But Tebaldo, whose first care was to fulfil the wishes of his dead wife, made it a condition that any damsel that might be offered to him in marriage should first try his wife's ring on her finger to see whether it fit. But finding no one who met the condition – the ring being always too big for this one or too small for that one – he was forced to dismiss them all without further negotiation.

Then it happened that Doralice, Tebaldo's daughter, sitting at table with her father, espied her mother's ring lying on the board and slipped it on her finger, whereupon she cried out, 'Look, father, how well mother's ring fits me!' The prince looked on and saw that it was quite true.

Not long after this, Tebaldo's mind was assailed by a strange and diabolical temptation to take to wife his own daughter, Doralice. For many days thereafter his thoughts wavered between yes and no. But at last, overcome by the force of this devilish intent, and fired by the maiden's beauty, he one day called her to him and said, 'Doralice, my daughter, while your mother was yet alive, but fast nearing the end of her days, she urged me never to marry any woman whose finger would not fit the ring she herself wore throughout her lifetime, and I vowed on my life that I would observe this last request of hers. Thus, when I felt the time was come again for me to wed, I made trial of many maidens, but I could not find one who might wear your mother's ring, except you alone. So I have decided to take you for my wife, for in this way I shall satisfy my own desire without violating the promise I made to your mother.'

Doralice, who was as pure as she was beautiful, when she heard the evil designs of her wicked father, she was sorely troubled in her heart. Distressed by his sinful proposition, and fearing the effects of his anger, she kept up her happy appearance, but retired without making an answer. In such matters, there was no one she could trust more than her old nurse, so she went straight to her as the surest bulwark of her safety to seek advice about what she should do. When her nurse had heard about the felonious designs and malicious intent of her father, she offered words of comfort to Doralice, for she was well acquainted with the girl's steadfast and constant nature and knew that she would be ready to endure any torment rather than accede to her father's desire, promising then to aid her in keeping her virginity unsullied by so foul a disgrace.

Then she set herself to thinking about how she might bring the girl to safety, jumping from one thought to another, but nothing sure or trustworthy came to her mind. To take flight, putting the girl at a great distance from her father, was an appealing prospect, but the nurse dreaded his cunning and feared that Doralice might fall into his hands and be slain. That disturbed her the most.

At last, while frantically turning over her thoughts, the faithful nurse hit upon a fresh scheme. In the deceased mother's bedroom there was a handsome wardrobe chest, magnificently carved, in which Doralice kept her richest dresses and her most precious jewels. This chest, the nurse alone could open, so she removed from it by stealth all the robes and ornaments it contained and hid then away in another place. Afterwards, she placed inside a good quantity of a special liquor of such great virtue that whoever took a spoonful or even less could live for a long time without other nourishment. She then called Doralice and enclosed her in the chest, and told her to remain in hiding until such time as God sent her better fortune or her father relinquished his cruel resolution. Obedient to her beloved nurse's command, the maiden did as she was ordered. The father, meanwhile, still fixed upon his lecherous desires, and making no effort to restrain his unnatural lust, demanded every day what had become of his daughter. But finding no trace of her, and having no idea where she might be, his rage became so terrible that he threatened to have her killed in some horrible fashion.

A few days later, it came about one morning at sunrise that Tebaldo went into the room where the chest was kept, and as soon as his eye fell upon it, he could no longer endure its sight, such old associations it brought to mind. So he gave orders to have it immediately taken away, stowed, and then sold, to rid himself of its offending presence. The servants were quick to obey their master's command and, taking the great chest upon their shoulders, they bore it away to the marketplace. It so happened that at that moment there was in the city a rich merchant from Genoa, who, as soon as he caught sight of the sumptuously carved wardrobe, he greatly admired it, and decided then and there that he would not lose it, however much he might have to pay for it. To achieve his end, he approached the servant in charge of selling it, found out the asking price, bought it outright, and gave orders to a porter to carry it away to be placed on board his ship. The nurse, who stood at a distance watching the transaction, was very pleased with the way things turned out, although she grieved sorely at losing the maiden. Yet she found some comfort in the thought that whenever there is a choice to be made between two evils, it is always wiser to avoid the greater of them.

Having set sail from Salerno with his carved chest and other valuable wares, this Genoese merchant voyaged to the island of Britain, which we now call England, and landed near a wide plain. Before he had been there long, Genese, the recently-crowned king of the island, happened to be riding at breakneck speed along the seashore in pursuit of a beautiful doe, which, running in fear, at last plunged into the waves of the sea.

The king, weary and worn out by the long chase, was happy to rest awhile. Seeing the ship, he sent word to the master to give him something to drink. The merchant, pretending he didn't recognize the king, greeted him in familiar fashion, gave him a hearty welcome, and prevailed upon him to go aboard his vessel. The king no sooner saw the exquisite chest with its fine carving than he was taken by a great desire to possess it and became so impatient to call it his own that every hour seemed like a thousand before he was able to claim it. In due course, he asked the price of the merchant and discovered that it was a very hefty one. But being even more taken with this precious object, the king would not leave the ship till he had arranged the matter with the merchant. Once he had sent for enough money to pay the demanded price, he took his leave, ordering the wardrobe to be borne to the palace and placed in his chamber.

Genese, still quite young, had not yet taken a wife, but rather found his chief delight in setting out early each day for the hunt. Now that the wardrobe was transported into his bedroom with the maiden Doralice hidden inside, she heard all that went on in the king's chamber. Thinking all dangers were now past, she began to hope that a happier future was in store for her. As soon as the king had departed for the hunt, as was his custom, Doralice issued from the chest and with the greatest care put the chamber in order, sweeping it and making the bed. Then she adjusted the bed-curtains and replaced the coverlet, which was cunningly embroidered with fine pearls, and arranged two beautifully ornamented pillows. After this, the fair maiden sprinkled the bed with roses, violets, and other sweet-smelling flowers, mingled with Cyprian spices that exhaled a subtle, sleep-inducing odour. Day after day, Doralice continued to arrange the king's chamber in this pleasant fashion without being seen of anyone. In doing so, she gave Genese much pleasure, for every day when he came back from the hunt, it was as though he was met by all the perfumes of the Orient. One day he asked his mother, the queen, and all the ladies attending her, which of them had so kindly and graciously adorned his room and decked the bed with sweet-scented roses and violets. One and all answered that they had no part in any this, for every morning when they went to put the chamber in order they found the bed already strewn with flowers and perfumes.

Hearing this wondrous tale, Genese determined to clear up the mystery once and for all. The next morning he proclaimed that he was going to visit a castle some ten miles away, but instead of leaving, he quietly hid himself in the room, keeping his eyes steadily fixed on the door, waiting to see what might happen. He had not been long on the watch before Doralice, looking more beautiful than the sun, came out of the great chest and began to sweep the room, straighten the carpets, deck the bed, and diligently set everything in order, as had become her custom. No sooner had the fair maid ended her kindly and thoughtful office than she made ready to return to her hiding place. But the king, who had taken careful note of everything, suddenly caught her by the hand and shoulders and seeing that she was very fair and fresh as a lily, asked her who she was, whereupon the trembling girl confessed that she was the daughter of a prince, but that for all that, she had forgotten his name because of her long imprisonment in the chest. Nor would she reveal anything of the reason that she had been hidden inside. The king, after he heard her story, fell violently in love with her, so that, with the full consent of his mother, he made her his queen and had two beautiful children by her.

Meanwhile, Tebaldo remained under the control of his wicked and treacherous passion. Unable to find any trace of Doralice, no matter where he searched, he began to believe she must have been hidden inside the coffer which he had caused to be sold and that, having escaped his power, she might be wandering about the world. With his rage still burning against her, he set about trying whether he might by chance discover her whereabouts. After attiring himself as a merchant, he collected together a great store of precious stones and jewels marvellously wrought in gold, left Salerno without anyone knowing, and began searching through all the nations and countries round about until by chance he met with the same trader who had originally purchased the chest. He demanded of him whether he had been satisfied with his bargain and into whose hands the chest had fallen. The trader replied that he had sold the piece to the king of England for double the price he had given for it. Tebaldo rejoiced at this news and took the road to England. There, after his entry into the royal city, he spread out his goods under the wall of the palace, not only jewels and golden ornaments, but spindles and distaffs most cunningly made, whereupon he began to cry his wares, 'Spindles and distaffs for sale, ladies.'

It so happened that one of the ladies of the court was looking out the window, heard the street cry, and saw the merchant with his goods. Then she ran to the queen and told her there was a merchant below who had the most beautiful golden spindles and distaffs for sale that she had ever seen. The queen commanded him to be brought into the palace and he came up the stairs into her presence. Doralice did not recognize him in his merchant's guise, never thinking to behold her father again, but Tebaldo recognized his daughter at once.

When the queen saw how fair the workmanship of these spindles and distaffs was, she asked the merchant what price he was asking for them. 'The price is great,' he answered, 'but I will make you a gift of all this merchandise if you allow me to satisfy a caprice of mine, which is to sleep for one night in the same room with your children.' The good Doralice, in her pure and simple nature, never suspected the accursed design of the false merchant. Yielding to the persuasion of her attendants, in time she granted his request.

But before the merchant was led to the sleeping chamber, certain ladies of the court deemed it wise to offer him a cup of wine well-drugged with opium to make him sleep more soundly. So when the night came and the merchant seemed overcome with fatigue, one of the ladies conducted him into the chamber of the king's children where a sumptuous bed had been prepared for him. Before she left him, the lady said, 'Good sir, are you not thirsty?'

'Indeed I am, lady,' he replied. Herewith she handed to him the drugged wine in a silver cup, but the crafty Tebaldo, while pretending to drink, let it spill over his garments and then lay down to rest.

In the children's room there was a side door through which it was possible to pass into the queen's apartment. At midnight, when all was still, Tebaldo stole through this door and, going up to the bed beside which the queen had left her clothes, he took away a small dagger which he had noticed the day before hanging from her girdle. Then he hastened back to the children's room and killed them both with the dagger, which he then returned to its scabbard all covered with blood. Afterwards, he opened a window and let himself down by a knotted cord. As soon as the shop men of the city were astir, he went to a barber and had his long beard shaved off for fear he might be recognized, put on new long clothes, and walked about the city without apprehension.

In the palace, meanwhile, the nurses, as soon as they were awake, went to suckle the children. But when they came to the cradles, they found both infants lying dead, whereupon they began to scream and weep bitterly, to tear out their hair and rend their garments, laying bare their breasts in grief. The dreadful news came quickly to the ears of the king and queen, whereupon they ran barefooted to the place and upon seeing the dead bodies of the babes they wept bitterly. Soon the report of the murder of the two children was spread throughout the city, just as a new rumour circulated that a famous astrologer had arrived – a man who, by studying the courses of the stars, could understand the past and foretell the future. When this report came to the ears of the king, he had the astrologer summoned immediately to ask him, once he had arrived in the royal presence, whether or not he could name the murderer of the children. The astrologer replied that he could. Whispering secretly in the king's ear, he said, 'Sire, let all the men and women of your court who are inclined to wear a dagger at their side be summoned before you and if among these you find one whose dagger is smeared with blood in its scabbard, that same person will be the murderer of your children.'

At once the king commanded that all his courtiers should present themselves. When they were assembled, he diligently searched with his own hands to see if any one of them might have a bloody dagger at his side, but he could find none. Then he returned to the astrologer – who was no other than Tebaldo himself – and told him that his quest had been in vain, and that everyone in the palace had been searched, except his mother and the queen. To this the astrologer replied, 'Your Majesty, search everywhere and respect no one and then you will surely find the murderer.'

So the king searched first his mother, followed by the queen, and when he took the dagger that Doralice wore and drew it from the scabbard, he found it covered with blood. Convinced by this proof, the king turned to the queen and said to her, 'O, wicked and inhuman woman, enemy of your own flesh and blood, traitress to your own children, what desperate madness has led you to dye your hands in the blood of these babes? I swear to God that you shall suffer the penalty of such an iniquitous crime.'

But while the king in his rage would gladly have sent her immediately to a shameful death, a desire for lingering vengeance prompted him to dispose of her in ways that would prolong her suffering and cruel torment. He thus ordered that she be stripped and buried naked up to her chin in the earth, and that she should be well fed with savoury food to sustain her life so that worms might devour her flesh and bring her to extremest agony. The queen, used to misfortune in the past and conscious of her innocence, contemplated her terrible doom with calmness and dignity.

The astrologer inwardly rejoiced as soon as he learned that the queen had been judged guilty and condemned to a cruel death. Afterwards, when he had taken leave of the king, he departed from England satisfied with his work and returned secretly to his palace, where he told the old nurse the whole story of his adventures and how Doralice had been sentenced to death by her husband. As she listened, the nurse showed outward signs of joy, but in her heart she was sorely grieved, overcome by the love she had always felt towards the princess. Early the next morning she departed from Salerno on horseback and rode day and night until she came to England. Immediately, she got herself to the palace and went before the king, who was giving public audience in the great hall, and throwing herself at his feet she demanded a private interview on a matter which concerned the honour of his crown. The king granted her request and took her by the hand, requesting her to rise. Then, when the rest of the company was gone and they were alone together, the nurse addressed the king in these words: 'Be it known to you, Sacred Crown, that your wife Doralice is my child. She is not, indeed, the fruit of my womb, but I nourished her at these breasts. She is innocent of the deed that is charged to her, for which she has been sentenced to a lingering and cruel death. As for you, when you have learned everything and laid your hands upon the impious murderer, when you have understood the reason that moved him to slay your children, you will surely show her mercy and deliver her from such bitter and cruel torments. But if you find that I speak falsely in this, I offer myself to suffer the same punishment now endured by the wretched Doralice.'

Then the nurse set forth from beginning to end the entire history of Doralice's past life. The king, when he heard it, had no doubt of its truth and right away gave orders that the queen, who was now more dead than alive, be taken out of the earth. Doralice, after a short while, with the careful nursing and ministrations of the court physicians, was restored to health.

Next, King Genese stirred up mighty preparations for war throughout his kingdom and gathered together a great army which he dispatched to Salerno. After a short campaign, the city was captured and Tebaldo, bound hand and foot, was taken as a prisoner back to England where King Genese, wishing to know the whole sum of his guilt, had him tortured, whereupon the wretched man made a full confession. The next day, he was conducted through the city in a cart drawn by four horses, then tortured with red-hot pincers like Gano di Magazza, and after his body had been quartered, his flesh was thrown to ravenous dogs for food.

Such was the end of the impious wretch Tebaldo. King Genese and Doralice his queen afterwards lived happily together for many years and left at their deaths many children to fill their place.

All the listeners were both amazed and moved to pity by this pathetic story. Once it was brought to an end, Eritrea, without waiting for the Signora's word, presented her enigma:

I tell you of a heart so vile,
So cruel, and so full of guile,
That with its helpless progeny
It deals as with an enemy.
And when it sees them plump and sleek,
It stabs them with its cruel beak.
For, lean itself, with malice fell,
It fain would make them lean as well.
So they grow thin with wasting pain,
Till nought but plumes and bones remain.

The ladies and gentlemen gave various solutions to this enigma, one guessing this and another that, finding it hard to believe there could be an animal so vile and cruel as thus barbarously to maltreat its own progeny. But at last, the fair Eritrea said, with a smile, 'Nay, good sirs, don't be astonished, for assuredly there are parents who hate their children as virulently as the rapacious kite hates its young. This bird, being by nature thin and meagre, seeing its progeny fat and seemly – as young birds mostly are – stabs their tender flesh with its hard beak until they too become lean like itself.'

This solution to Eritrea's sharp enigma pleased everybody and won the applause of all. Then Eritrea, having made due salutation to the Signora, resumed her seat. After it became Arianna's turn, who, when prompted by a sign from her Mistress, rose from her chair and began her fable as follows.

I.4 Commentary

Straparola's story of Doralice and her incestuous father assumes a central and key position in a narrative tradition that spans from its presumed origins in early medieval legend, saints' lives, and the Byzantine tale to its final literary reshaping in the Grimm Brothers' 'Allerleirauh' or 'All-Fur,' after passing through Perrault's pages in which, as 'Peau d'Asne' or 'Donkey-Skin,' it becomes one of the most beloved fairy tales of all time. The story is representative of several folklore motifs around the central theme of the persecuted daughter, whereby a charming, loving, and patient adolescent is driven from her paternal home, often after the death of her mother, by the unwanted sexual demands of her father. The nature of her destiny varies from treatment to treatment, but includes incarceration in chests and near starvation, cruel mothers-in-law, trumped-up accusations of giving birth to monstrous children, periods of exile with her hands severed followed by divine or magical healing, or live burial as in the present tale, invariably reversed by a princely lover or husband who, after dispatching his wicked mother (or Doralice's monstrous father) reconstitutes his family. A charming fairy tale may be imagined in and through these story elements, but that transition is barely begun in the frank and brutal version offered by Straparola. Doralice has no protective fairies.

This story lends itself to several interpretive inclinations. In its generic profile, the reader may be satisfied to discover therein a vision of the dysfunctional family, including the sexual targeting of children by family males, or the malicious envy and controlling machinations of a domineering mother-in-law. No wisdom of the 'folk' could be more archetypal. Or in an equally emblematic way, Doralice may represent a Proserpina figure, a beleaguered virgin and chaste mother, whose purity, patience, loyalty, and willingness to engage in menial tasks earns for her, though sinless, exoneration and redemption after untold suffering, the entire design carrying overtones of elemental strife and ancient ritual, all of which was apt for medieval elaboration into a saint's life. Both readings of the heroine's dilemma, domestic or mythological, depend upon the temporary loss of her identity, for while she is nearly always well born, yet in her exile she often allows herself to be thought a commoner. Thus, the story tradition vacillates between the rise of a charming 'servant-class' girl hated for her lowness by the haughty mother-in-law and the restoration of a high-born heroine after a period of labour and initiatory wandering. These stories are likewise fantasies of extreme suffering. Doralice is fed well to prolong her life while being consumed by worms, while other heroines remain up to seven years in appalling circumstances, fed on garbage or wandering in wilderness areas with severed hands, often attempting to care for their children. Yet all these tales of torment are tragi-comedies and cyclic in design, as romances invariably are, driven by a faith in deliverance after near despair, the recovery of the nuclear family, and nostalgia for home.

Straparola does not shy away from representing cruel fathers or wicked step-mothers (as in 'Biancabella,' III.3) in their nastiest incarnations, followed by harsh and fell vengeance. No sequel to this tale will surpass it for unusual punishment: Tebaldo is hauled back in bonds to the scene of his crime where he is tortured by hot pincers and dismembered by quartering before being fed to ravenous dogs. And no subsequent version will have the heroine interred up to her chin for slow consumption by worms. Such fantasies are not exclusive to Straparola's age and are not necessarily witnesses to a more rigorous and unfeeling sense of justice. Yet a softening does take place from Basile's treatment of the tale in the *Pentamerone* onwards. This is one of the features that positions Straparola's rendition between the ritual brutality of his sources and the ethos of the fairy tale. His matter-of-fact handling of attempted incest, paternal vengeance, infant murder, and royal justice is a reminder of just how much violence is buried in the narrative genes of these wonder tales, soon to be tamed for more delicate sensibilities. The tale, as it is configured by Straparola, has a chilling as well as a heart-warming capacity to touch our deepest emotions in its 'tone poem' treatment of family betrayal; the residual charms and optimism by which an anonymous girl, by arranging the prince's room like an oriental hideaway, wins instant love, marriage, and children in a single sentence; a father's murderous treachery; the heroine's powers of endurance; a nurse's unfailing loyalty; the final recovery of truth after time; and the execution of savage justice, followed by years of happiness and the arrival of many more children to replace those which were lost. Such a tale is shot through with archetypal concerns, including the irrational act of murdering children directly in the gene line, against all the design features of the human brain selected and phylogenetically installed to protect progeny even more than the self. There is a sense in which Tebaldo treats his own fantasy-bride daughter as an adulterous wife, and in a carefully plotted act of revenge, slays her legitimate royal children and his heirs out of spite and jealousy, almost in the manner of the historical William Calverley of York who becomes 'The Husband' perpetrator of infanticide in the anonymous play *The Yorkshire Tragedy* (1608).

How Straparola came by his version of the story remains something of a mystery, but of a kind that will become commonplace by the time these commentaries are completed. The long history of a story type to follow, one of the most complex to be met with in relation to the tales in the *Notti*, is offered in the broadest of contextualizing terms – a history worth consideration in its own right. But admittedly, there are significant 'missing links' separating this sprawling medieval and Renaissance literary heritage – the stories associated with such heroines as Oliva, Hélène, Constance, and Dionigia – from the more immediate sources inspiring

Straparola. In a manner that will become more familiar with each new story, an interim source must be imagined through retro-engineering from the present tale in order to account for the variation and reconfiguration of folkloric motifs whereby the tale of Doralice may be affixed to a vast virtual stemma comprised of a multitude of second and third cousins. Straparola's tale is patently a member of the group, but that membership can only be understood by reducing to its component parts the common profile of the self-banished daughter who finds a royal marriage on her own terms, only to meet with betrayal that involves her children and her own life. New to the Doralice group, and hence without precedent, is the suppression of the monstrous birth and treachery of the queen-mother motif, featured in so many of the analogues to follow, and their replacement with the vindictive father who gains entry by posing as a merchant (a folklore motif in its own right), the request to sleep in the infants' bedroom, the planting of the murder weapon to implicate the heroine as murderer of her own children (Motif-Index, K2155.1.1), the stratagem of the astrologer with his inside information used as a portent, and the expedition of revenge to bring back the malefactor.[80] All of these elements have independent histories of their own, which through some anonymous process have been substituted and interpolated into the ancient tale of incest and the beleaguered queen. That this process is so entirely endemic to the procedures of the oral culture and not to single literary authorship presents further evidence that the present tale was the immediate product, not of the works forming the literary history to follow based on the surviving literary record, but on the folk tale tradition that evolved in parallel to those texts. Any other explanation is difficult to imagine without special pleading. Evolution there has been, and the present tale is a record of that progress, distancing it from all of the surviving literary analogues, yet, as already stated, in its sensibilities it remains relatively 'primitive' in its preoccupations with violence and justice, while carrying the lighter spirit of subsequent tales in the sexual rectitude, charm, angelic domesticity, and resilience of a heroine who is no longer billed as historical or a saint.

80 One such tale of the merchant who insinuates himself into a forbidden place through the irresistibility of his wares (Motif K139.1.3) is 'King Gallafro's Vain Precautions' in the present collection (IX.1), in which Prince Diego of Castile seduces the queen of Spain by assuming the disguise to gain entry to her tower where the lady was incarcerated by a jealous husband.

Turning now to that huge preliminary literary record, the generic story type was richly represented in verse romances, folk tales, the Breton *lai*, and the *novella.* For the reasons set out above, of the many examined, none stands out as the clear parent to the present rendition. Significantly, Straparola does not follow the precedent set by Ser Giovanni some century and a half earlier in his *Il pecorone* (X.1), where this material is displaced to a contemporary 'novelistic' setting and subjected to the limits of natural cause and effect. His maintains the folkloric characteristics of the wonder tale. Doralice makes her escape in her mother's carved chest by living for weeks on magic food, most conveniently the chest falls directly into the hands of the king of England, and as a matter of course, once it is placed in his room, Doralice comes out from time to time to domesticate this bachelor king by arranging his furniture and plumping up his pillows like a household angel. The conventions of fantasy prevail, even though there are no supernatural creatures who take charge of the heroine's survival or arrange for her return. Unique to this version, too, is the angry pursuit by Doralice's father, who walks all the way from Salerno to London to frame his daughter by implicating her in the crime of infanticide, which he performs upon his own grandchildren. The nurse makes the same trip on horseback a short while after. It was these fantastic and implausible features of the folk tale that no doubt suggested to Giambattista Basile the story's further potential for development in the direction of the 'classic' fairy tale. It is fascinating, at the same time, to see just how many of the 'primitive' concerns of the story, from Doralice's saintliness and suffering to the dark imputations of incest, that persist in the signature design of the story type preserved by later writers.

Incest in literature is a topic much under discussion, whether in its mythical, psychological (including Freudian), or historical dimensions. Given that it is the behavioural intentionality that initiates the action of what may be referred to as the 'Belle Hélène' narrative group with which the story of Doralice is associated, it situates her experiences squarely within the debate.[81] But which debate? If incest is a universally acknowledged taboo, a violation that pertains to the wicked imaginings of illicit

81 Further to this, see Claude Roussel, *Conter de Geste au XIVe siècle: inspiration folklorique et écriture épique dans La Belle Hélène de Constantinople* (Geneva: Droz, 1998), pp. 142–80. All the current theories are treated, whether it is a trace memory of ancient rites concerning the concentration of dynastic power within the family, the harmless expression of a universal subliminal craving, or simply the expression of social inversion (p. 143).

sexuality, its usage here can be treated largely as functional – a situational imperative that motivates her flight and sets the rest of the plot in motion. No one is suggesting that the father has an entitlement, even though he was prompted to choose her in accordance with conditions set by the girl's dying mother. But ambiguities remain, for in later versions, the girl lingers for a time by placing material demands upon her father, making his sexual urgings the grounds for 'daddy' negotiations. As a precondition to putatively granting him favours, she seeks elaborate dresses as gifts, raising the ante each time with the intent of surpassing his financial means, meanwhile acquiring elaborate clothes with which she later hopes to win a more suitable man. Is this another of the discontents of civilization? In making a father's incestuous intentions the motive for the girl's escape, the topic is consciously raised, whether as a trace of ancient rites, as psychological sublimation for repressed desires, as diabolical energy that must be contained through ritual cleansing, or an unfortunate byproduct of the concentration of patriarchal power. Doralice is decisive in her conduct, but the fact admits of alternate readings. In this regard, Straparola's tale is among the harshest in its judgment, for in many other versions both before and after, even though 'no' means 'no,' time purges the father of his drives and the denouement often includes him into the family reunion. This same shift is seen through a comparison of the finale to Greene's *Pandosto* with Shakespeare's *The Winter's Tale.* In the former, the heroine's father, upon her incognito return to his court, takes an incestuous interest in her which, when discovered, leads to his suicide, whereas in the latter, the incest motif is suppressed.

There are further troubling complications in Straparola's representation of incest. In the narrative prototype, *La Belle Hélène de Constantinople,* a fifteenth-century romance (based on much earlier sources), the Emperor Antoine of Constantinople not only falls in love with his daughter, but applies to and receives from the Pope a dispensation permitting the marriage, thereby placing the work in the context of a debate concerning consanguinity and the realization of dynastic ambitions through close intermarriage.[82] Of these matters, the study *Incest, Drama and*

82 Jean Wauquelin, *La Belle Hélène de Constantinople, roman en prose* (1448), trans. Marie-Claude de Crécy, in *Splendeurs de la cour de Bourgogne*, ed. Danielle Régnier-Bohler (Paris: Robert Laffont, 1995). The matter of papal dispensation is a prominent feature in the version of the story from late medieval Germany entitled, 'Deu tochter des küniges von Reuzen' (The daughter of the king of Reuzen) in which the pontiff is bribed with gold and silver. This heroine is then sent all manner

Nature's Law 1550–1700 by Richard McCabe sets out the historical context.[83] Theologians, jurists, reformers, and philosophers would expend considerable lamp oil during the period on setting the boundaries. But with or without dispensation, Hélène was horrified by the thought, and that was enough to launch her epic wanderings from Constantinople to Syria to England.

The most troubling element, however, is an associated fairy-tale motif that justifies the father's choice, for in Straparola's tale, as in others before and after, he is happily wed to a wife who, among her final wishes, specifies the conditions she would have her husband meet in choosing a future mate – conditions to be treated as sacred. In related tales, one dying spouse demands that her replacement have a finger size that fits her ring, another that the new wife's feet fit her shoes, and another that her successor is equal to her in beauty. In all such instances, after a prolonged search, it is discovered that the daughter alone can meet the criterion, hence spawning the father's interest. It is as though the girl's own mother sets up the unique conditions whereby her daughter is subsequently drawn into adversity. If these tales convey truths, we are challenged to understand why a mother's wish is subliminally calculated to redound so disastrously upon her daughter. Is the incestuous desire born of some probative test, some ritual procedure that marks the girl for her particular fate? What incest means is not easily determined, but at least the heroine's response is categorical. The eroticization of the parent towards the child meets total resistance, for intuitively the child knows she is born to a different destiny. Yet in so defining the source of conflict, the story reflects a dimension of conflict within the family.

La Belle Hélène de Constantinople has been evoked as a convenient prototype for the Doralice story type by dint of its early appearance (going back at least to the twelfth century), as well as its success and wide

---

of costly gifts and clothes from her father, but when she divines their significance she is distraught, cuts off her hair, throws down the bride's clothes, and disfigures herself till the blood runs down. She is placed in a boat which takes her to Greece and there in time she finds a royal partner, but is traduced by the evil queen mother; thereafter her story resembles the destiny of the queens in the 'Biancabella' (III.3) and 'Truth-speaking Bird' (IV.3) cognate stories. Friedrich Heinrich von der Hagen, *Gesamtabenteuer: Hundert Altdeutsche Erzälungen* (Darmstadt: Wissenschaftliche Buchgesellschaft, 1961), vol. II, pp. 595–613.

83 *Incest, Drama and Nature's Law 1550–1700* (Cambridge: Cambridge University Press, 1993).

circulation, including chapbooks still current in the nineteenth century.[84] This is but one, however, of the several analogue traditions, a scant few of which can be described here by way of indicating Doralice's rich literary ancestry and complex overlay of motivic materials.[85] *La Belle Hélène* is a sprawling and episodic tale of inaugural incest and the heroine's two royal marriages, in Syria and in England, each betrayed by a mother-in-law. In subsequent versions, however, the Syrian prelude leading to the conversion of Muslims is gradually jettisoned. Hélène is the daughter of an emperor who, in her exile, loses her identity, yet by her innate charms attracts Henry of England for her husband. During the king's absence, her twins are born. The queen mother forges letters to and from her son, the first one telling him that his children were born monsters and the second one, putatively in the king's name, telling his agent, the duke of Gloucester, to execute both mother and children. The unexpressed presumption is that the monstrous births entail sorcery or bestial conception. The duke, however, shows compassion and arranges for her severed hand to serve as proof of her death, which is no doubt a residual detail from the legend of Santa Uliva of the severed hands. (That story may have given rise to the many fairy tales involving handless maidens, including Biancabella, III.3.) Hélène's severed hand, curiously, is placed around the neck of one of her two exiled and wandering sons. After the queen mother is executed, a search by all parties continues for some time before Hélène is reunited with her husband, sons, and father, thanks to the tell-tale hand around the boy's neck, which is miraculously restored to her use through the offices of Martin, Archbishop of Tours. This ending has an affinity with the version told by Ser Giovanni in 'Dionigia and the

84 This *chanson de geste* probably originated in northern France and is known from three complete manuscripts and one fragmentary fifteenth-century manuscript. Prose versions are also known, one of them stemming from Jean Wauquelin's 1448 work for Philippe le Bon.

85 Others for consideration include, 'De Alixandre, Roy de Hongrie, qui voulut espouser sa fille,' in *Nouvelles françaises inédites du quinzième siècle*, ed. Ernest Langlois (Paris: H. Champion, 1908), pp. 61–7. In this version the heroine is put to sea with her ward, having already sought to dissuade her father by severing her hands. The motif also occurs in a fourteenth-century version entitled *Fabula romanensis de rege Francorum, cujus nomen reticetur, qui in filia sua adulterium et incestum committere voluit* (Paris: Bibliothèque Nationale, 1370). See also 'Ystoria regis franchorum et filie in quo adulterium comitare voluit,' ed. Hermann Suchier, *Romania* 39 (1910), pp. 61–76 (fourteenth-century *chanson de geste*); and Jehan Maillart, *Le Roman du Comte d'Anjou* (Paris: Champion, [1316], 1931).

King of England' (*Il pecorone* X.1), in which the heroine is reunited with her brother, husband, and children in Rome through the offices of her friend, the Pope.[86] These are the common motifs establishing the form of the narrative. But there is no simple account to be offered concerning the relationship of this tale to the many others in existence, including Straparola's.[87]

The 'Belle Hélène' prototype was clearly far more ancient than this fifteenth-century romance, which has many elements in common with the English tales on the Constance theme appearing as early as the mid-thirteenth century. Regarding even earlier sources, we may retreat behind the conclusion of a leading expert, that 'from the XIIIth century, a legend spread throughout all of Europe, the origins and filiations of which remain relatively obscure.'[88] The earliest written version to survive in any language is the Latin *Vitae Offarum*, formerly attributed to Matthew Paris around 1250.[89] Very likely it too was adapted from a folk tale and interpolated into the life of this eighth-century English king. In this

86 Giovanni Fiorentino, *The Pecorone*, trans. W.G. Waters, illus. E.R. Hughes (London: Society of Bibliophiles, 1898), X.1, vol. II, pp. 73–95; Giovanni Fiorentino, *The Pecorone*, trans. W.G. Waters, illus. E.R. Hughes (London: Lawrence & Bullen, 1897), pp. 127–33.

87 Others in that ancient tradition, vacillating between pseudo-history and folk tale, include lines from *Der Keiser und der kunige Buoch oder de sogenannte Kaiserchronik* (a poem of the twelfth century in 18, 578 lines), here edited by Hans Massmann from 12 complete and 17 incomplete manuscripts (Quedlinburg: Leipzig Basse, 1849), ll. 11, 36 7*ff*; see also the *Istoria de la fiyla del rey d'Ungaria*, a work in Catalan of undetermined antiquity, ed. Pasquale Morabito (Reggio Calabria: Mendionali Nuniti, 1974). There is also a Slavonic tale entitled 'The Miller's Daughter Becomes Queen,' in *Tales from Twelve Tongues*, ed. Henry B. Wilson (London: Burnes & Oates, 1883). These may provide further hints concerning the rise of the *Belle Hélène* group.

88 Claude Roussel, *Conter de geste au XIVe siècle: inspiration folklorique et écriture épique dans La Belle Hélène de Constantinople* (Geneva: Droz, 1998), p. 17. The Anglo-Saxon origin of the Offa-Constance legend related to *La Belle Hélène* has been questioned since the 1930s in favour of folkloric and Eastern origins. See Alexander Haggerty Krappe, 'The Offa-Constance Legend,' *Anglia* 61 (1937), pp. 361–9.

89 Roger of Wendover and Matthew of Paris, *Flowers of History: Comprising the History of England from the Descent of the Saxons to A.D. 1235, Formerly Ascribed to Matthew Paris*, trans. J.A. Giles (London: H.G. Bohn, 1849; reprint, New York: AMS Press, 1968). For the *Vitæ duorum Offarum*, Matthæi Paris, see *Historia major*, ed. William Watts (London: A. Mearne, 1684), cited in John Colin Dunlop; *History of Prose Fiction*, ed. Henry Wilson (New York: Burt Franklin, [1896], 1970), vol. II, p. 169; and Alfred Bradley Gough, *The Constance Saga* [*On the legend contained in the 'Vita Offæ primæ' and other MSS. including the Chronicle of N. Triveth*] (Berlin: Mayer & Müller, 1902).

account there is no sea journey, but it tells of a girl escaping an incestuous father, the king of York. She is sent to the woods to be mutilated and left to the animals, but the servants take pity on her. It is King Offa of Northumbria who rescues and later marries her. Somehow the king of York is drawn into an alliance, finds out about the marriage, and falsifies letters to have her treated as a sorceress, which again results in having her taken, during her husband's absence, into the forest with her children, there to have both hands and feet cut off. The queen is spared, the children's limbs are miraculously restored by a hermit, refuge is granted in the hermitage, and eventually they are found by her grateful husband. In this story, a revengeful father performs the offices of the wicked mother-in-law. Thus the story begins its literary journey, tellingly with the father as the villain of the intrigue, as he is in the tale of Doralice.[90]

90 Edith Rickert, 'The Old English Offa Saga,' *Modern Philology* 2 (June, 1904), pp. 29–77, and *Modern Philology* 2 (January, 1905), pp. 321–76. Other important early versions include the seminal, anonymous German romance, *Mai und Beaflor*, studied by Otto Wächter, *Untersuchungen über das Gedicht 'Mai und Beaflor,'* (Erfurt: Druck von F. Kirchner, 1889). This work is Austro-Bavarian and dates to 1257–9, which the author claims to have found in a prose chronicle, a work rather different from the *Life of Offa I*, but quite similar to Philippe de Beaumanoir's *La Manekine*, trans. Christiane Marchello-Nizia (Paris: Stock-Plus, 1980). In *La Manekine*, the king is Hungarian and the incestuous marriage is urged by the barons and endorsed by the clergy in the interests of begetting a male heir. His daughter, Joïe, is horrified and cuts off her own hand which falls into the river. The king, outraged because he is unable to marry a mutilated woman, asks to have her burned alive, but she is sent away instead in a ship. She is discovered by and marries the king of Scotland against the queen mother's will. Again there are falsified letters and orders to have her burned with her son, but manikins are burned in their places and she is set to sea again in the same boat in which she had arrived. The final reunion takes place in Rome and includes both the repentant father and the loving husband, who must first be forgiven for his presumed crimes against his wife. As a byway here, the stories of self-mutilating heroines in order to avoid incest, often by cutting off their own hands or disfiguring themselves in various ways, are also legion. The motif is found in the exempla of Jacques de Vitry, no. 57, which tells of a nun beloved by a prince who was praised for her beautiful eyes, whereupon she tore them out and sent them to the prince saying that she would rather lose her eyes than her soul. Thomas Frederick Crane traces the story back to the *Vitae patrum*, bk. X, chap. 60, in the *Patrologiæ cursus completus ... Patrologia Latina*, ed. J.-P. Migne (Paris: Migne, 1967), vol. 74, p. 148. Étienne de Bourbon, thirteenth century, in his *Tractatus de diversis materiis predicabilibus* (Turnhout: Brepols, 2002), no. 248, tells the story of Richard I, king of England, who provokes the same response from a nun. When he sought to ravish her, she asked what it was that had so moved his passions, and when Richard replied that it was her beautiful eyes, she blinded herself to rescue her

It is an instance of the conversion of folklore into pseudo-history, with overtones of the saint's life simultaneously present in the actions of the blessed hermit.

It may be added here, parenthetically, that the story, from its earliest years, was also assigned to other historical figures. Hans Wilhelm Kirchhof in his *Wendunmuth* most inconveniently recreates a parallel plot in the name of Charlemagne and his queen, Hildegard. In this version the king sets off on a war mission leaving his queen in the care of an untrustworthy bastard brother, Talandum. In 773, hence within a year or two of the young girl's marriage to the king, he bares his heart to her and, being refused, converts his desire to vicious hatred. Accused of shameful acts, she is tried by being cast into water and then sent to the forest to have her eyes put out. Hildegard's sister sends her a helper in her highest need and he advises her to send a dog's eyes to the court as proof of her death. Then one of her handmaidens appears and together they make their way to Rome where the queen lives a life of such piety that her fame spreads as a healer, thereby maintaining the intimations of saintliness. Talandum, by God's divine justice, is meanwhile stricken by a disease. He convinces the king to join with him in a pilgrimage to Rome to consult with the famous healer in hope of a cure. Rosina the handmaid recognizes him immediately and urges Hildegard to ignore his pleas unless he makes a complete confession of every sin from his youngest age. The healing she then performs amazes everyone, including Pope Adrian, who requests to meet her. The king goes to St. Peter's and is there reunited with his queen, while Talandum is made to know the source of his healing. Once again dynastic history is conflated with hagiography, based on the legend of indeterminate origins.[91]

virginity. *Anecdotes historiques, légendes et apologues*, from an unedited collection of Étienne de Bourbon, ed. A. Lecoy de la Marche (Paris: Librairie Renouard, 1876), fifth part, nos. 500 and 248, pp. 431, 211–12.

91 Just how this version of the tale originated and how it came down to Kirchhof is work for other scholars, but other works worth consulting from Oesterley's annotations will be mentioned following the main entry. 'Von König Carolo mango eine ware histori' (Of King Charlemagne, a true story), in *Wendunmuth*, ed. Hermann Oesterley, 5 vols. (Tübingen: Litterarischen Verein in Stuttgart, 1869), bk. II, no. 23, vol. II, pp. 47–52. Among the many references, Oesterley includes Vincent of Beauvais, *Speculum quadruplex*, vol. IV. *Speculum historiale* (Graz: Akademische Druck und Verlagsanstalt, 1965), [VII, 90]. *Nicodemus Frischlini Hildegardis magna: comoedia* (Tübingen, 1579), but frequently published thereafter in his

The story of Constance, far better known as Chaucer's 'Man of Law's Tale' – or 'The Tale of Constance of Rome' to coin a name – among his *Canterbury Tales*, came to him from the *Chronicles* of Nicolas Trevet, written between 1328 and 1335 for Mary Plantagenet, the sixth daughter of Edward I.[92] This 'romanced' history founded on legend originating in folklore contains the Syrian preamble of the *Belle Hélène* tradition, her marriage to a Sultan, his conversion to Christianity, the hatred of the Sultaness and the persecution of the Christians, and Constance's trip to England in a rudderless boat – the equivalent of Straparola's chest aboard a merchant's vessel. There she resumes her work of conversion, meanwhile beloved by a knight whom she rejects. In retaliation, the knight murders her hostess and throws the blame on the innocent girl by hiding the bloody knife under her pillow. This is in parallel to Doralice's father's murder of her children and the planting of the guilty knife.[93] Tellingly, this motif has an early association with the story tradition. Constance,

---

Operum poeticorum. Juan de Timoneda, *El Patrañuelo*, ed. Federico Ruiz Morcuende (Madrid: Espasa-Calpe, 1958), no. 21. Jean Gobi, *Scala celi of Joannes Gobbi junior* (Ulm, 1480; reprint, Chicago: University of Chicago Press, 1928), no. 32.

92 On the man, see Ruth Josephine Dean, 'Nicolas Trevet, historian,' in *Medieval Learning and Literature, Essays Presented to Richard William Hunt* (Oxford: Oxford University Press, 1976), pp. 328–52. For the text, see 'The Man of Law's Tale,' in *Sources and Analogues of Chaucer's 'Canterbury Tales,'* ed. Margaret Schlauch (New York: Humanities Press, 1958), pp. 151–81; or see 'The Man of Law's Tale,' *Chaucer's Major Poetry*, ed. Albert C. Baugh (New York: Appleton-Century-Crofts, 1963), pp. 313–33.

93 The episode of the bloody knife placed by the queen in order to incriminate her in the death of her children (a vestige of earlier tales of actual cannibalism on her part [see the notes to IV.3]) is an ancient European folk motif that is associated with a number of accused queen stories. It is not employed by jealous sisters or hostile mothers-in-laws; they resort to substituting animals for newborns and the letter exchange device, also included in this story, as in 'The Truth-speaking Bird' (IV.3). Rather this pertains to those tales in which the queen is traduced by a brother-in-law or, as here, by her own father. The motif may be Eastern, for it occurs in the *Tooti-nameh*, but there are early examples of it in the West, as in *La conte de la femme chaste convoitée par son beau-frère*, ed. Axel Wallensköld in *Acta societatis scientiarum Fennicae* 34, no. 1 (Helsinki: Finska Vetenskapssocieteten, 1907). The bloody dagger appears in literary versions of the tale as early as the mid-twelfth century in *Crescentia* (of Rome), ed. Friedrich Heinrich von der Hagen in *Gesamtabenteuer* (Darmstadt: Wissenschaftliche Buchhgesellschaft [1850], 1961), vol. I, pp. 129–64. It is also known in *La bone Florence de Rome*, ed. Albert Knobbe (Marburg: Elwert, 1899).

however, makes a prayerful appeal to Saint Anne in the presence of the king, a sacred book is produced, and a miraculous hand descends to smite the guilty knight. Romance and the saint's life are still working in parallel. What fairy tale conventions will later bestow upon the heroine is still produced here by the intervention of heaven. Yet much suffering will follow as the plot of this famous tale unfolds. She will marry the king, but in his absence the queen mother will report monstrous births, forge letters, facilitate the young queen's banishment, and condemn her son to years of fruitless searching before he can restore his family. This shaping of events was destined to enjoy a long literary history in variations down to the time of Straparola.

Chaucer tells this story with only minor deviations from the original narrative facts, but with a great deal of rhetorical proclamation and moralizing, in earnest or in parody. John Gower tells 'The Tale of Constance' in the *Confessio Amantis* in those same years – the end of the fourteenth century (scholars are still debating the relationship between the two versions).[94] Here there is no incest plot or ring fitting test, but there are two marriages (the first husband is massacred as in the Trevet account) and a long and frightening sea voyage, following which the heroine becomes a castaway in England (the voyage in the Trevet original lasts exactly three years and eight months). There are two treacherous mothers-in-law, a lecherous knight, a frame-up plot with a bloody knife, exile, surviving children, and the final reunion, the entire story embellished by Christian miracles.

A fourth English version may predate both Chaucer and Gower, but only by a few years. It is the 1,000-line Breton *lai* entitled *Emaré*, a conventional but most charming poem which, in its brevity, contains most of the motifs to be found in Chaucer and Gower.[95] Yet there are certain little features rather more like those in Straparola, including the king's

94 John Gower, *Confessio Amantis*, ed. Russell A. Peck (Toronto: University of Toronto Press, and Cambridge, MA: The Medieval Academy of America, 1980), pp. 108–36. For a summary of the Chaucer, Gower, and Trivet controversy in relation to this tale, see Margaret Schlauch, *Chaucer's Constance and Accused Queens* (New York: Gordian Press, [1927], 1969), pp. 132–4.

95 The text may be found in *Romancing the Goddess: Three Middle English Romances about Women*, ed. Marijane Osborn (Urbana: University of Illinois Press, 1998). See also *The Romance of Emaré*, ed. Edith Rickert (London: Kegan Paul, Trench, Trübner & Co., 1908).

incestuous desires brought on by his wife's death – traces, arguably, of the originating folk tale. The princess Emaré's nurse, as in our fable, provides her with counsel and she is sent off to sea in a wooden chest that tosses about directly in the water, in which the heroine nearly starves to death – thus the subsequent motif of the magic nourishing potion. In this version, she is spared the burial up to her chin that figures in Straparola's 'Doralice,' and in the end is not only reunited with her loving husband, but reconciled to her offending father as well. These English variants are as useful as any for illustrating the founding narrative cluster, hinting at the underlying tradition, variations upon which inspired Straparola.

Turning now from England to Italy, there were other emanations from this same ancient legend which form a large part of its legacy. One in particular is important for the echoes it contains of an ancient saint's life that is closely aligned with the Constance-Hélène group, namely the life of Santa Uliva. *L'Historia de la regina Oliva* is an Italian verse romance that dates to the beginning of the fifteenth century; it was in turn adapted for theatrical production towards the middle of the century as the *Rappresentazione di santa Uliva*. The Emperor Julian, discovering that his daughter was the only girl as beautiful as his first wife, demands a dispensation from the Pope. The resisting daughter severs her hand as a deterrent and sends it to her father, for which she is exiled to Brittany, there to perish. Eventually, she is taken into the service of the king and queen, and while carrying the royal child in her arms, she is accosted by a knight, drops the child, and is then blamed for its death. Her death sentence is pronounced but commuted to exposure in the forest, the one where she had been initially discovered. (Forests will remain a feature of the story as a place of obscurity, exile, primordial fear, refuge, and rediscovered faith.) There she prays to the Virgin who appears in person to restore her hand and direct her to a monastery. Yet sanctuary evades her. Falsely accused of the theft of a chalice, she is put to sea in a box. Then the king of Castile finds and marries her and it is only then that the double exchange of letters takes place, accusing her of giving birth to a monster. A poor woman and her baby are burned in the place of the royal mother and her child (reminiscent of the manikin motif), and again she is set adrift, ultimately arriving in Rome where, after twelve years, she is rediscovered, the queen mother slain, and the family rejoined. This is a nearly baroque proliferation of banishments and symmetrical episodes, but the play (Florentine) and the romance undoubtedly served to familiarize Italians with the outline of events and the motivational mechanisms, many of which may have passed back into the tales of the folk.[96] Santa Uliva carries the story back to the popular imagination, superimposing a saint upon the miseries of the traduced queen.

Brief mention has already been made of the story of Dionigia as told by Ser Giovanni in his *Pecorone* (X. 1), a work compiled during the last quarter of the fourteenth century.[97] This tale takes up the history of Chaucer and Gower as an Italian *novella*. A French princess, to escape an enforced marriage to an old German prince, disguises herself and escapes by sea to England, there to enter a convent. When the English king passes by, sees, and falls in love with her, marriage follows and the saga begins of alleged monster births, the queen mother's countermanding of her son's orders to care for the young queen and her twin offspring until his return, the forged letter calling for their execution, escape through the offices of the good Viceroy, and Dionigia's departure for Genoa by sea. When at last she arrives in Rome, the heroine there leads such a pious life that she comes to the attention of the Pope. Meanwhile, the king discovers the truth of his mother's deed, has her slain, and sets out in search of his family. When Dionigia learns of her husband's arrival in the company of her brother, now the king of France, she tells her story to the Pope, and the Pope arranges for the grand reconciliation after much explanation on all sides. This version remains patently closer to 'The Man of Law's Tale' than to Straparola's, telling more about the state of this pan-European tale in the fourteenth than in the sixteenth century. Yet it serves as a point of orientation for imagining the interim variations required to produce the Straparolan variation. As set out above, the leap from Dionigia to Doralice is unlikely to have been due to Straparola's own genius; traces of folk motifs from earlier records gainsay that hypothesis, including the ploy of the travelling merchant, the planting of the murder weapon, and the astrologer's disguise. Rather, as the folklorists made their adjustments, older versions prevailed among authors borrowing from the literary record. One further, predating Straparola's by a scant year or two, provides evidence of that kind, this story taken from a literary source of the mid-fifteenth century in the Chaucer/Ser Giovanni mode.

96 *Rappresentazione di santa Uliva*, in Alessandro d'Ancona, *Sacre rappresentazioni del secoli XIV, XV e XVI* (Florence: LeMonnier, 1872), vol. II, pp. 235–315.

97 *The Pecorone*, trans. W.G. Waters (London: Lawrence & Bullen, 1897), pp. 127–33: from Waters' own copy, no. 5 of 110 printed.

Francesco Maria Molza (1489–1544) was a Roman writer with a reputation for being the new Boccaccio. In fact, he left only a few *novelle,* which were written during his youth and published only after his death. Among them was a story based on the King Offa tradition, originally appearing in an edition of 1547 of which no copies survive. (It is known to us today through the rediscovery of Molza's original manuscript in the nineteenth century.)[98] There is no particular novelty in his development of the materials. The dying queen tells her husband, the king of England, to marry someone who carries her looks; their daughter alone qualifies. Enter the incest motif. The matter is referred to the pope for a dispensation, in accordance with the 'Belle Hélène' group. Meanwhile, her uncle, the duke of Lancaster, helps the girl flee to a French monastery where the Dauphin sees, falls in love with, and marries her. The Constance-Dionigia story ensues. (Of interest is that the story begins in England and moves to France, reversing the familiar direction.) Accused of infidelity by the wicked mother-in-law during the king's absence, she becomes the victim of a palace intrigue. A false letter is sent to the king; his measured reply is intercepted and altered. The young queen is condemned to die, but is rescued by her guardians and allowed to escape to Rome where she becomes a nurse in a royal household. When her husband returns and discovers the treachery, his mother is punished and he goes in search of the lost queen. Molza's source was Bartolomeo Facio's *De origine belli inter Gallos et Britannos historia* in which the children of the beleaguered English princess and the French prince inherit the kingdoms of France and England, which, when separated, gives rise to the Hundred Years War.[99] Facio (1400–57) takes the old pre-conquest legend and turns it into pseudo-fourteenth-century history in a work that Poggio translates into the vernacular; Molza, meanwhile, turns this pseudo-history back to fiction.

98 Molza's '[Fille du Roi de Bretagne]' is included in *Novellieri del cinquecento* (Milan-Naples: Ricciardi, 1971), vol. I, and in *Conteurs italiennes de la Renaissance,* ed. Giancarlo Mazzacurati, Georges Kempf, and Anne Motte-Gillet (Paris: Gallimard, 1993), pp. 761–80. Others of his *novelle* came to print in 1549 in Lucca under the title *Quattro novelle dell' onoratissimo Molza.*

99 *All' origine della Guerra dei cento anni; una novella Latina di Bartolomeo Facio e il volgarizzamento di Jacopo di Poggio Bracciolini,* ed. Gabriella Albanese (Rome: Storia e letteratura, 2000).

Francesco Sansovino published a version bearing a certain affinity with Straparola's in *Cento novelle scelti da i piu nobili scrittori,* 1561.[100] The reason for the resemblance is usually because the 'noble author' from whom the stories were taken is Straparola himself, whom Sansovino frequently appropriates or closely imitates. A daughter of the king of France, to avoid marrying an old man, flees her country, becomes a monk, and is discovered by the king of England whom she weds. She is later accused by her wicked mother-in-law of murdering her own children – an accidental throwback, perhaps, to a primitive version involving infanticide or even cannibalism, equally germane to the tale of 'Doralice.' The mother then escapes to Rome where she is found by her husband and taken back to England. The deviations from Straparola, however, are probably no deviations at all, but are due to a much greater debt to Ser Giovanni.

Only with Basile's 'The Bear' (*Pentamerone* II.6) do we come to a further demonstration of the later folk developments within the story type, the contrasts with Straparola now to be accounted for by regional diversity and advancing years.[101] His tale begins with a dying queen who exacts a promise from her husband to marry a new wife at least as beautiful as she is. The king conducts an elaborate search, but can only settle upon his own daughter. The female helper organizes her escape, which Basile embellishes with a rather splendid satire on the vanity of women. The proposal made to Preziosa, for such is the new heroine's name, was rather matter-of-fact, but she screams and flies into a rage that only heaven could describe. So the old woman gives her a magic stick to place in her mouth that would instantly turn her into a bear. With that the story strikes out on its own, more in the manner of a folk tale than ever. Even though 'The Bear' contains many of the 'Doralice' episodes, the story is radically transformed. Rather than take to the seas, she takes to the woods, there to meet the neighbouring prince who leads her into his private quarters, not as a housekeeper in a chest, but as a pet bear. Nevertheless, she can take the stick from her mouth when no one is around and, as a girl, do a bit of favour-currying housework, in Doralice fashion. This stooping to menial labour further develops the Straparolan motif and will become increasingly central to the fairy tales to follow. In

100 (Venice: Francesco Sansovino, 1561), pp. 78v–83r (from the copy once belonging to the Pontifici Biblioteca di Bologna).

101 Giovanni Battista Basile, *The Pentamerone,* trans. Richard Burton (New York: Boni & Liveright, 1927, 1928), pp. 150–7.

parallel fashion, the queen mother takes a profound disliking to this bear, no longer Christian or lower class as such, and orders it to be killed, regenerating the now familiar motifs in a new key. The preposterousness of it all is that the prince has fallen in love with his bear to the point of lovesickness, taking to his bed in a state of decline that only the bear's presence can reverse. He asks her to cook for him and feed him in this monstrous parody of domesticity, and when he also insists upon the healing kiss, it proves to be the transforming kiss as well because she is obliged to remove the stick from her mouth. The tale remains that of a beleaguered virgin in disguise, but employs a fantastic form of metamorphosis from bear to human, and generates a curious trial of the companionable emotions coupled with a pre-marital demonstration of the girl's home economics, ostensibly elaborating upon features in ovo in the Straparola tale. But his departures do not encourage us to think that Basile drew directly upon Straparola; undoubtedly he based his version upon a variant folk tale belonging to the same group, now most fancifully altered into a form of 'beauty and the beast' in reverse.

The story tradition was known to English readers in chapbook form throughout the eighteenth and early nineteenth centuries (Worldcat lists some sixty editions) under the title *The Crafty Princess; or the golden Bull; in four parts.*[102] They follow the divisions of the conventional tale: how the king wanted to marry his daughter and threatened to kill her; how she concealed herself inside a golden bull to be transported to the prince she loved; how her arrival and her affection came to the prince's attention; and how, in the final part, her death was planned by three women during the prince's absence, how she was rescued, and how the lovers were finally married. Such was the literary sequel to a story that reaches far back into English literary history, independent of the 'Peau d'Âne' group, one that has now shed its historical overtones to serve as a children's romance. It is a clear remnant of the folk tradition that made up the pan-European phenomenon of which Straparola's 'Doralice' provides an early impression.

Perrault modifies the story considerably in 'Peau d'Asne' by sending his little heroine out into the world at the instigation of her fairy nurse, disguised no longer as an animal, but inside an animal's skin, and more pointedly the skin of her father's precious gold-excreting donkey

102 One such was published in Worcester, MA, by Isaiah Thomas, 1787. There were many American as well as British and Scottish printings.

(borrowed from a tradition that Straparola employs in 'Adamantina's Magic Doll,' V.2). Her adventures take her to a neighbouring farm where she performs degrading and menial tasks and where she is known only as 'Donkey-Skin.' But in due course, a passing prince sees her and sickens with love. Once within his domain, she wins him over with her domestic skills, in the manner of Doralice. Then like Cinderella she is pursued. Eventually, after disappearances and searches, her finger is found to fit the ring she had formerly baked in a cake (a now dislocated feature), and by that means she is discovered and selected out for all the usual marital realignments that conclude such tales. Moreover, her once incestuous-minded father now reappears purged and purified. This is merely a quick sampling of the metamorphoses that seized upon the Straparola heritage, in illustration of the rebalancing and invention that both preserves and yet modifies these tales according to the shifting mores of successive times, the court milieu, and the preciosity of the new readership, particularly in France at the very end of the seventeenth century.

The Grimm brothers, in 'All Fur' (No. 65 of the *Kinder- und Hausmärchen*), also offer a tale of incest averted, flight in the disguise of animal skins, entry into the initiatory forest, and adoption as a poor girl dressed all in fur. She too did menial work, but found her way into the pots-and-pans world of a royal kitchen, there alternating between her rough disguise and her three fine dresses, extracted from her father in hopes of delaying their union, now serving perfectly for slipping into the royal balls incognito where she could steal hearts and flee. She played hide and seek with all who tried to find her until the ring in the soup gives her away. Then her golden hair is revealed, linking her to yet another tale tradition. She is elevated to a royal marriage and finally makes contact with a penitent father, bringing the fairy tale to an end, while marking the great distance it has come from the medieval tale of the beleaguered virgin accused of giving birth to monsters.

By the end of the nineteenth century, researchers had recorded dozens if not hundreds of regional versions of this tale. They represent a rich array of mutilations and metamorphoses, some of them quite imaginative, yet each preserves the defining feature of the threatened heroine, whose female helper equips her with a means to escape, with or without the fanciful dresses she has requested in order to delay the unwanted incestuous union. The version entitled 'Wooden Maria,' assembled from several versions by Calvino in his *Folktales* (No. 103), recounts the initiating story of the ring, the stalling tactic of having several fine wedding gowns made, and a wooden outfit constructed for the girl by her nursemaid in which she makes her escape with her other gowns tucked into the skirt.[103] Like Doralice, she wins the heart of the king or the prince (it is not at all clear), through her domestic skills in baking pizza. There is some confusion whether it is the same girl in the beautiful dresses as in the wooden dress, but this is resolved when the gift tokens appear in the pizzas she bakes for the king's son, at which moment she is liberated for the last time from her wooden prison, again combing her hair.

A variation on the story appears in 'Fair Wood Maria,' collected by Thomas Crane, in which the girl is actually married to her father before she makes her escape in the wooden dress.[104] Yet another variation comes from Lorraine in the north of France, recorded by Emmanuel Cosquin, in which the get-away vehicle is a golden bull in the story entitled 'Le tareau d'or' (I.27).[105] A dying wife sets the tale in motion with her request

---

103 Italo Calvino, *Italian Folktales*, trans. George Martin (New York: Pantheon, 1980), pp. 378–82.

104 Thomas F. Crane, 'Fair Wood Maria,' in *Italian Popular Tales*, ed. Jack Zipes (Santa Barbara, CA: ABC-Clio, 2009). Giuseppe Pitrè collected the story in Tuscany as 'La donnina di legno' (The little wooden girl), pointing out in his notes that the story was known throughout Italy. *Novelle popolari toscane, parte seconda* (Rome: Casa editrice del libro italiano, n.d.), pp. 101–2. The opening of the story is also represented in 'Il trottolin di legno,'in *Le novelline di Santo Stefano*, ed. Angelo de Gubernatis (Turin: A.F. Negro, 1869), no. 3, pp. 19–21. A dying woman asks her husband to remarry someone upon whose finger her ring is a perfect fit. After an unsuccessful search, the daughter tries on the ring and is caught doing so, with devastating results. An old woman advises the girl to stall the wedding by making impossible demands – a dress of gold, for example – but with the help of a magician, every demand is met. The girl makes her escape in a wooden 'trottolin' which embarks her upon a round of adventures in which she uses her splendid gowns on a series of Cinderella-like occasions remote from the present story. English readers will find the story most readily as 'Kari Wooden Gown' in which all the parts are present from the incest opening to the clothes exchange by which a prince is bamboozled and then drawn in by the heroine's craft and charm. *The Red Fairy Book*, ed. Andrew Lang (London: Longmans & Co. [1890], 1912), pp. 189–201.

105 Emmanuel Georges Cosquin, *Contes populaires de Lorraine, comparés avec les contes des autres provinces de France et des pays étrangers, et précédé d'un essai sur l'origine et la propagation des contes populaires européens* (Paris: F. Vieweg, 1886), no. 28, vol. I, pp. 273–80. Cosquin provides a check list of cognate versions, several of which have already been included. But in general, his tales are those in which there is a long romance sequel of the 'Peau d'Âne' (Donkey skin) variety, which does not appear in Straparola. Others resembling Straparola's in pronounced ways are the versions recorded by Bernhard Schmidt, 'Der Drache,' in *Griechische Märchen, Sagen und Volkslieder* (Leipzig: B.G. Teubner, 1877), no. 12, pp. 93–8, and by Eugen Prym and Albert Socin, *Der neu-aramæische Dialekt des Tûr 'Abdin* (Göttingen: Vandenhoek

that her husband marry another as marvellous as she is, leading to a fruitless search and the sealing of the daughter's destiny. Now in addition to the gowns, the daughter requests a piece of furniture in the form of a bull in which she can hide (a curious parody of the Trojan horse substituting for the wardrobe). There is no helping nursemaid. As with Doralice's chest, this is given away, now to a sickly prince. The princess is discovered when she slips out to eat the prince's food, for he lies in wait to find the culprit. They become close friends before he is forced to leave. He tells her to hide again in the bull until she hears a tapping code signalling when she should come out. Her rival for the prince's hand comes into the room, by chance imitates the code, and so the truth of the secret favourite is revealed.

Patrick Kennedy collected an Irish analogue entitled 'The Princess in the Cat-Skins,' a Hiberian 'peau d'âne.' It begins exactly as the story of Doralice: the good mother dies leaving her daughter to a bad husband (not her father) who takes a mind to marry her against her will. The distraught girl is driven to seek counsel and to launch delaying tactics involving elaborate gowns. She ends up in flight to take up the life of a shepherdess, remarkable in her cat-skin disguise. She handles her prince coyly with her transformations into and out of gowns. Everyone at the princely residence laughs at her, but some flirt and she slaps those who try to kiss her. If you want a prince, you have to manage the riff-raff. The closure is pure 'Cinderella' with a ball, an escape, and the sartorial disclosure of the phantom princess.[106] The Highland tale collected by Campbell entitled 'The King Who Wished to Marry his Daughter' belongs to this same tradition, along with so many more.[107] There is a Syrian

& Ruprecht, 1881), no. 52 (121), vol. I, pp. 145–9, with a translation in the second volume. In the latter, the heroine, a Jewish merchant's daughter besieged, emerges from her transported coffer to make coffee and is caught by the prince. She tells her story and he marries her.

106 *Fireside Tales of Ireland* (Dublin: McGlashan & Gill, 1870), pp. 81–7; new ed. (Norwood, PA: Norwood Editions, 1975).

107 J.F. Campbell, 'The King Who Wished to Marry his Daughter,' in *Popular Tales of the West Highlands, Orally Collected* (Paisley: Alexander Gardner, 1890; reprint, Edinburgh: Birlinn, 1994), no. 14, vol. I, pp. 269–77. This is a charming adaptation of the fairy tale to the conditions of the highlands, where the girl meets the king's son in church with her various gowns on, and whose shoe left behind is the means for finding her as the dirty serving wench – the girl whom the king has vowed to marry because the shoe fits her alone. An incestuous father launches this version as well because only his daughter fitted perfectly into his deceased wife's clothes.

version in which a rich Jew seeks a new wife by sizing each candidate's feet with his wife's shoes, only to find that his daughter alone can wear them; he then seeks to ravish her. She too escapes in a coffer with provisions and is also sold to a prince whose room she not only tidies up, but for whom she makes coffee.[108]

Another type of folk tale that connects intimately to the Doralice, *Belle Hélène,* Biancabella (III.3), and King Ancillotto (IV. 3) groups pertaining to traduced queens and girls with severed hands is equally well represented among the tales collected by the nineteenth-century ethnographers. Sebastiano Lo Nigro, in his study of the Sicilian folk tale, includes among his categories 'La fanciulla dale mani mozze' (The girl with the severed hands), for which he provides a generic profile of potentially many tales. A young girl, locked in her room, is seen by the king, induced to flee, marries him and lives in his palace. When he leaves for the wars, she is left in the care of his mother, pregnant. Apparent here are the features from the Biancabella and King Ancillotto groups mentioned above. The false letters are exchanged, her hands are severed, and she is sent into the woods where San Giuseppe restores them – a lingering hint of the hagiographical tradition of yore. When the king returns and

---

Campbell also reports other versions such as the one on the island of South Uist in 1859, from his companion, who had gotten it from a girl at the inn at the Sound of Benbecula, etc. (vol. I, pp. 273–4). He then mentions 'Peau d'Âne,' 'Katie Wooden Cloak,' 'Finette Cendron' by the Contesse d'Aulnoy, and the present tale by Straparola. To this list may be added 'La fille du roi d'Espagne' (The king of Spain's daughter), collected by Luzel for his *Contes populaires de la Basse-Bretgne.* This heroine is chosen to replace her mother in her father's bed, which forces the girl to consult with an old woman who sets up the delay tactics in terms of sartorial demands. The girl flees with her dresses, takes service as a pig keeper, and there, through a series of up-class, down-class, clothes shifting, she mystifies then wins the young master. (Rennes: Presses universitaires de Rennes, 1996), vol. III, pp. 175–83.

108 Three further versions appear as 'Maria di legno,' in *Roman Legends: A Collection of the Fables and Folk-lore of Rome,* ed. R.H. Busk (Boston: Estes & Lauriat, 1877), pp. 66–90. These were collected in Rome in the late nineteenth century. In the first version, the devil himself is the undesirable suitor and a fairy aids the princess in delaying his advances and making her escape with the three traditional dresses and a wooden disguise. In the third version, the recalcitrant daughter, refusing her incestuously minded father, is first imprisoned in a tower, and then abandoned in a chest in the middle of a forest where she is recovered by a prince. Nearly all the conventional motifs of baking the ring into a cake or putting it into a broth are represented as well. They bear all the essential markers of the story type, clearly in wide circulation throughout Italy.

comes to understand the treachery against his wife, he goes in search of her in the woods. As Lo Nigro states, such stories represent an uninterrupted tradition going back to the twelfth century, where the motif appears in England for the first time. That point is still open to demonstration as discussed above. His principal source for the type is the story collected by Laura Gonzenbach in Catania.[109]

But if this is not dizzying enough, in Calvino's collection of *Italian Folklore*, there is the tale of 'Olive,' (No. 71), which casts an entirely new light upon the story tradition, picking up many of its major motifs from Hélène's struggle to maintain the Christian faith to the punitive lopping off of hands of the persecuted girl. It is an extraordinary tale in its preservation of so many motifs of the ancient story tradition. Born Jewish, but raised a Christian, the girl at eighteen is reclaimed from foster parents by her wandering father and forced to renounce her adopted faith. After the burning of her secret prayer book, she is led to his workshop where her hands are cut off. She is then sent out into the forest to die. There she wanders unable to feed herself except through a miracle that causes the boughs of a pear tree within the walls of a palace to bend down to nourish her. His majesty discovers the thief, but takes pity on the mutilated girl instead. What were once miracles for this proto-saint – not by accident bearing the name of Saint Uliva – are now interpreted as sorcery by the queen mother and so the persecution resumes. Olive bears two children to the king, which makes the old woman furious, so that during the king's absence she is again exiled to the woods with her

109 Sebastiano Lo Nigro, *Racconti popolari siciliani: Classificazione e bibliografia* (Florence: Leo Olschki, 1957), pp. 140–1. Laura Gonzenbach, *Sicilianische Märchen* (Leipzig: Engelmann, 1870; reprint, Hildesheim: Olms, 1976), no. 24. Further to this motif, Thomson, *Motif Index* S 12, K 2117, see Johannes Bolte and Jiří Polívka, *Anmerkungen zu den Kinder- und Hausmärchen der Brüder Grimm* (Leipzig: Dietrich, 1913–18, 1932), vol. I, pp. 298*ff*, and Aurelio M. Espinosa, *Cuentos populares españoles* (Madrid: S. Aguirre, 1947), vol. II, p. 376. Yet another was collected by Auguste Dozon: 'Les souliers,' in *Contes albanais* (Paris: Ernest Laroux, 1881), no. 6, pp. 41–8. In this tale, the dying wife specifies shoes, which only her daughter can fill. This girl plays along with her father's incestuous proposal until she can escape hidden inside of a grand chandelier. It is purchased, to be sure, by a prince, whose food she mysteriously consumes in the middle of the night like a 'phantom lady.' Once discovered, the prince is charmed, yet must leave for a year, urging her to resume her hiding place in his absence. She is caught, however, by the mother of the prince's fiancée, who arranges to have the girl thrown into a briar patch – well, 'nettles.' She is rediscovered by hiding her wedding ring under a plate of vegetables she made up for the prince's table.

two babes under her arms. In her desperation she attempts to drink from a pool, which an old crone advises her to do, even though she may drop her babies. When they fall, the girl thrusts her hands into the water where they are instantly healed, enabling her to rescue her children. Olive dwells in a forest villa for three years before the mourning king, deceived by his mother, happens upon the little household and, as their guest, is told the story of Olive's life until he finally recognizes her. When he offers to slay his mother, however, Olive intercedes asking for mercy, and so they all return to a peaceful life once the mother-in-law is resettled in a nunnery. Here is a version long after Straparola's that returns to the roots of the narrative tradition that produced the story of Doralice, in a sense completing the circle.

Doralice had spent time buried in the ground and gnawed by worms before she is disinterred and miraculously nursed back to health, having lived a life of patience entirely worthy of a saint. Clearly the formula spoke to the imagination, for it passed through many metamorphoses, making the transition from romance to fairy tale. The overlay and comparison of versions is assurance that Doralice is a story not only for an age, but for all time. Just how many of Straparola's choices in the compiling of his version were reflections of his particular social concerns is an eternally moot point, but the fundamental narrative pieces belong to a legacy the origins of which are lost in antiquity.

Of note, in closing, is the extent to which, in this story, Straparola indulges his penchant for quoting phrases and images from Boccaccio. There is no apparent reason except the pleasure he found in replacing phrases that might have been his own with wording from a favourite source that served his purposes. Characteristically, the bits are randomly chosen from throughout the *Decameron*. When, in the middle of the second paragraph, he explains that it would have been better if Doralice had never been born, he states 'molto meglio ... sarebbe stato se quella avuta non avesse,' which is far too similar to Day IV.1.3 of the *Decameron* to be mere coincidence: 'e più felice sarebbe stato se quella avuta non avesse.' Later we find from Boccaccio's *Decameron* (X.8.17), 'raffrena il concupissibile appetito,' echoed by Straparola's 'raffrenando il concupissibile appetito.' Boccaccio's 'fiero proponimento' (*Decameron*, IV.1.48) Straparola repeats, and his 'di fargli vituperosamente morire' (*Decameron*, II.6.38) is echoed by 'di farla vituperosamente morire.' There are several others, but these few reveal Straparola's peculiar practice, of little consequence as the stories go, but indicative of his stylistic habits in paraphrasing these popular tales.

I. Fable 5
Polissena and the Priest

ARIANNA

Dimitrio the merchant, disguising himself as a certain Gramotiveggio, surprises his wife Polissena with a priest and sends her back to her brothers, who put her to death. Dimitrio afterwards marries his serving-woman.

We often see, dear ladies, great inequality in the degrees of love. How often the husband fondly loves his wife and she cares little for him, while at other times the wife loves her husband only to receive hatred in return. In conditions like these, the passion of sudden jealousy is often born, the destroyer of all happiness. It renders a decent life impossible; it leads to dishonour and untimely death, with all attendant reproach and disgrace to our sex. I say nothing of the headlong perils and the numberless ills into which both men and women hurl themselves by reason of this accursed jealousy. It would weary rather than divert you were I to recount them all to you one by one. But as it is my task to bring to an end this evening of pleasant discourse, I will tell you the story of Gramotiveggio, not heard in former times, and from which I am certain you will gather as much pleasure as you do instruction.

The noble city of Venice, famed for the integrity of its magistrates, for the justice of its laws, and for receiving men from every nation of the world, is situated in the highest inlet of the Adriatic Sea and is named the queen of cities, the refuge of the unhappy, and the asylum of the oppressed. Her walls are the sea and her roof the sky. And although nothing grows there, yet all things needed for the life of a great city are to be had in abundance.

In this rich and magnificent metropolis there lived in former days a merchant named Dimitrio, a good and trustworthy man of upright life, albeit he was of low degree. Because he greatly desired to have children, he married a fair and graceful girl named Polissena, whom he loved as ardently as ever a man loved a woman. He let her clothe herself so sumptuously that there was no lady in that entire city, except among the nobility, who could outbrave her in raiment, or rings, or costly pearls. Besides, he was careful to let her have all the best things to eat in abundance, which, though far above the usual fare of one of her class, made her softer and more delicate than ever.

Now it came about that Dimitrio – the nature of whose business often compelled him to travel overseas – determined to take ship with a cargo of goods for Cyprus. Once his apparel was ready and the house was stocked with provisions and all that would be required, he left his dear wife Polissena with a fair and buxom serving-maid to keep her company and set forth from Venice on his voyage.

After his departure, Polissena went on living in her luxurious ways and indulged herself with every delicacy. Before very long, she found herself unable to resist the prickling of her amorous desires, so she cast her eyes upon a priest of her parish and became hotly enamoured of him. For his part, the priest, being young, lively, and well-favoured, finally guessed at the meaning of her glances tossed in his direction, and seeing that she was blessed with a lovely face and a graceful shape, and that she was likewise endowed with all the charms that men desire in a woman, he began to return her loving glances. A mutual love thus arose between their faithful and devoted souls, so that not many days passed before Polissena, without being seen by anyone, brought the young man into the house to take her pleasure with him. And so, during several months, they secretly enjoyed the delights of love in close embraces and sweet kisses, leaving her poor husband to fare as well as he might through the perils of the swollen sea.

Now after Dimitrio had been some time in Cyprus and had made a reasonable profit on his goods, he sailed back to Venice. Once disembarked, he went to his home and to his dear Polissena, who, as soon as she set eyes on him, burst into tears. When Dimitrio asked her the reason for her weeping, she replied, 'I weep because of bad news that came to me recently and also for the great joy I feel in seeing you again, for I've heard tell by many that several of the ships destined for Cyprus were wrecked and I was desperately afraid that some misadventure had happened to you. But now, seeing that by God's mercy you have returned safe and sound, for the joy I feel I can't keep back my tears.'

The trusting Dimitrio, thinking to have returned to Venice to make up to his wife for all the solitary time she had spent in his long absence, took her tears and sighs as a sign of her warm and constant love for him. But the poor dupe never suspected that all the while she was saying in her heart, 'Would to heaven he had been drowned at sea so that I can, with even more security and ease, enjoy this lover of mine who dotes on me so completely.'

Before a month had passed, Dimitrio was forced to set out on his travels once more, which filled Polissena with more joy than can be imagined, allowing her soon thereafter to send word to her lover, who was as keen and alert in the matter as she was. When the time agreed upon for their rendezvous came around, he went secretly to her. But the comings and goings of the priest could not be kept sufficiently hidden to escape for long the eye of a certain Manusso, one of Dimitrio's friends who lived opposite them. Manusso, who held Dimitrio in high esteem because he was a pleasant companion and always ready to do a friendly service, began to grow suspicious of his young neighbour, turning the matter over and over in his mind. He came to understand and predict that when certain signs were given at certain hours, the door would always be opened to the priest, and that after this the lovers would disport themselves, often with less caution than prudence demanded. He decided that such business, till then still held a secret, should remain so in order to avoid scandal. Better to give his project time to ripen and to wait for Dimitrio's return – which came about well before he was expected.

For as soon as the merchant found himself free from his duties, he took ship for home, sailing back to Venice with a favourable breeze. Having disembarked, he went straight to his own house and knocked at the door. The serving-maid, when she had seen from the window that it was her master, ran quickly to let him in, nearly weeping with joy. Polissena, hearing her husband's return, came downstairs forthwith, taking him in her arms, embracing and kissing him as though she were the most loving wife in the world. And because he was weary and worn with the sea voyage, he went to bed without supper and slept so soundly that the morning came before he had taken any amorous pleasure with his wife. With the night passed and the arrival of full daylight, Dimitrio awoke. Then leaving his bed without so much as a kiss for his wife, he went to fetch a little box from which he drew certain small objects of no little value. Returning to bed, he presented them to her. But she set little value in such gifts, given that her thoughts were elsewhere.

Not long after, Dimitrio had occasion to go into Apulia to purchase oil and other merchandise. Having announced this to his wife, he began to make ready for his journey. Cunning and wily of heart as she was, she pretended to be heartbroken at his departure, kissed him lovingly and urged him to tarry a few more days with her. But in her heart of hearts, she reckoned one day of his presence like a thousand, for it prevented her from finding delight in the arms of her lover.

Manusso, who had many times seen the priest courting Polissena and doing such things with her as are not to be named, felt that he would be doing his friend a wrong if he failed to let him know all that he had seen. So he decided, come what may, to tell him everything. He invited him one day to dinner and said to him as they sat at table, 'Dimitrio, my friend, you are surely aware that I have always held you in great affection and will continue to do so for as long as there is breath in my body. There is no task you could name, no matter how difficult, that I wouldn't undertake for the love I bear you. And if you promised not to take it ill, I could divulge to you certain matters which you would find most unpleasing. I'm only worried about disturbing your peace of mind. But if I tell you, you must take it in the spirit intended, with circumspection and prudence, without letting your anger master you and blind your eyes to the truth.'

'You should know,' answered Dimitrio, 'that you can say anything to me you please. Even if by some accident you had killed a man, you could tell me and fear nothing.'

Manusso answered, 'I have killed no one, but I have seen another man slay your honour and your good name.'

'Speak your meaning clearly,' said Dimitrio, 'and don't beat about the bush.'

'Do you want me to tell it to you in a single word?' asked Manusso. 'Then listen and hear patiently what I have to say. Polissena, your wife, whom you hold so dear, all the time you're away, sleeps every night with a priest and takes her pleasure with him.'

'How can this be possible,' replied Dimitrio, 'seeing that she loves me so tenderly? She never fails to shed floods of tears on my chest and fill the air with her sighs every time I leave her. Even if I were to see this thing with my own eyes, I would never believe it.'

'Well, if you're as wise as I take you for,' said Manusso, 'you won't close your eyes to this, like so many besotted fools. I'll let you see with your own eyes and touch with your own hands everything I've told you.'

Dimitrio replied, 'I'm willing to do whatever you recommend to see in person what you've promised.'

Manusso continued, 'Well, you'll be convinced that everything I've said is true. But you have to be careful to keep your secret and to put a good face on the matter. Otherwise, you'll spoil the pheasant's tail. The next time you have to go abroad, just make believe to set sail, but instead of leaving Venice, come to my lodging as secretly as you can and I'll let you see everything.'

As soon as the day had come for Dimitrio to leave on his journey, he embraced his wife tenderly, bidding her to look after the house. Having said his goodbyes, he pretended to go aboard his ship, but returned and hid himself secretly in Manusso's house. As fate would have it, before two o'clock had struck, there was a great storm with rain so heavy that it seemed as though the heavens themselves would burst – rain that kept pouring the whole night long. The priest, who had already been notified of Dimitrio's departure and didn't worry a bit about wind and rain, was waiting for the time when he could visit his little sweetie. On giving the sign the door was opened, and as soon as he was inside, Polissena greeted him with a sweet and most savoury kiss. Her husband, concealed in the passage across the way, saw all that went on and, no longer able to contradict his friend's assertion, was completely overcome, bursting into tears with grief and indignation.

His friend then spoke to him, 'What do you think, now? Have you not seen something you'd never have believed? But stay collected and don't say a word, for if you hear what I have to say and do exactly as I direct you, you'll see something more. Take off the clothes you're wearing now, put on these beggar's rags, and smear your face and hands with dirt. Then go over to your own house as a tramp and in a disguised voice ask for a night's lodging. Very likely the servant, seeing how bad a night it is, will take pity on you and let you in. By doing this, you'll see other things you'd rather not have seen.'

Listening to his friend's counsel, Dimitrio doffed his clothes and put on the rags of a poor man who might well come to a house and, in the name of God, beg for lodging. Although rain was still pouring down, he went over to the door of his own abode; there he knocked three times, lamenting and sighing bitterly all the while. The serving-maid opened the window. 'Who's knocking down there?'

Dimitrio, in a broken and counterfeit voice, replied, "I'm a poor old man nearly drowned by the rain in need of a night's lodging." With this, the good-hearted girl, who felt as kindly towards the poor and miserable as her mistress felt towards her priest, ran to Polissena and begged her to grant the petition of this poor beggar all soaked with the rain and to give him shelter until he was warm and dry. 'He can draw some water for us,' she continued, 'make up the fire, and turn the spit so the fowls will be roasted sooner. Meanwhile, I can put the pot on, get the soup-plates ready, and attend to more pressing matters in the kitchen.'

The mistress agreed to this and the girl opened the door, called him in, and invited him to sit by the fire to turn the spit. At that time, the priest and Polissena came down from the bedroom into the kitchen holding one another by the hand and right away started to make fun of the poor old gent with his dirty face. Going right up to him, Polissena asked him his name.

'I am called Gramotiveggio, Signora.'

Polissena, when she heard this, began to laugh so heartily that you could have extracted her teeth. Then she threw her arms around the priest, crying out, 'Come, dear heart, let me kiss you.'

So poor Dimitrio had to look on while they embraced each other – leaving to your imagination what he must have felt in seeing his wife kissed and fondled in his very presence by the priest.

When the time had come for supper and the lovers were seated, the serving-maid returned to the kitchen and said to the poor man, 'Well now, father, I must tell you that my mistress has for a husband as good a man as you'll find in all Venice, one who gives her all she desires. God only knows where the poor man is in this dreadful weather, while she, the ungrateful hussy, cares nothing about him or his honour, blinded as she is by this lecherous passion – always cuddling with her lover and shutting the door to everybody except him. Well, I ask you, let's go softly over to the door of the next room and see how they behave themselves at the table.' Arriving at the door, they looked on as the two of them put tidbits into each other's mouth and engaged in all sorts of love play.

When the time came for going to bed, the two lovers retired to their room, launched into their playful dalliance, and at last took their harvest to the mill in earnest, breathing heavily and tossing their legs. Poor Dimitrio, all the while in bed in the adjoining chamber, could easily hear everything, never closing his eyes throughout the livelong night. As soon as morning had come, he warmly thanked the housekeeper for her company and the hospitality she had offered, and with that took his leave. Without being seen, he crossed over to the lodgings of his comrade Manusso, who said to him, laughing, 'Well, my friend, how goes the business? Maybe you've seen things you weren't looking for?'

'For certain I did,' answered Dimitrio, 'things I'd never have believed if I hadn't seen them with my own eyes. But I must be patient, since that's the way my rotten luck would have it.'

Manusso, who was a crafty fellow, then said, 'My friend, I think you should do what I'm about to tell you. Get yourself cleaned up and put on your own clothes. Then go right back to your house and make believe that luckily you hadn't set sail before the storm broke. Be careful that the priest doesn't get away, for as soon as you enter, he'll surely hide himself somewhere and stay put until the coast is clear. Meanwhile, invite all your wife's relations to a banquet at your house and then, once you've dragged the priest out of his hiding place in their presence, you can do whatever seems right to you.'

Greatly pleased with Manusso's advice, as soon as he could get himself out of his ragged clothes and into his own, he went over to his own house and knocked at the door. The servant, when she saw it was her master, ran quickly to Polissena, who was still in bed with the priest, and said to her, 'Signora, the master is back.'

When she heard these words, the mistress was beside herself with fright. Getting up with all the speed she could, she hid the priest, still in his nightshirt, in the coffer where she kept all her best clothes and then, in her fur-lined cloak and her bare feet, she ran to open the door to Dimitrio. 'My dearest husband,' she cried, 'you are so welcome back. I haven't closed my eyes for love of you, wondering always how fortune might be treating you. But God be praised, you have come back safe and sound.'

As soon as he entered the bedroom, Dimitrio said, 'Polissena, my love, I barely slept a wink last night on account of the bad weather, so I'm in dire need of a little rest. In the meantime, have the servant go to your brothers' house and invite them in our name to dine with us today.'

To this Polissena replied, 'Not today, but for another day we might invite them, seeing that it rains so heavily and the girl is busy calendering our shirts, tablecloths, and other linen wear.'

'Tomorrow the weather may improve and I will have to set forth,' said Dimitrio.

Polissena then said, 'But you might go yourself, or if you are too weary, go ask your friend Manusso to do you this service.'

'That's a good suggestion,' said Dimitrio and, having sent for his friend, he carried out the affair exactly as it had been agreed upon.

The brothers of Polissena then arrived and they all dined jovially together. When the table was cleared, Dimitrio declared, 'Good brothers-in-law of mine, I have never properly let you see my house, nor the fine apparel I have given to Polissena, my wife and your sister, so that in seeing it all you can judge how well I treat her. Now Polisenna, my dear wife, get up and show your brothers all around the house.'

Dimitrio then rose and showed them his storehouses full of wheat and timber, oil and other merchandise, butts of Malmsey, Greek, and other choice wines. Next he said to his wife, 'Bring out the rings and the pearls which I've bought you. Look at these fine emeralds in the little casket and the diamonds and rubies and other rings of value. What do you think of these, my brothers? Have I not treated your sister well?'

'We know it for a truth,' they replied together, 'and if we had not been satisfied with your worth, we would never have given our sister to you in marriage.'

But Dimitrio hadn't yet finished, for next he directed his wife to open all her coffers and to bring out her beautiful clothes. Polissena, her heart sinking with dread, replied, 'What need is there to open the coffers and show my clothes? Don't my brothers know well enough that you always let me dress myself most honourably and more sumptuously than our social condition requires?'

But Dimitrio, looking rather angry, insisted, 'Open straightway this coffer and that other one,' and while he spoke he went on showing all her wardrobe to her brothers.

When they came to the last of the coffers, the key to it was nowhere to be found for the good reason that the priest was hidden inside. Dimitrio, seeing the key was not forthcoming, took up a hammer and beat the lock so forcefully that it gave way and then he opened the lid.

It was impossible now for the trembling priest to go on hiding himself or escape being recognized by all the bystanders. The brothers of Polissena, when they saw how matters stood, were so angry that they would have knifed them both then and there, for the weapon was in their hands. But Dimitrio wouldn't allow it, thinking it too shameful to kill a man in his shirt, no matter how stout a fellow he was. So turning to the brothers he said, 'What do you all think now of this trull of a wife of mine, who was all my hope and happiness?'

Then to Polissena, 'Have I deserved any of this from you, vile woman? Who would stop me from cutting your miserable throat?' The wretched creature, who had nothing to offer by way of excuse, remained silent, because her husband told her to her face all he had seen of her doings the night before so clearly that there wasn't a word to say in defence.

Then turning to the priest, who stood there with his head bent down, 'Take your clothes, get out of my sight, and may evil fortune go with you. Don't let me ever see your face again, for I have no wish to dirty my hands in your accursed blood for the sake of a strumpet wife. Just get out of here, fast. Are you waiting for something more?' The priest, without opening his mouth, stole away, imagining as he went that Dimitrio and his brothers-in-law were right behind him with their knives drawn.

Dimitrio turned to his two kinsmen and said, 'Take your sister wherever you want, for I can't bear to look at her any longer.' The brothers were inflamed with rage. They took her home with them and instantly put her to death. When news of this was brought to Dimitrio, he cast his eyes upon the serving-maid, who was in fact a very comely woman, having kept in his mind her compassion for him. Soon after, he made her his wife, gave to her all the jewels and apparel of his first wife, and lived many a long year with her in joy and peace.

As soon as Arianna had brought her story to an end, the company all together declared that the virtue and self-control of the unlucky Dimitrio were most commendable, particularly when he had before his very eyes the priest who so palpably dishonoured him. Quite as noteworthy was the terror of the culprit, who, clad only in his nightshirt, and seeing the husband and brothers of his mistress close upon him, trembled like a leaf shaken in the wind. The Signora, perceiving that any discussion of the case might be long and excessive, called for silence and directed Arianna to give her enigma, whereupon, with a gracious manner and pleasant smile, she set it forth in these words:

Three jolly friends sat down to eat,
A merrier crew you could not meet.
They tried and emptied every dish,
For better fare they could not wish.
The valet next before them placed
A dish with three fat pigeons graced.
Each ate his pigeon, bones and all,
But pigeons twain were left withal.

This enigma seemed to the company to be too difficult to solve, and finally it was judged to be impossible, for no one saw how, after each had eaten his pigeon, two of the three could still remain on the board. But they didn't look for the snake that was hidden in the grass. Wherefore, seeing that the secret of her enigma had not been grasped and that the solution had escaped them all, Arianna turned with a subtle countenance towards the Signora and said, 'It seems to me, dear lady, that my enigma is not to be solved, and yet it is not so difficult that it can't easily be disentangled. Here is the answer: Out of the three jolly friends, one bore the name of Each. As they sat together at the same table, they ate as if they had been famished wolves, so that when, at the end of the feast, the valet brought them three roast pigeons, setting one before each, two out of the three revellers were so full they could eat no more, but the one whose name was Each finished his off, so there were two pigeons left when they rose from the table.'

The solution to this obscure riddle was greeted with great laughter and applause, for not one of the company could have solved it. The last story of the night now having been told, the Signora directed everyone to go home to rest, but to return again the ensuing evening under pain of incurring her sore displeasure. Then the torches were lighted, shedding their snow-white glow, by which the revellers were conducted down to the landing.

The End of the First Night

I.5 Commentary

Such a choice of subjects must invite the reader to wonder whether the principle dictating the ordering of the tales is not mere chance, for this little work is as fastened to the everyday events of the contemporary piazza as the preceding narrative is to the wonder tale. This story is pitched as a recent event, putatively at least, that took place in Venice. The extraordinary that happens to ordinary people told with realistic economy is characteristic of the *novella*. The plot deals with the painful but compulsive need to know the truth about the sexual fidelity of a spouse and the gathering of the incontrovertible evidence of betrayal. This story is memorable largely for the means by which the husband, alerted by a nosey neighbour (or genuinely true friend), seeks that confirmation by sheltering as a tramp in his own house. We think his thoughts for him as he endures all he witnesses with an excess of self control. Despite the contrast with the preceding tale, this one too was perhaps a part of the folk culture of the Veneto. That thesis is strengthened by analogous works collected in the late nineteenth century, for such a storytelling tradition necessitated historical roots. By circular reasoning, Straparola's work indicates that the story was at least as old as the sixteenth century, this becomes a necessity on the assumption that such tales do not have multiple origins – but how much older is a moot point, for nothing resembling it precedes it, and mention is made that it was 'not heard in former times.'

That vacuum allows for a return of Straparola the author. But a problem may arise when several such tales in the *Notti* lacking prior sources are also discovered to have folkloric sequels, for that, by default, grants a founder's status to Straparola for them all. In short, if Straparola did not borrow from story types current in his time that were themselves the narrative antecedents to those collected in the nineteenth century, then he must be the author of the sources to all those nineteenth-century tales, giving all of them literary origins in the image of the folk tale. That would entail a rather elaborate hypothesis about Straparola as author, for the present story preserves several folk tale characteristics. The language of interiority is not easily generated by the oral culture and Straparola shows no apparent inclination to improve upon what he putatively found, despite ample opportunity. Dimitrio's feelings while witnessing his wife's inconstancy are left largely to innuendo. Even his intentions in gathering evidence against his spouse are unspecified. It is the neighbour who assumes the responsibility for the plot to call in the brothers, corner the priest, bring him out into the open through a sham house inspection in the presence of the kin, and let the raw instincts of the clan take care of the outcome. Dimitrio is a mere bystander to the fell and final justice administered in the name of family honour, although an assumed thirst for revenge makes him complicit in the deeds while avoiding personal responsibility. Meanwhile, the celerity with which the loyal maid, outraged by her mistress's sexual cavorting, and the liberated husband discover their mutual attraction is characteristic only of folk narratives. Such rapidity exceeds the contractedness of the most efficient *novella.*

The resulting tale is one of raw instinctual justice, a ritual performance by family members in the name of honour. Such a ritual is reiterated in the tale of Malgherita Spolatina, who likewise dares death for love (VII.2), although in a rather different key, and perishes in the name of family honour. Tellingly, her story wins pity, an emotion that Aristotle imposed upon the definition of tragedy. Malgherita is purified by her death, although she had fallen in love with a hermit living on an island; she manages to steal the point of view as a Hero swimming to meet her Leander, whereas Polissena is a false-teared hypocrite, an ungrateful wife, whose hedonism knows no limits. That she is married to a merchant whom she does not love, that he is often away, that he encumbers her with expensive gifts, rich clothes, and precious jewels, brings her no redemption. Dimitrio is a consummate provider and it is on these grounds that he justifies his marital entitlements in the eyes of her brothers. Polissena has been sold to a dynastic union, yet she is able to fashion herself as no more than a little vixen. The tale, from the outset, assumes a moral stance in those terms – an expression of male anxiety in the name of marriage and the clan. Must subversive love always find justification? Must the language of the emotions concerning exclusive partners and family honour always be denied? After all, Polissena is no worse than the many wives who do successfully hide their lovers, dupe their husbands, and even run away. Erminione will outwit Hippolito and prevail (IV.2), just as Genobbia does her husband Raimondo (IV.4), and Tia does Cecato (V.4). All three are stories of adultery, all three deal with cuckolded husbands and scotfree lovers, and not one is concerned with the demands of justice and social order, or the entitlements of matrimony and its solemn oaths. They deal with other economies of desire and the erotic rewards for cunning and wit. But Polissena has simply had all her options denied. The deeds of the priest are known, his presence is beyond equivocation, and his hiding place is revealed. Her empirical world is without ambiguity, the witnesses are present, and they have an emotionally charged involvement with her deeds, for her brothers can barely prevent themselves from murdering her on the spot. That manifestation of human emotions is as true to the species in its phylogenetic programming as all the longings of love and escape. In that regard, the story profiles a bold truth.

The tales replicating the narrative design of the present story, as gathered by the nineteenth-century folklorists, imply a history presumably centuries old, one that includes, arguably, the version upon which the present story is based through whatever field notes or memory and transcription processes Straparola employed. One is entitled 'Li dui cumpari' (two close friends [as close as godparents]) in Giuseppe Pitrè's collection of Sicilian fables. Another from Sicily and a third from Venice or the Veneto imply the existence of the many others required to fill in the narrative and geographical spaces that separate them from Straparola's lone early version.[110] There may have been hundreds of

110 *The Collected Sicilian Folk and Fairy Tales of Giuseppe Pitrè*, ed. and trans. Jack Zipes and Joseph Russo, 2 vols. (New York: Routledge, 2009), vol. I, pp. 619–22. In this version it is the husband's apprentice who makes the bet with his master who says to him as he hides in the chest, 'And you who are there inside, You can hear the whole story, So give me the money and the mule.' See also, *The Collected Sicilian Folk*

variants on the story type. 'The Two Close Friends' has a substantial preamble that is not part of Straparola's rendition. These buddies and near neighbours, one childless, one with many children, discuss their wives with their contrasting displays of affection. He who was without a large family was pampered and bussed, whereas the other was largely ignored by a wife preoccupied with the duties of raising a big family. Envious of his mate, the latter began to abuse his wife, even making pretexts to beat her before explaining his sense of privation. But the woman came to her own defence with a knock-out blow in revealing that her neighbour's wife's show of affection was merely a smokescreen to her illicit affair with the priest, while she, loyal to the core, felt no need to practice the hypocrisy of show-love. Her husband needed to witness this with his own eyes, and he was not disappointed when the jolly fat priest showed up. Thereafter, the priest and the neighbour's wife made their amorous proceedings audible to him for hours. Not much time went by before this man was again listening to his friend gloating over the affections of his wife, making it impossible for him, with his ocular proof, to refrain from laying a bet with his *cumpari* over his wife's fidelity and the attentions of a member of the clergy. At that juncture, the story proceeds as in the present tale when the cuckolded husband is advised to have himself transported into his own house, this time in a chest. Here, it is the friend who disguises himself as a beggar in order to prompt and witness the showdown. At this juncture, a number of toasts spoken aloud and laced with double meaning provide the beggar with an opportunity to remind his friend hidden in the chest that he has lost the bet and that he will soon be paying up what he owes, both money and a mule. In this tale, the dynastic revenge and the husband's marriage to the maid have disappeared. This cuckolded husband exacts his own revenge by erupting from the chest, his cane in hand, beating everything hard about the priest into soft pulp ('e zoccu avia duru cci lu fici moddu') before levelling similar attentions upon his wife. In this rustic setting, the adultery is taken more in stride, in the spirit of the *fabliaux*, while paying off the bet becomes the sorest point. In spite of

and Fairy Tales of Giuseppe Pitrè, vol. II, p. 916. The second Sicilian version was published by Pitrè: 'Li trii brinnisi' (The three toasts), in *Otto fiabe e novelle siciliane raccolte dalla bocca del popolo* (Bologna: Fava & Garagnani, 1873). The Venetian version, entitled 'La mugier d'un pescaor' (The fisherman's wife), was collected by Domenico Giuseppe Bernoni in *Fiabe e novelle popolari veneziane* (Venice: Fontana-Ottolini, 1873), pp. 33–6; new ed. (Venice: Filippi, 1969).

these many alterations, the core of the narrative known to Straparola is entirely visible three centuries later.

Bernoni's transcription in Venetian dialect tells of a priest who waits his turn with the wife, asking her often when her husband would be going fishing. Once the priest is in the house and food is cooking, a storm blows up and an old man comes along begging for shelter. He is taken in for pity and treated to scenes of kissing and squeezing between the lovers. When the husband also turns up, the wine, cheese, and rabbit are stashed here and there and the priest goes under the bed. When the old one is asked for a story in the presence of the husband and wife, he makes predictions, as though by divination, just where such things as wine, cheese, and meat might be found, each prediction proving amazingly true. Ultimately he comes to the priest under the bed, who is driven out with a sound thrashing before the stick comes down on the wife. Then the food goes down the hatches of those for whom it was not intended. This is Straparola's story retold with economy if not haste. It follows in the tradition concerning which Straparola's version is the only witness prior to the nineteenth century.

This story contains examples of those striking literary quotations that characterize Straparola's style, manifesting his peculiar capacity to draw out verbatim from a nearly photographic memory, or from a commonplace book of quotable quotes, or directly from their literary sources, phrases of varying lengths which serve the text as though they were written specifically for it. This subtle little intertextual game, Straparola plays for his own secret reasons, for the cited bits hardly exceed what he could easily have paraphrased for himself. When Polissena heard the name of Gramotiveggio (Gramo ti veggio 'misery, you I see'), she laughed so that her teeth appeared, then she called to her lover-priest, 'Deh, anima mia dolce, lasciatimi basciare' (come, my sweet soul and let me kiss thee), a line taken from Boccaccio's *Decameron,* Day IX, story 5, sect. 59 (IX.5.59). The lovers, once in the room 'cominciorono macinare a ricolta' (start taking their harvest to the mill), an echo of the *Decameron* VIII.2.23, while the very next phrase, 'forte soffiavano e menavano le calcole' (breathing heavily and shaking the legs), may relate to the *Decameron,* VIII.9.26. Straparola, without borrowing narrative ideas, makes use of this work as an encyclopedia of phrases and not-so-quotable quotations. The opening discussion on the frequent disparity and asymmetry between lovers and the arrival of sudden jealousy that torments lives and gives no rest seems to have taken its inspiration from Pietro Bembo's *Gli*

Asolani.[111] This is, moreover, the first of several *novelle* in the collection in which eating is a prelude to love making (see III.5, V.4, VIII.3, and XII.1 for further examples). In the present story, however, it is the husband in his beggarly guise who prepares the food. This work also calls for a second meal which serves as a tribunal; it is the wife's last before being slain by her brothers for her infidelity.[112]

---

111 *Gli Asolani*, ed. Carlo Dionisotti (Turin: Einaudi, 1966), bk. I, sect. 12, where Straparola's 'disavaglianza' is echoed by Bembo's 'disagguaglianze,' p. 22, and bk. I, sect. 30, where Bembo speaks of the trials of 'subita gelosia,' p. 50.

112 See Corinne Lucas, 'De la chronique à la nouvelle: l'art de faire taire la faim,' in *La table et ses dessous*, ed. Adelin Charles Fiorato and Anna Fontes Baratto (Paris: Presses de la Sorbonne Nouvelle, 1999), pp. 168–9.

The Second Night

Already Phoebus had dipped his golden chariot wheels in the salt billows of the Indian Sea and withdrawn the splendour of his shining rays from the earth, already his sister the crescent moon had shot her clear and flashing beams in sovereign wise through the dusk of night and the gay, sparkling stars had patterned the heavens with their points of light when the same honourable and courtly company made their way once more to the accustomed meeting to continue their pleasant recreation. And when they were all seated according to their several degrees, Signora Lucrezia set out the terms for this night in the same order as before. Because five of the young ladies still had their stories to tell, the Signora asked the Trevisan to write their names on pieces of paper and place them in the golden vase and then to draw them out one after the other as they had done the previous evening. The Trevisan was quick to follow her command. As it turned out, the first slip that was drawn from the vase carried the name of the fair Isabella, the second that of Fiordiana, the third of Lionora, the fourth of Lodovica, and the fifth of Vicenza. Then the flutes struck up a melody and they all began to dance in a circle, Antonio Molino and Lionora leading the revels. The men as well as the women were laughing so merrily it's as though I can hear them still. The dancing once ended, they all sat down and the damsels sang an affectionate *canzone* in praise of the Signora.

What once we sang we sing today,
And ever will we tune our lay
To praise thee, lady, as the queen
Of beauty and of all our scene;
The loftiest theme the poet sings,
The sweetest chord that shakes the strings,
The fairest shape the painter gives,
The peer of all in thee survives.

He who never owns the spell
Which moves us now thy praise to tell,
Wins no kindly word from me.
He the bliss shall never see

That flows on earth from faithful love,
And waits on spirits blest above.

At the end of this most pleasant song, Isabella, chosen by lot to start the second night's revels, began her relation of the following story.

II. Fable 1
The Pig Prince

ISABELLA

Galeotto, king of Anglia, had a son born in the shape of a pig. This son marries three wives, and, in the end, having shed his swinish appearance, becomes a handsome young man and is afterwards known as King Pig.

Fair ladies, if a man were to spend a thousand years in rendering thanks to his Creator for having made him in the form of a human being and not of a brute beast, he could not say enough in gratitude. This thought brings to my mind the tale of one who was born a pig, yet afterwards became a handsome youth, and was known ever after by all men as King Pig.

You may well remember, dear ladies, that Galeotto, king of Anglia, was a man equally blessed with worldly wealth and with gifts of the mind. His wife was Ersilia, the daughter of Matthias, king of Hungary, a princess who outshone all the other ladies of her time in virtue and beauty. Galeotto was a wise king, so ruling his land that no man could reasonably raise a complaint against him. But though they had now been married several years, still they had no child, which caused considerable unhappiness to them both. One day, as Ersilia was walking in her garden plucking flowers, suddenly she felt overcome with weariness, and seeing nearby a place covered in fresh green grass, she sat herself down and, soothed by the sweet singing of the birds in the trees, she fell asleep.

Then by good fortune, while she slept three splendid fairies flew past. Beholding the sleeping queen, they halted and gazed upon her beauty, and then advised among themselves how they might render her both inviolable and enchanted. Once in agreement, the first spoke out, 'I will that no man shall ever do her harm, and that the next time she lies with her husband, she conceives and bears a son who will have no equal for beauty in the entire world.'

Then the second chimed in, 'I will that no one shall ever have power to hurt her, and that the prince she bears shall be gifted with every virtue and charm under the sun.'

The third then added, 'And I will that she shall be the richest and wisest among women, but that the son she conceives will be born all covered with a pig's skin, with a pig's looks and manners, and that he remains in this condition until he has been three-times married.'

As soon as the three fairies had flown away, Ersilia awoke, quickly arose, and went back to the palace, taking with her the flowers she had plucked. Not many days had passed before she knew she was with child, and when the time of her delivery had come, she gave birth to a son whose members were those of a pig. When news of this prodigy came to the ears of the king and queen, they sorely lamented such an event, and the king, bearing in mind how saintly and wise his queen had been, and hoping to spare her the shame of this monstrous birth, felt moved on many occasions to have this offspring of hers killed and cast into the sea. But after debating this in his mind, and considering that this son was of his own blood and begetting, whatever he might be, he put aside the cruel intent he had been harbouring. Seized with pity and grief, he decided that the son should be brought up and nurtured like a rational being and not as a brute beast.

The child, therefore, being nursed with the greatest of care, would often run up to the queen and put his little snout in her lap and his little paws on her knees, and she would always caress him, stroking his bristly back with her hand, embracing and kissing him as though he were human. Then he would wiggle his tail and by clear signs show that his mother's caresses were much to his liking.

The pigling, when he grew older, began to talk like a child and to wander abroad in the city. But whenever he came near any dirt or filthiness, he would always wallow in it in the manner of pigs and so return home all befouled and covered in mire. Then, running up to the king and queen, he would rub his sides against their fair garments, defiling them with all manner of dirt and filth. Yet, because they had no other son but him, they took it all in good patience.

One day he came home covered with mud and muck, in his customary way, and lay down on his mother's elegant dress and said with a grunt, 'Mother, I want to get married.'

When the queen heard this, she replied, 'Don't talk nonsense. What maiden would ever take you for a husband? Do you think that any noble or knight would give his daughter to such a dirty and unsavoury thing as you?'

But he kept on grunting that he must have a wife of one sort or another. Not knowing how to manage him in this matter, the queen asked the king, 'What on earth should we do about this? Our son wishes to marry, but where shall we find anyone who will take him for a husband?'

Not long after, the pig came back once more to his mother, snorting loudly, 'I must have a wife, and I will never leave you in peace until you get me the one I saw today, because she's the one I really like.'

This girl was the daughter of a poor woman who had three on her hands, each one of them a miracle of loveliness. When the queen heard this, she had the poor woman brought before her, along with the eldest daughter, and said, 'Good mother, you are poor and burdened with children. If you will agree to what I shall say to you, you will become rich without more ado. I have this pig son you see here, who yearns to marry your oldest daughter. Pay no mind to the fact that he's a pig, but think of the king and of me, and remember that your daughter will inherit this entire kingdom when the king and I are dead.'

Upon hearing the queen's words, the maiden's thoughts were greatly troubled, and blushing as red as a rose for shame, she said that on no account would she listen to the queen's proposal. But the poor mother urged her so pressingly that at last she yielded. So when the pig came home all covered with filth as usual, his mother said to him, 'My son, we have found you a wife just as you desired.' And then she had the bride brought in, who, by this time, had been dressed in sumptuous regal attire, and presented her to the pig prince. Seeing how lovely and desirable she was, he was filled with joy. All foul and stinking as he was, he jumped round and about her, attempting by his pawing and nuzzling to show some signs of his affection. But when she found he was soiling her beautiful dress, she thrust him aside, whereupon the pig said to her, 'Why do you push me away? Have I not had these garments made for you myself?'

But she answered disdainfully, 'No, neither you nor any other of the whole kingdom of hogs could ever have made this for me.'

And when the time for going to bed was come, the young girl said to herself, 'What am I to do with this foul beast? This very night, while he lies in his first sleep, I will kill him.'

The pig prince, who was not far away, heard these words, but said nothing, and when the two retired to their chamber he got into the sumptuous bed, stinking and dirty as he was, lifting up the delicate sheets with his filthy paws and abominable snout. At last, after befouling everything with stinking muck, he lay down by his wife, who very soon fell asleep. But the pig, only pretending to sleep, presently gave her such savage blows on the breast with his sharp hoofs that he killed her instantly.

The next morning he got up early, as usual, and went into the pasture to eat and get dirty. The queen, meanwhile, went to visit her daughter-in-law, and to her great grief found that the pig had killed her. After returning from feeding and wandering about the city, he said in reply to the queen's bitter reproaches that he had only dealt with his wife as she had intended to deal with him, and then departed in a mightily bad humour. Not many days had passed before the pig prince again began to beseech the queen to allow him to marry one of the other sisters, and when the queen refused at first to listen to his petition he persisted in his purpose, threatening to smash everything in the whole palace if he couldn't have her for a wife. When she heard this, the queen went to the king and told him everything, and he answered that perhaps it would be wiser to kill their ill-fated offspring before he created more fatal mischief in the city. But the queen felt all the tenderness of a mother towards him in spite of his brutish nature and could not endure the thought of doing away with him. So once more she summoned the poor woman to the palace, together with her second daughter, and held a long conversation with her, begging her to give her daughter in marriage. At last the girl assented to take the pig prince for a husband. Yet her fate was no happier that her sister's, for the bridegroom killed her as he had killed his first bride, and then fled headlong from the palace.

Upon his return, dirty as usual and smelling so foully that no one could get near him, the king and queen severely reprimanded him for the evil deed he had done, but again he cried out boldly that if he hadn't killed her first, she would have killed him. As had happened before, in a very short time the pig began to importune his mother to let him have the youngest sister for his wife, who was much more beautiful than either of the others. And when his request was repeatedly refused, he became more insistent than ever, and with violent and bloodthirsty words he began to threaten the queen's life unless he could have the young girl in marriage. The queen, when she heard this shameful and unnatural speech, was nearly broken-hearted and half out of her mind. But putting all other considerations aside, she called for the poor woman and her third daughter, named Meldina, and said to her, 'Meldina, my child, I desire that you should take the pig prince for a husband. Pay no heed to him, but think of his father and me. Then, if you will be prudent and bear patiently with him, you may be the happiest woman in the entire world.'

Meldina answered this speech with a serene and grateful smile on her face, saying how perfectly content she was to do as the queen had asked, and thanked her humbly for consenting to choose her as a daughter-in-law. Seeing that she had nothing of her own in the world, it was indeed great good fortune that a poor girl like her should become the daughter-in-law of a potent monarch. When she heard this modest and amiable reply, the queen could not keep back her tears for the happiness she felt. But she was afraid nevertheless that the same fate might be in store for Meldina that had fallen to her sisters.

Now when the new bride had been clothed in rich attire and decked with jewels, and was waiting for the dear bridegroom, the pig prince came in filthier and muddier than ever. But she spread out her rich gown and besought him to lie down by her side. Even the queen urged her to thrust him away, but she would not consent to this and said:

> 'Your most pious and venerable majesty,
> There are three wise sayings that I remember to have heard.
> The first is that whatever cannot be found,
> It is the greatest folly to go searching for.
> The second is that we should not believe everything we hear,
> But only those things which bear the marks of sense and reason.
> The third is that if you've gotten hold of some rare and precious treasure,
> Cherish it, and never let it slip from your hands.'

The pig prince was wide awake all this while and heard everything she said, so that when her speech was finished, he got up and kissed her on the face and neck and bosom and shoulders with his tongue, nor was she backward in returning his caresses, thereby arousing in him a warm love for her. As soon as the time had come for retiring for the night, the bride went to bed and waited for her dear spouse, in spite of his dirt and stench, and with his coming she lifted up the coverlet and invited him to lie near her and put his head upon the pillow, covering him carefully with the blankets and drawing the curtains so that he would feel no cold. When morning came, the pig prince got up, leaving the mattress all covered in manure, and ranged abroad to pasture. Soon after, the queen went to the bride's chamber, expecting to find that she had met with the same fate as her sisters. But when she saw her lying in the bed all defiled with filthiness and rot yet looking pleased and contented, she thanked God for this favour – that her son had at last found a spouse to his liking.

One day not long after, when the pig prince was in pleasant conversation with his wife, he said to her, 'Meldina, my beloved wife, if I could be entirely sure that you can keep a secret, I'd tell you now one of mine – something I've kept hidden until now. I know you to be very prudent and wise, and that you love me truly. For that reason I wish to share my secret with you.'

'You may tell it to me in all safety, if you're so inclined,' said Meldina, 'for I promise never to reveal it to anyone without your consent.'

Being now certain of his wife's discretion and fidelity, straightway he shook off the foul and dirty pig's skin from his body and revealed himself to be a handsome and well-shaped young man, and all that night he remained closely enfolded in the arms of his beloved wife. But he charged her solemnly to keep silence about this wonder she had seen, for the time had not yet come for delivery from his miserable state. So whenever he left the bed, he donned once more the dirty pig's hide. I leave you to imagine for yourselves how joyful Meldina was when she discovered that, instead of a pig, she had won for herself a handsome and gallant young prince. Not long thereafter she proved to be with child, and when the time of her delivery had come, she gave birth to a handsome baby boy. The king and queen were overjoyed, especially when they found that the newborn child was indeed entirely human in form and not a beast.

But the burden of the strange and ponderous secret that had been confided to Meldina began to weigh upon her, so that one day she went to her mother-in-law and said, 'Gracious queen, when first I married your son, I deemed that I was married to a beast, but now I find that you have given to me as my husband the handsomest, worthiest, and most gallant young man ever born into the world. For I can assure you that when he comes into our bedroom to lie by my side, he casts off his dirty hide and leaves it on the ground and is changed into a graceful and comely youth. No one would believe this unless they saw it with their own eyes.'

When the queen heard these words, she thought that her daughter-in-law must be jesting, but Meldina persisted in the truth of her words. The queen demanded how she might witness this thing with her own eyes, and Meldina replied, 'Come to my bedroom tonight after we've fallen into our first sleep. The door will be open and you will find that what I tell you is true.'

That same night, when the appointed time had come and all were gone to rest, the queen had torches lit. Accompanied by the king, she went to her son's room, and when she had entered, she saw the pig's skin lying on the floor in the corner of the room. Then, going to the bedside, she found therein a handsome young man with Meldina lying in his arms. When they saw this, the king and the queen were both greatly delighted and the king gave an order that before anyone left the chamber, the pig's hide be torn to shreds. They were so pleased by their son's recovery that they nearly died for joy.

King Galeotto, when he saw that he had so fine a son and a grandchild as well, laid aside his crown and his royal robes and placed his son in his own stead after having him crowned with the greatest pomp. Yet he was ever afterwards known as King Pig. Thus, to the great contentment of all the people, the young king began his reign and he lived long and happily with Meldina, his beloved wife.

No sooner was Isabella's story finished than the whole company broke into laughter at the notion of the pig prince, all foul and smeared with mud as he was, kissing his beloved spouse and lying by her side. 'But let us cease our laughter,' cried Signora Lucrezia, 'so that Isabella's enigma may be duly propounded.' There and then Isabella set forth her riddle with a smile.

I prithee, sir, to give to me,
What never did belong to thee,
Or ever will, what though thy span
Of life exceed the wont of man.
Dream not this treasure to attain,
Thy longing will be all in vain;
But if you deem me such a prize,
And pine for me with loving eyes,
Give me this boon, my wish fulfil,
For you can grant it if you will.

When Isabella had thus set forth her subtle enigma, the listeners were all bewildered, for no one could understand how a man could give what he didn't possess or ever could possess. But Isabella, when she saw that they were greatly puzzled, finally said with much good taste and judgment, 'Don't be astonished, my good friends, for without any doubt a man can give to a woman that which he has not or ever will have, and that is a husband, which no man will ever have, but which is easy for him to give to a lady.'

The whole company received this solution with much applause, and when silence had once more been imposed upon the assembly, Fiordiana, sitting next to Isabella, arose from her seat and said with a merry smile, 'Signora, and gentle folks all, doesn't it seem appropriate to you that Signor Molino, our good friend, should enliven this honourable company with one of his merry conceits? I say this not because I want to escape the task of telling my own story – for in fact I have more than one ready – but because I feel that a tale told with all his customary grace and style would give the company the greater delight. As you well know, he is ingenious and full of wit, and gifted with all those good parts which pertain to a man of breeding. As for ourselves, dear ladies, it is better that we should ply our needles than be always telling stories.'

All agreed with Fiordiana's thoughtful and timely words and applauded them warmly. Then the Signora cast her eyes towards Molino, saying, 'Come, Signor Antonio, it is now your turn to favour us with an example of your graceful wit.' With this, she signalled him to begin. Molino, who had not reckoned on being called to recite on that evening, first gave his thanks to Fiordiana for the flattering words she had spoken of him, and then in obedience to the Signora's wishes he began his fable.

II.1 Commentary

The story of the pig prince enters the literary record as a Brahmin tale of metempsychosis in which a human soul enclosed within a beast recovers its human body through a process of ritual, magic, or expiation. That fact is a reminder that ancient Aryan mythmakers framed the human condition in close proximity with the animal kingdom and imagined as possible all manner of literal metamorphoses from higher forms to lower and back again, in keeping with the doctrine of metempsychosis or the transmigration of souls. The traditional direction was the relocation of the souls of the deceased into the bodies of animals, which in turn gave birth to the beast fable in attempting to imagine the inner lives of such composite creatures, sometimes driven by human desires and sometimes by the instinctual natures of the host. Thus King Pig, the enchanted prince, longs for a wife, yet rolls himself compulsively in the mud. As the story type progressed through time from myth to fable to the 'novelistic' fairy tale, the meaning of the husband as beast in relation to his parents, wife, or wives likewise progressed. Invariably, however, his nature is conceived as a curse because, as Straparola's narrator states at the outset, if a being is made in human form rather than that of a brute beast, it is worth a thousand years of thanks to the Creator – an interesting variation on such Jewish benedictions as, 'Blessed are You, Lord our God, King of the Universe, Who did not make me a slave, a gentile, or a woman.' The story's imperative is to find liberation for a human soul from the curse of animal incarnation. Andrew Lang notes that 'there is no Hellenic tradition on the subject of a human mother bearing a beast-child,' but that 'German and Romaic stories on the theme abound.'[1] He describes such a myth as being natural to primitive men, but 'revolting to later feeling.' Stories of that nature demonstrate their antiquity in reflecting traces of totemism; they predate the myths of the higher elemental, seasonal, and sky gods. Among the surviving tales within the genre is 'The Frog-King,' which relates how a king's daughter marries a frog who is ultimately changed into a handsome young man – a comedy of self-recovery. The myth is remarkably old in that it was 'made before the separation of races,' after which time it was carried to all parts of the world.[2] Embedded in the narrative genes of Straparola's tale is a memory of the struggle for purgatorial purification and redemption; in its future is the struggle for the psychological reform that makes a man fit company for female society. One is vestigial, the other in ovo. A moment of crux in its history came about when all such misfortunes were attributed to the capricious interference of the fairies.

Max Müller found absurd the central concept of the prince as a frog and struggled to find a more emblematically dignified reading by associating the frog with the sun.[3] But this is no help in explaining why the same story also employs serpents, donkeys, wild boars, domestic pigs, and hedgehogs. By Straparola's time, the fable still retained the generic birth curse and concluding deliverance from beast to man through the destruction of the animal covering, but in further imagining the domestic component at a 'lower,' more realistic, mimetic level, it also fostered

1 *Peasant Customs and Savage Myths: Selections from the British Folklorists*, ed. Richard Dorson, 2 vols. (Chicago: University of Chicago Press, 1968), vol. I, pp. 199–200.

2 Andrew Lang, in *Peasant Customs and Savage Myths*, vol. I, p. 201. Its diffusion is marked by a Zulu version reported by Henry Callaway, *Nursery Tales, Traditions and Histories of the Zulu* (1868; reprint, Nendeln: Kraus Reprints, 1970), pp. 241–8.

3 Friedrich Max Müller, *Chips from a German Workshop* (London: Longmans, 1875), vol. II, p. 46.

a certain delight in picturing a ménage between a girl and a barnyard animal in which filth is introduced into the marriage bed as a kind of love test – one that entails a mastery over disgust that Freudians might interpret as overcoming sex nausea. Less pointedly, it is about coming to terms with the immediate physical earthiness of cohabitation in terms rather unflattering to males, but the onus of accommodation for which is placed on the girls by overcoming their prissiness. This can be turned into one of real psychological barriers to a happy union, as it is for Amoret and Scudamour in bk. III of Spenser's *Fairie Queene.* Just when this feature appeared in the folk tradition is impossible to say, but Straparola confirms its presence, along with the fairies, by the early sixteenth century. More generally, the tale served as an emblematic depiction of the necessary adjustments within the couple whereby wifely tolerance and compassion ultimately reform the savage beast, allowing him to escape from his arrested self. That feature was later enhanced in the 'Beauty and the Beast' tradition in which the beast with a potential for kindness finds his better self through the ministrations of a sympathetic woman. Regarding the construction of gender roles from 'The Pig Prince' to 'Beauty and the Beast,' the subservient wife and the brutal husband, feminist readers may find more to loathe than to love. In Lewis Seifert's words, 'Straparola insinuates that this hero is always already a man waiting for a woman to assume her rightful submissive place beneath him so that he can assert his dominance.'[4] The deadly pig has been compared to Bluebeard and called a 'serial killer' ('meurtrier "en série"'), even though for Straparola's protagonist it was kill or be killed. But not every 'Beast' is a spoiled pig with a brutal streak and animal appetites struggling to become human; some are true gentlemen merely cursed by ugliness and deformity. On a comparative basis, our story is somewhere in between.[5]

The present story type is referred to by folklorists as the 'beast-bridegroom' (ATU 425A), with its counterpart or mirror reversal in the

4 'Pig or Prince? Murat, d'Aulnoy and the Limits of Civilized Masculinity,' in *High Anxiety: Masculinity in Crisis in Early Modern France*, ed. Kathleen P. Long (Kirksville, MO: Truman State University Press, 2002), pp. 203–4.

5 For an engaging discussion of the early French fairy tales as free creations in dialogue with related stories, in opposition to the historico-geographical approach of the folklorists and the confinement of these works as extended folk tales, see Ute Heidmann and Jean-Michel Adam, *Textualité et intertextualité des contes* (Paris: Garnier classique, 2010), esp. pp. 33–80. For the allusion to serial killers, see p. 127.

tales of serpent wives, melusines, and swan maidens who are captured, submit themselves to domesticity and motherhood, but regain their freedom and their original animal forms when their husbands violate the conditions by which they are held.[6] The beast-bridegroom type was apt for diverse development along thematic lines, whether in emphasizing the liberation from ugliness (as in the 'Beauty and the Beast' group), from fairy enchantment (as in the 'Frog Prince' group), the imposition of a taboo (as in the 'Bluebeard' group), or the wife's expiatory quest (as in the 'Cupid and Psyche' group). The present tale's relationship to stories in this last group is implied by the injunction to secrecy which the third wife ignores without consequence – a non-sequitur quite out of keeping with the logic of folk tales unless her betrayal leads to adverse consequences – which, of course, it does in Psyche's arduous pursuit of her absent mate. There are narrative reasons, however, for suppressing the sequel to the broken taboo, creating a rebalanced tale that concludes with the wife's contribution to the removal of the hideous animal covering. It becomes the moment of redemption in the emerging 'Beauty and the Beast' group. This development within the folk tradition had produced concurrent forms of the story by the sixteenth century, which is apparent through a simple comparison of the stories by Straparola and Basile (outlined below). In brief, closure in the burning or shedding of the skin (as in the Eastern tales), rather than in 'Psyche's Quest,' was a recentring of the story that would attract the fairy-tale writers, whether directly or through Straparola's literary mediation.

An inaugural sub-motif is that of the barren parents desperate for a child. It expresses a desire and hence a vulnerability that provokes a reaction from the sub-world of magic, devils, or fairies, three of whom appear in Straparola's tale to offer two blessings and a curse. That was new to his source tradition and a singular feature, for it is one of the few times in Straparola in which the benevolent and malevolent wills emanating from the fairy kingdom set the terms for the ensuing action and its plot. For some, such as Jan Ziolkowsky and Ruth Bottigheimer, Straparola's wonder tales also qualify as 'fairy tales,' but this one, by dint of actual fairies, takes the lead in that campaign. even though the fairies do not return to protect the queen as promised, or preside over the removal of

6 For this tradition, see Barbara Fass Leavy, *In Search of the Swan Maiden: A Narration on Folklore and Gender* (New York: New York University Press, 1994). 'The serpent prince' is ATU type 433.

the curse. Sometimes the spell is shaped out of the parent's own words, as when, in the Grimms' tale, 'Hans My Hedgehog,' a father will accept a son on any terms, adding rhetorically and figuratively 'even if he's a hedgehog' – which, of course, is the form in which his son is born by dint of the magic power of the words in the curse. Typically, the mother leaves the palace, wanders into nature, falls asleep, dreams, and meets with apparitions who determine the destiny of the child and who are sometimes themselves the agents of conception, as in the story of Biancabella (III. 3), whose father and twin sister are both serpents (chthonic creatures representing the good earth). Spenser adapts the myth in *The Fairie Queene* (III. vi) when Chrysogonee exposes her womb to the sun and gives birth to Amoret and Belphoebe. This fairyland accretion is a continuing part of the process that distances the tale from its original myth, for it is the idiosyncratic logic and playful conditions of the fairies, operating outside the Christian world order, that define the terms of reversal: the pig prince must marry three times before he can be released from the spell. Little wonder this story was taken up later by the founders of the French *conte de fées*; the fairies were already there.

In relation to these conditions, the tale becomes for the characters a set of adverse circumstances and contrary natures, a test of character, an initiation rite, and a riddle to be decoded through creative provisional thinking. It takes three sisters to get it right, as in the casket game in which those who choose incorrectly must forfeit their lives. The tale proceeds as a failed *Bildungsroman* of sorts in which the pig is nurtured by a loving mother, indulged in his filthy ways, and remains so arrested in his development that he is not only a monstrous birth but a monster child. There follows another archetypal contest between paternal deception leading to the child's near destruction and the mother's instinctual right to nurture her child, however deformed. With the prince's maturation comes the crisis of puberty, sexuality, and marriage in the context of a royal dynasty. The kingdom is used as bait to attract wives from the poorest class because no aristocratic woman would marry a pig. That motif too is new to Straparola's sources, thereby creating another of his tales of rising fortunes from poverty to riches – although at fatal risk to the first two candidates, who are insensitive, ambitious, and cruel. Thus the tale is not only a contest between an affection-craving male and vain, exploitative brides, but a tale of unequal marriage and the continuity of a royal household brought down to an awkward fairy tale in which the royals are obliged to pledge their kingdom to paupers. Meanwhile, in the marriage bed itself, there is a fight to the finish for control within the couple, symbolized by attempted assassination and sharp retaliation. Amusingly, our sympathy is on the side of the pig. The fairies may be women's helpers, but they create the conditions for the massacre of two aspirants in the rags to riches game of marrying with a prince. In that regard, this tale is a more calloused version of 'Cinderella.' Two aspirants pioneer at the cost of their lives.

The resolution of the tale demands that the pig prince recover his human form by fulfilling prescribed conditions. To satisfy the fairies, he must marry three times – an odd provision – and in keeping with the ancient sources, his outer covering must also be destroyed. Both conditions are met, leading to a kind of conflated denouement.[7] Just why Pig swears his wife to secrecy about his ability to shed his skin at night is, in that regard, a mystery, because her breach of that taboo alone leads to his liberation. But a glance at both source and analogue tales reveals that a second set of conditions prevails, and that without the skin and animal form, the beast-man protagonist is compelled to leave his wife and venture to other worlds where he will be eternally lost or from which he must be retrieved. It should follow that, in divulging his secret, a curse about to end would be prolonged, and that Meldina would be compelled to endure years of separation and a sorrowful quest in search of her mate.

7 The destruction of the discarded skin is a motif shared with the fox wife stories telling of the mother who can be made to remain at home to bear a man's children only by finding and destroying her fox skin. This is a wife-taming tale rather than a husband-taming and liberation tale, again closer to the Melusine group. The destruction of the animal skins was the precondition to domestication. Raymond Jameson, *Three Lectures on Chinese Folklore* (Peking [Beijing]: San Yu, 1932), pp. 94–6. Another complex tale having only this trait in common with Straparola is Anthony Hamilton's 'The History of Pertharite and Ferandine' in which a brother and sister seek to restore their father, the archduke, to sanity. They are transformed into a fox and a crocodile, although Ferandine also appears as a singing fish who by that means gives instructions to the prince on how to rescue her from the enchantment. The Prince and Princess of Lombardy come to their aid using a magic comb and necklace, but initially the prince does not comprehend the urgency of burning Ferandine's outer crocodile skin. Once burned, Ferandine is far closer to the recovery of her former self, while Pertharite is liberated from his enchantment as a white fox by placing the magic necklace, once an object of fear, around his neck. This story deals with the paradoxical requirement of love in full romantic register between animals and humans, for the princess is in love with the ingratiating fox, and the prince is compelled by his mysterious desire for the sea creature. *Select Tales of Count Hamilton, Author of the Life and Memoirs of the Count de Grammont,* 'translated from the French,' 2 vols. (London: J. Burd, 1760), vol. I, pp. 33–117.

But this does not ensue. The story, in fact, deviates towards a rival myth in which complete liberation for the prince comes about only through the shredding of the hide. Straparola had to slip through these vestiges of three narrative orders: the triple marriage and the end of the curse, the broken promise and the curse prolonged, and the ritual destruction of the skin leading to deliverance. Both the truncated comedic versions and the longer suffering romance versions, as stated earlier, were both current in the sixteenth century. Arguably, only by shedding the long coda – the search for the lost spouse – could this story tradition have transformed itself into the fairy tale versions of Madames d'Aulnoy, de Villeneuve, and de Beaumont.

By dint of having chosen to elaborate a story about a pig marrying below his social station and about a monster birth, arguments have been made that Straparola was seeking to address specific issues of his own time and place in social history. An intriguing perspective offered by Suzanne Magnanini is that the story participates in the scientific investigations into monstrosity that absorbed scientific thinkers from Ambroise Paré to Ulisse Aldrovandri (whose collection can still be seen today in Bologna in Palazzo Poggi). The story of a pig child who could marry and be reformed stands in stark contrast to the mothers of deformed offspring who, in that superstitious age, were sometimes burned as witches for having children that could only have been sired by an incubus devil. Such projected associations with concurrent scientific issues cannot be denied, but there is not much about the shaping of the story that plays to them in any particular way. In the first instance, Straparola seems intent merely upon recycling a current folk tale as he found it, but there may have been latent interests implicit in the process of selection.[8] By a different optic, the tale is a potential reminder that young men in the patrician households of Venice outnumbered the available eligible women in their class and were reduced to diluting the dynastic blood by marrying down. But in that regard, the tale can be no more specific than any tale of rising fortunes when members of the lower classes, by wit, magic, or bravery, manage to marry into royalty. 'The Pig Prince' is not very comforting on the topic in that it costs the lives of two of the sisters before a member of the elite finds marital happiness with a commoner –

8 Suzanne Magnanini, *Fairy-Tale Science: Monstrous Generation in the Tales of Straparola and Basile* (Toronto: University of Toronto Press, 2008), pp. 96–104.

hardly a form of assuaging the fears of those who might so fantasize themselves into upward mobility.[9]

Auguste Loiseleur Deslongchamps, in his study of ancient Indian literature in the West, mentions (without providing references) a version of the 'Pig Prince' in Pahlavi, presumably from the period of Persian translations from the Sanskrit *Panchatantra* (ca. third century AD), in which this story finds its earliest literary form.[10] How this narrative type came to the West remains moot. It was not included in the Arabic *Kalila wa Dimna*, which otherwise – through translations into Hebrew and Latin, not to mention Spanish, Italian, German, and English by 1570 – brought a goodly part of this Indian classic (the *Panchatantra*) to Europe as 'The Fables of Bidpai.'[11] According to the Persian tale, a royal wife becomes pregnant at last through the employment of magic words, but gives birth to a serpent son. The substitution of a pig for the serpent may have come early or late during the intervening 1,200 years, but the serpent version also persisted in the West, as in the story told by Basile in the *Pentamerone* (1634). Against all counsel, the mother keeps the monster child, nourishes it, and finally demands that a marriage partner be found. Her husband, Déva-Sarma, sets out on a long trip to find a man willing to marry his daughter to a snake. The Brahmin returns with her and, having gotten it right the first time, the marriage was a happy one, for the girl took great care of her husband. One night she found a man in her bedroom and attempted to flee, but in the end she was convinced that it was her husband without his serpent's skin. The Brahmin father, meanwhile, had witnessed the entire transaction, took the skin, and burned it, and so ensured his son's complete transformation.[12] Tellingly, there is no quest coda. The story is little more than a tale of metamorphosis. The marriage is quasi-allegorical, the wife's role minimal, the domestic and social nuances almost invisible, and the sense of a curse

9 Magnanini, *Fairy-Tale Science*, pp. 112–16. See also Stanley Chojnacki, *Women and Men in Renaissance Venice: Twelve Essays on Patrician Society* (Baltimore: Johns Hopkins University Press, 2000), pp. 53–75.

10 Viṣṇu Śarma, hereafter Vishnu Sarma, *The Panchatantra*, trans. Chandra Rajan (London: Penguin, 1993), p. 159; Auguste Loiseleur Deslongchamps, *Essai sur les fables indiennes et sur leur introduction en Europe* (Paris: Techener, 1838), p. 39.

11 See the 'Introduction' to Sir Thomas North, trans., *The Moral Philosophy of Doni Popularly Known as The Fables of Bidpai*, ed. Donald Beecher et al. (Ottawa: Dovehouse Editions, 2003).

12 From *Le trône enchanté, conte indien traduit du persan*, trans. Daniel Lescallier (New York: J. Desnoues, 1817), vol. I, pp. 4*ff*.

or of the initiatory conditions of deliverance imperceptible. Thus, in all the accretions evident in Straparola's tale, we can see the phases of the folk mind at work, adding the conventional motifs whereby such stories were more plausibly motivated, humanized, socialized, localized, and 'untied' or brought to their denouement.

Something of the process is seen at work in a late Sanskrit variation in which the snake has become a donkey. This occurs in the birth tale of the Vikramaditya in *Vikrama's Adventures, or the Thirty-Two Tales of the Throne,*[13] a story added to the *Vikramacarita* sometime after the thirteenth century – a modified version of which may have been known in the Latin West at an earlier date as the source of the *Asinarius.*[14] This story is a strange tale of an invisible god, wailing near the river, who offers threats to the king unless he will give him the princess in marriage. Disasters follow which force the king to an offer and the girl to obedience. She goes to a new palace with her husband and for many years enjoys him at night as a handsome man, to her great delight and contentment. But when her mother visits and sees the abandoned skin, she burns it in the fire, breaking the curse placed upon the donkey god for his former lechery but now enabling him to return to the heavens, abandoning his pregnant wife. In this tale of a god longing for congress with a mortal maiden before making his escape, the skin is all that holds the visiting husband in the human world. The identifying markers are clear, but Straparola's version, by comparison, is separated from this story's thematic orientation by many variations and accretions.[15]

13 Trans. Franklin Edgerton, 2 vols., Harvard Oriental Series 26–7 (Cambridge, MA: Harvard University Press, 1926), vol. I, pp. 263–6. The story is more readily available in *Simhasana Dvatrimsika: Thirty-two Tales of the Throne of Vikramaditya*, trans. A.N.D. Haksar (New Delhi: Penguin, 1998), pp. 181–4.

14 Jan M. Ziolkowski, *Fairy Tales from Before Fairy Tales: The Medieval Latin Past of Wonderful Lies* (Ann Arbor: University of Michigan Press, 2007), p. 219–20.

15 It may be mentioned in passing that the story survived into modern times in the East as well as in the West. One such was collected by Maive Stokes: 'The Monkey Prince,' in *Indian Fairy Tales* (London: Ellis & White, 1880), no. 10, pp. 41–50. This version retains all the principal features of the story, including the burning of the monkey's skin at the end, with the parents invited into the bedroom to witness the transformation. The hero was born a monkey, but he was a true prince inside and could, on occasion, remove his own skin and dress up as a prince. Such details as these, however, suggest that at this juncture, the Eastern makers were now under the spell of the Western fairy tale, including Straparola's own contribution.

The Latin *Asinarius*, translated as *The Donkey Tale* and dating to around 1200, is an important link between the Eastern and Western stories of a hero enclosed in a removable skin.[16] Its existence confirms the success of this cluster of story motifs in a version potentially compiled from a composite tradition some 350 years before Straparola. The Latin tale, thought to have been written for the Hohenstaufen dynasty then in power both in Germany and in Sicily, contains no fairies, no grime, and no murders in the marriage bed. Rather, the donkey, as an 'adolescent,' goes visiting foreign courts in the guise of a minstrel and there proves himself to be the epitome of politeness. After proper courtship and an elegant wedding, the bridegroom enters the bedchamber and takes off his skin to share in the marital embrace. Of note is the same unexplained transition from donkey to a man in a donkey's skin that constitutes a metamorphosis back to human form before the fact. That slippage is implicit in the pig prince, born a pig, but who, at an unspecified moment, is described as a man in a removable skin. This feature persists throughout the story tradition and allows for an enactment of his release to which the wife can also make a contribution. She, for a time, keeps his secret, but in the *Asinarius* seems to be under no vow to do so. When the skin is burned, the son-in-law grieves and thinks of flight, as though he had a higher calling (as in Vikramaditya's case), but the king blocks his way and offers him half the kingdom, bringing the tale to a happy close. That there are overtones of secrecy, and that the bridegroom is at first miserable and thinks of escape suggests palimpsest-like traces of a longer version (as in the Straparola tale), necessitating an expiatory quest by the bride for her lost husband. The relationship of 'The Pig Prince' to this almost courtly or chivalric rendition is open to assessment on a motif-by-motif basis, as Ziolkowski does with the Sanskrit tale and 'The Donkey Tale,' the differences due to the work of more than two centuries of non-linear oral transmission by intricate stages.[17] As matters stand, the *Asinarius* is the only text marking the passage of the generic tale of the

16 Trans. Jan M. Ziolkowski in *Fairy Tales from Before Fairy Tales*, pp. 341–50. This work provides a comparative study of the tale in relation to the Sanskrit 'Vikramaditya's Birth' and Grimm's 'The Donkey' on pp. 200–30.

17 Jan M. Ziolkowski, *Fairy Tales from Before Fairy Tales*, pp. 220–5. Ziolkowski is concerned with finding tales that qualify as true fairy tales before the time of Straparola and Basile, and cites the *Asinarius* as a prime example. Yet disagreement remains whether or not fairy tales can actually be defined independently of the folk tale at any time.

'beast-bridegroom' from the ancient and Eastern worlds to the Latin and vernacular West before Straparola.

Although the early record of the story type is slight, we can nevertheless be certain that the tale existed among the folk in the early sixteenth century and that hence the discovery of further versions dating to that era would come as no surprise. But for now, further insights into the story's history can only be gained by retro-engineering from the many 'King Pig' tales collected in the nineteenth and twentieth centuries. A complete assessment of the late sequels would be an arduous undertaking, but a few examples will suffice to circumscribe the territory. The book *Beauty and the Beast: Visions and Revisions of an Old Tale* reproduces some twenty-seven versions from as far as Indonesia, Jamaica, Norway, and the American Southwest, in addition to those from the central Eurasian regions.[18] One place to begin might be 'King Crin,' revised by Italo Calvino (from a tale collected by Pitrè in the Piedmont) for inclusion in his book of Italian fables.[19] It confirms the survival of the compound tale that includes the quest for the lost spouse now linked to supplemental motifs. In this folk tale, the story moves quickly to the serial murders of the intolerant and disgusted sisters, maintaining the same 'folk' brutality evinced by Straparola – brutality which rapidly disappears in the fairy-tale versions of the French salons. True to formula, the youngest sister detects some hidden principle, but rather than wallow in the filth she decides to do a bit of tidying up, including a gentle scrub up of Mr. Crin himself, before accepting his affections – to which her pig husband poses no objections. But a taboo remains in place, which is broken by the wife when she spills hot wax on her husband while attempting to see his true appearance during the night, initiating a long period of mourning and searching before the pair is reunited and the final transformation takes place. The spilled wax, the equivalent of Straparola's vow to secrecy, is without doubt a legacy from a tale in the 'Cupid and Psyche' tradition.[20]

18 Betsy Hearne, *Beauty and the Beast: Visions and Revisions of an Old Tale* (Chicago: University of Chicago Press, 1989).

19 *Italian Folktales*, trans. George Martin (New York: Pantheon, 1980), pp. 57–60.

20 An example of the continuity of the tale, despite wide diffusion and diversification, may be demonstrated in a clumsy variant collected by Francis Hindes Groome among the gypsies of Romania. 'The Snake who became the King's Son-in-law' entails many substitutions: a snake for a pig, and a marriage into a royal family as opposed to being born into a royal family. This snake protagonist, raised as a pet,

All that follows is something of a hodgepodge of errantry motifs that include wearing down a pair of iron shoes and the acquisition of three nuts, each with its magical properties, provided by the housekeepers of three hostile elemental beings: the sun, moon, and winds. With her newly gained power, the wife is able to purchase time with her prince, ward off the pursuit by other princesses who seek him in marriage, and so provide for a reunion. The horseshoes are linked to the horse-women tales in which, as night riders, they are captured and shoed, only to awake in human form with the telltale shoes still attached to their hands and feet. This long coda is also associated with tales in which the wife serves out her husband's sentence in the underworld, often returning just in time to prevent him from marrying someone else. These and many related skill-testing circumstances are imposed upon the pitiable but resilient heroine in all of these compound 'Psyche' tales, which together represent the narrative road not taken by Straparola and his predecessors back to the *Asinarius*.

Andrew Lang's 'The Enchanted Pig' in *The Red Fairy Book* is a clear corroboration of the currency of Calvino's tale. Again, little is made of the opening birth tale. The youngest daughter prevails, shows compassion, and receives consideration in return. The couple lives in seclusion and the wife is cognizant of an enchantment that is the cause of her husband's suffering. The princess therefore seeks the help of a witch to break the spell, but by mischance lands upon the mother of the slain dragon whose death at the hand of the hero had brought about his cursed transformation in the first place. She is told to tie the pig's foot while he is asleep, but the string breaks and the husband awakes to the dreadful realization that her meddling has cost him a lengthy prolongation of the spell, otherwise destined to end in three days. To win him back, she too must wear out a pair of iron shoes and build a ladder, the final rung of which is supplied by her amputated little finger. The variations are suggestive but incidental to the underlying structure, which retains the two parts: the birth and marriage and the expiation of

demands the king's daughter. After many feats, the match is made and the snake consoles his bride by assuring her on their wedding night that things are not as they seem. With that, he flips a somersault and becomes a golden youth. The king sends a man to see how the pair is faring and he returns with a happy report. Many narrative parts are damaged or truncated, but the defining features are evident: marriage to a beast and escape from a spell through the ritual faith implicit in so contrary a union. *Gypsy Folk Tales* (London: Herbert Jenkins, 1963), no. 7, pp. 21–4.

a broken taboo. These complementary tales reveal something of the substitutions, accretions, and accidents typical of oral transmission.

Basile's tale 'The Snake,' from the second book of his *Pentamerone*, may be passed over briefly insofar as the story differs significantly from 'the pig prince' type and evinces no debt to the *Piacevoli notti*. Yet it is important as an early witness to the survival of the 'Psyche' branch of the story involving the final wandering and the snake as husband. Such differences are typical of their cognate stories, indicating that Basile very likely knew nothing of Straparola's collection, or at least took little from it, thereby necessitating that many of Straparola's story types were known in variant versions in and around Naples.[21] When, in Basile, the father burns the sloughed skin of the serpent, the snake prince is resentful and makes his escape, injuring himself in the process. The princess, during her expiatory wandering, hears the history of her husband's enchantment from a white fox, a creature she must then kill as part of her 'labours.' She ultimately approaches her prince incognito with a magic potion requisite for his second liberation, testing his fidelity at the same time. Nothing of this could have been derived from Straparola. In sum, the implied history of this folk tale is intriguing – a mental tease. Apuleius and Basile tell related stories, separated by more than one-and-a-half millennia. The 'Asinaria' and 'The Pig Prince' are the lone intermediary versions, apart from the Eastern tales that hint at origins, but are documented in the West long after the Apuleian folk source was in circulation in ancient Rome. Because all are part of the 'same' story type, we must imagine the modes of literary memory and oral memory by which it was transmitted throughout several centuries down to recent times, various manifestations of which are recorded in these four transcriptions, each one a version of the tale current in its respective time and place. Of these few surviving pre-modern literary versions, Straparola's alone features a pig, and in that regard stands as the literary ancestor to an entire tradition of pig princes within the 'beast-bridegroom' group.

The true sequel to Straparola, and the mediating tale between his *Nights* and Madame de Beaumont's *Beauty and the Beast*, is Madame Marie-Catherine d'Aulnoy's 'Le Prince Marcassin' from her *Suite des contes*

---

21 Giovanni Battista Basile, *The Pentamerone* (II.5), trans. Richard Burton (New York: Boni & Liveright, 1927), pp. 141–9. A later handling of this tale may be seen in Madame d'Aulnoy's 'Serpentin vert,' in *Cabinet des fées*, ed. Élisabeth Lemirre (Arles: Picquier Poche, 1994), vol. I, pp. 253–86.

nouveaux ou les fées à la mode.[22] The tale incorporates the entirety of Straparola's plot in design and detail, but converts it into a salon tale of courtship and sentiment. This is undoubtedly one of the creations to which Henriette-Julie de Castelnau, comtesse de Murat, refers in her address to her readers concerning not only her own borrowing from *Les facetieuses nuits du Seigneur Straparolle*, but 'Les Dames who have written in this genre before me.'[23] To be sure, D'Aulnoy deviates in adding a rival for the hand of the first sister and replaces her murder by an angry husband with the lovers' mutual suicide in the next room. Nevertheless, the second sister does scheme against the prince's life with a supposed accomplice and is gored by the boar's tusks. After this second failure, the poor defeated beast takes to the woods to run with his confreres, but there meets the third sister, who is gentle and playful with him, inviting yet coy, so that through a kind of consenting abduction they live together in a forest grotto sealed from view, but where the princess can nevertheless hear her distraught mother calling for her in the woods. Eventually in the night she perceives the prince's arms and legs and at last detects the abandoned skin, which, once hidden, brings liberation. These episodes, including the concern for the mother and the enforced but willing captivity, provide the clues to new developments reflected in Beauty's relationship to her father and her isolation with Beast in his lavish country estate, there by degrees to work his transformation.

---

22 *Suite des contes nouveaux ou les fées à la mode*, 2 vols. (Paris: Théodore Girard, 1698); *Contes II, Contes nouveaux ou Les Fées à la mode*, ed. Philippe Hourcade and Jacques Barchilon (Paris: Société des Textes Français Modernes, 1998), pp. 429–71.

23 Quoted from the unpaginated edition of 1699 of her *Histoires sublimes et allégoriques* in Ute Heidmann and Jean-Michel Adam, *Textualité et intertextualité des contes* (Paris: Garnier classique, 2010), p. 51. Ute Heidmann seeks, in her discussion surrounding the passage, to deliver Perrault and others from the literary larceny to which De Murat would seem to be confessing in her avowed use of Straparola. But it is really a non-question in the post-humanist world of amplification upon ancient and contemporary texts as the default method of literary 'work,' of the kind that Straparola was doing in 'authoring' folk tales, and Shakespeare in authoring plays built incontestably upon known and intertextually accessible literary sources. The fact remains, as one famous commentator excusing Shakespeare said, that some authors 'invade' those texts with greater transformational genius than others and thereby clear their names. The irony in the case of Straparola is that his value to us may be the greater because he appears to have been content with rather faithful transcriptions of his sources, to the extent that memory, however furnished or fortified, would allow him.

Just a year later in 1699, Henriette Julie de Murat published 'Le roy porc' (The pig king), which opens with the wish for a child, the intervention of the three fairies, and the birth of a twice-blest but once-cursed pig son, raised until age fifteen by a fairy in a shelter remote from the court.[24] Thereafter, the departures are so pronounced as to constitute a new story, for the prince spends his time courting a water undine in secret, managing in the end to win her away from the river god who holds her in thrall. In much those same years Charles Perrault published his 'Riquet-à-la-Houppe,' which plays upon the contrast between beauty and ugliness, the whole of the tale motivated by the designs of the fairies.[25] This too is a tale about the transforming power of love, provided one is a believer in a future time when someone ugly will seem beautiful to the beholder. Riquet is also enchanted from birth and cursed with striking ugliness, but he is otherwise human. Hence the themes are related and some of the motifs belong to a common repertoire, but the order of the narrative strikes out entirely on its own.

Madame Gabrielle de Villeneuve's 'Beauty and the Beast,' published in *La jeune amériquaine et les contes marins*, appeared in 1740[26] and provided the basis for Madame Jeanne-Marie LePrince de Beaumont's more famous story of the same name, appearing in *Le magasin des enfans* in 1756. The English translation followed only three years later in *The Young Misses Magazine*.[27] Too many substitutions and alterations to ethos and theme have taken place to warrant a comparative approach between these and Straparola's tale. Belle or Beauty is a far more developed portrait of the conflict between duty to a parent and duty to a prospective mate, and a study in the limited range she enjoys for self-expression and auto-determination. Beast, meanwhile, has become an ogre, unloved, yet pathetic and even suicidal. He is under a spell that can only be broken

24 *Histoires sublimes et allégoriques* (Paris: Florentin Delaulne, 1699).

25 *Popular Tales*, ed. Andrew Lang (New York: Arno Press, 1977), pp. 50–9.

26 Madame Gabrielle de Villeneuve, *La jeune ameriquaine et les contes marins*, ed. Élisa Biancardi (Paris: Champion, 2008). (The earliest edition of this work was published in The Hague in 1740.)

27 The English version is readily found in Iona and Peter Opie, eds. *The Classic Fairy Tales* (New York: Oxford University Press, 1974). The French version appeared in *Le magasin des enfans, ou dialogues entre une sage gouvernante et plusieurs de ses élèves de la première distinction* (London, 1756). *The Annotated Classic Fairy Tales*, ed. Maria Tatar (New York: W.W. Norton, 1999), pp. 58–78.

when a person consents to marry him without constraint. It is a gender inversion of the tale told by Chaucer's Wife of Bath concerning the young knight compelled to marry an old hag who also escapes a spell to become beautiful when the terms of the curse are met – an ancient story in its own right. Thus Beast, like the pig prince, is not free to liberate himself from his own animal covering. As for the comparative relationship between Madame de Villeneuve's and Madame de Beaumont's tales, a good place to begin is with Jerry Griswold's *The Meanings of Beauty and the Beast: A Handbook*.[28]

Burning the skin of an alligator liberates a beautiful nymph in the 'Histoire de Pertharite et Férandine' of Count Antoine Hamilton, but how deeply his debt remains to the 'Pig Prince' group remains open to discussion. More demonstrably in the group is the story of 'Hans My Hedgehog,' reconstructed by the Grimm brothers.[29] This is a fresh reconfiguration of the entire structure, now with the father so keen for a son that even a hedgehog would do. He is then provided with one in precisely that form – as though Tyl Eulenspiegel were filling in for the fairies. By helping two kings find their way out of the forest, Hans is promised by each the first thing he sees upon his arrival at their respective courts; thus he finds himself with two princesses pledged to him

28 *The Meanings of Beauty and the Beast: A Handbook* (Peterborough, ON: Broadview Press, 2004). There is also an extensive discussion of the intertextual relationships implicit in Perrault's *La barbe bleue* which suggests, among many intriguing interconnections, that the motif of the slain wives locked away in the forbidden room has something in common with the two wives brutally slain by the Pig Prince of the present story. See Heidmann and Adam, *Textualité et intertextualité des contes*, pp. 126–8. The motives of the two murderers were somewhat different, however, in that Blue Beard was a sadist and enjoyed setting his wives up by piquing their insatiable curiosities, while King Pig was seeking companionship and found himself the object of intended murder. They are quite different stories.

29 Count Antoine Hamilton, 'Histoire de Pertharite et de Férandine,' in *Contes: Avec la suite des Facardins* (Paris: A.A. Renouard, 1820), vol. I, p. 72. Brothers Grimm, *Kinder- und Hausmärchen* (Göttingen: Dieterich, 1857), no. 108; 'Hans My Hedgehog,' in *Grimm's Complete Fairy Tales* (Garden City, NY: Nelson Doubleday, n.d.), no. 155, pp. 484–8. A further exploration of this motif in German literature must include Josef Haltrich's 'Das Borstenkind' (The child with bristles), in *Deutsche Volksmärchen aus dem Sachsenlande in Siebenbürgen* (Hildesheim: Olms [1856], 2007); and Johann Wilhelm Wolf's 'Das wilde Schwein' (The wild boar), in *Deutsche Märchen und Sagen* (Leipzig: Brockhaus, 1845).

who, in the manner of Jepthe's daughter, had come out to meet their fathers. But when Hans returns for the first, he discovers her deceit, spikes her all over with his quills, and leaves her in disgrace. The second, however, remains true to her word and leaves with Hans to be married. On the wedding night, Hans himself instructs his father to burn the skin which he removes at night and, with a few more touches, becomes white-skinned and handsome. Even a hedgehog can find happiness through metamorphosis. You have to have seen one to enjoy the joke.

Related tales in the group include the Sicilian 'Lu sirpenti,'[30] 'Vom re porco,' translated from the Sicilian,[31] 'Il re porco,' from Florence or its surroundings,[32] and 'Zelinda and the Monster,' also translated from the Italian.[33] There are versions in Angelo De Gubernatis's *Novelline de Santo*

30 'Lu sirpenti' (The Serpent), in Pitrè, ed., *Fiabe, novella e racconti*; *The Collected Sicilian Folk and Fairy Tales of Giuseppe Pitrè*, trans. Jack Zipes and Joseph Russo (New York: Routledge, 2009), no. 56, p. 855–6. In his commentary, Pitrè included close analogues collected in Ficarazelli, Montevago, and Noto, while mentioning many others including versions collected by Vittorio Imbriani, *La novellaja milanese* (Bologna: Fava, 1872), no. 6; 'Il re porco,' in Imbriani, *La novellaja fiorentini con la novellaja milanese*, ed. Italo Sordi (Milan: Rizzoli, 1976), no. 12, pp. 168–82; 'La fola dèl Rè Purzèl,' in Carolina Coronedi-Berti, *Favole Bolognesi* (Bologna: Arnaldo Forni, 1883; reprint, Forni, 1981), no. 10, pp. 34–7; 'Der Prinz mit der Schweinshaut,' in Arietti Widter, Georg Widter, and Adam Wolf, eds., *Volksmärchen aus Venetien*, with 'Nachweisen' by Reinhold Köhler (Leipzig: F.A. Brockhaus, 1866), no. 12. See also 'Bellindia,' in Gherardo Nerucci, *Sessanta novelle popolari montalesi*, ed. Roberto Fedi (Milan: Rizzoli, 1977), no. 16, pp. 128–33. Yet another version occurs in Rachel Harriette Busk, *Roman Legends: A Collection of the Fables and Folk-lore of Rome* (Boston: Estes & Lauriet, 1877), pp. 115–18.

31 'Prince Scursini,' in *Sicilianische Märchen*, intro. Otto Hartwig, ed. Laura Gonzenbach, 2 vols. (Leipzig, 1870), no. 42. Giuseppe Pitrè records another version of 'Il re porco' in his *Novelle popolari toscane parte seconda* (Rome: Casa editrice del libro italiano, n.d.), pp. 129–40, with further variants, pp. 140–2. This story features the long quest for the lost husband suppressed in Straparola in which the wife must weep vials of tears. The story follows the familiar order through the death of the first two wives.

32 'Maestra,' in *La novellaja fiorentina*, ed. Vittorio Imbriani (Leghorn: Francesco Vigo [1871], 1877), p. 168; Imbriani, *La novellaja fiorentini con la novellaja milanese*, ed. Italo Sordi (Milan: Rizzoli, 1976), no. 21, pp. 271–80.

33 *Italian Popular Tales*, ed. Thomas Frederick Crane (Santa Barbara, CA: ABC Clio, 2001), pp. 7–11. This story's affinities are closest to 'Beauty and the Beast,' for it is about trespassing in a rose garden and being forced by a monster to give him the eldest daughter in marriage, while her two younger sisters were only too glad to betray her.

Stefano,[34] Andrew Lang's 'The Enchanted Pig' from Romanian origins,[35] and, further east, a version in *Cossack Fairy Tales*.[36] One of the most amusing was collected by Domenico Comparetti, 'Il figliuolo del re,' in which the brat pig jumps up and down, shaking the entire palace each time he wants a wife, and kills the first two because they stick him with forks when he tries to feed off their plates. The third wife is more compliant and

34 'Sor Fiorante mago,' in Angelo De Gubernatis, ed., *Le novelline di Santo Stefano* (Turin: A.F. Negro, 1869), no. 14, pp. 36–7. This is a strange but demonstrable analogue in which three daughters of a woodsman are invited to marry a serpent, only the third of which graciously accepts. The serpent becomes a handsome prince with minimal ado and they live in a fine castle. The girl is forbidden to mention his name, however, but is, like Psyche, enticed to share confidences. The rest of the story is taken up with the trials of her quest involving vials of tears, wearing out iron shoes, and the loss of years in regaining her husband.

35 Andrew Lang, ed., *The Red Fairy Book* (1890; reprint, London: Longmans & Co., 1912), pp. 104–15. The third daughter of the king discovers her fate when the three girls go snooping in a forbidden room. When the pig comes courting, she marries him, indeed, wipes and kisses his dirty snout by day, but is treated to a transformed prince by night. This story explains the confusion in Straparola, for in attempting to break the spell by tying a string to his foot the princess prolongs it by three years, leading to the long sequel (suppressed in the *Piacevoli notti*) in which the bride, in Psyche fashion, must seek her husband, walk in iron shoes, climb a ladder of bones, chop off her little finger, and more, assuring a happy ending.

36 'The Serpent-Tsarevich and His Two Wives,' in *Cossack Fairy Tales and Folk Tales*, ed. R. Nisbet Bain (London: A.H. Bullen, 1902; reprint, Millwood, NY: Kraus Reprints, 1975), pp. 191–200. In this tale, the son of the Tsar is born a serpent, lives in a stone hut, and when grown, asks to be married. The twelfth daughter of an old woman, thought to be too young to meet the prince, begs to go along. She puts on twenty suits of clothes, accepts the prince in marriage, then enters into a clothes-shedding contest with the tsarevich until his last serpent skin is shed and burned. His new human form is to be kept a solemn secret, as in the present tale by Straparola, but she breaks her promise, and again there is a long sequel of expiation and searching not in the present tale. But it is of a very particular kind, being closely related to 'Fortunio, the King's Daughter, and the Mermaid' (III.4). On her journey, she begs for lodging in frightening fairy tale places such as ogres' castles, but in each instance comes away with a little silver, gold, or diamond apple. When she at last finds her husband, now remarried, she disguises herself as an old woman and displays her precious wares outside his house. These the first wife barters in exchange for closer and longer periods of time with her husband, much as Fortunio's wife barters her apples to see more and more of her husband's body, until he is at last freed from the mermaid's clutches. When the tsarevich discovers his first wife watching over him and comes to understand that the second has 'sold' her that privilege for trinkets, he reclaims her for her loyalty and has the second quartered between wild stallions.

that very night gets a handsome young man for her partner who simply stays that way for the rest of his life – true narrative celerity and compression.[37] Other versions have been collected in Spain by Aurelio Espinosa; these are discussed under the heading, 'El principe encantado' (The enchanted prince).[38] The list could be greatly extended, but the sample is sufficient to demonstrate the vigour and staying power of this folk creation recycled continuously from the very beginning of the modern era. If folk tales 'symbolize the aspirations, needs, dreams and wishes of the people, either affirming the dominant social values and norms or revealing the necessity to change them,' the widespread success of this tale suggests that in situation, design, and theme it conveys particular pleasures and fantasies and reflects abiding truths of pertinence to each generation of its reciters and their audiences.[39]

37 'Il figliuolo del re' and 'Federika,' in Domenico Comparetti, *Novelline popolari italiane* (Rome: Loescher, 1875), vol. I, nos. 9 and 36, pp. 38–9, 146–50.

38 *Cuentos populares españoles* (Madrid: S. Aguirre, 1947), vol. II, p. 487.

39 Jack Zipes, *Breaking the Magic Spell: Radical Theories of Folk and Fairy Tales* (Austin: University of Texas Press, 1979), p. 5.

II. Fable 2
Filenio Sisterno's Revenge upon the Three Ladies

ANTONIO MOLINO

Filenio Sisterno, a student of Bologna, having been tricked by certain ladies, takes his revenge upon them under pretence of a feast to which he invites them.

I should never have thought or imagined, gracious ladies, that the Signora would have laid upon me the task of telling a story, seeing that, according to the drawing of lots, we should be calling upon Fiordiana to give us hers. But since it is the pleasure of the assembly, I'll take it upon myself to tell you something that may by chance fit your humour. And God forbid that my narrative should prove tiresome to you all, or that it crosses the bounds of civility. If so, I must simply crave your indulgence, for the blame is to be laid upon Signora Fiordiana. She is the cause of it all.

In Bologna, the chief city of Lombardy, the parent of learning and a place furnished with everything needed for its high and flourishing condition, there lived a young scholar of graceful and amiable parts named Filenio Sisterno, born on the island of Crete. One day it happened that a magnificent feast was given to which were invited the most beautiful and distinguished ladies of the city, together with many gentlemen and certain of the scholars, among whom was Filenio. After the manner of gallants, he went dallying first with this fair dame and then with that one, and finding no difficulty in suiting his taste, he decided to lead one of them for a dance. His choice fell upon Signora Emerenziana, the wife of a certain Messer Lamberto Bentivogli. She didn't turn him down either, for in addition to being sprightly and beautiful, she was gracious as well. During the dance, which Filenio made sure was a slow and gentle one, he pressed her hand softly and whispered these words to her: 'Ah, Signora, how great is your beauty, for it surpasses all others my eyes have ever seen. There is no lady alive who could ensnare my heart as you have done. If only I could hope you felt the same, I'd be the happiest man in the world. But if you prove to be cruel, you'll soon see me lying dead at your feet, knowing yourself to be the cause of my demise. Because I love you so dearly – for indeed I couldn't do otherwise – you should accept me as your servant, disposing both of my person and of the little I can call mine as if they were your own. I couldn't win a higher favour from heaven than to find myself subject to such a mistress, for you've captured me in the snare of love as though I were a bird.'

Emerenziana listened earnestly to these sweet and gracious words and, like a modest gentlewoman, made as though she had heard nothing and kept her peace. When the measure came to an end, Emerenziana sat down and immediately Filenio led out another lady as his partner. The dance had barely begun before he spoke to her in much the same way. 'Truly, most gracious Signora, there is no need for me to be lavish of words in setting forth the depth and ardour of the love I have for you and ever will have for as long as this soul of mine inhabits and rules my unworthy body. How blessed I would be if I might possess you as the lady of my heart and my very own mistress. Loving you as I do and being wholly yours, as you may easily understand, I beg you to accept me as your most humble servant, seeing that my life and all I have to live for depends on you and you alone.' This fair lady, whose name was Panthemia, although she understood his meaning perfectly well, made no reply, but in all modesty kept on dancing. When it was over, she sat down with the other ladies, a little smile creeping over her face.

Little time went by before our gallant scholar took a third partner by the hand, this time the most attractive, gracious, and fairest lady in Bologna, and lead her through the steps of the dance, forcing the others who crowded around her in admiration to make way. And before the dance had ended, he addressed her as follows: 'Lady, perhaps I may seem to you presumptuous beyond all measure to reveal the secret love which I have borne and still do bear you, but please don't blame this offence on me, but on your own beauty, which raises you high above all the others and makes me your slave. I'll say nothing of your delightful manners, nor of your surpassing virtues, which are great enough to bring down the gods from the heavens. So if your loveliness, the work of nature and not of art, can allure the immortal gods, no marvel that it should constrain me to love you and to keep your image in my inmost heart. I beg you then, sweet lady, the only comfort of my life, to reserve some tenderness for the one who dies for you a thousand times a day. If you grant me this grace, I'll owe my life to you, and so I can only recommend myself to your kindness alone.'

This fair lady, who was called Sinforosia, when she heard the sweet and loving words that flowed from Filenio's ardent bosom, could not prevent a sigh, but taking care for her honour as a married woman, she made him no reply, but returned straight to her seat once the dance was ended.

Soon thereafter, by chance all three of these ladies found themselves sitting together in a close circle and engaged in a lively conversation when Emerenziana, the spouse of Messer Lamberto, in a spirit of pleasant humour and not at all for spite, said to her two companions, 'Dear friends, I have to tell you of a diverting adventure that happened to me this evening.'

'And what was that?' they enquired.

Emerenziana continued, 'While we were dancing this evening, I had for my partner a real cavalier, handsome, trim, and gracious beyond anyone you could imagine, who protests that he is so hotly enamoured of my beauty that he can find no rest day or night.' Then word by word she related all that the scholar had said to her. As soon as Panthemia and Sinforosia heard her story, they told her that the same thing had happened to them, and before they left the feast, they had determined among themselves that it was the same gallant who had made love to all three of them. So his words didn't arise from true feelings, as they had each at first believed, but merely from deceit and feigned love. Now they lent no more credence to him than one gives to the delirious babblings of a sick man or the mad heroes of romance. So before they parted company, they came to an agreement among themselves that they would trick him in such a way that he would never forget that he had made such a mockery of them.

Filenio, meanwhile, kept up his amorous pursuit and continued making love to one lady after another. Judging by their gestures that they were not unkindly disposed to him, he set himself the goal, if it were possible, to convince each of them to grant to him the highest favour of love. Yet despite his best-laid plans, not one of his pursuits produced for him the fulfillment of his desires.

Emerenziana, who had no patience for the mock love-making of this silly scholar, called in a fetching and buxom maid of hers and told her to make up some excuse for talking to Filenio so that she could disclose to him the love her mistress had conceived for him, and to let him know that whenever he desired, he might spend the night with her at her own house. When Filenio heard this he was elated beyond all measure and said to the maid, 'Hurry back home right away and commend me to your mistress, and tell her on my behalf that she can expect me this evening at her house, provided of course that her husband is not at home.'

When this message had been brought to Emerenziana, she had a big quantity of prickly thorns collected and brought in to her. These she had strewn under the bed where she slept and awaited her gallant's arrival. When the night had come, the scholar took his sword and stole towards the house of his fair enemy, and the door was immediately opened to him, once he had given the password. Then, after the two had made a little conversation and taken a light supper, they retired to the bedroom for the night.

But no sooner had Filenio taken off his clothes to get into bed than Messer Lamberto was heard outside, and with that the lady feigned to be at her wits' end about where she should hide her lover, telling him to get under the bed. Seeing the great danger they were both in now, Filenio made all haste to go where he was directed without putting on more clothes than the shirt he was wearing, in consequence of which he was so miserably pricked by the thorns prepared for him that there was no part of his body, from the crown of his head to the soles of his feet, which was not running with blood. In this dark hole, the more he tried to defend himself from the spines, the more grievously he was wounded, yet he didn't dare make a sound lest Messer Lamberto should hear and slay him. I leave you to imagine further the plight of the poor wretch that night, as likely to end up an amputee as he was speechless. When the morning finally arrived and the husband had left the house, the wretched scholar put on his clothes as best he could and made his way back to his lodging, bleeding and in great fear of dying outright. But diligently treated by his physicians, his body mended and he recovered his former health.

Not many days had passed before Filenio attempted yet another round of love-making, casting amorous eyes on the other two ladies, Panthemia and Sinforosia. One evening he went so far as to engage Panthemia in conversation, repeating to her his continued woes and torment, and beseeching her to take pity on him. Panthemia, who was full of tricks and mischief, then feigned passion for him, at first excusing herself that it was beyond her power to answer his desires, yet at the last, as though vanquished by his tender prayers and ardent sighs, brought him into her house. When he was undressed and ready to go to bed with her, she urged him to go into a little room adjacent where she kept her orange water and perfumes so that he could spice himself up a bit before going to bed. The silly scholar, never suspecting the craft of this lady trickster, went into the little room, set his foot on a board barely attached to the joists, and fell with all his weight into a warehouse below wherein merchants kept their store of cotton and wool, the floorboards along with him. Easily he could have broken his neck or his legs had not good fortune been on his side, letting him off without injury. Now finding himself in this dark place, he began to search for some door or ladder to make his escape, but finding none, he cursed the hour and the place where he had first set eyes on the woman. When the morning dawned at last and the unhappy scholar finally discovered on one side of the storehouse certain holes in the wall through which a dim light streamed in through the old and moss-grown masonry, he set to work with all his might to pull out the stones from the places in greatest decay and so make a gap big enough to get himself through. Outside he found himself in an alley not far from the public thoroughfare, barefoot and clad only in his shirt, from whence he crept back to his lodging without anyone seeing him.

Next it happened that Sinforosia, having heard about the tricks the two others had played on the scholar, resolved to treat him to a third as noteworthy as the former. So the next time she saw him, she began to ogle him from the corners of her eyes to let him know of the passion for him that was burning inside. Inveterate lover that he was and forgetting already his former perils, he began to walk up and down in front of her house playing the amoroso. Sinforosia, seeing how smitten he was for her, sent him a letter by an old woman to let him know that his fine person and gracious manners had so captured her fancy that she could find no rest night or day and that whenever it pleased him, he could come and speak to her. Filenio took the letter and, once he understood its full import, he was suddenly filled with more glee and happiness than he had ever known before, forgetting entirely all the other injuries and setbacks he had already suffered. He took pen and ink and wrote to say that as much as she might be in love with him, on his side he was as much in love with her, or even more so, and that at any time she might appoint, he would be at her service and command. As soon as she read these words, Sinforosia set about to find the first occasion to bring the scholar to her house. Upon his arrival, after many feigned sighs she said, 'O my Filenio, truly I know of no other gallant who could have brought me into so sore a plight except you. Your comeliness, your grace, and your discourse have kindled such fire in my heart that I burn like dry wood.'

The scholar, as he listened to her, took it for certain that she was melting with ardour for him. For some time longer the poor simpleton kept on bandying sweet and loving words with her, till it seemed to him the time had come to go to bed and lie down beside her. Then Sinforosia said, 'Before we go to bed, sweet friend, we should have a little bite to eat.' And taking him by the hand, she led him into an adjoining room where there was a table spread with sumptuous cakes and the finest wines, into which the mischievous dame had caused to be mixed a certain drug strong enough to put her gallant to sleep for a fair time. Filenio took a cup and filled it with wine, and suspecting no fraud he emptied it to the last drop. Enlivened by the banquet and having washed himself in orange water and dainty perfumes, he got into bed. But then the drug began to work and he slept so soundly that even the roar of the loudest artillery in the world couldn't have awakened him. When Sinforosia saw that he was in a heavy slumber and that the drug had taken well, she called one of her maids, a strong wench whom she had let in on the prank, and the two of them lugged Filenio by the legs and arms down to the door, which they softly opened, and put him in the street about a stone's throw from house and there they left him.

It was about an hour before dawn when the drug had spent its force and the poor wretch came to, thinking all that while that he had been in bed with the lady, only to find himself barefoot, clad only in his shirt, and half dead with cold from lying on the bare ground. His arms and legs were so nearly helpless that he found it hard to get to his feet, and once he'd managed this, it was with difficulty that he kept from falling down again. As best he could, he managed to regain his lodging without being seen and there he took the best means he could to recover his usual health. Had it not been for his lusty youth, he would surely have been maimed for life. At last, though, he regained his former health, and when he ventured out again, he showed no signs of remembering the injuries and vexations that had been practised upon him. Rather, he conducted himself towards the three ladies as if he loved them as well as ever, pretending to be enamoured of one and then of another.

Meanwhile, never suspecting malice on his part, the ladies put a good face on the matter and treated him graciously, as if they were dealing with a real lover, although he was nothing to them but an ongoing pastime. Filenio was many times tempted to give his hand free play and to mark their faces for them, but wisely he considered their stations in life and the shame that would be cast upon him should he offer violence to three weak women. Hence he restrained his wrath. Day and night he thought about how he might best wreak his vengeance on them, and when he couldn't hit upon a ploy, he was in great perplexity. But in the course of time, he devised a scheme by which he might easily carry out his purpose and, as it turned out, fortune was on his side.

In the city of Bologna he rented a very fine palace containing a magnificent hall and many dainty chambers. There he proposed to give a great and sumptuous feast to which he would invite a company of gentlefolk, including Emerenziana, Panthemia, and Sinforosia. They accepted the scholar's invitation without demur, suspecting nothing malicious. When they had arrived at the feast, the wily scholar, with many courteous words, led them into a room and urged them to take some refreshment. As soon as the three ladies had entered the chamber – foolish and imprudent as they were – Filenio locked the door and said, as he advanced towards them, 'Now wicked ladies, the time is come for me to take my revenge upon you for your mischief and naughtiness, and to give you some repayment for all the ills you put upon me for having loved you so well.'

When they heard these words they seemed more dead than alive and began to repent wholeheartedly that they had ever abused him, while at the same time cursing their own folly in having trusted the word of one they ought to have treated as a foe. Then, with fierce and threatening looks, the scholar commanded them, if they placed any value upon their lives, that they should strip themselves naked. When they heard these words, the ladies exchanged glances and began to weep, begging him the while, not only for the sake of love, but also for the sake of his natural gentleness, that their honours might be respected. Filenio, exulting in his deed, was exceedingly polite to them, yet informed them nevertheless that he could in no wise allow them to remain clothed in his presence. Hereupon, the ladies cast themselves at Filenio's feet and with piteous weeping humbly begged him not to heap such terrible disgrace upon them. But now that his heart had grown as hard as a diamond, he told them that there was nothing to blame in what he intended to do, that it was nothing but just revenge. So the ladies were forced to take off their clothes and stand before him as naked as the day they were born – in which condition they were just as fair as when they were clothed. Only then, looking them over from head to foot and seeing their beautiful and delicate bodies in their whiteness surpassing even the snow, the scholar began to feel some pity for them. But recalling his recent wrongs and the nearly mortal perils he had undergone, he chased away his pitying humour and once more hardened his heart. Then most astutely he carried all their clothes and linens they had lately worn into a neighbouring closet and with a menacing tone ordered them all to get into one bed.

Although astounded and shaking with terror, the ladies cried out, 'Wretched fools that we are! What will our husbands and our friends say when they are told how we have been found here naked and foully murdered in this bed?'

Seeing them lying beside each other like married folk, the scholar took a large and very white sheet of linen, not too thin, but transparent enough for their flesh to be seen. This he took and covered them from head to foot. Then he left the chamber, locking the door behind him to go find their three husbands, who were dancing in the hall. The dance coming to an end, Filenio took them with him into the chamber where the ladies were lying on the bed and said to them, 'Gentlemen, I have brought you here for your diversion, for I intend to show you the prettiest sight you've ever seen.' Having then led them up to the bed with a torch in his hand, gently he began to lift up the covering at their feet, turning it back far enough to reveal the pretty limbs beneath it as far as the knees – their husbands now gazing upon their white limbs and dainty feet. When he had done this, he then uncovered them to the middle and thus displayed their legs whiter than alabaster, which seemed like columns of polished marble, and their bellies rounded in so shapely a fashion that nothing could be finer. Next, uncovering their fair bodies yet a little more, he showed their gently swelling bosoms with the two round breasts so fair and sweet that they might have constrained the great god Jupiter to kiss and fondle them. I leave you to imagine the diversion and pleasure of the three gentlemen, as well as the distressing plight of the poor unhappy ladies when they heard their own husbands join in making fun of them. There they lay quite still, not daring so much as to cough lest they be discovered, while the husbands kept on urging the scholar to uncover their faces. But more careful in other men's wrongs than in his own, he would not in the least agree to this. Still not yet satisfied, he brought out their garments, which he showed to their husbands, who, when they looked at them, were astonished and not a little distressed at heart. After examining them closely, on said to another, 'Isn't this the gown that I once had made for my wife?'

'Is this not the headpiece I bought for her?'

'And isn't this the pendant that she hangs around her neck? Are these not the rings she wears on her fingers?'

At last, Filenio led the three gentlemen out of the chamber and invited them to remain for supper in order not to break up the party. Learning that the repast was ready and everything set in order by the wise majordomo, the scholar gave the word for everyone to be seated. Then while the guests were setting their teeth to work, Filenio returned to the chamber where the three ladies were and said, as he uncovered them, 'Good evening, fair ladies. Did you hear what your husbands said? They are now outside impatiently waiting to see you. So get up. Surely you have slept long enough. Stop yawning and rubbing your eyes. Take your clothes and put them on without delay and go into the hall where the other guests are waiting for you.'

With such words as these he mocked them, while they, for their part, were disconsolate, despairing, and terrified that this adventure might come to some fatal end, and so they wept bitterly. Full of anguish and terror, and looking for nothing less than death at his hands, at last they arose and turned to the scholar, saying, 'Filenio, you have taken more than vengeance upon us. Now nothing remains but for you to draw your sword and make an end of our lives, for we desire death beyond any other thing. But if you will not grant us this request, at least allow us to return unobserved to our homes so that our honours may be saved.'

Seeing that he had carried the affair far enough, Filenio gave them back their garments and told them to quickly get dressed. When this was done, he sent them out of the house by a secret door and back they went to their houses. No sooner inside than they removed their fine clothes which they had been wearing and put them away in their closets, and with careful prudence they sat down to work instead of going to bed. When the feast had come to an end, the three husbands thanked the scholar for the fine entertainment he had given them, and in particular for the sight of the lovelies arranged in the chamber for their benefit – more beautiful than the sun himself. Having taken their leaves of him, they returned to their homes, where they found their wives sewing at the fireside in their bedrooms. The sight of the clothes, the rings, and the jewels which the scholar had exhibited to them had made them somewhat suspicious, so each one now demanded of his wife where she had spent that evening and where her fine clothes were. To this questioning, each lady boldly replied that she had not left the house all evening. Then, taking the keys of the coffers in which her apparel was arranged, she showed this to her husband, with the rings and other jewels that he had given her. When the husbands saw these, they were silent and had no idea what to say. But after a little while, they told their wives word by word what they had seen that evening. The ladies made as though they knew nothing of the matter and, after jesting about it all, they undressed and went to bed.

In after times, Filenio often met the three ladies in the streets and would always enquire of them, 'Which of you was in the greatest fear? Did I suffer more from your tricks, or you from mine?' But they always turned their eyes down to the ground and said nothing. And in this fashion, the scholar avenged himself the best way he could of the pranks he had endured without ever resorting to blows.

When they had listened to the story of Molino, the Signora and all the other ladies declared that the revenge taken against the three gentlewomen by the scholar for the tricks they had played on him was as revolting as it was cowardly. But when they came to consider the severe punishment which the poor fellow had suffered in couching upon the thorns, the great danger he had incurred in falling from high to low, and the biting cold he had been exposed to when lugged out into the open street to sleep on the bare earth in only his nightshirt, they admitted that his vengeance was no heavier than was due. The Signora, although she had excused Fiordiana from telling her story, in due order now demanded of her at least to give her enigma, which should have some reference to the story of the scholar. In obedience to this request, she said, 'Albeit the enigma which I have to submit to the company has nothing to do with deeds of grave and terrible vengeance such as the ingenious Signor Antonio has set out in his fable, still it will be of interest to every thoughtful young man.' So without further delay, turning toward the noble company, she propounded her riddle.

From two dead blocks a living man
Gave life to one whose spirit ran
To vivify another wight,
Who thus from darkness rose to light.
Two living ones together bite
The creature by the maker's side,
And by the creature's radiance led,
The master communes with the dead.

Signora Fiordiana's subtle riddle was interpreted in various ways, but not one of the company could hit upon its exact meaning. Now seeing that Fiordiana kept on shaking her head at the attempts made by the company, Bembo remarked with a quiet smile, 'Signora Fiordiana, it seems like folly to me to waste our time in this fashion. Tell us what you will and we shall be contented.'

'Well, then,' replied Fiordiana, 'since this noble company requests that I be my own interpreter, I'll gladly do this, not because I deem myself in any way competent for the task, but because I wish to oblige everyone here, to whom I am bound by so many kindnesses. My enigma, ladies, means simply that a student who rises from bed early in the morning, and he, a living thing, by the working of two dead things, the flint and the steel, gives life to the dead tinder, and this in its turn enlivens the dead candle. Thus the first living one, the student, by the help of these other two living ones who lately were dead, sits down to converse with the dead, that is, with the books writ by learned men of times long past.'

The explication of this most ingenious riddle by Fiordiana pleased the company greatly. But seeing midnight was drawing nigh, the Signora requested Lionora to begin her tale at once – which she did in the words to follow with a gladsome and assured countenance.

II.2 Commentary

Straparola's tale of Filenio and the three ladies is a novelistic farce in which the 'polygamous' courting of a young scholar arouses collective female disdain – the amoroso forgetting the efficiency of gossip in detecting those deemed to be cheaters in love. Their subsequent humiliation of his masculine pretensions, however, leads to countermeasures that cost the women a great deal in terms of peace of mind and self-esteem – a narrative of rigorous quid pro quo. The story's 'moral' can hardly be self-evident, because in the battle of the sexes the sinned against and the sinning are often difficult to distinguish. That is perhaps the genius of this narrative, which turns the meaning over to the audience for discussion in a way that perpetuates the 'battle' in the playful ambience of the court or the salon to which such stories were initially read, for the concluding question tendentiously asks which of the parties had been brought to the most acute suffering. Otherwise, in the earliest versions (French), the 'moral' appears in the form of a warning to men not to try to match wits with women, whereas the *novellieri* to follow seek to warn women that students are far too clever and should never be humiliated and scorned. That is due to an inversion of the main episodes, as a look at the principal sources will reveal, for in the inaugural *fabliau* it is the woman who has the final word, whereas in the later *novelle* the scholar has his revenge.

By all appearances, the story is of French provenance, originating in a tale of the twelfth or thirteenth century. But Straparola, for his principal ideas, may have relied upon the version created by Ser Giovanni Fiorentino late in the fourteenth century, a version in which *fabliau* slips into *novella*, while preserving much of the robust psychology and folk combativeness of the original genre. The spirit of the *novella* is equally apparent in the present tale, for Straparola chooses a setting in contemporary Bologna and designs events as a town-gown adventure involving an amorous student and no less than three citizens' wives – a feature found in related French versions. By tripling the love interests of his protagonist and having him duped not once but three times as a result, the story becomes more schematic, as though derived from a folk tale – which indeed it may have been. The question of sources will often bring us to this crux. Straparola's gain is in involving all three women at once in a common denouement, making their exposure both more 'public' and more humiliating.

The principal identifying feature common to this story type is the invitation of a husband to view his wife naked up to her neck in the bed of another man, playing upon his inability to identify her without the benefit of seeing her face. In the gesture there is both titillation and revenge, while preserving a sufficient degree of ambiguity to allow the woman to escape by brazenly outfacing her husband with denials and counter-accusations. Straparola's invention is memorable for its brinkmanship in exposing the bodies of three married women to the semi-public gaze of all their husbands at once and having his hero go so far as to show them their wives' clothes as well. The tricks put upon Filenio are more conventional, whether invented or adapted from other tales, and are easily interchanged: rolling him about naked among thorns under the bed; dropping him into a cellar through a trap door; and dragging him out of the house drugged to spend the night in a frozen street. Straparola concludes his tale with a final encounter between the spouses, once the women have regained their own houses and composed themselves. In certain of the cognate tales, the women even confront their jealous husbands and counter-accuse them, by their own confession, of gawking at naked women in a neighbour's house in an effort to secure their reputations, if not their inner self-respect. This coda is not a feature of Ser Giovanni's tale, which ends abruptly as the wife scurries home through a small back door while the husband is made to go around home the long way. In all the reconfigurations of episode, motif, and setting in the present story, we are presumably seeing Straparola's creative imagination at work, barring the existence of later sources which have escaped attention, or the intervention of the oral culture.

A brief glimpse at the principal sources reveals that in the founding *fabliau*, 'Les deux changeurs,' the narrative logic is inverted, for it is the lover in bed with his friend's wife who begins the sport. It is he who invites in the husband to show off his conquest by revealing to him all but his mistress's face,[40] risking the husband's dawning awareness that he is seeing his own wife. Incensed by so mean a trick, the wife determines upon revenge by dissimulating her anger until she can turn affairs to her advantage. In due course, Béranger, the lover, is coaxed into her house during her husband's absence. There he is induced into the bath and deprived of all escape for want of clothes when the husband's return is announced. The wife bars no holds in telling her husband to climb into the tub to frighten the person cowering under the cover, identified to him as an ugly female neighbour. When he at last leaves, Béranger is treated to every insult – coward, poltroon – and warned never again to mock a woman's favours or to underestimate her vengeance.

A further tale resonating with ours is by Geoffrey de la Tour-Landry from his *Livre du chevalier de la Tour-Landry*, dating to 1381.[41] The wise Boussycault (the spelling used by Caxton in his translation 'Of thre ladyes that aresonned Boussycault') flirts with three women, as in the Straparola tale, who later meet to gossip, only to discover that they are all admired by the same man. When they call him to account, refusing him even a stool to sit on, he scorns them all as unequal to his wants and desires, leaving them abashed and ashamed. The familiar moral is that of the *novellieri*, not to match wits with the sages of the world. The most curious feature, however, is the number of women pursued by the protagonist, perhaps reflecting a concurrent folktale which may have served as a template for Straparola's triple design.

This story reappears in Italy in the tale of Buondelmonte and Nicolosa (II.2) in Ser Giovanni Fiorentino's *Il pecorone*, mentioned above, the composition date of which is still under debate, but which is traditionally assigned to dates between 1378 and 1390.[42] The action takes place in Florence and the would-be lovers are a husband and a wife from feuding households whose palazzi are opposite each other in the same street. Buondelmonte sees and falls in love with Nicolosa, negotiates through a maidservant, sends gifts, and ostensibly wins the lady's acquiescence. The bath scene now comes first, and as the moment of bliss approaches,

40 In *Fabliaux ou contes du XIIe et du XIIIe siècle*, ed. P.J.B. (Paris: Le Grand d'Aussy, 1781), vol. IV, pp. 173–8; (reprint, Geneva: Slatkine Reprints, 1971), pp. 385–6.

41 William Caxton, trans., *The Book of the Knight of the Tower*, ed. M.Y. Offord (London: Early English Text Society and Oxford University Press, 1971), pp. 41–3.

42 Trans. W.G. Waters, 3 vols. (London: Privately Printed for Members of the Society of Bibliophiles, 1898), vol. I, pp. 52–73.

Nicolosa cries out for help, bringing not only her husband into the room but armed men from the city as well. Buondelmonte, like his predecessor, cowers in the bath and manages to avoid detection, although he is so unnerved by the shock that he will hear no more of the lady's subsequent enticements. (Are we surprised?) His love goes cold and he broods over his revenge while dissimulating his continued favour. The feud once over, lover and husband become the best of friends. The lady is invited to a tryst in the Buondelmonti household where she is put to bed in a locked room, while Buondelmonte retires to spend the night with his own wife upstairs. The next morning, Nicolosa's husband returns and is called in by his friend to view his jolly mistress in bed, her face excluded, of course. There the story ends, leaving the audience divided along gender lines in its assessment of the question concerning which of the two suffered the greatest fright and humiliation. We see in this the general design of the present story, but a low coincidence of detail.

That Straparola's scholar spent a cold night in the street by the design of the lady he affected may owe something to Boccaccio's tale of Elena and Rinieri in the *Decameron* (VIII.7), for she too scorns an amorous scholar to whom she has given a rendezvous by locking him overnight in a snowy courtyard while she and her lover spy on him from inside the house.[43] Rinieri reserves a cruel fate for her by leaving her naked on the top of a turret to endure both a cold night and a day of burning sun, which leave her in a nearly ruined state of health. The trick and revenge design is evident, but Elena is a widow and there is no lifting of the covers to expose her body.

It is unlikely that Straparola used this story as a principal narrative source, but he was certainly aware of its cognate design, given the extent to which he pillaged it for diction and phrasing. This is by far his most ambitious ventriloquizing of Boccaccio's work because he borrows from half a dozen passages in scattered fashion. That he was working in a cut-and-paste mode, as elsewhere, is less evident here, for the sporadic patterning suggests rather that he read Boccaccio extensively, fixing numerous passages in mind of which he availed himself as his own narrative situations permitted. Boccaccio's 'serrò dentro al petto suo ciò che la non temperate volontà s'ingegnava di mandar fuori; e con voce

43 Trans. Edward Hutton (London, 1620; reprint, New York: The Heritage Press, 1940), pp. 389–406. This story is also 'Mistresse Helena of Florence,' in Painter's *Palace of Pleasure*, ed. Joseph Jacobs (New York: Dover, 1966), pt. II, no. 31, vol. III, pp. 329–53.

sommessa, senza punto mostrarsi curcciato' thus becomes Straparola's 'chiuse dentro del petto le passate ingiurie, e senza mostrarsi crucciato e di portarle odio ... ' There is a noticeable degree of remodelling as though the act of writing was stylistically primed by a single story, but from which he borrowed in a rather plastic manner.[44]

Les cent nouvelles nouvelles, a kind of French *Decameron* written around 1460 for the Burgundian court, contains a well-told version of the tale, worthy of remark for our purposes because it incorporates a long final scene between the suspicious husband and his astonishingly self-composed wife. At first she pretends not to recognize him when he arrives at the door and refuses him admittance – a stock comedic device. Upon entry, he casts aspersions on her fidelity, but she so works him that he ends up begging her forgiveness. If Straparola required a model for his own closing tiff and reconciliation, he could have found it here.[45]

From such materials as these, Straparola compounded his story, interpreting this *novella* according to his own insights as a raconteur (or those of intervening raconteurs), emphasizing what he undoubtedly found to be a memorable moment of suspense and escape. The story unfolds as though it were on a conventional stage set of the *commedia erudita*, with the lover gaining entry to the three ladies' houses before bringing the women to his own for the dramatic climax, all the while criss-crossing the central piazza in anticipation and in defeat. That inherent dramatic ambience accounts perhaps for the fact that several of the story's sequels are adaptations for the comic stage.

The potential structural parallels have long since been pointed out between this story as it was translated in William Painter's *Palace of Pleasure* (No. 49)[46] and the tricks put upon Sir John Falstaff in Shakespeare's

44 A complete citation of all the relevant passages of both authors may be found in Straparola, *Le piacevoli notti*, ed. Donato Pirovano (Rome: Salerno, 2000), pp. xxxix–xli.

45 [Antoine de la Salle], *Les cent nouvelles nouvelles*, ed. Roger Dubuis (Lyons: Presses universitaires de Lyon, 1991), pp. 31–5.

46 This is a significant fact, for Painter's very influential collection of tales and *novelle* by Boccaccio, Bandello, Cinthio, and others contains but this one story by Straparola – proof that he was known. It constitutes one of the few Straparola tales appearing in a close translation into English before the end of the nineteenth century – there are six or seven others mentioned in the commentaries to follow. *The Palace of Pleasure* was published in parts, the first in 1566, the second in 1567,

Merry Wives of Windsor.[47] Mistress Page and Mistress Ford, to whom Sir John has made independent propositions, collaborate in his humiliation by luring him into a series of amorous rendezvous, there to smother him in piles of dirty laundry before dumping him into the Thames, to have him beaten as the supposed witch of Brentford, and to have him pinched by fairies in the forest in an elaborate, nearly communal tormenting of the old lecherous knight. But there is no turnabout in which the women are exposed to their husbands in the buff, leaving the debt to Straparola a rather general one, if it exists at all. A far greater correlation of motif and detail exists between Shakespeare's play and Ser Giovanni's story of Bucciolo and the Master's wife (I.2), in which an apprentice in love tells his teacher of his exploits without realizing that the lady in question is his wife.[48] In this same general vein, Mr. Ford in disguise as Master Brook is party to Sir John's boastful accounts of his exploits with his wife. How Shakespeare acquired this plot from *Il pecorone*, which was not translated into English before the nineteenth century, is work for Shakespeare specialists, but poses no harder a problem than the playwright's access to Ser Giovanni for the materials (IV.1) he rewrote as *The Merchant of Venice.*

For readers interested in further exploring the present story's fortunes in subsequent literature, the five following works may serve as a point of departure: *Les comptes du monde adventureux* (1595) No. 37, taken from Ser Giovanni;[49] Giovanni Sagredo's *L'Arcadia di Brenta* (1667);[50] *Les amants*

---

in London by Henry Denham and Henry Binneman, respectively. It was edited by Joseph Jacobs for publication by David Nutt in London, 1890, and later reprinted (New York: Dover Publications, 1966), vol. II, 18–28.

47 See Giorgio Melchiori, 'Introduction,' *The Merry Wives of Windsor* (Walton-on-Thames: Thomas Nelson and Sons, 2000), pp. 13–15, and Geoffrey Bullough, *Narrative and Dramatic Sources of Shakespeare*, 5 vols. (London: Routledge & Paul, 1957–75), vol. II, pp. 3–58.

48 Straparola also developed this story in the present collection as the first story of the fourth night.

49 *Les contes du monde aventureux, où sont récitées plusieurs belles histoires mémorables, par A.D.S.D.* (Paris: Estienne Groulleau, 1555); the initials indicate, perhaps, one of the three following: Antoine de Saint-Denis; Abraham de Saint-Dié; or André de Saint-Didier.

50 *L'Arcadia di Brenta* (1667), ed. Quinto Marini (Rome: Salerno, 2004); according to the editor, Sagredo's source is Bandello, *Novelle*, pt. I, no. 3, outlined below, but the differences are striking. Sagredo tells a lively tale of a student who pursues a married woman, only to find himself tricked and stuffed into a trunk in anticipation of her husband's return. He is further terrified when she invites her husband to change shirts, which he does by poking about in the trunk for another. The trial

heureux; and the French comic opera *Souliers Moëre-Dorés*, in which the story is retold in Bowdlerized form. Brantôme altered the tale in his *Vie des femmes galantes* by making the protagonist not a student but Louis d'Orléans.[51] Admittedly, however, these sequels are few and minor compared to the influence cast by other tales in this collection. Arguably, as sensibilities in the early modern period came to demand less frank and robust representations of the battle between the sexes, a tale such as this, with its very particular acts of malice and its resistance to modification, may well have fallen from favour.

Also worthy of mention is a version of the tale contemporary with Straparola's, 'The Joke of a Woman played on a Man for which She was Repaid in Double Measure' by Matteo Bandello.[52] The young Pompeio, living in an unspecified Lombard city, falls in love with Eleonora, a married woman known to all for her beauty, her fetching manners, and her jesting ways by which she would bring on, then ward off suitors. Persisting in his campaign, Pompeio went so far as to go right into her house, having heard her husband was away. Upon the husband's unexpected return, the would-be lover is hidden under a pile of clothes beneath a coffer or chest. Eleonora invents a game with her husband to have him cut some of this clothing in two with his newly purchased sword, both to distract

---

and teaching by fear was complete. Nevertheless, intent upon a turnabout, this student manages to entice the lady to visit him in a garden pavilion outside the city. There her husband arrives as well, but this time she is caught in bed with nowhere to go and takes herself for dead. The student covers her up and goes out to meet the husband to whom he offers to reveal the subject of his delight up to her breasts. All present ask to see the lady's face, but the séance comes to an end and the door is locked shut behind him. All concerned are then left to ponder their respective encounters with fear.

51 Pierre de Bourdeille Brantôme, *Vies des dames galantes* (Paris: Gallimard, [1666], 1981), pp. 80–2. Also, *Lives of Fair and Gallant Ladies* (New York: Liveright, 1933). The list might also have included no. 21 in Nicolas de Troyes' *Le grand parangon* which, according to Krystyna Kasprzyk, dates to the 1530s. *Le grand parangon* (Paris: Marcel Didier, 1970), p. ix. But this work seems to have remained in manuscript form for some time and may never have gained real currency before the edition by Émile Mabille, first published in 1866. *Les amants heureux* (Amsterdam: Le petit David, 1695).

52 Matteo Bandello, *Le novelle*, ed. Giochio Brognoligo, 3 vols. (Bari: Laterza, 1928–31), pt. I, no. 3, vol. I, pp. 44–55. These stories may be found in other Italian editions, such as in *Tutte le opere*, ed. Francesco Flora (Milan: A. Mondadori, 1952); the five-volume edition, ed. Bruno Cagli (Bologna: Sampietro, 1967); as well as in the English translation by John Payne, *The Novels of Matteo Bandello* (London: Villon Society, 1890).

him and to frighten Pompeio in the extreme. This is a new device altogether. The lad escapes but now seeks both sex and revenge, or rather sex as revenge, by feigning sickness in a way that will draw the woman into the trap. As arrangements would have it, Eleonora is a friend of Pompeio's sister, Barbara, who becomes the means and messenger – and who provides the drinks and refreshments for the twenty-five men who are called in to stare at Eleonora's fair body up to her neck, after Pompeio leaps up from his sick bed to compromise her as Amnon does his sister Tamar, before installing her in bed in an adjoining room for the viewing. The lack of coincident detail suggests that each storyteller came by the narrative from independent and unspecified sources, thereby making his own version neither source nor sequel to the other. Assertions to the contrary entail placing these men, with their respective careers, in proximity, thereby enabling an exchange of materials before publication. Bandello's *Novelle* were first published in 1554, but both men had been at work on their collections for some time prior to their respective publications. If Bandello borrowed from Straparola during the brief window following the publication of the first volume of the *Notti* in 1550, he would have to have excised a great deal of episodic play concerning every material detail of the story.[53] The comparatist's enterprise is therefore to imagine how concurrent versions of the same story type might appear simultaneously in the work of artists unlikely to have relied on each other.

The answer no doubt resides in the kind of concurrent borrowing from literary sources that includes the version by Hans Wilhelm Kirchhof, whose *Wendunmuth* (1563) contains the charming tale of the beautiful shoemaker's wife who is having an affair with the priest. The shoemaker suspects nothing. Hence for a joke the priest invites him in while his own wife is there in bed. He turns up the sheets to her knees and asks the craftsman to measure the woman for a new pair of shoes. When the wife returns home, her husband tells her that he had just measured a foot identical to hers, but never does he put all of the evidence together. We must imagine that she will continue to rise early and make her visitations.[54] Here the leading motif is deployed to different ends, yet

53 Ernest Hatch Wilkins, *A History of Italian Literature*, rev. ed. Thomas Bergin (Cambridge, MA: Harvard University Press, 1974), p. 233.

54 *Wendunmuth*, ed. Hermann Oesterley, 5 vols. (Tübingen: Litterarischen Verein in Stuttgart, 1869; reprint, Hildesheim: Georg Olms, 1980), bk. I, sect. 2, 65, vol. II, pp. 528–9. This tale makes its first appearance in the English-speaking world in 'A Tael of a Freer and a Shoemakers Wyef' in Thomas Churchyard's *The First Parte of*

proves, simultaneously, that it was floating free in the European imagination at precisely the time Straparola was writing. This may be the same tale in its German emanation, derived from a widespread and diversified oral tradition. Against that hypothesis in the present case is that the story type did not come down to recorded times in oral form, perhaps because it died out as tastes changed, or because it was an entirely literary tradition.

Straparola's story may reflect something of the mentality of the times – a social climate in which a story of this kind could still find favour. Its pretext is a search for non-invasive revenge, not only through the voyeurism of the three husbands, but by what is suffered in the minds of the women. The story examines the levels of shame, identity, honour, humiliation, and privacy associated particularly with the female body, largely because of the cultural and emotional values attached to the erogenous zones. To expose them to public gaze may be more deleterious to self-esteem than an assault in private. The response to this story, read as it were by the collective emotions of the women in the Signora's circle, is telling, for their first reaction is anger at the dastardliness of it all as viewed from a female perspective, although their view is mollified in remembering the dirty tricks played upon the student that set him scheming in the first place. This is brilliant *novella* material, the signature components largely represented in sundry sources, but not all of them in any one source, French or Italian. How Straparola came to his own formula remains open to speculation. He could have read those several versions and made his synthesis. It is more likely in this case than in many another. Yet, given his habit of relying on the treasury of local tales, this one too may be a product of the synthesizing habits of oral recitation.

Churchyardes Chippes (London: Thomas Marshe, 1575), pp. 84–92. In this parallel rendition, a worldly friar seduces the cobbler's wife after taking her to his cell for the night. Early the next day he leaves her, eager to avoid punishment for missing the morning prayers. Then he sees the cobbler and invites him to his cell to measure his own wife's feet for shoes, placing the woman in a terrible fright. Several weeks later, to pay him back for so dastardly a trick, she invites the friar to her own house, gets him ready for bed, sends her houseboy to the shop to fetch her husband, feigns alarm over his arrival, and bundles the churchman into a trunk. Then she makes as if she were overcome by a terrible pinch in her vitals and calls for aqua vita, which is kept in the trunk, whereupon her trusty husband beats at the sturdy lock with a hatchet until it is about to break. Only then does she tell him to desist because her stitch had now passed. To be sure, once her husband is out of the house, she triumphantly announces her revenge.

I. Fable 3
Carlo da Rimini among the Pots and Pans

LIONORA

Carlo da Rimini loves Theodosia, but she doesn't love him, having promised her virginity to God. Striving to embrace her by force, he finds himself embracing pots, cauldrons, spits, and other kitchen utensils, instead of the girl. In this manner, his face becomes all foul and blackened, for which reason he is soundly beaten by his own servants.

Dear ladies, the clever story just told to us by Molino has made me give up all thought of the one I had in mind and induced me to offer another in its place, which, if I'm not mistaken, will be equally pleasing to you ladies as Molino's was to the gentlemen. And to the degree that his was rather long and obscene, to the opposite degree mine will be brief and upright.

I must tell you then that Carlo da Rimini, as I think many of you may know, was a man whose trade was fighting. He was a despiser of God, a blasphemer of the saints, brutal, and a cutthroat, while at the same time given over to all kinds of inordinate luxury. So great was his malignity and the corruption of his nature that his equal could not be found. Now in the days when he was a handsome and polite young man, it chanced that he fell passionately in love with a certain maiden, the daughter of a poor widow. Yet, though she was nearly destitute and only with great difficulty contrived to make a living for herself and her child, she would rather have died of hunger than to have lived off the wages of her daughter's sin.

The maiden, whose name was Theodosia, was very pretty and graceful in manner, and no less honest and discreet in her conduct. In addition to this, she was prudent and sober tempered, and had already determined to devote herself to the religious life and to prayer, holding all the things of the world of small account. Carlo was burning with lascivious passion and pestered her time and again with his entreaties. On the days when he couldn't see her, he felt near mortal vexation.

He made frequent trial of her with his flattery, gifts, and solicitations, trying to win her consent to do his bidding, but all his efforts were useless. Like a good and wise creature, she would accept none of his presents, but prayed every day to God to turn his heart away from his dishonest desires. At long last there came a time when he could no longer keep his ardent lust and bestial longings within bounds. Feeling grievously affronted by these continual rebuffs by one whom he craved more than his own life, he made up his mind to ravish her and satisfy his lecherous appetite, let the consequences be what they may. Still, he was afraid to stir up any public scandal, for fear that the people, who held him in great hatred, would rise up and slay him.

But at the last, overcome by his unbridled lust, with a mind distempered as though he were a mad dog, he made a plan involving two of his subalterns – both desperate ruffians – to carry her away and rape her. One evening at dusk he armed himself and made haste with the two desperadoes to the young girl's house, the door of which he found open. But before going inside he charged his men to stand guard and stay alert to make certain, if they valued their own lives, not to let anyone else enter the house or to come out until he rejoined them. The two bullies were entirely willing to obey their leader's commands and promised that whatever he ordered, they would carry it out. Theodosia, meanwhile, by means unknown to me, had gotten news of Carlo's intent and straightway shut herself up in a little kitchen. When he had mounted the staircase of the house, Carlo found the old mother there at her spinning, suspecting nothing. He demanded where her daughter was for whom he had such amorous fixations. The poor old woman, as soon as she realized that this oversexed cavalier was armed and more intent upon doing evil than good, her mind lapsed into confusion, her face turned as white as a corpse, and she was ready to scream. But seeing that such outcries would be entirely useless, she resolved to hold her peace and to place her honour in the keeping of God, whom she altogether trusted. Then, plucking up her courage, she turned and spoke to Carlo, 'I don't know what twist of mind or insolent spirit may have brought you here to defile the soul of a girl who desires only to live an honest life. If you have come with a righteous intent, then may God grant you the fulfillment of every just and honourable wish. But should it be otherwise – may God forbid – you're guilty of great wickedness in trying to attain by force what can never be yours. You should have done with this carnal itch and stopped seeking to ravish from my daughter something you can never return – I mean her chastity. The more you lust after her, the more she'll hate you, for her mind is firmly set upon dedicating herself to a life of virginity.'

Upon hearing the aging mother's impassioned words, instead of being awakened to pity or turning away from his evil intentions, Carlo went into a madman's rage and began to search for Theodosia in every corner of the house, finding no trace of her until he came to the little kitchen. There, seeing the door locked fast, he thought, and rightly so, that she must be hidden inside. Spying through a crack in the door, he saw Theodosia fervently praying. So in sugared words he started begging her to open the door to him, 'Theodosia, light of my life, you can be sure that I'm not here to stain your honour, which is dearer to me than my own self and my own good name. I'm here to take you for my wife, provided that my offer is acceptable to you and to your mother, as well. What's more, I swear that I'll kill anyone who affronts your honour in any way.'

Theodosia listened attentively to Carlo's speech and answered him directly, 'Carlo, I beg of you to abandon this obstinate yearning. I can never marry you, because I have dedicated my virgin self to the service of Him who sees and governs us all. But if cruel fortune permits you to violently defile my body, at least you are powerless to blacken the purity of my soul, which I have given to my Creator from the hour of my birth. God has given to you a free will to know the difference between good and evil and the ability to do that which you know to be right. Therefore, follow after the good, turn away from evil, and men will think well of you.'

When he saw that his flattery was to no avail and that the maiden had no more to say to him, he could no longer contain the fire burning in his heart. More maddened now than ever, he put all words aside and, to his great delight, with little difficulty smashed down the door, which was not all that strong or secure.

When Carlo entered the little kitchen and cast his eyes upon the girl, so unbelievably graceful and fair, his passion turned to white heat. He could only think of satisfying his unruly lust. Then he threw himself upon her from behind like a famished greyhound upon the trembling hare. The ill-fated Theodosia, with her loose golden hair about her shoulders, grew pale as Carlo grasped her tightly around the neck and felt so deadly a languor coming over her that she could scarcely move. She commended her soul to heaven and called for God's help from above.

Hardly had she finished these prayerful thoughts in her mind than her body miraculously melted away out of Carlo's grip. At the same time, God so clouded the light of his reason that he no longer knew the objects around him. For while he thought he was holding the maiden in his embrace and covering her with kisses and endearments, in truth, he was hugging nothing better than pots and pans, spits and cauldrons, and other kitchen implements lying about the room. Though his lust was in some measure satisfied, he soon felt his wounded heart stirring again, and once more he rushed to embrace a huge kettle, thinking all the while to be holding the fair form of Theodosia in his arms. By handling the kettles and cauldrons in this way, his face became smeared with soot, so that he looked more like the Devil than Carlo da Rimini. Finally, his desires for the moment satiated and aware that it was time to retreat, he found his way out by the staircase, all blackened as he was. But the two ruffians, who were keeping guard near the door to prevent anyone from entering or leaving the house, when they saw him thus transformed, with his face all disfigured and looking more like a beast than a man, imagined that he must be some ghost or evil spirit and were inclined to take to their heels. But looking closely at his face in its disfigured and ugly condition, they took heart. Standing up to him, they began to drub him with their cudgels and their fists, which were as hard as iron, so that they cruelly mangled his face and shoulders with a hearty goodwill and left him without a hair on his head. Still not satisfied, they threw him down on the ground, tore the clothes from his back, and dealt him so many kicks and blows that Carlo had no time to open his mouth to ask the reason for this cruel treatment. Finally, he made a manoeuvre that freed him from their hold and then ran for his life, convinced all the while that the tough guys were right behind.

Carlo was so soundly bastinadoed by his servants, his eyes all swollen and discoloured, that he ran towards the piazza shouting and complaining in a loud voice of the ill-handling he had gotten from his own men. The town guard, when they heard these cries and lamentations, approached him, and when they saw his foul and disfigured state they took him for a bedlamite. Because no one recognized him, the whole crowd started to make fun of him and to yell out, 'Give it to him, give it to him, he's a lunatic.' Then some began to shove him, others to spit in his face, while others took dust and threw it into his eyes. They kept up this maltreatment for quite a long time before the uproar came to the ears of the Provost. He got up from his bed and went over to the window overlooking the piazza, demanding to know the cause of such a tumult. When one of the guards answered that there was a madman at the centre of this ado, the Provost gave order that he should be bound hand and foot and brought before him. His command was carried out immediately.

Now Carlo, who up to this time had been the terror of all, found himself bound, ill-treated, and insulted without any idea of the cause. He was so utterly confounded in his mind that he broke into a violent rage, nearly breaking the ropes that held him. As soon as he was brought before the Provost, the latter recognized him straightway as Carlo da Rimini. When he witnessed the filthy condition of his prisoner, he knew that it was the work of Theodosia, for he was in on the secret of Carlo's enflamed passion for the girl. His speech then turned all soft and soothing, promising Carlo that he would punish those who had brought him into such a state of disgrace. Carlo was at first astonished, having no idea that his face resembled that of an Ethiopian. But when at last he was brought to understand the filthy condition he was in, and how he resembled a brute beast rather than a human, he, like the Provost, attributed his disfigurement to Theodosia. Giving his anger free vent, he swore an oath that unless the Provost punished her, he would revenge the outrage with his own hand. When the morning came, the Provost sent for Theodosia, convinced that she had done the deed through magic. But wise and discreet as she was, she knew full well the danger she was in and fled to a convent of nuns of the holy life where she dwelt in secrecy, there serving God with a good heart for the rest of her days.

At a later time, it happened that Carlo was sent to lay siege to a castle. There, eager to perform bolder and mightier deeds than were in his power, he ended up like a rat caught in a trap, for as he clambered up the walls of the citadel to fix the banner of the Pope on the battlements, he was struck by a huge stone which crushed his body; death took him off before a word of confession was uttered. Thus the wicked Carlo made a wretched end of his days in keeping with what he deserved, without having plucked the fruit of love he so ardently desired.

Before Lionora had come to the end of her short but engaging story, all her companions began to laugh over Carlo's stupidity, what with kissing and embracing the pots and kettles and thinking all the while that he was enjoying his beloved Theodosia. Nor were they any less amused by the cuffs and blows he got from the hands of his own men, and then from the town guard. After a good spell of laughter, Lionora, without waiting for further word from the Signora, set forth her enigma:

I am fine and pure and bright,
At my best I'm snowy white.
Maid and matron scourge and flout me,
Yet they cannot do without me,
For I serve both young and old,
Shield their bodies from the cold.
A mighty parent mothered me,
Mother of all mothers she,
And, my time of service past,
I'm torn and beaten at the last.

This cleverly-worded enigma won the praise of all the company, but as it seemed beyond the power of anyone to solve it, Lionora was requested to divulge its meaning, whereupon she said with a smile, 'It is scarce becoming that one of my slender talents should presume to teach you, ladies and gentlemen, who are so much more versed in knowledge. But given that it is your will, and your will to me is law, I'll tell you outright what my riddle means. It signifies merely linen cloth, fine and white, which is pierced by ladies' scissors and needles, and afterwards beaten. Such cloth serves as a covering to us all and comes from the mother of all, the earth. Moreover, when it grows old, we straightway send it to the fuller to be torn up into small pieces to be made into paper.'

Everyone was pleased with the interpretation of this clever enigma and commended it highly. Lodovica had been chosen to tell the next story, but when the Signora was advised that she was troubled with a bad headache, she turned to the Trevisan and said, 'Signor Benedetto, it is indeed the duty of us ladies to provide the stories tonight, but seeing that Lodovica's head is bothering her so, we beg you to take her place this evening, granting to you a free field to tell whatever would please you the most.'

To this the Trevisan replied, 'Although I have little skill in these matters, Signora, yet because your wish is my command, I'll put forward my best effort to satisfy you all, begging at the same time to be held excused if I fail.' Having made his due salutation, he rose from his seat and began his tale in the following words.

II.3 Commentary

This vignette from the lives of the saints, here turned into a little 'historical' *novella*, is to be found in hagiographical literature under the heading

'Agape, Chionia, and Irene.' They were martyrs in Salonika in 304, their feast day is April 3, and it is among the 'April' saints that they appear in the *Acta sanctorum*.[55] In their generic story, there is no attachment to Saint Anastasia or to Theodosia and no delusional rampage among the pots and pans on the part of their assailant. But there is a continuity of accretions and associations that link their story to Straparola's. In the earliest accounts, two of the girls, for refusing to sacrifice to the gods, were taken before the governor of Macedonia, Dulcitius, and were subsequently burned. The third of the three, Irene, had kept Christian books and had fled to the mountains. The governor ordered her to be stripped and exposed in a brothel, although she remained unmolested. Refusing to conform, she too was burned.[56] Out of these simple and unremarkable relations came the story of the sexually motivated prefect under whose charge they had been placed, and the serio-comic miracle of his mental derangement during which he made love to the pots and pans, taking them for the three beautiful women.

That amplification was undoubtedly traditional by the time the story was dramatized in the mid-tenth century play *Dulcitius*, written by Hrotsvitha, the celebrated Saxon nun of Gandersheim. The play, despite its theatrical treatment, Terentian milieu, and homiletic dialogue, preserves a clear version of the hagiographical narrative.[57] The apparent new setting of the play is Rome, for the first scene takes place at the court of Diocletian. (Although she is not mentioned, the story now accords with the place and date of the martyrdom of Saint Anastasia.) When all three, in their entrenched piety, sass the emperor seriatim, he turns them

55 Ed. Bollandi, 'De sanctis sororibus Agape, Chionia et Irene,' vol. I, pp. 245–50. Hippolyte Delehaye describes the main events from the *Légendier romain*, stating that Anastasia accompanied the three sisters to prison after their arraignment by Diocletian in Aquileia. Dulcitius, the prison keeper, was to torment them for refusing to sacrifice to the Roman gods. Upon entering their cell, however, he was taken by a madness which led him to a kitchen where he began embracing the pots and pans, leaving him all covered in soot. In this way, the three sisters were temporarily spared. *Étude sur le légendier romain: Les saints de novembre et de décembre* (Brussels: Société des Bollandistes, 1936), p. 152.

56 Donald Attwater, *The Avenel Dictionary of Saints* (1965; reprint, New York: Avenel, 1981), p. 34.

57 The play is known by the name of the Macedonian governor, but its given title is *Martyrdom of the Holy Virgins, Agape, Chionia and Hirena. The Plays of Hrotsvit of Gandersheim*, trans. Katharina Wilson (New York: Garland Publishing, 1989), pp. 37–49.

over to Dulcitius the governor who attempts to rape them. But Dulcitius finds the women singing hymns and suddenly goes insane. The women then comment upon his folly among the pots and pans, mocking his absurd erotic antics. Curiously there is no dialogue in which they plead for their virginity and sanctuary, nor is the event profiled as a miracle. The governor, covered in soot, is mistaken by his men for a devil. He goes to the emperor to complain and there he is beaten by the guards. He then seeks revenge by having the women stripped naked and put on public display, but their garments cling to their bodies while Dulcitius, himself, falls into a profound and miraculous sleep. They are accused of witchcraft and the eldest two are burned, although after the departure of their souls even their clothes and hair are not consumed by the fire. Count Sissinus then attempts to deal with Irene by exposing her to view in a brothel, but undaunted in spirit she escapes miraculously to the mountains, only to be captured and slain by an arrow. The story has grown, the ridiculous appears alongside the miraculous, the violence has increased, and in the process the tale of the virgin martyrs becomes more pointedly gendered, more dramatic, and more ideological.

We are able to check in on the progress of the fable three centuries later in the *Legenda aurea* (The golden legend), arguably the most successful of all the medieval anthologies of saints' lives. It was compiled by Jacobus de Voragine (from Varazze near Genoa) around the year 1260.[58] By that time, a number of further amalgamations had taken place. In this version, the three martyred women have become the beautiful serving maids and sisters of Saint Anastasia, a woman born into a noble Roman family who died under Diocletian in 287. A prefect falls in love with the three sisters and has them locked into a kitchen when they refuse his advances. There he goes in secret, but loses his senses and starts kissing the utensils and cookware before re-emerging covered in soot. In making his exit, he is taken for a devil by his own men, as in Hrotsvitha, but this time he is beaten for good measure. He goes to complain to the emperor, but before he gains entry, the guards beat him again and throw mud (dirt, dust) on him, as in Straparola, thinking him a madman. He accuses the maidens of magic and demands that they be stripped nude

58 Jacobus de Voragine, *The Golden Legend*, trans. William Granger Ryan, 2 vols. (Princeton: Princeton University Press, 1993), vol. I, pp. 43–4. No doubt created as a manual for preachers, it survives in over 1,000 manuscripts and was translated into all the languages of Western Europe. Caxton produced his English version in 1483.

in front of him so he can at least feast his eyes, but their clothing clings fast to them and he falls into a deep sleep. Immediately thereafter, without further ado, the virgins are crowned with martyrdom. But the other part of their story is now attributed to Anastasia (rather than to Irene). After she refuses to worship the pagan gods, the prefect tries to seduce her in a bridal chamber and is turned blind. Another prefect offers her freedom if she agrees to give him all her worldly wealth. She is then thrown into prison where she is fed by Saint Theodora with food from heaven; ultimately, however, she too is bound to a stake and burned alive. In certain ways the ensemble has been further fragmented, but in making Saint Anastasia the central figure, it becomes inevitable that the episode of the pots and pans is told of her as well, thereby unifying the elements around a single protagonist. By the time these materials come to Straparola, either he or a predecessor, under the influence of the *novella* with its secular and social orientation, has given even greater prominence to the comic miracle of the pots and pans, the signature 'beffa' (or miracle) of the story. Moreover, the self-preserving protagonist is no longer the patrician Anastasia, but Theodosia, the daughter of a poor widow. Nor does she come to a saint's martyrdom, but seeks sanctuary in a convent, an option for girls without material prospects or family protection.

Regarding the process whereby a thirteenth-century saints' tale becomes a sixteenth-century *novella*, there is but one further hint. The prefect is given an ambiguous historical identity as Carlo Malatesta. The story is told as a real event in the life of this celebrated mercenary who died in 1429 after a lifetime of warring and campaigning. The details given of Carlo's death in Straparola's tale, however, do not coincide with the life records of this famous warrior, leaving open to speculation that the Carlo intended may be the far more shadowy Carlo of Rimini who died in 1508 at the age of 28 after a few years of military service for the Venetian Republic. If this Carlo died during a siege on behalf of the Pope and was slain by falling stone, he is certainly the man inspiring the adaptation, but in principle the Venetians were rarely if ever on the side of the Pope. By contrast, the Carlo of our tale is a well-known public figure, which alone gives ironic piquancy to the abuse he receives in the course of the story. The early Carlo was Lord of Rimini, a respected statesman, learned, grave to the point of austerity, not noted for social abuses, but hated by his foes. He did fight for the Papal States, but did not die in battle, although he had the reputation of a blasphemer for having thrown a statue of the virgin into the river to mock the piety of the Mantuans. In Straparola's tale he is said to be brutal, a cutthroat, and blasphemous, as well as a philanderer. But perhaps the portrait is a composite one based on the remote but lasting reputation of the family. That there were stories maligning or making fun of the Malatesti is no surprise, given the number of their enemies. This story is indeed tame compared to those once circulating about Sigismondo, said to have had incestuous relations with his daughters and to have attempted sodomy with one of his sons before being warded off at knifepoint. There is hence a well-established context for telling unflattering stories of the sexual predation of this family's members in general. The more specific question is when and by whom the old legend was appropriated to those ends, a question that is likely to evade all answering.

That the development of this tale passed through *The Golden Legend* seems assured given the many synonymous details, such as the crowd that declared Carlo a lunatic and cast dirt in his eyes until he was rescued by the praetor. Only the end is truncated when, after being summoned, Theodosia suddenly escapes into the holy life of a nun. Meanwhile, the violence of the tale has increased with the abuses compounded against the witless and defeated Carlo. It is the tale of a historical bully who gets his own back again from a pious virgin. But the vengeance wreaked upon the person of Carlo is broadened in its application by Straparola's chosen storyteller, Lionora, to constitute vengeance against men in general by abused women everywhere. Lionora, in fact, exchanges her intended story for this one in answer to Molino's relation of the cruel revenge against the three wives when the angered protagonist exposed them naked up to their necks to their gawking husbands. Through this exchange of stories, a little controversy over women turns into a full-scale battle of the sexes by reducing males to predators and females to seekers of sanctuary, piety, and escape. Lionora's point is carried when her women companions burst into laughter over the ludicrous scene in the pantry with the pots and kettles and at the lambasting Carlo receives from his own men. On the whole, the tale is rather low comic fare of an entirely farcical nature, no doubt influenced by the *lazzi* performed in the theatres. Lionora was not to have the last word, however, for the Trevisan, Signor Benedetto, is about to regale them all with the fable of Belfagor, taken for one of the most misogynistic stories of all time.

By all appearances, Straparola's was the last literary treatment of this motif. It might have been acceptable to him in a collection that featured the mechanisms of fairy tales from the world of magic. Nevertheless, as a tale intimating divine intervention in the lives of the perfect, it would find a diminishing place in the literature of contemporary social motivation and natural causation. Even so, the social design of the tale could have its sequels. In Barnabe Riche's *Farewell to Military Profession,* in the tale 'Of Nicander and Lucilla,' a poor but beautiful maiden, nobly born but fallen upon hard times, is betrothed to Nicander. Her desires are impeded only by the lack of a dowry.[59] Thus she lingers, exposed to the sexual ambitions of Don Hercules, whose erotic cravings increase with his frustrations in the face of Lucilla's firm and virginal resistance. At that point in the narrative, the two stories would seem to diverge beyond all relationship. But curiously, Straparola mentions a hypothetical alternative in passing: that Theodora's mother would rather have died of hunger than to have lived off the wages of her daughter's sin. Who would have entertained the idea that she might? And yet the prostituting of children to unwanted marriages, if not to pure sexual exploitation for cash, is common literary fare. This is precisely what follows in Riche's story, for Lucilla's mother, in her poverty, enters into collusion with the Don to sell her daughter's sexual favours by admitting him secretly into her room to view her naked body and take his pleasure with her. Whereas the girl's mother preaches the sanctity of virginity in Straparola, now it is Lucilla herself who must use all of her verbal skills to make the Don desist. In the end, the story of the impoverished girl targeted for rape by the lord of the city finds its mirror reversal in exchanging raging lust for noble magnanimity. It is as though the same story had been rewritten, but by a flatterer of Gonzaga virtue as opposed to a despiser of Malatesta brutality. And that is indeed the case, for Riche's source was a tale about Duke Alfonso of Ferrara written by Giraldi Cinthio for Duke Ercole II, his patron and the son of Alfonso (*Hecatommithi* VI.3). Cinthio turns the ridiculous assault into a story about the sublimity of self-mastery. Each story is a reminder that the sexes have their social roles and instincts and that the very prospect of the civilized life is based upon negotiation, repression, and self-control. Both stories explore those terms, but Straparola's, in the interest of pointing blame, tells of an all-out assault

59 *His Farewell to Military Profession,* ed. Donald Beecher (Ottawa: Dovehouse Editions, and Binghamton, NY: MRTS, 1992), pp. 202–17.

met by the defiance of death in chastity – negotiation at its deafest, most intransigent, and futile extreme. The women prevail and get revenge, but at a certain cost. Meanwhile, the bizarre sublimation of sexuality in embracing pots and pans and in mistaking them for the body of the beleaguered virgin is hilariously thought-provoking. Curiously, this was no mere rampage, but a violent hallucination in which one act is experienced as another. Carlo thinks he is having her. The hedonics of lust are, after all, a thing of mental constructions and dripping dopamine on the nucleus accumbens. Hence, Straparola's narrative is an allegory for the treatment of sexual maniacs. Give them delusions from an induced surfeit of neurotransmitters in their padded cells.

This story contains a further instance of Straparola's inclination, at select but unpredictable moments, to ventriloquize passages principally (though not exclusively) from Boccaccio's *Decameron*. To be sure, it is a testimony to his reading and to the humanist habit of building by *imitatio* upon the works of the great forebears. But with Straparola, the question is always why – why at particular moments, when all the surrounding materials appear to be of his own devising, and why in so literal a fashion? Moreover, there is the question of actual procedures, whether he held these passagettes in memory and called upon them spontaneously, or whether he was conducting a rather more studied and esoteric exercise in collateral functions and substitutional phrasing. Here is the material to reflect upon. When Carlo emerges from the kitchen all blackened from the pans and his own servants take him for the Devil, we are told that they pounded him with 'their fists, which were as hard as iron, so that they cruelly mangled his face and shoulders with a hearty goodwill, and left him without a hair on his head,' and then, still not satisfied, they threw him down on the ground and 'tore the clothes from his back.' Just why Straparola would feel the compunction at this moment to lift words from the *Decameron* (IX.8) is an intriguing question. The latter reads, 'con le pugna, le quali aveva che parevan di ferro, tutto il viso gli ruppe né gli lasciò in capo capello che ben gli volesse: e, convoltolo per lo fango, tutti i panni indosso gli stracciò,' echoed by Straparola's, 'con le pugna, che di ferro parevano, tutto il viso e le spalle li ruppero, né li lasciorono in capo capello, che bene gli volesse, né contenti di ciò, lo gittorono a terra, stracciandogli e' panni da dosso ... ' The story would hardly be changed if Carlo's servants had harmed him in any way imaginable with their fists and cudgels, but for reasons known only to the author, he relies upon Boccaccio's precise words – a nifty bit of secluded intertextuality, surely for reasons other than a dearth of inspiration of his own, for even children can come up with words for beating an adversary's face to a pulp, yanking all the hair off his head, and ripping the clothes off his back.[60] Surely there was a pleasure here of a more subtle kind in fitting the words of the master into a text that is otherwise of a different stamp and ethos.

60 See Donato Pirovano, *Le piacevoli notti* (Rome: Salerno, 2000), p. xxxvii; for the corresponding passage in Boccaccio, see *The Decameron*, trans. J.M. Rigg (London: Navarre Society, ca. 1900), vol. II, p. 300.

II. Fable 4
The Devil's Marriage to Silvia Ballastro

BENEDETTO OF TREVISO

The Devil, having heard diverse husbands railing over the humours of their wives, makes trial of matrimony by espousing Silvia Ballastro, taking for his best man one Gasparino Boncia. But finding himself no longer able to endure his wife, he enters into the body of the duke of Malfi, from which his companion, Gasparino, presently casts him out.

The frivolity and want of judgment that is nowadays to be found among most women – I'm speaking of those who heedlessly let the eyes of their intellect feed their fancies with unbridled desires – gives me occasion to tell this noble assembly a story which may not be familiar. Although you may find it a little on the short side and not well put together, nevertheless I hope it may serve as a wholesome lesson to you women to be less irksome to your husbands and less demanding than before. And if I seem rather too biting, don't blame me who remains a humble servant to you all, but make your complaint to the Signora, who, as you've all heard, has given me leave to set before you any story that commends itself to my taste.

I will explain first, gracious ladies, that many years ago the Devil, becoming weary of the endless clamour and accusations made by husbands against their wives, determined to try out marriage for himself. So that he might better accomplish this design, he took the shape of a goodly young man of courtly manners, well furnished with lands and gold, one Pancrazio Stornello by name. As soon as the news of his intentions made the rounds of the city, various matchmakers attended upon him with a plentiful choice of attractive and well-dowered women. Among them was a very fair damsel named Silvia Ballastro who was presented for his inspection. It was she who found favour in the Devil's eyes and was chosen to be his most beloved wife.

Never had the city witnessed such magnificent nuptials and celebrations. The kinsfolk of the bride came from far and near, and for his best man and companion the bridegroom chose a townsman of repute, a certain Gasparino from the house of Boncio. After the solemn and sumptuous ceremony, he led his delightful Silvia home. Not many days passed before the Devil addressed her, saying, 'My dear wife, I hardly need to tell you that I love you more than I love myself, seeing that I have already given you many tokens of my affection. For the sake of this love of mine, I'm about to ask of you a favour easy for you to grant in that whatever you should ask is wholly acceptable to me. It is nothing else but that you ask of me now all that you want and ever are likely to want by way of clothes, jewellery, pearls, and other accessories loved by ladies, for, given my great love for you, I've decided to give you everything that you may demand, though it may cost me a kingdom. But I make only one condition, which is that you never trouble me with these matters again. Hence, be careful that you request all that you will possibly need for the rest of our married life, and be careful likewise never to demand anything further of me, for you will ask in vain.' Silvia begged for time to consider this proposition and, going directly to the worldly-wise old lady, her mother, Signora Anastasia, she laid her husband's offer on the table and asked for advice. Anastasia, who knew well enough how to play this sort of game, weighing the proposal, took pen and paper and wrote out a list of articles so long that it would require an entire day for one tongue to cover the mere essentials. Then she said to her daughter, 'Take this paper, return home, and ask your husband to give you everything that is written therein. And if he agrees, you may well accept his terms.'

With that, Silvia left her mother, walked back to the house, and finding her husband she asked him to give her all that was written on the list. When he had read it over carefully, he said, 'Now are you certain, my dearest Silvia, that you have put down here all you want, that there is nothing missing for which at some time in the future you may have to ask me? For if you have, I'm warning you now that neither your prayers, nor your sighs, nor your tears will suffice to get it for you.'

Silvia could think of nothing else to add, saying she was content with what had been written, and that nothing more would follow. Therewith, he ordered up the vast store of rich clothes studded with large pearls, and rings, and all sorts of jewels, the most sumptuous and dear that had ever been seen. Over and above these things, he gave her headdresses and girdles embroidered with pearls, and all sorts of dainty trinkets, more than were on the list and finer than can be told. When Silvia was arrayed in all these and aware of being the best-dressed woman in the city whom no one could equal, she was as joyful as could be. Nothing remained for her to ask of her husband, so well had he cared for all her needs.

About that time, the city was all abuzz with excitement concerning a great feast to which all the nobles and dignitaries were to be invited, and among them Silvia was not forgotten, for she was one of the most beautiful and distinguished ladies in the city. In order to celebrate this festival with even greater honour, the other ladies met and devised all sorts of new fashions, altering the old ones so much that there was no resemblance left between them. Just as if it had happened today, there was no mother's daughter in the town who was not bent upon gracing the festival in the newest fashion, each one vying to outdo the other in pomp and magnificence.

When this news came to Silvia's ears that the matrons of the city had altered all the dress fashions, she was suddenly overcome with fear that her recently acquired hoard of clothes provided by her husband would be found so out-of-fashion as to be unfit for wearing to the feast. In consequence, she fell into an unpleasant and melancholy tantrum. Then she could neither eat nor sleep, filling all the house with sighs and groans drawn up from the very bottom of her heart. The Devil, who came to understand the trouble in his wife's breast, pretended to know nothing of the matter, and one day addressed her, 'What is troubling you, Silvia, that you look so unhappy? Have you no heart for the coming festival with all its pomp and solemnity?'

Seeing her opportunity, Silvia plucked up her courage and said, 'What is the festival to me? How can I go there in these old-fashioned clothes of mine? I'm sure you'll not force me to go, only to endure the mockery of the others. I could hardly believe it of you.'

Then Pancrazio said to her, 'Didn't I give you everything you wanted for the rest of your days? How is it that you now ask me for more?'

Seeing now that she had no suitable clothes for the occasion, Silvia wept even more over her unhappy fate. Then the Devil said, 'I gave you at the first all that you needed from henceforth, but I'll once more gratify your wishes. Ask me for anything you want and your request will be granted, but never again. If, after this, you make a similar request, the results will be something you'll never forget.' Right away, Silvia abandoned her peevish humour and made out another list of braveries as long as the last. All of these things Signor Pancrazio got for her without delay.

Not many months passed before the ladies of the city once more set to work to make changes in the fashions, and once more Silvia found herself dressed in outmoded garments. No other lady could boast of jewels so costly or robes of such rich and sumptuous a weave, but this was no solace to her. All day long she went about moping in sorrow without daring to make another appeal to her husband. He, noticing her sorrowful face for a second time and knowing full well what was vexing her (although again pretending ignorance), said to her, 'Silvia, my love, why are you so sad?'

Then she plucked up her courage, 'Is there not cause enough for me to be sad, seeing that I have no clothes in the new fashion, and that I can't even show my face among the other ladies of the city without them making fun of me and bringing reproach on you as well as on me? I tell you, the respect and fidelity I have toward you don't merit this return of shame and humiliation.'

At these words, the Devil was fiercely angry and said, 'What reason do you have to complain? Haven't I twice given you everything you asked for? Your desires are insatiable and beyond my power to fulfil. I'm leaving immediately and you'll never see my face again.'

The Devil was as good as his word. After he had given Silvia a goodly store of new garments, all after the latest fashion, he left her without saying goodbye and went to Amalfi. There he entered into the body of the duke and tormented him grievously. The poor duke was gravely afflicted by this malign spirit, yet there was no man in Amalfi of a sufficiently good and godly life that he could drive the spirit out of his body.

By chance, shortly thereafter, Gasparino Boncio, the gallant who was best man at Pancrazio's wedding, was forced to flee from his city for a certain crime. To escape arrest and judgement, he got himself to Amalfi where no one knew his secret and there he took up gambling, at which he was a master. For this and other trickery, he gained a reputation throughout the city as a clever and accomplished fellow, although his dealings were nothing but fraud. One day, while gaming with gentlemen of the place, he went a step too far and angered them all so much that only fear of the law stopped them from murdering him on the spot. One of them, in a rage over his losses, vowed that he would bring Gasparino into such grief that he wouldn't forget it for the rest of his life. Without further delay, he went before the duke, made a deep bow before him, and said, 'Your Excellency, there is a man named Gasparino here in town who boasts that he can cast out evil spirits which have gotten into the bodies of men, whether they're of the earth or the air. It seems to me,

Your Excellency, that you would do well to ask him to try his skill in delivering you from your present torment.' Upon hearing these words, the duke sent forthwith for Gasparino, who, being summoned, made his appearance.

'Signor Gasparino,' the duke said, after looking him in the face, 'they tell me you profess to be an exorcist of evil spirits. Well, as you've no doubt heard, I'm sorely tormented by one of these, and I pledge my faith to you that if you'll liberate me from this devil that incessantly tortures me, I'll favour you with a gift that will bring eternal happiness.'

Gasparino, who had never uttered such words, stood as one dumbfounded. As soon as the duke was silent, he began to protest that he knew nothing of such matters and had never boasted of any such power. But the gentleman who was standing by came forward and said, 'Don't you remember, Signor Gasparino, how on a certain day you told me all about this?'

Gasparino persisted in denying any such speech, and while they were both arguing about it, the duke broke in and said, 'Come, come, hold your peace, both of you! As for you, Master Gasparino, I give you three days to work up your charms, and if you can deliver me from this misery, I promise you the most beautiful castle in my dominions. In fact, you can ask of me whatever you will. But if you fail in this, before eight days have passed I'll have you suspended by the neck between the two columns of my palace.'

Upon hearing the duke's stern conditions, Gasparino was completely stunned and sorrowful. Leaving the presence chamber, he began to ruminate day and night as to how he might accomplish the task laid upon him. On the day fixed for the incantation, he went to the palace. There he requested that a large carpet be spread on the floor, after which he began to conjure the evil spirit to come out and to cease his torments. The Devil, who was quite at his ease in the duke's body, made no reply, but breathed so strong a blast of wind through the duke's throat that it nearly choked him. When Gasparino renewed his conjurations, the Devil cried out, 'Companion of mine, you enjoy your life, so why can't you leave me at peace where I'm very comfortable? You're tormenting me to no purpose.' Then the Devil began to deride him. But Gasparino was not to be daunted and for the third time called upon the Devil to come out, asking him so many questions that at last he discovered that the evil spirit was none other than his old friend Pancrazio Stornello. 'I'm compelled to confess the truth that I'm Pancrazio, married to Silvia Ballastro,' the Devil went on, 'and don't I know you? Aren't you Gasparino Boncio, my very dear friend and best man? Don't you remember those merry nights we spent together?'

'Alas, my friend,' said Gasparino, 'why have you come here to torment this miserable duke?'

'That is my secret,' answered the Devil. 'Why do you refuse to go away and leave me here where I'm more at my ease than before?'

But Gasparino went on with his questioning so long and so adroitly that he induced the Devil at last to tell him the story of his wife's insatiable greed, of the violent aversion he had conceived for her, how he had fled from her and taken up his abode in the body of the duke, and how no consideration could ever induce him to return to her. Having learned so much, Gasparino said, 'well, my dear friend, now I want you to do me a favour.'

'And what may that be?' the Devil enquired.

'Nothing more than to leave the body of this poor man.'

'Friend Gasparino,' said the Devil, 'I never took you for a wise man, but this request of yours tells me you're a downright fool.'

'But I beg you, I implore you for the sake of the great times we had together to do this one request for me,' said Gasparino. 'The duke has heard that I have power to cast out spirits and has imposed this task on me. Unless I fulfil it, I'll be hanged and you'll be charged with my death.'

'Nonsense!' said the Devil. 'The meanest and sorriest faith in the world is the one between close friends. Anyway, the suffering will be yours, not mine. What can I desire more than to see you at the bottom of the infernal abyss? Why didn't you keep your tongue between your teeth instead of going about boasting of powers you don't possess?'

'Tell me,' replied Gasparino, 'who was the one who gave you all this trouble?'

'Have patience,' the Devil replied, 'because I have nothing more to say to you, so take your leave and expect no more answers.' And so, in a state nearing rage, he caused the duke to feel more dead than alive.

After a little time the duke came to himself and Gasparino addressed him, 'Take courage, my lord, for I see a way of ridding you of this evil spirit. I must ask you to command all the musicians in the city to assemble at the palace tomorrow morning and at a fixed moment to play upon their instruments while the bells all ring loudly and the gunners fire their cannons as a sign of rejoicing for victory. The more noise they make the better for my purpose. The rest you may leave to me.'

The next morning, Gasparino went to the palace and duly began his incantations. Now, as had been settled, the trumpets and cymbals and tambours gave out their music, and the bells and artillery clanged and roared so loudly and long that it seemed the world must be coming to an end. At the last, as Gasparino was proceeding with his conjurations, the Devil asked him what was meant by this medley of instruments and cacophony the likes of which he had never heard before. 'Nay, but you know as well as I do,' replied Gasparino.

'No, I don't,' said the Devil.

'Is it possible,' cried Gasparino, 'that you know less than we mortals who are wrapped in a fleshly body, and who can know and hear nothing because our earthy substance is too dull and gross? I'll tell you in very few words,' said Gasparino, 'if, in the meantime, you let the duke have a little ease.'

'It shall be as you wish,' said the Devil. And then Gasparino brought out his story.

'You must know, my dear friend and companion,' he began, 'that it has come to the duke's ears how you were forced to run away from your wife on account of the woes you suffered through her greed for attire and so he has invited her to Amalfi. The noise you hear is part of the rejoicing of the city over her arrival.'

'I see your hand in this, honest Signor Gasparino,' said the Devil. 'Well, you have outdone me in cunning. Was there ever a loyal friend? Was I not right in belittling the claims of gossip? However, you have won the game. The distaste and horror in which I hold my wife are so great that I will do your bidding and betake myself elsewhere. Rather than set eyes on her again, I prefer to head for the nethermost part of hell. Farewell, Gasparino, you will never see or hear of me again.'

Immediately after these words were exchanged, the poor duke began to throttle and choke and his eyes rolled about in ghastly ways, but these frightening signs only gave warning that the evil spirit had at last taken flight. Nothing remained to tell of his presence except an appalling stench. Gradually the duke came to himself and, when he had regained his former health, he sent for Gasparino. Not to be accused of ingratitude, he gave him a stately castle and a great sum of money, along with a crowd of retainers to do him service. Though assailed by the envy of certain of the courtiers, Gasparino lived happily and in prosperity for many years. But Madam Silvia, when she saw all the clothes, jewels, and rings consumed to smoke and ashes, after a few days lost her wits and died most miserably.

The Trevisan told his story with great wit and the men greeted it with hearty applause and laughter. But the ladies demurred somewhat, so that the Signora, hearing them murmuring amongst themselves while the men kept up their merriment, commanded silence and directed the Trevisan to give his enigma. He began thus, without a word of excuse to the ladies for the sharp goads directed at their sex by his story.

In our midst a being proud
Lives with every sense endowed.
Keen his wit, though brainless he,
Reasoning with deep subtility.
Headless, handless, tongueless too,
He knows our nature through and through.
Born but once and born forever,
Death shall touch or mar him never.

The abstruse riddle of the Trevisan was no light task for the wit of the company and it was in vain that each one tried to unravel it. At last, the Trevisan, seeing that their guesses were all wide of the mark, said, 'It doesn't seem right for me to perplex the ingenuity of this honourable company any longer. With your permission, I'll now unfold its meaning, unless you prefer to wait for some cunning wit to unpack it.' With one voice, they urged him to reveal its significance, which he did in the following terms: 'My enigma signifies nothing other than the immortal soul of man, which, being spiritual, has neither head nor hands nor tongue, yet makes its working known to all, and, whether it is ultimately consigned to heaven or doomed to hell, it lives eternally.' The Trevisan's erudite explanation of his obscure riddle vastly pleased the company.

Inasmuch as the night was now far spent and the crowing of the roosters was announcing the dawn, the Signora made a sign to Vicenza, assigned to tell the final story of the second night, to begin her task. But Vicenza, still red in the face, not from bashfulness but from her indignation at the Trevisan's story, spoke out, 'Signor Benedetto, I looked for a better turn from you than this. I thought you would aim at something higher than to be a mere railer against women. But since you take so bitter a tone, it seems you must have been vexed by some lady who has asked of you more than you could give. Besides, it's unfair of you to judge us all alike. Your eyes should tell you that some of us, although all of the same flesh and blood, are gentler and more worshipful than others. If you berate women in such a way, beware that someday they don't get their teeth into you so that all your pretty words and merry songs will be useless to you.'

'No, no,' replied the Trevisan, 'I didn't tell my story to hurt the feelings of anyone, nor for spite of my own, but to give counsel and warning to ladies contemplating marriage to be modest and reasonable in what they demand of their husbands.'

'I don't give a fig what your intentions may have been,' said Vicenza, 'nor do any of these ladies. But I won't sit silently here and let it be thought that I allow these charges of yours against women to carry any weight. I'll tell you a story which you may find to be for your own edification,' and with a little curtsy, she began.

II.4 Commentary

Straparola's stories are presented in a social setting by ten young ladies insufficiently differentiated to allow for a meaningful correlation of narrative contents to specific personalities. But the case is altered with the story of Pancrazio and his marriage to Silvia Ballastro, for not one of the women, judging by their collective anger at the end, could ever have been induced to tell so unflattering a tale as this. It could only be assigned to someone willing to assume the stance of a misogynist, and that lot fell to the playful Benedetto of Treviso, who, in the end, had to hide behind the thin rationale of intending no slander, but only a cautionary tale to the ladies to be kind and fair to their husbands. The story begins and ends as a complaint against women, although the nature of those accusations varies from version to version; in one tale the wife is an argumentative and physically abusive termagant; in Straparola's, she is a pouting and extravagant follower of the latest fashions, while in Machiavelli's the promotion of her impoverished family bankrupts Belfagor and sends him fleeing from his creditors. Whatever the topical motivations, however, the rhetorical effect of bringing a fallen archangel to failure and defeat in his attempts to manage a wilful wife is so transparently satirical as to require little explication. To be sure, the story plays between particularity and universality, for the characters are given names, locales, and individual identities, but readers and audience members, whether women in anger or men in glee, tend to read these individuals as categories and classes – that all women are shrews and all men helplessly henpecked. In Straparola's rendition, however, there is the more subtle matter of misunderstanding between men and women concerning the nature of changing fashions and Silvia's compelling need to participate in the game of sartorial fitness and social survival, which includes its own ante-raising mechanisms in the periodic alteration of styles. In effect, the story profiles the psychology that drives the fashion trade as an arms race among women in the incessant modification of their adornments, coupled to matters of social status by which they might lure their husband financiers into the contest. Of that social economy, Pancrazio understands precisely nothing at all – or so he pretends.

The many stories in this generic narrative tradition differ from one another in matters of morphology, tone, and detail, but all of them include the two-part career of a demon or devil who first tries and escapes matrimony, then turns to a career of demonic possession in conjunction with a person who plays the exorcist and is, at the end, able to drive out the Devil only by threatening him with the arrival of his wife – thereby linking the two parts together. Despite these identifying motifs, however, there are important sub-groupings, for in critical ways Straparola's fable does not fit with the 'Belfagor' group made famous by Machiavelli. In terms of influence, given the presumed chronological precedence of the stories in kind by Machiavelli, Brevio, and Doni, Straparola's variant would appear to be a faulty and imperfect derivation, even an intentional corruption. But one must ask how, in relation to a literary prototype, Straparola's work could deviate so radically in structure and theme. His hero does not even bear the telltale name of Belfagor. In this, the usual construction of literary debt to Machiavelli comes into question. In fact, Straparola's tale has more in common with versions collected in the nineteenth century than it does with those written by his literary contemporaries, suggesting that he took his work independently and directly from the oral tradition available to him, as, no doubt, did Hans Sachs in much these same years. Hence, while Straparola may remain in the running for the first to have written out the tale for publication, the dating question no longer has bearing upon his presumed debt to the literary Belfagor.

In the contest for the earliest composed, it would appear that Straparola's was later by dint of its publication date, some thirty years after Machiavelli is thought to have written his *Belfagor*. Probability is in Machiavelli's favour, even though Straparola had published his first work in 1508 and, hence, any time thereafter could have begun his collecting for the *Nights*. Traditionally, priority settles upon the respective claims of Brevio and Machiavelli.[61] Their work is of a piece and Doni's makes a

61 A letter by Anton Francesco Doni to Francesco Ravesla, 10 March 1547, speaks of the *novella* (*Belphagor*) and other prose Brevio was about to publish that was copied from Machiavelli and that was rightfully the latter's. In the annotations to 'Belphagor' (III.3), in Gabriel Chappuys, *Facétieuses journées*, ed. Michel Bideaux (Paris: Champion, 2003), p. 841. When Machiavelli's *novella* was published two years later, accompanying letters from his son expressed the desire to re-establish

third – having acknowledged, albeit ambiguously, his debt to the other two. All of them tell the same story of the Devil who marries, endures mistreatment, is brought to bankruptcy, and escapes to go on the road as a confidence game practitioner to possess royal family members in order to gain high rewards. All deal with multiple episodes of possession, the Devil's order to the exorcist to desist, and the rustic trickster's escape from death by coercing the Devil's cooperation through fear of his wife's imminent return. Axon concludes that 'Brevio may have derived his materials from the same source as the Florentine secretary.'[62] But what source did he have in mind? By contrast, Straparola's Devil, on two occasions, offers to his wife all she might desire by way of clothes, jewels, and furnishings, each time warning her that it would be the last. It is her pouting and insinuations that drive him out of the house. This variation presumably belongs to his popular source, for it is unknown in any of the literary versions. The financial distress suffered by Belfagor in Machiavelli's story is transferred to Gasparino, who is the Devil's one-time bridegroom and now his desperate new companion in the exorcism game. Straparola's devil, Pancrazio, feels no debt to him and refuses to leave even his first host until Gasparino comes up with the ruse of the returning wife. In effect, Straparola's source has reversed the design of the story, elaborating the opening and truncating the second part. Nothing in this points to a rewrite of the Brevio-Machiavelli model. That probability is further confirmed by the publication dates of all the works concerned. Machiavelli may have written *Belfagor* as early as 1518, but it was not published until 1549, only months before the publication of the *Nights* in 1550, while Brevio's *Belfagore* preceded that date by only five

Machiavelli's claim to his work. Doni then published his own version in 1551, a year after the first volume of the *Piacevoli notti* appeared. In light of this little controversy, one must choose between another plagiarism on Straparola's part with his many changes introduced to disguise his debts, or a creation indebted only to a popular tradition from which Machiavelli himself drew his materials.

62 William Axon, 'The Story of Belfagor in Literature and Folk-Lore,' *Transactions of the Royal Society of Literature* 23, no. 2 (London: Asher & Co., 1902), p. 118. Omitted from the approach to sources is the brief 'fabula' on the topic outlining the telltale action of the Devil taking a wife, but without dialogue, names, or episodes in Lorenzo Abstemio's *Hecatomythium* (Venice, 1499), no. 194. Yet it may have been a vehicle of inspiration. The work was frequently published together with Aesop throughout the sixteenth century.

years.[63] We do not know when Straparola wrote his individual stories, or the order in which he wrote them, but there is much to suggest that the first twenty-five, those appearing in the first volume, were collected, transcribed, or revised years before the publication date. However the dating issue resolves itself, the story is older than any of the named writers, necessitating that Machiavelli and Straparola, directly or indirectly, derived their matter from the folk. The two sub-groups represented by these writers, in fact, maintained their respective identities down to the nineteenth century, their distinguishing features undoubtedly reflecting the differences between the oral versions then current in Tuscany and the Veneto from which these authors respectively drew.

This appraisal of the matter will not be agreed to by all. Michel Bideaux, no doubt seconded by many, held that Straparola made off with the *Belfagor* of Machiavelli, thinking that he could create a new work by making the changes listed above – 'modifications malheureuses' (unhappy changes), avoiding accusations of plagiarism only by mutilating the work.[64] But the matter of dating and Straparola's predilection for popular rather than literary sources in the early part of the collection campaign against this theory.[65] The question of plagiarism has become critical here only because the author in question is Machiavelli. Straparola, in the

---

63 Giovanni Brevio published his 'Belfagore' in *Rime et prose volgari* (Rome: Antonio Blado, Asulano, 1545) an unspecified period of time after it was written. It may be found in English in *The Italian Novelists*, ed. Thomas Roscoe (London: F. Warne [1824], 1880). Niccolò Machiavelli's *Novella di Belfagor* was published posthumously in 1549, but was very likely written as early as 1518. Anton Francesco Doni's recension, with ambiguous acknowledgment to both writers, could not have predated the Secretary's, for in 1518 he was but five years of age, although he was born in Florence and did not leave until 1538. His collection entitled *Novelle* was edited by G. Petraglione (Bergamo: Istituto italiano d'arti grafiche, 1907). See also Giuseppe Calligaris, *Anton Francesco Doni e la novella di Belfagor* (Turin: Unione tip.-editrice, 1889).

64 Gabriel Chappuys, *Les facétieuses journées*, ed. Michel Bideaux (Paris: Champion, 2003), p. 843. Chappuys published his collection in 1584, with a version of the story based on Brevio, taken from the 1566 edition of Sansovino's *Cento novelle scelte* in which Straparola's story (since 1562) had been replaced. Straparola's was no. 64 in the 1561 edition.

65 Marziano Guglielminetti sides with the mainstream of opinion concerning Straparola as a plagiarist when regarding his handling of some twenty-three tales from Morlini's *novelle*, but is among the few to recognize the folkloric origins of the present story for all of these writers. *La cornice e il furto: studi sulla novella del '500* (Bologna: N. Zanichelli, 1984), pp. 63–9.

end, appears to have created no more new stories than Shakespeare – about two each, and neither mentions sources. But in Straparola's case, there is every indication that he had done his fieldwork and that what is taken for mutilation is simply his disinclination to enhance his materials in the direction of the *novella*, for which reason his legacy is all the greater as a documenter of popular culture.

That versions of the story were collected in the nineteenth century in such diverse regions as the Punjab, Turkey, Cairo, Serbia, Poland, Bohemia, and Sicily, among potentially many others, implies that we are dealing with a tale that migrated during centuries from the Indian subcontinent and the Indus Valley to nearly all parts of Europe, and that began not with the incarnation of a fallen angel, but with the demons and devils in trees and wells who lived in close proximity to humans and shared in their relationships. A point of departure is the tale of Mohamed Bux, collected in the upper Indus Valley by Charles Swynnerton (1892). Bux decides to push his termagant spouse into a well.[66] There she lands on a demon's back and in time, after their attempt at domestic cohabitation fails, he too takes flight. As a sweeper in a mosque he meets Bux, now a dervish. Both realize they are victims of Fuzzle Noor and so the devil arranges to marry his new friend to a princess in compensation for his troubles. It is, of course, managed through the confidence game of possession and exorcism, although again, the devil gets comfortable and refuses to leave not once but twice before being threatened with the return of the dreaded wife. In common with contemporary Italian versions, the reward is royal marriage rather than the monetary rewards of the earlier literary versions. The imperative of romance has taken precedence. As a measure of the transformations and stabilities that affect folk tales over time, this story may be compared to the version in the *Suka saptati* (The seventy tales of a parrot), which dates to the sixth century or earlier.[67] A Brahmin had a wife named Karagarâ (poisoner) whom

66 *Indian Nights Entertainment* (London: E. Stock, 1892), pp. 298*ff.*

67 *The Enchanted Parrot*, trans. B. Hale Wortham (London: Luzac, 1911), nos. 56 and 57, pp. 92–4. This story is the source of the adjusted version in the Persian *Tooti nameh* described below. One might well ask if Machiavelli knew the *Suka saptati* given that Story 61 (pp. 113–15) features the whole of the plot of the *Mandragola*. A glowering and disagreeable merchant and his good-looking and light-hearted wife Tejuka live in a village. She wants a lover and finds one in a religious procession. She makes signs and tells him to throw a pot into the house containing a serpent. When it gets out, she'll claim to be bitten. He, meanwhile, will be loitering in the streets disguised as a doctor. The husband finds him, of course, is told the diagnosis is

everyone feared, including a pesky goblin who lived in a tree nearby. The Brahmin, eager to get away from her, set out on his travels and along the way met the goblin, who attached himself to his old master, and together they cured a king's daughter in anticipation of great rewards. The tree demon then promised to go his own way, yet lingered on, dissatisfied. After the Brahmin married the princess as his promised reward, the goblin abducted her. When the Brahmin finally caught up with them, he merely threatened the goblin with the imminent arrival of Karagarâ and the goblin fled in a trice. For want of an earlier version, this story may be cited as the fountainhead of a millennium-long elaboration upon the type that culminates in Machiavelli, Straparola, and Riche.

A.H. Sayce collected a similar tale in Arabic from a professional storyteller in Cairo, in which a wife, following her husband to Mecca, is, for her malice, drowned in a well where she disturbs a demon (ifrit or djinn). She so annoys him, in fact, that he too flees her company to join the husband in a series of adventures involving demon possession and exorcism. This story, as in the Machiavelli tradition, entails three victims, the third liberated only by threatening the demon with the imminent arrival of his wife Bakhtiya.[68] Perhaps the critical recension linking the East to the West is that found in the *History of the Forty Vezirs*, in which a woodsman's shrewish and wilful wife falls into a pit. When her husband lets down a rope, however, an ifrit or demon escapes first, complaining of the 'scolding ill-starred woman' who had tormented him verbally and physically. The two then engage in the game of possession and cures whereby the demon might reward the woodsman for his liberation. When the woodsman is sent to cure the second princess, however, the ifrit has had a change of heart and refuses to leave until the return of the scolding

---

grave, and is given an ointment for it that is toxic. The husband is told to administer it himself, but it makes his eyes burn, so the doctor has to take over. The lovers then enjoy their bliss, while the merchant is pleased by the cure and opens his house to the doctor for a good many visits thereafter. Is this close enough?

68 Archibald Henry Sayce, 'Cairene Folklore,' *Folk-Lore* 9, no. 4 (1900), pp. 354–95; see p. 374. A similar version was collected for the same number of this review beginning on p. 213. It is related to a version traced to the *Tales of a Parrot* (*Tooti Nameh*), telling of a demon driven out of his pipal tree by a scolding wife, sending the demon and the Brahmin, her husband, on the road to repeat the exorcism game until the demon refuses to emerge before being threatened with the wife's return. Further to the surviving Eastern versions, see William Axton, 'The Story of Belfagor in Literature and Folk-Lore,' *Transactions of the Royal Society of Literature* 23, no. 2 (London: Asher & Co., 1902), p. 114.

wife is announced, whereupon he takes his flight.[69] Given the structural precision with which the Eastern and Western versions coincide, it must be presumed that some form of the compound tale, having both the marriage and the confidence game of possession and exorcism, persisted among the folk throughout the pre-Renaissance period. How much personal genius Machiavelli and Straparola exercised respectively upon their adaptations of those sources is a moot point, but such popular sources there must have been.[70]

It is a long way from the tale in the *Forty Vezirs* to Machiavelli's eminently more sophisticated *novella*. But there are traces of its progress along the way among the medieval writers. Jacques de Vitry appears to have made an adaptation from the folk in the tale of the 'devil worsted.' This demon served a rich man for some time and was rewarded by marriage to his daughter. But she was so argumentative that the demon told his father-in-law that he wanted to return home. The rich man asked where that might be and was told that it was in hell, where he preferred to live without her, and then he disappeared.[71] A version of the Eastern tale may likewise have appeared in the *Hecatomythion secundum*, a collection of 100 fables by Lorenzo Abstemio (Lorenzo Bevilacqua of Macerata), first published in Venice in 1495, plausibly bringing traces of the story

69 Sheykh Zada 'The Twenty-seventh Vezir's Story,' in *History of the Forty Vezirs or the Story of the Forty Morns and Eves*, ed. E.J.W. Gibb (London: George Redway, 1886), pp. 288–94. This is the nineteenth-century translation of the Turkish *Qirq Vezir Tarikhi*, a translation from the Arabic dating to the earliest years of the fifteenth century. Of the Arabian original little is known, but it seems to have shared features with the Sindibad group. See W.A. Clouston, *Popular Tales and Fictions*, ed. Christine Goldberg (Santa Barbara, CA: ABC Clio, 2002), p. 280.

70 Michel Bideaux (pp. 844–5) has an intriguing explanation of how Machiavelli came, through his investigations into Florentine history, to employ the name 'Belfagor,' which he derives from Roderigo-Belfagor, a name arising in Spain in association with Americo Vespucci's sojourn there in 1491. Luigi Pulci, however, employed the name in his *Morgante*, trans. Joseph Tusiani (Bloomington: Indiana University Press, 1998), bk. IV, strophe 97, and there the matter may rest, for scholars otherwise are inclined to attribute the name to the Moabite idol Ba'al-Peor.

71 Jacques de Vitry, *Sermones feriales et communes*, sermon 17, sect. 7, in Goswin Frenken, *Die Exempla des Jacob von Vitry* (Munich: C.H. Beck, 1914), no. 60, pp. 127–8; it is also in Carolyn Müssig, *The Faces of Women in the Sermons of Jacques de Vitry* (Toronto: Peregrina, 1999), pp. 154–5.

closer to Straparola both in time and location.[72] In Hans Sachs's jester tale, 'Der Teufel nahm ein altes Weib zur Ehe,' the Devil marries an ugly, rich, old, and quarrelsome woman, but ends up running away to join forces with a physician in the forest. Their exorcism game is now turned into anti-clerical satire and the Devil is beaten out of his portion of the winnings. It is dated 1557, entailing either that the Italian written sources had travelled rapidly and had been greatly modified to accord with national character and humour, or, far more likely, that a parallel folk tradition had been in circulation in southern Germany.[73] That probability helps to confirm the presumption of folk versions in Italy that served both Machiavelli and Straparola.[74]

Machiavelli, Doni, and Brevio style their narratives as *novelle* by adding local detail, fuller motivations, the dynamics of the extended family, strategies of escape, and bantering dialogue. The name of the Devil is taken from the Assyrian or Moabite idol Ba'al-Peor who appears in Numbers 25:3. Whether as a single or composite literary creation, the story had many imitators, in whose works the misogynous tones are frequently tempered, moralized, and mitigated. A few of these are worth citation as witnesses to the full literary heritage inaugurated by this ancient story tradition. But of greater relevance to the present study are those few that are in direct or indirect debt to Straparola; they stand out by the offer

72 This work came too late to my attention to investigate. Versions of the Eastern tale are reportedly to have been written by Lafebvre de Thérouane in 1488, and by Abstemius in 1495, according to S. Prato in 'Quelques contes littéraire dans la tradition populaire,' *RTP* 4 (1889), p. 174. But the certainty of their existence and their potential relationship to Straparola remain to be determined. The *Hecatomythion* appears to have been joined to the *Fabulæ ex græco in latinum per Laurentium Abstemium* (Venice: Ioannem de Cereto de Tridino, 1495).

73 *Ausgewahlte poetische Werke*, ed. and rev. Karl Pannier (Leipzig: n.p., n.d), pp. 163*ff.*

74 The Straparolan motif of the wife driven to nagging by her longing to keep up with the latest fashions has an important prototype in the tale of the 'Burgess of France' in *The Novellino*, a collection originating in the late thirteenth century known as *Lo cento novelle antiche*; a wide-ranging assembly of tales and vignettes predating all the other collections of *novelle*. Whether it is a source or a cognate version stemming from the same generic folk tradition that gave rise to Straparola's tale remains moot, but clearly both enjoy a common inheritance, for in the early tale a citizen's wife, vexed by her inability to rival the other women in the village in matters of dress, drives her husband to usury, earning for herself the reprimand of no less a figure than the wise prophet Merlin, who inspired her to remove her 'wicked robe.' *The Novellino*, intro. Janet L. Smarr, trans. Roberta Payne (New York: Peter Lang, 1995), no. 25, pp. 48–9.

made to the young wife, in consultation with her mother, to purchase once and for all her lifelong supply of clothes and accessories upon the understanding that she might never again trouble her husband in the matter. That is the signifier of his sub-group.

In the 1562 edition of his *Cento nouvelle scelte,* Sansovino incorporates a version of the story from Brevio, thereby replacing the Straparola story that had appeared in the edition of 1561.[75] A further modified, more gentle, and edifying rendition is thereafter contributed by Carlo Casalicchio in *Utile col dolce* (1578; 1671).[76] In the eighteenth century, the story appeared in versified form as 'Il matrimonio del diavolo: novella faceta de Giambattista Fagiuoli a sua moglie' (The marriage of the Devil: newly composed by Giambattista Fagiuoli for his wife).[77] Not surprisingly, he tempered the tone even more, claiming as sources all the above authors, including Straparola and Casalicchio, while excluding Machiavelli. In France, Gabriel Chappuys included the tale in his *Facétieuses journées* (1584).[78] Equally indebted to Machiavelli was Tanneguy Lefebvre's 'Le marriage de Belphégor' (1665).[79] *Roderic ou le Démon marié* appeared in 1694, likewise derived from The Secretary, but much swollen with detail.[80] The history of the story in France is capped by Jean de La Fontaine's *Belphégor,* appearing in 1682.[81] Straparola's works were first translated by Jean Louveau in 1560 and completed by Pierre de Larivey in 1576; the edition went through many printings in all subsequent centuries, offering up the entire collection to the formation of the French literary consciousness.

75 Francesco Sansovino, *Cento novella scelte* (Venice: [Francesco Sansovino], 1561), no. 64, pp. 267v–272r.

76 *L'utile col dolce* (Naples: Giacinto Passaro, 1578); *L'utile col dolce* (Venice, 1733), cent. I, pp. 85–6.

77 Giambattista Fagiuoli, *Il matrimonio del diavolo.* The author died in 1742 and the first two printings are rare. It was reprinted in Venice in 1820. For more on this reference, see Giambattista Passano, *Il novellieri italiano in verso* (Bologna: G. Romagnoli, 1868), pp. 174–5.

78 *Facétieuses journées* (Paris: J. Heuzé, 1584); Gabriel Chappuys, *Facétieuses journées,* ed. Michel Bideaux (Paris: Champion, 2003), pp. 370–9.

79 In *Vie des poètes grecs* (Paris: C. de Sercy, 1665).

80 This work claims to be a historical novel translated from the Italian by Charlotte Catherine Patin (later attributed to Machiavelli, despite its 119 pages) (Paris: A. Baratropolis, 1745).

81 *Poème du quinquina et autres ouvrages en vers* [Belphégor] (Paris: chez D. Thierry, 1682); *Oeuvres,* ed. Louis Moland, 7 vols. (Paris: Garnier frères, 1872–86), vol. IV, pp. 443*ff.*

The story made its first appearance in England in the epilogue to Barnabe Riche's *Farewell to Military Profession* (1581), where, according to common practice, the story is given a local setting. Now in London, Balthazar the Devil makes a trial marriage with Mildred and she makes trial of his patience.[82] His flight takes him first to Dover, but not finding passage, he turns towards Scotland where he takes demonic possession of King James VI, the author of a book on demonology and witchcraft and the butt of English humour. For this bit of mockery Riche paid dearly, for after 1603, when James VI became James I of England, Riche was without all hope of a pension until he grovelled for many years in apology. In this incarnation of the tale, Persinus the exorcist, compelled to cure the king or die, was no other than the physician-father to the detested wife. Important for our purposes is that Riche relies entirely upon Straparola's design, raising the question of how he came by his materials. Riche plays vague about his sources, saying that he heard the story long ago, he can't remember where, but we might guess that it was in Louveau's translation.

The Tudor play *Grim the Collier of Croydon*, attributed to William Haughton and written close to 1600, owes something to Riche – not only for materials from the story of Balthazar, but from the fifth story in the collection, 'Of Two Brethren and Their Wives,' along with material directly from Machiavelli, the legend of Saint Dunstan, the anonymous play *A Knack to Know a Knave*, tales of Robin Goodfellow, and somewhat more. Straparola, in this way, makes a contribution to a vignette that found its way onto the Elizabethan stage.[83] Ben Jonson, in *The Devil Is an Ass*, made a beginning with the Machiavelli plot and conceit, but soon abandoned it to explore the tribulations of marriage in alternate terms. An anonymous pamphlet in the British Library that appeared in 1647 contains a translation of Machiavelli's *Belfagor*. There is no title page, but inside it is called 'The Divell a married man; or the Divell hath met his match.' The pamphlet had some influence upon the parliamentary wrangling of the day. John Wilson wrote a tragicomedy called *Belphegor, or the Marriage of the Devil* for the Queen's Theatre in 1691, claiming to have

---

82 *His Farewell to Military Profession*, ed. Donald Beecher (Ottawa: Dovehouse Editions, and Binghamton, NY: MRTS, 1992), pp. 315–22.

83 The full title is *Grim the Collier of Croydon; Or, The Devil and His Dame: With The Devil and Saint Dunston*, first printed as *Gratiae Theatrales, or, A Choice Ternary of English Plays* (London: R. D[odsley], 1662; reprint, Binghamton, NY: MRTS, 1984; ed. William M. Baillie).

relied upon both Machiavelli and Straparola, a knot to be untied by specialists in Restoration Theatre.[84] There are many versions of the story appearing at later dates, duly listed by William Axon, and without exception indebted to Machiavelli rather than to the *Nights* of Straparola.[85]

If turning the stories of the folk into *novelle* is the goal of the literary enterprise, clearly Machiavelli takes the prize. The form in which he found his material is unknown, although he attributes his knowledge of it to an old holy man in Florence. By the same token, Straparola has a clear debt to antecedent forms arguably going back through a long period of oral transmission to an ancient source. His version seems literary, yet adheres to a folk design, presumably because he went directly to the folk for this as for so many other stories in the collection.

Italo Calvino provides us with a version from Palermo, collected by Giuseppe Pitrè late in the nineteenth century, entitled 'Lame Devil,' in which all of the essential narrative parts are present, but in a form that requires no more than two pages.[86] The first half is all about clothes and

84 *The Dramatic Works of John Wilson*, ed. James Maidment and W.H. Logan (Edinburgh, 1874), pp. 287*ff.*

85 'The Story of Belfagor in Literature and Folk-lore,' *Transactions of the Royal Society of Literature* 23, no. 2 (London: Asher & Co., 1902), pp. 110–11. This work contains a 'first' translation of Brevio's *Belfagore*, discounting that which was made by Thomas Roscoe in *The Italian Novelists*, 1825. Robert Browning, in the nineteenth century, developed the basic materials in his own way in 'Doctor——,' one of his 'dramatic idyls' told by a rabbi, in which Satan is sent to earth as the representative of Death, but who nevertheless agrees that 'A Bad Wife' is an even greater power. When the Devil's offspring comes of age, the father declares that he will become a doctor, and that the two of them will work together to kill off the patients, with the explanation that their arrival came too late. When the Emperor falls sick and the doctor (of death) is called in, the Emperor promises him his 'only daughter, fair beyond belief! Save me – to-morrow shall the knot be tied!' The son desires such a marriage and asks his father to desist long enough for him to win the prize. But Satan replies, 'Fool, I must have my prey!' So the boy asks to have his mother sent for and with that, the Devil goes through the roof cursing, leaving only a whiff of sulphur behind. Death is again defeated by a bad wife and so the son is married. *The Poems and Plays of Robert Browning*, ed. Saxe Commins (New York: The Modern Library, 1934), pp. 1086–9.

86 Italo Calvino, *Italian Folktales*, trans. George Martin (New York: Pantheon Books, 1980), pp. 586–8, from G. Pitrè, *Fiabe, novelle e racconti popolari siciliani*, no. 54; 'Lu diavulu Zuppiddu,' in *The Collected Sicilian Folk and Fairy Tales of Giuseppe Pitrè*, ed. and trans. Jack Zipes and Joseph Russo, 2 vols. (New York: Routledge, 2009), vol. II, p. 854. A similar story was collected by Domenico Giuseppe Bernoni, 'El diavolo,' in *Fiabe popolari veneziane* (Venice: Fontana-Ottolini, 1873). An amusing version of this

fashions and the gala social events that provoke the wife to ask for more and newer gear, precisely as in Straparola. Again, there can be no certainty whether Straparola himself provided the motif, or whether this tale depends entirely upon the generic folk tradition. When the wife, Rosina, asks Lame Devil for more clothes, he 'exploded like a firecracker, "Zounds! So it's true that men all go to Hell through the fault of you women!"' With that he returns to hell and meets with another devil with whom he returns to earth. The second wants to try marriage as well; he chooses the daughter of the king of Spain, and then the two devils set off together to play the exorcism game – but only once, as in Straparola. True to form, Lame Devil doesn't want to leave, so Brother Devil arranges for the fanfare to announce Lame Devil's wife. There are variations, but the informing structure is that of our author and not of Machiavelli. Because Straparola, by all appearances, reflects a similar folk source, we are invited to think that this Sicilian tale belongs to the same tradition of tales that first entered the literary record in 1550, confirming our author's independent literary reconstruction of the tale.

The Judeo-Christian archangel makes his appearance, but in taking a wife, in short order he must submit himself to a more integrated place in a culture of local incarnations and transmigrations. In the West, the story's humour relies upon whittling the demon of medieval culture down to a defeated husband, and in imagining demonic possession as a casual confidence game. The gothic mind could somehow allow for the burning of witches for having trafficked with the same creatures (the devils) who played the clowns in the Last Judgment plays. It is all a matter of adjusting the level of mimetic representation. To a different point,

---

tale appears as 'The Devil Who Took to Himself a Wife,' in *Roman Legends: A Collection of the Fables and Folktales of Rome*, trans. Rachel Harriette Busk (Boston: Estes & Lauriat, 1877), pp. 343–5. This devil wins a contest in hell and his prize is liberation, whereupon he heads for earth to marry. True to form, he finds a pretty, argumentative spendthrift who drives him out of house and home. But he offers her one last good turn to set her up before leaving, which was to allow her to play doctor to a possessed queen, the first time with his collaboration. After a three-day charade of ointments and hocus pocus, the devil departs. But the wife takes to the game and follows the reports of the newly possessed. 'What! you here again!' says the devil, and each time tells her to scram, but she is under a death threat and thus can do no other than nag and screech until he acquiesces, perpetuating the domestic spat by instalments until the devil escapes back to hell. That she was under a death threat to perform is again redolent of Straparola, and of the many stock folktale employments of this device, as in 'Livoretto,' III.2 and 'Costanza,' IV.1.

rumour holds that Machiavelli was unhappily married, but he alone cannot account for the story's lasting appeal as a form of narrative compensation for abject male defeat in domestic battles. The look of it is overtly anti-feminist, a secular sermon – albeit a hollow one – counselling women to modify their frivolous demands in marriage, with the story serving as an exemplum. So it is presented, a little maliciously, by Straparola's narrator. But such simple stories are often polyvocal. There is, in the old tale, an emerging comedy of manners dealing with the eternal incompatibility between men and shrewish wives, including the strategies on both sides for maintaining a working truce. Thus, in spite of the sermonizing in the dark, and the sniggering of men in corners, controlling women may take comfort in the Devil's incapacity to quell their voices, even though they must take care that their imperious feeding does not kill off their hosts. And that is precisely the line of scrimmage at which the story deposits its version of the gender wars. Thereafter, it is all a matter for readers, one by one, to correlate the verities of literature with the verities of life.

II. Fable 5
The Beating of Simplicio de' Rossi

VICENZA

Messer Simplicio de' Rossi is enamoured of Giliola, the wife of Ghirotto Scanferla, a peasant. Being caught with her in her own house, he is beaten and in every way grievously mishandled by her husband before returning to his own house.

One cannot deny, dear ladies, that Love has a gentle nature, yet rarely does he grant happy and glorious results to his followers. That's how it turned out in the case of the lovesick Messer Simplicio de' Rossi, for just as he was flattering himself that he was about to enjoy the woman he so ardently desired, he had to make his escape carrying about as many bruises as any man possibly could. I'll relate this entire story if you'll listen intently, as it is your gracious custom to do.

In the village of Santa Eufemia, situated just below Camposempiero in the territory of the famous and illustrious city of Padua, there lived some years ago one Ghirotto Scanferla, a man rich and influential enough for one of his station, but at the same time a factious, wrangling fellow. His wife was a young woman named Giliola, who, although she was born a peasant, was most attractive and graceful. This Simplicio de' Rossi, a citizen of Padua, fell violently in love with her and, as it happened, had a house that stood not far from Ghirotto's. Often it was his custom to roam around the neighbouring fields in the company of his wife. She was very beautiful and possessed of such fine qualities that her husband might have devoted himself to her in love and loyalty, but instead, he held her in small esteem. Rather, his love for Giliola was robbing him of his rest both day and night, although he kept this passion hidden in his heart, partly because he was afraid of arousing her husband's wrath, partly on account of Giliola's good name, and partly for fear of giving offence to his own wife. Close to Messer Simplicio's house there was a fountain gushing out streams of water that attracted people from the surrounding areas – water so clear and delicious that not only the living but the dead might drink of it to their benefit. Giliola made her way there every morning and evening with a copper pail to fetch water for her household needs. Love, meanwhile, in sparing no man, spurred on Messer Simplicio's passions, yet he found comfort merely in gazing now and again upon her beauty, for in consideration of her good name, he could bring himself to show no outward signs of his love. For her part, she knew nothing of all this, nor had any clue of his admiration. As became a woman of honest life, she gave attention only to her husband and her household affairs.

One day it came about that Giliola, going to fetch water as was her custom, met Messer Simplicio, and in her simple, courteous way, as any woman might, said 'Good day, sir' to him, to which he replied with the word 'Ticco.' His idea was to amuse her with such jesting and to acquaint her with his sense of humour. But she paid no attention to him, said nothing more, and went right on about her business.

As time went on, the same thing happened over and over again, Simplicio always giving back the same word in response to Giliola's greeting. She gave no thought to Simplicio's stratagems and always returned home with her eyes cast down upon the ground. But after a time, she decided to tell her husband what had happened. So one day when they were conversing pleasantly together, she said to him, 'O, my husband, there is something I'd like to tell you, something that perhaps will make you laugh.'

'And what might that be?' enquired Ghirotto.

'Well, every time I go to the well to draw water,' said Giliola, 'I meet Messer Simplicio, and when I tell him "Good morning," he always answers me with "Ticco." Over and over again I've pondered this word, but I can't get at its meaning.'

'And what answer did you give him?' said Ghirotto, and Giliola replied that she had made no answer at all. 'Well,' said Ghirotto, 'the next time he says "Ticco" to you, take care that you answer him "Tacco." Pay close attention to what I'm telling you and be sure not to say another word to him, but come back home as you usually do.'

So Giliola went to the well to fetch water at her usual time and met Messer Simplicio, gave him good day, and as before, he answered her with 'Ticco.' Then Giliola replied 'Tacco,' according to her husband's directions. Thereupon, newly inflamed by his passion, and thinking that he had at last made it known to her, and that she was consenting to his desires, he took courage and said, 'And when shall I come?'

But Giliola, as her husband had instructed her, uttered no further word, made her way home, and being questioned by her husband how the encounter had gone, she told him that she had done exactly as he had ordered, that Messer Simplicio had asked her when he might come, and that she had made him no reply.

Although Ghirotto was merely a peasant, he was still shrewd enough to grasp the meaning of Messer Simplicio's watchword, which perturbed him a great deal, for it was clear to him that it meant something more than stringing pearls in the dark. So he said to his wife, 'The next time you go to the well, if he should ask you again, "When shall I come?" you say to him, "This evening." The rest you can leave to me.'

The next day, when Giliola went to draw water at the well in her customary way, she found Messer Simplicio there, waiting for her with ardent longing, and greeted him with her accustomed, 'Good morning, sir.'

To this, the gallant answered 'Ticco,' and she followed suit with 'Tacco.' Then he added, 'When shall I come,' to which she replied, 'This evening.'

'I'll be there,' he said.

So when Giliola returned to her house, she said to her husband, 'I've done everything just as you directed.'

'What did he answer?' Ghirotto asked.

'That he'd come this evening.'

Now Ghirotto by this time had got a bellyful of something besides lasagna and macaroni. So he said to his wife, 'Giliola, let's go now and fill a dozen sacks of oats, for I'll pretend that I'm going to the mill. When Messer Simplicio arrives, you must make him welcome and give him an honourable reception. But before this, get an empty sack ready beside those that are full of oats, and as soon as you hear me come into the house, make him hide himself in the sack and leave the situation to me.'

'But we don't have enough sacks in the house,' said Giliola, 'to carry out this plan you're proposing.'

'Then send our neighbour Cia to Messer Simplicio,' said the husband, 'and have her beg him to lend us two, and at the same time she can let him know that I have business at the mill this evening.' So all of these directions were diligently carried out. Messer Simplicio had listened carefully to Giliola's words, and now, noting that she had sent Cia to borrow two of his sacks, he believed all the more firmly that the husband would be going to the mill that evening. He was then at the highest pitch of felicity and the happiest man in the world, fancying all along that Giliola was as hotly inflamed with love for him as he was for her. But the poor fool hadn't an inkling of the conspiracy that was being hatched for his undoing, for otherwise he would have gone to work with far greater caution.

Messer Simplicio had a good number of capons in his poultry yard. Of these he took two of the best and sent them by his servant to Giliola, urging her to have them cooked by the time he should come to her according their agreement. When the dark of night arrived, he stole secretly out and made his way to Ghirotto's house, where Giliola gave him a most gracious reception. Seeing the oat sacks standing there, however, he was rather surprised, for he expected that her husband would have taken them to the mill. So he asked Giliola, 'Where is Ghirotto? I thought he had gone to the mill, but I see the sacks are still here, so I don't know what to think.'

Then Giliola replied, 'Don't complain, Messer Simplicio, or have any fear. Everything will be fine. It's just that at vesper time my husband's brother-in-law came to the house and brought word that his sister was seriously ill with a persistent fever and probably wouldn't live to see another day. So he mounted his horse and rode away to see her before she dies.' Living up to the sense of his name, Messer Simplicio took all this for the truth and said nothing more.

While Giliola was busy cooking the capons and getting the table ready, lo and behold Ghirotto her husband appeared in the courtyard, and Giliola, as soon as she saw him, feigned to be grief-stricken and terrified, and cried out, 'Woe to us, miserable wretches that we are! We're as good as dead, the both of us,' and without a moment's hesitation she ordered Messer Simplicio to get into the empty sack that was lying there. Mightily unwilling to do it, still he got inside the sack and she set it behind the others full of oats and waited for her husband to come in. When Ghirotto entered and saw the table duly set and the capons cooking in the pot, he said to his wife, 'What's the meaning of this sumptuous supper you've prepared for me?'

To which Giliola answered, 'I was certain that you'd be coming back towards midnight all worn out and tired, so I wanted to have something ready to restore you after all your fatigue, something really tasty for your dinner.'

'By the looks of it,' said Ghirotto, 'you've hit the spot, because I'm not feeling my best, so I can hardly wait to take some supper and go to bed, and anyway, I have to be up really early tomorrow morning to go to the mill. But before we sit down, I want to check the sacks we got ready for the mill to make certain they're all properly weighed and in order.' Having spoken these words, he went over to the sacks and began to count them, and finding there were thirteen, he feigned to have made a miscount of them and began to count them over again, and still he found there were thirteen of them. So he said to his wife, 'Giliola, what's the meaning of this? How is it there are thirteen sacks here when we only got twelve ready? Where does the odd one come from?'

And Giliola answered, 'Yes, that's true enough that when we put the oats into the sacks there were only twelve, and how this extra one got here I'm sure I don't know.'

Inside the sack, meantime, Messer Simplicio, who knew well enough that there were thirteen sacks on account of his being there, kept silent as a mouse although he continued muttering paternosters under his breath, at the same time cursing Giliola, his passion for her, and his own folly in having put his faith in her. If he could have gotten out of his present mess by flight, he'd have taken to his heels in a second, for he was more afraid of the shame than the losses that might ensue. Ghirotto, who knew perfectly well what was inside the sack, took hold of it and dragged it outside the door, which he'd left open on purpose, so that once the poor wretch inside had been well drubbed he would have free field to go wherever he wanted. Then Ghirotto, having caught up a knotty stick he had set aside for the purpose, began to belabour him so soundly that there wasn't a limb of his carcass that wasn't broken or bruised. A little more would have put an end to Messer Simplicio. But moved by her pity or the fear of seeing her husband an outlaw, Giliola stepped in. Had she not wrenched the cudgel out of her husband's hand, he easily could have killed him.

Finally, after Ghirotto had ceased his labour and disappeared, Messer Simplicio slunk out of his sack and made his way home, aching from head to foot and dreading all the while that Ghirotto was close behind him with his stick. Ghirotto and his wife, meanwhile, after eating a good supper at Messer Simplicio's cost, went to bed. Giliola, a few days later, when she went to the well, saw Simplicio, who was walking up and down the terrace in his garden, and with a merry glance greeted him with 'Ticco.' Still feeling the bangs and bruises he had received on account of this word, he only replied:

'Neither good morning, nor tic nor tac,
Will e'er again get me inside your sack.'

When Giliola heard this, she was struck silent and went back to her house with her face red for shame, and Messer Simplicio, after the sorry abuse he had received, changed his humour and gave the most complete and loving service to his own wife, who formerly he'd disliked so much, in order never again to be treated to such an experience.

No sooner had Vicenza ended her story than all the ladies cried out with one voice, 'If the Trevisan treated badly the women he dealt with in his fable, Vicenza has given the men even worse in hers in letting Messer Simplicio be so beaten and mauled in the treatment he got.' And while they were all laughing about one thing and another, the Signora made a sign for silence so that Vicenza could propose her enigma. She, feeling that she had more than avenged the insult put upon her sex by the Trevisan, gave her enigma in these terms:

I blush to tell my name aright,
Rough to touch, and rude to sight.
Wide and toothless is my mouth,
Red of hue my lips uncouth;
Black all round and from below
Ardour oft will make me glow;
Rouse my passion closely pent,
Make me foam till I am spent.
A scullion base may e'en abuse me,
And all men at their pleasure use me.

The men were hard pressed to keep from laughing when they saw the ladies cast down their eyes into their laps, although smiling at the same time. But the Signora, to whom modest speech was more pleasing than anything that savoured of ribaldry, sent a stern and troubled glance at Vicenza and said to her, 'If I had not too much respect for these gentlemen, I would tell you to your face what the meaning of this lewd and immodest riddle of yours really is. I'll forgive you this once, only take heed that you don't offend again in such fashion, for if you do, I'll let you feel and know how great my power is over you.' Then Vicenza, blushing like a morning rosebud at hearing herself so shamefully reproved, plucked up her courage and answered, 'Signora, if I've uttered a single word to offend your ears or those of any of the modest gentlewomen I see around me, I would most certainly deserve not only your blame, but severe chastisement to boot. But my words were simple and blameless in themselves and hardly meriting such a bitter rebuke, for the interpretation of my riddle, which you have all taken in the wrong sense, will prove my words to be true and demonstrate my innocence at the same time. The thing my enigma describes is a stockpot, which is black all around, and when fiercely heated by the fire boils over and scatters foam on all sides. It has a wide mouth and no teeth, and takes everything that may be thrown into it, and any cook may take out what he wants while the dinner is being prepared for his master.'

On hearing Vicenza's modest solution to the riddle, all the listeners, both men and women, gave her hearty praise, deeming that she had been wrongfully reproved by the Signora. And now, because the hour was late and the rosy tint of the morning was already visible in the sky, the Signora, without excusing herself in any way for the scolding she had given Vicenza, dismissed the company, bidding them all to assemble in good time the following evening under pain of her displeasure.

The End of the Second Night

II.5 Commentary

This story by Straparola has no apparent or acknowledged literary sources, although its several identifying motifs bring many parallels to mind. There are *fabliaux* and *novelle* by the dozens featuring wives sought out and solicited for sex by their neighbours, many in which the women make rendezvous in bad faith to lure the lovers into a trap, some in which the wives are faithful from the outset and collaborate with their husbands in duping the suitors to teach them a lesson, and a few in which the suitors are lured into sacks for a drubbing. In short, all the generic parts requisite to the formation of Straparola's tale were in circulation, but no particular tale is so closely aligned as to propose itself as the narrative source. This allows that he may have elaborated his own story, compiled it from a version current among the folk, or rewrote it from a simplified written version that has disappeared or escaped attention. Of interest, too, is that it is a kind of inversion of the story of 'Tia Rabboso or the Ruses of an Adulterous Wife' (V.4), in which a burgher of Padua casts eyes upon a rural wife, makes his pitch and receives an invitation, takes a fine meal to their rendezvous, and enjoys the woman in her own bed before her peasant husband returns from the mill. It is Tia who designs the ruse, deceives her husband, and motions her lover to leave and never show his face around there again.

Particular to this (folk) *novella* is the 'ticco-tacco' game, in which the would-be seducer makes innuendoes with a greeting that invites a second verbal response. This is likely a folk motif already circulating in the sixteenth century, for it is to be found in popular tales from diverse regions at later dates and therefore appears to have been traditional. The wife is baffled, but her husband understands and prompts his wife with its counterpart, one which Messer Simplicio then misinterprets as the lady's own amorous reciprocation. It is a game of ambiguous signifiers to which its inaugurator falls prey. Among the intriguing features of this exchange are the overtones of measure for measure, or tit for tat, for while Simplicio thinks only of pleasure, the wife's husband thinks only of revenge, doling out a rather heavy measure for Simplicio's unrealized ambitions. That the outraged husband nearly kills him and must be dissuaded by his wife is, in its own right, a measure of the husband's sense of his injury in terms of the sanctity and exclusivity of his marriage.

Such rough justice as beating a helpless man trapped in a sack aligns the story with the *fabliau*. It is simple village fare, transferred to Santa Eufemia near Composempiero, an agricultural centre in the Paduan countryside some nineteen kilometres from the city, which may or may not suggest something about its origins. The tale has the marks of oral culture in its simplicity and generic design. Both the means and the ends are subject to considerable variation, for not only could the lover be placed in a sack, but in a coffer, under the bed, up the chimney, or inside a cupboard, while the justice could be administered not only in the form of a beating, but in dragging him over cobblestones, scorching him with hot water, dousing him in a river, chasing him naked through a public place, or seducing his own jolly wife. Revealingly, Straparola has this story told by an angry woman, Vicenza, still smarting from the implications of the misogynistic tale just related by the Trevisan. Her 'tacco' is in the form of the most generic of all tales in which an undesired amoroso is beaten black and blue, as though Simplicio's destiny would settle the score against the entire male race. The symmetry is proximate at best, for the revenger is also a male in this story, and given the victim's name, Simplicio, the revengeful assault is brought to bear upon a naïve and foolish man. It is the sanctity of marriage, not womankind, which is exonerated.

The following analogues – a finite sampling – display some of the motifs, but none I think that can be said to form part of a line of direct sources eventuating in Straparola's tale. Following the publication of the *Notti*, however, there are stories in kind, particularly in France, that owe their origins directly to Straparola, no doubt through the influence of the Louveau translation of the *Nights* appearing first in 1560. A predecessor meriting particular attention is an anonymous twelfth- or thirteenth-century *fabliau*, 'Constant du Hamel' or 'De la dame qui attrapa un prêtre, un prévôt et un forestier.'[87] This story has a rather political prelude in which the priest, the magistrate, and the forester abuse their public trust in using their offices to gain access to the intended woman by excommunicating and discrediting her husband. When he becomes alarmed, it is his wife who takes matters in hand, cheerily certain that in working in close collaboration, they can lure each of the would-be suitors into a snare. After sending for each, she places them in the preliminary bath traditionally enjoyed by lovers, then steals their clothes, as in the stories related to 'Filenio Sisterno' (II.2), displays her alarm when her husband stages his return, and urges each one to hide himself – one on top of the other, as it turns out – in a barrel of feathers.[88] With all three in hiding, their respective wives are called in and molested on top of the barrel where the husbands can hear the proceedings, grumbling amongst themselves the while. Later, the husband, armed with an axe, lights the feathers on fire, forcing the naked men to flee for their lives. As they try to escape, he beats them, then turns the dogs on them, and finally sends them running through the town covered in feathers with the entire village in pursuit. Duhamel and his wife end up not only revenged against men from the empowered classes, but also in possession of their money and jewels. This early work has the suitors in triplicate, the collaboration of the wife and husband, the deceptive assignations, the enclosure within

87 Pierre Jean-Baptiste Le Grand d'Aussy, *Fabliaux et contes du XIIe et du XIIIe siècle* (Paris: Eugene Onfroy, 1781), vol. III, pp. 226–40; (reprint, Geneva: Slatkine Reprints, 1971), pp. 398–401. It is also found in Etienne Barbazon, 'Constant Duhamel,' in *Fabliaux et contes des poetes francois des XIe, XIIe, XIIIe, XIVe, et XIe siecles* (Paris, 1808), vol. III, p. 296; (reprint, Geneva: Slatkine Reprints, 1976).

88 This *fabliau* shares a design in common with 'The Three Hunchbacks' upon which Straparola's story of that title (V.3) is closely affiliated. The hunchback visitors are not lovers, they all perish while in hiding, and the rest of the story is concerned with getting the bodies out of the house without the wife's husband finding out. Nevertheless, there are close affinities with the *Estormi* type, as well as a tale in the *Mishle Sendebar,* in which the wives work in conjunction with their husbands, as here, to dupe the lovers out of their money before killing them, for which see the Commentary to V.3. Another early version is included among the *Anecdotes historiques, légendes et apologues, tirés du receuil inédit d'Etienne de Bourbon, Dominicain du XIIIe siècle,* ed. Albert Lecoy de la Marche (Paris: Renouard, 1887), no. 469, p. 404.

a container, and the final compound humiliation which includes physical abuse. In these terms, it establishes a signature sequence to which the story of Simplicio belongs. Speculation is free, however, as to whether this work participated in an early elaboration upon a paradigmatic tale that made a linear descent down to the sixteenth century and after, from which Straparola, arguably, devised his own literary representation.

A sequel to the *fabliau* is Jakob Ayrer's *Fastnachtsspiel* about the goldsmith, the tailor, and the shoemaker. Each is in love with the miller's wife. In collusion with her husband, each is invited to her house, and each is enclosed in a meal sack. Once they are tied in, the miller gives them all a harsh ride to market, drubbing them along the way. Ultimately, each man is sold to his own wife, which makes the punishment complete.[89]

One further and more elaborate variation upon this narrative group is Boccaccio's eighth story of the eighth night, telling of the exchange between two neighbours, Spineloccio Tavena and Zeppa di Mino.[90] When it is discovered that Spineloccio is cuckolding his friend Zeppa, instead of berating his wife, Zeppa asks for her cooperation. He wants his revenge in kind by having her lure Spineloccio into the house, but this time to shout the alarm of his return and so frighten Spineloccio into a chest. This much accomplished, she invites his wife in for supper, after which Zeppa takes over by seducing her on top of the very chest in which her husband is hiding. The poor woman acquiesces out of fear that her lack of cooperation would make it far worse for her husband, asking only that it not jeopardize her friendship with Zeppa's wife. Thus injury is met by injury, obviating the need for further revenge, and thereby allowing the two couples to maintain their friendship as before – all of which brings the closure of this tale in line with Straparola's story of the 'Two Friends who Held Their Wives in Common' (VI.1).

Sabadino degli Arienti, secretary to the Bentivoglio family in Bologna in the fifteenth century, published in 1483 a collection of sixty-one tales loosely in the manner of Boccaccio and bearing the title *Novelle Porrettane.* The thirty-seventh tells of Francescotto and his wife Bellencina, who is pursued relentlessly by the rector of San Giorgio in Poggiale, to the point that her jealous husband is ready to leave or kill himself. When he shares his dilemma with a jurisconsult, he is advised to be patient. 'Do you have

89 *Opus theatricum* [including thirty-six] *Fassnacht oder Possen Spiel* [by Ayrer] (Nuremberg: B. Scherssen, 1618), pp. 84b–89g.

90 Giovanni Boccaccio, *The Decameron,* trans. Edward Hutton (New York: Heritage Press, [1620], 1940), pp. 406–10.

a barrel in the house? Excellent. Tell your wife to invite the priest, pretending you are going into the city. You hide, let him enter, then stage a return, whereupon your wife will get the rector into the barrel. Put on a lid and bring him to me in a cart.' All is carried out to plan, and a rough ride it is for the priest, for the husband looks for every pothole that will make him hit his head on the lid of the barrel. Upon arrival, a domestic starts pouring hot water over the thing until the wretch is forced to confess his presence, then tell the entire story of how he got there from the beginning, and say whether he is still inclined to chase the woman, to which he replies that he would rather die first. Then he is turned over to his fellow friars. Although lacking both the 'tit-for-tat' greeting and the fatal sack, the order of the story is much of a piece with Straparola's and a cognate sampling of the story type. Nevertheless, given the traces of oral features in the present tale, Straparola's likewise, may have come to him as an interim product of the memories of local raconteurs.[91]

The first to draw upon Straparola's story, or at least to exploit its principal narrative feature of enticing an importunate suitor into a sack and having him beaten by the lady's husband, was Francesco Sansovino in his *Cento novella scelte*.[92] In this version, the bourgeois lover is invited to an elegant meal. The husband then arrives and the wife hides her suitor in a sack. There he is tied in by the husband, beaten, and then left aside to taste his misery during the long supper which the husband and wife enjoy together.[93]

Also derived from Straparola through Sansovino is the eighth story of the ninth day of *Les facétieuses journées* of Gabriel Chappuys, who names the wife Libre and places his story in Trissigol.[94] The story was popular and is to be found in variant representations in *Les Serées*, published by

91 *Novelle Porrettane*, ed. Giancarlo Barnabei (Bologna: Santarini, 1992), pp. 169–73. Giovanni Forteguerri tells the story of Guerra Filippini who sought to seduce Lisa Rustichi, but found himself robbed by her husband instead and compelled to give over his mission. *Novelle* (Bologna: G. Romagnoli, 1882), pp. 177*ff.*

92 *Cento novella scelte* (Venice: Francesco Rampazetto, 1561), vol. IX, p. 8.

93 Also apt for comparison is Matteo Bandello's forty-third *novella*, featuring two gallants rather than three, who end up in a barrel which is then carried into public and opened, exposing the cavaliers to view. *Tutte le opere*, ed. Francesco Flora (Verona: Mondadori, 1952), vol. III, pp. 142*ff.*

94 ed. Michel Bideaux (Paris: Champion, 2003), pp. 764–70. The original work of *Les facétieuses journées* was first published in Paris by J. Houzé in 1584.

Guillaume Bouchet in 1585;[95] the *Courier facétieux, ou recueil des meilleures rencontres de ce temps* (1650);[96] and *Les divertissements curieux, ou le thresor des meilleures rencontres et mot subtils de ce temps* (1650).[97] The tale in the *Courier facétieuses* resembles that of Boccaccio in which the lover is locked in a trunk and his wife is called in for seduction on top of it. Jean de La Fontaine in 'Les Remois' joins motifs together in ways suggesting that he knew several of the stories in the group, from Boccaccio to Straparola's French imitators. The tale is set in Rheims and tells of the loyalty of a painter's wife who, in her clever intrigues for trapping her unwanted suitors, does credit to all the women of that city. She prepares an elegant supper for her two suitors, whom she hides upon her husband's unexpected return. Seeing the fine meal, the husband poses questions, only to learn that it is for the two wives of her suitors. Once there, the painter's wife takes each of the women separately to the wine cellar while her husband seduces the other within earshot of the hidden husbands, who can barely restrain themselves. It is a direct descendant of the *fabliau* of Duhamel. But it follows from Boccaccio that neither man has the fortitude or desire to carry through with his previous designs upon the painter's wife.[98] The tale revels in the same notion of poetic justice, namely seduction as revenge for intended seduction, having now left the world of sticks and axes behind for more subtle forms of retaliation. But the law of talion is still at work through the complicity of the targeted couple. Straparola's story is a cousin to this plotline and handling of poetic justice.

One final story loosely related to this narrative group is Barnabe Riche's 'Of Two Brethren and Their Wives,' a further variation upon the original *fabliau* telling of a wife's clever employment of a new lover, instead of her husband, to manage unwanted suitors. Dorothy, disappointed by her ailing husband, takes on three lovers, but finds the first two possessive and jealous. She thus invites them to her house, the first to be hidden in a box, the second dressed as a porter to carry the box away, believing that Dorothy is inside. Once in the fields, the third lover,

95 Guillaume Bouchet, Sieur de Brocourt, *Les Serées* (Poitiers: Guillaume Bouchet, 1585), no. 32, p. 592; *Les Serées du librairie-imprimeur G. Bouchet*, ed. Jean-Claude Arnould (Paris: Champion, 2006).

96 (Lyons: C. La Rivière, 1650), p. 326.

97 (Lyons: J. Huguetan, 1650). The relationship between these two final citations requests further investigation.

98 *Oeuvres complètes* (Paris: Garnier, 1872–6), vol. IV, pp. 27–36.

a soldier, dogs them, challenges them, and flogs them both, enjoys the lady for a short while longer, and then is called off to the wars, leaving her free to return to her husband. True to the formula is the clever wife, unwanted lovers, false assignations to lure them in, a feigned report of the husband's return, concealment, and beatings, revealing a common vocabulary of motifs obliquely related to those in the tale by Straparola, but unlikely to have been derived from it in any direct way. Instead, we are invited to think of some great chest of interchangeable parts from which all of these stories are composed – a virtual chest, the contents of which can be known, paradoxically, only through the comparing of motifs in the hundreds of stories then in circulation. Straparola's tale is about an unwanted suitor who is trapped in a sack and beaten by the husband – such is its distinguishing trait – but it also belongs to all those in which married women, indisposed to requite such desires, connive with their husbands in setting up false hopes and in administering justice according to a homemade version of quid pro quo. The drubbing in a sack is but one such mode in the generic story type.

On the basis of a limited sampling, we may conclude that the story remained in circulation down to the nineteenth century in the oral tales of the folk. Giuseppe Rua knew of a Romanian poem that contained the 'tric tracco' phrase and told of an unfaithful wife and her lover in a sack, while in later years Teófilo Braga collected in Portugal the tale of a friar who constantly harasses a lady by saying 'Tic-taco' to her, until at last she tells her husband. He too instructs her to answer in kind, and after that, to invite the friar to the house. Then the husband intrudes and subjects the padre to a beating in a sack. When the woman sees him later and repeats the familiar greeting, he replies in a grim manner that he would say nothing that would bring him again into such a sack ('Nâo sou gorgulho que vá ao seu saco').[99] This story type of the ambiguous greeting and the drubbing in a sack, so patently cognate with Straparola's tale, enjoyed a long afterlife, entailing a history of transmission accounting for its wide dissemination. Given that Straparola's tale is unlikely to be the father of them all, its very existence can only be accounted for by a sixteenth-century ancestor carrying the 'ticco-tacco' motif that inspired Straparola, making his the first recorded version of the type. Can there be any other explanation?

99 *Contos tradicionais do povo português* (1883; reprint, Lisbon: Publicaçôes Dom Quixote, 1987), no. 116, vol. I, pp. 265–6.

The Third Night

Already the sister of the sun had begun her reign in the sky above the forests and the gloomy gorges of the hills, there displaying her golden circle over half the heavens. Already the car of Phoebus had sunk beneath the western waves, the wandering stars had lighted their lamps, and the pretty birds, ceasing their tuneful songs, had sought repose in their nests amid the green boughs when the ladies and their gallants met once more at the customary time to renew their storytelling. As soon as all were seated according to their ranks, Signora Lucrezia commanded that the golden vase be brought out as before, putting into it the names of five damsels who, according to the order determined by lot, should tell their stories that evening. The first name drawn from the vase was Cateruzza, the second Arianna, the third Lauretta, the fourth Alteria, and the fifth Eritrea. Then the Signora gave the word for the Trevisan to take his lute and Molino his viol, and for all the rest to follow Messer Bembo's lead in the dance. When the measures had come to an end, and the sweet lyre and the divine strings of the tuneful lute were fallen silent, the Signora directed Lauretta to sing a song. Anxious to obey the Signora in everything, she took hands with her companions, and after making a respectful bow, they struck up the following *canzone*:

When I look upon that beauteous face,
Where love smiling holds his court,
There from your resplendent eyes
Light so radiant doth arise,
That it shows us paradise.

All my sighs and all my tears,
Foolishly I shed in vain;
All the anguish of my heart,
All my hidden woe and smart,
With my faint desire have part.

Then to love's last mood I fly,
Making no account that earth and sky
Stand beneath me and above;

So my soul is drawn by love
To the heights of passion free,
And I yearn that fate's decree
Shall bind me, whatsoe'er betide,
Dead or living, to thy side.

After Lauretta and her companions, by their silence, had signalled the end of their song, the Signora, bending her gaze upon the fair and open countenance of Cateruzza, requested her to begin the storytelling of the third night. Blushing a little and laughing lightly, Cateruzza began in these terms.

III. Fable 1
Pietro the Fool and the Magic Fish

CATERUZZA

Pietro the Fool gets back his wits by help of a tuna fish whose life he had spared after taking it in his net. He wins for his wife Luciana, the daughter of King Luciano, after getting her with child by magic means.

There is ample proof, dear ladies, both in the chronicles of the past and in the doings of our own day, that a fool, whether by lucky accident or by sheer force of blundering, may sometimes score a success where a wise man might fail. For this reason it has come into my mind to tell you the story of one of these fools, who got for his wife the daughter of a king and became a wise man into the bargain through just such an incredibly foolish deed.

In the Ligurian Sea there is an island called Capraia, which, at the time of my story, was ruled by King Luciano. Among his subjects was a poor widow named Isotta, who lived there with her only son Pietro, a fisher boy. But alas, this Pietro was so witless that everyone who knew him called him Pietro the Fool. Although he went fishing every day, he never caught a thing. Yet, in spite of his ill-success, he would always come up from his boat shouting and bellowing so that everybody could hear him, 'Big and little, big and little tubs and buckets and pails – Pietro has caught a whole boatload of fish!' His poor mother always believed her son and would get everything ready to process the catch, only to find herself jeered at by this nitwit of a lad, who would stick out several inches of tongue at her just to mock her.

Now the widow's cottage stood just opposite the palace of King Luciano, who had only one child named Luciana, after her father – a pretty and graceful girl of about ten years old. Every time that Pietro raised his silly cry of 'big buckets, little buckets, big pails, little pails,

Pietro has caught a whole mess of fish,' the child would run to the window where she took such delight in his antics that she nearly died of laughter. When he saw that he was made sport of, Pietro would grow very angry and hurl nasty words at her. But the more he uttered his mean words, the more she laughed and made fun of him – as wilful children will do.

Even so, Pietro went on with his fishing day after day, and upon his return he repeated to his mother the same silly words. But at last fortune favoured him, for he caught a very fine, big, fat tuna. Overjoyed at his good luck and leaping about on the shore, he began to shout and cry out repeatedly, 'Mother and I will eat well tonight; mother and I will eat well tonight.' Then, to his amazement, the fish he had taken, instead of trying to get away, said to simpleton Pietro, 'Hey, my friend, I'm asking as a favour that you spare my life. What were you planning to do with me anyway, little brother? Once you've eaten me, what further benefit do you think to gain from me? If you let me live, there is no telling what service I may be able to render you.' But our simple Pietro wanted to eat more than he wanted to talk, so he hoisted the fish onto his shoulders and set off for home, happy as he could be to share with his mother in their need. But the tuna kept on imploring his captor to spare his life, promising him first as many fish as ever he could carry, and finally to do him any favour he might demand.

Well, he might have been a fool, but Pietro's heart was not made of stone. So out of pity, he decided to spare its life; first with his feet he ran and then with his arms he tossed it back into the sea. Mindful of the favour and not wanting to seem ungrateful, the fish said to him, 'Climb into your little boat and, with your oar and your body, tilt it over to let the water run in.' Pietro followed his advice so that leaning over on one side he half filled the boat with water, which brought in with it such a huge quantity of fish that the vessel was in danger of sinking. Seeing this, Pietro thought nothing of the risk, but was beside himself with joy. So taking as many fish as he could possibly carry, he hastened for home, crying out while he was still a long way off, in his usual way, 'Big buckets, little buckets, big pails, little pails, big tubs, little tubs, Pietro has taken a big haul of fish.'

Thinking he was only playing his old game again, Isotta paid no attention at first. But finally, hearing him cry out louder than ever and afraid that he might commit some greater folly if he didn't find the containers prepared as usual, she got them all ready. Imagine her surprise to see her blockhead of a son at last coming back, praise be to God, with a bountiful catch.

Princess Luciana was at the palace window, and hearing Pietro bellowing louder than usual, she laughed outright as never before. Not knowing how to react, the poor simpleton went almost mad with rage. Leaving his fish, he rushed back to the seashore and called out for the tuna to come and help him. Hearing Pietro's voice, he swam up to the shore, put his nose out of the salt waves, and asked what he had to complain of.

'All I want for the moment,' said the fool, 'is for the king's daughter, Luciana, to get pregnant.' And so, in less time than an eye's wink, it was done.

Not many days or months went by before her virginal belly began to swell with all the signs of a pregnant woman, even though she was not yet twelve years old. When her mother noticed this, she was beside herself with alarm, for she couldn't believe that a child of eleven could show all the signs of a mother-to-be. At first, she attributed the swelling to the effects of some incurable disease, but when she brought Luciana to be examined by certain women who were experts in these cases, no sooner had they seen the girl and inspected her by all their secret arts, but they declared her beyond all doubt a very pregnant little girl. The queen, overwhelmed by the terrible report, told it to the king who, unwilling to endure such ignominy, commanded that her life be taken. A close and rigorous enquiry was made to discover who could have violated the girl, but nothing was ever found out. So Luciano, to hide this terrible scandal, determined to have his daughter secretly killed.

On hearing this, the queen begged her husband to spare their daughter, whom she fondly loved, at least until her baby was born, and then he could do with her as he wished. The king, moved with compassion for his only daughter, accepted to wait that long. When the time for the birth arrived, Luciana was delivered of a fine baby boy. The king, upon seeing so beautiful a child, could no longer harbour the idea of putting them away, but instead gave the order to the queen to have the boy nursed and well cared for until he was a year old. By the end of that period, the child had become beautiful beyond compare, and so it came again into the king's mind to try to find out who the father might be. He issued a proclamation that every man in the city above fourteen years of age, under pain of losing his head, should present himself at the palace, carrying in his hand some fruit or flower that might attract the child's attention. On the appointed day, in obedience to the proclamation, all those summoned came to the palace, one man bearing fruit and another man a flower, one this, one that, each passing before the king and taking his seat according to his social rank.

It happened that as a certain young man was on his way to the palace, he met Pietro the Fool and said to him, 'Pietro, why aren't you going to the palace like all the others in obedience to the king's command?'

'What should I do in such a crowd as that?' said Pietro. 'Can't you see that I'm a poor naked fellow with hardly a rag for my back, and you ask me to thrust myself in amongst all those gentlemen and courtiers? O no, that's not for me.'

Then the young man, laughing at him, said, 'Come with me and I'll give you a coat. Who knows but what the child may turn out to be yours?' In the end, Pietro let himself be persuaded to go to the young man's house. There he put on a decent coat and they went together to the palace. He climbed the stairs and sat down in a seat near the exit where he was barely visible. By this time all the men had presented themselves to the king and were seated in the hall. Then Luciano commanded the child to be brought in, thinking that if the father were present, a natural bond would move the child to make a sign. As the nurse carried the infant down the hall in her arms, everyone, as she passed, began to caress the child and offer him gifts, this one a fruit and that one a flower. But the little boy refused them all. After the nurse had gone past fifty or more men, she turned towards the exit door, and as she approached, the child began to laugh and crow, throwing himself forward so vigorously that he almost jumped out of the nurse's arms. Not knowing that anyone was there, she walked on down the hall. But when she came back to the same place, the child was even more delighted, laughing and pointing at the door with his finger, such that the king, who had taken notice of the child's actions, called to the nurse and asked her who was behind the door. And the nurse said, 'Oh, it's some beggar or other.'

When he was called and commanded into the presence, the king knew that it was Pietro the Fool. And when the child, which was close to him, continued to stretch out its arms and clasp Pietro around the neck, the king knew the sign and was stricken to the heart with grief. Having discharged the assembly, he commanded that Pietro, his daughter, and the child should be put to death immediately.

But the queen, in a more prudent manner, reflected wisely that if they were decapitated and burned in the king's presence, his own shame and dishonour might arouse the people. So she persuaded him to have a huge cask made into which the three might be placed and then cast into the sea to drift at random, thus reducing their suffering. The king agreed to this, so that when the cask was made, all three were put inside with a basket of bread, a flask of wine, and a drum of figs for the child, and tossed out into the rough seas, expecting that the waves would soon dash them to pieces against the rocks. But things turned out differently from what the king and queen had planned.

Pietro's poor old mother, upon hearing of her son's misfortune, died of grief within a few days. Meanwhile the unhappy Luciana tossed about by the cruel waves and seeing neither sun nor moon, lamented her great misfortune. Because she had no milk to give to her child, it cried incessantly and had to be soothed to sleep with the occasional fig. But Pietro seemed not to have a care in the world; he thought only of the tasty bread and good wine. 'For crying out loud, Pietro, you don't care at all about this evil you've brought upon me; you don't care how innocent and miserable I am. You eat and drink and laugh without giving a thought to the danger around us.'

'Why, this disaster is a whole lot more your own fault than mine,' he replied. 'If you hadn't made such fun of me it wouldn't have happened. But don't lose heart; our troubles will soon be over.'

'I can believe that,' cried Luciana, 'because any moment now this cask will be split on a rock and then we'll all be drowned.'

'Nay, hush,' said Pietro, 'for I have a secret, and were you to know what it is you'd be amazed and really delighted too.'

'What secret could you know?' said Luciana. 'What could you do of any use to us in a mess like this?'

'I'll tell you right now,' Pietro replied. 'I have a faithful servant, a great fish, and he'll do for me anything I ask of him – and there's nothing he can't do. I may as well confess it; he's the one who got you pregnant.'

'That would be pretty amazing if it were true,' said Luciana. 'So what would this fish of yours be called?'

'His name is Signor Tuna,' replied Pietro.

'Well, have him give me your power over him,' said Luciana, 'so that from now on he'll do what I tell him to do.'

'If that's what you want,' said Pietro. Without more delay he called the tuna, which rose up right near the cask, and ordered him to do everything that Luciana might ask of him. Then she exercised her power over the fish by telling him to make the waves cast the barrel ashore on one of the safest and most beautiful of all the rocky islands in her father's entire dominion. As soon as the fish had done her bidding up to that point, she laid yet more tasks upon him. One was to change Pietro from the ugly fool that he was into the handsomest and wisest man in the whole world. Not content with that, she wanted a sumptuous palace to be built on the island with lofty corridors and many halls and chambers surrounded by a fair and pleasant garden full of trees bearing pearls and precious stones, and in the middle of it to place two fountains, one of the freshest water and the other of the finest wine. And she wanted all of this done without delay.

All this while, the king and queen were in a state of deep misery, for now they were regretting how they'd sent Luciana and their grandson to their deaths, and how they must by now be eaten by fish. To find some solace to their woes, they decided to go to Jerusalem and visit the Holy Land. So they commanded a ship to be put into readiness for them and provisioned with all the appropriate things. They then set sail with a favouring wind, and before they had travelled fifty leagues from the island of Capraia, they came in sight of a stately palace built above the cliffs of a small island. Seeing that this palace was so rich and fair, and erected within Luciano's kingdom, they were taken with a strong desire to inspect it more closely. So, having put into a harbour, they landed on the island and disembarked. Before they had reached the palace, Luciana and Pietro saw and recognized them and, going out to meet them, greeted them with a cordial welcome. But the king and queen did not know their hosts, so great was the change that had come over them. The guests were first taken into the palace, which they examined in every part, praising aloud its great beauty. Then they were led down a secret staircase into the garden, the splendour of which pleased them so exceedingly that they vowed they had never looked upon so delightful a place.

In the centre of this garden there stood a noble tree which bore on one of its branches three golden apples. The keeper of the garden was charged to guard them jealously against robbers. But now, in a most mysterious way, the finest of these apples was slipped into the folds of the king's robe and hidden away in his bosom. Luciano and the queen were about to take their leave when the keeper approached Luciana and said, 'Madam, the most beautiful of the three golden apples is missing and I can find no trace of the thief.'

Luciana directly gave orders that the members of the entire household should be searched one by one, for such a loss as this was no light matter. After looking and looking again, the keeper returned to Luciana to report that the apple was nowhere to be found. At these words, Luciana, pretending great distress, turned to the king and said, 'Your majesty must not be angry with me if I ask that even you allow yourself to be searched, for the golden apple that is lost is of inestimable worth and the most precious thing I have in the entire world.' The king, not suspecting any trick, and certain of his innocence, straightway loosened his robe, and lo the golden apple fell from it to the ground.

Seeing this, the king stood there as one dazed, ignorant as to how the golden apple could have come into his robe. Luciana said, 'Sire, we have welcomed you to our house with all the honour befitting your rank, and now, as recompense, you would secretly rob our garden of its finest fruit. It seems to me that you have proven yourself most ungrateful.'

In his innocence, the king attempted to prove to her that he could not have taken the apple. Seeing his confusion, Luciana knew that the time had come for her to speak and reveal herself to her father. 'My lord,' she said, with tears in her eyes, 'I am Luciana, your unlucky daughter, whom you sentenced to a cruel death, along with my child, and Pietro the Fool. I am that Luciana, your only child, who without ever knowing a man found myself pregnant. And here is the most innocent of children, by me conceived without sin.' Then she presented him with the child. 'Over here is Pietro the Fool, who, by the virtue invested in a certain fish called Tuna, has become exceedingly wise. In the same manner, the palace you see here has been built. Moreover, it was by the enchantment of this fish that I became pregnant. And if for that reason you are innocent of the theft of the apple, I am doubly innocent of my pregnancy.'

Then weeping for joy, they all embraced each other and made great jubilation. After spending a few days on the island, they all embarked, returning together to Capraia, where a great triumph and feast were celebrated in their honour. Pietro was duly married to Luciana and lived long with her in great esteem and consideration according to the high rank he had been given. When Luciano arrived at the term of his life, Pietro was named heir to the realm.

The story of Cateruzza, having been told many times before, still brought tears to the other women's eyes. But when they knew it would have a good and happy ending, they rejoiced and rendered thanks to the Lord for his mighty favours. Seeing Cateruzza had concluded her tale, the Signora required of her to follow the prescribed order, and she, not willing to hold her hearers any longer in suspense, with joy and a good heart proposed the following enigma.

Sir Redman stands behind a tree,
Now hidden, now in sight is he.
To him four runners speed along,
Bearing a warrior huge and strong.

Two darts into the trunk he wings,
And Redman from his lair upsprings
And smites him from behind with skill;
Thus ten little men one giant kill.
Now he who shall this speech unfold
Must be a witty rogue and bold.

Cateruzza's graceful and ingenious enigma was received by the whole company with applause. Many interpretations were proposed, but none came so near the mark as Lauretta's, who said, with a covert smile, 'Our sister's enigma can have but one meaning – which must be the wild bull. He has four runners to carry his huge bulk. The sight of a red flag maddens him, and thinking to tear it, he strikes his horns into the tree. Straightway, the huntsman who was hiding behind the trunk comes forth and kills him with a dart released by ten little men, which are the ten fingers of his two hands.'

This speedy solution to her riddle made an angry red arise in Cateruzza's cheeks. She had hoped that it might prove too difficult for all present, but she hadn't reckoned on Lauretta's adroitness. Seeing that the two were likely to exchange a lot of words, the Signora called for silence and gave the floor to Arianna to begin her tale. Not a little bashful, the girl began as follows.

III.1 Commentary

Stith Thompson identifies this story as a member of 'The Lazy Boy' group (ATU 675), because the protagonist, as in Basile's 'Peruonto,' is notoriously lazy, a complete ne'er-do-well, in addition to being a simpleton. Pietro is, moreover, a representative of the lowest classes, a pauper and the unproductive son of an impoverished widow. Nevertheless, it is his destiny to acquire through magic (and very little effort of his own) a place in the ruling dynasty. Not only is this a story of magic empowerment and wonderful luck, but a tale of unimaginable upward mobility. The story is hence told under the heading of foolish deeds that turn out well, or of lucky accidents that bring amazing good fortune. Critical to the story type is an animal endowed with supernatural powers which, when the hero spares its life, offers to perform essentially anything the poor simpleton may ask. Such are the conventions of fairy tales. There follows a cluster of narrative events that forms the core of the story type. The antics of the simple boy attract the attention of a young princess, typically the only child of the reigning king and queen. It is her role to laugh at him, mock his character, and to make fun of his condition in life. The protagonist, provoked by her derision, then seeks out his animal benefactor to enact his revenge by merely wishing that the princess, at her tender age, should become pregnant. Thereafter, her situation is discovered by her parents: a wrathful and intransigent father, and a mother begging for time and leniency. In due course, a handsome boy-child is born, or even twins, again as in 'Peruanto.' The king is prevailed upon to search for the father, beginning with prospective candidates from the highest social echelons. The search from highest to lowest is, in fact, a constant feature of the story type. But the king's blue-blood hopes are quelled when the baby responds with interest, laughter, affection, or the presentation of a gift, to the lowly father – a character who is often present at the inquest dinner, ceremony, or convocation, merely by chance. Moved by Pietro's inferior standing and meagre intelligence, the king gives in to his wrath. The final sequence of the story begins with the incarceration of the young mother, the child, and the fool in a box or barrel to be carried to the mountains or set adrift in the sea, as in Straparola's tale. Now the haughty little princess meets the perpetrator of the curse face to face, complaining about her fate. She is sometimes forced to feed him to gain access to his magic power, or negotiate for that power in order to escape from the barrel. The magic fish or dolphin is now called up to carry out a sequence of wishes, whether to convert the barrel into a fine sailing ship, or simply to land them all safely on an island. In all versions, a palace and garden are erected by simply making a wish, and the homely hero is transformed into a handsome and sociable prince. Thus the story might have concluded, except that the innocent princess has a score to settle with her father over his calloused indifference to her life and safety. Her chance arrives when the parents are moved to travel, to make a pilgrimage of expiation, and by mishap are brought to the palace to seek refuge. Not recognizing their daughter, they are entertained until arrangements are made to conceal an object of value in the king's garments whereby he may be accused of theft. There follows the inevitable *anagnorisis* or revelation of identities, recrimination, and *peripeteia* in the reunification of the royal family and the eventual elevation of the lazy boy to king of the realm. These are the narrative features that define the story grouping and that are present to some degree in each of its retellings throughout the past four centuries.

The story type is well known throughout Europe and as far east as Siberia, as well as in some parts of America where it was carried by both

French and Portuguese settlers and there disseminated among the natives. Tellingly, however, it is not known in India or Africa, so that by default it seems to have originated in southern Europe.[1] This surmise on the part of Thompson arises largely from the fact that Straparola's fashioning of the tale remains the earliest in the literary record, followed by the tale of 'Peruonto' in Giambattista Basile's celebrated *Pentamerone*, first published in 1634.[2] That Basile comes second does not give assurances in itself that he knew and borrowed from the Straparolan 'prototype.' Both contain the defining narrative features set out above, but there are telling differences in the details. Peruonto, for example, wins his power to make wishes come true merely by thinking them to himself for having built a shelter in the woods for three sleeping fairy children, while Straparola's Pietro, in sparing the life of a great tunny or tuna fish, is invited to call upon the creature to enact his wishes. The departures are significant, for they indicate divergent strains of the story type already present in the early modern period which persist down to the modern era in the culture of the folk. Those which favour the tradition of the sea creature as helper used by Straparola are, in fact, in greater number. At the same time, insofar as Peruonto made the princess laugh and mock him by leaping about under her window on a self-animating bucking log, it is clear that his story is closely aligned with all those subsequent tales in which there are self-cutting saws or other magically automated objects. Hypothetically, Straparola could have invented the story that persisted in the magic animal tradition, while in modifying that story, Basile could have launched the alternate tradition, with possibilities for all manner of subsequent modification. But the more plausible scenario is that both borrowed directly from a folklore tradition of indeterminate origins already diversified throughout the storytelling regions of Italy. Straparola appears to be saying as much in adding, at the story's conclusion, that it still had power to bring tears even though the story had 'been told many times before.' By implication, it was a traditional tale, and hardly of recent devising.[3]

1 Stith Thompson, *The Folktale* (Berkeley: University of California Press, [1946], 1977), p. 69.

2 'Peruanto,' in *Lo cunto de li cunti* (The pentamerone), trans. Sir Richard Burton (New York: Boni & Liveright, 1927), Day I, Diversion 3, pp. 24–31.

3 Coming too late to my attention to explore further is the suggestion by Letterio di Francia that Pietro is the same character as one to be found in Cinthio degli Fabrizi's sprawling *Libro della origine delli volgari proverbi*, dating to 1526, his tale in

The tale of 'Aladdin and his Wonderful Lamp,' nights 515 to 591 of the *Arabian Nights*, is far too divergent in its nature to form a direct ancestor to the 'lazy boy' group, but there are a number of tell-tale parallels. Aladdin is a poor tailor's son and a worthless wastrel who would do no work to support his widowed mother. He too acquires a magic object which he employs to attain marriage to the incomparable princess Badr al-Badur, thereby creating his own crossing of the social barriers from the lowest to the highest. He too is transformed from a lout to a prince, and the story faces head-on the question of how the sultan could possibly marry his daughter to a pauper's son. Both stories feature the erection of sumptuous palaces to which the older generation is invited to meet the younger generation on their own turf. The stories thus follow a common profile of social climbing from the lowest to the highest echelons on the part of the least promising of social creatures through magic powers of nearly limitless scope available for the asking. The most that can be said regarding influence, however, is that there are motifs within the vast closet of story elements that were in circulation throughout the late Middle Ages and Renaissance, many arriving in the West through contact with Arab culture; such circulation of motifs fortifies the plausibility of a pre-existing folk source upon which Straparola relied. But in the case of the *Arabian Nights*, the final report is still not in concerning the scope of its circulation in Europe before the early eighteenth-century translation by Galland, and just when such components as the tale of the wonderful lamp actually became a part of *The Thousand Nights and one Night* collection in the first place. Segments of this work have been assigned dates of origin from the eighth to the fourteenth centuries, but

---

turn taking its origin from another by Antonio Cornazano in *De proverbiorum origine* (Milan, 1503), entitled 'Leggenda del pescatore e del pesce fatato' (Legend of the fisherman and the magic fish), in illustration of the proverb (no. VII) 'Se ne accorgerebbi gli orbi' (Even a blind person would recognize that). By all indications, di Francia is providing a potential source, or an analogue story, based on a generic narrative tradition that predates Straparola. But the matter still requires further investigation. He also recommends a perusal of Ser Giovanni Forteguerri's *Novelle edite ed inedite* for another early version, although my cursory glance did not turn up the story. Di Francia, *Novellistica* in *Storia dei generi letterari italiani* (Milan: Casa editrice Dottor Francesco Villardi, 1924), vol. I, 'Dalle origini al Bandello,' pp. 716*ff.* Fabrizi's *Libro* has been recently republished (Milan: Spirali, [1526], 2007), Cornazano's *De proverbiorum origine* (Milan: Martire Mantegazz, 1503), Forgteguerri's *Novelle*, ed. Vittoria Lami (Bologna: Presso l'Editore Gaetano Romagnoli, 1882).

such early dates do not guarantee their widespread familiarity to writers in the West during the late Middle Ages and Renaissance.[4]

It would be supererogatory here to attempt a full history of the tale subsequent to Straparola, and particularly so when so few can be attributed directly to his influence. The outstanding exception, however, is *Le Dauphin*, published in 1698 by the Countess Marie-Catherine d'Aulnoy in *Suite des contes nouveaux ou les fées à la mode.*[5] That as many as six of her fairy tales can be traced directly to Straparola is further corroboration that *The Dolphin* constitutes an interpretation and amplification of 'Pietro the Fool.'[6] To be sure, she changes Straparola's tuna fish to a speaking dolphin and, for the benefit of her aristocratic salon audience, she

4 For more on the problem of the influence of *The Arabian Nights*, see Robert Irwin, *The Arabian Nights: A Companion* (London: Penguin, 1994), p. 99 and surrounding pages. There he states 'other reflections of the *Nights* and other Arab anthologies continued to appear in European story collections of the sixteenth and seventeenth centuries, such as the *Piacevoli notti* by Gianfrancesco Straparola, the *Heptameron* by Marguerite of Navarre and Giambattista Basile's *Pentamerone*.' This would seem to bode well for some form of influence, but with such disparities as those represented in the stories of Aladdin and Piero, the most that may be said is that *The Nights* nourished a story type that as folklore had an indirect influence upon Straparola in this case.

5 *Suite des contes nouveaux ou les fées à la mode* (Paris: Théodore Girard, 1698). Another version, drawn from Straparola, based on 'the lazy boy' (Type 675), and laundered for the salons, was written by Henriette-Julie de Castelnau, Comtesse de Murat, entitled 'Le Turbot,' first published in *Histoires sublimes et allégoriques ... dédiés aux fées modernes* (Paris: Florentin & Pierre Delaulne, 1699), pt. II, pp. 66–212. As in Mme. d'Aulnoy's version, the hero, such as he was represented in the pages of Straparola, remained entirely unacceptable, yet she wished to follow the original, providing the illusion that Mirou was a perfect fool, thick, and vengeful. He, with a princess and their child, end up in a barrel, but it washes up on a happy isle where Mirou's tutelary fairy makes him beautiful and bright and renames him Fortuné. And now, by some miraculous slippage, it is Fortuné the prince who is the true father of the child; the idiot fisher boy has been entirely forgotten and thus the problem of blue blood origins of the royal child is resolved. The child was conceived by this prince during a nocturnal caprice in a convenient trysting palace furnished by a fairy. Even though the father is now an aristocrat, the morals are little better. This is one of the eight tales assigned directly to Straparola's influence among the authors of the early French fairy tale by Raymonde Robert, for which see the following note.

6 This number (i.e., as many as six from Straparola), however, would be contested by Raymonde Robert. For Mme. d'Aulnoy, she accepts his influence only in this story and 'Le Prince Marcassin' (II.1), and credits to him only eight of the thirty-six which are based directly or indirectly on folk tales among the 115 fairy tales

abandons the tradition of the pauper turned king by making Alidor a born prince, although he is ugly beyond redemption, the laughing stock of the smug but beautiful princess he adores, and sensitive to the point of inflicting melancholy despair upon himself at a moment's notice. Moreover, among the powers granted by the dolphin to Alidor for having saved his life is self-metamorphosis. A new direction is taken when Alidor flies to his beloved as a canary. This ancient motif, here redeployed, is carried to even greater lengths when the princess engages in a mock marriage to her songbird companion, hardly imagining that its devotion is Alidor's, and that it might wish pregnancy upon her. The *récit* is too delicate to speculate on the details concerning how such a thing might come to pass; the ritual marriage in an ambiance of magic is explanation enough. Clearly in this way Mme. d'Aulnoy avoids the distasteful and intolerable fact of a pauper idiot getting a princess with child out of mere spite. The tale evolves further with the invention of a wicked fairy, Grognette, who, because Alidor has disrespectfully perched on her rock, has free rein to bring both Alidor and the princess mother to the nadir of their respective fortunes. The girl must endure four years of imprisonment in a tower without her child, while the looks-impaired prince goes completely mad with despair (curiously no longer employing his transformational abilities).[7] The power of the dolphin has entirely waned as Grognette works her will. In this manner, all of the misfortunes of the original tale are replicated: intransigent patriarchal wrath, the mental weakness of the protagonist, the suffering of the princess at the hands of her family, the probative measures to find the father through the natural sympathy felt by the child, and the cruel delivery of the innocent little family to the perils of the sea. True to the spirit of Straparola's tale, even four years of prison do not cure the disdain and shrewishness of the princess, so that in the company of the ugly prince she remains as peevish as ever. In the manner of Luciana, Livorette also demands

catalogued by Delarue and Tenèze. *Le conte de fees littéraire en France de la fin du XVIIe à la fin du XVIIIe siècle* (Nancy: Presses universitaires, 1982), p. 132. Nevertheless, cases for several more have been made in the present commentaries.

7 That Alidor flies to the beloved as a bird, that the princess is enclosed in a tower, and that Alidor becomes desperately morose suggests that Mme. d'Aulnoy was looking simultaneously at the story tradition epitomized by Marie de France's *Lai de Yonec*. In 'Fortunio and the King's Daughter' (III.4), Straparola also employs the motif in having Fortunio turn himself into an eagle in order to fly up to his beloved, although once in her room he converts himself back again.

control over the magic helper, and Alidor, like Pietro, assigns it to her without reservation, at which point she converts him into a trophy prince consort and builds a royal castle. Yet they are still not married, for in keeping with her aristocratic biases, not only does the author hold out for a protagonist who is born a prince rather than a pauper, but in the name of Grognette, she demands parental permission before Alidor and Livorette can marry. In the end, proper protocol must be observed; the egalitarianism and 'class' plasticity of Straparola are written out of the tale. In this much expanded redaction, romance and fairytale enjoy a fragile coexistence; it becomes a story of magic agency and wonder combined with the tribulations of courtship. Fairyland logic allows for a polarization of the good and evil forces, but the tastes of the salon and late seventeenth-century French social values dictate the interpretation of the fable.

Although this story type is known in France as a folk tale, it is not as frequently found as many others. In *The Types of the Folktale,* Aarne and Thompson list only thirteen.[8] Nevertheless, in a version collected in Lower Brittany as late as 1953 known as 'Ugly Yann,' a few of the story elements are well remembered. At the opening, the favour offered to a special creature, such as the tunny fish, is missing. Yann simply has the powers as a gift from God. He commands his faggots to carry him as in the 'Peruanto' tradition, and he punishes the princess for her taunting by asking 'by the grace of God' that she become pregnant. She too has a boy child and her father demands to know its paternity. As soon as the boy begins to walk he is given a ball and all the men in the kingdom must file past in the detection ceremony. Yann receives the ball, the princess is banished, they marry, and one day he explains his powers. There is no special palace constructed and no royal parental visit, followed by score settling and reconciliation. The princess merely asks Yann to make himself handsome. And there the story ends with so many of the familiar parts missing. But there can be no doubt that it is a truncated version of the familiar tale.[9]

8 Paul Delarue and Marie-Louise Tenèze, in *Le conte populaire français: Un catalogue raisonné* (Paris: G.-P. Maisonneuve and Larose, 1976), vol. II, pp. 358, 584, 649. Here they list twenty – still not a substantial number.

9 *Folktales of France,* ed. Geneviève Massignon, trans. Jacqueline Hyland (London: Routledge & Kegan Paul, 1968), pp. 14–16, 278. It was heard from an old peasant woman who was the rival of the famous informant from Plouaret so frequently recorded by F.M. Luzel in his *Contes populaires de la Basse Bretagne.*

Two remarkably brief versions of the story from the nineteenth century serve to bookend the many more available to folklorists and ethnographers during that era. Number 62 of the *Kinder- und Hausmärchen* published by Jacob and Wilhelm Grimm in 1812 – but dropped from subsequent editions – is 'Hans dumm,' or 'Simple Hans.'[10] The telling is reduced nearly to a plot summary, and details are streamlined. There is no fish, dolphin, or favour bestowed that explains his magic powers; Hans possesses innately the ability to realize his wishes merely by thinking them. The story begins with the pregnancy of the princess and moves on quickly to the search for the father, beginning with the highest born and descending to the lowest. Hans is chosen, marking him out for inclusion in the barrel to be cast into the sea. The princess blames him for her fate because he forced his way into the church, ugly and hunchbacked as he was, thinking the child's choice was a random one. Only then does Hans confess that he had wished her pregnancy, and that whatever he

10 (Berlin: Realschulbuchhandlung, 1812). As stated at the outset, the number of variants in this narrative group is legion and a comparative study could grow to considerable length. The following three are offered as openers, representing Scandinavia, Brittany, and Greece. In the first, a lazy boy named Lars is taunted by a princess, who tells him that he needs a 'boy' to help him, to which he replies that she should have one too. Gifted with the power to make spoken wishes come true, he got her pregnant. The king, baffled by this turn of events, was furious and even more so when, upon demanding that the infant bestow an apple upon its father, the child gave it immediately to Lars. All three are put to sea in a boat, whereupon the princess takes over, using Lars' powers to build a palace on an island as well as overhaul Lars himself. All ends up in reconciliation and the acceptance of Lars as an heir. Klara Stroebe, *Nordische Volksmärchen* (Jena: Eugen Diederichs, 1915), vol. I, no. 30. A version in which the king refuses to accept the boy as his successor is found in F.M. Luzel, *Légends chrétiennes de la Basse-Bretagne* (Paris: Maisonneuve, 1881), vol. I, pp. 59*ff.* See also Johann Georg von Hahn, *Griechische und Albanische Märchen* (Leipzig: W. Engelmann, 1864), no. 8. 'Der halbe Mensch' (The half-man), vol. I, pp. 102–9. This is an unusual version in which the princess laughs at the hero and mocks him because he has only half a head, one arm and one leg, although he is able to hew wood in the forest. His tutelary fish, which fulfilled wishes when called upon for having its life spared, first loaded the boy's mule, to the amazement of the princess. When she becomes mysteriously pregnant, the story flows along in the expected order. The 'father' is discovered by the child's gift of the apple and death is pronounced for all three, which is commuted to exposure at sea. The princess feeds the half man figs and gains his secret, they build a palace, and the king finds them while out hunting. A spoon is hidden in the king's coat and he is accused of stealing, and so father and daughter are reconciled. But in the end, the half man is not converted into a prince and is given one of the king's slaves in marriage, rather than the mother of his child.

wishes always comes true. She then asks for food and gets potatoes. As in Basile, the barrel is converted to a ship. Hans is then told to wish for a palace and, at the same time, to enact his own conversion from a hunchback to a young and clever prince. In the end, of course, Simple Hans becomes king.

Italo Calvino took his story of 'The Cloven Youth' for his *Fables* from the *Fiabe popolari veneziane* (Venice, 1893) collected by Bernoni.[11] The framing device tells of a protagonist cloven in half whereby he becomes the object of laughter and derision, but who is repaired in the end through the wish-fulfilling mechanisms of the traditional story. The fable otherwise resembles that of Pietro in consistent and faithful ways, suggesting either that Straparola's was a not-too-distant source, or that this nineteenth-century Venetian rendition was faithfully preserved from a folk tale of the Veneto that had served Straparola. The latter prospect is a corroboration of sorts that Straparola lived and worked in that same region, as Ruth Bottigheimer has argued.[12] Such an example would illustrate, at the same time, the remarkable continuity of tales within the oral tradition.[13] Even so, Bernoni's version has been somewhat scrubbed

11 *Italian Folktales*, trans. George Martin (New York: Pantheon Books, 1980), no. 34, 'The Cloven Youth,' pp. 99–102, taken from Domenico Giuseppe Bernoni, *Tradizioni popolari veneziane* (Venice: Filippi,[1875], 1969). James Bruyn Andrews found 'Le Naïf' (The simpleton) along the Ligurian coast between Menton and Genoa, which tells of a fool who has the power to realize all his dreams. His first wish is a wagon full of wood upon which he rides under the window of the princess. Upon hearing her raillery he wishes her pregnant, and from that point onward the story unfolds in the expected manner. The child goes from man to man and picks out the Naïf for his father. They too, as a little family, are subjected to life in a barrel until the boy wishes their escape. *Contes ligures, traditions de la rivière recueillis entre Menton et Gênes* (Paris: Ernest Leroux, 1892), pp. 266–70.

12 *Fairy Godfather: Straparola, Venice, and the Fairy Tale Tradition* (Philadelphia: University of Pennsylvania Press, 2002), pp. 45–81.

13 The story circulated widely in a variety of forms throughout Italy. Comparatists will wish to consult 'La favola del falchetto,' in Giuseppe Pitrè's *Novelle popolari toscane*, ed. Laura Regina Bruno (Palermo: La Palma, 2005), no. 30, pp. 227–9, in which the hero rides into town on a bundle of wood, passes under the window of a princess, and sets up the mockery that leads to the rest: the curse, the baby, the laughing response to everything, the grand palazzo, Falchetto's remake, and the arrival of the king; 'Lu cuntu di Martinu,' in Giuseppe Pietrè's *Otto fiabe e novelle siciliani* (Bologna: Fava & Garagnani, 1873), no. 3; 'Lu loccu di li passuli e ficu' in Pitrè's *Fiabe, novelle e racconti popolari siciliani* (Palermo: Luigi Pedone Lauriel, 1875), no. 188; 'Scioccolone' in Rachel Harriette Busk's *Folk-Lore of Rome* (London: Longmans, Green & Co., 1874), p. 119; and 'Il matto della Tegna,' in Isaia Visentini's *Fiabe*

up and simplified. There is no nagging princess who takes control, and her counterpart is a perfectly attentive and protective husband, making the rags to riches less problematic, the family more functional, and the class conflict invisible. The baby is supplied with gold and silver apples to present to the grandfather and father, respectively, and the king holds two parties at the palace, one for the rich and one for the poor, the latter of which the half boy most joyfully attends. All of the trials and tribulations of the narrative follow suit, but the story as we know it is far less troubled in this telling.

Concomitant to the suggestion that oral versions may sometimes simplify the social problems and crises elaborated upon in literary versions is the suggestion that complex issues are at other times embedded in the elements of narrative conflict. Pietro belongs to a tradition of simpleton protagonists who impose pregnancies upon unwitting and mystified young girls. In the world of natural causation, a father is a prerequisite to the condition, and the laws of nature provide grounds for a rigorous interrogation into the paternity of the child, one that involves shame, family honour, responsibility, and revenge. Immaculate conceptions are a violation of both the natural and social order; they demand explanation. Even when Pietro is identified as the father through the principle of empathetic response to a natural father, the matter of the pregnancy is not entirely resolved merely by attributing it to the power of wishing or the agency of a magic sea creature. This piece of mental dissonance is passed along to the king and queen, causing the

---

mantovane (Turin: E. Loescher, 1879), no. 47, pp. 208–11. In this last, Matto goes into the country to gather a bundle of wood. Weary of his burden, he throws it on the ground, climbs on, and says that whoever carries it will now carry him home. When it moves on its own, he passes before the palace where the princess cries out, 'Look, it's Matto del Tegno.' He warns she will fall in love with him, which she does. They marry in secret, have a child, arouse the king's wrath, and provoke a huge festival to find the father by passing the child about until it gives the apple to Matto. To hide his shame, the king thinks only of getting rid of all three. When they are set adrift in a boat, Matto wishes for bread and it appears by virtue of his unexplained magical powers. Once on the uninhabited island, through these same powers Matto builds a palace with servants, horses, carriages, and all. The king somehow finds himself hunting on this remote island and seeks shelter from a storm, only to be confronted by his as yet unrecognized daughter with charges of theft. Her stratagem leads to recognition, reconciliation, family acceptance, and a recall home. This is Straparola's story in truncated form without the magic tunny fish and infected with a few alternate folk tale motifs, but still in possession of all the critical parts of the compound narrative.

patriarch to seek compensation for such defamation of his high honour, while the matriarch asks for time and consideration. In the end, vengeance, even against his own flesh and blood in the destruction of his daughter and his only prospective heir, takes precedence over pity. That is a matter for consideration, particularly because the princess demands redress. The king's resolve has parallels in Greene's *Pandosto,* a story better known through Shakespeare's *Winter's Tale,* in which a sole surviving daughter, thought to be the love child of a now hated enemy, is put to sea with small provision in a tiny craft to meet her destiny by drowning. That story, too, moves through a long period of grief and expiation before the daughter reappears with a prospective mate to bring her father to contrition for his former cruelty (passing over the very great differences that separate the milder version by Shakespeare from the far more troubling one by Greene). Such tales deal head-on with the abuses perpetrated in the name of honour and the premises of the patriarchy concerning wives and children as chattels under exclusive control.[14] In this tale, a father is brought face to face with the injustice of his rigour.

Yet the young girl victimized by her father is not all sweetness and good cheer. Luciana is initially characterized by her superiority complex, which is confirmed through her mockery and disdain for the lower social and intellectual echelons. Pietro's wish is merely quid pro quo in taking down by a notch or two this sanctimonious little snob, a wish which presumably backfires when he is bound to her through his ersatz paternity and thus compelled to share in her punishment. At that moment, a little family

---

14 In a more archetypal sense, the princess shares her initial condition with all the princesses who have been locked away in towers, immured and imprisoned, in order to keep them free of unwanted impregnation. These were measures taken by a threatened king in order to control the acquisition of a son-in-law on his own terms. Invariably, in each of those tales, all measures fail, whether the princess is visited by a bird who turns lover, or the rays of the sun peering through a chink, or, as in the present case, by a low-lifer who commands the verbal magic whereby mere wishes may be turned into fact. These stories are related, in turn, to all those concerned with the delaying tactics of riddles, quests, or menacing chests (as in Shakespeare's *The Merchant of Venice*), whereby the weak will eliminate themselves or fortune will intercede. A concomitant solution is for the king to marry his own daughter – hence the incest crises plots already seen – and thereby create a bloodline male heir in the next generation. Historically, kings have had cause to fear sons-in-law who inherited their power through marriage to daughters, as King Lear's story attests. The matter becomes acute in matriarchal cultures where power is transmitted through marriage and may be passed on before the old king is dead.

under duress suddenly emerges, with all the overtones of the holy family with their miraculous boy-child taking flight. Nevertheless, Luciana remains a little nag to the end, assuming control over the magic fish not only in search of sanctuary but in the realization of her inflated nesting requirements and over-the-top decorating demands. Little princess seems not to have learned a great deal, being reconciled to her fool only because he could be converted into a little trophy prince by imperious command. At that juncture, Pietro passes out of the picture, settling for remote insemination of his child and a henpecked future as a royal family adjunct; he has been overhauled perhaps, but he has still not escaped the stigma of his birth. Pietro may rise to dynastic power, but in effect he makes one foolish wish and then his imagination fails him. If, in this profile of the protagonist of a rags-to-riches tale, the downtrodden see any gratulatory wish-fulfillment trajectory for themselves, the more power to them.

Despite her mysterious pregnancy and the acquisition of an unsatisfactory mate, Luciana manages to salvage some righteous anger and put on a great material show that brings her alienated parents back under her roof on her own terms. The balance of the story deals with the dynamics of the royal family, the passage of time, and the work of reconciliation. The magic helper is merely an accessory now as the story drifts from the lazy boy to the determined princess, and from social-echelon conflict through the rising tale of the poor boy to the turnabout assertion of the injured child. When the ladies in Straparola's audience heard this tale, they were moved to tears, suggesting that for such auditors there was a sufficient substance of character or emblematic activity to arouse empathy and a genuine outpouring of spontaneous emotion. This is hardly to be associated with the motifs of pauper-fools made powerful, trickery, or revenge, but with innocence abused, the prospects of certain death, deliverance, and the eternal drama of the family and its centrality in our psychic lives. The story, then, introduces several thematic modes, drifting with clear narrative purpose from one to another in a way that makes the assembled parts appear fully motivated, sequential, and necessary. If these thematic hints and social perspectives are valid inferences from the tale as it stands in the *Notti*, they represent the insights of that age that are expressed, as it were, through a tale still preserving its archetypal dimensions, magic transformations, and implicit mysteries. But because it comes into the record only with Straparola, to say what it was throughout its pre-history and back to its origins is work of the most speculative kind.

Worthy of mention is Giuseppe Rua's discovery of the close relationship between Straparola's description of the fairy castle and a similar passage from Boccaccio. Straparola writes: 'con logge e consale e con camere bellissime.' Boccaccio: 'e con logge e con sale e con camere.' Straparola: 'una fontana di acqua freddissima ed una volta di preziosi vini' compared to Boccaccio's 'e con pozzi d'acque freschissime, e con volte di preziosi vini.' Rua thinks Straparola was simply giving himself less trouble, but the more striking fact is that the passages are so conventional in both and hardly presenting matter that Straparola could not have approximated on his own. But there is a phenomenon at play not easily accounted for, that from time to time, such passages are tipped into Straparola's text from readings not otherwise associated with the story type in hand.[15]

15 Rua, *Tra Antiche fiabe e novelle: Le 'Piacevoli notti' di Messer Gian Francesco Straparola* (Rome: Ermanno Loescher, 1898), pp. 99–100.

III. Fable 2
Livoretto and His Wonderful Horse

ARIANNA

Dalfreno, king of Tunis, had two sons, one called Listico and the other Livoretto, afterwards known as Porcarollo. Livoretto, after many adventures, wins Bellisandra for his wife, the daughter of Attarante, king of Damascus.

It is no easy matter for the helmsman, no matter how wise, if he is troubled by envious and contrary fortune and driven amid hard and jagged reefs, to bring his tempest-tossed vessel safely into a sheltered harbour. So it happened to Livoretto, son of the great king of Tunis, who, after many dangers, heavy afflictions, and tiring ventures hardly to be believed, succeeded at the last, through the fortitude of his spirit, in trampling under foot his wretched fortune, and finally to reign peacefully over his kingdom from the great city of Cairo. I will make all of this abundantly clear in the fable I'm about to tell you.

In the royal city of Tunis on the coast of Africa, not long ago, there reigned a famous and powerful king named Dalfreno. He had for his wife a beautiful and wise lady, and by her two sons, prudent, virtuous, and obedient to their father in everything, the elder being called Listico and the younger Livoretto. Now it happened that by royal ordinance and the approved customs of the state these young men were barred from the succession to their father's throne, because by right it was reserved for the female line. The king was much troubled and grief-stricken in his heart, knowing that by ill fortune he had been deprived of a female heir and that he had come to the end of his days when he might expect more children. His sorrow was all the heavier because he was haunted by dread that after his death his sons might be looked at askance, unjustly treated, and ignominiously driven out of the kingdom.

The unhappy king, held fast by these painful reflections and ignorant of where remedy might be found, turned to the queen, whom he dearly loved, and spoke to her: 'Madam, what shall we do with these sons of ours, seeing that, according to the law and ancient custom of the land, we are powerless to make them heirs to our kingdom?'

The queen, with her prudence and discretion, answered him in the following manner: 'Sire, it seems to me, given that you possess numerous and inexhaustible treasures, that you should first give to each of them a generous supply of money and jewels and then send them away into some foreign country where no one knows them. Then, with luck, they may find favour in the eyes of some nobleman who will make certain that no evil befalls them. But if they must suffer, may God forbid, at least it will not be known whose sons they are. They are young, handsome, well mannered, high-spirited, and on the alert for every honourable and knightly enterprise. Let them go where they will. Hardly a king, prince, or great lord will be found who would not love them and prize them on account of the rich talents that nature has lavished upon them.'

The prudent queen's reply accorded perfectly with the humour of King Dalfreno, so he called his sons Listico and Livoretto into his presence and spoke to them in the following manner: 'My sons, source of my greatest delight, after I am dead you will have no hope of succeeding me, by no means because of any vices or ill manner of living, but because it is determined by the law and ancient custom of the country. Because you are male rather than female, such as you were created by nature and your parents, you are barred from all claim. Therefore your mother and I, for the benefit and advantage of you both, have determined to let you travel into foreign lands, taking with you a ready supply of jewels, gems, and money to help you in finding some honourable position whereby you will be able to sustain your lives. In this way you will make us happy and fulfill all our desires.'

Listico and Livoretto were as pleased with the proposal as the king and queen, because they shared an ardent interest in seeing new lands and enjoying the pleasures of the world. Now the queen was partial to the younger son, loving him more tenderly than the elder – as is often the way with mothers – and before they made their departure, she called him aside and gave him a spirited horse, a prancer flecked with spots, with a small shapely head and stalwart courage shining in its eyes. In addition to these good qualities, it was a fairy horse – of which fact Livoretto was fully aware.

As soon as the two sons had received their parents' benediction and secured the treasure prepared for them, they departed in secret together. After they had ridden many days without finding a place that pleased them, they were greatly disappointed. 'All this while we've been riding in one another's company and closely searching the country, but we haven't found anything worth the effort.' Then Livoretto spoke up, saying to his brother, 'Perhaps, if you're in agreement with this, it would be wiser for us to go our separate ways, so that each of us can search out his own adventures.'

The proposal was pleasing to them both, so after they had warmly embraced and kissed each other, they bade farewell and went their respective ways. Listico made his way towards the West and was never heard from again, while Livoretto journeyed into the East. There he rode from country to country finding nothing to his advantage until the money, jewels, and treasure given to him by his father were entirely depleted and only his magic horse remained. He found himself at last in the great city of Cairo, the royal capital of Egypt, which at that time was under the rule of a sultan named Danebruno, a man wise in all the secrets of statecraft, powerful through his wealth and high estate, but heavily stricken in years. Yet despite his advanced age, he was enflamed by his ardent love for Bellisandra, the daughter of Attarante, king of Damascus. To win the princess in marriage by love or by force, he had sent a powerful expeditionary army against the city with orders to set up camp around it, lay siege, and take it by storm. But Bellisandra was already aware of just how old and ugly the sultan of Cairo was, and had made up her mind once and for all that she would rather die by her own hand than be forced to marry with such a man.

As soon as Livoretto arrived in Cairo and entered into the city, he set about exploring every part, where he found many marvels and realized just how much this metropolis suited his tastes. Knowing too that he had by then lavished all his substance in satisfying his pleasures, he made up his mind that he would not leave from there without taking service with some master or other. One day, finding himself near the palace of the sultan, he looked into the courtyard where he saw a great number of sanjaks, mamelukes, and slaves, asking them whether the sultan's court lacked any kind of servant, for he would willingly serve. They told him all the posts were filled. But after a time, one of them recalled that there was a place in the household for a man to tend the pigs and shouted after him, asking whether he would be willing to be a swineherd, to which

Livoretto answered 'Yes!' So the man told him to climb down from his horse, whereupon he led him to the pigsties, asking at the same time his name. 'I'm called Livoretto,' he told him, although in after years all men knew him by the name of Porcarollo.

His only job was to fatten up the pigs, and in this duty he showed such great care and diligence that he easily achieved in two months what would have taken another man six to accomplish. Thus it came about that he found service at the court of the sultan. When the sanjaks, mamelukes, and slaves saw what a serviceable fellow he was, they persuaded the sultan that it would be good to find other employment for him because his diligence and cleverness deserved something better than the low post he now held. So by the decree of the sultan, he was put in charge of all the horses in the royal stables, with a large increase in his wages, all of which pleased him greatly because he reasoned that as master of all the other horses, he would be better able to look after his own as well. Then he settled to work in his new post, rubbing down and currycombing the beasts so well and with such an expert hand that their coats shone like velvet, for they were in excellent condition.

Among the horses there was an animal of low value, but very high-spirited and exceedingly beautiful. Being so handsome a steed, he gave it special attention, training it perfectly, so that everywhere it went, the palfrey would curve its neck, dance, and stand straight up on its hind legs pawing the air so fast that every movement seemed like the flight of a bolt from a crossbow. When they saw what Livoretto had taught the palfrey by his careful training, the mamelukes and slaves were struck with amazement, for it seemed to them that such things were scarcely possible in the course of nature. Hence, they decided to tell the whole matter to the sultan so that he too could witness and enjoy the marvellous skill of Porcarollo.

The sultan always bore about him an appearance of great melancholy, whether from the torture of his amorous passion, or by reason of his advanced age. He cared little or not at all for any kind of recreation. Weighed down by these troublesome humours, he would pass his time in thinking only of his beloved mistress. But the mamelukes and slaves made such ado over the matter that before long the sultan was persuaded to stand one morning at his window in order to take in all the amazing and dexterous feats of horsemanship that Porcarollo could perform on his trained palfrey. Taking notice of this handsome and well built youth, attractive beyond his expectations, he concluded that it was mismanagement on his part – a decision he now came to regret – to have used so much talent in no higher office than the feeding and tending of animals. After he had reflected upon the hidden virtues of this gracious youth, he resolved forthwith to remove him from his current post and to place him in a higher one. Porcarollo was then summoned into his presence and addressed: 'Porcarollo, it is my intention that you serve no longer in the stables, but that you attend me at my own table in the role of cupbearer, tasting everything that is placed before me.'

The young man, after he had duly entered upon the office of cupbearer to the sultan, carried out his duties so artfully and skillfully that he won the approbation not only of the sultan but of all those at the court. But among the mamelukes and slaves there arose such a bitter hatred and envy against him by reason of the great favour accorded him by the sultan that they could scarcely bear the sight of him. Had they not been kept back by the fear of their master, they would assuredly have taken his life. Therefore, in order to deprive the unfortunate youth of the ruler's favour, and to have him either slain or driven into perpetual exile, they contrived a most cunning and ingenious plot for the advancement of their design. One morning a slave named Chebur, on duty that day in attendance upon the sultan, said, 'Sire, I have some good news to give you.'

'And what may that be?' enquired the sultan.

The slave replied, 'It's that Porcarollo, whose real name is Livoretto, has been boasting that he could perform anything for you, that he could even get Attarante's daughter for you to enjoy.'

'How could such a thing be possible?' asked the sultan.

To which Chebur replied, 'It is indeed possible, O my lord. But if you will not put faith in my words, enquire of the mamelukes and of the other slaves, in whose presence he has boasted more than once of his power to do this, and then you will easily know whether the tale I am telling you is false or true.'

After the sultan had duly assured himself that what the slave had reported was so, he summoned Livoretto into his presence and demanded of him whether the report circulating at the court about him was actually true. The young man, who knew nothing at all of what had taken place, stoutly denied it and spoke so bluntly that the sultan, now fully aroused with rage and animosity, gave him his orders, 'Get yourself there immediately, and if you haven't brought the Princess Bellisandra, the daughter of Attarante, king of Damascus, into my power within the space of thirty days, I will have your head taken off your shoulders.'

The young man, upon hearing this cruel speech of the sultan, withdrew from the presence overwhelmed with grief and confusion and set off for the stables. No sooner had he gone in than the fairy horse, after noting the sad looks of his master and the scalding tears falling so plentifully from his eyes, turned to him and said, 'Alas, my master, why do I see you so afflicted and so full of grief?'

The young man, weeping and sighing deeply all the while, told him from beginning to end all that the sultan had required him to perform. Whereupon the horse, tossing his head and imitating the gestures of laughter, managed to comfort him somewhat and told him not to fear, but to be of good heart because all his affairs would come to a prosperous end. Next he told his master, 'Go back to the sultan and beg him to give you a letter patent addressed to the captain-general of his army, commanding him that as soon as he reads the letter sealed with the great seal, he should immediately raise the siege of Damascus and give you money and fine clothing as well as arms so that you may be able to prosecute with vigour and spirit the great enterprise that lays before you. And if it should happen, during your voyage there, that any person or animal of whatever kind or condition should entreat you to do them service, take care that you perform the favour that is required of you, for if you hold your life dear, you must not refuse to do the service asked for. Next, if you should meet with any man eager to purchase me from you, tell him that you are willing to sell me, but then demand so extravagant a price that he will give up all thought of the bargain. However, if at any time a woman should wish to buy me, conduct yourself gently towards her and be as kind to her as you can, giving her full liberty to stroke my head, my forehead, my eyes and ears, my flanks, or do anything else she may have a mind to, for I will let them handle me as they wish without doing them the least mischief or injury of any kind.'

Hearing these words, the young man, now full of hope and spirit, went back to the sultan and requested of him the letter patent and for everything else that the fairy horse had named to him. Thereupon, he mounted the horse and took the road that led to Damascus – his departure giving great delight to all the mamelukes and slaves, who, because of the burning envy and hatred they bore him, thought it a certainty that he would never return alive to Cairo. Now it happened that when Livoretto had been a long time on his journey, he came one day to a certain body of water, and as he passed by he remarked that the shore gave off such a horrible stench that no one could come near the place without great difficulty. There upon the bank he saw a fish lying half dead. The fish, when it saw Livoretto approaching, cried out, 'Alas, kind gentleman, I beseech you of your courtesy to set me free from this stinking filth, for as you may see, I am very nearly dead because of it.'

The young man, clearly remembering what the fairy horse had told him, right away got down from his saddle and drew the fish out of the ill-smelling water and washed it clean with his own hands. After it had returned thanks to Livoretto for his kindness, the fish said to him, 'Take from my back the three biggest scales you can find and keep them carefully by you, and whenever you should need any help, put down the scales by the bank of the river and I will come to you immediately and provide you with instant help.'

Livoretto accordingly took the three scales, and once he had tossed the fish, all clean and shining, into the clear water, he remounted his horse and rode on until he came to a certain place where he found a peregrine falcon which had been frozen into a sheet of ice as far as the middle of its body and could not get free. The falcon, when it saw the young man, cried out, 'Alas, fair youth, take pity on me and release me from this ice wherein, as you see, I am imprisoned, and I promise that if you deliver me from this terrible plight, I will lend you my aid at any time you should chance to need it.'

The young man, overcome by compassion and pity, went kindly to the succour of the bird. He drew the knife that he carried attached to the scabbard of his sword and with the point he struck and chipped the hard ice round about the bird so that it broke in pieces. Then he took out the falcon and held it close to his chest in order to bring back some heat to its body. When it had recovered its strength and was itself again, the falcon thanked the young man profusely for his kindness and, as a recompense for the great service he had wrought, it gave him two feathers which he would find growing under its left wing, begging him to guard and preserve them most carefully for the sake of the love it bore him, so that if, in the future, he should happen to be in need of any aid, he might take the two feathers to the river and stick them into the bank, and immediately it would come to his assistance. Having so spoken, the bird then suddenly took wing and flew away.

After Livoretto had continued his journey for some days, he came to the sultan's army camped before the city, and there he found the captain-general waging his merciless combat against the city of Damascus. Once brought into the general's presence, Livoretto drew forth the sultan's letter patent, and as soon as the general had mastered the contents, he immediately gave orders that the siege should be lifted. This done, he marched back to Cairo with his whole army. Livoretto watched the departure of the captain-general and then made his way into the city alone the next morning. Having taken up his lodging at an inn, he attired himself in a very fair and rich garment all covered with rare and most precious gems which shone brightly enough to make the sun pale with envy. He mounted his fairy horse and rode straight to the royal palace. There he made the horse go through all the exercises he had taught it, and with such great readiness and dexterity that everyone who beheld him stood still in amazement and could look at nothing else.

Now it happened that the noise of the tumultuous crowd in the piazza below roused the Princess Bellisandra from her sleep and drew her forth from her bed. Having gone out on a balcony, which commanded a view of the entire square beneath, she saw the handsome youth and the prowess of his spirited horse. So taken was she by this magnificent animal that she fell in love with it in the same manner that a young man is seized with love for a charming maiden. So she went to her father and besought him most urgently to buy the horse for her, because ever since she had looked upon its beauty and grace she had come to feel that she could not live without it. Now the king loved this daughter most tenderly and thus to please her, he sent out one of his chief nobles to ask Livoretto whether he would sell his mount for a reasonable price, because the king's daughter had fallen passionately in love with it. On hearing this, Livoretto answered that there was nothing on earth precious and excellent enough to meet the price for the horse, and for that reason he demanded a sum of money greater than the riches to be found in all the dominions which the king had inherited from his forefathers. Hearing so enormous a price, the king called his daughter and said to her, 'My daughter, I cannot bring myself to lavish the value of my whole kingdom in satisfying your desire in the purchase of this horse. Have just a little patience, live happily and contentedly, for I will go in search of another horse to buy even better and more beautiful than this one.'

But the king's words merely enflamed Bellisandra's ardent longing to possess the one she had seen, and so she urged her father more insistently than ever to buy it for her, no matter the price he had to pay. Yet, after much praying and beseeching, the maiden found that her entreaties were to no avail with her father, so she left him and went to her mother and fell into her arms, feigning to be downcast and half dead with despair. The mother was filled with pity at seeing her child so grief-stricken and pale, giving her what gentle consolation she could and begging her to moderate her sorrow. As soon as the king should be out of the way, she suggested that they two would seek out the young man and bargain with him for the purchase of the horse. Because they were women, perhaps he might then let them have it at a more reasonable price. The maiden was somewhat comforted when she heard these kind words of her beloved mother. The king being called away, the queen despatched a messenger to Livoretto, requesting him to come right away to the palace with the horse. When he heard the message, Livoretto rejoiced greatly and made his way there. The queen then asked him what price he would really accept for the horse which her daughter so much desired to own, and he answered her in these words, 'Madam, if you were to offer me all you possess in the world for my horse it could never suffice to purchase it for your daughter, but if she would be pleased to accept it as a gift, she can have it for nothing. Before she accepts the gift, however, I would prefer that she make a trial of it, for it is so gentle and well-trained that it will allow anyone to climb upon it without difficulty.'

With these words, he got down from the saddle and helped the princess to mount, and when she had the reins in her hand she made it go here and there and managed it perfectly. But after a little time, when the princess had gone some stone's throw distant from her mother, Livoretto suddenly sprang upon the crupper of the horse and struck his spurs deeply into the flanks of the beast and pricked it so sharply that it sprang away as swiftly as a bird flying through the air. The maiden, bewildered by this strange conduct, began to cry out, 'You wicked and disloyal traitor. Where are you taking me, you false-hearted dog?' But all her cries and reproaches were to small purpose, for there was no one near to give her aid or even to comfort her with a word.

Now as they rode along, they came to the bank of a river, and in crossing over the maiden drew from her finger the finest of the rings she wore and cast it secretly into the water. After they had been for many days on their journey, they arrived at last at Cairo, and as soon as Livoretto came to the palace, he took the princess and presented her to the sultan. When he saw how lovely and graceful she was, he exulted within himself and welcomed her with all sorts of kindly speeches. After a time, when the hour for retiring to rest had come, the two of them, being in a richly appointed chamber, the princess spoke thus to the sultan, 'Sire, do not dream that I will ever yield to your amorous wishes unless you first command that wicked and rascally servant of yours to find my ring which fell into the river as we were travelling here. Whenever he will have recovered it and brought it back to me, then I'll be ready to comply with your desire.'

The sultan by this time was all on fire with love for the damsel, but she prevented him from troubling her more for the present, so he turned to Livoretto and told him to set out directly in quest of the ring, threatening that if he should fail in his task that he would have him put to death.

Livoretto, as soon as heard the words of the sultan, perceived that these were orders which must be carried out at once, and that he would put himself in great danger by opposing his master's wishes. So he left the presence deeply troubled and went out to the stables where he wept long and bitterly, for he was altogether without hope that he could ever recover the princess's ring. The fairy horse, when he saw his master so cast down with grief and weeping piteously, asked him what evil afflicted him that should cause him to shed such bitter tears. After Livoretto had told him the cause, the horse addressed him, 'Ah, my poor master! Be still. Don't you remember the words of the fish? Open your ears to what I'm about to say and take care to perform everything just as I direct you. Go back to the sultan and ask him for all you will need for your enterprise, and then set about it with full confidence; have no doubts.'

Livoretto did exactly as the horse commanded him, no more and no less. After travelling for some time, he came at last to the very spot where he had crossed the river with the princess and there he laid the three scales of the fish on the green turf of the bank. With that, the fish could be seen gaily darting hither and thither in the water before swimming up to Livoretto, whereupon he produced from his mouth the precious ring and delivered it into his hand, took the three scales, and dived back again into the river.

No sooner had Livoretto gotten the ring back safely than all his sorrow turned to gladness, and without any delay he made his way home to Cairo. When he had come into the sultan's presence and made obeisance to him, he presented the ring to the princess. Seeing that her wish had now been fulfilled by the restoration of the precious ring she had so ardently desired, the sultan began to court her with the most tender and amorous caresses and flattering speeches, hoping thereby to induce her to lie with him that night. But all his supplications and wooing were in vain, for the princess said to him, 'Sir, do not think to deceive me with your fine words and false speeches. I swear to you that you shall never take your pleasure of me until that false rascal who entrapped me with his horse and carried me here has brought me some of the water of life.' The sultan was so enamoured of this lady that he was anxious to do all in his power to please her. Therefore, Livoretto was summoned immediately and told that if he valued his life he must go and fetch some of the water of life.

Livoretto was mightily distressed to hear this impossible command and began to complain bitterly that the sultan his master should offer so wretched a reward for all his faithful services, for all the long and arduous fatigue he had undergone, placing his own life all the while in imminent danger. But still burning with love, the sultan was in no mind to abandon his intent to satisfy the wishes of the lady; he would have the water of life found for her at any cost. So in his customary way, Livoretto left his master's presence and went to the stables, cursing his evil fortune and weeping bitterly all the while. The horse, seeing his despair and hearing his sad laments, said to him, 'O, my master, why do you torment yourself like this? Has a new evil now befallen you? Calm yourself and remember that a remedy is to be found for every evil under the sun, except death.' And when the horse had heard the cause of Livoretto's sore weeping, it comforted him with gentle words, urging him to recall the precious gift of the two feathers and what the falcon had said upon being delivered from its icy bonds.

This unhappy youth, remembering perfectly well, mounted the horse, taking with him a small phial of glass which was well sealed with a stopper. This he tied to his girdle and rode on until he came to the place where he had set the falcon at liberty. There he planted the two feathers in the bank of the river according to the directions he had received and suddenly the falcon appeared in the air and asked what his need might be. To this Livoretto answered, 'Some of the water of life.'

When it heard these words, the falcon cried out, 'Alas, alas, gentle knight, the thing you seek is impossible. You will never get it by your own power because the fountain from which it flows is always closely watched and guarded by two savage lions and two dragons which roar most horribly and incessantly both day and night, and which pitilessly mangle and devour all those who seek to approach the fountain to take the water. But in gratitude for the great service you once rendered me, take the phial which hangs at your side and fasten it under my right wing, and make certain not to leave this place before I've returned.'

When Livoretto had done everything just as the falcon had ordered, the bird rose up from the earth with the phial attached to its wing and flew away to the region where the fountain of the water of life was to be found, and having secretly filled the phial with the water, it returned to the place where Livoretto was waiting and gave him the flask. Then he took up his two feathers and flew away out of sight.

Livoretto rejoiced greatly that he had actually procured some of the precious water. So without further delay, he returned to Cairo in haste and, once he was there, presented himself to the sultan, who was passing the time in pleasant conversation with his beloved Bellisandra. The sultan took the water of life and with great glee he presented it to the princess. As soon as she could call this precious fluid her own, he renewed his entreaties that she yield herself to his pleasure. But as firmly as a strong tower beaten by the raging winds, she declared that she would never consent to gratify his desires unless he first cut off the head of Livoretto with his own hands, who had been the cause of all this mischief. But when the sultan heard this savage request of the hard-hearted princess, he was not moved in the slightest to comply, because it seemed to him a most shameful thing that Livoretto should lose his life in so cruel a manner for all the great labours he had accomplished. But the treacherous and wicked princess, resolutely determined to carry out her evil purpose, seized a naked dagger and, with a rash and intrepid spirit, stabbed the youth in the throat while the sultan stood by looking on. Since no one was there with valour enough to help him, the boy fell to the earth, dead.

Still not content with this vicious outrage, the wicked damsel hacked his head from his shoulders. Once she had chopped his flesh into small pieces, torn up his sinews, broken his hard bones and ground them to a fine powder, she took a large copper bowl into which, little by little, she tossed the pounded and cut-up flesh, mixing it with the bones and sinews, as housewives do when they make a pasty in a leavened crust. After it was well kneaded and the dissected meat thoroughly blended with the powdered bones and the sinews, the princess fashioned out of the mixture a fine and shapely image of a man, and this she sprinkled with the water of life out of the phial, and immediately the young man was restored to life from death more handsome and graceful than he had ever been before.

When the sultan, who was feeling the heavy weight of his advancing years, saw this amazing feat and the extraordinary miracle performed before his very eyes, he was struck with astonishment and stood as one confounded. Then he felt a great longing to be made a youth again, so he begged Bellisandra to treat him in the same way as she had Livoretto. The princess wasted no time in obeying the sultan's command. Taking up the sharp knife still wet with Livoretto's blood, she seized him by the throat with her left hand and held him firmly while she dealt him a mortal blow in the breast. Then she commanded the slaves to throw the body of the sultan out of the window into the deep moat of the palace, so that, instead of being made young again like Livoretto, he became food for dogs. Thus did the wretch end his life in a very sorry fashion.

By reason of these wondrous feats, all men greatly feared and honoured the princess. Moreover, when she learned that the young man was a son of Dalfreno, king of Tunis, and that his rightful name was Livoretto, she wrote a letter to the old father, giving him a full account of all the amazing accidents that had befallen his son and urgently begged him to come at once to Cairo so that he might be present at the celebration of her marriage to Livoretto. King Dalfreno delighted in receiving this good news about his son, of whom he had heard nothing since he left Tunis with his brother. Having once put all his affairs in good order, he travelled to Cairo where he was welcomed by the entire city with the most distinguished marks of honour. Soon afterwards, Bellisandra and Livoretto were married while the entire population rejoiced. Thus, with the princess for his lawful spouse, Livoretto was made the sultan of Cairo amid sumptuous feasts and triumphs, and with the happiest of omens, where, for many years thereafter, he governed his realm in peace and lived a life of pleasure and tranquillity. Dalfreno tarried in Cairo a few days after the nuptials and then took leave of his son and daughter-in-law and safely made his way back to Tunis.

As soon as Arianna had come to the end of her moving tale, keeping to the rules they had all agreed upon, she placed her hand on an enigma and pronounced it as follows:

Small though my compass might be,
A mighty furnace engendered me.
The covering which around me clings,
Is what from marshy plain upsprings.
My soul, which should be free as air,
Is doomed a prisoner close to fare.
It is a liquor bland and sweet,
No jest is this which I repeat,
All silken are my festal clothes,
And man will put me to his nose
To make me all my charms disclose.

All those assembled listened with the keenest attention to the ingenious enigma set forth by Arianna and they made her repeat it over and over again, but not one of the entire company had wits sharp enough to disentangle it. At last, the fair Arianna gave the solution in these words: 'Ladies and gentlemen, my riddle means only a little flask of rose water which has a body of glass born in a fiery furnace. Its covering comes from the marshes, for it is made of straw, and the soul which is contained within is the rose water. The gown that surrounds it is the envelope or covering, and whoever sees it puts it to his nose to enjoy the sweet smell.'

As soon as Arianna had given the solution to her enigma, Lauretta, who was seated next to her, remembered that it was her turn to speak. So without waiting for a further prompt from the Signora, she began in the following manner.

III.2. Commentary

The story of Livoretto and his wonderful horse is yet another of Straparola's tales that crosses into the domain of the fairy tale according to criteria more readily intuited than defined. Among the tell-tale elements are the supernatural capacities of a talking horse, the timely interventions of animals under obligation to the hero for his former kindnesses, the quest imposed upon the hero to find the beautiful princess, and the employment of magic elements such as the miraculous water of life by which the story is brought to resolution, followed by the formulaic marriage of the prince-in-disguise to an imperious princess who takes him on her terms.[16] It simply features materials intrinsic to the genre. Detectable in the background are vestiges of tales about oriental rulers and the predatory entitlements of harem culture, the eroto-politics of an old sultan, and the shrewd delaying tactics of a princess determined not to sacrifice herself to his unsavoury demands. The story is set, moreover, in Tunis, Cairo and Damascus.[17] Livoretto, on his side, in consultation

---

16 On the medieval fascination with automatons, flying horses, wonderful mechanical devices, tales of speaking brass heads and their Byzantine origins, see Karen Jolly, 'Medieval Magic: Definitions, Beliefs, Practices,' in *Witchcraft and Magic in Europe in the Middle Ages*, ed. Bengt Ankarloo and Stuart Clark (Philadelphia: University of Pennsylvania Press, 2002), p. 67.

17 Faouzia Demnati Chaïeb is interested in this and related stories, such as 'Costanza' (IV.1), in terms of their settings in Africa and the Near East and the political climates of the times. This story begins in a dynastic dilemma which detaches the son from his homeland (in violation of the principle of male primogeniture). His direction is towards the East in a landscape half political and half romance geography. Straparola creates decadent sultans in Cairo and Tunis, while Livoretto's quest is for the daughter of the king of Damascus through a series of palace intrigues. The historical overtones concern the excessive political power of the mamelukes in Cairo. Such tyranny began in the thirteenth century and ended in

with his equine counsellor, has risen from keeper of the pigs to the sultan's seneschal, performing all the tasks imposed upon him in loyal service to his master in a tale of rising fortunes based on merit, only to be slain, decapitated, and dismembered by the captive princess. As strange as this procedure may seem, it is an established part of the tale's tradition, for just as the quests are tantamount to rites of passage testing the personal courage and courtesy of the hero, so his death becomes a ritual prelude to resurrection and transformation through the water of life – a transaction that barely resists interpretation in terms of some vestigial rite of rebirth and renewal, particularly because the sultan, who is thrown into the moat and fed to the dogs, may simultaneously symbolize the expulsion of the dying season. The ending is so stark and abrupt in its murderous *peripeteia*, however, that a child might protest its violence even by comparison with Hollywood action films. In a more gently emblematic way, however, the story is about the perseverance of the hero, fortitude in adversity, cunning mixed with kindness, and the enactment of an archetypal destiny in the idealized coupling with a member of the opposite sex – although, paradoxically, the hero of this tale plays no actualizing or desiring role in the matter. Until the last moment, the princess wants him dead, and after that she wants him refashioned entirely by her own hands, although even those facts can be turned to insight by psychoanalytical critics. It is a simple tale of near destitution as a prelude to a royal restitution, but in the melding of motifs it is a fable of considerable complexity.

One way of disentangling the compound thematics is to separate the distinct narrative parts, insofar as there are at least five recognizable motifs which can stand alone as stories. Such a diversity of motifs suggests that Straparola's version is derived, presumably without much motivic variation, from a folk source current in the early sixteenth century, and that his prototype was itself a conflation of narrative elements from

---

1517 after the campaign of Selim Soliman II against Egypt. Thus, the time frame of the story must date to the mameluke era. These are interesting correlations, although any particularity of interest on Straparola's part in the sociological and political realities of these areas may be questioned. It is true that the motivating circumstances of these stories depend upon the willful absolutism and predatory luxuries of the 'oriental' ruler as imagined by Western storytellers in the age of the Ottomans. That stories created in this ambience also represent a social critique of 'oriental' court culture is a debatable extra measure. *L'altérité orientale-mauresque dans la culture du quotidian en Italie à l'époque de la Renaissance* (Manouba, Tunisia: Publications de la faculté des letters, 2000), esp. p. 303.

diverse backgrounds which, through success with their audiences, settled into a relatively fixed tradition, while coexisting simultaneously with alternate descendants of that same tradition scattered throughout many parts of Europe. Only some such theory can account for the remarkable variety of similar tales in concurrent circulation in the nineteenth century. That generic tale incorporates all or several of the following: a prince disguised or displaced, a magic horse, jealous associates, an eroticized and threatening ruler, helper animals, the search for a princess (often with golden hair), death and resurrection rituals, and the fairy tale ending. Stated differently, by linking the episodes within 'Livoretto' to their parallel episodes in related stories, it will be discovered that this tale is a point of confluence in the circulation of some of the most salient motifs of the Eurasian folk tale.

The first to be mentioned is the framing device whereby the prince is detached from his place of birth, launched upon his road of life, and challenged to find his fortune in alien climes by skill and understanding combined with innate goodness. That his father's kingdom is matrilineal and therefore excludes both Livoretto and his older brother from the succession is an odd pretext, especially in light of their father's (masculine) kingship, but it does the job. Livoretto's mother equips him with a magic horse when he leaves home, its special powers known to the boy but put to the test only later in the story. True to a folk tale tradition – see also Straparola's story of the three brothers (VII.5) – the brothers go their separate ways. Arriving in Cairo, Livoretto takes on the lowliest of employments before rising to a high and enviable position through his merit. He then falls victim to the jealousy of mamelukes and slaves who wish him dead on the one hand, and to the capriciousness of an amorous sultan who threatens death should he fail in his quests on the other. In related tales, the horse may be acquired later, either by taming it or by stealing it from the stables of a giant. In Livoretto's story, the helper animals are acquired en route to fetch the princess, but in other versions, the hero wins their support during his initial outward journey. An important variant appears in those stories in which the hero takes his rival with him when he leaves home, or meets him shortly thereafter, whether as a treacherous relative, schoolmate, or a hunchback. There are versions devoid of this segment entirely, but most include the circumstances that launch the young prince into the world.

A second distinct marker is the enchanted horse, which in some tales has remarkable speed, power and intuition, in others it can speak and reason, as in the present story, while in still others it can fly, whether as a mythological animal or as a mechanical simulacrum of a flying horse, as in *The Arabian Nights*. The mechanical horse directed by pins on its head and neck had wide dissemination in Europe from as early as the fourteenth century. It may be said to have had its origins in the first book of the Sanskrit *Panchatantra* (as early as the third century AD) in the story of the amorous weaver whose friend creates for him a flying machine in the form of a golden eagle 'made of wood and gaily painted in different colours [with] cleverly devised pegs to operate it in an unusually novel manner.' With this splendid contraption, he not only wins his princess by impersonating Lord Visnu, but defeats her father's enemies.[18] Notably, in the Straparola version, there are two horses, the speaking steed given to Livoretto upon his departure, and the wild one in the sultan's stables which the hero alone succeeds in taming, the latter suggesting a vestige from a variant version of the story retained in the source. There are just such tales in which the horse itself agrees to be tamed only by a hero it deems sympathetic and worthy, just as Livoretto's horse agrees to remain tame and docile when ridden by the princess. Not far removed are the flying horses of the Arabian tales, including the mechanical horse made of ebony and ivory that ascends and descends by manipulating the pins fixed to its head, as well as the spirited and intelligent creatures of the chivalric romances. Livoretto's horse cannot fly, but it can run as swiftly 'as a bird flying through the air,' and carry both prince and princess on its back, just as Bayard carries all four of the sons of Aymon. This horse is not only a remarkable means of transportation, but it can also be a wise and sage counsellor, with a prescience that enables it to anticipate the end of each exploit and to prepare the hero for every eventuality – it is the boy's fairy godmother in the pre-fairy age – connecting this story to a sizeable repertory of magic horse narratives. Nevertheless, there are subsequent tales in the 'Livoretto' mode similar in all respects except for this miraculous animal, just as there are others without the helping creatures or the ritual death and resurrection motifs.

A third identifying feature, widespread in the folk literature of the world, is the reciprocity established between the hero and a number of animals he meets along the way. It presupposes on their part the ability to speak and reason, as in all beast fables, and to feel a sense of obligation to the hero for having come to their rescue (ATU 554). Their pledge

18 Vishnu Sharma, *The Panchatantra*, trans. Chandra Rajan (London: Penguin, 1993), p. 81.

of future aid is materially signalled in the talismanic tokens they present to the hero in the form of expendable items from their own bodies such as an insect's leg, a rat's whisker, a fish's scale, or a bird's plume. Each acquisition anticipates an episode to follow, one in which the hero is baffled by a challenge that only one of these helpers can execute, either through its ability to perform tasks involving small or numerous objects, or through its locomotive capacities in water and air. Readers keep tabs on such foreshadowing features and mark the imperfections when narrators fail to include episodes for all of the gathered parts. This motif was deployed in the previous tale (III.1) of Pietro the Fool and his tunny or tuna fish whose obligation to the boy for sparing his life is the organizing principle of the entire story. Here the episode of the ring accidentally falling or being strategically thrown into the water and fetched by the obliging fish is an ancient oriental motif widely redeployed in European romance and folklore. The magic fountain on the top of a mountain, guarded by ferocious animals and to which a bird alone has access, is likewise, in its many variants, a widespread motif. These features link Straparola's story to 'the animal brothers-in-law' group (Type 552), in which, as the result of a reckless promise, a man indebted to these animals must bestow his daughters upon them in marriage. The girls' brother, however, receives from them pledges of aid and retains those obligations in the form of feathers, hairs, or scales. Thus, behind the beast fable is an illustration of the indebtednesses accumulated through marriage and the extended family. It is revealing, as in the story of Livoretto, however, that when the favour is once granted, the animals collect their feathers and scales like coupons and thereby limit their services to a single episode. This story type, in turn, becomes associated with the dragon rescue stories wherein, through the magic powers of the helpers, a princess is rescued from a land or sea monster (as in Cesarino, X.3).[19] An assessment of this motif as a rite of passage and a plot-enabling device might be extended to include a significant number of folk and fairy tale types.[20]

19 Thompson, *The Folktale* (Berkeley: University of California Press, [1946], 1977), p. 56.

20 A small anthology of resumes of tales involving 'thankful beasts' appears in W.A. Clouston, *Popular Tales and Fictions: Their Migrations and Transformations*, ed. Christine Goldberg (Santa Barbara, CA: ABC Clio, [1887], 2002), pp. 93–107. One in particular stands out, collected among the Slavs, in which two brothers seeking their fortunes curry the favour of ants and fish and take the water of life to

The bride quest motif, a form of aristocratic exogamy often replicated in these tales, is carried out by the prince-in-disguise on behalf of an aging but sexually motivated potentate – a classic case of marital asymmetry. The means whereby the sultan first becomes attracted to her is absent in Straparola's tale, and perhaps defectively so, insofar as there are many closely paralleling stories featuring a golden strand of hair which has become detached and which is carried by water to a remote place where it is retrieved and presented to the ruler, thereby inciting him to adore, search for, and possess its original owner. The motif is known among folklorists as 'the princess with the golden hair.'[21] In a typical version, a horse gives advice to a young protagonist – living in a pigsty, with or without a wife, and employed as the king's gardener – about how to rise in status while avoiding the wiles of his rivals. The story also contains magic elements that become obstacles to a pursuing enemy, such as a comb which, when thrown down behind the horse, becomes an instant forest. Of the generic connections between 'the golden hair' group and 'the magic horse' group, there can be little doubt. The question is whether the tale of Livoretto was once a 'golden hair' tale as well. There are many variants, for the girl sought is sometimes the king's abducted daughter, or even the queen held in captivity, with appropriate adjustments to the story's denouement. What remains clear is the 'crossroads' nature of this story, for there are several 'golden hair' tales both before and after Straparola's that are very similar indeed.[22]

---

an ailing princess, thereby uniting two of the leading 'Livoretto' features. When she refuses to marry the designated hero and imposes impossible tasks upon him, he meets them with the aid of his loyal animal friends, including the fish that tosses back to him a pearl lost in the sea. Louis Paul Marie Leger, *Recueil des contes populaires slaves* (Paris: E. Leroux, 1883), no. 25, p. 102.

21 Thompson, 'Goldener Märchen' (ATU 314), in *The Folktale* (Berkeley: University of California Press, [1946], 1977), p. 59. This story type he lists under the heading of 'Helpful Horses' because the enabling hero, although not always, is usually accompanied by his magic horse. Further to the motif of golden hair and the significant role it has played in folklore, see Marina Warner, *From the Beast to the Blonde: On Fairy Tales and Their Tellers* (London: Vintage, 1995), pp. 362–3.

22 In the later literary record, the tale perhaps best epitomizing this group is 'La belle aux cheveux d'or' of Madame Catherine d'Aulnoy in which Beauty with the golden hair rejects the advances of a great king and becomes the object of the enforced quest of a courtier named Avenant. The hero must perform impossible tasks, which he accomplishes with the aid of animals indebted to him for former favours: the carp who fetches the ring; the crow who helps him behead an ogre; and the owl who leads the way to the water of eternal youth and beauty. Given the similarity of

The fifth motif is constituted of all that pertains to fountains of youth, the water of immortality, or the waters of life and death. This liquid of resurrection or oblivion must also be obtained from an enchanted region accessible only through preliminary training in how to circumvent its dangers, or through the aid of an animal helper. The water becomes an instrument in a tale of the death and transfiguration of the hero, in Livoretto's case administered by the princess herself, described as 'treacherous and wicked,' for not only does she stab him but beheads him and cuts his body into small parts in a rather ghoulish fashion. Not unlike the child princess in 'Pietro the Fool,' Bellisandra refashions her eventual mate according to her wishes and now with her own hands. This beheading and resurrection motif is met with again in Straparola's tale of the boy who seeks death and meets new life (IV.5), while the water of life is featured again in 'Dancing Water, Singing Apple, and the Truth-Speaking Bird' (IV.3). In each story of this type, the young protagonist must be the first to venture his life, meeting his death by surprise attack or by voluntary courage; only then can the old king or villain rival be enticed to seek his own rejuvenation and thereby collaborate in his own death. There are many variations on the mechanism, however, for in related tales the two submit to being boiled in a cauldron, or having their heads severed, the one refitted, the other not, or to being baked in an oven – the hero basted in his own sweat and thereby preserved, the old king basted in grease and thereby fried.[23] Particular to the present story is the

---

details, it would appear that she is again drawing directly upon Straparola, yet reworking the several motifs to her own ends. Madame d'Aulnoy, *Contes des fées*, ed. Nadine Jasmin (Paris: Honoré Champion, 2004), pp. 175–87. This story includes the motif of the unwanted king or ogre who, in seeking to rejuvenate himself, accidentally takes the wrong liquor, or is intentionally beheaded but not brought back to life. The minor details in common, such as the three scales and the two feathers, give further assurance that d'Aulnoy was drawing on Straparola's version, although the eternal question remains concerning the availability of folk tales to members of the French aristocracy.

23 The antiquity of this motif may be demonstrated by a story in *Alberuni's India*, originating circa AD 1030. A practitioner working with the oil of immortality and invincibility brings it to a boil and invites the king to take first advantage of it by climbing in, promising that he would pour in the packets of ingredients that would lead to his perfection. The king declined, inviting the other to do as he wished, so in he went. But when the king came to the last packet, he grew fearful of producing a superior rival and hence allowed the practitioner in the vat to dissolve and become consolidated into a silver bar. *Alberuni's India*, ed. Dr. Edward Sachau (New Delhi: Tupa & Co., 2002), p. 179.

idea of life itself as an essence contained in a magic water, that mystery by which inanimate matter is made animate. Only by the most ritualized of processes can it be obtained and employed as an elixir of youth.

All of these elements appear with near seamless continuity in the story of Livoretto, as though no part of the ensemble had ever had an extraneous existence – such are appearances – but a glance at the subsequent cognate tales with their recombined motifs argues otherwise. The present tale is merely the earliest in the literary record of what must have been a well-established and already diversified folk narrative type – in fact a version already showing signs of modification away from a more conventional form. That the story of Livoretto is lacking the motif of the golden hair, that the princess must graduate from a spoiled child wanting a horse to a murdering priestess and ultimately to a submissive bride in order to perform all the operations of the plot, and that the hero must liberate a falcon frozen in the ice en route from Cairo to Damascus, suggests that it is already somewhat 'late,' both as a truncated version of 'the golden hair' group (ATU 314), and as a story carrying vestiges of former versions from remote geographical areas. Meanwhile, the oriental setting might suggest that it is closer to its Arabic origins than most to follow. By way of demonstration, of the many tales having close affinities with Straparola's fable both before and after 1550, only a small sampling can be afforded, leaving moot the exact channels whereby the signature motifs were assembled initially into relatively stable patterns. Merely to generate a provisional stemma of tales adequate to account for the relationship of this story to its two closest chronological cousins, that published in Basel in 1602, and that written by Basile in the 1630s, already confounds the critical imagination.

In 1852 an Egyptian papyrus dating to 1250 BC was translated and published; it once belonged to King Seti II and contained the story entitled 'The Two Brothers.'[24] The tale was a lengthy account of a younger brother, Batu, who escapes the wrath of his elder brother through the advice of a talking cow. He marries a beautiful woman with golden hair, a strand of which floats down a river and comes to the attention of the pharaoh. The ruler fetishizes this golden strand and demands possession of its original owner, leading to the murder of her husband, Batu. Yet, through a series of transformations, he is brought back to life to revenge

24 An account of this discovery is given by Thompson, *The Folktale*, p. 275 without benefit of a reference, but according to him translated by M. de Rougé.

her and become the next pharaoh. To be sure, there is no wonder-working horse (no doubt an Arabian accretion), nor any trick-performing animals (undoubtedly added from the Sanskrit tales), and no water of life, per se, yet there are rival brothers and an exodus, a speaking animal, the motif of the golden hair, a search for the beloved lady, and a murder and resurrection plot leading to the recovery of the lost bride and the death of the amorous magistrate. The tale predates Straparola's by some 2800 years, yet the affinities are transparent. There is no stretch in thinking of this work as the Ur-text to the entire 'Livoretto' group. But the intervening tales hardly form a linear history.

Consider the following story from the Sanskrit *Sinhâsana-dvâtrinçikâ* (The Thirty-two Tales of the Throne) in which a divine princess offers to marry the one who would sacrifice himself by leaping into a cauldron of boiling water. Thereupon King Vikramâditya, without hesitation, leaps in. All those watching the proceedings shout in horror, but the princess arrives with 'amrita,' the water of immortality, and sprinkles it on the king who is, by that time, a mere blob of flesh. He then returns to life more beautiful than ever. In this, the water of life makes its appearance as a groom selection mechanism for a divine woman searching among mortals for a worthy husband made fit by ritual death. The power and authority of the 'princess,' with her control over life, death, and marriage, seems to have been an integral part of the tale.[25] All the elements of the final episode of Livoretto's tale are here and ready to be added to a related tale of questing and return.

Emmanuel Cosquin, in his annotations to 'La belle aux cheveux d'or' from the *Contes de Lorraine*, profiles an ancient tale of the Kamaoneins, a people from the Himalayas whose stories were collected by a Monsieur Minaef – a story remarkably close to the twenty-first tale of the Persian *Tooti-nameh* – in which a péri, a graceful and beautiful female genii, loses a hair and thus touches off the erotic longings of a prince determined to find its owner. When she is taken away, her husband follows her with a frog and serpent as helpers, both in debt to him for former services, one in the form of a Brahmin, the other disguised as a barber. The king wishes to get rid of the young man by sending him on dangerous or impossible missions, including the search for a ring retrieved by the

25 'The Heavenly Nymph and the Kettle of Boiling Oil,' in *Vikrama's Adventures or The Thirty-two Tales of the Throne,* trans. Franklin Edgerton, Harvard Oriental Series, vols. 26–7 (Cambridge, MA: Harvard University Press, 1926), no. 15, vol. 26, pp. 140–5.

Brahmin turned frog. At last, the king and the young man are to face one another in battle, but the serpent stings the ruler, thus reuniting the péri with her husband.[26] In this tale, the helping animals appear, envy and obsessive love motivate the quest, metamorphoses take place, but the enchanted water and the rejuvenation of the hero are not included, and the Arabs must add the wonder horse.

A variant tale of indeterminate age bears a close affinity to the Himalayan story; it has been traced to the Tartars of Siberia. An orphan with a very fine horse becomes the object of jealousy. He is sent out to bring back the daughter of the 'King of the Péris,' and the adventure turns around the matter of how a mortal can kidnap such a beautiful and enchanted woman. Once captured, as in the tale of Livoretto, she delays her fate by first demanding the recovery of a lost ring – a feat thought to be impossible. The tale ends with the trial of the boiling cauldron from which the prince escapes, protected by his magic horse, but in which the king loses his life. This tale has countless cousins throughout the Balkans, serving as a point of entry into Western folklore.[27] Its affiliations with the 'Livoretto' type are manifest.

Just what kind of reinforcement may have been provided to the generic tale of the wonderful horse in Western literature by the tale of Kamar al-Akmar, or 'The Magic Tale of the Ebony Horse,' nights 414–32 of *The Arabian Nights,* is no matter for easy assessment, for in itself, it is not a tale necessarily independent from the more than two-millennia old stories from Egypt and India outlined above. That the Persian king in the tale has three beautiful daughters and a son, Kamar, who rides the magic flying horse to advantage in finding his 'foreign' bride follows generic lines. But the story belongs, not to those of the exiled prince, but to those of the rash promise made to evil magicians disguised as friendly helpers, and to whom, in consequence, he must marry his daughters. These husbands are both jinni as well as ancient, hideous old men. This patterning of events suggests affinities with the 'animal-husband' tales

---

26 *Contes populaires de Lorraine,* 2 vols. (Paris: F. Vieweg, 1886), vol. II, p. 303. The *Ṭūṭīnāma* hereafter the *Tooti-nameh* (Tales of a parrot) by Ziyā al-Dīn Nakhshabī, ed. Francis Gladwin (London: J. Debrett, 1801), pp. 108–12; this is a Persian work dating to AD 730, derived from the Sanskrit *Couka-saptatī* (The seventy stories of the parrot). The work by Minaef is entitled *Indiiskia Skaski y Legendy* (St. Petersburg, 1877).

27 W. Radloff, *Proben der Volksliteratur der Türkischen Stämme Süd-Sibiriens,* 4 vols. (St. Petersburg: L'Académie imp. des sciences, 1866–72), vol. IV, p. 373.

in which the animals lend their respective talents to their questing brother-in-law. But Kamar protests the old wizard's marriage to his youngest sister, incurring his secret anger, whereupon the jinn produces a magic horse of his own crafted from wood and ebony with a twin set of pins in its head to make it rise and descend. The prince is tricked into mounting it without understanding the mechanisms and hence rises into the air supposedly never to return. Yet he locates in time the second pin, descends to a foreign court, and through many adventures induces the willing princess to quit her homeland to return with him on the back of the magic steed. The parallels, so far, are but generic at best. In a second long episode, however, the princess is abducted by the magician, deposed at a foreign court where she feigns madness to delay the amorous desires of the ruler, is discovered by her prince, who brings her into proximity with his horse, rescues her by a ruse, leaves the magician to be executed, and flies home with his bride. The more specific markers are all absent: the prince is not exiled to a foreign court, the horse does not speak, there are no helping animals, and no quest on behalf of an amorous sultan. Yet the tale is known to have come early to Europe through Andalusia and to have played a distinct role in fostering European tales of wonder horses.[28]

28 *The Book of the Thousand Nights and One Night,* trans. J.C. Mardrus and Powys Mathers, 4 vols. (London: Routledge & Kegan Paul, 1964), vol. II, pp. 458–88. Stith Thompson in *The Folktale* has a section on 'Helpful Horses' where he discusses them in relation to the 'golden hair' tales, which in turn relate to the giant and wild man helpers who furnish the young hero with a magic horse for his exploits, as in Straparola's own story of 'Guerino and the Wild Man of the Woods' (V.1), which also includes such helper animals as the hornet that buzzes around the head of the right girl, 'Potentiana of the golden hair.' Once again crossroads form. He too rides into the city, as Livoretto does, and attracts the attention of the court with his performance on horseback. As Thompson says, 'The tales of helpful horses have a tendency to merge into one another in many of their details, sometimes in the way in which the magic horse is acquired, sometimes in the remarkable deeds accomplished' (p. 61). In the 'goose girl' type (ATU type 533), the girl is given a speaking horse who continually warns her and, as in the identity exchange framing motif, the heroine is forced to cede her identity to a false princess who kills the horse, the head of which is mounted over the castle gate. The goose girl has power over animals which she can call to her aid, and so the parallels accumulate once again in a closely related tradition with the magic horse in common. The earliest European reference to the mechanical horse of *The Arabian Nights* appears in *Cléomandès et Claremonde,* a romance by the minstrel Adenès of Brabant, no doubt written for Mary of Brabant who married Philippe the Bold in 1277. The poem was composed before 1283. An imitation of the original was made by Count Tressan at the end of

Perhaps the most intriguing and frustrating allusion to the Arabian mechanical horse in European literature appears in Chaucer's 'Squire's Tale' from *The Canterbury Tales* in which the Tartar king Cambyuskan receives as a gift a horse of brass with a pin that enables him to fly in the air (ll. 190–224). But now there are references to magical objects such as a ring that gives access to the language of birds and a mirror that reveals enemies and foretells the approach of armies. These added details, not a part of the romance tradition, imply that Chaucer relied upon a folk tale variant in which the Arabian tale has been 'contaminated' by sundry folk motifs. According to Albert Baugh, it is doubtful, in any case, that Chaucer could have known *Cléomadès*, the early romance through which the Arabian mechanical horse was introduced to Western literature. Partially set out in 'The Squire's Tale' is a story of bride-winning by the elder son of a king after perils through which he passes with the aid of the brass horse. A second tale follows the fortunes of the younger son, Cambalo, who fights in the lists to win Canacea, at the outset said to be his younger sister with the rings. Confusion sets in early as Chaucer exposes the rhetorical enthusiasm and narrative inadequacy of the squire, who is seeking to outdo his father as a raconteur. No doubt the rings were to have been lost and recovered, there were to have been

---

the fifteenth century, said to have been derived from the Spanish. It circulated at the time of Straparola under the title *Cheval de Fust*, or *Celinde et Meliarchus*. On how this story came to Europe and made its way north, see Thomas Keightley, *Tales and Popular Fictions: Their Resemblance, and Transmission from Country to Country* (London: Whittaker & Co., 1834), pp. 42*ff.* Tressan's story is described in 1481 in Caxton's translation of *Reynard the Foxe*, chap. 32, when Reynard enumerates all the jewels he had lost, thus giving an account of the ebony horse originating in *The Arabian Nights*. Caxton's King Crompart, who made a horse from a tree, is derived from the magician villain Crappart in *Cléomadès* who, in the tradition of the *Nights*, steals the lady away by working the magic horse. Keightley traces the story to Persian roots, given its Persian setting in *The Arabian Nights*, and given the tale of the Indian who appears on his wonderful horse before Shah Chosroe and his son Firooz during the festival of the new year (Noo Rooz), celebrating the return of the vernal equinox. The motif is found again in Cervantes' *Don Quixote*, pt. II, chap. 40, the episode in which the Don is sent to release the bearded women on Clavileño, the wooden horse operated by pegs in his head. Here Cervantes had a memory slip that led generations of annotators to assume that Pierre de Provence also flew through the air with his beautiful lady Maguelone on a magic horse, for the materials he undoubtedly found in *Cléomadès* or one of its derivatives he erroneously attributed to *Pierre de Province et la belle Maguelone*; none of his editors bothered to verify the fact before the nineteenth century.

conversations with birds already begun with the lovesick and fallen falcon, and some episode must have included the magic mirror. The very complexity of the tale appears to have exceeded the squire's wits, bringing the Franklin to his rescue by cutting off the tale with high praise when the squire gets lost in an endless detour. But the innuendoes point to a romance modified into a folk tale, with a setting in Tartary and a king's name suggesting a variation upon Cambalù Khan, derived from an unimaginable source. It is the only hint that during the late Middle Ages the tale of the mechanical horse had been integrated into the folk tradition that produced Straparola's model.[29]

One might well ask whether the folk tradition that produced 'Livoretto' did not place some pressure for adaptation upon the wonder horses of French romance. In the well-known thirteenth-century *chanson de geste, Les Quatre Fils Aymon* (The four sons of Aymon), Reynaud of Montauban, one of Aymon's valiant sons, receives the fairy horse Bayard from Charlemagne. It can neither fly nor speak, but exercises its animal intelligence in such marked ways as to evince human-like understanding. It responds to language and human emotions, signals its comprehension with its paws, intuits situations, performs noble and extraordinary feats, and thereby influences nearly every episode of the tale. Bayard is there-

29 It is for these reasons less likely, as J. Burke Severs suggests, that 'in writing the *Squire's Tale* Chaucer apparently had no one source before him but worked freely with elements from the legends of Prester John, the *Cléomadès* of Adenès li Rois, and *The Arabian Nights*' – indeed which *Arabian Nights*? 'The Tales of Romance,' in *Companion to Chaucer Studies*, ed. Beryl Rowland (New York: Oxford University Press, 1975), p. 275. 'The Squire's Tale,' *The Canterbury Tales*, in *Chaucer's Major Poetry*, ed. Albert C. Baugh (New York: Appleton-Century-Crofts, 1963), pp. 459–70. Baugh's comments are on p. 459. See W.A. Clouston, *On the Magical Elements in Chaucer's Squire's Tale* ([London]: Chaucer Society, 1890), no. 26. In 'Valentine and Orson' there is the dwarf Pacollet of Toledo who made a wooden horse by enchantment with a pin in his head that made him fly through the air. Finally, King Gradasso, in Matteo Maria Boiardo's *Orlando Innamorato*, III. vii. 24–8, cuts down an enchanted tree and from its wood a fine horse leaps forth, which, when the king mounts it, rises up into the air and then plunges into the Fiume del Riso, the River of Laughter. Trans. Charles Stanley Ross (Berkeley: University of California Press, 1989), p. 824. As stated above, all of these tales have as their remotest ancestor, concerning pin-operated horses, the tale of the amorous weaver in bk. I. of the *Panchatantra*. Therein, the weaver is set astride the Garouda bird, made of wood, and taught how to manipulate the pin to make it fly. He is en route to rescue a princess in the palace of the seven stories, who will mistake the flying artisan for Vishnu himself. *Pañcatantra*, trans. Édouard Lancereau (Paris: Gallimard, 1965), pp. 97–8.

fore both the most superior of all the battle-trained palfreys of medieval lore and an enchanted steed on the threshold of language, the edge of folklore and mythic status. From the early *chanson de geste* onward the conventions surrounding the horse were subject to expansion so that in subsequent versions the horse begins to speak to Reynaud. In ways parallel to the tale of Livoretto, the horse is bartered for but never exchanged and declared to be of inestimable value. It begins to express emotions of its own and to remain in tune with the world of magic causation, becoming an auxiliary character to the narrative, as though destined to merge with the magic horses of the folk tale. Yet Bayard, as an emblem of freedom and of necessary insubordination, as a liberated spirit who returns to nature and disappears into the unknown, he remains grander than his folk tale counterparts. He had his own epic destiny to fulfill.[30]

The vital parts of the 'Livoretto' nucleus were largely in evidence in fragmentary and partially assembled forms among the tales of ancient India, Persia, Egypt, and Tartary, but Chaucer's tantalizing fragment aside, there seems little promise in the medieval 'horse' romances for recapturing the narrative thread. But an established and complex narrative tradition there must have been, for there appears in the *Maase Buch*, published in Basel in 1602, an analogue close to Straparola's tale in its general profile, yet clearly an ethnic adaptation of a source bearing significant variants.[31] In this late sixteenth-century creation, a wicked king has been encouraged by his people to take a wife – a motif seen in the 'Griselda' group – and the king sets his heart upon finding the girl whose golden hair has been dropped by a bird. The bride search is conducted by the court favourite, Rabbi Chanina, who sets out with the help of a crow, a dog, and a fish. The remarkable substitutions would indicate that this author owed nothing to Straparola, but everything to the tradition his story represents, with the golden hair and animal helpers, but without the magic horse. The fish returns the missing ring, while the crow goes after the vial of the water of paradise and the water of hell, the first of which brings the slain rabbi back to life, the second of which

30 *Quatre Fils Aimon, L'épisode ardennais de 'Renaut de Montauban,'* ed. Jacques Thomas, 3 vols. (Bruges: Sinte-Catherina Drukkerij, 1962). See Sarah Bandelle-Michels, *Les Avatars d'une chanson de geste de Renaut de Montauban aux Quatre Fils Aymon* (Paris: H. Champion, 2006), p. 363, on Bayard as a speaking horse.

31 Little information on this intriguing book is available in English sources. See Jakob Meitlis, *Das Ma'assebuch: Seine Entstehung und Quellengeschichte* (Hildesheim: Georg Olms, 1987).

burns the king to a cinder. The rabbi and the princess marry. The story permits us to imagine two models converging backwards towards a common source, giving further evidence of the kinds of tales then current, one of which was given literary representation in the present work.

That exercise is complicated, however, by the source implicit in the creation of 'Corvetto' (III.7) in Giovanni Battista Basile's *Il Pentamerone: or the Tale of Tales.*[32] In this story, there is no introit episode of separation, travel, and rise at a foreign court, nor does the protagonist set out with a horse or accumulate animal helpers along the way. But he is a king's favourite so envied for his position that his rivals, true to the tradition, seek his destruction by so praising his prowess that the king sends him out on a series of suicide missions. The order of narrative remains that of Straparola, and there are tell-tale coincidences of detail. The first task is to steal the talking horse of a neighbouring ghoul who lives near 'Scotland' on a high mountain (the name derived from the creature of Muslim folklore who preys upon corpses), thereby placing this tale squarely in the tradition that becomes 'Jack-in-the-Beanstalk,' complete with the ghoul's signature curse, except that in some, the giant himself becomes the prince's friend, comforter, and guide, and accompanies him on his quest to find the princess, replacing the role of the talking horse. Basile's Corvetto goes on to steal the ogre's counterpane by hiding under the bed. He is no whimpering prince, but a cocksure one who goes up the mountain a third time to enter service in order to cut off the ghoul's head. He then lures the ghoul into a pit and stones him to death, brings back the key to the castle, and at last is married to the king's daughter. It could almost be said that Basile's story is different entirely and might be passed over, except that it represents the earliest manifestation of a type that is joined, or rejoined, to the Livoretto type in many subsequent renditions.

Consider the compound tale collected by Emanuel Cosquin in Lorraine in the second half of the nineteenth century entitled 'Le roi d'Angleterre et son filleul' (The king of England and his godson). In this tale, the hero's identity is usurped by a hunchback who masquerades as the true godson. The abased hero, to his intended peril, is sent to steal the mule of the giant (a miraculous beast able to cover great distances

32 Trans. Sir Richard Burton (New York: Boni & Liveright, [1893], 1927), pp. 247–52. The more standard edition, however, is *The Pentamerone*, ed. N.M. Penzer, trans. Benedetto Croce, 2 vols. (Westport, CT: Greenwood Press, 1932), III.7, vol. I, pp. 271–7.

with ease). The giant lives across a body of water in a place accessible only when the blackbird (merle) sings (do blackbirds sing?), and he has his comic oath as in Basile. The hero is then sent back to fetch the singing bird (not the bedcover), followed by the magic lantern (redolent of the many tales featuring miraculous light-producing objects), and finally the lost princess. She lives in a silver chateau which also must be taken to the king. This is Basile's tale. But successful entry to the silver mansion requires elaborate provisions such as fabric and three hundred weaver maidens, all by way of attaining the abducted girl. Now, grateful animals enter the action, offering enchanted body parts as tokens of aid. We are back in the tale of Livoretto. The hero does not have a horse for counsellor, but the giant himself, and he carries with him an ant's leg, a rat's whisker, a crow's feather, and the king of the giants' beard, as the story grows more prolix. Ultimately, the wicked queen acquires the water of life and the water of death, but they are used to restore and beautify the abducted princess and to slay the evil crone. The hunchback presents himself for marriage to the princess but is discovered and slain, while Adolphe (the hero), the rightful godson, is restored. By the nineteenth century the two traditions featured respectively in Straparola and Basile were joined, in fact, superimposed one upon the other. Whether they had been separated from whole cloth in the late Middle Ages is a more difficult question to resolve. Of stories in this category there are many from all parts of Europe.[33]

33 *Contes populaires de Lorraine*, ed. Emmanuel Cosquin (Paris: F. Vieweg, 1886), vol. I, pp. 32–49. Cosquin provides many analogues in his annotations, including one collected in Greece by J.G. von Hahn, 'Der Königssohn und der Bartlose' (The king's son and the beardless one), in *Griechische und albanische Märchen* (Leipzig: W. Engelmann, 1864), no. 37, vol. I, pp. 233–9, in which a horse becomes the prince's confidant and in which he learns the language of animals, and another collected in Sicily by Laura Gonzenbach in *Sicilianische Märchen* (Leipzig: W. Engelmann, 1870), no. 30; 'The Story About Ciccu,' in *Beautiful Angiola: The Lost Sicilian Folk and Fairy Tales of Laura Gonzenbach*, trans. Jack Zipes (London: Routledge, 2006), no. 5, pp. 28–40. Only the second half of this story pertains to the Livoretto type. Ciccu becomes a favourite at court, but his jealous brothers report that he can fetch the ogre's sword, always taking counsel from his horse. He brings in the ogre, only to be sent for the most beautiful woman in the world to marry the king. This requires the labours of his animal friends. The horse fetches the princess from the castle when the princess asks to ride it. The means for slaying the old king was for Ciccu to go first into the tile oven, but secretly covered by the horse's sweat. The order of the narrative is very similar to that of the present tale. Another, equally close, is from Brittany, the story of Petit-Louis, in which the boy

One last of this genre was collected by Domenico Comparetti in his *Novelline popolari italiane*, called 'Granadoro' (No. 5), which, once again, tells of a traveling prince forced to exchange his identity with a rival and to take up his residence in the king's stables where, to help him, a wild horse tells the boy how it might be tamed. One challenge along the way is to kill another horse with a sabre by distracting the animal with mirrors. But ultimately it is the tale of the search for Queen Granadoro. Well provisioned, the hero sets out on horseback, collecting tokens on the way from a fish, a swallow, and a butterfly. Granadoro refuses to return without finding her lost ring, and then demands water from the spring of life, which was sought by the swallow. Finally, she had to be identified among three identical sisters (a motif appearing in Straparola's fable of Guerrino, V.1), duly accomplished by the butterfly. The false prince, in anger at the hero's successes, kills him in the stables, but Granadoro uses the water of life to restore him while the false nephew is slain instead.[34]

---

sets out to find his godfather, the king, and along the way is robbed of his magic horse and his identity by a leper who throws him into a well. Destitute, he makes his way to the court, becomes a keeper of the horses, and rediscovers his old mount, along with its vital counsel. The leper tells the king that the boy has boasted of his ability to bring to court the princess with the golden hair, hoping he would perish in the attempt. But with the help of his animal friends he performs many feats and convinces the girl to accompany him. She too holds out by making requests involving her chateau and its keys thrown into the water. Each time Petit-Louis is compelled to perform until at last he fetches the waters of life and death whereby the old king is slain. The story forgets to deal with the leper or to employ the water of life, but we can imagine how they are handled in a more complete version. François-Marie Luzel, *Veillées bretonnes: moeurs, chants, contes et récits populaires des Bretons armoricains* (Morlais: J. Mauger, 1879), pp. 148*ff*; new edition (Rennes: Presses univertaires de Rennes, 2002). The number of related stories collected by the folklorists is impressive to say the least. Cosquin profiles several more in his annotations (vol. II, pp. 295–304), including the Russian tradition of tales concerned with the hero's quest for the firebird.

34 *Novelline popolari italiane* (Bologna: Forni Editore, [1875], 1968), vol. I, pp. 18–22. A closely related tale was collected by James Bruyn Andrews in Liguria, no. 2, 'Le roi d'Angleterre.' A boy en route to visit his family is the victim of identity theft by a man who makes him his domestic and assumes his place at the court of England. The real godson of the king is compelled to work in the stables where he has the company and advice of a talking horse. The imposter has him sent on demanding missions, including the rescue of the abducted princess. The horse is a flawless advisor and the boy makes his way towards royal marriage after proving himself the actor of the audacious deeds by which the girl is retrieved. A ship is prepared with food for the beasts along the way who then promise their loyal service. Rats and

To complete the fortunes of this most successful and widespread of story types, the following four, because of their celebrated and familiar sources, have been chosen from the hundreds possible. Among the tales collected by the Grimm brothers, there are three of particular interest, No. 63, 'The Water of Life,' No. 81, 'The Queen Bee,' and No. 98, 'Ferdinand the Faithful and Ferdinand the Unfaithful.'[35] In the first, of the three brothers who set out to find the water of life to heal an aging father, only the younger succeeds by gratefully following the advice of the dwarf. He finds a princess into the bargain. On the return trip he does favours for neighbouring rulers and wins their support. When the envious older brothers steal the water and set up the younger one to be killed, debts are called in to rescue him. Finally, each brother seeks to ride up to the princess's castle to claim her, but only the youngest wins

---

ants perform magic tasks and the wedding follows, along with the incineration of the imposter. *Contes ligures, traditions de la rivière recueillis entre Menton et Gênes* (Paris: Ernest Leroux, 1892), pp. 8–15.

35 *Grimm's Complete Fairy Tales* (Garden City, NY: Nelson Doubleday, n.d.), pp. 162, 239, 324. 'Ferdinand the Faithful' also appears as No. 126 in *Grimm's Fairy Tales*, ed. Elizabeth Dalton and Ludwig Emil Grimm (New York: Barnes & Noble, 2003), pp. 366–9. The commentary by Johannes Bolte and Jiří Polívka on the story of 'Ferenand getrü und Ferenand ungetrü' includes a substantial bibliography of further analogues. They examine those in the 'talking horse' group and those in the 'golden-haired maiden' group. *Anmerkungen zu den Kinder- und Hausmärchen der Brüder Grimm*, 5 vols. (Leipzig: Dieterich'sche Verlagsbuchhandlung, 1913–32), vol. II, pp. 18–37. A late discovery, and altogether closer to Straparola, is 'Willy Faith' from *Danish Fairy Tales*, ed. Svend Grundtvig (London: G.G. Harrap & Co., 1914), pp. 9–26. Willy has a talking horse which counsels him as he makes his way to a foreign court. He picks up three magic feathers against the animal's advice, which together form the face of a beautiful princess. Once installed as a groom in the king's stables, the portrait comes to the king's attention. He falls in love and the enforced adventures to find her ensue. This tale involves the crossing of a body of water and provisions for the beasts and fish along the way. The princess, when found, must be 'disenchanted' by capturing a feather from the golden bird. On the way back, she throws the keys to her castle into the sea, but the fish return them. With that obstacle to an unwonted marriage removed, she demands the waters of life and death. This was the third quest, the result of picking up the third feather. Willy, dismayed, consults his horse and completes the quest with a little help from his friends. He is then made the object of the first trial of the magic waters and returns to life more handsome than ever. The king insists upon two round trips in this fountain of youth, but in the middle of the second the water of life runs out. Alas, poor king; welcome to matrimony, rich Willy Faith. Now the speaking horse is 'disenchanted' too and is transformed into the brother of the princess. The entire story as it was known to Straparola remains intact with several agreeable accretions.

her by riding straight up the golden road. In the second tale, a younger son goes in search of his two wild and reckless older brothers. Travelling together, only the youngest gains credit with the animals, whereas the elder boys would have wantonly destroyed the ants, ducks, and bees. They arrive at stables filled with horses turned to stone. There the elder brothers, failing in their tasks, are likewise turned to stone, while the younger succeeds with the help of the animals. Ultimately, the real princess must be identified among three, as in the story of Queen Granadoro, a task accomplished by the bee, whereupon young Witling wins the bride and becomes king.

But it is the third that carries the greatest number of correspondences with the story of Livoretto. A boy's godfather gives him the key to a castle in which he finds a white horse. During his travels, he picks up a pen, rescues a fish, and gains a flute. A rival displaces him and he is sent questing for the girl beloved of the king. The real Ferdinand seeks counsel from his horse, Schummel. He must cross a sea to find a giant who in turn helps him carry the princess to the ship. He loses his pen in the water, the sense of which is unclear, but with his flute he summons his fish to fetch it. In the end, the princess removes and replaces the hero's head, but cannot refit the old king's head, and so he perishes. An added feature is the true identity of the horse itself, for when Ferdinand the Faithful rides it three times up the hill, it returns to its former self as a young prince – hence the enchanted horse. It is a naïve retelling of a story bearing most of the motivic markers defining the Livoretto type, with several substitutions and borrowings from sundry analogues. In comparing the correspondences and departures, a glimpse is to be had into the accidents and transformations that characterize tales orally transmitted through decades and centuries, while once again providing hints through retro-engineering of the tale that informed Straparola.[36]

36 Giuseppe Pitrè provides another, No. 34, 'The Enchanted Horse,' in which three brothers set out, the eldest two impoverishing themselves through gambling, while the third, through his prudence, makes a fortune, leading to the invidious jealousy of his brothers. The king of the country is obsessed by the golden hair he sees caught in a tree in the middle of the sea. First he wanted the hair, and then, of course, its owner, always upon pain of death for the hero. With each new challenge the hero consults his talking horse and confidant, and always the horse knows what to do. The hero first builds up good will with a variety of animal helpers, finds the queen of the golden hair in a court entirely of gold, and abducts her, as in Straparola, by luring her onto the horse's back before leaping on behind her and taking her to the king's court. Along the way she throws precious possessions into the

In Calvino's rendition of the tale called 'Body-Without-Soul,' No. 6 in his *Fables*, Jack the hero leaves home to seek his fortune. He comes to a kingdom where there is an untamed horse which he alone can master. Thus he rises at court, becomes the envy of those around him, and hence is sent on a hopefully fatal mission, which is to find the king's abducted daughter. In this tale, Jack wins the pledged support of four animals by solving a dispute among them over the equitable distribution of food (a motif with wide circulation, including its appearance in Straparola's III.4). With the body parts they give to him, he is able, not only to call upon them, which he does later, but to change himself into their forms. Jack rides on to the castle on his horse, Rondello, and there changes shape to reach the princess and deceive the sorcerer who holds her in thrall. Only the animals can help him carry out the complex formula required to kill the sorcerer, culminating in the breaking of a black egg on his forehead – the office of the princess. The fairy tale ending follows. The departures towards the end are particularly notable, entailing both loss and invention. Yet even this variant preserves many of the generic features of the Renaissance prototype. That Straparola's specific tale had a part in guiding any that came after it is, in this case, to be doubted. Rather, it is a literary elaboration upon a tale he deemed worthy of his attention that has proven its worth through generations of subsequent oral transmission and alteration.[37] In the final analysis, the story of

---

water, true to the present story, which must be fetched with the help of the talking animal helpers. Much as the opening is a significant variant upon Straparola's circumstances of the hero's departure, so the finale is a variation, employing not the magic water, but the sweat and grease solution as the hero sits in boiling water for three days, protected by the sweat of his horse, while the king is fricasseed in grease. The queen and hero then marry. The story comes from Noto. It may or may not owe something to the literary tradition, but clearly bears a close, though abbreviated, kinship with Straparola's tale. *The Collected Sicilian Folk and Fairy Tales of Giuseppe Pitrè,* ed. and trans. Jack Zipes and Joseph Russo, 2 vols. (New York: Routledge, 2009), vol. I, pp. 180–3.

37 The story restored by Calvino was initially collected in Liguria by James Bruyn Andrews for publication in his *Contes ligures* (Paris, 1892), no. 46. *Italian Folktales Selected and Retold by Italo Calvino,* trans. George Martin (New York: Pantheon Books, 1980), pp. 18–21. Other stories of speaking horses who guide their princely riders through challenging adventures with magical clairvoyance include 'El Príncipe Español' in which the prince sets out on his adventures and collects helping animals as he goes, a whale and an ant among them, in his search for 'La Belleza del Mundo.' The horse provides complex and detailed instructions throughout the story, which is a series of quests to faraway castles including, along the way, the

Livoretto participates, as one of the earliest recorded versions, in a folk tale tradition, the origins of which are ancient and archetypal in spirit, again intimating initiation rites, death and resurrection motifs, and the quest of the hero, not to mention matters of courage in the face of treachery, lost family relationships, spirit guides, the world of magic, totem animals, and bride selection.

Finally, the materials of the Livoretto group begin to lose their identity in a twentieth-century folk version from France that begins with a poor boy who is blinded by his family in order to become a pathetic beggar, who is abandoned in the forest by his brothers, and who accidentally urinates and defecates on the heads of giants from his perch in a tree, before they find him and give him three wishes, one of which is to heal his sight, the second of which is to meet a mule, and third of which is to find a golden feather. Little of this pertains to the conventional tale.[38] Yet the mule turns out to be the wonderful talking quadruped and mentor, while the golden feather is the magic object that arouses jealousy at court where the lad is employed, which, in turn, is the cause that he is sent on a series of 'impossible' missions, all of which the boy, with the aid of his mule, is able to perform. These missions have to do with a captured queen who frustrates her captor's wedding plans by making outlandish requests. She demands that her castle be brought intact and placed opposite her captor's palace before considering marriage. That feat miraculously accomplished, she demands her keys, which she had tossed into the water. The fish now perform on the hero's behalf. With each deed, the Peers of France grow ever more jealous of Gold Feather. At last they accuse him of being in love with the captive queen and so he is to be burned. But the mule instructs him to wrap himself in the seventh layer of a blanket, the other six of which have been worn away by riding on it for endless days. This is related to the stories in which

---

location of the tree with the golden apples and the three golden horseshoes. *Cuentos populares Españoles*, ed. Aurelio M. Espinosa, 3 vols. (Madrid: S. Aguirre, 1946), vol. I, pp. 326–31. See also John Francis Campbell, *Popular Tales of the West Highlands*, 4 vols. (Edinburgh: Edmonston & Douglas, A. Gardner, 1890–3), vol. II, pp. 344–76; Patrick Kennedy, *The Fireside Stories of Ireland* (Dublin: McGlashan & Gill, 1870), pp. 47–56; Genero Finamore, *Tradizioni popolari abruzzesi* (Lanciano: Carabba, 1882), vol. I, *Novelle*, no. 11; and Reinhold Köhler, *Kleinere Schriften*, ed. Johannes Bolte, 3 vols. (Weimar: Feiber, 1898–1900), vol. I, pp. 541–72, and vol. II, pp. 328–46, containing a Jewish version similar to Straparola's.

38 *Folktales of France*, ed. Geneviève Massignon, trans. Jacqueline Hyland (London: Routledge & Kegan Paul, 1968), pp. 49–54.

animal sweat protects from the effects of the fire. When the hero comes out more handsome than ever, the king requests the secret and enters the flames, but designedly he is misinformed and burns to ashes, freeing the queen and the young hero to marry. The opening features are almost as though the storyteller were warming up, coming at last to the type (ATU 531, 'Ferdinand the True and Ferdinand the False'). This story, recorded in Upper Brittany, just after the middle of the twentieth century, shows how long-lived these folk designs were, this one recorded some five centuries after the version copied down by Straparola. There have been many substitutions, all of them familiar from interim versions, but the story design stands out in strong relief.

Affiliated with this branch of the tale is the version collected and retold by Josef Haltrich in his *Sächsische Volksmärchen aus Siebenbürgen* (Vienna, 1882), in which the story of the *Ross* or talking charger is preceded by a tale of dragon slaying in an enchanted forest which enables the young initiate to heal a blind man who, in gratitude, gives him the magic horse with which he is to ride forth into the world to seek his fortune. This story follows closely the prescribed order, which includes ingratiating himself with his new royal employer while the others in envy slander him with false boasting about feats he would perform for the king. On the way to the court, the boy had picked up three feathers, copper, silver, and gold, and the king demands to have the birds from which they came brought to court. There is a grand council of the entire bird kingdom at which the king of birds disclaims all knowledge of the wanted creatures until news is at last brought of these birds and their accompanying dragons near the end of the earth. To be sure, the dragons must be sacrificed to bring the birds back to court. Then upon pain of death, the boy is sent after the beautiful mermaid, who is lured from the depths with white bread and wine and caught by her foot. She is scornful and imposes delaying tactics which again jeopardize the young hero's life. She demands the capture of her stallion and stud-horse (Gestüt), all of which is accomplished through the brilliant stratagems of the boy's own charger. Once brought to court, the mermaid demands that they be milked and that the king bathe himself in their milk before she would marry him. There are images enough here to keep the happy hermeneute preoccupied. In keeping with the great tradition going back to Straparola, the boy must go first. He is saved from harm as his charger breathes cold air on the milk from its left nostril, while during the king's bath it breathes hot air from its right nostril and scalds him to death. Curiously, however, the boy, now king, chooses the king's sister for his bride, as promised to him, and rejects the mermaid who is made the new queen's lady-in-waiting. But this formula seems to have pleased everyone, and so they were 'reich und mächtig, glücklich und zufrieden' (rich and mighty, happy and satisfied). Nothing short of extraordinary is the variety of substitutions within a narrative frame that holds its complex shape during centuries. Moreover, this is clearly a story of initiation, adventure, and deep symbolism that appealed to generations of auditors and left them musing over the implicit motivations of the human heart that launched each new challenge. And always it was the ingenuity of the horse and the trajectories of the adventures, invested with the well-wishing for a maligned hero, that commanded ready attention.

III. Fable 3
Biancabella, or the Damsel and the Snake

LAURETTA

Biancabella, daughter of Lamberico, marquis of Monferrato, is sent away by the stepmother of Ferrandino, king of Naples, to be put to death. But the assassins only cut off her hands and put out her eyes. Afterwards, she is healed by a snake and returns happily to Ferrandino again.

It is most laudable and necessary that a woman, no matter what her condition might be, should bear herself with prudence in everything she does, for without prudence, nothing will come to a commendable issue. If a certain stepmother, of whom I'm about to tell you, had used it with due moderation when she wickedly plotted to take another's life, she would not herself have been cut off by divine judgment in such fashion as you shall now hear.

Once upon a time, now many years ago, there reigned in Monferrato a marquis called Lamberico, who was a man of great power by reason of his titled estates and great wealth. But he had no children and was exceedingly anxious for progeny – a bounty which heaven had denied him. Now one day it happened that the marchioness was walking for her pleasure in the palace garden when suddenly she was overcome by sleep, whereupon she sat down at the foot of a tree and there fell into a deep slumber. While she gently slept, a little serpent crept up to her side, slipped beneath her clothes without her taking the least notice, and entered by her vagina. By subtle windings, it penetrated right into her womb and there secretly lay very quiet. Before a long time had passed, the marchioness discovered she was with child to her no small pleasure and to the greatest delight of the entire city. When the time arrived for her delivery, she gave birth to a girl child around whose neck a serpent was coiled three times. When the midwives who were in attendance upon the marchioness saw this, they were terrified. But without doing any harm whatsoever, the snake untwined itself from the infant's neck. Slipping down and gliding along the floor, it made its way into the garden.

The nurses washed the child clean in a bath of clear water and clothed it in snow-white linen. When it had been duly cared for and dressed, they began to see, little by little, that around its neck there was a collar of gold, fashioned with the most subtle handiwork. It was so fine and lovely that it seemed to shed its lustre from between the skin and the flesh, just as the most precious jewels might shine out from an enclosure of transparent crystal. Moreover, it encircled the infant's neck the same number of times as the little serpent had done. Because of her exceeding loveliness, the child was named Biancabella, and grew up in such goodliness and beauty that it seemed she was more divine than human. When she arrived at her tenth birthday, it happened one day that she went with her nurse upon a terrace from whence she saw a fair garden full of roses and all manner of lovely flowers. Turning towards the nurse, she asked whose garden it was, given that she had never seen it before. The nurse replied that it was a place her mother called her own garden, where she often came for recreation. The child then said to her, 'I have never seen anything so attractive before. I have a mind to enter and walk there.'

The nurse then took Biancabella by the hand and led her into the garden. Allowing the child to go a small distance apart from her, she sat down in the shade of a leafy beech tree and settled into sleep, letting the little girl take her pleasure all the while in roaming about the garden. Charmed with the prettiness of the place, Biancabella ran about, now here and now there, gathering flowers until, at last, feeling somewhat tired, she too sat down under the shadow of a tree. But hardly had she seated herself upon the ground when there appeared a little snake which crept up close to her side. Biancabella, as soon as she saw the creature, was reasonably frightened and was about to cry out when the snake spoke to her in these words: 'Hush, I beg you. Don't be afraid and run away, for I want you to know that I'm your sister, born on the same day as you were, at the same birth, and that my name is Samaritana. If you obey me in all that I ask you to do, I will make you happy all your life. But if you do to the contrary, you'll become the most luckless and wretched woman the world has ever seen. You are free to go now without cause for any fear, but tomorrow I want you to return to the garden with two containers, one of them filled with pure milk and the other with fine rose water. Make certain that you bring no companions and are entirely alone.'

When the serpent was gone, the little girl got up from her place and went back to seek her nurse, whom she found still sleeping. When she had aroused her, they returned to the palace without a word being said of what had happened. When the morrow came, Biancabella found herself alone with her mother in the chamber, who noticed the child's sad and pensive look. 'Biancabella, what distresses you to make you put on such an unhappy face? You're not your usual lively and merry self, for today you look all sad and gloomy.'

Biancabella replied, 'There is nothing amiss with me. I just need to carry two containers into the garden, one of which must be filled with pure milk and the other with fine rose water.'

'Why, that's a small matter that troubles you, my child. You know that everything here is at your disposal.' Then the marchioness had two very beautiful vessels brought and filled, the one with milk and the other with rose water, and had them carried into the garden.

When the hour appointed by the serpent had come, Biancabella, all alone, hastened to the garden, opened the door, went in and fastened it behind her. Then she sat down on the ground beside the two vessels. Almost as soon as she was settled, the serpent appeared and came near her, ordering her to remove all her clothes and then, naked as she was, to step into the vessel filled with milk. This done, the serpent twined itself about her, bathing her body in every part with the white milk and licking her all over with its tongue, rendering her pure and perfect in all those places where by chance anything faulty was found. After stepping out of the vessel of milk, the serpent had her enter the one filled with rose water, whereupon all her limbs were scented with sweet odours that made her feel fresh all over. Then the serpent bade her put on her clothes once more, at the same time ordering her expressly never to tell anyone what had taken place, not even her father or mother. For it was the serpent's intention that no woman in the world should be found to equal Biancabella in beauty and grace. After she had bestowed upon her every good quality, the serpent crept away.

When all this was done, Biancabella left the garden and returned to the palace. Her mother was astonished beyond measure and didn't know what to say when she saw how much more gracious and lovely her daughter had become, and prettier than any other girl in the world. So she asked her what she had done to make herself so lovely. But Biancabella had no answer to give her. With that, the marchioness took a comb and began to comb and dress her daughter's fair locks, and immediately there fell pearls and all kinds of precious stones from the girl's hair, and when Biancabella went to wash her hands, roses, violets, and all sorts of lovely flowers fell from them, and with such odours arising that all the place became like an earthly paradise. Seeing this marvel, her mother ran to find Lamberico her husband and in full maternal pride said to him, 'My lord, heaven has bestowed upon us a daughter who is the sweetest, the loveliest, and the most exquisite work that nature has ever produced. For besides her divine grace and beauty, which is manifest to all who look upon her, pearls, gems, and all kinds of precious stones fall from her hair, and something even more marvellous to name, round about her white hands roses and violets tumble down which give off the sweetest odours to all those who should come to marvel at the sight. I would have believed none of this had I not seen it with my own eyes.'

Her husband, who was sceptical by nature, at first put no faith in his wife's words, treating them as matter for laughter and ridicule. But she went on plying him ceaselessly with accounts of what she had witnessed, so that he made up his mind to see for himself how matters really stood. Summoning his daughter into his presence, he found about her things even more marvellous than his wife had described. Elated by reason of what he saw, in his pride he then swore a mighty oath that in the entire world there was no man worthy to be united to her in marriage.

Soon thereafter the fame and glory of the supreme and immortal beauty of Biancabella began to spread itself throughout the world, and many kings, princes, and nobles came from all parts to win her love and favour and to have her to wife. But not one of these suitors was considered worthy to enjoy her, inasmuch as each one of them proved to have shortcomings of one kind or another. But at last, Ferrandino, king of Naples, came wooing, who, by his prowess and illustrious name, blazed out resplendent like the sun in the middle of the smaller lights. Presenting himself to the marquis, he demanded his daughter's hand in marriage. The marquis, seeing that the suitor was handsome, well built, and full of grace besides being a prince of great power, possessions, and wealth, gave his consent to the nuptials. Summoning his daughter, without further negotiations the two were betrothed by joining hands and kissing one another.

Scarcely were the rites of betrothal completed when Biancabella called to mind the words that her sister, Samaritana, had so lovingly spoken to her. Therefore, she withdrew from the presence of her spouse under pretext that she had pressing business to attend to. Once arriving at her chamber, she fastened the door from the inside and then passed along by a secret passageway into the garden. There, she began to call upon Samaritana in a low voice. But she no more appeared as before. When Biancabella perceived this, she was greatly surprised. After searching through every part of the garden without finding a trace of Samaritana, she was overcome by a deep sadness, for she knew that this had happened to her because she had not been duly obedient to her commands. Grieving and bewailing this mischance that had befallen her, she returned into her bedroom. There she opened the door and rejoined her spouse, who had been waiting a long time for her, and sat down beside him. The marriage ceremonies at last completed, Ferrandino led his bride away with him to Naples, where, with great pomp and festivity, they were joyfully welcomed by the entire city.

Ferrandino's stepmother was also living in Naples with two rather mean and ugly daughters of her own, one of whom she had set her heart on marrying to the king. But now that all hope was removed of ever accomplishing her design, her rage and anger against Biancabella became so savage that she could hardly endure to look upon her. Yet she was careful to conceal her animosity, pretending all the while to hold Biancabella in all love and affection. Meanwhile, as fortune dictates, the king of Tunis had launched a mighty military force both by land and by sea to make war on Ferrandino – whether because he had won Biancabella for his wife or for some other reason. Already, this king, at the head of this powerful army, had passed into the territories of the Kingdom of Naples. Urgently, Ferrandino took up arms to defend his realm, hurrying to the field to confront his foe. Having settled his affairs and made provision of all things necessary for Biancabella – especially now that she was with child – he gave her over to the care of his stepmother and set forth with his army.

Ferrandino had not been gone long before the spiteful and ill-spirited stepmother formed a wicked plot against Biancabella's life. She summoned two of her most loyal retainers and charged them to take Biancabella with them to some place of recreation and not to leave until they had slain her. Moreover, so she might be fully assured that they had carried out their duty, they were to bring back to her some sign of Biancabella's death. Ready for any ill-doing, these ruffians prepared themselves to carry out their mistress's orders. Under pretence of conducting Biancabella to some place of amusement, they took her away into a wood where they planned to kill her. But when they saw just how lovely and gracious she was, they were moved to pity and hadn't the heart to take her life. So they cut off both her hands and tore the eyes out of her head, and carried them back to the stepmother as certain proofs that Biancabella was dead. When the hateful and ill-natured woman beheld these tokens, her joy and satisfaction were unbounded and her servants were paid. But the scheming of this malicious woman was not yet at an end. She sent a report throughout the kingdom that both her own daughters were dead, the one of a continuous fever and the other of an imposthume which had caused her death by suffocation. Afterwards, she made proclamation that Biancabella, distraught by grief at the king's departure, had suffered a miscarriage and was then seized with a tertian fever that had wasted her so cruelly that there was more reason to fear her death than to hope for her recovery. The scheme of this wicked and cunning woman was to place one of her own daughters in the king's bed, maintaining the while that she was Biancabella, shrunken and distempered by the fever.

Ferrandino, after he had attacked and put to rout the army of his foe, marched homeward in the full triumph of victory, hoping to find his beloved Biancabella in a state of joy and happiness. But instead, he found her lying in bed shrivelled, pale, and disfigured. Then he went up to the bed and gazed closely at her face. He was overcome with amazement when he saw the wreck she had become and could hardly convince himself that the woman he saw there was Biancabella. Afterwards, he requested her attendants to comb her hair, but in place of the gems and precious jewels which had once fallen from her fair locks, there was nothing but lice, which devoured her unceasingly, and from her hands there came forth, not the roses and the sweet-smelling flowers that had always fallen, but only filth and a foul stench that turned the stomach of all who saw her. Yet the wicked old stepmother kept up the words of consolation to him, declaring that all this distemper had arisen only from the long course of the ailment that possessed her.

Meanwhile, the ill-fated Biancabella, bereft of her hands and blind in both eyes, was left alone in that solitary place. Finding herself in such cruel affliction, she called over and over to her sister, Samaritana, pleading with her to come to her rescue. But no answer came to her except the resounding echo of her own voice reverberating through the air. While the unhappy creature was left in this agony of despair, aware that she was cut off from all human aid, there came into the woods a venerable old man, kindly of aspect and no less kindly in his heart. Her voice of sorrowful lamentation falling upon his ears, he advanced a slow step at a time to find a blind girl, her hands cut off, bitterly mourning her sad fate. When the good old man looked at her and saw how piteous her condition was, he could not bear to leave her all alone in this wilderness of thorns and brambles, but overcome by fatherly pity, he led her home with him to his house and placed her in the care of his wife, commanding her very strictly to take good care of her. Then he turned towards his three daughters, who in radiance gleamed like three stars, and earnestly exhorted them to keep her company with all due affection and look to all her needs. But the wife, who had a hard heart and none of the old man's pity, was violently moved to anger by these words. Turning towards him, she shrieked, 'Husband, what is this you'd have us do with this woman, all blind and maimed as she is? No doubt she's been punished for her sins, and not for any good that she's done.'

But the old man only answered, 'Do what I tell you, and if you refuse, you may never expect to see me here again.'

Now while the wretched Biancabella was left in the charge of the wife and the three daughters, conversing with them of many things, and meditating over her misfortunes, she asked one of the maidens as a favour to comb her hair. The mother, hearing this, grew angry, not wanting her girl to act as a servant. But the daughter's heart was more compassionate than her mother's, for she called to mind her father's commands. Moreover, she was sensibly aware of Biancabella's air of grace and nobility. Straightway, she unfastened the pure white apron from her waist, spread it on the floor beside Biancabella, and then began softly to comb her hair. Scarcely had she passed the comb through her tresses before there fell out pearls, rubies, diamonds, and all sorts of precious stones. The mother, seeing this, was seized with dread and stood as one struck dumb; suddenly all her former ill will was transformed into friendliness. When the old man came back to the house, they all ran to embrace him, greatly rejoicing with him over the stroke of good fortune by which they were to be delivered from their present state of poverty.

Then Biancabella asked them to bring her a bucket of clear water and bade them wash her face and her maimed arms. From these, while all were standing by, roses, violets, and other flowers fell down in great abundance, whereupon they deemed she could be no mortal woman, but some divine personage.

It came to pass, after a time, that Biancabella felt a desire to return to the place where the old man first had found her. He, his wife and daughters, seeing how great the benefits were which they derived from her presence, loaded her with endearments and begged her most earnestly not to leave them on any account, putting forward many reasons not to carry out her wish. But she had made up her mind most resolutely, determined at all hazards to go her way, promising at the same time to return. The old man, when he saw how firmly she was set on her departure, without further delay took her with him back to the place where he had found her. She then requested the old man to leave her there, bidding him to come back when evening had fallen so that she might return with him to his house.

No sooner had he gone his way than poor Biancabella began to wander up and down the gloomy wood calling loudly upon Samaritana and making her cries heard as far above as the high heavens. But Samaritana, although she was all the while nigh to her sister and had never for a moment abandoned her, refused as yet to answer her call. Finding her words were scattered in vain, the wretched Biancabella cried out, 'Alas, what further concern do I have with this world, seeing that I have lost my eyes and my hands, and now that all human help is denied me in the end?' As she spoke, a sort of frenzy came upon her which took from her all hope of deliverance from her present evil, in her despair urging her to lay hands upon her own life. But because there were no means available to her by which she could bring her miserable being to an end, she made her way to a pool of water not far distant, thinking to drown herself. But when she came to the shore of the pool and stood there ready to cast herself into the water, a loud voice sounded in her ears, 'Alas, what would you do? Take not your life, but keep it for some better end.'

Biancabella was alarmed by the mysterious voice and felt her hair stand on end. But thinking there was something familiar about the voice, she plucked up a bit of courage and asked, 'Who are you that wander about these woods?'

The voice replied, 'I am Samaritana, your sister, for whom you've been calling so long and painfully.'

Hearing these words, Biancabella answered in a broken voice through her agonized sobs, 'O, sister, help me I beg of you. If I have ever been disregardful of your counsel at any time in the past, I pray you to forgive me. I'm sure I've erred and I confess my fault, but my misdeed was the fruit of my ignorance and not of my wickedness, for if it had come from evil, divine justice would not have permitted me, as its author, to have lingered so long upon the earth.'

When Samaritana heard her sister's woes set forth in this pitiful story and witnessed the cruel wrongs that had been done to her, she uttered some comforting words. Then she gathered various medicinal herbs of wondrous power and virtue, which she spread over the places where Biancabella's eyes had been. Then she joined hands once again to her arms and straightway made all sound again. Once this was done,

Samaritana threw off the foul serpent's skin and revealed herself to be a maiden of lovely aspect.

The sun had already begun to hide its glittering rays and the evening shadows were creeping up when the old man returned to the wood with anxious and hasty steps. There he found Biancabella sitting beside a forest nymph. He gazed into her face, all the while standing like a man struck with wonder, scarcely able to believe it was the girl he had once found. But when he was certain it was she, he cried, 'My daughter, were you not blind and bereft of your hands this very morning? How is it that you have been so speedily healed?'

Biancabella answered, 'My cure is due to nothing that I have done myself, but by the virtue and the kind ministering of my dear sister sitting here beside me.' Then both sisters arose from the place where they were seated and, basking in their joy, they went together with the old man to his house, where the wife and the three daughters gave them a most cordial welcome.

Some time later, Samaritana and Biancabella, with the old man, his wife, and their three daughters, left their cottage for the city of Naples, intending to take up residence there. When they had entered the city, they happened upon a vacant space close to the king's palace, where they decided to take up quarters. When the dark night had fallen, Samaritana took in her hand a twig of laurel and with it she struck the earth three times, uttering at the same time certain mystical words. Almost before her voice had ceased, there sprang up forthwith a palace, the most beautiful and sumptuous that was ever seen. The next morning at an early hour King Ferrandino looked out of the window and when he beheld the rich and marvellous palace standing where there had been nothing the night before, he was completely overcome with amazement. He called his wife and stepmother to come and see it, but they were greatly disturbed at the sight of it, for a boding came upon them that some ill was about to befall them.

Ferrandino stood by closely scanning the palace before him, examining all its parts. Lifting his eyes to a certain window he beheld inside the chamber two ladies of a beauty more rich and dazzling than the sun. No sooner had his eyes fallen upon them than he felt a tempest of passion rising in his heart, for he was certain that he recognized in one of them a resemblance of that loveliness that had once been Biancabella's. When he asked who they were and from what land they were come, he was told that they had been exiled from their home, and that they had journeyed from Persia with all their possessions to take up their abode in the noble city of Naples. When he heard this, Ferrandino sent a messenger to enquire whether he and the ladies of his court might pay them a visit of welcome. To this gracious message they sent an answer, saying that it would indeed be a most precious honour to be thus visited by him, but that it would be more respectful if they, as subjects, should pay this duty to him, rather than that he, as lord and king, should visit them.

Hereupon, Ferrandino asked for the queen and the ladies of the court to be called, and although at first they refused to go, fearing their impending ruin, nevertheless they accompanied him to the palace where the two ladies gave him the reception due to a highly honoured guest, with all signs of friendly welcome and modest bearing, showing him the wide galleries, the roomy halls, and richly ornamented chambers, the walls of which were lined with alabaster and fine porphyry, while all around them there were carven figures so finely wrought as to appear alive. When they had exhibited to the king all the parts of the sumptuous palace, Biancabella approached Ferrandino and most gracefully invited him to come one day with his queen to dine at their table. The king, whose heart was not of stone, but of a most magnanimous and liberal nature, graciously accepted the invitation. After thanking the ladies for the warm welcome they had received, he and the queen returned to their own palace. When the day fixed for the banquet arrived, the king and queen, with the stepmother, dressed in their royal robes and accompanied by some of the ladies of the court, went to do honour to the magnificent feast set before them. After the seneschal had given them water to wash their hands, he led the king and queen to a table apart, set somewhat higher, yet still near the others, and having done this, he had all the rest of the guests seated according to their rank. In this fashion they all feasted merrily and joyfully together.

When the stately banquet had come to an end and the tables were cleared, Samaritana rose from her seat and turned towards the king and queen saying, 'Your majesties, so that the time may not become tedious, let one or other of us propose something in the way of a diversion that will let us pass the day with enjoyment.' When the guests heard what Samaritana said, they all agreed that she had spoken well, yet no one was found bold enough to make a proposal. Whereupon Samaritana, when she perceived that they were all silent, went on, 'Because it seems that no one of this company is prepared to suggest something, with your majesty's leave I will ask one of our own maidens to come out whose singing may well provide you with considerable pleasure.' The damsel, whose name was Silveria, was called into the banqueting room. Samaritana then asked her to take a lyre in hand and sing to it something in honour of the king that would be praiseworthy in every way. Obedient to her lady's command, the damsel, standing before the king, took up her lyre, and touching the sonorous strings with her plectrum, she recited the story of Biancabella in a sweet and delectable voice from beginning to end without once mentioning her name. When the entire story had been set forth, Samaritana again rose to her feet and asked the king what would be an appropriate and fitting punishment for those who committed so abominable an atrocity. Then the stepmother, who deemed that she might hide her own misdeeds by a prompt and ready reply, did not wait for the king to give his answer, but called out defiantly, 'Why, I should think that casting them into a red-hot furnace would meet the case.'

Then Samaritana, with her countenance afire with anger, answered, 'You are the woman by whom this scandal has come about. Cursed creature that you are, you are condemned out of your own mouth.' Then, with a look of joy upon her face, Samaritana turned to the king and said, 'Look carefully, for this is your Biancabella, this is the wife you loved so dearly, this is she without whom you could not live.' Then to prove the truth of her words, Samaritana asked the three daughters of the old man to comb Biancabella's hair in the presence of the king. They had hardly begun when pearls and precious stones began to fall from her tresses, while from her hands there fell sweet-smelling violets and morning roses. And for even greater certainty, she pointed out to the king how Biancabella's snow-white neck was encircled by a fine chain of the most delicately wrought gold growing naturally between the skin and the flesh and shining out as though through crystal.

The king, perceiving by these manifest and convincing signs that she was indeed his own Biancabella, began to weep for the joy he felt and to embrace her tenderly. But before he left the palace, he had a red-hot furnace kindled into which he ordered to be cast the stepmother and her daughter. This is how they received just and meet punishment for their wickedness. After this was done, the old man's three daughters were given honourably in marriage, and thereafter King Ferrandino lived long and happily with his beauteous Biancabella and Samaritana, leaving behind heirs, lawfully begotten, to inherit the kingdom.

During the telling of Lauretta's story, several of the listeners were moved to tears. When she had come to the end, the Signora asked her to follow the example of those who had gone before her and to set forth her enigma. This she did most gracefully in the following words:

A proud and cruel maid I spied,
As through the flowery meads she hied.

Behind her trailed a lengthy train,
Upreared her head in high disdain,
And swiftly on her way she took,
And sharp her touch, and eke her look.
What though her tongue moves all around,
She utters neither voice nor sound.
She is long, and thin, and wise,
He can tell her name who tries.

All the company listened attentively to the enigma which Lauretta gave them, and she, seeing little likelihood that anyone would find the solution to it, said, 'Dear ladies, so as not to keep you any longer in suspense, or to weary your minds, which must feel harassed by the pathos of the story I just recounted, I will tell you the answer right away if that is your pleasure. The damsel I described is nothing other than the serpent which, when it goes through the flowery meadows, keeps its head erect and its tail trailing on the ground behind it, frightening all who see it with its baleful eye.'

Everyone was surprised that no one had guessed the solution to the riddle. And when she had resumed her seat, the Signora made a sign to Alteria to begin her fable. She, having risen and made her reverence to the Signora, began immediately.

III.3 Commentary

The story of Biancabella, by the time it had reached Straparola, represented a rich amalgamation of established story motifs, and most notably those associated with tales concerning 'the maiden without hands' (ATU 706).[39] It begins with an animal birth tale in which a serpent sister becomes the heroine's animal helper, upon conditions. From a different tradition, the calumny of a wicked mother-in-law and her blood daughter by another marriage provides the motor to the intended murder of the beautiful heroine bride, commuted to mutilation and abandonment in the forest through the pity of the executioners. The tale concludes with

39 On this motif, see Heinrich Däumling, *Studie über den Typus des Mädchens ohne Hände innerhalb des Konstanze-Zyklus* (Munich: C. Gerber, 1912), and Stith Thompson, *The Folk Tale* (Berkeley: University of California Press, [1946], 1977), pp. 120–2. See also Count Théodore Joseph Boudet de Puymaigre, 'La fille aux mains coupées,' *Revue de l'histoire des religions* 10 (1884), pp. 193–208.

a restoration sequence bearing the features of an oriental tale in which the retribution imposed upon the wicked mother and daughter is suggested by the wicked woman herself. These and related features had come together by the sixteenth century – and arguably earlier – to form a narrative type about a banished bride who, by her resilience and good nature, is restored to a loving husband who had been deceived by his wife's female household rivals. (The story, in these regards, bears many resemblances to 'the truth-speaking bird' group featured in IV.3.) Presumably it was the archetypal 'truth' of this situational tragi-comedy that confirmed the order of the narrative and made it one of the most widely circulated of tales in after years – from Ireland to eastern Russia and the Near East (but apparently excluding India) – in all of folklore.[40] In the words of Italo Calvino, 'Biancabella' is simply 'one of Straparola's finest.'[41]

That Biancabella is an abandoned queen who is falsely exiled due to slander (and in related versions the misrepresentation of the birth of her children) by a jealous queen mother, and a heroine who must be restored by her misinformed husband, aligns her story with the tradition of *La Belle Hélène* and its many cognates represented by Straparola in the story of Doralice (I.4). Much of the commentary on that story applies to 'Biancabella.' But several new motifs are introduced, giving Biancabella's story a very particular cachet of its own. Clearly it is related to the Greek tradition of 'the maiden who laughs roses and weeps pearls,' for the heroine is endowed with hair that sheds precious jewels when combed and with hands that drop roses and violets. This configuration of graces hovers between the emblematizing of her charms and the very real production of wealth that serves her for protection during her exile, as well as proof of her identity when she is found. The story begins with a remnant from ancient myth concerning the chthonic snake goddess in which twin sisters are born, the one human and superlatively beautiful, the other a serpent who is later metamorphosed into a forest nymph. The metamorphosis of a woman into a snake and back again is a cousin motif to the stories of Mélusine who, as a wife, embodies a taboo which, when broken by her husband, allows or compels her to return to her serpent origins. Biancabella's sister is likewise a totem protectress who beautifies her in a secret garden by washing her in milk and rose water and licking

40 Stith Thompson, *The Folktale* (Berkeley: University of California Press, [1946], 1977), p. 121.

41 *Italian Folktales*, trans. George Martin (New York: Pantheon Books, [1956], 1980), p. 718.

her limbs. Moreover, there is an unspecified taboo inadvertently broken by Biancabella which separates her from her sibling protectress, even though Samaritana is always invisibly present. A long period of suffering and expiation (brought about through betrayal and the severing of her hands) must follow, which is resolved not by the quest of a disabused husband as in the Doralice tradition, but by the healing powers of the sister with whom she is reconciled at an extreme moment of despair. That Samaritana has meanwhile become a woodland maiden liberated from her snake-body prison (the remnants of a tale all its own) puts the final touches upon a compound overlay of mythic elements pregnant with significance but almost beyond definitive interpretation.

Biancabella as a 'white beauty' or blonde goddess, the 'Snow White' victim of a jealous stepmother figure, also re-enacts a kind of ritual death and resurrection motif involving expiation for the violation of an implicit code. In that regard, the story is wonderfully complex. It is, meanwhile, a bride selection tale in which Ferrandino, king of Naples, chooses an outsider for her beauty over local contenders, creating a figure not unrelated to the pauper bride Griselda. The envious stepmother inaugurates a substitute bride plot in which there are some innovative touches, as when the combing of the false bride's hair produces lice rather than jewels. The pool of despair where Biancabella's sight and hands are restored is yet another motif with echoes in a number of later tales. In the final sequence, all seven members of the woodland household go to Naples – the healed Biancabella with her sister and the woodsman who has given shelter to the heroine, together with his wife and three daughters – there to construct a magic palace through Samaritana's fairy powers, in keeping with palace creations familiar from *The Arabian Nights*, leading to the banquet of truth through the recitation of Biancabella's story. It is a fable of innocent beauty, betrayal and victimization, marriage fraud, real and symbolic mutilation, the recovery of the nuclear family temporarily threatened, as well as a tale of sibling loyalty under stress, each featuring elements of the human condition in general that have no doubt contributed to the enduring resonances of this story over centuries.

'Biancabella' has many cousin narratives featuring one or more of the motifs making up the fable, including the many medieval stories of maidens and saints with severed hands. But there are no apparent literary analogues from Straparola's time or before featuring the full configuration of episodes and motifs he presents. Nevertheless, the many folk tales collected in the nineteenth century about abandoned wives and maidens blinded or with their hands severed attest to a folk narrative type stretching far back into time, of which Straparola's is the earliest version on record. Before that time, we can only imagine a gradual assembly of parts through the collective efforts of the folk 'mind.' Such a process there had to have been, resulting in the folk tale that served Straparola as his source and that represented one variant of a type which achieved abundance unto saturation three centuries later. In sum, given the ancient and well-known elements embedded in the story, and given its massive and diversified survival in later centuries, it is inconceivable that Straparola was its author. Rather, the tale in a representative sixteenth-century version passed through his hands and first came to literary attention while pursuing its destiny as a folk tale on a pan-European scale.

Reading the story for its 'meanings' poses certain challenges, because the parts making up the whole individually appeal to different registers of interpretation, as though the tale had emerged as a kind of Darwinian creation in which independent elements were brought together to strengthen one another through a process of natural selection, thereby leaving traces of primitive encoding beneath the displacements eventuating in 'lower' and more transparent mimetic fields of representation. The fertility serpent that creeps into a desiring woman's womb creating twins intertwined at birth, the one bearing a marker of her sister in the form of a golden necklace glowing through the skin, pertains to a zoomorphic order of its own only obliquely related to tales of wicked stepmothers. Such a miraculous birth, with its animal to human transformations, may ultimately depend upon myths of the chthonic gods living part of their lives as reptiles below the earth and part as mortals above the earth, embodying the alternatives between sun and moon, light and darkness, or summer and winter in the agonistic drama of the changing seasons. At the same time, Samaritana the snake goddess has become a fairy nymph as well as the animal helper of later fairy tale creations. Biancabella, in this, is defenceless beauty and grace while Samaritana has unlimited powers but is confined to her serpent shape. The relationship is an unsteady one, for in cognate versions the serpent becomes the rival sibling who viciously turns on her sister. Just why Samaritana ignores her sister's cries for help for so long, yet professes to have been near her throughout her agony, is a question to ponder, for just how Biancabella broke faith with her sister or breached a sacred taboo is not entirely clear, yet remains one of the story's salient motifs.

That the snake-birth element contained here, within the context of Renaissance thought, might serve at the same time as a reflection upon nature and monstrosity is an inferential and collateral possibility at best, insofar as these fabulous metamorphoses are far older than Renaissance science and served mythological ends long before they were put to empirical investigation. Yet just such matters as snake births in related contexts were investigated phenomenologically because, in the words of Ambroise Paré, 'marvels are things which happen that are completely against Nature as when a woman will give birth to a serpent, or to a dog, or some other thing that is totally against Nature, as we shall show hereafter through several examples of said monsters and marvels.'[42] But how these events, such as they appear in wonder tales, might be deemed to intersect with ostensibly similar events reported to have arisen in the phenomenological world is a challenging question. Paré's interest in the reported monstrosities of nature, as when children born to women are said to resemble the person or creature held in the mother's imagination at the time of conception, emerged as part of the debate over received medical ideas then under empirical investigation. The question is whether Paré would have considered the story of 'Biancabella' as *natural* evidence of a monstrous birth. We are told that a serpent had entered her mother's womb and presumably fecundated her, thereby giving its characteristics to their hybrid children as major traits in the one and as minor traits in the other. Surely, not even Paré could subscribe to such a form of miscegenation in the natural world. Samaritana, in any case, leaps free from the curse of her father's 'genetic endowment' by the story's end in true fairy tale fashion as though she had been a human child all along, cursed to endure a spell which had reduced her to serpent form. This is not natural history, but a tale of emblematic transformations, a tale in which girl is born a serpent because she was cursed at birth and then liberated.

Yet in a more popular sense, the story may have had a chilling appeal because the insinuation of a serpent into the body through the female sex organs is so easily imagined. Paré entertains the report out of Lycosthenes 'that in the year 1494 a woman of Krakow, [living] on the square called Holy Spirit, gave birth to a dead child who had a live snake attached to its back, who was gnawing on this little dead creature.'[43] This turns out to be an instance of monstrosity because Paré believed that

42 *On Monsters anad Marvels,* trans. Janis Pallister (Chicago: University of Chicago Press, 1982), p. 3.

43 *On Monsters and Marvels,* trans. Janis Pallister, p. 58.

rotting flesh could engender snakes, not because humans beget them, or because they had crept in from the outside. Yet where fairy tale and fact may find common ground arises with the case of the woman from Normandy who believed 'that she had a snake in her belly which had gotten into her while she was asleep in a hempfield.' Tellingly, however, the physicians would not rally to her claim, but treated her as an impostor, as though she had been hearing too many fairy tales.[44] Yet her delusion may have reflected a current obsession concerning wombs and serpents, predicated upon a fear that alien creatures might introduce themselves through the body's vulnerable orifices. These intersections are studied at greater length by Suzanne Magnanini in *Fairy-Tale Science: Monstrous Generation in the Tales of Straparola and Basile.*[45] But genuinely hard work still remains to be done in aligning the modern scientific mind with the Renaissance scientific mind in relation to literary wonders and the empirical world as they knew it. Part of the difficulty resides in the inclusiveness of the Renaissance mind in deference to authority: we are never certain with them where imagination and belief began and ended because of their own partiality to correspondences whereby analogies result in category conflation. Even Conrad Gesner in his *Historia animalium* (1551) created a compendium including all that was said by the ancient Greeks and Romans 'with factual truth and falsity as, at best, a minor criterion for emphasis,' placing empirical information, fables, proverbs, and practical lore side by side.[46] But we must move on.

That the motif of the severed hands so successfully met the criterion for 'meme' survival is perhaps to be explained merely by the hold it has upon the imagination. The story compels the pity and fear associated with the loss of such life-sustaining organs as hands and eyes, the perfect correlative to the inward helplessness and suffering felt by a nurturing mother in exile after the loss of her children. Coupled with this is the wasteland of the forest, the alien place of isolation and self encounter, and the eventual meeting with the humble woodlanders. At that juncture, the story suddenly leaps again to social relations in generic form as the compassionate woodsman takes pity on Biancabella but is obstructed in his intentions by a grasping wife and her mistrusting daughters,

44 *On Monsters and Marvels*, trans. Janis Pallister, p. 83.

45 (Toronto: University of Toronto Press, 2008). See pp. 96 and 100 for commentary on the present story.

46 Stephen Jay Gould, *The Hedgehog, the Fox, and the Magister's Pox: Mending the Gap between Science and the Humanities* (New York: Harmony Books, 2003), p. 2.

paralleling the hostile household from which Biancabella had been banished. Here, at least, Biancabella becomes cherished for her jewel-shedding hair, while such charms back at court served merely to enrage the stepmother and further incite her aspirations for her ugly daughters. Perhaps there is little mystery at all in the persistence of wicked stepmother tales, given the composition of the medieval and early modern household in which older members and their offspring lingered in insecurity after being attached to the households of inheriting sons and their encroaching new brides.[47] Intergenerational conflict, jealousy of the new wife, and fear of her control over the household are predictable results. At the same time, at an even more generic level, the mother's stratagem to insinuate her own daughter into the king's bed is a barely disguised expression of a mother's raw instincts for furthering her own genetic bloodline by securing the highest grade of seed for her own daughters – mythic drives with undercurrents of primal competition and violence motivated by 'selfish genes.' Not only does the old biddy want to control the household and the young man's affection, but she wants the royal sperm reserved for her own progeny. We cannot, by the criteria of plausibility, ask how an ugly daughter without any of Biancabella's features might pass herself off for the banished bride. The truth lies in the emblematic gesture of bride replacement whereby the strategies of exogamy are temporarily defeated by endogenous scheming and fraud. Fairy tales such as this merely turn into emblematic narratives the social negotiations within extended kinship groups and the psychological dangers for the outsider bride with her enviable charms and radiant complexion who must integrate herself into a hostile family environment. Worth noting, however, is that while Biancabella was the chosen one for the royal bed, and was well advanced in her dynastic role by her pregnancy at the time of her expulsion and mutilation, she does not subsequently bring forth a child. Her condition is simply forgotten. Such narrative defects can only be attributed to competing versions of the story which have been imperfectly joined by a forgetful raconteur, suggesting most instructively that, despite the remarkable power of the story, Straparola was working with a version somewhat decayed and already several narrative generations from its *oikotype.*

---

47 On the sociology of wicked stepmothers, see Marina Warner, *From the Beast to the Blonde: On Fairy Tales and Their Tellers* (London: Vintage, 1995), pp. 226*ff.*

Just how interwoven the motifs were by Straparola's time is evidenced by his tale's nearest analogue, the story of 'Penta the Handless' (III.2) in Basile's *Pentamerone.*[48] Their similarities point to a story type with many integrated parts, but their contrasts indicate a tale already widely diversified by time and geographical distance. In effect, Basile's creation represents a parallel group sharing only a few central identifying features. Such matters of taxonomy are difficult to resolve. Basile's tale is closer to the *Belle Hélène* and *Santa Uliva* groups, for his heroine cuts off her own hands in flight from her brother's incestuous advances. She is put to sea in a chest, is cast up on foreign shores, endures the misery of her mutilation, is hated by the wife of the fisherman who finds her, is put to sea again, re-emerges to marry a king only to endure for a second time the malice of Nuccia, the fisherman's wife. After many trying mishaps, she is recovered by her penitent brother and her husband. Associations with the romance of *Emaré* are particularly marked. Nuccia, rather than the protective queen mother, forges the letter that turns newborn infants to monsters in the imagination of the king as well as the letter that gives the command, as though from the king, to have the queen banished or slain. In Basile, a magician rescues the wandering girl and ultimately restores her hands, while the confession gained from Nuccia brings her to a slow roasting. There is no serpent sister, no jewels and flowers, but the severed hands, the menacing of legitimate offspring, the exile to the forest, the healing, and the restoration of the family remain common features. Both are tales of envied and mutilated beauties, but the differences separating them represent, in a sense, bookends to the variety of motifs in the handless maiden tales collected in the nineteenth century.

Turning to the literary record before 1550, there are only stories bearing a select few features in common; there are none with anything like the full complement of motifs that compound to form the story of 'Biancabella.' In that sense, Straparola's is the first. Yet the circulation of related motifs during earlier periods suggests a story-making process that can only be retro-constructed from the present work. Ser Giovanni Fiorentino's *Pecorone,* dating to 1378–88, offers a case in point. It contains a version of the *Belle Hélène* story (X.1) that significantly predates both Straparola and Basile. That story relates paradigmatically to certain plotting features

48 Giovanni Battista Basile, 'Penta the Handless,' in *Il Pentamerone: or The Tale of Tales* (1534–6), trans. Sir Richard Burton (New York: Boni & Liveright, 1927), III.2, pp. 206–16.

of Biancabella's story, while at the same time linking it to Straparola's 'Doralice' (I.4).[49] Dionigia, daughter of the king of France, flees from an unwanted marriage by crossing over to England. There she marries the king, is gotten with child, and is placed in the care of her mother-in-law. The story follows, as in Basile, with reports of two monster children, orders to have all three slain, and the mother's escape by sea to Genoa and to Rome where she raises her boys up to service in the papal court. But there are no rival sisters, no severed hands, and no serpent birth, leading again to the conclusion that the 'Doralice' type, before it could serve as the centre of the 'Biancabella' type, would require a massive sea change.

Tales of daughters, princesses, and queens with severed hands were widespread in ancient and medieval literatures and the motif appears to have passed early into the folk culture if it did not arise there.[50] Several later versions of the type will appear in subsequent pages. The late medieval story of 'Uliva' is among the most prominent of story traditions bearing this feature. Italo Calvino, in his anthology of fables, provides the tale of 'Olive' (No. 71), which is a late Tuscan variant upon the *Istoria de la Regina Oliva* and the popular Florentine mystery play *Santa Uliva*.[51]

---

49 *The Pecorone of Ser Giovanni*, trans. W.G. Waters, 3 vols. (London: Society of Bibliophiles, 1898), vol. II, pp. 73–90. A mere byway to the history of this narrative is the story of 'La serva fidele' in Tommasino Reppone di Gnanopoli's (Pompeo Sarnelli's) *Posilecheata*, ed. Enrico Malato (Florence: Sansoni, 1962), pp. 77–107. Yet the story bears mention because of the displaced employment of so many common features. This is the tale of a sweet girl-child cursed at birth by the sixth of seven fairies, the last serving to mitigate somewhat the spell cast by her predecessor. The sixth, angry at the world, condemns Pomponia to three years, months, days and hours of life as a serpent, following a transformation on her wedding night. During this time the heroine must find an alter ego who will be flawlessly faithful in her service. The resonances inhere in the heroine's departure on her wedding night, the location of a sister-like double, the conversion to serpent state, the menace posed by the three sisters, the period of expiation, and the eventual restoration to human state. This story may owe something to the story tradition that gave rise to Straparola's 'Biancabella.'

50 Linda Dégh, for example, describes eleven Hungarian and central European versions of ATU 706, involving young daughters threatened by paternal incest who, in their flight, become victims with severed hands. *Studies in East European Folk Narrative* ([Indiana]: American Folklore Society, 1978), pp. 340–59.

51 Italo Calvino, 'Olive,' in *Italian Folktales*, trans. George Martin (New York: Pantheon Books, [1956], 1980), no. 71, pp. 255–61. The two Renaissance works have been profiled in the commentary on the story of Doralice (I.4). They are, respectively, an early fifteenth-century verse romance and a play adapted from it at mid-century under the title *Rappresentazione di Santa Uliva*. When the Emperor Julian discovers

Again, we are reminded of the profile of a saint's life behind the story of Biancabella, the innocent and pure child cursed, mutilated, and sent into the wilderness to die. In the tale from Montale Pistoiese, the girl is born Jewish but raised a Christian. When she is taken back by her father, she is persecuted for her religious practices, first with beatings, then by cutting off her hands and abandoning her in the woods. There are no jealous sisters, but as in the Grimm tale, there is a garden with pear trees with branches that miraculously bend down enabling her to eat the fruit. Taken for a thief, her stumps nevertheless win the king's pity; true to tradition he relents and then falls in love. A status-conscious queen mother grows angry and the king agrees to go in search of a finer bride but finds none as fine as Olive. War and pregnancy then coincide; the king is called away, forcing the mother and her two infants to take refuge in the woods. There the heroine encounters a pool and in seeking to drink from it drops her infants into the water. A washer woman nearby refuses to help, but tells the heroine to plunge her stumps into the healing water and thereby save her children with her own restored hands. It

that his daughter alone matches his first wife for beauty, he demands a papal dispensation, but the girl severs her hand in resistance. She is exiled, marries a king, gives birth, drops the child by accident and is accused. In exile she prays to the Virgin, who restores her hand. She is then found by a second king and marries, leading to the monster birth accusations and the forged letters. These narrative elements were hence well known in Italy and must feature in the consciousness of storytellers, although there is a distance to be crossed between a saint's life play and a fairy tale only a century later. See *Sacre Rappresentazioni del secoli XIV, XV, e XVI*, ed. Alessandro d'Ancona (Florence, 1872), vol. II, pp. 235–315. In a late version, the girl is promised to the devil in marriage, but avoids her fate by crossing herself. So her greedy father, paid by the devil, punishes her by having her hands severed and sending her into the forest. All the familiar features follow: marriage to a king, his absence, the birth of her children, the letter exchange by an evil witch, the exile to the forest, the restoration of her hands in the water, the magic castle, and her rediscovery by the king. Dietrich Jecklin, *Volkstümliches aus Graubünden* (Zürich: Olms, [1874], 1980), vol. I, pp. 111*ff.* The story was well-established in German-speaking areas, for it survives in a late medieval version entitled 'Deu tochter des küniges von Reuzen' in which the daughter cuts her hair and disfigures herself to avoid an incestuous union approved by the Pope which had been purchased with gold and silver. Her escape is to Greece where she marries into royalty but falls prey to the wicked queen mother. A substitution of letters by getting the messenger drunk sends her again into exile, this time to Rome where the reunion of the family eventually takes place. Friedrich Heinrich von der Hagen, *Gesamtabenteuer: Hundert Altdeutsche Erzählungen* (Darmstadt: Wissenschaftliche Buchgesellschaft, 1961), vol. II, pp. 595–613.

is a story of miracles, of maternal devotion under duress, of pious hope and despair, with an eventual return, whereupon, in saintly fashion, she pardons the malicious mother who then enters a convent. But the circumstances of this loss and restoration in Biancabella's story are still far removed from the present tale.

In *La Belle Hélène de Constantinople*, a *chanson de geste* probably originating in northern France as early as the twelfth century, the mother-in-law betrayal motif is prominent. The forged letters and the call for the queen's execution are likewise featured. Hélène's life is spared, but her hand is severed as proof of her death, and it is through this hand, attached to the neck of one of her sons, that the mother is reunited with her children. Likewise, in *La Manekine* of Philippe de Beaumanoir, the Hungarian king's daughter severs her own hand, which falls into the river, in order to avoid an incestuous marriage.[52] The story remains related to that of Santa Uliva, which likewise tells of a hand cut off to avoid an incestuous union. These three works with their repertory of motifs – severed hands, exile, miraculous healing, royal marriages, and kin betrayal – profile an extensive narrative tradition in which the elements are conjoined in a signature association. Whatever its immediate or distant relationship to the folk tales in the Santa Uliva group,

52 *La Manekine*, trans. Christiane Marchello-Nizia (Paris: Stock-Plus, 1980). The king wants his daughter, Alegría, burned alive when she refuses him and cuts off her left hand. A seneschal comes to her aid and she manages her escape to Scotland where she marries a king and falls victim to her wicked mother-in-law. When the false letters are exchanged about a monster birth, her husband now putatively seeks her death by fire, forcing yet again her escape by sea, this time to Rome. Her hand is found in a fountain and rejoined by the prayers of the Pope. This is a story of the thirteenth century. There are many useful notes on the handless girl tradition by Hermann Suchier in his edition of the *Oeuvres poètiques de Philippe de Remi, Sieur de Beaumanoir* (Paris: Firmin Didot, 1885). He cites nineteen versions from the twelfth to the sixteenth centuries. Closely related is the *Historia de la hija del rey de Hungría: Legendas en prose catalana-provensal* (Palma: Guasp & Vicens, 1873), which takes place in Marseille and features a heroine who hides in a convent where the Virgin miraculously heals her. Not far removed from these stories of beleaguered wives are the stories of chastity, refusal, and mutilation in the lives of the saints. Saint Agatha, for refusing to marry the consul or to renounce her faith, has her breasts seared or severed. When she is offered medical help, she refuses, placing her trust in the healing powers of Christ alone – and indeed Saint Pierre restores them, much as the maiden's hands are miraculously restored in some stories by the Virgin herself. Jacques de Voragine, *La légende dorée*, trans. Teodor de Wyzewa (Paris: Perrin, 1920), no. 33, pp. 146–50.

Straparola's tale clearly bears a generic kinship to all such early stories about maidens with severed hands.

Our tale likewise bears a kinship to the handless maiden tales from the Islamic world. The tale of 'The Woman whose Hands were Cut off for giving Alms to the Poor' from *The Arabian Nights* is concerned with a forbidden act of charity, that of giving two small loaves of bread. The king responsible for the mutilation of the apprehended girl nevertheless marries her, only to arouse the jealousy of his other wives. Accused of infidelity, she is exiled with her child, but in her attempt to drink from a pool her child falls into the water. Two men happening by see her weeping and not only rescue the child but offer prayers to Allah, who restores her severed hands. These men were the two scones of bread she had given in charity, returning as though from the dead to aid her in her deepest distress. (See the related motifs in the commentary to XI.2.) This is a truncated version of the tale in which the handless maiden is restored to her husband, he now disabused of the calumny spoken against her. Moreover, in keeping with the narrative order of 'the grateful dead' group, it should have been the soul of the beggar to whom the alms were given that came to her rescue.[53] Although the date for which the tales of *The Arabian Nights* first exercised their influence upon European culture remains contested, the coincidence of details regarding bride selection, jealousy, severed hands, exile, and restoration suggests that the entire tradition might have had its origin in Arabic folklore. By the same token, it is equally plausible that the motif of the pearl tears and golden hair, linked with tales of royal children born as dogs and cats according to the malicious reports of jealous sisters, is Arabic as well. Margaret Schlauch, consulting the *Supplemental Arabian Nights*, relates a story that is closely cognate with Straparola's tale of 'Singing Apple, Dancing Water, and the Truth-Speaking Bird' (IV.3). In the Eastern tale, a younger sister marries a king and reaps the hatred of her two older sisters who plot her ruin.[54] They substitute dead and live animals and bits of wood in the

53 *The Book of a Thousand Nights and a Night*, trans. Richard Burton (London: The Burton Club, 1884), vol. IV, pp. 281–3.

54 Margaret Schlauch, *Chaucer's Constance and Accused Queens* (New York: Gordian Press, [1927], 1969), pp. 48–9. Schlauch is concerned with the false accusations of queens and the many motifs pertaining to the *Emaré*, *Belle Hélène*, 'Doralice' group, of which Biancabella is one, but now in a tradition of her own. The story is the same as, or similar to, the 'Histoire des deux soeurs jalouses de leur cadette' which, in *Les milles et une nuit* (Lyons: Briasson, 1717), Antoine Galland claims to have collected

birth bed and spirit away the royal children until, in exasperation, the credulous Persian king has his wife walled into a space at the door of the chief mosque where every good Muslim is compelled to spit on her upon entering the place of worship. The three children, meanwhile, enact the story told by Straparola concerning the speaking bird, the singing tree, and the dancing water, the disastrous quests by the two brothers, the redeeming quest by the faithful sister, and the means whereby the speaking bird reveals the truth about the exiled mother, leading to her restoration. The story is somewhat removed from 'the handless maiden' group, but features the promise of a son who would weep tears, the envious sisters, and close confinement rather than mutilation. The 'meme' of the handless maiden passed from tales of punishment to sainthood to gratuitous mutilation of innocent brides in association with rising tales of beauty rewarded by marriage, the happiness of which is delayed by calumniation, treachery, and mutilation often by the nearest of kin.[55] But whether that movement was from East to West remains a moot point,

---

from a Maronite Christian Arab from Aleppo named Youhenne Diab, and for which there is no written Arabic source. It is nights 667 to 688 of *The Arabian Nights*. See also Jack Zipes in his notes to *The Collected Sicilian Folk and Fairy Tales of Giuseppe Pitrè*, ed. and trans. Jack Zipes and Joseph Russo, 2 vols. (New York: Routledge, 2009), vol. I, p. 841.

55 Stith Thompson provides an overview of the conditions that bring about the heroine's loss of hands from incest avoidance to breaking a taboo or giving birth to monsters. He traces the motif back to '1200 in southern England,' naming seventeen variants. It had become universal by the seventeenth century. Thompson links the story to 'Our Lady's Child' narratives concerned with the loss and regaining of the protection of a fairy godmother or the Virgin Mary herself, claiming that the motif 'first appeared in polite literature through Straparola.' *The Folktale* (New York: Holt, Rinehart & Winston, 1946), pp. 120–2. In a parallel tradition, there is the motif of blinding, as in the legendary story of Hildegarde, one of the wives of Charlemagne, who, falsely accused of scandal, was sent to the forest to have her eyes put out. She is rescued, the eyes of a dog are sent back to the court as proof of the deed, and the accused lady escapes to Rome where she becomes a famous healer. Ultimately, she cures her accuser, Charlemagne's brother Talaud, of his blindness, as reported by Vincent de Beauvais. See F.-M. Luzel, *Légendes chrétiennes de la Basse-Bretagne*, 2 vols. (Paris: Maisonneuve, 1881), vol. II, pp. 262–3. The notes correspond to 'La bonne femme et la méchante femme' (The good woman and the wicked woman), in which there is a rich mixture of elements from the 'Biancabella' tradition, including the girl abandoned in the woods with her arms severed and fed by a little dog. She too is taken up by a seigneur who marries her, only to have her children substitued by animals and false letters sent to her husband – all the work of a wicked sister-in-law. She too is exiled with her

for the version in *The Arabian Nights* is in a decayed state in relation to the folk tale already fully formed in Europe by the beginning of the thirteenth century. Such are the early tales closest in their features to 'Biancabella,' yet in so many crucial ways still distant from the folk tale made manifest by Straparola.

Far more valuable information about the 'Biancabella' type may be distilled from its later descendents, of which there are many. Turning to the nineteenth-century renditions, a story from Lower Brittany, 'La fille qui naquit avec une couleuvre autour du coup' (the girl born with a serpent around her neck), reveals a clear vestige of the serpent sister tale incorporated by Straparola, preserving many cognate details, while at the same time illustrating its aptness for transformation.[56] A queen, longing for a child, in a reckless rhetorical flourish vows that even a toad or a grass snake would be acceptable. In due course, she gives birth to a baby girl with a grass snake about her throat. The snake, as in Straparola, slithers away leaving a red mark behind. When Lévénès (Happiness), the princess, reaches her twelfth birthday, she meets the snake under clandestine circumstances and learns that it is her sister. Milk, at the snake's bidding, is then taken to the garden into which the snake dips itself before offering it to the princess as a rinse that eliminates the red mark on her throat. Following this strange rite, Lévénès is married to a stranger from a far land in whose palace she one day discovers, in a forbidden room, the corpses of eleven pregnant women. The story now follows the course of the Blue Beard group. Before her destiny is fulfilled, however, the princess gets word to her parents, the grass snake warns the king and queen, and all rush to her rescue. The serpent bites the ogre's heel just as the axe was to have fallen on the princess's neck. Lévénès then gives birth to a son, who is immediately slain by an angry mob for fear that he would become like his father, while priests refuse to baptize the serpent sister. With this idiosyncratic configuration of motifs, this tale testifies not only to the continued circulation of the serpent birth story featured by Straparola, but to the malleability of all such tales as they add and subtract motifs and alter their meanings – a clear caveat to those who

children, still without arms until they are restored by a woman who is none other than the Blessed Virgin. She remains in the forest in a nice thatched cottage until her penitent husband rediscovers her.

56 François-Marie Luzel, ed., *Contes populaires de Basse-Bretagne*, 3 vols. (Paris: G.P. Maisonneuve & Larose, [1887], 1967), story 6, vol. II, pp. 341–8.

undertake deep readings of such narrative clusters based on a single, late, literary recension.

In Lorraine, Emmanuel Cosquin collected the story of 'Marie de la chaume du bois,' a bride-selection tale in which a younger and prettier sister of rural cottage origins marries the king. The fortune of her beauty, however, outrages a jealous older sister whose part is taken by her mother.[57] The substitutions are easily worked out whereby the tale of sisters is again combined with the tale of the wicked older woman seconding the ambitions of a favourite child. As Marina Warner points out, such tales of women against women are often macabre in their violence,[58] for in this highly 'folkloric' tale, the sister herself performs the mutilations, not only removing her sibling's eyes and severing her hands, but her feet as well, before knocking out her teeth. While the older sister substitutes the younger at the palace, the derelict heroine is rescued by an old man in the woods who, in magician fashion, offers her a series of wishes (as the serpent will do in the Comparetti tale recounted below). Characterizing this group of stories is the negotiation for body parts back at the palace by offering precious commodities to the mother and daughter. Item by item, such things as a golden spinning wheel and distaff are exchanged one by one for the precious limbs and organs required to restore the heroine to her former self. As in Basile, a beggar tells the tale of the mutilated girl to the prince, leading to the *anagnorisis*. The true bride is reinstated and the cruel blood kin are fed to the beasts – such primitive and summary justice being a typical part of the tradition. Again, the serpent tale and the jewel-shedding *chevelure* are absent, but the mutilation motif has been augmented, the rival sister becomes a real sister, while the order of exile, rescue, magic healing, and restitution remain in their customary sequence. Marie and Biancabella share a common heritage without much contest, but Cosquin's tale has been transformed by the selective processes of folk transmission.[59]

---

57 Emmanuel Cosquin, *Contes populaires de Lorraine*, 2 vols. (Paris: F. Vieweg, [1887]), no. 35, vol. II, pp. 44–6.

58 Marina Warner, *From the Beast to the Blonde: On Fairy Tales and their Tellers* (London: Vintage, 1995), p. 226.

59 Cosquin in turn directs readers to many cognate tales featuring the little boy who goes to the château to recover teeth, hands, and eyes in exchange for rich goods produced by magic in aid of the heroine by her magic helper. See Josef Wenzig, *Westslawischer Märchenschatz* (Leipzig: F.A. Brockhaus, 1845), p. 45. This is related to the trick employed by the husband of Doralice to gain entrance to her palace by masquerading as a peddler. See the commentary to I.4.

Perhaps the latest tale of this genre to be collected in France, 'The Woman with Her Hands Cut Off,' from the Lower Marche, although much compromised during its transmission, nevertheless 'remembers' a goodly number of the archetypal features. A brother and sister, once very close, are made enemies by a wicked sister-in-law (the brother's wife), who plants the evidence that inculpates the innocent girl for heinous crimes. Her brother, in anger, severs her hands and turns her out to wander. Helpless, she seeks to eat apples in a king's garden by catching them in her mouth. The king, true to the fable, spies, discovers the girl. dressed in rags, provides her with clothes, and marries her against his mother's wishes. She bears the king two sons while he is away at war and is led off to the forest with her little twins by command of the king's mother. The story takes a turn when St. John and St. Paul become the boys' godfathers and the Holy Virgin their godmother. Thus her hands are restored and the boys are promised castles. Seven years later the king goes searching for them in the woods and in due course arrives at the castle where the family is rejoined. The heroine then goes in search of her brother who had been for seven years laid up in bed with a splinter in his knee which only his sister could heal. In the end, they burn the spiteful sister-in-law, although the mother-in-law is forgotten. The story has fallen into fragments and the longer episodes are reduced to resumes, but the principal design persists. Several variants of this story were collected by the same editor, Geneviève Massignon, in Corsica as well as in French Nova Scotia around the middle of last century.[60]

60 *Folktales of France*, ed. Geneviève Massignon, trans. Jacqueline Hyland (London: Routledge & Kegan Paul, 1968), pp. 116–20, 267. A tale similar to this was included by Jean Fleury, 'La fille sans mains' (The girl without hands), in his *Littérature orale de la Basse-Normandie* (Paris: G.-P. Maisonneuve & Larose, 1967), no. 3, pp. 151–60. This story begins with the vain mother of a beautiful daughter who wants the girl disfigured or slain, demanding that the assassins bring back not only her heart but her two hands. They spare her, but not her hands. The girl then wanders, attempts to eat fruit, is taken in by a noble family, is loved by the son, hated by the mother-in-law, gives birth to two sons, is driven out during her husband's absence, nearly loses a child in the water but recovers her hands while saving it, retires to a house for twelve long years, and is ultimately found by her husband. The old mother is placed underground where she is eaten by beasts. We think of Doralice up to her neck in worms.

Giuseppe Pitrè collected a Sicilian tale, 'Li dui soru' (The two sisters), in which the heroine's aunt and her daughter become the rivals.[61] En route to marry the king, the girls are exchanged; the young bride is blinded and abandoned in the woods. There she helps an old man fill his baskets with roses that fall from her own lips when she speaks, and with these she bargains for her eyes and eventually recovers her fiancé. The competing women have been distanced, yet remain kin to the heroine. The falling flowers return to the story, while maintaining the motif of the exchange of commodities for the stolen body parts not present in Straparola. The impression is now of a story that could be constructed in kaleidoscopic fashion from a cupboard of exchangeable narrative parts.

An even more intriguing variant for our purposes originates in Monferrat, where it was collected by Domenico Comparetti.[62] There may be significance in the fact that Straparola's own story is also set in the city of Monferrat, the common region suggesting more than incidental relationships between the versions. The three sisters, out in the woods with their father, are frightened by a serpent, but only the youngest does not spurn it, thereby gaining a lifelong helper. The snake awards her with three gifts, tears that make pearls and silver, laughter that makes golden flowers, and hands that, when washed, produce fish! When the king's son passes, he collects her golden flowers and, like the maid with the golden hair, he seeks the girl, finds her in the attic and offers marriage. The jealous sisters cut off her hands, remove her eyes, and toss her in the bushes. One of the sisters then impersonates her with the prince, carrying out the substitute bride plot. A stableman rescues the mutilated girl for whom she cries rich pearls. The snake returns to her in the garden telling her of the queen's pregnancy, her craving for figs in winter, and how she might herself barter the fruit at the palace for her eyes, along with peaches for her hands. The queen gives birth to a monster in a way redolent of the Doralice monster birth tales, again rejoining the two traditions. Of interest is the sister-in-need motif and the presence of an unrelated serpent helper. The reversal comes about when, at the birth festivities, the prince recognizes his true bride in attendance whose

61 *The Collected Sicilian Folk and Fairy Tales of Giuseppe Pitrè*, ed. and trans. Jack Zipes and Joseph Russo, 2 vols. (New York: Routledge, 2009), no. 62, vol. I, pp. 287–9.

62 'Le tre sorelle' (The three sisters), in *Novelline popolari italiane*, ed. Domenico Comparetti (Bologna: Forni Editore, [1875], 1968), no. 25, vol. I, pp. 103–6.

identity is confirmed by her laughter, crying, and hand washing. There have been substitutions and borrowings, but the high incidence of common motifs suggests a closer affiliation with Straparola's source tale than any of the others collected at that same time.

A Tuscan version appears in the *Novelline di Santo Stefano*, collected by Angelo de Gubernatis (No. 13).[63] This story features the mother-in-law relationship and her hatred for the queen. When the king departs, she orders two servants to take the heroine to the woods and kill her. Moved by her tears, they blind her and take her eyes to the queen mother as proof of the deed. The heroine is sheltered by an old man, while a serpent

---

63 Angelo de Gubernatis, 'La cieca' (The blind girl), in *Le novelline di Santo Stefano* (Turin: A.F. Negro, 1869), no. 13, pp. 35–6. A similar tale, 'La niña perseguida' (The persecuted girl), appears in the *Cuentos populares españoles*, ed. Aurelio Espinosa (Madrid: S. Aguirre, 1947), vol. II, pp. 376–90. See also Gherardo Nerucci, 'La bella Giuditta e la su' figliola Maria' (Beautiful Judith and her daughter Maria) and 'Uliva,' in *Sessanta novelle popolari montalesi*, ed. Roberto Fedi (Milan: Rizzoli, 1977), no. 17, pp. 134–65, and no. 39, pp. 324–34, respectively. See also Heinrich Pröhle, 'Die schöne Magdalene,' in *Kinder- und Volksmärchen* (Leipzig, 1853), no. 36, pp. 122–6. This is a composite tale in which a widow shepherdess has a beautiful daughter, but when a lover comes for the girl, the mother is jealous and wants him for herself. So Magdalene is sent to the forest with executioners who cut off her arms. She wanders the forest and into the garden of a castle on top of a mountain where she is found by the king. He marries her and all is well until letters to the king about the birth of their son fall into the hands of her own cruel mother who sees that her daughter has become a queen. The false letters cause her to be sent once more into the forest of tribulation with the baby now strapped to her back. She entrusts the baby to a lion with a thorn in its paw, seeks healing in a pond, returns to extract the thorn, and together they settle down in a house belonging to a 'white' man. The king discovers her in time and the wicked shepherdess is punished by being rolled down a hill in a barrel driven full of nails. This same device was used against mean queens in stories in the Ancillotto group (IV.3). A very similar story, 'La fille du marchand de Lyon' (The daughter of the merchant of Lyons), appears in the *Contes populaires de Lorraines*, ed. Emmanuel Cosquin, 2 vols. (Paris: F. Vieweg, 1886), no. 78, vol. II, pp. 323–8. A dog's heart is brought back by the servants sent out to kill the girl on her mother's orders. She hides in a tree, is found by a count, marries, has a child, is hated by the mother-in-law, and again is taken out, this time by coachmen, who insult her and kill her child. She escapes and, in male disguise, is overheard by the count as she tells her tale and is thus restored. It is much decayed, but has for its narrative ancestor *Le roman de la manekine* of Philippe de Beaumanoir, the famous thirteenth-century jurist. The same story was collected in the Tyrol by Christian Schneller for his *Märchen und Sagen aus Wälschtirol* (Innsbruck, 1867; reprint, Hildesheim: Olms, 1976), no. 50.

offers her three marvellous objects, one for each eye, and one for permission to sleep in the palace in a room near the queen, as in the tale by the Grimm brothers and in the Comtesse d'Aulnoy's *L'oiseau bleu.* The serpent's gifts link the story to that of the serpent helper and the bartering at the palace, but the device for entering the palace is a reminder of the relationship to the Doralice group (I.4). Now, in a technical sense, the tale of the severed hands restored by magic healing has been transformed, for there are many others cited by Cosquin from Catania and Epirus in Greece, for example, in which eyes are lost and restored by bartering, and in which there is no serpent helper, no rivalry for the king's bed, and no wicked stepmother.[64] The stories remain similar in outline, yet lack increasingly a synchronicity of motifs. Another tale collected by Pitrè (No. 62) tells of a girl with the remarkable ability to disburse flowers from her extremities. En route to meet her fiancé, she is so driven by thirst that she gives first one eye and then the other for water, allowing the stepmother to supplant her with her own daughter. The fraud is detected when the second bride lacks the flower power of the first, and the true beloved is restored. The story is nearly transformed, but the essential markers remain in clear view.

A quite remarkable reconfiguration of these many motifs appears in the *Légendes chrétiennes de la Basse-Bretagne* (no. 14) in a tale entitled 'L'oiseau bleu.'[65] A king and queen marry, each having a daughter, one beautiful and charming, the other ugly and unpleasant. Marie, the beauty, is sent away to be disfigured by a sorceress, but the sorceress, like the snake sister in Straparola, makes her even more beautiful and causes diamonds to fall from her lips when she speaks. Jeanne, the daughter of the queen – the ugly one – is likewise sent for beautification, but she is so haughty and imperious that she remains hideous with tadpoles falling from her lips. When the king departs, Marie is ostensibly slain in the woods, her heart returned to the court as proof, although she escapes

64 Cosquin, *Contes populaires de Lorraine* (Paris: Vieweg, 1886; reprint, Marseille: LaFitte, 1978), vol. II, p. 45.

65 Ed. F.M. Luzel, 2 vols. (Paris: G.-P. Maisonneuve & Larose, [1887], 1967), vol. II, pp. 292–308. The story was collected from a carpenter in Tonquédec in 1873. Further versions of the handless girl stories are known in simpler narrative forms. Paul Sébillot, *Contes populaires de la Haute-Bretagne* (Paris: G. Charpentier, 1880), vol. I, pp. 105*ff.* See also Gherardo Nerucci, ed., *Sessanta novelle populari montalesi* (Florence: Le Monnier, 1880), pp. 348*ff*; and 'Uliva' in *Sessanta novelle popolari montalesi*, ed. Roberti Fedi (Milan: Rizzoli, 1977), pp. 324–34.

to a convent where, in due course, she is discovered by a rich lord. At their wedding, with the royals in attendance, the king rediscovers his daughter. The story continues in the usual way, but with a curious conflation of motifs, for instead of mutilating the girl, the evil queen mother consults a sorceress who turns her into a bird by driving a pin into her temple. The heroine is now entrapped in an animal prison while the ugly half-sister is placed in the lord's bed. The folk tale has taken over motifs from Madame d'Aulnoy's *L'oiseau bleu,* itself a recreation from Straparola's tale, conflated with the aviary elements of the ancient romance of *Yonec.* A series of 'pathetic' scenes follows in which the bird seeks to revisit her child and to complain of her woes, tantamount to the banquet recitation of the heroine's tale by which her identity is recovered. Expeditious and fell justice ensues with the conflagration of the mother, daughter, and sorceress in a giant oven.

Another important rendition of this folk tale is 'The Maiden without Hands' (No. 72) among those collected by the Brothers Grimm.[66] This one too belongs essentially to the *Belle Hélène* group of handless maidens, the dismembering now the work of her own father to protect her from a wizard. In this rendition, episodes are reversed, for the girl first goes wandering, grows hungry, seeks fruit from a royal garden, is aided by a fairy, and eats the fruit without the benefit of her hands. She then meets the king who becomes her friend and has silver hands made for her, marries her, and finally goes off to battle leaving her in his mother's care. The motifs are all familiar. When the child is born, however, the wicked wizard intercepts the letters, altering the outbound one to tell of a monster birth and the inbound one to have the mother and child slain. The heroine is allowed to escape to the forest where the good fairy rescues her, installs her in a cottage, and restores her hands. Seven years of searching by the king transpire before the little family is reunited.

66 *Grimm's Complete Fairy Tales* (Garden City, NY: Nelson Doubleday, n.d.), pp. 205–10. The stories of girls with severed hands are among the most widespread in the world. It appears among the *Contes grecs,* ed. Émile Legrand, *Recueil de contes populaires grecs* (Paris: Leroux, 1881), p. 24, drawn in turn from a book of pious tales written in the seventeenth century by a Cretan monk. In a Lithuanian version, the opening of the story also has an affinity with the Cinderella group when the girl seeks to delay her fate by asking for lavish clothes before being whisked away as the rat girl. August Leskien and Karl Brugmann, eds., *Litauische Volkslieder und Märchen* (Strassburg: Karl J. Trübner, 1882), no. 24.

Straparola's 'Biancabella' had a direct influence upon the emergence of the French *conte de fée.* Of the many 'Blanche Belle' sequels, the most seminal to the later tradition are those by Jean de Mailly in *Blanche Belle* (1698) and Mme. d'Aulnoy in *L'oiseau bleu.* That de Mailly locates his story in Monferrat is the first of many features that tie his story directly to Straparola. To be sure, he replaces the serpent sister with a sylph, who carries out the magic impregnation, no doubt following the rise in the status of sylphs following the publication of the *Entretiens sur les science secretes* by Montfaucon de Villars known as Le Comte de Gabelis. De Mailly, in keeping with a parallel tradition, has the pearls and rubies fall from the heroine's lips as she speaks. As in Straparola, she weds Ferdinand, king of Naples. In this elaboration upon the narrative, the heroine is sent to the woods for protection along with the queen mother and her daughter by another marriage. The queen mother has a fairy confidant with whom she hatches the substitution plot. Blanche Belle is imprisoned in another chateau, comfortable, unmaimed, isolated, but still accompanied by her faithful sylph. This time it is the scheming daughter who receives beautification from the fairies in order to match her rival, careful to maintain the deception by spreading about rubies and pearls.

The prince, though deceived, nevertheless grows despondent and in his melancholy wandering happens upon the chateau of his true love. The mutilation plot, too cruel for the salons, has been exchanged for psychological torment, poignant emotions, and tender melancholy. In the end, the queen mother and her daughter are simply banished from the inner circles of the court – punishment enough for the elite of the *ancien régime.* With the demolition of the fairy castle, the whole menacing ethos of dynastic ambition is once again contained, introducing a period of tranquillity around the royal couple. In this way, Straparola's creation is both transformed yet confirmed as a fairy tale through the sentimental ambience of the French court.

That refitting of the Straparolan prototype is reenacted in Mme. d'Aulnoy's *L'oiseau bleu,* at least in its overall design, now featuring the substitution of an ugly half-sister for the chosen bride, the treacherous ambitions of the queen, and the employment of fairy guardians. The story takes an alien turn, however, when the prince, for being deceived by a false bride, is made to spend seven years of expiatory transformation as a blue bird. In its investigation of subtle seduction and gallantry, the deployment of sentimental language in a milieu of the marvellous, and in blaming the prince named Charmant for his failure to recognize the true graces of his chosen wife, Catherine d'Aulnoy seizes upon undercurrents implicit but undeveloped in the more schematic renditions of the folk. Blanche Belle, meanwhile, as Florinne, persists in her role of innocent beauty in a world of social intrigue and invidiousness.[67]

The story recorded by Straparola is remotely related to medieval tales of handless maidens and wicked in-laws joined to an early folk tale concerned with serpent births, curses, and guardian spirits coming to early light only through the present tale. Presumably it too was found among the tales of the folk raconteurs of his era. Stated otherwise, his tale of 'Biancabella' is the earliest literary record of a remarkably successful narrative type composed of diverse elements including serpent births, the severing of hands, bride selection among commoners, scheming queen mothers, mutilated saints, substitute brides, exile to deserted places, magic helpers, miraculous healings, and romance closures accompanied by harsh justice. Straparola's rendition looks in both chronological directions in summarizing and disseminating the story of the mutilated princess at a moment marking the dawn of the Western fairy tale.

67 'L'oiseau bleu' was first published in 1697 in the initial volume of *Les contes des fées*, but survives only in the collection entitled *Le cabinet des fées*. See *Contes des fées* (édition critique), ed. Nadine Jasmin (Paris: Champion, 2004). Jasmin indicates the pointlessness in collecting the many 'oiseau bleu' sequels that appeared throughout the nineteenth century, for they are all folkloric reductions of the literary original (p. 1091), except insofar as they reincorporate motifs through a process of *contaminatio* corresponding to those in the Straparola tale, in a sense returning to the proto-narrative group through alternate sources, as in the story of 'La bonne femme et le méchante femme' collected by Luzel in Lower Brittany, as recounted above, in turn related to the entire group of tales of the kind and unkind girls, for which, see Warren E. Roberts, *The Tale of the Kind and the Unkind Girls* (Berlin: W. de Gruyter, 1958; reprint, Detroit: Wayne State University Press, 1994).

III. Fable 4
Fortunio, the King's Daughter, and the Mermaid

ALTERIA

Fortunio leaves his supposed mother and father perceiving himself to have been wronged by them. After much wandering up and down the world, he comes to a wood where he finds three animals who are guided by his judgment. Afterwards, being at Polonia for a tourney, he wins Doralice, the king's daughter, as his wife.

It is a common proverb in the mouths of men, often repeated among them, that we should never be the cause of affliction nor make light of the truth, for whoever keeps his eyes and ears open and holds his tongue is not likely to harm his fellow men and will always live at peace.

Once upon a time there lived on the frontiers of Lombardy a man called Bernio. Although he was not overly endowed with the gifts of fortune, yet he was generous of heart and very intelligent. This man married a worthy and amiable woman named Alchia. She was of lowly origin, but was nevertheless of goodly parts and exemplary conduct, and loved her husband as dearly as any woman could. They greatly desired to have children, but such a gift of God was not granted to them, perhaps because man in his ignorance often asks for things that would not be to his advantage. Yet, inasmuch as this desire for offspring preoccupied them continually, and because Fortune obstinately refused to grant their prayer, they decided at last to adopt a child, whom they intended to nurture and treat in all ways as though he were their own legitimate son. Early one morning they went to a certain place where young children were often left, abandoned by their parents. Seeing one who appeared to them more graced and attractive than the rest, they took him home with them, named him Fortunio, and brought him up with the utmost care and discipline. Then, according to the good pleasure of Him who rules the universe and adjusts everything according to His will, after a time Alchia grew great with child, and when her time of delivery had come, she was brought to bed with a boy who was the very image of his father. On this account, both father and mother rejoiced exceedingly and called their son Valentino.

The infant was well nurtured and grew to be strong, healthy, and well-mannered. Moreover, he loved his brother Fortunio so dearly that he could in no wise live without him. But Discord, the foe of all that is good, became aware of their warm and loving friendship and, being no longer able to tolerate their mutual affection, one day interposed between them, creating such feelings that before long the two friends began to taste her bitter fruits. On one occasion, when they were playing together in the manner of boys, they became somewhat excited over their game, and Valentino, who couldn't bear that Fortunio should get the advantage over him, flew into such a passion of anger that he called the other a bastard and the son of a whore.

Fortunio, when he heard these words, was beyond measure astonished and distressed. Turning to Valentino, he said, 'What, am I a bastard?'

Valentino replied, muttering angrily between his teeth, what he had already said bluntly enough. In a state of grief and alarm, Fortunio ceased his play and went straight to his supposed mother and asked her whether he was in truth the son of Bernio and herself. Alchia answered that he was, and when she understood that Fortunio had been insulted by his brother, she took Valentino to task, berating him soundly and declaring that she would chastise him severely if ever he should do the like again. But the words which Alchia had spoken aroused fresh suspicion in Fortunio and made him all the more certain that he was not her real son. To discover this truth became his obsession. When Alchia saw Fortunio's stubborn determination, and that she could not bring him to stop his importunities, she acknowledged that he was not her true child, but that he had been adopted and brought up in their house for the love of God and for the alleviation of the misfortune which had been visited upon herself and her husband. These words were like so many dagger thrusts into the young man's heart, only adding to his misery. In the end his grief grew beyond endurance. Seeing that he could not bring himself to seek refuge from his trouble in a violent death, he determined to leave Bernio's roof to wander up and down the world until he should happen upon a better fortune.

Alchia, perceiving that Fortunio's desire to leave home had grown stronger every day, and that nothing would serve to dissuade him, heaped all sorts of curses upon him, praying God that if ever he should venture upon the sea that he might be engulfed in the waves and swallowed up by the sirens, or meet the worst perils of ships venturing on the high seas. In his tempestuous wind of anger and rage, Fortunio paid no attention to Alchia's malediction, but without a word of farewell to either of his parents, he departed and took the road leading westward. He travelled on, passing by lakes, valleys, mountains, and all kinds of wild and desert places, and at last one day between noon and three o'clock he came upon a thick and densely-tangled forest in the centre of which he found a wolf, an eagle, and an ant, all of them engaged in a long and sharp quarrel over the body of a dead stag – unable to agree among themselves how the meat should be divided. When Fortunio came upon the three of them, they were in the middle of their stubborn dispute and no one was disposed to yield to the others. After a time, they agreed that this young man, who had come among them unexpectedly, should decide the matter in question and assign to each one of them the portion he deemed appropriate. When they had all assented to this and had promised to be satisfied with whatever award he should make and observe the terms however unjust they might seem, Fortunio readily undertook the task. After carefully considering the case, he divided the prey among them in the following manner. To the wolf, as to a voracious animal and one very handy with his sharp teeth, he gave all the bones of the deer and all the lean flesh in reward for his toil in the chase. To the eagle, a rapacious fowl though devoid of teeth, he gave the entrails and all the fat lying around the lean parts and the bones. To the provident and industrious ant, who had none of that strength that nature had bestowed upon the wolf and the eagle, he gave the soft brains as her share of reward for the labour she had undergone. When the three animals understood the terms of this just and carefully-considered decision, they were fully satisfied and thanked Fortunio as well as ever they could for the courtesy he had shown them.

Now insofar as ingratitude, of all vices, is the most reprehensible, all three were of one accord that the young man should not depart until they had rewarded him properly for the service he had done them. Wherefore the wolf, speaking first, said, 'My brother, I give you the power to instantly become a wolf, if ever you should desire to become one, merely by saying the words, "Would I were a wolf!" and then return to your former shape whenever you desire.' In the same manner, both the eagle and the ant endowed him with the power to assume their forms and similitudes.

Then Fortunio, extremely pleased by their gifts, offered his thanks as best he knew how and took his leave. He wandered far abroad till at last he came to Polonia, a populous city of great renown, which at that time was under the rule of Odescalco, a powerful and valorous sovereign, who had but one child, a daughter called Doralice. Now the king was eager to find a noble mate for this princess, and it chanced that, at the very time when Fortunio arrived in the city, he had made a proclamation throughout his kingdom that a grand tournament should be held in the city, and that the Princess Doralice should be given in marriage to the man who became victor in the jousts. Already many dukes, marquises, and other powerful nobles had come together from all parts to contend for this noble prize. But on the first day of the tourney, which had already taken place, the honours of the tilting were borne off by a foul Saracen of hideous aspect and ungainly form, and with a face as black as pitch. When the king's daughter saw the deformed and filthy figure of the day's conqueror, she was overwhelmed with grief that fate should have awarded the victory of the joust to such a man. Her face, all crimson with shame, she buried in her tender, delicate hands, sorely weeping and lamenting, execrating her cruel and malignant destiny, and begging that death might take her rather than that she should become the wife of this misshapen heathen.

Fortunio, upon entering in at the city gate, noted the grand pomp on all sides, the crowds, and the great competitions among the contestants. When he learned the cause of these glorious tournaments, he was immediately possessed by an ardent desire to prove his valour in the jousts. But when he realized that he was lacking in all the apparel needed in such honourable contests, his heart fell and he grew exceedingly sad. While he was lamenting his situation, he happened along before the king's palace. Raising his eyes to the sky he caught sight of Doralice, the daughter of the king, who was leaning out of one of the windows of her apartment. She was surrounded by a group of lovely and highborn ladies and maidens, but she shone out among them all by reason of her beauty, as the bright and radiant sun among the tiny stars.

By-and-by, when dark night had fallen and all the ladies of the court had retired to their rooms, Doralice, restless and sad at heart, went alone to a small and beautifully ornamented chamber. As she stood there alone near an open window, behold there was Fortunio below. No sooner had he caught sight of her than he began to say, 'Ah, if only I were an eagle.'

Scarcely had these words issued from his lips than he found himself transformed, whereupon he flew as an eagle directly in through her chamber window. Then, by wishing to become a man again, he was restored to his own shape. He went forward with a light and joyful air to greet the princess, but as soon as she saw him, she was filled with terror and began to cry out in a loud voice, as though she were being attacked and torn by savage dogs. The king, who happened to be in an apartment not far from his daughter's, heard her cries of alarm and ran immediately to discover the cause. When she reported that there was a young man in the room, he forthwith ordered it to be searched in every part. But nothing of the kind was found because Fortunio had once more changed himself into an eagle and flown out of the window. Hardly had the father gone back to his chamber, however, when the maiden began to cry aloud the same as before, because Fortunio had once more come into her presence.

Fearing for his life again when he heard the girl's terrified cries, Fortunio immediately changed himself into an ant and crept into hiding beneath the blond tresses of the lovely damsel's hair. Odescalco, hearing his daughter's loud outcries, ran to her aid, but when he found nothing more this second time than he had before, he was greatly angered and threatened her sharply that if she should cry out again and disturb him, he would perform a deed which would not be to her liking. With such menacing words he left her, suspecting that what had caused her trouble was some vision of one or other of the youths who, for love of her, had met his death in the tournament. Fortunio listened attentively to what the king said to his daughter. No sooner had he left the apartment than Fortunio put off the shape of an ant and stood revealed in his own form. Doralice, who in the meanwhile had gone to bed, was so terror-stricken when she saw him that she tried to spring from her couch and give the alarm, but she could not because Fortunio placed one of his hands on her lips and spoke to her, 'Princess, fear not that I have come here to despoil you of your honour, or to steal anything that belongs to you. I am come rather to help you to the best of my power and to proclaim myself your most humble servant. But if you continue to cry out, one of two misfortunes will befall us: either your honour and fair name will be tarnished, or you will be the cause of your death and mine. Therefore, dear girl of my heart, do not at one and the same time stain your own reputation and imperil both our lives.'

While Fortunio was thus speaking, Doralice was weeping bitterly, her presence of mind completely overthrown by this frightening declaration. The young man, seeing how terrified she was, went on addressing her in words so gentle and persuasive as to have melted a heart of stone. Won by his words and tender manner, she at last softened towards him and was pacified. Meanwhile, seeing how handsome he was in face and how strong and well knit in body and limb compared to the ugliness and deformity of the Saracen, she felt again the torment of bestowing herself upon the latter should he gain the victory in the tournament. While this thought was passing through her mind, the young man said to her, 'Dearest heart, if I had the means, I would willingly enter the jousts to tilt on your behalf, for if I venture, I'm sure to win the prize that belongs to the victor.'

Whereupon the damsel said in reply, 'If only this were to happen, be assured I would give myself to you, and you alone.' And seeing what a well-disposed youth he was and how ardent he was in her cause, she brought out a great quantity of gems and a heavy purse of gold urging him to take them. These Fortunio accepted with his heart full of joy, inquiring of her what clothing she wished him to wear in the lists on the next day. 'Of white satin,' she replied, and he did just as she had commanded.

On the following day, clad in polished armour over which he wore a surcoat of white satin richly embroidered with the finest gold and studded with jewels most delicately carved, Fortunio rode into the great square, a stranger to all who were present there. He was mounted on a powerful and fiery charger which was caparisoned and decked in the same colours as its rider. The crowd was already assembled to witness the grand spectacle of the tournament and as soon as they caught sight of the mysterious new champion with his lance in hand and ready for the fray, they were lost in admiration of so brave a sight. Then everyone began to inquire of his neighbour, 'Ah, who can this knight be in such splendid array that no man knows and who rides so gallantly into the lists?'

Having entered the tournament, Fortunio called upon his rival to advance, whereupon the two champions, lowering the points of their trusty lances, rushed one upon the other like two uncaged lions. But Fortunio dealt his stroke so adroitly upon the Saracen's head that the latter was driven right over the crupper of his horse and fell dead upon the bare earth, mangled and broken like a glass thrown against a wall. No matter who went up against him that day, Fortunio always came away the winner. The damsel was elated by this happy turn of events and kept her eyes steadily fixed on him in deepest admiration, thanking God in her heart for having thus graciously delivered her from the bondage of the Saracen, all the while praying to Him that this brave youth might be the final victor.

When evening had come, Doralice was called to supper with the rest of the court, but she declined their request, instead ordering them to bring certain rich foods and delicate wines to her chamber, feigning to have no hunger for the moment, but that she would eat later on should her appetite by chance return. Then, having locked herself in her room and opened the window, she watched with ardent desire for the coming of her lover. When he had gained entry by the same means he had used the previous day, they supped together joyfully. Then Fortunio asked her in what fashion she wished him to array himself on the morrow, and she answered, 'You must wear green satin all embroidered with the finest thread of silver and gold, and your horse in the same manner.'

On the following morning, Fortunio appeared attired as Doralice had directed, and having duly presented himself in the square at the appointed time, he entered the lists and proved himself to be as valiant a champion as on the day before. So great was the admiration of the people at his prowess that the shout went up with one voice that he had most worthily won the gracious princess for his bride.

Once again as the night approached, the princess, full of joyous expectation, made the same pretext for excusing herself from supper as she had made the day before. Then, locking the door of her chamber and opening the window, she awaited the valorous Fortunio and supped most pleasantly with him. Upon asking once more the colours he should wear the following day, she answered, 'A surcoat of crimson satin, all worked and embroidered with gold and pearls, and the trappings of your horse as well, because tomorrow I'll dress myself in the same manner.'

'Lady,' replied Fortunio, 'if by any chance I should delay somewhat in making my entry into the lists, don't be astonished, for I shall not be late without good cause.'

The third day being come, and the hour of the jousts, all the spectators awaited the outcome of the momentous strife with the utmost of anticipation, but by reason of the inexhaustible valour of the gallant and mysterious champion, there was no opponent found to enter the lists against him, while he himself, for some hidden reason, did not appear. After a time the spectators grew impatient at his absence and began to utter insults. Even though Doralice had been warned by Fortunio himself that his arrival might well be delayed, she was overcome by so much anxiety that she fainted and tumbled to the ground. But as soon as she heard that the unknown knight was advancing into the great square, her failing senses began to revive.

Fortunio was clad in a rich and sumptuous garb, with the trappings of his horse made of the finest cloth all embroidered with shining rubies, emeralds, sapphires, and great pearls, which all agreed was sufficient, more than sufficient, to purchase a kingdom. As soon as Fortunio came into the lists, everyone began to shout, 'Long live the unknown knight!' and applauded vigorously. Then the jousting began. Fortunio once more carried himself so valiantly that he brought to earth all who dared oppose him and so won the victory. When he had descended from his noble horse, the chief men of the town carried him aloft on their shoulders into the presence of the king to the sound of trumpets and all other kinds of musical instruments, shouting all the while so loudly that it reached the heavens. When they had taken off his helmet and his shining armour, the king beheld a proper and becoming young man. Then he called his daughter into his presence and betrothed them forthwith and celebrated the nuptials with the greatest pomp, keeping open table at the court for the space of a month.

After Fortunio had lived for some while with his fair wife, he was seized one day with the thought that he was playing the part of an unworthy sluggard in thus passing his days in indolence, merely counting the hours as they sped by in the manner of fools and of those who make nothing of their lives. So he made up his mind to go abroad into regions where he might find scope and recognition for his valour. After preparing a galley and taking aboard a large treasure given to him by his father-in-law, he took leave of his wife, embarked, and set sail. Wafted by gentle and favourable breezes, Fortunio advanced into the Atlantic Ocean. But before he had gone more than five or six leagues, there arose from the waves the most beautiful siren that had ever been seen. Singing softly, she made her approach. Fortunio, who was leaning over the side of the ship and listening to her song, presently fell asleep, and while he slept, the siren drew him gently from where he lay. Then bearing him into her arms, she sank with him headlong into the depths of the sea. After trying to save him, but in vain, the mariners broke out into loud lamentation. Weeping and despairing, they decked the galley with black ensigns and returned to the unhappy Odescalco to tell him of the terrible mischance that had befallen them during their voyage. When the sad news was brought to them, the king and Doralice, with the entire city, were overwhelmed with the deepest grief and put on the black garments of bereavement.

At the time of Fortunio's departure, Doralice was with child, and when the day of her delivery was come, she gave birth to a beautiful boy, who was gently and carefully nurtured until he came to be two years of age. At this time, the sad and despairing Doralice, who had always brooded over her unhappy fate in losing the company of her beloved husband, began to abandon all hope of ever seeing him again. So she, like a brave and great-souled woman, resolved to put her fortune to the test and go seek him upon the deep, even though the king her father would not consent to let her depart. For her voyage she had an armed galley prepared, well fitted for such a purpose, and she took with her three apples, each one a masterpiece of handicraft, of which one was fashioned out of brass, another of silver, and the last of fine gold. Then, having taken leave of her father, she went on board with her child and sailed away into the open sea before a prosperous wind.

Sailing over calm waters, this sad lady requested of the mariners to take her to the very spot where her husband had been carried off by the siren, to which they agreed. When the vessel had been brought to the exact place, the child began to cry fretfully and in no manner would he be pacified by his mother's endearments. So she gave him the apple which was made of brass to appease him. While the child was sporting with it, he was seen by the siren, who, coming near the galley and lifting her head out of the foamy waves, said to Doralice, 'Lady, give me that apple, for I have the greatest longing for it.' But the princess answered that she would not give it to her because it was her child's toy. 'If you will give it to me,' said the siren, 'I will show you the husband you have lost as far as his breast.' Doralice, when she heard these words, at once took the apple from the child and gave it courteously to the siren, because she longed to get sight of her husband. The siren was faithful to her promise and after a little time brought Fortunio to the surface of the sea and showed him as far as the breast to Doralice as a reward for the gift of the apple before plunging with him once more into the depths of the ocean and disappearing from sight.

After watching all this most attentively, Doralice longed even more to see her husband again. Not knowing what to do or say, she sought comfort in the caresses of her child, and when the little one began to cry once more, the mother gave it the silver apple. Again the siren was on the watch and spied the silver apple in the child's hand. Raising her head above the waves, she begged Doralice to give her the apple, but she shrugged her shoulders saying that it served to divert the child and could not be spared. Whereupon the siren said, 'If you will give this apple, which is far more beautiful than the other, I promise I will show you your husband as far as his knees.' Poor Doralice, who was now consumed with desire to see her beloved husband again, put her love for him before even that which she bore her child and cheerfully handed the apple to the siren, True to her promise, once more she brought Fortunio to the surface, exhibiting him to Doralice as far as his knees before plunging again beneath the waves.

Meanwhile, the unhappy Doralice watched in silence, having no notion how she might liberate her husband. She caught up her child in her arms and sought comfort for herself in attempting to still his weeping. The child held in memory the fair apple he had been playing with, so that to calm his crying, his mother gave him the fine golden apple. When the covetous siren, still watching the galley, saw this apple and perceived that it was much fairer than either of the others, she at once demanded it as a gift from Doralice. She begged long and persistently and at last made a promise to the princess that in return for the gift of this apple, she would bring Fortunio once more into the light and show him from head to foot. So Doralice took the apple from the boy, in spite of his protests, and gave it to the water nixie. Coming quite close to the galley, the siren, bearing Fortunio upon her back and rising somewhat above the surface of the water, showed him to her from head to foot. Now, as soon as Fortunio felt that he was quite clear of the water and resting free upon the back of the siren, he was filled with great joy in his heart. Without hesitating for a moment, he cried out, 'Ah, if only I were an eagle.' Scarcely had he ceased speaking when he was forthwith transformed into a bird, and taking flight, he alighted on the mast of the ship. From there, before the eyes of all the crew, he descended into the ship and returned to his proper shape, kissing and embracing his wife and child, and greeting the mariners one and all.

Rejoicing at the rescue of Fortunio, they set sail back to King Odescalco's kingdom, and no sooner were they entered into the harbour than they began to play upon trumpets, nakers, drums, and other musical instruments. The king, hearing the noise, was greatly amazed and waited to find out the cause of it all with the utmost suspense. Shortly thereafter, a herald came before him and announced to the king how his dear daughter had arrived with her husband, Fortunio. When they were disembarked from the galley, they all made their way to the royal palace, where they were welcomed with triumphant celebrations.

After some days had passed, Fortunio left for his old home and there, after changing himself into a wolf, he devoured Alchia his adoptive mother and Valentino her son in revenge for the injuries they had done to him. Then, after he had returned to his rightful shape, he mounted his horse and rode back to his father-in-law's kingdom. There with Doralice his dear wife, he lived in peace for many years to the great delight of them both.

As soon as Alteria had brought her moving and sympathetic story to an end, the Signora asked her to set forth her enigma, which command she obeyed without delay:

> Far from this our land doth dwell
> One who by turns is fair or fell;
> Springing from a twofold root,
> One part woman, one part brute,
> Now like beauty's fairest jewel,
> Now a monster fierce and cruel,
> Sweetest song on vocal breath,
> To lead men down to shameful death.

This notable riddle of Alteria's was answered in divers fashions by the listeners, some giving one interpretation and some another, but not one of them came upon its exact meaning. Therefore, seeing they could not solve it, she said, 'Gentlefolks all, the real subject of my enigma is none other than the siren, which is fabled to dwell in the deep sea. She is very fair to look upon, for her head, breast, body, and arms are those of a beautiful damsel, while all the rest of her form is scaly like a fish, and in her nature she is cunning and cruel. So sweetly she sings that mariners by her song are soothed to slumber, and while they sleep she plunges them into the sea.' One and all commended Alteria for her pleasant and subtle interpretation. Raising her bright face, she duly thanked all present for listening so graciously to her tale and returned to her place. This done, the Signora asked Eritrea to follow in due order with her story, which she began in these words.

III.4 Commentary

This is another of Straparola's grand proto-fairy tales featuring a conflation of motifs with individual histories so extensive that to pursue each in terms of its cognates and analogues would again constitute a community (or an 'ocean') of tales. In placing the story of Fortunio within that community of narrative parts, there are the conventional questions of propinquity and influence in relation to the vagaries of transmission and accretion during a period from which a scant few literary transcriptions and adaptations remain outside of Straparola's own pages. That sparseness is nearly absolute where the full configuration of parts making the 'Fortunio' tradition is concerned (ATU 316). But such a community seems reasonable to assume, given the antiquity of the contributing motifs. Moreover, the large number of cognate tales collected in the nineteenth century throughout Europe lends credence to the belief that a version of this tale served Straparola as a template in the sixteenth century. That belief is strengthened by the iterative and formulaic nature of the telling and by the curious lapses in story logic characteristic of the oral tradition, as when Fortunio arrives on the third day of the tournament and no one is brave enough to confront him, yet he puts in another good day of jousting and comes out the victor, or when Doralice, denied permission to travel by her father, makes secret preparations for her voyage, yet takes leave of him when she sets sail, not to mention the repetition of the relationships between the characters. This is surely Straparola faithfully following his source rather than forgetting himself or imitating oral style right down to its lapses. The only alternative is to grant sole authorship of this story to Straparola, necessitating that he built it exclusively from recombinant folk motifs, and that he single-handedly launched this story tradition in the oral culture to follow throughout the Eurasian world. That would appear to be the less likely of the two scenarios.

One feature of the tale is the folk motif of the longed-for child by an aging couple, as in the 'pig prince' group (II.1), but with a trajectory of its own. There is first an adopted child followed by a natural child, then the breakdown of the bond between the boys by the discovery of their contrasting status. Fortunio, 'the bastard,' feels the injury, seeks his true origins, and sets off into the world, cursed by his adoptive mother to fall prey to the allurements of a mermaid.[68] The second major motif is the encounter of the animals in dispute over the distribution of their fallen prey. It is a stock folk tale motif with an extensive history relating to the many stories featuring animal helpers. For having settled their argument,

68 For those seeking to create a mental geography for this tale, it begins in Lombardy and proceeds West towards Polonia, which is counterintuitive if the country is imagined. Rather, Polonia is a city belonging to the Matter of France, mentioned by Andrea da Barberino (1370–1431) in his *I reali di francia* (The royal house of France), ed. Giuseppe Vandelli et al. (Bari: Laterza, 1947), first published in 1491 and dealing with adventures from the age of Charlemagne and Roland.

each creature – wolf, eagle, and ant – offers to the hero the power to transform himself into its form (ATU 665).[69] This feature is redolent of Livoretto's acquisition of animal helpers (III.2), but with the added dimension of self-metamorphosis (see the Lattanzio group, VIII.4). The animals, in effect, display a gratitude which Fortunio refuses to grant to his adoptive parents, for it is as a wolf that he will round out the tale's essential symmetry by returning to settle scores with his mother and her birth son. Such magical powers will likewise enable him to win a princess and escape the clutches of a water nixie, thereby holding the subsequent episodes together under a common mother's curse and a common set of magical powers. These are precisely the elements of the folk tale – the opening curse and the helpful companions – that will be foregrounded in the fairy tales to follow with evil curses and the restorative powers of the good fairies.

The hero is now equipped to arrive in a foreign city, the third major folk motif, where he will compete for the prize princess through a combination of martial prowess, self-transformational magic, and gallantry. As in most bride-winning fairy tales, the hero either performs remarkable feats or solves riddles, with or without meeting the princess in advance. (This is not always the case, however, as in Pietro's rise as the 'lazy-boy' (III.1), or Constantino's fortune (XI.1) gained entirely through the agency of his cat.) Fortunio might very well have won his princess simply by jousting for her, as in some versions at lower mimetic levels in the trajectory from myth to realism. But Straparola arranges for the hero to meet the princess by soaring into her room as an eagle before returning to his human shape. Nothing could be less realistic than Fortunio hiding from the girl's father by crawling under her hair as an ant. Yet this is the very scene that Jean de Mailly develops as a tender, delicate, and sentimental exchange at a level of far greater social realism for his French readers in the age of *préciosité* and the salons. At the same time, as with bride-winning in *The Merchant of Venice*, Straparola's tale preserves the tri-partite design and the social rituals of selection by riddle, fortune, and gaming skills. Victory in the tournament over such adversaries as the swarthy Saracen, representing for the princess the horrors of a booty marriage, is a telling, quasi-allegorical episode. Fortunio secures the

69 Stith Thompson, in *The Folktale* (Berkeley: University of California Press, [1946], 1977), p. 58, speaks of the metamorphosis into animal shapes, a motif he identifies closely with 'the grateful dead' stories, although it does not pertain to Straparola's 'Bertuccio' in the present collection (XI.2).

marriage by martial prowess; nevertheless, as a sociable hero, he demonstrates a profile of manly gallantry in the field and the boudoir. This was of precious concern in later years to the likes of Mme. d'Aulnoy, who repeatedly fanticized her metro-man as hero.

After the completion of the romance in union and fecundity, the matter of the mother's curse still remains. That malediction is tantamount to an assault upon her adopted son's marriage through the enticements of an enchanted mistress, the proverbial mermaid whose irresistible singing waylays the vulnerable male. Only through the cunning and constancy of his wife, determined to protect her household and her maternal entitlements, is he released from this insidious rival. Such a curse is quite particular in having come from the boy's own mother. Fortunio will thus be exposed to a siren who will capture him and keep him for years beneath the surface of the sea. This final episode, with a long, continuous, and diversified history as a folk motif, entails a seductress, an interrupted marriage, and the absence of a beloved spouse under circumstances variously psychological and symbolic. We are challenged to think through what it means for the princess, with her young child, to go in quest of her missing husband, armed with a stratagem apt to deceive a mermaid. According to this story type, typically three precious objects of incremental value are handed over to the water sprite in exchange for more complete glimpses of the hero's body until at last, clear of the water, he can trick the nixie and escape by self-transformation into a bird. There is a fifth and final motif, transformed or entirely abandoned in nearly all subsequent tellings, in which Fortunio employs his options as a wolf to return to his home city to devour in revenge both his mother and his offending brother. That Straparola retained this harsh motif of fell justice is further assurance that he is working in literal fashion from folk material, for writers trained up in the Italian *novella* were not inclined to replicate such matter without a sense of obligation to a wonder source. These four or five principal elements constitute the story type of 'Fortunio' and position Straparola's tale as the earliest among the many on record that contain the same configuration or formula of events.

Interpreting these motifs in relation to the human condition, the perceived truths of which are thought to have played a role in their survival as folk motifs, is always an engaging but speculative enterprise. The secrets of birth, legitimacy, sibling rivalry, initiation rites, kindness to animals, bride questing, marriage, rival women and the challenge to the nurturing nuclear family, along with instincts of revenge against hated family members, once they are identified as the informing instincts behind emblematic constructions, are nearly self explanatory. There are, of course, questions to ponder, such as the peculiar curse of the mother, namely that her son later fall prey to a seductive women; is she knowingly wishing devastation upon the boy's own chances to perpetuate his bloodline? Or is the nature of the curse a mere precondition interjected by an innovative storyteller in order to splice the virtually independent mermaid tale upon the completed tale of bride-winning? The 'rising' bride-winning tale ending in marriage and eternal happiness is, after all, of a different order than nixie seduction plots leading to long-term separation, questing spouses, imprisonment as though in expiation of former faults, and the nostalgic reunion after years lost and beyond recovery, as in the Psyche myth. The bittersweet feelings arising from this innovative combination are difficult to define. But the sub-motifs are perfectly clear. There is the hero on an initiatory quest who proves his sensibilities in gaining the gratitude of the animals, who demonstrates his self control in the bedroom of the beloved, and who masters his physical prowess in the games. His A+ performance as the complete gentleman wins the princess. More emblematically, as a child of ambiguous origins, he 'relegitimates' himself at the same time that he actualizes his fairy tale potential in the marriage – an anxiety that later tellers suppress through a recognition plot that restores the hero to his birth parents as the lost child of a king. Straparola's tale in that regard is more provocative in leaving the birth issue and the boy's status unresolved, as well as the reasons for the boy's hostility towards his adoptive mother and her son culminating in his metamorphosis into a devouring wolf. As for the hermeneutic potential of water nixie tales, I refer the reader to Marina Warner's examination of the motif with regard to such tales as Andersen's *The Little Mermaid* in which a figure, once a demon and seducer of sailors with her alluring song, struggles in her silence to become an angel, yet remains aligned with women who represent a seductive dream and a fatal attraction while in herself she is womanhood captive, oppressed, and physiologically ambiguous.[70] Mermaid stories are always about who they are, what they represent, their native element, and what they seek in luring men to an enforced and alternative life beneath the sea. At the same time, trips below water may indicate a process of psychological self-

70 Marina Warner, *From the Beast to the Blonde: On Fairy Tales and Their Tellers* (London: Vintage, 1995), pp. 396–408.

discovery for the hero. For Edzard Storck, the two women represent the archetypal struggle between the spiritual and civilized forces embodied in the wife and the dark, elemental forces of the nixie, while in more immediate social terms it is the story of a wife's struggle against the siren woman to preserve her marriage.[71]

By definition, the story of Fortunio has something to do remotely with sirens in Homer and jousting as in Boccaccio's *Teseida*. The one is about seduction and self discipline and the other is about competition for a bride through combat, both of them representing archetypes redeployed in Straparola's story. But a long investigation into potential sources has produced only remote treatments of the individual motifs, and nothing like the compound formula intrinsic to the folk tale. A century and a half prior to the publication of the *Piacevoli notti*, Ser Giovanni, in *The Pecorone* (IX.2), tells a long episodic story we might provisionally name 'Arrighetto and Lena, the king of Aragon's daughter,' in which a beautiful princess, although closely guarded by a royal father bent on refusing all suitors, is nevertheless looked upon by the eligible princes of the chivalric world as a prize catch.[72] The son of the German emperor makes a plan to get himself inside the girl's private quarters by enclosing himself inside a great golden eagle sent to her city on purpose to be sold in a shop just opposite the palace. It goes without saying that the object ends up in the princess's apartments. That the bird is an eagle may be coincidental, but that the suitor is chased back inside the bird for refuge when the girl cries out in dismay upon seeing a strange man approaching her has motivic specificity. She is scolded by her household staff and told to cease her false alarms, forcing her to deal with her suitor and to test his civility, just as Doralice is told by her father to cease her outcries, thereby allowing Fortunio to identify himself and express his honest devotion. Straparola may indeed have modified this segment of his fairy tale in the image of Ser Giovanni's wooing scene. But this is far from a complete source. Thereafter, the tales go their separate ways, for Ser Giovanni's lovers do not plan their coordinated wardrobe for the final day of the tournament, as in Straparola, but elope by sea, bringing the whole

71 Edzard Storck, *Alte und neue Schöpfung in den Märchen der Brüder Grimm* (Bietigheim/Württ: Turm Verlag, 1977), pp. 126–30.

72 *The Pecorone*, trans. W.G. Waters, illus. E.R. Hughes, 3 vols. (London: Society of Bibliophiles, 1898), vol. II, pp. 34–69; or (London: Lawrence & Bullen, 1897), IX.2, pp. 113–26.

of Europe into a massive war near Vienna over the 'abduction' of this willing maiden.[73]

Further tales predating Straparola with promising affinities to that of 'Fortunio' are tellingly few, except in the most generic of ways, such as Marie de France's *Lai of Yonec,* in which a lover from a neighbouring realm flies up to the window of a married woman incarcerated in a tower in the form of a bird, there to enjoy her until the suspicious husband sets a trap from which the creature escapes with grave injuries. For real cognates, one must turn to the folk tale collections of the nineteenth century where the Straparolan type in part or in whole is well represented. Emmanuel Cosquin includes two tales with clear connections in his *Contes populaires de Lorraine.* In 'Les dons des trios animaux' (The gifts of the three animals), three brothers set out on the road of life and soon part ways.[74] He who takes the middle way encounters a lion, an eagle, and an ant disputing their respective portions of a dead donkey. The launching tale has been reduced to this bare formula, but serves to take the cobbler protagonist to the animal feud which, in resolving, wins him their gratitude and their magic powers. Tokens of the kind encountered in the story of Livoretto (III.2) reappear: the lion gives a chin whisker, the eagle a feather, and the ant a leg, each one with transformational power. The hero's task is to liberate a princess kept by an ogre and a seven-headed beast (see Cesarino X.3). He enters the room of the princess as an ant and in becoming a man causes her considerable alarm. But in due course she instructs him in how to cut off the heads and to find the three eggs that will slay the giant (because one contains his soul), as well as generate a coach containing garments with which to cut a fine figure when they arrive back in the realm. The fairy tale ending seems nigh, except that the hero has a rival for the princess who, by kicking him into the water, is thereafter able to claim the hero's deeds as his own, meanwhile terrifying the princess into compliance. The mermaid is replaced by a whale, who is induced to reveal, incrementally, the body of the hero by a musician who plays on his violin for longer and longer periods of time – showing first the head, then down to the waist, then to the thighs, and finally the entire body, whereupon the hero assumes

73 Worthy of mention is that both stories parallel the courting of the princess in the story of Kamar al-Akmar, or 'The Magic Tale of the Ebony Horse,' nights 414–32 of *The Arabian Nights.*

74 *Contes populaires de Lorraine,* 2 vols. (Paris: F. Vieweg, 1886; reprint, Marseille: Lafitte, 1978), no. 15, vol. I, pp. 166–9.

his eagle form and makes his escape. This princess, tellingly, does not go in search of her spouse. Now with the gift of a gold-cornered handkerchief the hero reclaims his beloved and the king burns the pretender. How different the tale must seem with an ogre and hydra conquest instead of a joust, and with a whale in the place of a mermaid, and yet the three core elements – the grateful animal helpers, the bride quest, and the abduction by a sea creature – are sequentially intact and structurally paralleled, despite the substitutions.[75] This is a story in the Straparolan tradition, but which in its details and texture is quite far removed from 'Fortunio.' We are thus challenged to imagine a stemma by which this story and Straparola's might be connected to a common source.

In another, tellingly named 'Fortuné' (No. 50) and possessed of very particular echoes, the hero encounters the wolf, the eagle, and the ant and settles their argument, as in Straparola. From them he gains his shape-shifting powers. This princess, however, is held underground by a lion, at least most of the time, for on occasion she negotiates visits to see her sisters (as Beauty does in 'Beauty and the Beast'). When the hero appears, having entered as an ant, the princess cries out and brings Lion running (just as the king comes running at the cries of Doralice), but the hero has already recovered his ant disguise (precisely as in Straparola). So far so good, but this story ends rather abruptly when the hero simply goes in quest of the egg that will slay the lion as soon as it is broken over his brow, a coup administered by the princess. The return to marriage and silence ever after requires but one more sentence. Cosquin makes his observation, however, that the story is the same as that employed by Straparola and that a common prototype emerges through the retrofitting of the implicit substitutions, a thesis further intimated by the

75 A closely related tale, 'Le corps sans ame, ou le lion, la pie, et la fourmi,' in *Contes français*, ed. E. Henry Carnoy (Paris: Ernest Leroux, 1885), no. 8, pp. 275–80, tells of a boy who settles the spat of the bickering animals, gains from each the power of self-metamorphosis into their respective forms, and goes in quest of the princess held in thrall by the seven-headed monster Corps-sans-Ame (body without soul). He runs through his forms to dispatch the monster and deliver the princess, but is nearly drowned by his rival. He saves himself by turning into a bird, just as the hero of the present story. A wedding in the making with the wrong groom is interrupted by the arrival of Kiou-Cher the hero, who is claimed by the princess. The name Corps-sans-Ame suggests the link with stories in which a quest for the egg containing the monster's soul must be carried out, as well as with those in which the bird and the ant forms are employed respectively to secretly visit the princess in her room and to escape notice once there.

common name of the two protagonists.[76] The implications are that the name was also common to the folk source employed by Straparola, along with the types of animals, and that through three centuries of accidents and variations, these features, together with the signature configuration of episodes, persisted from narrator to narrator down to the mid-nineteenth century. The only alternative is that Straparola's own tale influenced the later oral tradition.

The same configuration appears in one of the legendary tales collected by Campbell in the West Highlands (no. 4, var. 1). In this version a father promises his son to a siren, much as the mother in Straparola curses her son to be abducted by one. Thus the tale has a similar course to run, but in very different colours.[77] In the interim, the boy settles a dispute between a lion, a wolf, and a falcon, thereby gaining transformational powers. He then delivers a princess from a dragon and marries her – an already familiar substitution. Later he is lured by an undine, and it is his loyal spouse who must surmise his fate, seek him out, and play her harp on the shore in order to see him brought to the surface in incremental fashion until he flies away as a falcon. Only then does the hero go on a quest to find the egg that will liberate his princess abducted in turn by

76 *Contes populaires de Lorraine* (Paris: F. Vieweg, 1887), vol. II, pp. 166–77. There was also an extensive tradition of such stories in Spain and Portugal, as reported by Aurelio M. Espinosa in *Cuentos populares españoles*, 3 vols. (Madrid: S. Aguirre, 1946). See, for example, nos. 141 and 142, two versions of 'La princessa encantada' (The enchanted princess), vol. III, pp. 33–43. In a version corresponding to that found in Cosquin (I.15), the hero achieves the power of self-transformation into the forms of the animals he has helped, thereby enabling him to slay the beast with the seven heads and rescue the princess. This is Type III of the tale. In the Vth type, the hero conquers only by finding the egg that determines the life of the monster. He cites Straparola III.4 as a cognate tale to Type III, along with several others.

77 J.F. Campbell, "The Sea-Maiden," in *Popular Tales of the West Highlands, Orally Collected*, 2 vols. (Edinburgh: Birlinn, 1994), vol. I, pp. 147–72. This work was first printed in 1890 by Alexander Gardner and Paisley. The story is told in Gaelic about a son promised to a mermaid at birth. It is a long and complex tale of heroic battles with beasts, abductions, and a double quest for the hero from underwater captors. The first is a water beast who reveals the husband's body by degrees to his wife who is standing on the shore enticing the creature with jewelry. The second concerns the mermaid, who is slain by the hero's brothers who go in search of him when his tree begins to wither in evidence of his distress. The first two brothers fail and are captured in their turn, but the third succeeds, rescues them all, and a substantial treasure as well. This story performs the same motif as found in Straparola, but the tale as a whole shows many accretions and variations. Campbell offers several variant tales in his annotations.

the same siren. Therein lies a most strange variation that cannot delay us here, but it is fascinating to see the re-admixture of elements and the doubling of episodes which may inspire ever-evolving readings. Straparola's story type was current as far as the edge of the Hebrides.[78]

It was also known among the East Indians, but of the story collected by Maive Stokes in the nineteenth century, its age and origins are difficult to determine. In the tale entitled 'How the Raja's Son Won the Princess Labam,' the young hero not only acquires the help of ants and tigers whom he has befriended along the way, but also the services of a magic flying bed, a water-producing bowl, and a beating stick.[79] With these he goes courting, secretly enters the princess's bedroom, and leaves mysterious gifts behind, such as betel leaves and a shawl. To win the princess, however, he had 'impossible' tasks to perform, such as getting oil from mustard seed and slaying two demons, all of which he accomplishes with the help of his animal friends. At the end, the young couple returns to the hero's homeland with the magic bag, bowl, bed, and stick.

Further instances in which settling a dispute among the animals provides the means for winning a princess and escaping some creature of the underworld through the tri-partite exposure of the hero's body in anticipation of his flight include the version in Heinrich Pröhle's *Kinder- und Volksmärchen.*[80] The protagonist, able to convert himself into a lion, an eagle, or an ant, employs all three in winning his bride and escaping the clutches of a mermaid. In a variant tale from Epirus, the hero encounters the same animals, rescues his princess, but is swallowed by a drakos in a fountain and must be liberated in steps by his wife.[81]

---

78 For parallels such as these, Campbell thought Straparola must have been known early at the Scottish court, and that David Rizzio is a likely candidate to have carried him north.

79 Maive Stokes, *Indian Fairy Tales*, annotations by Mary Stokes (London: Ellis & White, 1880), no. 22, pp. 153–63.

80 'Der Mann ohne Leib,' in *Kinder- und Volksmärchen* (Leipzig, 1853; reprint, Hildesheim: Olms, 1975), no. 6, pp. 24–9.

81 Johann Georg von Hahn, *Griechische und albanesische Märchen*, 2 vols. (Leipzig: Wilhelm Engelmann, 1864), no. 5, vol. I, pp. 85–9. This tale presents a fascinating compilation of three distinct narratives artfully conjoined. It begins with the miraculous birth of a son promised to a dragon, resembling the curse of the boy's mother in the present tale. After settling an argument among the animals, he gains the ability to metamorphose himself into a lion, an eagle, or ant. He fights battles for the king and marries the princess. 'Dragon slaying' elements appear (as in X.3) when he is sent to do battle with the water dragon. Usually this episode precedes the marriage (as in the Cesarino, Saint George tales), but here replaces the

M.R. Köhler collected another in the Upper Palatinate in which the hero is promised to an undine from the outset, as in the Scots tale. His helpers are a bear, a fox, a falcon, and an ant, and in place of golden apples or orbs, the princess liberates her man with a golden jewel, a comb, a ring, and a slipper.[82]

'La sirène et l'épervier' (The siren and the sparrow hawk) collected by F.-M. Luzel in lower Brittany in the nineteenth century is remarkable for the similarity of its motivic and episodic design to the tale of 'Fortunio.'[83] Throughout this long tale, Fanch, the fisherman's son, is destined to encounter a dangerous siren from whom his parents, in their need, had accepted both abundant fish stocks and gold. On his outbound journey of initiation, the boy comes across a wolf, a bumblebee, and a sparrow hawk fighting over a dead horse. Therein consists the conventional motif of the acquisition of animal helpers, for in solving their dispute, they grant to the boy the power to assume their forms. As he

---

mermaid episode. As in the 'Livoretto' group, as well as the 'dragon slaying' group, the hero is replaced by an imposter who is accepted by the king. But the princess knows her man and, like the devoted wife of the present tale, she goes to the dragon's well with her magic apples. With these gifts, she wins the sight of incrementally larger protions of her husband's emerging body. The protagonist now resorts to his animal forms, first that of an ant, and then of the eagle in order to fly away with the princess. This tale reveals the embedded resemblance of III.4 to X.3 and VII.5: the magic births, the helper animals, the slaying of dragons, and the ultimate enchantment of the hero liberated by brothers or his beloved wife.

82 *Orient und Occident* (Munich: Georg Müller, 1918), vol. II, p. 117–18. Another tale containing these characteristics is 'The Cobbler's Lad,' in *Danish Fairy Tales*, ed. by Svend Grundtvig (London: G.G. Harrap & Co., 1914), pp. 148–65. This hero learns the language of the animals, settles a dispute over food, and wins the power to metamorphose himself into any of their forms. As a falcon he flies to Spain where he meets a princess promised to a goblin if ever the sun should shine on her before a certain age. She lives in a castle with north-facing windows. The boy flies into her bedroom, hides from searchers by becoming an ant, and remains beside her as a pampered white falcon. He returns as Prince Falcon to fight in the tournament with his fine trappings. Now it is the princess who is abducted and the cobbler must assume his many magical forms to find her. At this juncture, the story links with others, for he finds her in a castle inside a mountain combing the goblin's hair with his head in her lap. She must find the secret to his powers – again it is an egg containing his soul – this one in a lake in Poland, and send her lover on the liberating quest. Many adventures follow and the ending writes itself.

83 F.M. Luzel, ed. *Contes populaires de la Basse-Bretagne,* 3 vols. (Paris: G.P. Maisonneuve & Larose [1887], 1967), vol. II, pp. 381–418.

continues on his way he wins, moreover, the help of the geese through flattery and the ants by sharing his lunch. Coming to an enchanted castle, Fanch encounters three witches who assign him tasks in which failure constitutes death, as in the Livoretto group. But the queen of the geese helps him find the silver ball while the queen of the ants summons her troops to separate grain according to their kinds. The bumblebee then helps him pick out the youngest and most beautiful of the three witches in a pitch-dark room – a variation on a motif that appears in Straparola's tale of 'Guerrino' (V.1). Through these feats, he delivers three Spanish princesses from their fates and is offered one in marriage in gratitude, but he continues on his way. Thereafter, he goes to Paris, falls in love with the king's daughter, enters her room as a sparrow hawk, returns to himself, gets the girl pregnant, performs his transformation before the king, and wins the girl largely through his intimidating powers of magic. A former suitor, a Turkish prince, is not charmed by the outcome, however. He lures Fanch to the seaside and shoves him over a cliff to the long-awaiting mermaid and to a sojourn of two years beneath the sea. Granted permission to swim, by degrees, closer and closer to the surface, he manages at last to put his face through the surface of the waves and convert himself to a sparrow hawk one last time – the motivic equivalent of the ritual liberation through gifts granted to the siren by a pining wife. As in many other such escape tales, he arrives in the home country just in time to impede the royal wedding. Fanch's rival is then done to death in an oven and they all live happily ever after. The addition of the rival who threatens the princess and claims the hero's deeds as his own links this tale to that of 'The Gifts of the Three Animals' collected in Lorraine by Cosquin cited above. Overall, it is a faithful structural replay of Straparola's narrative design.[84]

One final representative citation must complete the textual testimonial to the geographical scope and widespread success of this story cluster.

84 There is a parallel situation of extracting bodies held back by the elements in the Nordic tale of 'The Three Princesses of Whiteland.' Rather than give gifts to a mermaid to allow a body to emerge progressively from the waves, the hero must allow himself to be whipped by trolls on three successive nights, each time more fiercely, in order to bring the girls progressively out of the earth where they have been buried up to their necks. The youngest is won for a bride, following the harrowing ordeal – a rather graphic form of male testing in the bride quest. Peter Christen Asbjørnsen, *Popular Tales from the Norse and North German*, ed. George Webbe Dasent (London: Norroena Society, 1907), pp. 203–10.

Angelo de Gubernatis, among the *Novelline di Santo Stefano*, collected a Tuscan tale in which, with the help of the lion, the eagle, and the ant and the ability to assume their shapes, the protagonist slays with an egg the magician holding the princess in thrall – a further example of the many tales in which the magic egg is understood to contain the soul of the villain, whether giant or magician, and which must first be found through the gathering of secret information and through a ritual quest. This hero, rather than being taken to the bottom of the sea by a mermaid, is taken underground and the princess must strategically employ crystal, silver, and golden balls to allow first the head of her husband to emerge, then his body down to the waist, and finally to the feet before he can make his escape as an eagle, as in the present tale.[85] Cosquin makes mention of this tale and opines that it was the same employed in writing the *Piacevoli notti*, which is to say that the Tuscan tale was a direct descendant of the source used by Straparola.[86] Such was his solution to the source question.

The relationship between Straparola's 'Fortunio' and Basile's 'The Enchanted Doe' (The Charmed Hind) in *Lo cunto* or the *Pentamerone* (I.9) is altogether more complex than the relationship between 'Fortunio' and the many nineteeth-century cognates just surveyed, despite the mere eighty years or less that separate them. Just why this is so is usually to be explained either by Basile's creative liberties or by the wide variations separating their respective sources. But here the case may be even more

85 'La fanciulla e il mago' (The girl and the sorcerer), in *Le Novelline di Santo Stefano* (Torino: Negro, 1869), no. 23, pp. 47–8. Mention may be made here of a story collected initially in Liguria that is retold by Italo Calvino in his collection of *Italian Folktales*, trans. George Martin (New York: Pantheon Books, [1956], 1980), no. 6, pp. 18–21. The curious feature, apart from replicating all the familiar parts of the present tale, is that the elements are integrated into a story that contains the adventures of a boy with a horse in the Livoretto tradition. Jack meets the animals arguing over a dead donkey, solves their dispute, and wins their gratitude, but like Fortunio, Jack has shape-shifting powers into a lion, dog, eagle or ant, rather than promises of service. He then sets off to liberate a princess from an ogre, true to versions of both stories, first climbing into her apartment as an ant. His purpose is to gain instruction from the princess about how to kill the ogre by cracking the fatal egg over his brow. Jack's task is rather to go in quest of the magic egg, to slay the giant, and return with the princess. The tale is instructive in showing the migration of story elements and the reconfigurations that link materials into diverse patterns. The tale was first collected by James Bruyn Andrews, *Contes ligures* (Paris: E. Leroux, 1892; reprint, Marseille: Laffitte Reprints, 1979), no. 46.

86 Emmanuel Cosquin, *Contes populaires de Lorraine* (Paris: Vieweg, 1886), vol. II, p. 131.

strained. Basile appears to be on the same generic page in this story, at least at the outset, for his contains a complex launching episode that incorporates a birth tale, the early companionship of two boys, and the flight of the base-born son, as in Straparola. This queen is made pregnant by enchantment using a cooked dragon's heart so potent in its powers of fertility that the beautiful virgin who prepared it and the furniture in the room become fruitful and multiply. (The notion of reproductive furniture is hilarious.) Both the queen and the serving maiden give birth to boys nearly identical in appearance and raise them together until the queen grows jealous of the prince's love for his friend. She then attempts to kill Canneloro by striking him with a heated iron, leaving a tell-tale mark that serves as identification in the future. The hero, without exposing the queen's deed, immediately sets off for the world of adventure. It all seems like a variation on the opening of the 'Fortunio' group: the unequal births, insults and hostility over the differentiated levels, and the hero's escape. But there would seem to be little reason to pursue the tale further. To be sure, this story is one of five or six at the centre of the debate over Basile's dependence upon Straparola and the degree to which the earlier writer's work supplied him with plots and materials. Letterio di Francia in his *Novellistica XVI–XVII secolo* was of the view that Basile knew Straparola inevitably, that at least three of their stories are kin, and that he treated Straparola much as Straparola did Morlini, borrowing from him without acknowledgment.[87] Yet when he comes to the individual stories, such as III.1, V.2, and II.4 in particular, he expresses doubts, and rightly so, for the versions rely upon widely distanced sources. Rather, in all probability, Basile never laid eyes on Straparola's collection. That is surely the case here, for the entire story belongs to 'the three brothers' group, fully illustrated in this collection by the framing elements of 'Cesarino the Dragon Slayer' (X.3), including the life signs denoting the brother in distress, the night spent in bed with his brother's wife with the sword between them, and the liberation of his brother and

87 *Novellistica XVI-XVII secolo* (Milan: F. Vallardi, 1925), p. 372. Luisa Rubini shares this view, that Basile 'hat die PN sicher gekannt' (most certainly knew the *Piacevoli notti*). She lists the ten stories with cognate elements. Arguably, their differences may be accounted for by independent reliance upon local versions of common tales. That copies of the *Piacevoli notti* made their way to Naples is quite conceivable, but that Basile adapted those stories to create his own is far less so. 'Straparola,' in the *Enzyklopädie des Märchens*, ed. Rolf Wilhelm Brednick (Berlin: Walter de Gruyter, 2007), vol. VII, p. 1365.

his animals from captivity, before the final identification of the true husband by the wife. Relating this story to 'Fortunio' is a case of mistaken identity, altogether.[88]

Meanwhile, it is the Germans who specialized in water siren tales, including many that are closely cognate with the formulation employed by Straparola. One of the most accessible is 'Die Nixie im Teich' (The nixie of the millpond) in the famous collection of the Grimm brothers.[89] A miller saddened by indigence encounters a sympathetic nixie in the millpond who asks the cause of his grief and sings to him. He promises to her the most recently born creature in his household. We know it will be his newborn son, creating a destiny tantamount to a curse. Prosperity is received in exchange and things take a happier turn as the boy grows up. But as with all children born or promised to mélusines, this one is instructed never to go near the water. In later years he becomes a huntsman and marries a maiden beautiful and true. A hunting trek, however, leads him to the place of danger, and while washing his hands after the kill, he is drawn into the water. His loyal wife haunts the pond and waits

---

88 All commentators on Basile have had to grapple with the question of his relationship to the matter of the folk and the degree to which he transforms their stories. As Stith Thompson poses the question, how much 'was exerted on Basile by the actual form of the tales when he reworked them in the high-flown style of the *Pentamerone*?' His answer is that we shall probably never know, because there are no folk tales from the period with which to make comparisons. *The Folktale*, p. 459.

89 No. 151 in *Grimm's Complete Fairy Tales* (Garden City, NY: Nelson Doubleday, n.d.), pp. 470–4, but No. 181 in *Kinder- und Hausmärchen* (Göttingen: Dieterich, 1857). The following titles are suggested for readers interested in the German tales concerning nixies and mermaids. Closest to the Grimm brothers' tale is Ludwig Bechstein's 'Der Müller und die Nixe' [*sic*], in *Deutsches Märchenbuch* (Leipzig: Georg Wigand, 1855), pp. 210–15; new ed., *Märchenbuch* (Augsburg: Wettbild, 2008). A classic in the genre is Johann Karl Musäus' 'Die Nymphe des Brunnens,' in *Volksmärchen der Deutschen (1782–87)* (Munich: Winkler Verlag, 1961), pp. 279–325. But in this work the nixie of the fountain is no longer the siren who lures men to their deaths, but a fairy godmother to the little Mathilde, daughter of a Swabian robber baron. The girl's mother is told by the fairy that she will not live to raise her daughter, but that she will replace her, giving the girl a magic apple which will grant to her three wishes during her lifetime. Then even the nixie disappears, leaving the girl to make her way in the world, to marry Graf Konrad, and to endure many hardships in a context of sensibilities worthy of the pre-Romantic age of *Empfindsamkeit*. There are essentially no narrative features corresponding to the siren episode in Straparola. The same is true of Johann Christoph Matthias Reinecke's 'Der Nixen Eingebinde' in his *Eichenblättern* (Gotha: J. Perthes, 1793).

before going in search of the old woman in the mountain cottage where she is given a golden comb with instructions to comb her hair beside the pond before placing the comb at the edge. When the water moves and the comb is taken, her husband's head appears. Further trips up the mountain ensue and more costly gifts are given – a flute, then a golden spinning wheel – until, sufficiently free of the water, the hero leaps to safety. (The objects are reminiscent of those traded for Biancabella's hands and eyes in many of the tales cognate to Straparola's III.3.) The story takes place in a rustic setting and there are no urbane negotiations with the siren, but all the ritual enactments remain clearly intact. In shedding the animal helpers and the fanciful winning of the princess, this folk tale has less of the 'fairy' spirit than Straparola's. Yet even here, the sequence of the pledge to a nixie, the bride quest, and the liberation from the fairy creature of the waters remains in clear evidence (followed by a long coda of separation, life as shepherds, and an eventual bittersweet reunion).

Given the absence of true literary sources and the wide number of survivors of the story type among the 'folk' throughout nineteenth-century Europe, Straparola, in this tale, once again represents the entry point of an entire narrative tradition; he is this story's literary father. Intuition holds that such tales as these are not invented as whole cloth creations, but jostle their way to a generic stability of design through the accidents of oral transmission. This one stands alone in the context of the sixteenth century and might otherwise have been assigned to Straparola's own genius, if it could be allowed that from his story alone were derived the many variations appearing throughout Europe and the East some three centuries later. But more likely his tale is derivative, for the story consists of folk motifs from beginning to end. The question is whether such creations are ever conceived by an individual talent, or by necessity depend upon the slower collective genius of generations of raconteurs.

Meanwhile, as the folk tradition carried the matter of this tale forward from the sixteenth century, Straparola's version was openly employed for literary imitation, once again by the makers of the early French fairy tales. This is readily seen in Jean de Mailly's 'Fortunio,' which appeared in 1698 in *Les illustres fées, contes galans.*[90] It is a faithful recreation taken

90 (Paris: M.-M. Brunet, 1698); trans. Jack Zipes in *The Great Fairy Tale Tradition from Straparola and Basile to the Brothers Grimm* (New York: W.W. Norton, 2001), pp. 145–55.

directly from the *Piacevoli notti*, plausibly through the Louveau translation. The hero is found floating on a river like a little Moses by his adoptive and loving parents, who then have a child of their own. The boys become as brothers, but the younger's mind is poisoned by a meddling outsider, leading him to demand his aristocratic rights to the prejudice of his foundling brother. Class consciousness becomes a factor. Fortunio importunes his mother concerning his origins, has the truth confirmed, and exiles himself in chagrin. Yet there is an implicit assumption of his noble birth with a tale of identity recovery in the making. His interim course, however, is an escape from shame. Fortunio gains transformational powers into a lion, eagle, or ant, but granted to him now by a fairy – clearly a French predilection by which the random helpers of the folk tale become part of an organized parallel world of tutelary fairies. One such becomes his guide, counsellor, and gift giver, setting him up as a knight (in the manner of 'the grateful dead' stories). He arrives in a new city just in time to compete for a princess to whom he is presented, not by flying in through her window, but by being presented at court where he might display his refinement, conversation, and courtesy.

De Mailly follows Straparola, but makes more of the princess's fear of falling into the hands of a ferocious man, the prize of martial combat. The protagonist then takes to flying into the girl's apartments as an eagle to comfort her. There follows the sequence of triple alarms and impatient family members, leaving her no option but to hear out the hero and witness his integrity and trustworthiness. Marriage follows after the formulaic victory in the tournament. The fortunes of war now take Fortunio into the heart of the sirens' realm as a military commander. The queen of sirens desires a human lover – the sexual motif becomes clear – and so the husband is abducted. Guided by her good fairy, the princess does not lose hope. She outfits a ship and sets off with her young son, giving him the precious balls to quell his wailing. With the third one handed over to the queen mermaid, Fortunio's entire body rises above the waves on a triton and turns into an eagle. That de Mailly followed Straparola so closely is brought into further relief by a singular exception: he borrows for the final episode the motif of the wound inflicted over the boy's eye with the fire iron from Basile's 'The Enchanted Doe,' for it is by this mark that he is rediscovered by the king to be his son. In making his hero a royal whose origins are temporarily obscured by fortune, de Mailly satisfied the tastes of the salons; the princess has been married to a true prince, rather than to an aspiring pauper. Wish-fulfillment tales of rising to aristocratic status without the blue blood aroused resistance among the habitués of the salons, and in that regard, Straparola has been transformed. Nevertheless, this story remains one of the fourteen or more instances in which Straparola provided the tale writers of late seventeenth-century France with materials, as well as certain of the inaugural attitudes and transitional practices whereby the folk tale migrated into the fairy tale.[91]

In matters of style, Straparola appears to be his own man, although there are occasional passages in which his wording takes inspiration from other writers. He would not be the first to employ stylistic echoes; rather to the contrary, writers in that age were given to repeating phrases, proverbs, and touchstone passages gleaned from their fellows with a proficiency uncultivated by the modern stylist. In a sense, it is remarkable that in his choice of stories to imitate, Straparola was not a 'Boccaccian,' as were so many of his colleagues. Yet it is from Boccaccio that he would, from time to time, lift a stylistic passage. When Fortunio is newly arrived in Doralice's room, terrifying her with his full human presence, at one moment he places his hand over her mouth, saying: 'But if you continue to cry out, one of two misfortunes will befall us: either your honour and your fair name will be tarnished, or you will be the cause of your death and mine.' In Boccaccio's story of Ricciardo and Catella (III.6) in the *Decameron*, there is a similar passage in which he says to her, 'and if you keep crying out, two things will come about. The first is that your honor and good fame will be lost. After that, it will lead to our deaths, both mine and yours.' Turning to the originals, the wordings are as follows: 'gridarete' 'griderrete,' 'due cose averrà' 'due cose ne verrano,' 'vostro chiaro nome e buona fama fie guasta' 'vostro onore e la vostra buona fama fia guasta.' The sustained similarities would seem to leave little in doubt. The more perplexing question is why Straparola suddenly thought of or needed Boccaccio, or whether such passages simply floated about in the memories of Renaissance writers, ready for transcription when a parallel context arose. Do they represent buried echoes, secret intertextual pleasures, homage, or simply verbal tags that remained from his reading?

91 On the question of influence and the narrative order passing from the folk tale to the fairy tale, see Raymonde Robert, *Le conte de fées littéraire en France de la fin du XVIIe à la fin du XVIIIe siècle* (Nancy: Presses universitaires, 1982), esp. pp. 97–126.

III. Fable 5
Isotta and the Cowherd Travaglino

ERITREA

Isotta, the wife of Lucaferro Albani of Bergamo, devises how she may trick Travaglino, her brother Emiliano's cowherd, and thus prove him to be a liar. But she loses her husband's farm and returns home worsted in her attempt and full of shame, bringing with her a bull's head with gilded horns.

So great is the power of truth, our infallible guide, that according to the Holy Scriptures it would be easier for the heavens and the earth to pass away than for truth to fail. It has so far-reaching a character, according to the writings of the wise the world over, that truth conquers even time itself and not the inverse. As with oil, which ever rises when mixed in a vessel with water, so too will truth rise above lies. No one should marvel at this prologue of mine, for I have written it because I was moved by the malignity of a wicked woman who thought to lead a poor simple lad to tell a lie by her false words and cunning allurements, but only caused him to speak the plain truth to her own undoing. All this I propose to set before you in this fable of mine, which I hope, regarding both time and place, will prove more profitable than harmful to you all.

To begin then, noble ladies, in Bergamo, an ancient city of Lombardy, there lived not long ago a man of wealth and standing whose name was Pietromaria Albani. To this man were born two sons, Emiliano and Lucaferro. He possessed likewise two farms in a township not far away, one of them known by the name of Ghorem and the other by that of Pedrench. These two brothers, namely Emiliano and Lucaferro, divided the farms between them by lot after the death of Pietromaria their father, with Pedrench falling to the share of Emiliano, while Ghorem fell to Lucaferro. Now Emiliano owned a very fine flock of sheep, a herd of lusty young bullocks, and a second herd of productive cows, and one

Travaglino, his herdsman, had charge over all these cattle. He was a man of the most approved truth and loyalty, a man who would forfeit his life rather than tell a lie, and who kept watch over his herds with incomparable zeal. Beside his troop of cows, Travaglino kept several very fine bulls, among them one of particular beauty. With Emiliano, this bull was so great a favourite that he had its horns gilded over with the finest gold. And as often as Travaglino went to Bergamo to look after his affairs, Emiliano never failed to ask about the welfare of his favourite bull with the gilded horns.

It came about that while Emiliano was deep in conversation with his brother Lucaferro and his friends, Travaglino came near the gathering and made a sign to Emiliano his master that he would like to speak to him, whereupon he withdrew from his brother and his friends and went apart with Travaglino where they held a long conversation. Now this happened so often that at last Lucaferro lost his patience and on one occasion became so indignant and enraged that he blurted out his feelings, 'To tell you the truth, I'm surprised by your behaviour, Emiliano. You take more account of this rascal of a cowherd than you do of your own brother and your many trusted friends. Not once, but a thousand times I should say, you've gone away from us when we were together in the open street or playing games as if we had been so many animals only fit to be driven to the slaughterhouse, to go hobnobbing with that scruffy peasant Travaglino, your cowherd, launching into such long conversations that you'd have us believe you had matters of the greatest importance to discuss, while in fact you talk about things that aren't worth a straw.'

Emiliano replied, 'Lucaferro, my good brother, there is surely no need for you to fly into so hot a passion with me, heaping all these injurious words upon poor Travaglino, who, after all, is a very worthy young fellow and someone by whom I set great store both by reason of his efficiency in his calling and for his staunch loyalty to me. Moreover, he has yet another especially good quality, inasmuch as he would never tell a lie, not even to gain all the gold in the world, and he has other excellent traits besides for which I hold him in high esteem. Don't be amazed, then, that I should treat him kindly.'

This answer only served to rouse the other's bile, leading them first to bandy words in anger, and then to nearly put their hands to their swords. Finally, when Lucaferro saw how highly his brother praised Travaglino's qualities, he said, 'You speak loudly enough today of his efficiency, good faith, and truthfulness, but I tell you that this cowherd of yours is the most bungling, the most disloyal loon in the world, as well as the biggest liar that nature ever made. Moreover, I'll pledge myself to bring all this to your attention and to let you hear him tell a falsehood before your very face.' After they had spent a good deal of time wrangling, they ended by wagering their respective farms over the question, settling the affair in this fashion: that if Travaglino should be proved a liar, then Emiliano's farm should pass to Lucaferro, but that if he should be found truthful, Emiliano would become the owner of Lucaferro's. So, calling in a notary, they had a legal instrument drawn up and ratified by all the forms required in such cases.

After the brothers had parted from one another, and after their wrath and indignation had somewhat abated, Lucaferro began to regret the wager most intently, as well as the legal instrument enacted under the seal of the notary. He found himself haunted by the fear that in the end he might lose his farm, which was the only sustenance he had for himself and his family. One day, when he was in his house, Isotta his wife remarked that he was in a very melancholy mood. Not knowing the reason, she said to him, 'Heigh-ho, my good husband! What can be the matter with you that you are so sad?'

Lucaferro answered her, 'Wife, hold your tongue, for goodness's sake. Don't make my troubles any greater than they are already.'

With that, Isotta began to be very curious and handled her inquisition so well that at last her husband told her everything. Her face all radiant with satisfaction, she then said to him, 'Is that all there is to put you into such a state of fear and agitation? Keep up your spirits, for you'll see that I have enough wit about me to make this lout Travaglino tell lies to his master's face not only once but a thousand times.' When Lucaferro heard these words, he was much comforted.

Knowing full well that the beautiful bull with the gilded horns was a particular favourite with her brother-in-law, Emiliano, Isotta decided to lay out her lures in that direction first. So, having dressed herself in a provocative way and daintily painting her face, she made her way alone out of Bergamo and over to Pedrench. There she found Emiliano's farm and Travaglino at work making ricotta cheese inside the house. She greeted him, saying, 'Travaglino, I've come to pay you a visit, have a draught of milk, and eat some of your fine cheese.'

'Welcome, my mistress,' Travaglino replied. After seating her, he began to prepare the table, setting out his choice ewe's-milk cheese and other good cheer to honour the lady. Yet he was most surprised to see her there at the farm all alone and looking so jolly, for it was by no means her custom to visit him in that way, making him doubt that she was actually Isotta, the wife of his master's brother. Yet, because he had seen her many times before, he did his best to make much of her and to pay her the honour due her estate.

When the meal was over and the table cleared, and Travaglino was about to return to his cheese-making, Isotta said to him, 'Travaglino, my good fellow, let me lend you a hand in making your cheese.'

'Do whatever you'd like, Signora,' he replied. Without saying another word, she tucked up her sleeves as far as her elbows, thus laying bare her fair, wanton, well-rounded arms white as snow, and set to work with a will to help Travaglino make his cheese, letting him, now and again, get a glimpse of her swelling bosom, where he might see her little breasts like two fine apples. Besides this, she artfully brought her own rosy cheek so close to Travaglino's face that they almost touched one another. Now Travaglino, to be sure, was only a simple countryman and cowherd, but he was no dullard, and although he understood clearly enough from her looks and manner that she was all excited, he did what he could to distract her with words and glances that pretended to a complete ignorance of the ways of love. But Isotta, who began to persuade herself that the youth was on fire with love for her, felt herself suddenly so inflamed with amorous desire for him that she could scarce keep herself in bounds. But though Travaglino saw clearly enough the drift of her lascivious ways, he dared not venture a word about it, fearing that he might trouble and offend her unduly.

To put an end to Travaglino's bashful dallying, the impassioned lady said to him, 'Travaglino, what is the reason you stand there so mum and pensive and won't venture to say a word to me? Maybe you're thinking about asking me something? Go ahead, don't keep your desire a secret, whatever it may be. You'd only be injuring yourself, not me, because I'm entirely at your pleasure and command.'

Travaglino, when he heard these words, came alive and made show of a great desire to enjoy her. The silly woman, seeing him moved at last by his amorous urges, knew the time had come to set about the business in the back of her mind, so on she went, 'Travaglino, I'm going to ask you a very great favour, and if you are so churlish as to refuse it, I'll have you plainly know that it's because you hold my love for you most lightly. Moreover, your refusal would be the cause of my ruin or even of my death.'

To this speech, Travaglino replied, 'Signora, for the love I feel for you, I'm ready to devote my life and all I own in this world to your service. Were you to ask me to carry out some enterprise of great difficulty, yet by reason of my love, and that which you have shown for me, I will accomplish it with ease.'

Isotta then took courage from his words and said, 'And if you're indeed my friend, such as I take you to be, I will know soon enough.'

'Lay whatever command on me that you wish, Signora,' replied Travaglino, 'and you'll see quite readily whether I'm your friend or not.'

'All I want from you,' said Isotta, 'is the head of that bull of yours with the gilded horns. Give me that and you can do with me whatever you please.'

When he heard this request, Travaglino was nearly overcome with amazement, but he was so excited by the prickles of fleshly desire and the allurements of the lusty wench before him that he answered, 'Signora, can this be all you would want of me? Not only will you have the head of the bull, but the sack it comes in – all this I willingly hand over to your keeping.' Saying this, Travaglino plucked up heart and folded the lady in his arms and together they took part in the sweetest delights of love. When this was done, Travaglino cut off the bull's head and, having put it in a sack, he handed it over to Isotta. She then set off for home smug in her satisfaction that she had accomplished her purpose and seized her pleasure into the bargain, albeit with more horns than farms.

Now Travaglino, as soon as the lady had taken her departure, began to feel rather troubled in mind, casting about for some excuse he might put upon his master when called to account for the death of the bull with the gilded horns which Emiliano so greatly loved. The wretched youth was held by these tormenting thoughts, having no idea what to say or do, when it occurred to him at last to take the branch of a bare tree, to dress it up with some of his own poor garments, and to make believe that it was Emiliano. Then, standing before this scarecrow, he proposed to make trial of what he would do and say whenever he should be brought face to face with his master. After he had set up the branch in a room of the house with his own cap on its head and certain of his garments upon its back, Travaglino left the chamber, then turned and reentered, saluting the branch, 'Good day, my master.'

And then making answer to himself, he said, 'I'm glad to see you, Travaglino. How do you find yourself, and how are things going at the farm? It's been a long time since I've seen anything of you.'

'I'm very well,' replied Traviglino, 'but I've been so busy recently that I haven't found the time to come and see you.'

'How did you leave the bull with the gilded horns?' asked Emiliano.

Then Travaglino replied, 'Master, the bull wandered into the woods and the wolves got him.'

'So where's his hide and his head with the gilded horns?'

Then Travaglino stood still and couldn't think of a thing to say, and afterwards left the room all confused. After a little while, he came in again and started anew with his discourse, 'God keep you, good master.'

'And you too, Travaglino,' said Emiliano, 'and how prosper things at the farm? How is the bull with the gilded horns?'

'I'm very well,' said Travaglino, 'praise God, but one day not long ago the bull broke out of the yard, and then after fighting with some of the other bulls, he was so heavily mauled by them that he is dead of his injuries.'

'Then where are his skin and his gilded horns?' asked Emiliano.

But Travaglino had no better an idea what to answer to this question than he did before. Finally, having gone through the same conversation several times, he gave the matter up in despair, entirely unable to devise a reasonable-sounding reply.

Now Isotta, who had by this time regained her house, said to her husband, 'What will that poor lout Travaglino do when he sets about excusing himself to Emiliano for the death of the bull with the gilded horns his master is so fond of? How will he get out of this without telling a lie or two? Look, here's the head of the bull, which I've brought back with me for a testimony against him whenever he starts his fibbing.' But the lady didn't mention a word to her husband about how she had made two fine horns for his brow bigger than those of a royal hart. When he saw the bull's head, Lucaferro was overjoyed and could hardly contain his glee, certain that he now would win his wager. Yet, matters fell out rather differently, as you'll find out in a moment.

After he had tried out several rounds of questions and answers with his scarecrow man, talking exactly as though he were with the master, and finding that no answers would serve his purposes, Travaglino decided, without further delay, to go and find the owner, no matter what might happen. Hence, having set out for Bergamo, he presented himself to his master, giving him a hearty salute. After greeting his herdsman in return, Emiliano said to him, 'And what business has been on your mind lately, Travaglino, that you have let so many days go by without coming in, or without letting us have any news of you?'

Travaglino replied, 'Master, the many jobs I have had in hand have kept me fully occupied.'

'And how goes my bull with the gilded horns?' asked Emiliano.

When he heard these words, poor Travaglino was entirely overcome with confusion. His face flushed as red as fire with shame and he was tempted to find some excuse for his fault and to hide the truth. But in the end, for fear of losing his good name, he took courage in hand and launched into the story of Isotta from beginning to end, how she had beguiled him, and how his dealings with her had ended in the death of the bull. Emiliano, as he listened to the story, was amazed beyond measure, but however great his fault might have been, Travaglino at least proved to be a truthful fellow and good to his word. So in the end, Emiliano won the wager and got the farm and Lucaferro gained nothing but a pair of horns for his own head, while his good-for-nothing wife, Isotta, in trying to dupe another, was magnificently duped herself and got nothing but shame for her trouble.

Once the tale was ended, everyone in that worthy company was vociferous in blaming the dissolute Isotta and equally loud in commending Travaglino, holding the silly wanton woman up to ridicule who had given herself to a herdsman in such a vile way because of her pestilential avarice. But seeing that Eritrea had not yet propounded her enigma, the Signora, glancing at her, made a sign that she must not interrupt the procedure they had followed so far, whereupon Eritrea, without further delay, recited her enigma.

I saw one day in fine spring weather,
A head and a breech full close together.
Another breech I likewise found
Squatting at ease upon the ground.
And one, as strong as any mule,
Stood quiet, subject to the rule
Of two, who in the head shone bright,
And looked with pleasure at the sight.
Meantime the head pressed closer still,
And ten there were who worked with will,
With dexterous grasp now up, now down,
No prettier sight in all the town.

If the ladies had made merry over the fable, they were no less pleased with the riddle. But seeing there was not one of them who could solve it, Eritrea spoke as follows, 'My enigma, ladies and gentlemen, is intended to describe one who sits down under a cow and sets to work milking her. And for the same reason, he who milks the cow must keep his head close to the cow's breech while, for his convenience, sits with his own breech on the ground. Although she is incredibly patient, yet to restrain her she is watched by the two eyes of the person milking her, and is stroked by two hands and the ten fingers which draw the milk from her.' This enigma pleased them all greatly, including its interpretation. But seeing the stars had now disappeared from the heavens, except for the morning star, the Signora asked that the company should retire to rest, each and every one, but to return again the next evening under pain of fine and punishment.

The End of the Third Night

III.5 Commentary

This novelette is a meditation, not upon hypocrisy and the detection of lies through the course of time as taught by the proverbial sense of the opening figure, but upon the cognitive speculations entertained by rational creatures caught between the good of truth-speaking and the good of rationalized mendacity – the fashioning of information in the interests of self protection and self advancement. Travaglino vacillates, in fact, between his ability to entertain lies provisionally in his mind and his self-appraised inability to succeed in lying, labouring under the conviction that his mind would crumple under interrogation, or that his stuttering or facial expressions would give him away. This is a story about the expediency of the lie, the social costs in speaking the truth, and the lie detector factor that is built into the semiotics of the body itself. There is thus tension between the Travaglino touted as a man of principled truth, a man constitutionally incapable of lying, and the Travaglino who always opts for the truth only because he mistrusts his capacity to lie and get away with it.

In a more conventional thematic sense, this is a story about professional and personal integrity of such a high calibre that it is taken for remarkable, automatically imputing the counter-thesis that among humans in general, truth is a frail thing made relative to interest. The latter is what we expect of mere mortals. Thus all men, out of interest, are corruptible, and, moreover, when it comes to sexual opportunity, the male of the species is both gull to desire and a hypocrite born: he will copulate on the basis of attraction, accept risk in accordance with drives more basic than ethics, and prevaricate to cover his guilt according to the most plausible scenario. Where extraordinary virtue purports to render fellow mortals beyond temptation, it is felt as an injury to the lesser mortals of the fallen world who will be out to take them down. The story is archetypal in the nature of the proposed seduction; the protagonist must balance out his obligations to honour, duty, and ethical integrity with his drives as a biological being, sexual opportunism, and hedonic rewards. This story further destabilizes the reader by offering no clear option between the truth and the lie in light of the preliminary wager to which the protagonist is not made a party. What is truth in relation to a contest between a man willing to wager his farm, and in some versions even his life, to compel a lie and the intended victim who is reputedly incapable of lying, although he has every motive for doing so? Truth is both a condition of the ethical soul and a relation of fact as reported in the light of ultimate evidential demonstration. The story is a simple one, but one that merits reflection as a riddle concerning the options of the ethical man, veracity, and the drives of the natural man, self interest, and confabulation.

That moment of reflection concerning such matters is embodied in a mock dialogue with in inanimate object – a feature common to all versions of this story on record, indeed a defining and signature feature. It is the moment of simulated debate when the protagonist must come to terms with his options by pretending that his cap or his staff stuck in the ground is his king or patron to whom he must give account. He may even hold the trees in mock debate. In each instance, he projects a conversation, supplying both sides himself, in which he either tells lies and entertains the consequences, or tells the truth and entertains the consequences. This ability to create imagined drafts of future acts and to weigh their costs and benefits is one of humankind's greatest evolutionary endowments. The future may be partially planned, barring contingency, by forecasting multiple consequences and choosing from among them the best course of action. Such provisional thinking is, at the same time, calibrated according to the best reasonable assessments of the self with regard to capacities, entitlements, and limitations. Travaglino's advantage is not only controlled provisional drafts of future options, but knowledge of his own limitations and the preoccupations of his patron. Ultimately his greatest gamble is on the patron's capacity for empathy, his ability to imagine the world from Travaglino's point of view and to confess in all honesty that in the cowherd's place, he too would have been unable to resist temptation. Clearly, something of all this must have registered with auditors through the centuries who, through their approbation and ensuing discussions, confirmed the value of the story, thereby inciting its preservation in the memories of scops, *trouvères*, and raconteurs over a considerable period of time. The story is brilliant in all these regards, an object lesson in cognitive computations.

At the same time, the story is a vehicle of fantasy concerning seduction. This is a tale of unexpected sexual opportunity, of excitement and anticipated *jouissance*, exploited with great sensuality in its 'oriental' redactions – fables in which a veiled beauty enters the room, alone, whereupon she raises her veil to reveal pure enchantment, followed by all the arts of seduction as prelude to making her outrageous demands. It is a tale of the predatory and absolute power women hold over men as tricksters in the guise of seductresses. The social history of the world offers infinite variations upon this universal vulnerability – all to minimum cautionary effect. It is a tale of the assailable and defenceless male, programmed by hormones, anticipated pleasure, and fantasy to accept the rare sexual opportunities that come his way, against lingering intimations of the high wages for random carnal knowledge. The story is profoundly poetic in that regard. At the very centre of this economy is not merely the power of beauty or the blandishments and cajolery of the siren, but the whim of the female that must be met, the appetites of a pregnant woman, or the costly dare of slaughtering a 'fetishized' animal. It is about the absurd challenges imposed by women and assumed by men as their destiny in the game of 'show' prowess and sexual reward. The entire age of chivalry was built upon this principle of female biddings and challenges and male ritual exploits in a climate of danger and risk. Women are entitled to make demands in exchange for their favours, and the macho ego is too easily fired to calculate the risks. For some women, raising the ante in relation to the power of their own beauty becomes little more than a snare.

Evidence for the history of this undoubtedly ancient Eastern story is both scant and late, calling for further investigation. The tale appeared in the West in two closely related Turkish versions (they are actually the same tale) suggesting that it was born among the Ottomans and entered Europe at an unspecified moment, there to experience further elaboration and diversification. The story as a Turkish tale, per se, must be assigned to the reign of Amurath II (Murad II, 1421–51), according to the 'princeps' manuscript, eventually translated by François Pétis de la

Croix (1625–95), in which the ruler is named. But clearly the Ottomans were themselves literary retainers of a more ancient tradition, for the stories were not only in circulation in Europe before that date, but the Ottoman 'author' acknowledges his debt to Arabic originals from unspecified and possibly non-surviving works. Among these tales is the quite splendid 'History of Saddyq, Master of the Horse.'[92] Togaltimur-Can, king of Tartary, employed Saddyq (True) as his horse master because of his inability to lie. But Vizier Tangribirdi hated him without cause, apart from envy, and sought Saddyq's demise. As a force at court, he was proud of his ability to ruin courtiers at will and for that further reason he was miffed by the horse master's unassailable virtue. Taking up her father's cause, Hoschendan (Shapely) prepared herself for the mission both in matters of make-up and wardrobe. At the employee's door, she dismisses her slaves and enters alone to practice all her incomparable arts of seduction – a portion of the tale no doubt relished by tellers and hearers alike. Transported by desire, Saddyq becomes putty in her hands, but not without remonstrance and a long period of resistance. She craves a repast of horse liver and heart – an Ottoman delicacy – consisting of the organs of the most prized animal in the stable. Saddyq offers to buy a horse in its place, but she would accept no substitutions. He must acquiesce to her malicious conditions in order to satisfy his eroto-frenzy. After their mutual supper, she at least paid her debt throughout the night before repairing home to tell her father of her exploit – a dear price paid to appease a parent otherwise delighted by her success. The vizier then relates all to the king, leaping over the fact of his daughter's sexual involvement. The horse master is called to account. Meanwhile, stricken by the cognizance of his own folly, the protagonist carries out the mock

92 This story was translated into English from the edition of tales prepared by Thomas Simon Gueullette, 'The Mogul Tales; Turkish Tales…' in *Tales of the East; Comprising the Most Popular Romances of Oriental Origin*, intro. Henry Weber, 3 vols. (Edinburgh: James Ballantyne, 1812), vol. III, pp. 173–5. I signal here the connection between the Edinburgh edition and the *Turkish Tales* of Pétis de la Croix, trans. Dr. King and others, 2 vols. (London: W. Mears & J. Browne, 1714), vol. II, pp. 44–56. Pétis de la Croix, who died in 1713, left his French translation among his papers; it was published in 1722 under the title *L'Histoire de la Sultane de Perse et des Visirs*. It relates the same famous framing tale that first appears in the *Book of Sindibad*, and that reappeared in the *History of the Forty Vizirs*, and in the French *Dolopathos* of Johann de Alta Silva, as well as the English *Seven Wise Masters*. See also Auguste Louis Armand Loiseleur-Deslongchamps, *Essai sure les fables indiennes et sur leur introduction en Europe, suivi du roman des Sept Sages de Rome en prose* (Paris: Techener, 1838), p. 173.

interview, speaking to his cap as though it were King Togaltimur. After rehearsing both responses, he realizes that in mendacity as in truth he would be cut to pieces, and that truth is hence the better way to go. After the real interview, the king turns to the vizier and asks for an appropriate punishment, whereupon the latter recommends death by slow roasting. There has been no wager and no victory in which the king might have found consolation for his loss. Rather, as magistrate, he simply opts for mercy over justice because his horse master had told the truth, confessing that in his place he would have been equally tempted. As for the vizier, his dirty secret does not come out, and yet his disappointment drives him to his sickbed, realizing that his daughter had prostituted herself for nothing. Read in parallel with Straparola's 'Isotta and the Cowherd, Travaglino,' their association is undeniable – they are the same story. But clearly, though separated by perhaps no more than 100 years, they belong entirely to their respective worlds, the one of sultans and viziers, of veiled beauties and Ottoman court culture, the other of local farms and the craft of a libertine housewife. Were the Ottoman tale a presumed source, the comparatist must account for the substitutions during so short a period of time that would have permitted the one to have evolved into the other, or simply credit Straparola with the transformation. But, in fact, despite its important status as a survivor from the tradition, this remote analogue is best considered a late literary development from an earlier tradition, the existence of which is witnessed by a sole early European survivor. In brief, while the tale may be Eastern in origin, we cannot assume that the earliest surviving Eastern version is to be valued necessarily as a source.[93]

93 This same story came to the West both later in the *History of the Forty Vezirs, or the Story of the Forty Morns and Eves*, as well as earlier, whether singly or in a collection. This work is attributed to Sheykh Zada. It was retranslated in the nineteenth century by E.J.W. Gibb and published in London by George Redway (1886), and dedicated to W.A. Clouston. The story appears as the 'Thirty-ninth Vezir's Tale,' pp. 358–63. There are curious variants between the French translation taken from several manuscripts of the original, the earliest dating to the first half of the fifteenth century, and this translation from a version published in Constantinople between 1617 and 1623, given the dedication to Sultan Mustapha I. (Ultimately Gibb worked with five manuscripts containing 112 stories in which only thirty-five were common to all.) In his rendition, the black horse has become a bay, and under the pressure of romance, the king marries his master of the horse to the vizier's daughter who had seduced him, allowing him to become chief vizier in his turn. The most telling detail is that the horse master, in offering a sword to the king

Inversely, however, turning to the earliest version on record in the West can be equally baffling. It is No. 111 of the *Gesta romanorum*, 'Of Vigilance in our Calling,' in which a gentleman has a cow of such prize for its white colour and pure milk that he tips its horns with gold.[94] We are off to a good start, for in dating the *Gesta* to 1300 or shortly thereafter, we have a version that shares an important detail with Straparola's and thereby suggests a continuum over the intervening two and a half centuries linking the two together. Nevertheless, this early version of the tale of the cherished white cow is a diminished and 'contaminated' effort that can only have been extrapolated from a more coherent version, an oikotype that can be imagined only through reconstruction. Either the source tale employed by the *Gesta*'s compiler, or the compiler himself, conflated this miniature *novella* with the classical tale of Argus, Io, and Hermes, for the keeper of the herd is no other than Argus of the hundred eyes, while the would-be thief of the gold-tipped horns is Mercury who, with his music and recitations, puts the guardian to sleep a few eyes at a time before cutting off his head. It is a botched job of the first order, for Argos has, indeed, an opportunity to talk to his staff in an effort to rehearse his options (a feature maintained down to the nineteenth century), but he has no occasion for testing his choices or for confirming

---

ostensibly to behead him, had calculated rather more perspicaciously, after identifying the vizier's daughter as his seducer, that he might be a candidate for the king's protection. It is an important detail. E.J.W. Gibb professes that he is no student of folklore and notes the work that must be done by 'eminent scholars' in determining the place of *The Forty Vezirs* in the shaping of European folklore (p. xvii), but he ventures, nevertheless, to list the six stories by Straparola which are cognate with tales in the Turkish collection, along with those in the French *fabliaux*, Chaucer, the *Gesta romanorum*, the *Decameron*, and the *Cento novelle antiche* (which dates to the same era as the *Gesta romanorum*), thereby suggesting that these stories were in circulation generally throughout Europe as early as the thirteenth century. Such early dates, however, can only be in reference to Arabic tales predating the arrival of the Ottomans though whom, in the Near East, many are uniquely known. The question relates to the larger question of the arrival in the West of all that pertains to 'the seven sages,' 'the seven wise masters,' 'Sintipas,' and to this medieval phenomenon in general.

94 Trans. Charles Swan, rev. Wynnard Hooper (London: Bohn, 1876; reprint, New York: Dover, 1959), pp. 199–201. Edward Tripp in *The Meridian Handbook of Classical Mythology* (New York: New American Library, 1973), pp. 98–9, outlines the origins of the story of Argus Panoptes, referring the reader in turn to Apollodorus, 2.2.2–3 and to the *Metamorphoses* of Ovid, bk. I, ll. 622–723. See note 95.

his virtues in the presence of his patron. In refusing to sell the animal, he is simply slain. Yet the inclusion of these two critical details, the gold-tipped horns and the interview with the staff, some 250 years before the *Piacevoli notti*, implies the story's European lineage reaches back not only before Straparola, or before the Ottomans had gained a firm hold on their new homeland in Asia Minor, but before the *Gesta* itself, having fallen away from a prototype uncontaminated by the intrusion of such classicizing overlays. There is little other explanation for the existence of Straparola's version in the form we know it. This tale, thus, must have belonged to European folk literature for a period of 700 years, derived at an early date from the Arabic lore that contributed to the tradition of the Sages and Viziers.[95] The present tale is presumably a transcription of the version (or one of the versions) of this story tradition current in the Veneto during Straparola's lifetime. Such stories must have existed whereby the narrative type was carried from the thirteenth century down to the nineteenth.

These scattered and highly contrasting literary snapshots of a 'living' story produce more innuendo than hard inflections about the history of the tradition except to confirm its existence in three remarkably contrasting literary renditions from three distinct periods. Just when this oriental tale began its journey in the West is a matter for speculation, and the extent to which it was subject to the diasporic effects of oral culture must be sketched in from only a few disparate examples. Thus, Straparola's tale becomes a precious mid-point marker of the state of its passage from the Middle Ages to the modern era, where indeed it reappears, but in limited numbers.

Another intervening version, published in 1800 in the *Volcks–Sagen* of Johann Carl Christoph Nachtigal (Otmar), confirms the wide (and necessary) circulation of the story in the eighteenth century, this one coming from northern Europe. It has been enhanced in full comic, novelistic

95 This mixture of classical mythology and the European folk tale of the man who can never tell a lie, and who sets up his staff to carry out a provisional conversation with his master, are further represented in *Le violier des histories romaines*, ed. M.G. Brunet (Paris: P. Jannet, 1858), pp. 265–6, which is the *Ancienne traduction des gesta romanorum*. The story remains essentially the same. In resisting Mercury, Argus of the hundred eyes is slain and his head cut off so that, in effect, he has no opportunity to speak the truth to a magistrate. This is in turn related to the story of Mercury and Argus, the guardian of Io, in Ovid's *Metamorphoses*, trans. Rolfe Humphries (Bloomington: Indiana University Press, 1961), bk. I, 624, p. 22.

fashion and thoroughly laundered with regard to matters of sexual license and shameful conduct. This plot comes down to a wager between two friendly bishops, with a rather expensive wine cask at play between them. The local bishop, Heinrich, has a pet ram in the custody of his trusty herder, Conrad. The visiting bishop, miffed by Heinrich's familiarity with his rustic, whom he teases about getting married, and in whose categorical honesty he has an expressed confidence, makes up his mind to bring down the herder's credit. He puts a bad construction upon all such men in the service echelons before taking his leave; the visiting bishop is a snob. Back at home he calls upon his man, Peter, for advice, who is like a court fool and advisor to him. Peter proposes that they enlist Lise, Conrad's heartthrob, to purchase the ram from him or forswear their eventual marriage. Conrad offers her far more in its place, but she insists, saying that she had already promised that specific animal to another and then begins to shed tears, while hinting in accusatory tones at the explanatory lies he could employ. The herder then drives his crook in the ground and thereupon hangs his coat to represent the bishop. In a dialogue with himself he tries out all the excuses, realizing that he could never carry off such lies. So he decides in favour of the truth, gives the ram to Lise for her house money, and prepares to confront the two bishops, who are by that time waiting for him. The ram is in Peter's stall by then and he is gloating over his imminent victory. But Conrad tells the truth in every detail, leaving the home bishop both angered yet delighted, once the truth of it all is confirmed. The visiting bishop admits to their plot and its failure. So Bishop Heinrich offers to officiate at the herder's wedding and give the newlyweds half his flock. The visiting bishop returns the ram and has the great cask built that is still seen in Halberstadt today. This is a literary treatment in keeping with late eighteenth-century German sensibilities, but at the core is the signature action of the failed temptation, all speaking to the wisdom of the title: 'Erlich währt am längsten!' (Honesty is the best policy).[96] This literary adaptation does double duty as an exemplum upon a text and as explanatory lore about the origins of the Halberstadt cask.

But there are folk versions as well. The two to follow are both from Sicily, the one collected by the redoubtable Giuseppe Pitrè, and the other by Laura Gonzenbach, as retold by Italo Calvino. In the first, a king has

96 (Bremen: Friedrich Wilmans, 1800), no. 23, pp. 293–310.

a calf so beautiful he calls it 'Golden Horn.'[97] That vestige is all that now remains of the golden-tipped horns of Straparola. Its keeper is called 'Old Man Truth' who, as in the sixteenth-century tale, is frequently called to account, responding to the king in the same formulaic interview of questions and answers. This same incantation is repeated when the herdsman reviews his options in talking to the trees along the way to the palace. The king's ministers, hearing the boasts of the keeper's unfailing veracity, take this as a challenge and profess they will make him lie. Such is their motivation, without wager or envy. In lieu of the seduction plot, two of the ministers dress up as women, one of them padded out to look pregnant; together they go to the country to pay the keeper a visit. There the pregnant one puts up such a fuss about her craving for calf meat, accompanied by dizziness and swooning, that the keeper is brought to slaughter the prized animal. On the way to the palace, he repeats all the versions of the excuses with which he has been prompted, but rejects them because the king would demand evidence he could not supply. Upon hearing the truth, the king experiences a dual reaction: loss over the animal but rejoicing that he had won the wager, lifting the employee to even higher esteem. As for the ministers, there are no repercussions. The tale, collected in Palermo, simply is what it is, a memorable anecdote providing clear record of the survival of the story chosen by Straparola.

Gonzenbach found the tale, 'Massaru Verità,' in Catania which Calvino later rendered as 'Steward Truth.'[98] In this version, the king has four

97 'Lu Zu Viritati,' (Old man truth), in *Sicilian Folk and Fairy Tales of Giuseppe Pitrè*, ed. and trans. Jack Zipes and Joseph Russo, 2 vols. (New York: Routledge, 2009), no. 78, vol. I, pp. 346–8. The notes make little of this story, saying that it 'does not conform to any of the types listed in Aarne-Thomspon-Uther's "Anecdotes and Jokes." It is essentially a morality tale of honesty triumphing over deceit, but it shows that honesty needs the addition of wit in order to succeed' (p. 869). There is a pragmatic kind of folk wisdom in evidence, but it shows less of the complex ethical musing and paradox of the Turkish 'originals.'

98 'Massaru Verità,' in *Sicilianische Märchen*, ed. Laura Gonzenbach, anno. Reinhold Köhlers (Leipzig: W. Engelmann, 1870), no. 8, pp. 39–41; Italo Calvino, *Italian Folktales*, trans. George Martin (New York: Pantheon, [1956], 1980), no. 187, pp. 668–71. There are certain differences between Calvino's telling and Gonzenbach's original. In the original, he was instructed to say that the missing creature had hurled itself off the mountain. When he arrives at the palace, the entire court is present and he makes his reply in local dialect. Only the minister had wagered his life. Vittorio Imbriani offers a further folk version entitled 'Giuseppe 'a Veretà' in *XII Conti pomiglianesi* (Naples: Detken e Richoll, 1876), pp. 1–2, mentioning in his

prized animals kept by his steward who, every Saturday, must go to report on their well-being. During each trip, he rehearses the stock dialogue, talking to his hat as a stand-in for the king. A jealous minister vows to make him lie, but fails to hit upon the means until his wife comes along with a solution of her own. She too primps herself up for the occasion, and for the arrival of such a beauty the steward bustles over his hospitality. But in lieu of seduction, she too feigns pregnancy and craves roast beef that can only be provided by the slaughter of the choicest calf. Like her counterpart, she conducts a charade of moaning accompanied by predictions of imminent death unless she is quickly satisfied. Less sociable than her predecessors, she dines on the fatted calf and leaves in haste. In this tale, the staff as interlocutor makes a return to which the steward propounds one lie after the other concerning the fourth animal, after rehearsing the prevailing truth about the other three. On the way to the palace he repeats the formula, now with the trees, until he reaches a more satisfactory conclusion. We are not told which until he delivers the truth to his master, but we could have guessed. In this tale, both king and minister had wagered their lives, so that in speaking the truth, the king's life is spared and the minister's is forfeited. Each tale reveals the folk tale process at work, both in relation to each other, and in relation to a prototype recorded by Straparola predating these by more than 300 years.

Only two examples of the story's pan-European distribution can be cited here, the first one telling of 'Faithful Svend' from *Danish Fairy Tales*, in which two men wager their estates over Svend the cowherd's flawless loyalty and truthfulness.[99] Svend's calumniator in the matter takes the bet and sends him with a message to his wife. She gets him drunk, makes him gamble away his fine clothes lent for the occasion, and turfs him out. On the road back he engages in the mock interviews, setting his tattered hat upon his walking stick, rehearsing lies that he cannot trust himself to deliver. By telling the truth he wins the bet and gains the forfeited estate for himself. It is a rather trivialized and laundered version, lacking all erotic play, but shows the story's currency in the North. The second comes from Portugal. 'O boi Cardil' (The ox named Cardil)

---

notes (p. 3) two further works featuring the story: 'Don Peppino' in *La scuola italica*, II.5 (Aug. 23, 1874); and 'Le tre Maruzze,' by Signore Troja, in *Novella trojana*, 1875, of which I can locate no further information.

99 *Danish Fairy Tales*, ed. Svend Grundtvig (London: G.G. Harrap & Co., 1914), pp. 187–92.

is the story of the king's *criado* who could never tell a lie. When the king boasted of him, the hearer laughed and began to plot his downfall. His wife participated in the would-be sex scandal that involved boi Cardil's slaughter. The king's questions, the ritual answers, and then the pure truth all fall into place.[100]

This story must have been a traditional vignette by the time it came to Straparola, whether from an oral or a literary source. It is easy to imagine its transmission through late medieval jest books, or collections of *fabliaux*, or exempla, this one on the advantages of unflinching truthfulness, but none such have come to light. Should one turn up in the wake of the *Gesta romanorum* that has been overlooked here, it would come as no surprise. Inversely, just as the story was in circulation among the folk in the eighteenth and nineteenth centuries, it must likewise have been in circulation in the sixteenth, thereby supplying Straparola with his precise model. This is a wager story, a seduction plot, a tale of cuckoldry as the deceived wife carries away her gold-tipped horns to her husband, only to forfeit the farm. And always it is a tale about truth as the best policy with an amusing, ironic twist.

100 Téofilo Braga, *Contos tradicionais do poro portugues*, 2 vols. (Lisbon: Dom Quixote, 1987), pt. II, no. 1, vol. I, pp. 189–90. Braga follows the story to Madiera as 'Boi Bragado,' and it is 'O Rabil' in *Contos populares portugueses*, ed. Adolfo Coelho (Lisbon: Compendium, 1996), no. 56. There are several books bearing this title.

The Fourth Night

Already the golden-haired Apollo with his radiant chariot had left our hemisphere, plunged into the sea, and gone to the antipodes, and the folk who had been labouring in the fields, weary with their long toil, felt a desire only to repose quietly in their beds, when the worshipful and high-born company assembled themselves joyfully once more at the customary place. And after the ladies and gentlemen had spent some time in mirthful conversation, the Signora Lucrezia, once silence was restored, requested them to bring out the golden vase. Then, having written with her own hand the names of five of the ladies and tossed them into the vessel, she called to Signor Vangelista and told him to draw out the names one by one, so that they would know with certainty just which of their companions would be assigned the duty of telling stories that night. Then Signor Vangelista, breaking off the pleasant discourse he was holding with Lodovica, went obediently towards the Signora, and respectfully sinking to his knees before her, he drew out first the name of Fiordiana, then Vicenza, then Lodovica, next Isabella, and last the name of Lionora. But before they began their recitations, the Signora gave word to Molino and the Trevisan to take their lutes and sing a ballad – which they did, as follows.

Song

There is a face which is my sun of love,
  In whose kind warmth I breathe and move,
  Or faint beneath its scorching ray;
And when it shines amongst the fairest fair,
  My lady reigns beyond compare,
And all around her bend beneath her sway.

Happy, thrice happy, is that favoured one,
  Who sees no face but hers alone,
  And passion's nectar eager sips,
Who listens to the music of her tongue,
  More sweet than lays by seraphs sung,
In words that fall like jewels from her lips.

But happier still were I, if she benign
  Would place her lily hand in mine,
And make me worthy such a prize to claim.
  Dull clod of earth although I be,
  Then should I full fruition see
Of every hope and end of every aim.

Everyone of the company listened attentively and commended the song. And when the Signora saw it was ended, she asked Fiordiana, to whom the first turn of storytelling on the fourth evening had been assigned, that she should begin hers immediately, following the order which had been observed since the beginning of their entertainment. So the damsel, no less eager to speak than to listen, began her fable.

IV. Fable 1
Costanza, the Girl-Knight

FIORDIANA

Ricardo, king of Thebes, had four daughters, one of whom becomes a wanderer over the earth. She changes her name from Costanza to Costanzo and arrives at the court of Cacco, king of Bithynia, who, because of her doughty deeds, takes her as his wife.

I must tell you first, fair and gracious ladies, that the fable which Eritrea told to us last evening has so dashed my confidence that I don't feel much in the mood to play the storyteller tonight. Nevertheless, my sense of obedience to all the commands of the Signora and the respect I feel for the whole of this honourable and gracious company compels and encourages me to make an attempt with a certain story which, although it will assuredly not be found so pleasing as Eritrea's, I will give to you for what it is worth. You will hear how a certain damsel, endowed with a noble soul and high courage, one who in the course of her noteworthy adventures was far better served by fortune than by reason, held it preferable to become a servant rather than to fall beneath her station and dignity, and how, after enduring servitude for some time, she became the wife of King Cacco. All this will be set forth in the story I'm about to tell.

Thebes is one of the great and splendid cities of Egypt, a place richly ornamented with noble buildings, both public and private, situated in a country rich in cornfields and favoured with fresh water in abundance – having all those things that make for a glorious metropolis. In times past, this city was under the rule of a king named Ricardo, a man profoundly wise, of great knowledge, and of the highest valour. This monarch greatly desired to have an heir to his kingdom. His wife was Valeriana, the daughter of Marliano, king of Scozia (Scotland), a lady who was perfection itself, very fair to look upon and exceedingly gracious in manner.

To them were born three daughters, fine mannered, full of grace, and fair as rosebuds in the morning. Of these, one was called Valentia, another Dorothea, and the third Spinella. In the course of time it became clear to Ricardo that Valeriana his wife had come to the end of her child-bearing season and that his daughters were ripe for marriage. He therefore determined to dispose of the three princesses in honourable unions, and at the same time to divide his kingdom into three parts, in order to give one to each of his daughters, keeping for himself only as much as he deemed sufficient for the entertainment of himself, his family, and his court. All this he carried out according to his intent.

The three maidens were given in marriage to three powerful kings, one to the king of Scardona, another to the king of the Goths, and the third to the king of Scythia. To each of them was assigned, by way of dowry, a third part of their father's kingdom, Ricardo keeping back only a small portion thereof to satisfy his vital needs. Thus the good king, with Valeriana his well-beloved wife, lived righteously in peace and comfort. But lo, after some little while it chanced that the queen, of whom the king expected no further offspring, was brought to bed of a very beautiful little girl, whom the king welcomed with affection and caresses as warm as he had given to the other three. Yet the queen was not so well pleased with this last infant, not by reason of any dislike for the child, but because, seeing the kingdom was now divided into three parts and given away, she feared there would be no chance of furnishing this daughter with a dowry sufficient to win her a marriage worthy of their state. She desired at the same time that the child should receive the share due to a daughter of hers. Having handed the child over to the care of a very competent nurse, she gave strict orders to have the child well nurtured, to give her good instruction, and to train her in the gentle and praiseworthy manners and carriage becoming to a maiden of her condition. By the time Costanza – for such was this child's name – was twelve years old, she had already learned to embroider, to sing, to dance, to play the lute, and to do every one of those feats which are held to mark a princess of rank. Not content with these graces, she gave herself also to the study of polite letters, which were of so great pleasure and delight to her that she would spend not only her days over them but her nights as well, striving always to discover the exquisite beauties of the books she studied. Then, more like a valiant young man than a young lady, she devoted herself to the arts of war, learning how to tame horses, to handle arms, and to run in the lists. In jousting she was so skilled that she often carried the victory, as if she had been one of those valorous knights held worthy for their honour and renown. For all these reasons, Costanza was greatly loved by the king and queen and all those in the royal entourage; there was no end to their affection.

When Costanza came to a marriageable age, her father, the king, was greatly troubled because he had neither the state nor the gold required to match her with some potent monarch. In this matter he often took counsel with the queen, but the prudent Valeriana, in whose eyes the good qualities of the child appeared so superior that no other lady of the land was her equal, was by no means disquieted, consoling his majesty with gentle and loving words, urging him to keep a light heart and not to doubt but that in the end some powerful lord, fired with love by their daughter's many virtues, would not disdain to take her as a wife without a dowry.

Before many months had passed, the damsel was asked for in marriage by various gallant gentlemen, among whom was Brunello, son of the great marquis of Vivien, whereupon the king and queen called their daughter to them in their chamber. When they were all seated, the king announced, 'Costanza, my well-beloved child, the time is now come when it is right for you to marry, and for a husband we have found a youth who should please your taste. He is no other than the son of the marquis of Vivien, our good friend and neighbour. His name is Brunello and he is a promising and gallant youth. The report of his valorous deeds has already spread throughout the world. Moreover, he asks nothing of us beyond our own goodwill and your fair sweet self, upon which I put a value exceeding that of all the pomp and treasure of the world. You must know that, although you are a king's daughter, yet by reason of my poverty, I cannot find for you a more exalted alliance. Hence, you must be content with this arrangement and conform to our wishes.'

The damsel, who was most prudent and fully conscious that she was sprung from high lineage, listened attentively to her father's words and without a moment's delay answered him as follows: 'There is no need, father, for me to spend many words in replying to your honourable proposal. I will only say what the present question demands. First I utter my gratitude, the warmest I can express, for all the affection and benevolence you have shown me in seeking to provide me with a husband without consulting with me in the matter. Next, speaking still with all submission and reverence, I do not intend to let myself fall below the race of my ancestors, who throughout all time have been famous and illustrious, nor do I wish to debase the crown you wear by taking for a husband one who is our inferior. Dear father, you have begotten four daughters, of whom you have married three in the most honourable fashion to three mighty kings, giving with them great store of gold and wide domains. Yet you wish to dispose of me, who has ever been obedient to you and observant of your precepts, in an ignoble alliance. Wherefore I tell you, to end my speech, that I will never take a husband unless I can be matched like my three sisters to a king of rank equal to my deserving.'

Shortly thereafter, Costanza, after shedding many tears, took leave of the king and queen, mounted a gallant horse, and set forth from Thebes alone, determined to follow whatever road fortune might lay open to her. Travelling thus at hazard, she deemed it wise to change her name, so instead of Costanza, she called herself Costanzo and attired herself in men's clothing. She passed over many mountains and valleys, forests and rivers, saw many lands, heard the languages of men and marked their ways and manners, including those who lived their lives after the fashion of brutes rather than of men. One day, at the setting of the sun, she arrived at the famed and celebrated city of Costanza, the capital of all the surrounding country, at that time under the rule of Cacco, king of Bithynia. Upon entering, she began to admire the superb palaces, the straight and spacious streets, the running water, the broad rivers, and the clear, soft, trickling fountains. Then, coming to the great square, she beheld the king's palace, lofty and magnificent with its pillars of marble, porphyry, and other precious materials. Soon after, lifting up her eyes, she saw the king, who was standing upon a gallery commanding a view of the whole square, whereupon she doffed her cap and made him a deep bow. The king, seeing so gracious and fair a stripling saluting him from below, had him called up and brought into his presence. As soon as Costanzo stood before him, the king demanded from what country he had come and by what name he was called. With a broad smile, the youth answered that he had journeyed from Thebes, driven out by envious and deceitful fortune, and that his name was Costanzo. He declared, moreover, that he desired to place himself in the service of such a great lord, promising all the faith and affection that good service entailed. Meanwhile, the king found himself greatly pleased by the appearance of the youth and said to him, 'Seeing that you bear the name of my city, it is my will that you stay here in my court with no other duties but to attend upon my person.'

The youth, who looked for no better employment than this, first rendered his gratitude to the king and quite joyfully accepted service under him as his lord, offering at the same time to hold himself ready to discharge any duty that might be assigned to him.

So Costanza, in the guise of a man, entered into the service of the king, serving him so well and courteously that everyone who knew him was astonished by his talents. It happened, too, that the queen, when she had well observed and considered Costanzo's graceful bearing, pleasant manners, and discreet behaviour, began to fix her eyes more diligently upon him, so that neither by day nor by night did she turn her thoughts upon any other. The glances she was forever darting in his direction were so soft and loving that not only a youth, but even the hardest rock – even a diamond itself – might have been softened. Thus consumed with her passion for Costanzo, the queen yearned only for an occasion to be alone with him, and before long that opportunity arrived to ask him outright whether it would please him to enter into her service, making it clear that over and above the reward she would give him, he would be more than welcome, sought after, and honoured at the court.

Costanzo understood clearly enough the drift of these words coming out of the queen's mouth, which expressed no goodwill for his advancement, but only her amorous passion. Moreover, being a woman like herself, she could not possibly satisfy the unbridled lust that prompted them. Humbly, thus, she answered her, 'Signora, my bond of service to my lord, your husband, is so strong that I would feel it a base injury were I to withdraw myself from obedience to his will. Therefore, I ask you to hold me excused and to pardon me that I am not ready and willing to take service with you, asking you to accept as the reason of my refusal of your gracious offer my resolve to serve my lord even unto death, provided that he is pleased to retain me as his man.'

Having then taken leave of the queen, he withdrew from her presence. The queen, who understood very well that oak trees are not felled with a single stroke, made several attempts on subsequent occasions, using her deepest cunning and art to entice Costanzo into taking service with her. But the youth, as constant and strong as a high tower beaten by the winds, remained unmoved. When the queen became conscious of this, her ardent burning love turned to mortal, bitter hatred, so that she could no longer bear the sight of him. Being now anxious to work his destruction, she pondered day and night how she might best bring this about, although she was in great fear of the king because he held the youth in such high esteem.

Now in the land of Bithynia there was a strange race of beings having one half of their body, the upper part, in the shape of a man, but with ears and horns like those of animals, while the lower part resembled a rough shaggy goat with a little tail twisted and curled like a pig's. These creatures were called satyrs, whose mischievous activities caused great loss and damage to the villages and farms of the country dwellers. The king desired to have one of these satyrs taken alive and delivered into his keeping, but there was no one in the court with sufficient prowess to attempt the enterprise. The queen sought Costanzo's destruction by having him sent on such an errand, but the outcome of the matter was not at all what she desired, for as often happens, by the working of divine providence and supreme justice, the intended deceiver is cast under the feet of the one she most sought to beguile.

The treacherous queen, very well aware of the king's desire, happened one day to be in conversation with him over various matters, and while they were thus debating, she mentioned to him, 'My lord, have you never considered that Costanzo, your faithful and devoted servant, is a knight so strong and courageous that he might easily capture one of these satyrs for you and bring him back alive, without calling on anyone else to aid him. And if events should unfold in this way, as I believe they would, you might give it a try right away, so that within an hour you would attain the wish of your heart and, as a brave and valiant knight, Costanzo would enjoy the honour of the deed to his eternal glory and triumph.'

The cunning queen's speech pleased the king greatly, and so he had Costanzo called immediately into his presence and said to him, 'Costanzo, if you revere me as much as you make a show of doing, and as all people are led to believe, you will now carry out my heart's wish and earn for yourself the glory of fulfilling the deed. You know that more than anything else in the world I yearn to have a live satyr in my own keeping. Seeing how strong and active you are, I believe there is no other man in all my kingdom so well suited to accomplish this as you. Loving me as you do, I know you will not refuse me.'

Assuming this demand to have come from the king's own heart, the youth was anxious not to vex him and thus answered with a cheerful and amiable face, 'My lord, in this as in everything else you may command me. Weak as my best strength may be, I would never hold back from striving to fulfil your wish, even though in the task I should meet my death. But before I commit myself to this perilous adventure, I would ask you, my lord, that you have a large vessel with a wide mouth carried into the wood where the satyrs live, no smaller than the great bowls in which the maids wash their nightgowns and other personal linens. Beside this, have a large cask of good wine taken there, the best and strongest that can be had, together with two bags full of the finest white bread.' Without delay, the king made the request to prepare everything that Costanzo had mentioned, and then Costanzo set out for the satyr's wood. When he arrived, he took a copper bucket and began to fill it with wine drawn from the cask and this he poured into the other vessel standing nearby. Next he took some of the bread, and having broken it into pieces, he put these into the vessel full of wine. This done, he climbed up into a thick-leaved tree standing nearby and waited to see what might happen next.

No sooner was he in the tree than the satyrs, having smelt the scent of the fragrant wine, began to gather round the vessel, each one swilling from it a good bellyful of wine, like hungry wolves when they fall upon a fold of young lambs. After they had taken their fill, they lay down to sleep, falling into a slumber so sound and deep that all the noise in the world would not have awakened them. Then Costanzo, seeing that the time for action had come, descended from the tree and went softly up to one of the satyrs whose hands and feet he bound fast with a cord. Next, without making any noise, he placed him upon his horse and carried him away. While Costanzo was on his way back with the satyr tightly bound behind him, they came towards evening to a village not far from the city. By this time, the creature had recovered from the effects of the wine, woken up, and began to yawn as though getting out of bed. Looking about, he saw the father of a family bitterly weeping in the middle of a little crowd going to bury a dead child, accompanied by a chanting priest there to conduct the service. Seeing this spectacle, the satyr began to laugh so heartily that he couldn't stop himself. Later, when they had entered into the city and had arrived at the great square, the satyr beheld a large crowd of people who were staring, their mouths agape, at a poor wretch on the gibbet about to be hanged. This time he laughed more loudly than he had laughed before. Afterward, when they had come to the palace, all the people standing by were taken by a rush of joy and started shouting, 'Costanzo, Costanzo!' The satyr, when he heard this outbreak, laughed louder than ever.

When Costanzo was conducted into the presence of the king and queen with her ladies, he presented the satyr to the king, whereupon the creature laughed again, and so loudly and long that everyone present was astonished. Seeing with what diligence Costanzo had fulfilled his wish, the king held him in the highest affection and esteem ever extended to a servant by his lord, which only added fresh grief to the burden already lying heavily on the queen's heart. Intending to ruin him, she had done nothing but exalt him to even greater honour. Now the wicked queen, unable to endure the sight of Costanzo's great fortune, devised yet another snare for him, which was this. She knew that the king went every morning to the cell where the satyr was kept, attempting for his diversion to make the creature talk, but entirely without success. Seeking out the king, she thus said to him, 'Sire, you have gone repeatedly to the satyr's cell where you have worn yourself out in an effort to induce him to talk to you for the sake of your diversion, but the creature shows no signs at all of saying a word. So why should you worry your brains over this further, for it is certain that if Costanzo were willing, he could easily make the satyr talk and answer questions.'

Hearing these words, the king had Costanzo straightway summoned into his presence and said to him, 'Costanzo, I am well assured that you know the extent of the pleasure I take from the satyr you captured for me. Nevertheless, I am much annoyed to find him dumb, refusing to make any answer to the questions I ask. But I'm certain you could make him speak.'

'Sire,' Costanzo replied, 'if the satyr is dumb, it is by no means my fault. It is the office of a god and not that of a mortal like me to make him speak. If, however, the reason for his muteness is not the result of natural or accidental defect, but a stubborn resolve to keep silence, I will do all that is in me to make him open his mouth in speech.'

Then, going together to the satyr's prison, they gave him some dainty food and even better wine and called out to him, 'Eat, Chiappino' – for this was the name they had given to the satyr. But the creature only stared at them without uttering a word. 'Come, Chiappino, tell us whether that capon and that wine are to your taste.' But still he was silent.

Costanzo, perceiving how obstinate the humour of the creature was, said, 'So you will not answer me, Chiappino. Let me tell you that it's a mighty foolish thing you're doing, given that I could, if I wanted to, just let you die of hunger here in prison.' At these words, the satyr shot a sidelong glance at Costanzo. After a short while, Costanzo went on, 'Rouse yourself and answer me, my Chiappino, for if you speak to me, as I hope you will, I will liberate you from this place.'

Then Chiappino, who had been listening eagerly all the while, when he heard of this chance at freedom, replied, 'So what do you want of me?'

Costanzo then said, 'Tell me, have you eaten well, and drunk to satisfaction?'

'Yes,' said Chiappino.

'Now I want you, by your leave, to tell me,' said Costanzo, 'what exactly it was that moved you to laughter in the village street when we met the dead child on its way to be buried?'

To this Chiappino replied, 'I didn't laugh at the dead child, but at the so-called father, to whom the child in the coffin was in fact no kin at all, and I laughed at the priest singing the office, for he was the real father,' by which speech the satyr would have them understand that the mother of the child had carried on an intrigue with the priest.

Then said Costanzo, 'And now I want to know, my Chiappino, what it was that made you laugh even louder when we came into the square?'

'I laughed then,' replied Chiappino, 'to see a thousand or more thieves who had robbed the public purse of crowns by the million, who deserved a thousand gibbets, standing in the square to feast their eyes on the sight of a poor wretch on the gallows, who perhaps may have pilfered ten florins to buy bread for himself and his poor children.'

Then said Costanzo, 'Tell me how it was, likewise, that when we came here into the palace you laughed longer and louder than ever?'

'Ah, for that I'll beg of you not to trouble me more right now,' said Chiappino, 'but to go your way and come back tomorrow, and then I'll answer you and tell you certain things about which, by chance, you haven't an inkling.'

When Constanzo heard this, he said to the king, 'Let us depart and come back tomorrow and find out what this thing may be.' So the king and Costanzo took their leave and gave orders that Chiappino should be given of the best to eat and drink to put him in fine humour for speaking freely thereafter.

When the next day arrived, they went once more to Chiappino and found him puffing and snoring like a great pig. Going up close to him, Costanzo called to him several times in a loud voice, but Chiappino, with his belly well filled, was fast asleep and as dumb as a stone. Then Costanzo gave him a sharp prick with one of his darts, whereupon the satyr awoke, stood up, and demanded who was there. 'Now get up, Chiappino,' said Costanzo, 'and tell us the thing you promised yesterday that we should hear. Explain why you laughed so loudly when we came to the palace?'

To this question Chiappino replied, 'For a reason which you should understand far better than I. In truth, it was from hearing them all shouting "Costanzo! Costanzo!" while all the time you have been Costanza.'

When the king heard this, he couldn't comprehend what Chiappino's words might mean, but Costanzo, who understood their significance immediately, quickly changed the subject and posed a different question, 'And when you had been taken into the presence of the king and queen, what made you laugh then as if nothing could stop you?'

To this Chiappino answered, 'I laughed so outrageously then because the king thinks that the maidens in waiting upon the queen are truly maidens, as do you. But I know that the greater part of them consists of young men.' With this he fell silent again.

The king didn't know what to say when he heard these words, but leaving the cell where the wild satyr was confined, he took Costanzo with him and together they went to a place where they could learn the truth. When matters had been put to the test, he discovered that Costanzo was indeed a woman, and that the supposed damsels about the queen were agile young men, just as Chiappino had said. Immediately the king had a huge fire kindled in the middle of the square into which he had the queen cast, together with her paramours, in the presence of all the people. Keeping in mind the loyalty and faithfulness of Costanza, and taking full note of her great beauty, the king made her his wife in the presence of all his barons and knights. Moreover, when he found out who her parents were, he was enormously pleased and straightway despatched ambassadors to King Ricardo and Valeriana his wife, and to the three sisters of Costanza, telling them that she was now a king's wife – all of whom felt joy over such good news. Thus the noble Costanza, in reward for the faithful service she had rendered, became queen at last and lived long with Cacco her husband.

As soon as Fiordiana had brought her fable to an end, the Signora made her a sign to give her enigma. The damsel, who was somewhat disdainful, although more by chance than by nature, set it out in the following words:

Over savage lions twain
A spirit soft and mild doth reign.
By her side four damsels move,
Prudence, Valour, Faith, and Love.
She bears a sword in her right hand,
Before it calm the righteous stand,
But wicked men and souls unjust
It smites and lays them in the dust.
Discord nor wrong with her may rest,
And he who loves her wins the best.

This clever enigma won the praise of all, some finding its meaning to be one thing and some another. But there was no one who could really and truly divine the sense if it. When Fiordiana saw this, she said outright, 'Ladies and gentlemen, you are all labouring in vain, for my riddle signifies nothing other than justice, infinite and equal, which is erected and established to hold sway over humankind in the manner of the gentle tamer of savage and hungry lions, by which I mean men of arrogant and unbridled spirit. She holds in her right hand a sharp sword, accompanied by the four virtues, which is to say, Prudence, Fortitude, Faith, and Charity. She is gentle and kind to the good, but hard and harsh to the wicked.' When Fiordiana ceased speaking, the listeners were greatly pleased with the interpretation of her enigma. Then the Signora asked Vicenza to follow in her turn with a fable, which she did in the following words:

IV.1 Commentary

Three motifs or miniature stories meet to form the story of Costanza. The first is indebted to medieval romance and features a girl disguised as a knight who, for want of a dowry and in danger of being forced into an arranged marriage, proudly chooses to find a place in the world equal to her rank. That she marries a king in the end, after engaging in a dangerous quest for the satyr, is not only the completion of a romance-cum-fairy tale, but the confirmation of her aristocratic entitlement. The second plot is of Eastern provenance and deals with the erotic despotism of the queen who, when her advances are rejected by the girl-knight taken for a young man, seeks either to send 'him' to his death on a dangerous mission, or to have 'him' punished for attempted rape by bearing false witness to her husband.[1] Paralleling this is the equally archetypal tale,

---

1 Concerning the ancient tradition of the scorned wife, Angelo de Gubernatis goes back to the story of Anapu e Bitiu as well as to Joseph and Potiphar's wife and to theories of their origins in seasonal or cult myths in *Storia delle novelline popolari* (Milan: Ulrico Höpli, 1883), pp. 58–60. The story is told in the names of Anapou (Anubis) and Satou in the introduction to *Sindibad*, by W.A. Clouston ([Glasgow]: Privately Printed for Subscribers, 1884), pp. xxiv–xxvi. Two brothers work the fields. The elder sends the younger to his wife to ask for seed and she offers more. When the lad refuses her advances, she accuses him by staging a rape scene. The cows warn Satou that his brother awaits him in the barn to kill him and he flees, invoking the aid of the Sun-god Re. Crocodiles intervene, but Satou mutilates himself to prove his innocence and leaves his brother's company. The version best known to all readers of Eastern literature is that which forms the framing tales of the *Historia septem sapientum*, *The History of the Seven Sages*, *Dolopathos*, and the *History of the Forty Vezirs or the Story of the Forty Morns and Eves*, each one a variation on the tale of the wise young prince under a vow of silence and thus unable to protect himself against the false accusations of his stepmother, who, when he rejects her advances, accuses him of that which he refuses to do. Deemed guilty by his silence, his death at the hand of his own father is delayed only by the strategic storytelling

originating in ancient India, of an immodest queen whose activities are revealed to the king by a supernatural creature whose ironic laughter is the prelude to her exposure. The third story is ambiguously Mediterranean or Nordic, depending on whether the beast to be captured and returned to court is the southern satyr or the northern wild man of the woods.[2] In both cases, the creature has the human capacity for speech and in the end is brought to explain his enigmatic conduct by revealing

---

of the various sages and viziers who trust in his innocence. For further perspective on the scorned queen and her revenge, see N.M. Penzer's annotations to the *Ocean of the Streams of Story* (Kathā sarit sāgara), trans. C.H. Tawney, 10 vols. (Delhi: Motilal Banarsidas, 1923), vol. II, pp. 120–4.

2 Both are invoked here because while Straparola opts for a satyr, his nearest literary antecedents present Merlin in the guise of the wild man. The satyr in literature merits monographic treatment because the half-human creature of ancient Greco-Roman mythology passed into Christian mythology as a form of demon or devil. The satyr at one point was treated as a pre-Adamic creature, to be associated with the 'sons' who later begot monstrous offspring in the manner of incubi upon the daughters of men. They lived in desert or forest areas, in the manner of Pan and his troops, as wild creatures impossible to catch, but subject to human appetites. All this is reflected in Costanza's tactics for capturing one. At the same time, satyrs were thought to host the transmigrated souls of men, according to Pythagoras, so that while as beasts they were stubborn, enigmatic, secretive, and bent upon preserving their savage liberty, yet as enlightened spirits they were associated with soothsayers and seers. Moreover, although reluctant in its use, they are graced with the powers of speech. The creature is employed in the present tale as a prophet and soothsayer, an agent in a family intrigue, who is motivated, like Shakespeare's Ariel, by the promise of liberty. The Renaissance took an interest in such beings from a scientific perspective as hybridized monsters, so that it was only in the folk tale that they were kept alive as mythological beings. Hédelin d'Aubignac considered them to be entirely bestial, having no human part, but the satyr was studied by Pico della Mirandola and Paracelsus as proto-humans, thereby maintaining the debate over pre-Adamic creatures. Meanwhile, humanists kept alive the legacy of Pausanias, Pliny, and Plutarch, while Saint Jerome, in 'The Life of Saint Paul,' the first hermit (ca. 377), talked of Saint Anthony and the satyr demons. Hédelin d'Aubignac, *Des Satyres brutes, monstres et démons*, ed. Gilles Banderier (Grenoble: Jérôme Millon, 2003); *Les vies de saints pères des déserts*, trans. Arnaud d'Andilly (Paris: Louis Josse, 1701), vol. I, p. 78; Jean Miniac, *Vivre au désert* (Grenoble: Jérôme Millon, 1992), pp. 31–2. When Straparola wrote the tale, satyrs were still in the news. The story of the mortal who captures a woodland creature by tricking it with food and wine and then releases it when it has revealed secrets has its origins in antiquity. The capture of Silenus by the shepherds of King Midas, who induced the creature to tell secrets about the universe, is recorded by Aelian (Claudius Aelianus) in [*Various Histories*], *Books I–V*, trans. Alwyn Faber Scholfield (London: Heinemann, 1959), bk. III, sect. 18.

the truth concerning both the wicked queen's illicit pastimes and the girl-knight's true nature, in essence resolving two stories condensed into one. In this regard, the tale is an ingeniously opportune amalgamation of identifiable parts, which, in less investigative terms, produces a miniature romance in which the heroine as adventurer rises at a foreign court, finds herself unwillingly involved in a sexual intrigue, acquits herself honourably in the quest for the wild man, and secures her future through marriage – although Straparola makes less than some of his imitators in involving her indifferent sisters and helpless parents in the moment of her triumph.[3]

Readers will have their own intuitions regarding the staying power of this narrative configuration involving the cross-dressing of a royal heroine in quest, the Potiphar's wife motif, and the capture of the truth-speaking satyr. Each episode has its own independent history with claims to considerable antiquity, including parallels in Greco-roman mythology involving scorned and vengeful queens and the lore of semi-human creatures of the woodlands or desert places. Romance overtones are maintained by the choice of place names in Straparola's tale, for Costanza sets out from the court of Thebes and arrives at the court of Bittinia, which may safely be read as Bithynia.[4] This was one of the preferred places in the world for Western writers to pitch their fanciful romances,

3 Stith Thompson refers to this story type in generic terms as Type 514, in which a maiden in male disguise goes off to the wars or is involved in a seduction plot that leads to dangerous expeditions or to accusations forcing her to disrobe to prove her innocence. *The Folktale* (1946; reprint, Berkeley: University of California Press, 1977), p. 55. My own analysis of the story's parts breaks away from assigning the story to the 'Corvetto' type, ATU 328, which comes together more persuasively in Basile's *Pentamerone*, IV.1, in which a youth at court, disliked, is betrayed into performing impossible or life-threatening tasks with the help of a wild horse, or the advice of a wild man, thereby enabling him to return with the keys to an ogre's castle and so regain his credit. 'Costanza' takes over parts of this story, but its principle aspects are more clearly seen in 'Guerrino,' V.1, and 'Livoretto,' III.2.

4 Faouzia Demnati studies these stories in relation to their exotic African and Near Eastern settings as a retrospective on the rich, exotic, and marvelous cities of the Crusader era. 'Costanza, the Girl-Knight' involves a traveller who encounters the oriental city as a place of civilization, luxury, and leisure, pitched to a readership on the eve of the Counter-Reformation. These are intriguing perspectives, perhaps exceeding Straparola's intentions, but a reminder that such stories do encourage the imagination to wander, as in the romance settings of a great deal of Renaissance fiction. *L'altérité orientalo-mauresque dans la culture du quotidian en Italie à l'époque de la Renaissance* (Manouba, Tunisia: Publications de la faculté des lettres, 2000), p. 395.

in company with others such as Bohemia, Natolia, Mantinea, or Phrygia. In effect, it is as though Straparola had poured an entire *chanson de geste* into a *novella,* beginning with the search for a suitable partner in the world; the strategy for the protection of female chastity by assuming a male disguise, as with Spenser's Britomart in the third book of his *Faerie Queene* and all her forebears in the literature of female knights; the danger of predatory sexuality and related court intrigues; the redeeming (or initiatory) quest to a wild place to do battle with a monster or prodigy; and the escape from calumniators by reclaiming female status and the romance entitlements garnered through eligibility for marriage.[5] That is to say, Costanza is a heroine eliciting empathy. She is a narrative centre who redeems her destiny in a royal match through determination and intelligence.[6] Her long speech to her parents expressing her disappointments and ambitions, and her intention to find her rightful status by venturing through the world, shapes the well-wishing that guides the plot to its conclusion. Treacherous queens and evasive satyrs are but accessories and obstacles to her archetypal life trajectory. To be sure, she reveals no particular interiority in relation to her disguise, or in her unwavering and out-of-hand rejection of a desiring queen, nor do we have much indication that she feels emotional partiality to the king before the fact of the queen's execution.

Nevertheless, she progresses from episode to episode in precisely the order followed by Viola in Shakespeare's *Twelfth Night,* from seeking a place in male disguise at the court of the duke she will later marry, to erotic solicitations on the part of a commandeering woman, to a mock sword fight to protect her masculine honour, to liberating herself from the accusations of a scorned woman, to revealing the riddle of her sex in anticipation of marriage. The satyr's revelations obviate the need for Costanza to pull down her dress before the king to prove her innocence, but it is telling that in Shakespeare's source, 'Of Apolonius and Silla' in

5 It would be supererogation here to elaborate on the many tales both literary and folkloric that feature girls disguised as boys in order to circulate freely in a predatory world while preserving their chastity. On this topic, see Shahrukh Husain, *Handsome Heroines: Women as Men in Folklore* (New York: Doubleday, 1995).

6 For an extensive study of the tradition of sex changes in fiction in relation to 'La doncella guerrera' or the young female warrior, see the commentary by Aurelio M. Espinosa for story no. 155, 'El oricuerno,' which combines the romance stories of the female knight with stories of remarkable sex changes in his *Cuentos populares españoles* (Madrid: S. Aguirre, 1947), vol. III, pp. 97–107.

Barnabe Riche's *Farewell to Military Profession*, Silla is compelled to do just that in the presence of the accusing woman who was more than scorned, but actually pregnant by the heroine's lookalike brother.[7] Had Costanza been accused of sex crimes against the queen, she had her own sex as alibi. There is an interlocking narrative vocabulary linking these divergent unmaskings. Such is Costanza's micro-romance with its character-testing feats. But the origin of the story lies elsewhere, namely in the tale of the cheating queen whose secret is revealed by a supernatural creature with soothsaying powers, to which the many romance-inspired elements are added. The intriguing feature of Straparola's 'Costanza, the Girl-Knight' is that it preserves its folkloric elements in full view – an assurance that his version of the story was not scaled back from medieval romance, but was built up from ancient narrative parts forming a compound folk tale, again suggesting that Straparola worked principally from oral rather than written sources.

One of the telltale features of the plot, in this regard, is the continuation of the scorned queen's tale, not with the usual accusation of attempted rape, but with the request to send the now despised protagonist on a dangerous quest (a feature already seen in the Livoretto group, III.2). It derives from the ancient plot of the lecherous queen and the laughing animal by whose antics her infidelity is eventually made known. That ancient story was the core around which the Costanza prototype was built as the Indo-Arabic fable resituated itself in a European context. In the story 'Yogananda and his Queen' from the celebrated *Ocean of the*

7 Ed. Donald Beecher (Ottawa: Dovehouse Editions, and Binghamton, NY: MRTS, 1992), p. 199. Just as the spurned and vengeful queen may be said to belong to the Phaedra prototype, who, as the wife of King Theseus, fell in love with her stepson Hippolytus, accused him of attempted rape, and allowed him to be executed by the king, so the girl falsely accused of attempted rape may be said to belong to the Saint Eugenia prototype, for she, the daughter of a duke, joined a monastic community in the habit of a man and in time became abbot. When accused of rape before a judge (who was her own father), rather than allow herself to be executed, she tore open her robes to prove herself a woman and thereby expose the calumny of her accuser. Her story is to be found in *The Golden Legend* of Jacobus de Voragine and there is a fine carving of the breast-bearing scene on a capital along the north aisle of Vézelay Abbey (Basilique Ste-Madeleine). As for stories featuring the narrative motor provided by a scorned and despotic woman who accuses a male of attempted rape, the count might run very high; Boccaccio's story of 'The Count of Antwerp' (II.8) comes immediately to mind. *The Decameron*, trans. J.M. Rigg, 2 vols. (London: The Navarre Society, n.d.), vol. I, pp. 137–51.

Streams of Stories (*Kathā sarit sāgara*), assembled around 1100 from a rich treasury of tales then in circulation, a Brahmin is led off to execution by order of the jealous king for merely chatting with the queen.[8] On the way, however, a fish in a market stall, even though it was dead, began to laugh. The king was advised to stay the execution until he knew the reason why. His wise man, Vararuchi, is told to climb a palm tree and watch. A terrible female Rakshasa happens by in search of food for her children, having been promised the flesh of the executed Brahmin. The wise man overhears her explain to the children that because the fish laughed, their meal has been delayed. The children ask why and they learn that the king's wives are all unfaithful and that the harem is full of men dressed as women, while an innocent Brahmin is about to die. This irony amused the fish.[9] So the spy in the tree informs the king on

---

8 Somadeva, *Kathā sarit sāgara* (Ocean of the streams of stories), trans. C.H. Tawney, 2 vols. (Calcutta: The Asiatic Society, 1880; reprint, New Delhi: Munshiram Manoharlal, 1992), vol. I, pp. 24–5. One of the earliest students of this story tradition was Felix Liebrecht, in the first volume of *Orient und Occident* (Leipzig: J.C. Hinrichs, 1929), p. 341. The best known of the Arabian versions is found in the framing tale of *The Arabian Nights*, ed. J.C. Mardrus and E.P. Mathers (London: Routledge, 1964), vol. I. When Shah Zaman remains behind in his brother's (King Shahryar's) palace while the king is out hunting, he witnesses the queen's twenty slave girls, ten of whom turn out to be men, engage in an orgy while the queen herself enjoys the services of a hideous blackamoor who drops down from a tree in the courtyard. This spectacle is therapy for Zaman, who was melancholy over the infidelity and execution of his own wife, for he might now conclude that the vice is common to women and the way of the world. His sudden return to health intrigues the king, who forces an explanation. The two kings set off wandering, and from their vantage in a tree they see a Jinni with a girl locked away in a box who, when the Jinni falls asleep, demands and receives sexual gratification from the two men, bidden down from the tree and threatened unless they comply – all to spite the Ifrit who had taken such pains to keep her services exclusive. Disabused of all illusions concerning the sex, they return, and King Shahryar not only slays his queen, but sets about the routine execution of all the girls in the harem after deflowering them one by one. This version preserves the cross-dressed men hidden in the queen's entourage, but does not have the animal confessor, or the mocking laugh that arouses the curiosity that springs the denouement.

9 The motif of the laughing creature or deity in response to facts and events to which others are blind or misinformed is a motif that appears in Indian fairy tales down to the nineteenth century. One such is 'The Fakir Ninaksa Saves the Merchant's Life,' collected by Maive Stokes. The fakir understood the irony in situations particularly involving animals that contain the souls of humans. *Indian Fairy Tales*, annotations by Mary Stokes (London: Ellis & White, 1880), pp. 114–18. It also occurs in the *Folktales of Kashmir*, ed. James Hinton Knowles (London: Trübner, 1888), pp. 484*ff.*

the authority of the Rakshasa, bringing about the release of the holy man. The women are not punished, for the point of the story is the injudicious behaviour and caprice of all-powerful rulers in the handling of justice. That is demonstrated when Vararuchi, for having revealed his knowledge of a hidden mark on the queen's body, is himself executed. But in later versions of the story, the women, for their lechery, are destroyed.

The oldest source on record of the story of the immodest queen exposed by a supernatural creature through the instrumentation of a young girl reticent to reveal the truth directly to the king is the *Çukasaptati*, dating to the sixth century or earlier.[10] The Queen Kamalila one morning refuses to eat a certain fish because it is a male, causing the fish to laugh out loud. The king compels his Brahmin on pain of banishment to explain the phenomenon, and the chief Brahmin in turn relates his dilemma to his daughter, who goes before the king. But she merely stalls matters through her evasive answers. Meanwhile, a minister whose laughter causes roses to fall from his lips is imprisoned because he refuses to reveal the source of this special talent. The Brahmin's daughter tells the king to find out why, and the minister accounts for his disinclination in terms of the infidelity of his wife. When the king turns to the queen and gives her a playful tap regarding the matter, she falls into a swoon, which causes the minister to break out laughing – presumably because, as in the *Arabian Nights*' tale of the ruler and his brother, the victim of cuckoldry has found a fellow sufferer in the king. But why, specifically, does he laugh? Because when the queen's lover had beaten her the night before she did not swoon, the minister explains. The king then sets up a search both for the marks on her body and for the lover who is hidden in a chest, with appropriate punishments to follow. Even in this early version, it is seen how the accusation is redirected as an

---

Egyptian versions of the story of considerable antiquity may be found among the *Egyptian Tales Translated from the Papyri* by William Matthew Flinders-Petrie (London: Methuen, 1895), vol. II, pp. 107–18, 129–30.

10 *Die Çukasaptati*, trans. Richard Schmidt (Kiel: Brockhaus, 1893), pp. 11–23. *Suka saptati* of Gangādhar Sarangi (Kataka: Ke Malika, 1968), known in English as 'The Queen and the Laughing Fish,' in *The Enchanted Parrot*, trans. B. Hale Wortham (London: Luzac, 1911), no. 5, pp. 27–32. A related version is recorded by James Hinton Knowles in *Folk-tales of Kashmir* (London: Trübner, 1888), pp. 484–90. This work was reissued by Arno Press, New York, in 1977.

inquest which frees the intermediaries from danger; it has taken an evasive girl and an equally evasive minister to get the truth out.

It is around this nucleus that the entire story unfolds. We are to imagine that as the story progressed towards the West, each receiving culture had to provide the surrounding circumstances for exposing the queen, in accordance with the necessity that such a dangerous revelation be displaced among voices compelled to speak against their wills – a feature carried through in Straparola when the satyr refuses to speak, forewarning the king that he may not appreciate what he learns. In the Western oikotype of the tale, closely followed by Straparola, the Brahmin's daughter is replaced by the girl-knight who, in her adventures, encounters the lecherous queen, while the Rakshasa, an Eastern demonic figure with soothsaying powers, is replaced by a satyr or wild man (leading earlier to the many versions in which Merlin plays the role opposite Grisandole, the counterpart to Costanza). That the girl-knight and the satyr bring bits of their own lore into the story is a collateral part of the Western reconfiguration.

Speculation is free as to how this motif flourished in the Arabic-speaking world, but for our purposes, the important fact is that it was known in the West by the twelfth century.[11] There is the prospect that the story entered through the Iberian Peninsula, given its version in the *Scha'ascherim* of Yosef ben Me'ir ibn Zabara, dating to that period.[12]

11 The motif of the boys disguised as girls in the queen's entourage made its way to the West in the form it was given in the *Kātha Sarit Sāgara* of Somadeva (it was not included in the *Tooti Nameh* or the originating *Çukasaptati*).

12 Yosef ben Me'ir ibn Zabara, *Sepher Shaashuim: A Book of Medieval Lore*, ed. Israel Davidson (New York: Jewish Theological Seminary of America, 1914); *The Book of Delight*, ed. Merriam Sherwood, trans. Moses Hadas (New York: Columbia University Press [1932], 1960), chap. 3, pp. 75–6. A wise young girl, pleasing to the king's sight, offers to interpret his troubling dream. Having heard it, she is 'abashed' to tell him the truth, but tells him finally to search among his wives and maidservants where he would find a man in women's clothes – he who is the ape of the dream 'leaping on the necks of your women.' Vengeance follows: the king first butchers the man in the presence his womenfolk, then slays them all to the last one and marries the maiden. See also the 233rd story of Jacques de Vitry in *The Exempla or Illustrative Stories from the Sermones Vulgares*, ed. Thomas Frederick Crane (London: David Nutt, 1890), pp. 229–30. In this version, a demon named Guinehochet tells a man that he has only one son, not two, for the other is the priest's. The man demands to know which is the false son and the demon refuses, saying that he has to nourish both or neither. The parallel with the satyr's behaviour in the present story is clear. Just how the motif travelled and developed is work for others, but sources to consider,

Arguably more important than all the literary renditions to follow, however, including those embedded in the various lives of Merlin, is the formation of the folk tale designated 'X' by Lucy Allen Paton, namely a Western prototype which preserved the generic parts of the Eastern story as a 'living' tale that was orally disseminated throughout the following seven centuries. Admittedly, it is only through the complex literary adaptations based on that tale that we can reconstruct its passage, yet according to Paton it is the folk tale 'X,' as it continued to evolve and spread, that provided the models for all such literary treatments – including Straparola's and Basile's – and not the literary adaptations themselves. That thesis stands to reason in light of the difficulty in accounting for the derivation of the literary versions from each other. This is now a familiar crux and will remain so, given the priority accorded routinely to texts in the propagation of texts, and the work of scholars reasoning out how authors modify the work of others. In the case of 'Costanza,' one late-fifteenth-century text, in particular, is apt for assessment as a source and must not be ruled out. Thus, the following history of cognate tales treats the surviving literary evidence both as potential source material and as indirect evidence of the unfolding folk tradition that survived down the nineteenth century, of which the present tale offers itself as the earliest transcription. Ultimately, the choice is between a literary rendition somewhat dissimilar to the Straparolan tale, but from which he managed to extract his more generic version, and a current folk tale the nature of which cannot be independently corroborated for another three centuries. But a folk tale there was, from which the tale of 'Costanza' is borrowed, whether directly or indirectly, for what is patently clear is that no claim can be made for Straparola as author of any part of the story.

Valentin Schmidt was the first to claim the early Merlin adaptations of 'X' as Straparola's direct literary source, but it is difficult to imagine how he could have rediscovered the generic folk tale buried in such stylized and historicized materials. There is a better case to be made for a folk tradition which preserved the common tale that at one point gave

according to Thomas Crane, include Brit. Lib. MS. Harleian 463, folio 19, included in Thomas Wright's *A Selection of Latin Stories from Manuscripts of the 13th and 14th Centuries* (London: T. Richards, 1842), as no. 15, and another, no. 44 (p. 43) in that same work from MS. Arundel no. 52, folio 114. See also Theobaldus Anguibertus, *Mensa philosophica* (Cologne: Zyryckzee, 1508), p. 241.

rise to Grisandole and at another to Costanza.[13] To represent this early segment of the tale's literary history, I have chosen the thirteenth-century *Roman de Merlin* in which the author assigns to the celebrated Celtic shape-shifter and mage, Merlin, the role of the sage who sees into the queen's nature and the corruption of her entourage. But it is to be underscored that the folk material had been incorporated into the story of Merlin as early as 1150 in the *Vita Merlini*, attributed to Geoffrey of Monmouth. That work, in turn, draws upon Welsh legend concerning the suffering that drives men to seek refuge in the wolds and that grants to them the powers of prophecy. The episode in which Merlin returns to the court to laugh his mysterious laughter at his sister, Queen Ganeida with the leaf in her hair, the sign of her infidelity, is the earliest trace of the Eastern story refitted upon the Celtic king and mage.[14] The author redeploys such enigmatic laughter as a prompt for revealing hidden truths in several subsequent episodes. This work inspired the *Prose Lancelot*, from which arose *Arthur and Merlin* (ca. 1250), *Merlin* (1425), and the *Prose Merlin* (1450). In these last three, the famous soothsayer

---

13 Lucy Allen Paton, 'The Story of Grisandole: A Study in the Legend of Merlin,' *PMLA* 22, no. 2 (1907), p. 248: 'It is evident also that X is not a reworking of *Grisandole*, but that the latter must be a redaction of X, from which its important variations occur in those parts where Grisandole's career touches Merlin's.' Friedrich Wilhelm Valentin Schmidt, 'Die Prinzessin als Ritter,' in *Die Märchen des Straparola*, vol. I, of *Sammlung alter Märchen* (Berlin: Duncker & Humblot, 1817), p. 335: 'Diese romantische Erzählung hat Strap. entlehnt aus dem Roman von Merlin' (This romance tale Strap. borrowed from the Tale of Merlin).

14 According to John Matthews, Merlin the wild man is inspired by the semi-mythical madman Lailoken who lived in the lowlands of Scotland. Both are noted for their prophetic laughter in series of three. Merlin laughs at the wife of King Rhydderch with the leaf in her hair, at the beggar who is sitting over a pot of gold, and the youth who purchases shoes on the day he is destined to die. According to this account, Queen Ganeida is Merlin's sister who tests his sanity, not the unfaithful queen. Behind all these practices he sees the initiation rites of the shaman. *King Arthur: Dark Age Warrior and Mythic Hero* (New York: Random House, Gramercy, 2004), p. 47. See also J.S.P. Tatlock, 'Geoffrey of Monmouth's *Vita Merlini*,' *Speculum: A Journal of Mediæval Studies* 18, no. 3 (July 1943), pp. 265–87. This article deals with the causes behind his retreat to the Caledonian woods, his madness, his life among the beasts, as well as his powers of divination in dealing with his sister Ganeida's adultery, and his subsequent prophesies. Tatlock traced the detection of adultery by a leaf in the hair to the Celtic legend of Lailoken, dating to AD 603, but the enigmatic laughter is Oriental.

frequently appears in disguise, laughs ironically at human foibles, and makes devastating prophesies.[15]

In a brief retelling of the highlights, the elements in common with the story of 'Costanza' can be seen at a glance. The preoccupations of the Medieval storyteller are fully manifest, based though they are on a written source, for the setting is the Rome of Julius Caesar, and the heroine who comes riding to court disguised as the knight Grisandole is Avenable, daughter of the maligned and exiled Duke Mathum of Germany.[16] She becomes Caesar's cup-bearer. Thereafter, Caesar dreams of a pig with long shaggy hair and twelve young lions, all of whom he consigns to the flames. Tormented by its possible meaning, he offers his daughter in marriage to the person who resolves the riddle. Merlin appears in the form of a stag (or a herdsman so disguised) to explain that only a wild man could offer the solution. The task falls upon Grisandole to roam

---

15 For more on the Merlin tradition, see Christopher Dean, *A Study of Merlin in English Literature from the Middle Ages to the Present Day: The Devil's Son* (Lewiston: Edwin Mellen Press, 1992).

16 Robert de Boron is credited with incorporating the tales of Merlin the prophet introduced by Geoffrey of Monmouth into the order of romance. Geoffrey (by 1136) had already elaborated upon the war-mad northern bard attached to the court of Arthur, said to have fled civilization to live in the woods in the sixth century, by making him a prophet in the Romano-British era of Ambrosius Aurelianus. That would have encouraged his further displacement into the age of Julius Caesar to whom, in the story of Grisandole, he presents himself in the form of a stag. Only a few lines of Robert de Boron's original verse romance survive (ca. 1190), but his work was preserved in the prose *Estoire de Merlin* (mid-thirteenth century), which in turn nourished the post-vulgate versions, the *Suite de Merlin*, and the English prose romance *Merlin*. This latter was edited by Henry Wheatley for the Early English Text Society, Orig. series 10, containing the complete prose *Vulgate Merlin*, chapters 1–6 of which cover Robert de Boron's *Merlin*. *Merlin or the Early History of King Arthur: A Prose Romance (about 1450–1460 AD) from the unique MS. in the University Library, Cambridge V=112*, ed. Henry Wheatley and William Mead (London: Trübner, 1899). The story also appears in *Le Livre d'Artus*, ed. H. Oskar Sommer (Washington: Carnegie Institution, 1908–16). The earliest surviving French romance on Merlin has been frequently published, including the edition entitled *Merlin: roman en prose du XIIIe siècle, publié avec la mise en prose de poems de Merlin de Robert de Boron*, ed. Jacob Ulrich and Gaston Paris (Paris: Firmin Didot, 1886). There are variations in the details among these several editions, including interpretations of the various circumstances encountered by the wild man on his return to Caesar's court. The present résumé reflects the version in *Le roman de Merlin l'Enchanteur, traduit en français moderne* (Paris: Henri de Briel, Librairie C. Klincksieck, 1971).

the forests in search of the wild man. A wild boar counsels her to use salted ham, honey, milk, and warm bread to lure the creature, and to employ four strong men to contain him. Then Merlin appears in the form of the wild man, striking his club against the trees, yet allows himself to be captured, laughing his mocking laughter all along, while refusing to explain himself except to the king. On the way, there is further laughter when he sees the poor at an abbey seeking alms, when he sees a stable-boy striking his master three times on the ear, and when he sees the queen with her twelve dames. The wild man's explanations reveal that the alms-seekers were standing above buried treasure, the blows represented the three orders of the realm (there are variant explanations), the twelve women were men, and that he, himself, who had never been bound by a man, had now been bound by a woman. Merlin had played all the parts and had upheld his reputation as a seer; he had fulfilled the role of the truth-speaking wild man. In the process, by provoking the queen's execution, he had cleared the way for a romance closure in which the heroine is married to Caesar and her father is exonerated and recalled. The Merlin appropriation became a literary tradition of its own with specific characteristics (absent in Straparola), but had fed initially upon the folk tale that pursued a parallel history down to recent times.

The business of supernatural laughter at hidden vices otherwise concealed to mortals was an integral part of the story type, but such vices and their ironic relations held a simultaneous place in the compilations of the writers of medieval exempla. This is particularly true of the father weeping for his dead son who is in fact lamenting the priest's son gotten with his wife, thus exemplifying the anxiety over paternity and the legitimacy of children. The *Mensa philosophica*, first published in 1487, contains a fragmentary version about a man seeking the truth in such matters from the Devil. The Devil insists that he has but one son, while the man, knowing he has two, calls the Devil a liar. To his chagrin, however, the explanation follows that the other is by the priest.[17] This is no doubt derived from Exemplum 233 in the collec-

17 [M. Scotus], *Mensa philosophica*, ed Erwin Rauner and Burghart Wachinger (Tübingen: Max Niemeyer Verlag, 1995), p. 133. It was originally published in Antwerp in 1487.

tion by Jacques de Vitry in which a demon in France named Guinehochet reveals such secrets. When asked by a man about the number of his sons, the demon replies that he has but one. The man accuses him of telling lies, but the demon explains that the other is the priest's. When the man demands to know the bastard in order to turn him out of doors, the demon refuses to say: 'You must either drive both away or feed both.'[18] This motif prevailed for centuries as a topic of enigmatic laughter, one of the many ironic circumstances that might arouse the mockery of those privileged to see into the hidden nature of things. Straparola's representation of such topics in his version of the tale no doubt originated in his source.

The story of Grisandole the girl-knight is a chivalric episode that draws upon the Eastern motif of the lecherous queen, on the northern European motif of the wild man of the woods with his powers of divination, as well as upon the Talmudic story of Aschmedai or Asmodeus.[19] Just who assembled the parts is a moot point, but the tale that came to Straparola featuring the heroine in disguise, the lechery of an oriental queen, the divinatory powers of a creature of the wilds, and closure in marriage was, by all this evidence, current in Europe by the second half of the twelfth century. Straparola may have looked to the *Istoria di Merlino*, translated from the French into Italian in 1480, but the clarity of narrative logic in his own retelling necessitates either a full correction

18 *The Exempla or Illustrative Stories from the Sermones Vulgares of Jacques De Vitry*, ed. Thomas Frederick Crane (London: David Nutt, 1890), p. 133. A version occurs in which the man claims to have four sons, to which the devil replies that he has only two. He is likewise told that he cannot know which: 'non faciam, tu omnes nutrias. Et non ausus fuit aliquem expellere, quia timebat expellere suos.' *Neue Beiträge zur Erzählungsliteratur des Mittelalters (Die 'Compilatio singularis exemplorum' der Hs. Tours 468)*, ed. Alfons Hilka (Breslau: Grass, Barth & Co., 1913), p. 73.

19 It is not clear how this parallel material from the lore of King Solomon is to be incorporated into the formation of the oral or literary tales of laughing outsiders who thereby provoke devastating revelations. Wine was used to lure Asmodeus into captivity, from whom King Solomon sought information. He too, in being led into the presence of the king, laughs enigmatically on three occasions, thereby setting up prophetic revelations. Presumably the Talmudic writers took up the folk materials to their own ends, much as the Merlin writers had done. The story of Asmodeus would appear to have no direct bearing on the formation of Straparola's source. See Lucy Allen Paton, 'The Story of Grisandole: A Study in the Legend of Merlin,' *PMLA* 22, no. 2 (1907), p. 247.

of the Merlin episodes or, more probably, reflects his familiarity with the folk tale from which the Merlin episode had fallen away.[20]

There are other literary works in which segments of Straparola's tale are quite intact, as in the first half of the *Novella del Fortunato,* where events correlate perfectly with the opening of 'Costanza.'[21] Both stories begin in Thebes. King Ricardo, too, has three daughters, marries them well, divides his realm into three parts, and has a fourth daughter late in life – Prudentia, born to Valeriana, daughter of King Merlino of Scotland. This daughter has all the graces of a young girl, but also takes up martial arts, jousting, and horsemanship, and, like Costanza, develops skills equal to any cavalier. A long encounter with her father concerning a marriage offer to Brunello, the son of a household marquis, and her proud rejection in the name of her ancestors, thereby launching her career as a girl-knight, constitutes far too many similarities for this *novella* not to have been among Straparola's sources. Moreover, by the report of Giovanni Papanti, its nineteenth-century editor, the work seems to have been first published in Venice by 'Hieronimo Cesalpini,' who was active in the very years Straparola published his *Piacevoli notti,* although the story itself may be considerably older. Conceivably, Straparola seized upon this contemporary publication of a work of undetermined authorship and undetermined age, extrapolating his Costanza from Prudentia. He could have modified the folk tale in the image of the literary romance to produce his own *novella.* But his dependence upon a folk tale version *tout court* remains equally possible.

Yet another story worth consideration is the fifth of Giovanni Sercambi's *Novelle,* which tells of the infidelity of a queen who keeps her lover hidden

20 Robert de Boron, *I due primi libri della istoria di Merlino ristampati secondo la rarissima edizione de 1480* (Bologna: R. Romagnoli, 1884). One of the intriguing details regarding the transmission of episodes and features among the many literary sources is that in the English *Merlin,* the wild man, as in Straparola, laughs while passing a funeral, followed by the same explanation that the man weeping is not the real father, but rather the priest who is reading the service. 'Introduction,' *Roman de Merlin,* pp. 44–6. In some fashion, this version of the tale had come to the author of 'Costanza.' There are many early references to Merlin in Italian literature that do not include the prophecy by laughter episodes, for which see Donald L. Hoffman, 'Merlin in Italian Literature,' *Merlin: A Casebook,* ed. P.H. Goodrich and R.H. Thompson (New York: Routledge, 2003), pp. 186–96.

21 *Novella [Piacevole] del Fortunato,* ed. Giovanni Papanti (Livorno: Francesco Vigo, 1869).

among her female entourage. When the king falls ill, he offers any reward, except his crown or his wife, for a cure. A wise doctor, through a series of investigations at court, exposes the queen and thereby cures the king, for his illness originates from his nightmares over her offending conduct. A grand assembly is held to which all the nobility is invited to bestow the promised reward. The doctor arrives nobly dressed, followed by a crowd of female admirers. But he, in fact, is a nobly born young woman who claims the king as her prize. This story would require extensive adjustments to become Straparola's, but that it belongs to the 'Costanza' type is readily apparent.[22]

That many elements of the Grisendole story appear in Giovanni Battista Basile's 'The Three Crowns' in *The Pentamerone*, written some seven or eight decades after Straparola, merely adds another episode to the general enigma surrounding their literary relationship, or lack thereof.[23] Again, there is nothing about the retelling that would suggest that Basile had Straparola open before him in tweaking this folk tale further in the direction of a fairy tale through his inimitable baroque stylizing. Basile is clearly working with materials common to the second half of 'Costanza,' but they are removed by diversification due to time and geographical distance. In short, Basile does not begin with the tale of Costanza, but with fairy tale material of his own combined with the girl-knight motif derived from a folk variation known in the south of Italy.

Basile opens with the motif of the royal daughter who is fairy-cursed from birth and kept mewed up in a tower throughout her childhood to avoid her fate. But when at last the girl is allowed to leave her ancestral home to marry, a crosswind simply carries her away and sets her down

---

22 For Giovanni Sercambi's 'De magna prudentia,' see his *Novelle*, ed. Rodolfo Renier (Turin: Ermanno Loescher, 1889), pp. 22*ff.* The story is in direct line from the Eastern tales, without the laughing fish, but with the king's enigmatic dream calling for interpretation by his wise men, ultimately revealing the queen's lover disguised as a maiden. This tale, missing so many of the narrative add-ons, is an unlikely source for Straparola, who had the shape of his narrative available to him in the 'home' format of the folk tale tradition more fully represented by the *Novella del Fortunato.* Also see Giovanni Sercambi, *Novelle*, ed. Giovanni Sinicropi, 2 vols. (Bari: Laterza, 1972), no. 5, vol. I, pp. 26–36.

23 *The Pentamerone*, trans. Richard Burton (New York: Boni & Liveright, 1927), IV.6, pp. 329–38. From *Lo cunto de li cunti overo lo trattenemiento de peccerille*, 5 vols. (Naples: Ottavio Beltrono, 1634), IV.6.

in front of a ghoula's house where she is in danger of being cannibalized. The tale we are expecting is nowhere in sight. Marchetta, for such is her name, wins favour by secretly putting the ghoula's house in order, herself acting like a fairy. However, after breaking a taboo that sets the ghoula's three daughters at liberty (the Bluebeard motif) she is forced to flee, disguised as a man. The king she meets while out hunting takes pity on her and makes her a court page. Naturally, the queen falls in love with the page, then comes to hate him for scorning her, and then accuses him openly of attempted rape (a motif not employed in 'Costanza'). The king accepts the matter at face value and the girl is carried off to the gibbet. There is to be no quest and no satyr, but another mechanism familiar to folk and fairy tales serves in their stead. At the eleventh hour, a mysterious voice reveals the truth while emanating from Marchetta's magic ring, a gift presented by the ghoula, who had taken pity on the girl after frightening her away. Marchetta's true gender is thus revealed, the king asks for the whole story from her own mouth, compares her situation to what he had heard from a fellow king, casts the accusing wife into the sea after weighting her body, and of course marries Marchetta. The stories compare at the typological level but represent highly divergent forms of the folk tale, whatever their immediate sources. That Basile borrowed from Straparola is again difficult to countenance, given the impoverishment of Basile's source and the discrepancies that separate them.

The two remaining directions of the commentary pertain to stories derived directly from Straparola's tale, predictably in France towards the end of the seventeenth century, and stories evincing close narrative affiliations with the 'Costanza' type, collected by the folklorists of the nineteenth century. The French literary elaborations reveal the potential embedded in Straparola's tales for amplification in a new literary context framed by the formalization of the fairy tale, while the perpetuation of the generic tale through a seemingly infinite number of oral versions recorded some three centuries later is an implicit argument for the abundance of such tales in Straparola's own time and the increased likelihood of one serving him directly as his source.

Thomas-Simon Gueullette's debt to Straparola is little acknowledged, but his story entitled 'The History of the Blue Centaur' is another that points to inspiration from the *Piacevoli notti*, no doubt through the highly successful Louveau translation. Gueullette was working in the shadow of Galland whose assembly of tales into the 'European' *Arabian Nights* had created the fashion for oriental tales. Gueullette's mission in his *Tartarian Tales, or a Thousand and One Quarters of Hours* was to create new oriental stories by refitting European tales with oriental settings and trappings.[24] In his restyling of 'Costanza,' he surrounds the familiar episodes with a love relationship between young royals who become separated. The princess, thinking the prince dead, disguises herself as a man and goes to Nanquin, where, for her winning ways and handsome appearance, she becomes the object of the queen's sexual advances. The heroine's disinclination turns the queen's desire to hatred, for which reason she is sent on the perilous quest to capture the arrow-proof Blue Centaur. True to the Straparolan model, she baits a trap with wine and food, and when the creature falls senseless with drink, she binds him in chains and takes him home. Along the way, as in 'Costanza,' the creature rouses himself and begins to laugh first at a funeral, then at a hanging, and finally at the court, yet even with imprisonment he refuses to explain himself. Gueullette does not forget that the queen can still make her accusations of attempted rape, and so the calumniated princess finds herself in prison beside the centaur, which makes him laugh even more. Hope of deliverance and fear of death, however, conspire to make the creature speak, not only to explain his enigmatic responses but to plead for the heroine's release. His insights are precisely those of Straparola's satyr: that the priest at the funeral was the father to the boy; that those who were to be hanged were but petty criminals; that the heroine was in a male disguise; and that two of the queen's close 'female' attendants were male sexual partners. Gueullette completes his little romance by having the newly discovered Princess of Georgia marry, not the king, but her once-missing prince. This and similar creations are part of Straparola's legacy.

Even though the Comtesse d'Aulnoy's *Belle-Belle, ou le Chevalier Fortuné* predates Gueullette's rendition by nearly two decades, it is altogether a more fanciful and freer adaptation, but without obliterating its underlying debt to Straparola.[25] This heroine-chevalier is sent by her father to fight for their deposed king, but fairy tale mechanisms soon intrude, for

24 The English translation was published in (London: J. & R. Tonson, 1759) from the French *Les mille et un quart-d'heure* (Utrecht: Etienne Neaulme [1715], 1737). See *Contes*, 3 vols., ed. Jean-François Perrin (Paris: Champion, 2010), vol. I, pp. 394–9.

25 Marie-Catherine d'Aulnoy, 'Belle-Belle, or, The Chevalier Fortuné,' in *The Great Fairy Tale Tradition*, trans. Jack Zipes (New York: W.W. Norton, 2001), pp. 174–205, from 'Belle-Belle, ou le Chevalier Fortuné,' in *Contes nouveaux ou les fées à la mode*, 2 vols. (Paris: Veuve de Théodore Girard, 1698), vol. II, in 'Le nouveau gentilhomme bourgeois' series; *Contes II, Contes nouveaux ou les fées à la mode*, ed. Philippe Hourcade and Jacques Barchilon (Paris: Société des Textes Français Modernes, 1998), pp. 215–69. This story also had its imitators, as in the story of Fortuné

in showing consideration to an aged shepherdess she wins the favour of the fairy held inside. The fairy gives to her a speaking horse named Camarade which, in turn, encourages her to enlist seven helpers with extraordinary skills along the way. At this juncture, we have fallen back to the story of Livoretto with his magic horse and the animal helpers he befriends through acts of kindness. Once at the court, however, Fortuné (for such is the name she adopts) not only wins the king's favour but attracts the queen's amorous attention. Once rejected, the spiteful queen has the disguised heroine sent to fight a dragon, but through the counsel of her horse and the aid of her helpers Fortuné prevails. In a second act of rancour, the scorned queen sends her to the court of the conquering emperor, Matapa, but again, through help from her friends, she returns victorious. Only then is she accused outright of attempted rape and condemned to death. Her true sex is revealed not through the laughter of a wild man or satyr, but simply by revealing herself to be female. The queen dowager, meanwhile, is poisoned by one of her confidants and in the end the king marries Belle-Belle. The story was written to illustrate two social clichés: that the fury of a scorned lover should never be underestimated; and that the heavens always fight for the innocent. It is also a miniature replay of the kind and unkind daughters, insofar as Belle-Belle's two older sisters meet the same shepherdess in distress and in scorning her earn the displeasure of the concealed fairy, so that all the jewels they touch thereafter turn to glass. The Comtesse d'Aulnoy was the most influential among the authors of the modern fairy tale in preserving and extending Straparola's legacy through adaptation.

The same narrative recurs in 'The Savage' by Henriette Julie de Murat, although this writer underscores new themes pertaining to physical beauty and the power of the imagination to fashion the public self.[26] Proof of the debt to Straparola is made clear by the elaborate replay of the family situation that opens 'Costanza.' Richardin and Coiranthe of

---

included in *Tabart's Collection of Popular Stories for the Nursery* (London: Tabart & Co., 1809), vol. II, pp. 148*ff.* Still to be investigated is the relationship between the story of the French author and the *Novello del Fortunato* (Leghorn: F. Vigo, 1869).

26 'The Savage,' in *The Great Fairy Tale Tradition,* trans. Jack Zipes (New York: W.W. Norton, 2001), pp. 205–19. Taken from Henriette Julie de Castelnau de Murat, *Histoires sublimes et allégoriques* (Paris: Florentin & Pierre Delaulne, 1699), 'Le sauvage.' Further work for specialists is the relationship between this tale and the Comtesse d'Aulnoy's, but it would appear that Julie de Murat knew the work of her predecessor and advanced her own imaginative interpretations accordingly.

Terceres have three ugly daughters designated to marriages which promise to produce a race of monsters. Nevertheless, they are the recipients of all the family wealth. Then a fourth child is born to the aging parents, the beautiful and talented Constance. Dissatisfied with her father's choice in an arranged marriage, she flees dressed as a male. Her fairy helper is named Obligeantine and her talking horse is Embletin, although the latter's role is diminished considerably as counsellor and confidant. This retelling integrates a far greater number of tangential episodes, thereby extending the tale. There is a princess who is attracted to Constance, but she has an ugly suitor from the Canary Islands whom Constance must face and slay in a duel. The satyrs become an entire race that rises up against the king after the invasion of the canary birds is quelled. One of them descends literally upon the king and demands a position at court. This work concludes with a double marriage, for not only does the king take Constance for his bride, but the satyr takes the princess that Constance had rejected. To be sure, the satyr has been a prince in enchanted form all the while. The final twist is Obligeantine's role in having Constance's hideous family invited to the weddings, but transfigured into beautiful people in order to spare embarrassment to everyone concerned. Just how much this tale has become a commentary on the preoccupations of the French court and salons is work for others. But it is a testimonial to the narrative and thematic elasticity of the kinds of stories selected and recorded by Straparola, presumably with some degree of appreciation for their inherent and intrinsic force.

That so many versions of the Costanza type were collected by folklorists in the nineteenth century, and in forms closely approximating Straparola's tale, does not indicate influence so much as the strength of the folk tradition that supplied the many literary adaptations throughout the preceding centuries. There is comparative work to be done in calibrating the relationship of these variants to their ancient sources. The following are a few among the many that might be cited. In Italy the tale was collected in diverse regions by Laura Gonzenbach,[27] Antonio De Nino,[28]

27 'Zafarana,' in *Sicilianische Märchen*, 2 vols. (Leipzig: W. Englemann, 1870), no. 9, vol. I, pp. 47–53.

28 *Le piu' belle fiabe abruzzesi* (Cerchio: Adelmo Polla, 1990), no. 23; 'Il satiro,' in *Usi e costume abruzzesi, Fiabe*, ed. Antonio de Nino (Florence: G. Barbèra, 1883), no. 23, vol. III, pp. 133–6. In this tale a young girl in love, lacking her family's approbation of her choice, decides to elope. The night is dark, however, and she leaves with a trickster impostor. They arrive at an island belonging to her father where there is

Gennaro Finamore,[29] Domenico Comparetti,[30] Georg Widter and Adolf Wolf,[31] and Gherardo Nerucci.[32] In France, the story was found in Lower Brittany by François-Marie Luzel, one version being 'Le Capitaine Lixur ou le Satyre' in which the youngest daughter of an aging knight goes off to court in disguise and encounters the hostile queen who causes her to go in search of dangerous beasts, including the Satyr who laughs mysteriously and at last is brought to tell the truths concerning the queen's sexual predilections and the heroine's gender.[33] Versions of the tale were

---

treasure. Once the would-be thief is off the boat, she turns navigator and flees, cutting her hair and changing her clothes in order to take service as a boy in a royal palace. Then the Costanza events begin. Accused by the envious of boasting about her satyr-management skills, she is sent on a mission to bring the creature in. Her means are familiar: tempting the creature with food while she hides in a tree above with a rope. This 'Costanza' has no horse to help her. Once in the noose the beast-man begins to laugh and does so repeatedly on the way back to the palace. The creature refuses to speak for several days, chided repeatedly for its enigmatic laughter. Under force, he confesses the now familiar truths: that the heroine is a girl, that the priest was baptizing his own son, that beggars were sitting on a treasure, and that the damsels surrounding the king's daughter were all men. Once the indecencies are dealt with, the king is free to marry the girl to the prince and give her the hidden treasure as a dowry. The queen's illicit suitors are passed to the daughter and other minor adjustments are in evidence, but the fundamental story is remarkably intact, reflecting a stable narrative group going back to times before Straparola.

29 *Tradizioni popolari abruzzesi*, 2 vols. (Lanciano: R. Carabba, 1882–6), no. 5.

30 In the *Novelline popolari italiane* (Rome: Forni, 1875) is to be found the story of 'Frederica,' no. 36, pp. 146–51, in which a lusty queen is turned down by her valet, a girl in disguise (Frederica as Frederico) on the run from a former false accusation against her for infidelity. Reported to the king for attempted rape, she is on the run a second time and must assume several different disguises which, in the final scene, she reassumes to demonstrate her former roles, saving till the last her true identity as a girl. This is a clever amalgamation of several stories at once, including the *Roman de la Violette*, because a violet birthmark is removed from her breast to prove her infidelity by a jealous merchant early in the tale.

31 *Volkslieder aus Venetien* (Vienna, 1864), no. 79, which includes further notes on maidens in disguise as knights who fight at foreign courts while struggling but ultimately failing to keep their true sex undisclosed.

32 *Sessanta novelle popolari montalesi*, ed. Roberto Fedi (Milan: Rizzoli, 1977), no. 29, pp. 254–66.

33 *Contes populaires de la Basse-Bretagne* (Paris: Maisonneuve, 1881), re-edited and published in 3 volumes as *Contes populaires de Basse-Bretagne* (Rennes: Presses universitaires de Rennes, 1996), vol. II, pp. 314–40.

likewise recorded in Spain by Aurelio Macedonio Espinosa.[34] Among the German folk tales, there are many about wild men who in some cases are made of iron and can only be captured by fraud or enticements of food and drink. They are vestiges of the tradition that connected Merlin to the creatures of the forest and tend to have far more in common with Straparola's 'Guerrino and the Wild Man of the Woods' (V.1), where the captured creature is liberated by a boy who wins lifelong help in exchange. A case in point is 'Der Eise Hans.'[35] In a related tale, collected in France, a ravaging iron giant is captured by a young swordsman with his dog, cords, and an iron carriage. This creature is displayed in a cage from which he is liberated in exchange for returning a child's ball which had rolled into his cage. Many of the events follow the story of 'Guerrino.'[36] But these drift away from the defining type.

Finally, there is a delightful variation collected in Albania by Louis Auguste Henri Dozon which brings several tales together and introduces novel elements. It begins with the third of three daughters of a dying knight who sets off in male disguise to take her father's place in the royal service. She engages in a reversed-gender version of Cesarino's dragon slaying (X.3) by killing such a beast to rescue the prince, who in turn advises the girl warrior not to accept the promised realm for a reward,

---

34 *Cuentos populares españoles* (Madrid, 1946–7), vol. III, pp. 57–66. The generic name for the story type in Spain is 'La abijada de San Pedro' (The goddaughter of Saint Peter), for the girl disguised as a boy and serving in a foreign court where she is accused of attempted rape and sent on quests is delivered by her godfather, whether St. Peter or St. Anthony, in the place of Merlin or a satyr. Many elements of the Livoretto story type figure prominently, such as the animal helpers and the three tasks: sorting grain, finding a ring at the bottom of the sea, or returning a lost son or daughter to the king. In some versions there is a gallows scene and the girl's last-minute rescue. Espinosa links these stories to the Castillan romances featuring 'la niña guerrero,' the girl warrior, in turn connected to the many heroines on the Spanish stage who travel in boy's disguises to pursue their love interests. The story can be found in *Cuentos extremeños*, ed. Marcel Curiel Merchán (Madrid: Instituto Antonio de Nebrija, 1944), pp. 225–9, and in Joan Timoneda, *El Patrañuelo*, ed. Rafael Ferreres (Madrid: Clásicos Castalia, 1971), no. 20.

35 Friedmund von Arnim, *Hundert neue Märchen im Gebirge gesammelt* (Charlottenburg: E. Bauer, 1844); 'Iron Hans,' in *The Great Fairy Tale Tradition*, trans. Jack Zipes (New York: W.W. Norton, 2001), pp. 326–9. Other scholars in the German tradition who have collected and commented on versions of this story include Johannes Bolte and Jiří Polívka, *Anmerkungen zu den Kinder- und Hausmärchen der Brüder Grimm* (Leipzig: Dieterich, 1937), vol. IV, pp. 85–6.

36 Henry Carnoy, 'L'homme de fer,' in *Collection de contes et de chansons populaires* (Paris: Ernest Leroux, 1885), vol. VIII, pp. 43–50.

but only the king's talking horse. No romance element yet emerges. The magic horse and its rider set out on new adventures in other realms, in the course of which the heroine wins a bride by leaping a wide trench on horseback while catching a flying apple. This time marriage ensues, but the princess, dissatisfied with her 'husband,' tells her father. Rather than a scorned queen's wrath, it is a young bride's disappointment that provokes the sequence of dangerous missions with fatal intentions. In each, however, the heroine prevails, first bringing back a lamia captured with honey, then a man-eating horse after attaching special iron shoes on her own mount. Still unable to satisfy the princess in bed, however, the heroine is sent out to deal with a church full of serpents. Through a well-executed plan, these creatures are forced to pay tribute, but their power to curse remains and they impose a sex change upon the heroine, making an apparent male into an actual one. For the newly minted hero, their malediction is his blessing, however, for he now returns to consummate his marriage. The motivic drift is extraordinary insofar as several distinct tales are evident, but at the heart of the story is the girl-knight in disguise confronted by a gender crisis and sent on suicidal missions to deal by craft with menacing creatures in the wild through the counsel of a talking horse.[37] Such a conflation of parts, by structural comparison with related versions, reveals something of the computational imagination of the folk tale reciters at work.

These several late transcriptions by folklorists place their own demands upon an analysis of the present tale. They demonstrate the pan-European currency of a common story type that can only have arisen in relation to the ancient Eastern tale. It featured the girl-knight, the wicked queen and her disguised lovers, the quest for the satyr, and the enigmatic laughter that brings about multiple revelations. Traces of its passage are evident in literary appropriations going back to the twelfth century, but Straparola's version preserves the characteristics, not of a reduced romance, but of a folk tale per se, and thus promises to be the first quasi-transcription of Paton's 'X,' designating the 'Costanza' group of oral tales. And there the matter must rest.

37 'La fille changée en garçon' (The girl changed into a boy), in *Contes albanais* (Paris: Leroux, 1881), no. 14, pp. 109–20.

IV. Fable 2
Erminione and Filenia, or the Jealous Husband Outwitted

VICENZA

Erminione Glaucio, an Athenian, takes as his wife Filenia Centurione, and growing jealous of her, accuses her before the tribunal. But with the help of her lover, Hippolito, she is acquitted and Erminione is condemned.

Of a truth, gracious ladies, there would be no condition sweeter, more delightful, or more happy in all the world than the service of love, were it not for that bitter fruit that springs from sudden jealousy, the foe to gentle Cupid, the betrayer of kindly ladies, the enemy that, day and night, seeks their deaths. This brings to mind a fable in which you'll understand immediately the hard and piteous fate that befell a gentleman of Athens, who, because of his cold-hearted jealousy, sought to have his wife slain by the sword of justice, but was himself condemned in her place. This judgment ought to please you, though, because most of you are in love, if I'm not greatly mistaken.

Athens, that most ancient city of Greece, although now through her excess of pride is entirely ruined and overthrown, was in times past the veritable home and resort of all learning. There, once upon a time, resided a gentleman named Messer Erminione Glaucio, a man highly considered and of much repute in the city, well-to-do, but at the same time of mean intelligence. It came about that when he was advanced in years, because he had no children, he made up his mind to marry, taking for his wife a damsel named Filenia, daughter of Messer Cesarino Centurione. She was of noble descent, blessed with marvellous beauty and with numberless other good qualities. In that entire city there was no other maiden to equal her. But because of her remarkable beauty, he was also in great fear that his wife would be courted by various gallants of the city, leading to some disgraceful scandal for which the finger might be pointed at him. This made him resolve to confine her to a lofty tower in his palace well out of all men's sight. Yet before long, without knowing why, the wretched old dotard was overcome by such a streak of jealousy that he mistrusted even himself.

Now there was residing in the city at this time a certain scholar from Crete who was young in years, but very discreet and much loved and esteemed by all who knew him on account of his amiability and grace. This same youth, Hippolito by name, had paid suit to Filenia before she was married. Besides this, he was on intimate terms with Messer Erminione, who held him as dear as if he had been his own son. This young scholar, weary of his studies and in need of recreational travel, left Athens for Crete and remained there for some while. But upon his return, he was dismayed to discover that Filenia was married. Thereafter, he fell into a deep melancholy made more acute by his loss of all hope of seeing her at his pleasure. Least endurable of all was that a maiden so lovely and graceful should be bound in marriage to such a slavering and toothless old man.

The burning pricks and sharp arrows of love became intolerable to the love-stricken Hippolito and at last impelled him to find some hidden way to fulfil his desires. After he had considered carefully the many schemes that presented themselves to him, he fixed upon one that appeared to him the most suitable. To put this into execution, he first went to the shop of a carpenter, his neighbour, where he ordered two chests to be made of equal length, breadth, depth, and capacity, so that not a soul could distinguish one from the other. When this was done, he made his way to Messer Erminione's house. Pretending to be in need of a favour, he minced the following words: 'Messer Erminione, you know well enough that I love and reverence you as though you were my own father, and that for my part, if I were not fully convinced of your affection for me, I would never dare beg a favour of you with the assurance I now use. But since I have always found you well disposed towards me, I feel certain you'll grant me my heart's desire and the service my soul so greatly yearns for. You know I'm constrained to leave Athens for the city of Frenna where I have important matters of business to expedite and I must remain there until all has been completed. And because I have no one about me I can fully trust, being served only by menials and hirelings in whom I place no real confidence, I would ask you to keep in your charge, if you would, a certain chest of mine in which I keep my most precious belongings.'

Messer Erminione, suspecting no craft in the young scholar, replied that he was quite content to grant this favour, and that for greater security the chest would be placed and kept in the same chamber where he slept. Upon this reply, the scholar gave thanks to Messer Erminione, the warmest he knew how to render, promising to remember this great favour for as long as he lived. Then he begged the old man to honour him by going as far as his own dwelling so that he could show him the various articles he kept stored in the chest. So the two went off together to the scholar's house, where the young man pointed out a chest filled with rich garments and jewels and necklaces of considerable value. Then, summoning one of his servants and presenting him to Messer Erminione, he said, 'If at any time, Messer Erminione, this servant of mine should come to ask for my chest, give it to him. You can trust him fully, as though he were my own self.'

Then, as soon as Messer Erminione had taken his leave, Hippolito hid himself in the other chest – exactly like the one filled with garments and jewels – and having fastened it from the inside, he requested his servant to carry it to a certain place he knew. The servant, who was party to the whole plot and most obedient in his patron's service, called a porter, according to his master's order, hoisted the load on the man's shoulders, and ordered him to carry it to the tower containing the chamber where Messer Erminione slept every night with his young wife.

It fell to the lot of Messer Erminione, being one of the chiefs of the city and a man of great wealth and influence, on account of the honourable position he held, to go for a certain time to a place called Piraeus, a couple of leagues distant from Athens, in order to settle certain suits and conflicts which had arisen between the townsmen and the peasants nearby. So when Messer Erminione had gone his way, as tormented as ever by the jealousy that weighed upon him day and night, the young scholar, enclosed in the chest now standing in Madonna Filenia's bedroom, was waiting for the favourable moment. More than once he had heard the fair dame weeping and sighing over her hard lot and bemoaning the place and hour in which she had been given in marriage to this destruction of her life, longing only for the oblivion of sleep. When it seemed to him that she was in her first slumber, he got out of the chest and went to the bedside, saying in a soft voice, 'Awake my soul, for I, your Hippolito, am here.'

When she was fully aroused and recognized him by the light of the candle burning in the room, she nearly let out a cry, but the young man, putting his hand upon her lips, prevented her, saying to her in a voice full of agitation, 'Be silent, heart of mine! Don't you see that I'm Hippolito, your faithful lover? Truly, I can't live without you.'

The fair young woman was a little comforted by these words, and when she began to compare her old husband to the youthful Hippolito, she was by no means dissatisfied by this turn of events and lay all night with her lover, spending the time in love talk while ridiculing the impotent ways of her doltish husband. Before they parted, they agreed to meet together in the same manner. When the morning began to dawn, the youth hid again in the chest, while every evening he would come out to spend the night with the lady.

After many days had gone by, Messer Erminione, for the discomfort he felt and the rabid jealousy that never ceased to torment him, managed to bring to an end all the disputes he had been sent out to settle and returned to his home. Hippolito's servant, as soon as he heard the news of Messer Ermonione's return, lost no time in going to his house, according to the agreement that had been settled, and politely requested in the name of his master, Hippolito, the return of the chest, which Messer Erminione turned over to him without remonstration. Summoning a porter, the servant then had the chest conveyed home. Once out of his hiding place, Hippolito walked towards the piazza where he chanced to meet up with Messer Erminione, whom he embraced and thanked most courteously in the warmest terms he could muster for the great kindness he had received, declaring at the same time that he and all he possessed were always at Messer Erminione's service.

It came about that one morning Messer Erminione remained in bed with his wife somewhat later than usual, and lifting up his eyes, he noticed on the wall high above his head certain stains that looked as though someone had been spitting. Once again his inveterate jealousy got the best of him. Amazed by what he saw and churning it over in his mind, he reasoned that if there was spit up there it had to be his or someone else's. And since he couldn't convince himself that it was his own, his thoughts began to terrify him. Turning, he asked in an angry voice, 'Whose spit marks are those up there on the wall? I'm certain they're not mine, for I never spat up there in my life. I know you've been cheating on me.'

Filenia, laughing all the while, answered him, 'Is there no other charge you would like to bring against me?'

Messer Erminione, when he saw her laughing, grew even more infuriated, saying, 'Ah, you laugh, do you, wicked woman that you are? Just what is it that makes you laugh?'

'I'm laughing,' answered Filenia, 'at your own foolishness.'

At these words, Messer Erminione began to roar and stomp with rage, intent upon measuring his own ability to spit so high. After much coughing and gasping, with all his might he strained to reach the mark on the wall, but he wore himself out for nothing, for the spittle always fell right back in his own face, spattering it all over. After the miserable old codger made several more attempts, he found himself in a worse mess than before. His failure only convinced him the more that his wife was a cheat, whereupon he began to say the meanest and nastiest things one can say to a woman. Had he not been afraid of the law and his own neck, he would most certainly have throttled her then and there with his own hands, but he managed to restrain himself, deeming it better to deal with her by legal process than to stain his hands in her blood. Not satisfied with the berating he'd already given her, he went to the tribunal full of wrath and anger, where he placed the charge of adultery against his wife before the judge. But because it lay not in the power of the judge to pronounce condemnation upon her unless the legal statutes had been duly observed, he ordered Filenia to be brought before him so that he could closely examine her.

Now the law and custom of Athens was that every woman accused of adultery by her husband should be set at the foot of the red pillar around which was entwined a serpent. There she was to make an oath whether or not the accusation brought against her was true. After she had taken the oath, she was required to place her hand in the serpent's mouth. If she had sworn falsely, the serpent would at once bite off her hand; otherwise she would receive no injury. Hippolito heard rumours of this charge before the tribunal and understood that the judge had sent to fetch Filenia to place her on trial. Being a resourceful youth, he at once took action to make certain she would not run the risk of an ignominious death. To rescue her from condemnation, he first stripped off all his clothes and donned in their stead the rags of a madman. Then, without being seen by anyone, he left his own lodging and ran straight to the tribunal as though he had been out of his mind, acting the part of a madman to perfection.

While the officers of the court were haling the poor lady along towards the tribunal, all the people of the city gathered to find out how the procedure would end. In the middle of the crowd the feigning madman forced his way in one direction and another, working his way so well to the front that he found a chance to cast his arms around the neck of the woeful lady and to press a kiss upon her lips, a caress that, with her arms bound behind her back, she could in no wise escape. As soon as she was brought before the judge, he addressed her in the following words, 'As you may see, Filenia, your husband Messer Erminione is here to lay a complaint against you, which is that you have committed adultery, asking that I deal out to you the due penalty according to the statutes. Therefore, you must now make an oath and say whether or not the charge is true which your husband brings against you.'

Then the young woman, who was very astute and keen of intellect, confidently swore that no man had ever touched her except her husband and the madman who was now present before them all. After she had sworn her oath, the ministers of justice led her to the place where the serpent was. When Filenia placed her hand in its mouth, it did her no harm whatsoever, insofar as what she had sworn had been the truth, which is that no man had ever caressed her in any way except her husband and the presumed madman.

When they perceived this, the crowd and all her kinsfolk who had come there to see the solemn and terrible sight at once set her down as innocent and wrongfully accused and cried out that Messer Erminione deserved the same form of death required as penalty for the crime imputed to his wife. Because he was a nobleman and one of the chiefs of the city, the president would not allow him to be publicly burned – as provided according the law in such cases – yet to fulfil the duty of his office he sentenced Erminione to be thrown into prison for life, where, after a short space of time, he expired. In this way, the wretched jealousy of Messer Erminione was brought to its miserable end, and by these means the young wife was delivered from death. Within a short while after, Hippolito made her his lawful wife and they lived happily together for many years thereafter.

Vicenza's story once ended, the Signora asked her to propound her enigma. Smiling gaily, instead of a song, she gave the following riddle:

When hope and love and strong desire
Are born to set the world on fire,
That selfsame hour a beast is born,
All savage, meagre, and forlorn.
Sometimes, with seeming soft and kind,
Like ivy round an elm tree twined,
It clips us close with bine and leaf,
But feeds on heartache, woe, and grief.

Ever in mourning garb it goes,
In anguish lives, in sorrow grows;
And worse than worst the fate of him
Who falls beneath its talons grim.

Here Vicenza brought her enigma to an end. The interpretations of its meaning were diverse and no one of the company was found clever enough to fathom its true import. When the fair Vicenza saw this, she sighed a little impatiently, and then, with a smiling face, she explained, 'My riddle signifies merely that chilling jealousy, which, all lean and faded, is born at the same birth with love itself, and winds itself around men and women just as the ivy hugs the tree. This jealousy feeds on heartache, seeing that a jealous man lives always in sadness. He's dressed in black because he's always melancholy.' This explanation of the enigma pleased everyone, and especially the Signora Chiara, whose husband had a jealous temperament. But to stop people from thinking that Vicenza's enigma had been framed to fit his case, the Signora right away asked Lodovica to tell her tale, which ran as follows.

IV.2 Commentary

Love has its own imperatives – call them the sanctions of Cupid – over which law and custom have no sway, not to mention the legal and emotional entitlements of jealous spouses. This story was written to confirm the futility in seeking to control the amorous aspirations of those under even the closest of surveillance. It offers no ethical speculations except through the biases of its narrative order whereby the jealous are relegated to harsh justice, whatever their rights, and lovers are granted the desires of their hearts, however sinful or illegal. Thus wretched jealousy is defeated, the bane of a woman's existence. The story of Erminione and Hippolito is unapologetic in this regard, arousing animus against the crotchety, unsavoury, and superannuated husband and sympathy for the bullied and incarcerated young wife. The locale of the present story is Athens, a seat of learning, but one that has fallen into decadence. The protagonist is a student, pleasantly playful and a touch brazen, who devotes himself to the service of love. Moreover, he had courted the lady before his travels, when she was still single, but finds her, upon returning from abroad, miserably yoked in what appears to be an arranged marriage. Such extenuating circumstances serve to reconcile the reader to a plot of rescue through seduction. In the process, the hero displays a capacity for hypocrisy both in ingratiating himself with the lady and in using his friendship with her husband to gain entry into the house in a coffer allegedly filled with his prized possessions. The coffer trick is, to be sure, one of the preferred means in the plays and *novelle* of the Renaissance for moving lovers secretly from house to house, as opposed to the freedom of fairy tales in which lovers may fly in as birds.[38]

Readers, along the way, lend their emotional approbation to this tale of youth conspiring against age, hope against despair, stolen pleasures after suffering, and craft in overcoming material obstacles, for the young wife is not only in a psychological prison, but a tower where she has been

---

38 A history of entries by coffer and chest, as practised by determined lovers, could be extended to considerable proportions. It was simply a realistic solution of the times, one that Straparola adopted among alternative choices for his *novella*-like creations, given the coffer's place in the Renaissance household and the availability of porters in the streets. For a brief history, apart from the many stories in the *Piacevoli notti* itself employing this device, there are examples to be found in Boccaccio's *Decameron* II.9 and IV.10 (which has features in common with the present story), in Giraldi Cinzio's *Ecatommiti* III.10, and in Cardinal Bibbiena's carnival play *La Calandria*. See *Renaissance Comedy: The Italian Masters*, vol. II, ed. Donald Beecher (Toronto: University of Toronto Press, 2009), pp. 23–100. In Cinthio's story II.10 of the *Hecatommithi*, a lover is smuggled into the lady's chamber in a chest through the help of the lady's maid, Liscia. Later, she arranges to have the chest called for, but the lover is caught, at which point the husband plans to revenge himself with the intruder's wife, and the story moves in the direction of Straparola's VI.1. One of the finest among them is in the fifth *novella* of Barnabe Riche's *Farewell to Military Profession*, ed. Donald Beecher, 'Of Two Brethren and Their Wives' (Ottawa: Dovehouse Editions, and Binghamton, NY: MRTS, 1992), in which Dorothy has one unwanted lover stuffed in a coffer, a second unwanted lover called in as a porter to carry 'her' away, and a third lover, her preferred soldier, sent after to bastinado them both, after the 'porter' offers to go shares with the 'woman' in the coffer. Another of memorable design is the *Discours tres facetieux et veritable d'un ministre de Cleyrat en Agenoit, lesquel etant amoureux de la femme d'un notaire fut enfermé dans un coffre & vendu a l'anquant a la place dudit Cleyrat* (Toulouse: Par la veuve Colomier, 1613), pp. 3–10. A translation of the title tells all: 'The very delightful and true story of a minister of Cleyrat in the Agen region who, for being in love with the wife of the notary, was closed into a coffer and sold at auction in the central square of said city.' The husband had seen the loving glances at a dinner party and was pleased when his wife confessed everything to him, asking for his advice. He recommended the rendezvous and the trick, and his wife played her part perfectly, even pretending to have lost the key once the coffer was sold at auction. We hear all about his sleepless night before the morning meeting and the husband's staged return after a hug and kiss and an exchange of a significant sum of money. He was blackmailed for even more at the end and made to endure public humiliation.

placed in isolation from the world. The doors, the locks – and the spies, in related stories – are emblematic of male jealousy and the condition of women during the Middle Ages as protected property, forced to dwell in edifices that served both as family strongholds and as military fortifications. Straparola's tale also incorporates an episode based on probative tests whereby guilt or innocence was thought to be established by the occult reactions attributed to special waters, the properties of fire, animal behaviour, or occult machines. In matters of marital fidelity, a judicial system might well maintain faith in such engines of verity or trial by ordeal, given the absence of investigative means, or reliable witnesses, or diseases, or pregnancies, whereby the secret sexual conduct of both men and women might otherwise be demonstrated. Anxiety over the matter with regard to fidelity and paternity might well lead to the employment of such medieval inventions as the Virgilian mouth or the Bocca della Verità. At least it was a way of breaking the stalemate before a judge, insofar as a guilty candidate was damned by her own attempted perjury or by her refusal to submit to the test. It is around this quality of lie detection that the closing events of the tale unfold – lie detection that honours the literal wording of the oath, however, and not the hidden secrets of the heart. The story thereby turns upon a quibble, a play of words, in the interests of a romantic escape rather than the settling of Truth.

In no preceding work do all the elements found in the tale of 'Erminione' – the tower, the coffer, the spit on the wall, the lover in the guise of a madman, and the probative test – appear together except in the fourth *novella* of Cieco's *Mambriano*, 'La pietra della verità' (The rock of truth), even though this *novella* deviates from the serpent and post mechanism to be found in the *Virgilius* tradition and in Straparola. The story in *Mambriano* likewise takes place in Athens. Agrisippo is an extremely rich old man who marries the fifteen-year old Lipomena – her parents were greedy for the money. He becomes jealous and builds a tower to keep her, but Cupid always finds a way. There are many poetic flourishes that are suppressed by Straparola, including the tale of the young and handsome Filomerse, expert in the arts of chivalry and hunting. While out fishing, he wounds a dolphin sacred to Neptune with an arrow and earns the anger of the gods. It is Cieco's mechanism for bringing the lover under Lipomena's window, where the hunter, now the hunted, is shot by Cupid and afflicted with ardent love. Filomerse does not lay plans, however, but collapses into sobbing lovesickness, leading to his mother's intervention, the call for the doctor, the detection of the cause of his malady, and the mother's scheme to save her son's life. Her solution features but one chest, supposedly packed with the boy's earthly belongings, to be stored by Agrisippo. Expectations of success restore the hero to health, banquets follow, he leaves town as a pilgrim, and returns secretly to his mother dressed as a chambermaid. After much coming and going, he is at last carried to his beloved in the coffer. Their tryst lasts precisely thirty-two days, whereupon the lovers must light upon less stressful circumstances for expressing their love. The old man's suspicion increases meanwhile, but again over the sputum he notices high up on their bedroom wall. The husband's proof of a lover's presence by attempting and failing to spit as high, however, is Straparola's invention or part of an alternate source. Both stories end in the same manner, for the old husband wants his accused wife tried by the rock of truth. Meanwhile, Filomerse dresses himself as a madman to accost her in order to teach her the equivocation needed for her escape. Exonerated, she is released and her husband is imprisoned in his own tower where, after four months, he expires, freeing the lovers to marry. Barring any lost intermediaries of greater affinity, including oral tales, this *novella* from *Mambriano* is presumably Straparola's principal narrative source. The extensive reduction involved and the variations in major details may well give cause for doubt insofar as Cieco's *novella* could, itself, represent an extensive literary elaboration upon an elusive oral prototype. But in this regard, it is critical that this is one of the few instances in which the story type upon which Straparola based his work left no subsequent legacy in the oral culture.

The author of *Mambriano* is Francesco Bello, known as Cieco da Ferrara; he was in the personal service of Duke Ercole I as early as 1477. His immediate source may have been Sercambi's *novella*, 'De astutia in juvene.'[39] But the Ur-story upon which his *novella* is based appeared early in European literature in the Western version of *The Seven Wise Men*, or *The Seven Sages of Rome* in the story called 'Inclusa.'[40] The jealous husband

39 Giovanni Sercambi, *Novelle* (Bari: Laterza & Figli, 1972), no. 29, vol. I, pp. 132–9.

40 *The Seven Sages of Rome*, French Version A (MS. Paris, BN f.fr. 2137, folios 38b–42c), ed. Hans R. Runte, SSFrATrans.html. This story appeared in the West – the earliest version is the French K MS. – no later than 1150 and no earlier than the tenth century. The intermediary sources are not known, but it is clearly related to *The Book of Sindibad* (Sendebar), ed. W.A. Clouston (Privately Printed, 1884), pp. 178–81, and before that to such works as the Persian *Tooti Nameh*. See also A. Loiseleur Deslongchamps, *Essai sur les fables indiennes et sur leur introduction en Europe* (Paris:

of a young wife, uncertain how to keep her in isolation, builds a tower beside the sea. A young cavalier falls in love with her and to possess her begins by making friends with her husband. He enters his service, moves into a house near the tower, and then digs an underground tunnel with a trapdoor. When he appears suddenly inside the lady's quarters, she welcomes him with pleasure. The nightly encounters last for a time. She even gives him her lord's ring which he, in turn, shows to the lord, to his great amazement. But by the time the suspicious husband reaches his wife, the ring is already back in her custody, returned through the trapdoor. At last, the woman herself is brought out and presented to the lord as the young soldier's sweetheart, following which the jealous lord is tricked into giving his own wife to the young man, thinking her safely hidden away in the tower. He learns of his error only after the two have sailed away. There is, as yet, no coffer trick, no threatened judicial hearing, no instrument of probation or trial by ordeal, and no trickster lover playing the madcap. All those details are to be added during the intervening two-and-a-half centuries separating the earliest versions of *The Seven Sages of Rome* from the work of Cieco. One small consideration is that the *novella* in *Mambriano* calls for a test, but it is not that of the traditional Virgilian serpent; that substitution is supplied by Straparola or an alternate source relying on the Virgilian tradition. Further clarification may thus be had by looking at two interim representations of the story: the Tristan and Iseult group, in which the jealousy of King Marc leads to trial by ordeal; and the Virgilius group, concerning accusations and the use of probative devices.

Just as there are potentially hundreds of tales of ladies immured in towers by jealous husbands down to Celia in Ben Jonson's *Volpone*, so there are many stories that feature ordeals and probative tests as a means

---

Techener, 1838), pp. 159–61, on the origins of the story in the *Book of Sendebar*. There is a variant in the Arabic version of the *Seven Vezirs* in which a jealous merchant shuts up his wife in their house. There she is seen by the sultan's son, but he can find no way to reach her. He communicates by shooting arrows with messages, and finally shoots a key to a chest. An associate then negotiates with the merchant to store a chest of precious goods for him and in this way the prince enjoys seven days of bliss with the lady. When the sultan asks for his son, the vizier requests the chest, but the lid comes open and everything is revealed. Fearful of revenging himself against the prince, the merchant can do no more than divorce his wife and vow never again to marry. *Tales, Anecdotes and Letters Translated from the Arabic and Persian*, trans. Jonathan Scott (Shrewsbury: J. & W. Eddowes for T. Cadell & W. Davies, London, 1800), pp. 131*ff.*

for dealing with marital infidelity. Rua follows Comparetti in tracing both elements of the story – the wife imprisoned by a jealous husband and the ordeal for the determination of truth or falsehood – to ancient legends from the East involving the sun and moon that found full personification in the romances associated with Tristan, Iseult, and King Marc, such as the *Tavola ritonda o Istoria di Tristano* in which Iseult is obliged to make her oath with her hand on a holy relic and the *vertudiosa pietra della itropica.* In certain of these tales, Tristan disguises himself as a pilgrim in order to approach her, comfort her, or kiss her and thereby set up the now-familiar equivocation. The Tristan lore may be the principal European textual tradition to improvise upon the Virgilian motif, making the *Mambriano novella* a proximate re-enactment of one of its key episodes. There are telling variations within the Tristan tradition as well, for in the *Sir Tristrem; a Metrical Romance of the Thirteenth Century* by Thomas of Ercildoune, the ordeal is carried out with a red-hot iron which Ysonde carries without being burned because Tristrem had come to her in the form of a poor beggar and embraced her in the boat crossing the Thames before a crowd of observers, setting her up with the essential equivocation.[41]

Straparola alters the mechanisms of the ending by grafting upon the *novella* from *Mambriano* certain features from an episode found among those that together constitute the life of Virgilius. This compilation in the name of the great Roman poet may be traced back to the twelfth century, by which time Virgil had achieved the reputation of being a great mage and necromancer. Not unlike the life of Doctor Faustus in later centuries, Virgil's life was constituted as a cycle of wonder tales, magical feats, and divinations. Early references to this accretion of texts appear in the *Otia imperialia* of Gervase of Tilbury, dating to 1212, and in *De naturis rerum* of Alexander Neckham, circa 1180.[42] Henry Morley,

41 Edition from the Auchinleck MS. by Walter Scott (Edinburgh: James Ballantyne, 1804), pp. 123–6. In the French metrical romance of *Tristram l'amoureux,* Tristram asks Ysolt if she remembers the trial she had undergone for his sake, how he had embraced her in coming out of the boat before so many witnesses, and how she had been acquitted before all the court, p. 221. The tale was known in Germany in the fourteenth century, as the *Meisterlieder der Kolmarer Handschrift,* ed. Karl Bartsch (Stuttgart: Litterarischen Vereins, 1862), pp. 338, 604; new ed. (Hildesheim: Georg Olms, 1962).

42 *Otia imperialia,* ed. S.E. Banks and J.W. Binns (Oxford: Clarendon, 2002); *De naturis rerum* (ca. 1180), ed. Thomas Wright (1863; reprint, Nendeln: Kraus Reprints, 1967). John Webster Spargo, in *Virgil the Necromancer, Studies in Virgilian Legend*

in his introduction to his anthology of *Early Prose Romances*, suggests that the tradition began in Naples where the poet had achieved tutelary status to the city by the twelfth century, and that from there the stories, many of them Eastern in origin, spread first throughout Italy and then to the rest of Europe.[43] The most influential of these collections was the French *Les faits merveilleux de Virgille* for which no manuscripts survive and which is today known only from its extremely rare early sixteenth-century editions, although it is undoubtedly many decades or centuries older. It was from this work that subsequent translations were made into English, Dutch, and German. By contrast, however, Giuseppe Rua states that the oldest source for this particular legend of 'How Virgilius made in Rome a metal serpente,' to use the earliest English title, dates to the first half of the fourteenth century in a work entitled *Von einem pild ze Rôme daz den emprecherinnen die vinger ab peiz*. In this story, an empress, accused of infidelity with a knight, submitted herself to the customary test and avoided her deserved punishment through the help of the knight who, in embracing her and kissing her in the guise of a madman, enabled her to say that no one had ever approached her more closely than her husband and the fool.[44] That same story appears in the English translation entitled *This boke treatethe of the life of Virgilius and of his death, and many maravyles that he dyd in his lyfe tyme by witchcraft and nigromansy, through the help of the devylls of hell*.[45] It contains the essential features that Straparola had to have known to adjust the closure of his story. Whether this particular episode began in Germany, France, or Italy is a moot point, but

---

(Cambridge, MA: Harvard University Press, 1934), advances the theory that the English scholar Neckham, at the end of the twelfth century, was responsible for launching the legends of Virgilian magic in the late medieval world. In dividing sources between the Tristan group and the Virgilian group, a place is denied to a version which is, nevertheless, important to the formation of the story type. In the middle of the twelfth century appeared *Die Kaiserchronik* (ll. 10688–10819), which tells the story in the name of Julian the Apostate and the widow, a story that seems to have had a Syrian origin. The widow had entrusted Julian with her wealth to keep it secure. When he refused to return it, she had him tested by oath before the image of Mercury in the Tiber. When Julian placed his hand in the statue's mouth, it bit his hand and held him fast until the treasure was returned.

43 *Early Prose Romances* (London: George Routledge, 1889), pp. 19–20.

44 Giuseppe Rua, *Novelle del 'Mambriano' del Cieco da Ferrara* (Torino: Ermanno Loescher, 1888), p. 80.

45 This work was printed by John Doesborcke in Antwerp early in the sixteenth century and appears in *Early Prose Romances*, ed. Henry Morley (London: George Routledge, 1889), pp. 209–36. The story of the metal serpent is on pp. 232–3.

it is clearly the story that found its way, through any number of intervening versions, into Straparola's tale of 'Erminione.'[46]

According to this tale, she who places her hand in the mouth of the serpent, the creation of which is attributed to Virgil the poet turned necromancer, must swear to the truth of her cause, for in failing to do so the hand may not be withdrawn (will be bitten off).[47] In the English rendition, a man from Lombardy mistrusts his wife despite her explanations. To exonerate herself she consents to go to Rome to swear her oath with her hand in the mouth of the serpent of truth.[48] Her partner in sin

---

46 For further information on the growth and diffusion of the myth of Virgil and the cycle tales, see Domenico Comparetti, *Virgilio nel Medio Evo* (Leghorn: Francesco Vigo, 1872); *Virgil in the Middle Ages*, trans. E.F.M. Benecke (Princeton: Princeton University Press, 1997).

47 During the seventeenth century there remained a high degree of curiosity concerning wonders and rarities, including such 'wondrous machines' as the serpent of truth. Two writers who report on adultery detection by such devices include Giovanni Felice Astolfi in *Cento avenimenti meravigliosi, stupendi e rari* (Venice: Turrini, 1660), Deca I, 3, 'Una donna rea è costretta dal marito a porre il braccio in una fonte, e ne è scorticata' (Of the woman forced by her husband to place her arm in a fountain, by which it was badly scorched). In the Life of St. Gandolf, a dissolute woman is told to bring up a stone from the bottom of a fountain and if she is guilty of adultery the water will take the skin from her arm. 'Sé ci sìa alcun rimedio per iscuoprire le mogli adultere' (Whether there are any means by which an adulterous wife may be discovered), in Scipio Glariano [Angelico Aprosio] (Naples: Novello de Bonis, 1668), Grillo 22.

48 The tradition remains in Rome to the present day that the stone mounted in the vestibule of the Church of Santa Maria in Cosmedin called the 'Bocca della Verità' is invested with the Virgilian magic whereby it will determine the truthful (faithful) from the dishonest in biting off the hand of the unfaithful. No doubt the portrait of a river god originally sculpted for a fountain, this stone, since the Middle Ages, has epitomized the belief in such probative instruments. Conceivably, this very stone may have been associated with the Virgilian phenomenon from early times, for it is to Rome that the Lombard couple must go to test the woman's honour. A statue by Jules Blanchard of a young female nude placing her hand in the 'Bocca' can be seen in the Luxembourg Gardens in Paris. The motif has also been kept alive in film and fiction, and particularly in the 1953 film *Roman Holiday* featuring Gregory Peck and Audrey Hepburn, and in *Only You* with Robert Downey Jr. and Marisa Tomei. As with so many other elements of Western fiction, the concept of the probative beast may have originated in the East. Friedrich von der Hagen describes the traditions associated with the 'bocca' in his *Briefe in die Heimat aus Deutschland, der Schweitz und Italien* (Breslau: J. Max & Komp, 1821), vol. IV, p. 106. A sculpture of a lion said to bite those who swear false oaths while holding their hands in its mouth – a work of uncertain antiquity – is to be found in Mahabalipuram, Tamil Nadu, India. As a point of comparison, a chastity-detecting lion is featured in

is beside her in the cart and she tells him to put on a fool's coat and thereby disguise himself so that when the day for the ordeal arrives he can be there. Virgilius knew of her falsehood and advised her not to place her hand in the contraption, but she insisted and by equivocation regained her reputation. Once again, the madman in the crowd had come forward to embrace and kiss her, whereby she could freely declare that she had no more to do with him (meaning the man whom she was accused of sinning with) than with that 'fole, that stode hyr by.' Thus she spoke a sufficient truth. Virgil was so angry that the woman had escaped his cunning that he destroyed the serpent. The mage pronounces upon the deceitfulness of the entire sex, but the woman's husband is satisfied and thus she regains his trust. Behind the machinations of this tale is the lady herself, whereas in Straparola it is the lover who crafts the deceit and disguising. Moreover, there is no demise for the jealous husband. Straparola makes all the necessary adjustments to accommodate the two sources in a united production.[49]

Such trials by ordeal in literature, however, go back to the early tales from the East, of which one from the sixth century must represent an entire heritage. In the *Suka saptati*, the Sanskrit collection known as *The Seventy Tales of a Parrot*, which in turn became the Persian *Tooti-nameh*,

---

Thomas Lodge's horror romance *A Margarite of America* (1596), in which the virginal heroine is spared and fondled by the beast while her peccant maid 'was rent in pieces, in that she had tasted too much of fleshly love.' Ed. Donald Beecher and Henry Janzen (Toronto: CRRS Publications, 2005), p. 156.

49 A German version of the story of Virgil and the probative serpent close in time to Straparola, although unlikely to have had any direct effect upon him, is nevertheless further testimony to the spread of this lore throughout Renaissance Europe. It is no. 206 of Johannes Pauli's *Schimpf und Ernst*, 'Ein Keiserin stiess ir Hand in das Maul Vergillii' (An empress sticks her hand in the Virgilian throat). The stone is in Rome, and whoever swears a false oath with the hand in its mouth will have it bitten off. It is almost now a travel book entry. A Kaiser accuses his Kaiserin of adultery with a knight and often they argue over it until he proposes that she purge and purify herself through the ordeal of the stone. She agrees. On the way to Rome, surrounded by her ladies in waiting, the knight breaks through the ranks in fool's clothing and embraces and kisses her 'vor aller Welt,' before all the world, causing her to cry out and protest against such evil. When she comes to the stone she then swears her deceitful oath about the fool and her husband as the only men ever to have touched her. Taken from the earliest edition of 1522, ed. Johannes Bolte (Berlin: Herbert Stussenrauch, 1924; reprint, Hildesheim: Georg Olms, 1972), pp. 130–1. A similar story appears as 'Die kaiserin mit dem leben pild,' in Hans Sachs, *Sämtliche Fabeln und Schwänke*, ed. E. Goetze (Halle: Max Niemeyer, 1894), no. 342, vol. II, p. 504.

the woman accused of infidelity counter-accuses. To put an end to the debate, she is sent to the Yaksha (a shape-shifting forest deity of human size in Indian lore) for trial by ordeal.[50] Those found guilty are beaten or killed while the innocent go free. The woman arranges with her lover that he seize her around the neck along the way, without further explanation. In doing so, to be sure, he provided her with the now-familiar enigma of being touched only by her husband and the man recently driven away by the bystanders in view of all. The Yaksha saw through her cunning, but applauded her wit and allowed her to escape. This was a story in need of improvement, such as a disguise for the lover so that he could not be recognized, and such improvements it received as it made its way across the Arabic world to the West.

One of the most extraordinary tales in this tradition is 'How Haran Gerel swore falsely and yet told the truth' from *The Saga of Ardschi-Bordschi and Vikramaditja's Throne.*[51] Naran Gerel, daughter of a king, was so closely guarded that if any man went near her, his legs would be broken and his eyes put out. Yet she wanted to see something of the world, so orders were given that all must withdraw completely and leave the empty streets to her. But the minister Saran stole a glimpse, which she detected, and by subtle signs arranged for a meeting. The minister's wife agreed that if she made such gestures he must go. During their meeting they were captured, however, and both were slated to die. The clever minister's wife came bearing fruit as though on doctor's orders and was admitted, there changing clothes with the princess and sending her home. At the trial the couple professed merely to have entered the private garden where the guards took them by mistake. In light of such doubts, the princess's

50 *The Enchanted Parrot*, trans. B. Hale Wortham (London: Luzac, 1911), pp. 52–5. This Eastern tradition goes as far back as the Chinese Buddhist *Tripiṭaka*, dating to the third century of the Christian era, in which a lover, dressed as a fool, lays the accused woman on the ground, thus touching her in a way that enables her to pronounce the ambiguous oath sworn before a sacred or holy tree. See *Cinq cents contes et apologues extraits du Tripiṭaka chinois et traduits en français*, trans. Édouard Chavannes (Paris: E. Laroux, 1910–34; reprint, Paris: Maisonneuve, 1962), no. 116, vol. I, pp. 387*ff.* A similar tale appears in the *Kitab Hayāt ad-Hajawān* of Muhammad ibn Musa ad-Damīrī, written near the end of the fourteenth century, in which the lover touches the beloved by lifting her down from a donkey.

51 *Sagas from the Far East or Kalmouk and Mongolian Traditionary Tales*, ed. Rachel Harriette Busk (London: Griffith & Farran, 1873), pp. 315–23. See also Bernhard Jülg, *Mongolische Märchen: die neun Nachtrags – Erzählungen des Siddhi Kür und die Geschichte des Ardschi-Bordschi Chan* (Innsbruck: Wagner, 1868), p. 107.

innocence could only be resolved by a probative trial. She must swear in the presence of the barley corns which, in the case of lies, leap into the air and burst with a loud noise. But the princess would be taught what to do by the subtle facial expressions of the minister's wife. This wife then blackened her husband, told him to make grimaces, and had him carry an empty water pitcher like a beggar. The princess understood that she could swear her oath on such a beggar because he was a false beggar and so escape prosecution by this literal technicality. The moral of the story is that if you have a permissive wife who is this clever, go abroad; if not, stay home. The origin of this Siberian tale goes back to the stories of ancient India.

This narrative idea was employed by Achilles Tatius in *Leucippe and Clitophon*, for as the romance draws to a close, the young women travellers, Leucippe and Melite, are obliged to prove their innocence after so many chastity-threatening adventures outside their parental households. Two methods are employed, each associated with a founding myth that explains the probative powers of the trial site. One is the cave of Pan where, following his attempt at rape, he has been left with the reeds from which he made the famous pipe. Virgins entering the cave under oath are met with the sweet sounds of the pipe, whereas the soiled and fallen are met with screams and after three days mysteriously disappear and are heard of no more. Leucippe embraces the ordeal and prevails. Melite, falsely arraigned for adultery, is compelled to write her oath upon a tablet hung around her neck before stepping into the knee-high water of the spring that is the source of the holy river Styx. Innocence is met with calm, but the waters will rise up to cover the tablets of the guilty. She too is proven pure before a large crowd, while her calumniators flee for their lives as the multitude cries out for their punishment.[52]

Straparola's story, in its implementation of the Virgilian ordeal, is a further testimonial to the peculiar mentality that gives credence to occult signs associated with augury and trial by ordeal. On the one hand there is an aspect of ritual magic and superstition, while on the other there is a deep-seated belief in an occult ordering of the universe that is concerned with hidden justice, truth, and reciprocity (or God's intervention through miracles). At the centre of such practices are the particular anxieties concerning the matters of vital concern to the collective human

52 *Collected Ancient Greek Novels*, ed. B.P. Reardon (Berkeley: University of California Press, 1989), pp. 273–81.

enterprise which remain beyond human ken through forensic evidence or the reading of intentional states implicit in human behaviour and expressions. They are the ritual and divinatory means whereby truth penetrates hypocrisy. Nevertheless, such trials simultaneously capitulate to the occult in the establishment of innocence and guilt. Straparola's story, in that regard, remains as ambiguous as others in the tradition, whether for its credulousness concerning such devices or for its irony in presenting the deception of such devices by the clever. The practice of trial by ordeal was widespread among the ancient Celts and Goths who looked for evidence of innocence or guilt in the reaction of skin to hot irons or boiling oil. In time, holy relics were drawn into the practice. Thomas of Ercildoune's heroine seems to have been subjected to the Saxon ordeal of carrying a red-hot piece of iron. Walking over burning plough-shares, often blindfolded, was another.[53] This was imposed upon Queen Emma, mother of Edward the Confessor, when accused of adultery with the Bishop of Winchester. She prayed at the sepulchre of St. Swithen and when she passed the test, her accuser fled to Normandy.[54] The Virgilian serpent, because it is attached to stories of deception that defeat the lie detector, in effect introduces a note of scepticism. Straparola's story perpetuates the tale of equivocation, justified by the entitlements of young love over withering jealousy and old age. But in the Saxon tradition, it is God Himself who is deceived by the cunningly worded

53 These stories are told in relation to the practices of medieval ecclesiastical courts, which also relied upon the burning iron and cold water tests in cases where evidence was insufficient to determine innocence or guilt. Pope Innocent III banned such practices in 1215 after long debate in intellectual circles, including the Fourth Lateran Council, but the practices continued semi-officially down to the eighteenth century in certain parts of Europe and America. The sagas and romances featuring ordeals, and particularly those in which trickery deceives the engines of truth, participated in the debate, further calling the legitimacy of such practices into question. Gottfried von Strassburg for one, in his telling of the Tristan story, makes ironic and derogatory comments over the efficacy and validity of trial by ordeal. See Jeff Sypeck, 'Ordeal,' *Medieval Folklore: A Guide to Myths, Legends, Tales, Beliefs, and Customs*, ed. Carl Lindahl et al. (Oxford: Oxford University Press, 2002), p. 302.

54 Ranulf Higden, *Polychronicon Ranulphi Higden* from MS. Harleian 2261, in *Rerum Britannicarum Medii Aevi Scriptores*, no. 41, ed. Joseph Rawson Lumby (London: Longman & Co., 1879), bk. VI, chap. 23, vol. VII, p. 165. Queen Emma requested the test to clear her name; it consisted of 'iv passes on iv cultres of hoote yrne for hereselfe, and v for the bischop with owte eny hurte, sche schalle be excusede of this cryme.'

oath. The same stratagem appears in *Amis and Amylion* and in the *Tavola ritonda o l'istoria di Tristano,* as well as in *Flore et Blanceflor.*[55] Thus, embedded within the modest *novella* of Erminione and his unfaithful wife is a vast legacy of tales of sequestered women, jealous husbands, impregnable towers invaded by the cunning, scenes of illicit love justified by youth, torment, and love's entitlements, and the circumvention of the trial by ordeal. All of these tales are comprised of generic narrative traditions retained in their respective forms – forms that are faithfully re-inscribed in the present tale, thereby linking it to its many predecessors. Imitation of the 'Inclusa' produced a goodly number of medieval sequels, including the twelfth- or thirteenth-century story, 'Du chevalier à la trappe.'[56] Two young people dream of each other without either knowing the other in waking life. The chevalier sets out to find her and after a considerable journey sees her in the window of her tower, where she is kept by a jealous husband. He is a powerful duke and his tower features no less than eighteen doors separating the lady from her liberty. She sings a love song to him and, in keeping with the prototype, he goes to meet the lord of the house to offer his services, fighting against all the duke's enemies. In time, he builds a house beside the tower, hires a workman for the excavations, and then kills him in the interests of secrecy. The trap door is mysterious and well-disguised. Through it he reaches the lady. When she gives him her husband's ring, he sports it boldly in the

55 *Amis and Amylion* (English metrical romance), ed. H. Le Saux (Exeter: Exeter University Press, 1993); *La tavola ritonda,* ed. Filippo Luigi Polidoro (Bologna: G. Romagnoli, 1864–6, from the codex in the Biblioteca Medicea Lorenziana, Florence); 'Flore et Blanceflor,' *Poèmes du XIIIe siècle,* ed. Edélestand du Méril (Paris: P. Jannet, n.d.; reprint, Nendeln: Kraus Reprints, 1970), pp. 164*ff.* For further literary representations of the story, see Pio Rajna, *Le fonti dell' Orlando furioso* (Florence: G.C. Sansoni, 1876), chap. 19, pp. 504*ff.*

56 Le Grand d'Aussy, ed., *Fabliaux ou contes du XIIe et du XIIIe siècle* (Paris: Onfroy, 1781), vol. III, pp. 157–67; (reprint, Geneva: Slatkine, 1971), pp. 263–5. The story is also known as 'L'histoire de la femme enlevée du roi.' This is a variation upon the story 'Inclusa' from the tradition of *The Seven Sages of Rome.* The device of the underground tunnel had a long history, for it does service again in the *Contes Tartares* of Thomas-Simon Gueullette, where he tells the tale of the dervish who dupes the jealous Persian, once again to prove that no precaution whatever can deter a woman. (The Hague: Henri du Sauzet, 1715–17); ed. Jean-François Perrin (Paris: Champion, 2010), vol. I, pp. 560–73. In the *Novellino* of Masuccio of Salerno, the trick recurs wherein a man takes his own wife on his horse to meet her lover, thinking her safe at home. Trans. W.G. Waters (London: Lawrence & Bullen, 1895), pt. IV, novel 34, vol. II, pp. 167–76.

lord's presence, raising extreme suspicion, but by the time the jealous old master gets the eighteen doors unlocked to question his wife, the ring has already been returned. The young chevalier then invites the lord to a banquet to meet his beloved and presents to him his own wife, but the same ruse is employed to assuage the lord's suspicion. With a boat awaiting them, they are well at sea before the duke realizes the deception. In this still-remote way, Straparola's tale can be said to fit within a sizeable class of stories pertaining to jealousy, castle keeps, and the determination of lovers that includes Marie de France's 'Lay of Yonec' to 'The Lady of Shalott.'[57]

A further example in this tradition is 'De Pyralius, qui feit édifier le chasteau jaloux: avec la description dudict chasteau,' the first story in the *Comptes amoureux* of Madame Jeanne Flore.[58] But now the design of 'Inclusa' has been modified by features from the *Mambriano* group in a version significantly amplified by lengthy descriptions of the setting and the characters' sentiments, and by the addition of episodes that tend to impose a more medieval ethos upon the materials of the *novella.* Being nearly contemporary with the tale of 'Erminione,' this work invites comparison as a cognate tale based on a common source. Jeanne Flore (pseudonym) places the tale in Toulouse, names her couple Pyralius and Rosemonde Chiprine, and indulges her fancy in describing the old man's maladies and decrepitude as well as the young wife's miseries and lamentations. His jealously is so advanced that he even walls up windows in fear of the sun's impregnating powers. Rosemonde thinks only of escape by any means possible. Her saviour is Jean Andro of Lyons, a hunter and fighter who is led to the foot of her tower by the pursuit of a wild boar. When he falls in love, he too is afflicted by all the conventional symptoms of love melancholy, making him a successor to Filomerse in *Mambriano.* Long passages of dream description, speculations, apostrophes, and complaints against injustice add considerable girth to the narrative. The

57 One further example ties this medieval story from the Seven Sages tradition to later Arabic tales: 'Histoire de Kamaralzeman et de la femme du joaillier' (The story of Kamaralzeman and the jeweller's wife), in *Contes inédits des mille et une nuits,* trans. Guillaume Stanislaus Trébutien (Paris: Dondey-Dupré, 1828), vol. III, pp. 150*ff.*

58 (Lyons: Benoist Rigaud, 1574), but first published in 1531. The standard edition was published in Torino in 1870; (reprint, Geneva: Slatkine Reprints, 1971), pp. 9–48. See also *Comptes amoureux par Madame Jeanne Flore touchant la punition que faict Venus de ceulx qui contemnent et mesprisent le vray amour* (Lyons: Denis de Harsy, 1542), and the modern edition by Régine Reynolds-Cornell (Saint-Etienne: Publications de l'Université de Saint-Etienne, 2005).

hero preaches to himself his chivalric duty to rescue the imprisoned maiden despite her marital status. At this juncture, the story goes its own fanciful way that includes encounters with giants guarding the tower, the crossing of multiple drawbridges, and the slaughter of serpents until Pyralius appears on the battlements to ask for mercy before fleeing by a postern gate. There follows an extensive erotic and ritualized encounter with the lady beginning with salutations and kisses, followed by dancing, food, and the appearance of Venus herself who leads the lovers into the bedroom. It is a striking creation, full of fantasy and wish-fulfillment that, at the same time, empties the narrative of its contemporary social particularity, and represents sensibilities in stark contrast with Straparola's in recycling Cieco's *novella* or the tradition upon which it was built. Jeanne Flore exchanges the original's closing duplicities for dragon-fighting bravura and a romantic rescue.

By contrast, Malespini remains altogether more faithful in his redeployment of that same *novella* in his *Ducento novelle*, entitled 'Avenimento di Agrissippo Ateniese, che rinchiuse la moglie in una torrè per grandissima gelosia, che non le giovò punto' (The story of Agrissippo of Athens who, because of his very great jealousy, locked his wife in a tower so that not even Jupiter could prick her). In this version, the dilapidated old man is eighty while the girl is a mere fifteen. He builds a tower four miles from the city, near the sea, with thirty-two inner doors for which he alone has the keys. When Filomerse, the young knight, indulges himself in a fit of love melancholy over the girl, physicians are called in to diagnose his depression, and there is a long aside on Neptune's court and Cupid. The story concludes with a fidelity test in which the lover plays the fool in a way that sets up the prevarication by which the young wife escapes the rigour of the Temple of Truth. She then appeals to the Senate over her two-year incarceration, causing the husband to be put in her place, while the young lovers now go on a daily basis to visit him. With regard to Straparola, however, it has little bearing apart from underscoring the ongoing interest in the story type.[59] Nevertheless, stories based on trials

59 Celio Malespini, *Ducento novelle* (Venice: Al Segno dell'Italia, 1609), no. 98, vol. I, pp. 259r–64r. Many of its passages are merely translations of *Mambriano*'s poetry into prose. See the annotations by Giuseppe Rua to the *Novelle del 'Mambriano' del Cieco da Ferrara* (Torino: Ermanno Loescher, 1888), pp. 79, 81. There is a second order of denouement for such stories of jealous husbands and incarcerated wives, which is for the husband to confess in the end that Cupid is crafty, that no amount of strategizing to keep out lovers will prove efficacious, and that where the wife

by ordeal were nearing an end as the practice itself lost juridical credibility. Furthermore, the apparent absence of such tales among the raconteurs of the nineteenth century suggests that it was never a tale in the popular tradition, but a literary creation from beginning to end. That question remains for others to solve.

---

proves this through an act of infidelity, the husband, rather than seek revenge, is best advised simply to tear down the tower and leave her at liberty. Such stories possess no trial scenes at the end as with Straparola's, but may otherwise contain many common features. The third story, day eight, of Francesco Sansovino's *Cento novelle scelte da i piu nobili scrittori* is a case in point. Galastro, king of Spain, upon the advice of his chiromancer, builds a tower where he places his wife. But in spite of his precautions, he finds himself cuckolded by Galeotto, son of King Diego of Castile. The boy thinks about the angelic beauty of the queen and of her confinement. When the king is out hunting, he disguises himself as a merchant and gains entry to demonstrate his wares. (A similar tactic is employed to different ends in Straparola's I.4.) As he draws her to the window for better light he begins speaking to her with his eyes to communicate his desire. Thereafter, they find the means to enjoy one another in a neighbouring room, while the king, upon his return, pays the merchant for his goods. In the end, the queen confesses everything in anticipation not of the king's anger but of his resignation to the fact that towers are futile and that Cupid is omnipotent, thereby regaining her freedom. (Venice: Francesco Sansovino, 1561), pp. 301v–5v. The story is based entirely on Straparola's IX.1, 'King Galafro's Vain Precautions.'

IV. Fable 3
Dancing Water, Singing Apple, and the Truth-Speaking Bird

LODOVICA

Ancilotto, king of Provino, takes the daughter of a baker as his wife and has three children by her. After harsh persecution at the hands of the king's mother, these exiled babes, now grown to adolescence, are made known to their father through the strange working of a certain water, of an apple, and of a bird.

Gracious ladies, I have always understood that man is the noblest and cleverest of all living creatures fashioned by nature, insofar as God has made him in His own image and similitude and willed that he should rule and not be ruled. It is rightly said, therefore, that man is the perfect animal and of greater excellence than all others, because all of these, including women, are subject to him. For that reason, anyone who by deceit and cunning causes the death of so noble a creature commits a heinous crime. It is no wonder that such persons, seeking to work harm to others, run headlong into destruction, as did the four women I'm about to describe, who, in trying to destroy others, were themselves deceived and came to a miserable end. This will all become clear to you in the fable to follow.

In Provino, a very famous and royal city, there lived in ancient times three sisters, pretty to look at, gracious in manners, and courteous in bearing, but of base lineage. They were the daughters of a certain Messer Rigo, a baker, who used his oven to bake the bread of other folk. One of the girls was named Brunora, another Lionella, and the third Chiaretta. One day when the three sisters were in their garden enjoying themselves, it happened that Ancilotto the king passed that way with a large entourage on their way to the hunt. Brunora, the oldest of the sisters, seeing such a fair and noble company, said to her sisters Lionella and Chiaretta, 'If I were married to the king's major-domo, I flatter myself to think that I could quench the thirst of the entire court with just one glass of wine.'

'And I,' said Lionella, 'please myself to think that if the king's private chamberlain were my husband, I could make enough linen from one spindle of my yarn to provide shirts of the best quality for the entire court.'

Then Chiaretta added, 'Well, if I were the king's wife, I flatter myself that I would give him three children at one birth, two sons and a daughter. Each of them would have long hair braided below the shoulders and intermingled with threads of the finest gold, and a chain of gold around the throat, and a star on the forehead.'

These sayings were overheard by one of the courtiers who hastened to the king and told him of the young girls' chatter. When he heard the gist of it, the king asked that they be brought before him, and when they were present, he asked them one by one to repeat what they had said in the garden. After each one had repeated to the king what she had formerly said, and in a manner most becoming, Ancilotto was mightily pleased by it all. So then and there, he wedded Brunora to the major-domo and Lionella to the chamberlain, and took Chiaretta as his own wife. The hunting was called off, for that very day everyone was to return to the palace where the unions were celebrated with the greatest pomp.

But the mother of Ancilotto was greatly angered by his marriage, for no matter how fair Chiaretta might be in face and figure, graceful in her person, or sweet and modest in her conversation, the queen mother held it a slight to the royal dignity that her daughter-in-law should be of vile and common descent, nor could she endure the fact that the major-domo and the chamberlain should be brothers-in-law of her son, the king. These matters kindled so fierce a rage in the queen mother against Chiaretta that she could hardly endure her presence. Nevertheless, she hid her wrath so as not to offend her son. In due time, according to God's good pleasure, Chiaretta became pregnant, to the great joy of the king, who soon expected to see the lovely progeny he had been promised.

Just at the time Chiaretta was expecting to give birth, Ancilotto was forced to make a journey to a distant country and stay for several days. He gave out orders that during his absence, his mother should look after the welfare of the queen and of the children born to her, and this, in spite of her concealed hatred, she heartily pledged herself to do. As soon as the king had begun his journey, Chiaretta gave birth to three children, two boys and a girl, just as she had promised when she was yet a maid. All three had their hair braided below the shoulders, and they wore golden chains on their necks and had golden stars on their foreheads. But as soon as the queen mother cast her eyes upon the innocent children – her hatred for Chiaretta burning as malignantly as ever – she vowed to have them secretly slain. No one would know they had ever been born and Chiaretta would be disgraced in the eyes of the king. Beside this, Brunora and Lionella had come to regard their sister with violent hatred and jealousy because she had been made their sovereign queen. They too lost no chance to further inflame the queen mother's spite through their cunning wiles.

On the very same day that the queen had given birth, it happened that in the stable yard three mongrel pups were born, two males and a female, which had white stars on their foreheads and traces of frilled collars around their necks. When this came to the attention of the sisters, these two she-devils went and took the puppies away from their mother and, with all their malicious craft, brought them to the old queen, saying in their sycophantic manner, 'We know, madam, that your highness has little love for our sister, and quite justifiably so, for she is of humble stock. It is not becoming that your son and our king should have mated with a woman of such base blood as hers. Knowing the disposition of your mind towards her, we have brought you these three mongrel pups, which, as you can see, were all born with stars on their foreheads. We now await your instructions in the matter.'

These words greatly pleased the old queen, guessing plainly at their evil intent. She arranged to show these whelps to her daughter-in-law, who had not yet seen the children she had borne, and to have her informed that these were her own offspring. To fortify the deception, the old queen compelled the midwife to bear the news. Accompanied by the two sisters and the queen mother, she showed the mutts to Chiaretta, saying, 'See, O queen, the fine fruit of your womb! Cherish it well so that the king, when he returns, may rejoice in the fine gift you have presented to him.' With these words the midwife placed the mongrels by her side, consoling her and telling her that such misfortunes as these happened to high-born folk from time to time.

It only remained for these wicked women, now that this barbarous deed had been completed, to contrive a means to slay the three poor, innocent children. But mercifully, God held them back from soiling their hands in the blood of their kindred. Instead, they made a chest, well-pitched inside and out, and, having placed the children within, they closed it and cast it into the river to be carried away by the current. But God in His justice would not allow these innocents to suffer. As the box floated along, it was seen by a certain miller named Marmiato, who hauled it out and opened it and found the three laughing children inside. Seeing how fair and graceful they were, he presumed they were the little ones of some noble lady who, to hide her shame, had committed this crime. Thus, after closing up the chest again, he set it on his shoulders and bore it straight home to his wife, Gordiana, and said to her, 'Look here, wife, what I've found on the river bank. It's a present for you.' Gordiana received the children joyfully and brought them up as if they had been her own, calling one Acquirino, the other Fluvio, because they had been found on the river, and the little girl Serena.

When he came back from his journey, Ancilotto was in high spirits, for he fully expected to find that Chiaretta had given to him the three beautiful children he had been promised. But the outcome was not what he had hoped, for the cunning queen mother, when she saw her son approaching, went to meet him and told him that his beloved wife had given him three puppy dogs instead of three children. Then, leading him into the chamber of the unfortunate Chiaretta, she showed him the mongrels which were lying beside her. The queen began to weep bitterly and to deny resolutely that the dogs were any of her children, but her wicked sisters came and declared that everything the old mother had said was the truth. On hearing this, the king was gravely disturbed and all but fell to the ground in a fit of grief. At long last, after he had come to himself, he credited his mother's false tale. But Chiaretta's dignity and sweetness, and the patience with which she bore the insults of the courtiers, won him over to spare her life. Even so, he condemned her to be kept in a cell under the palace where she was to wash the cooking pots and pans and be fed on the rotten garbage that fell continually into this stinking place.

While the unhappy queen passed her life in that foul cell feeding upon garbage, Gordiana, the wife of Marmiato the miller, gave birth to a son who was christened Borghino and lovingly brought up with the three foundlings. Once a month it was customary for Gordiana to cut the long and knotted hair of the three royal children, whereupon rare stones and great white pearls fell in abundance from their tresses. By these means Marmiato was able to give over his humble milling trade and live a life of ease and affectionate tranquillity with his wife and four children. But when the three foundlings had come to years of discretion, they discovered that they were not the children of Marmiato and Gordiana, but had been found floating in a chest on the river. As soon as they learned this, they became very unhappy and resolved to go their way in search of fortune elsewhere, much to the chagrin of their foster parents, who saw they would soon lose the rich harvest of jewels which fell from the children's locks and starry foreheads.

The brothers and their sister left Marmiato and Gordiana and journeyed many long days until they came to Provino, the city of Ancilotto their father, where they hired a house and lived together, maintaining themselves by selling the jewels and precious stones that continued to fall from their hair. One day the king, riding into the country with some of his courtiers, happened to pass by the house where the three were living, and they, as soon as they heard the king was coming, whom they had never seen before, ran down the steps and stood bareheaded to give him a respectful salutation. The king, whose eyes were as keen as a peregrine falcon's, looked at them steadily and remarked that on their foreheads each had a golden star, and immediately his heart stirred, for he had an inkling that they might prove to be his children. He stopped and said to them, 'Who are you, and where do you come from?'

Humbly they replied, 'We are poor foreigners who have come to this city to live.'

'I'm pleased to hear this,' replied Ancilotto. 'So tell me now your names.'

Then one of them said, 'I am named Acquirino.'

'And I Fluvio,' said the other.

'And I,' said their sister, 'am called Serena.'

'Ah ha, very well,' cried the king, 'I invite you all to dine with me tomorrow.' Although they were daunted by his gracious invitation, these young people did not dare to decline. No sooner was Ancilotto returned to the palace than he said to his mother, 'Madam, while I was abroad today I came by chance upon two handsome youths and a lovely maiden, and all three had golden stars on their foreheads. It seems to me they must be the children first promised to me by Queen Chiaretta.'

The wicked old woman shuddered at these words as though a knife had been driven through her heart, and calling in the midwife who had been present at the birth, she said to her in greatest secrecy, 'Hear this my old friend, do you know that the king's children are far from being dead as we planned, but are alive and more beautiful than ever?'

'How can this be?' replied the old crone. 'Were they not drowned in the river? Who has told you this?'

The queen mother answered, 'As far as I can gather from the king's own words they're alive, so I'm in desperate need of your help, for otherwise we are as good as dead.'

'Don't be alarmed, madam,' said the midwife. 'I have a plan in mind that should work the destruction of all three of them.'

So the midwife immediately set off for the house of Acquirino, Fluvio, and Serena and, finding Serena alone, she saluted her and talked of many things. After a long conversation, she said, 'My daughter, might you by chance have any dancing water?'

'Why no,' answered the girl.

'Ah, my daughter,' said the old lady, 'what delights you would enjoy if only you had some. If you could but once bathe your face in it, you would become a thousand times more beautiful than you are even now.'

Her curiosity now aroused, the young girl said, 'And how could I possibly get it?'

'Don't you have brothers?' the old goody asked. 'Send them to fetch it. They will find it easily enough, for it is not far from here.' And with these words she departed.

After a short while, Acquirino and Fluvio came back, and right away Serena told them of the old woman's visit and began begging them, if they loved her, to get her some of the wonderful dancing water. But they laughed at her request as a silly fancy and refused to go on a fool's errand, seeing that no one could say where it was to be found. But persuaded at last by their sister's pleading words, they departed together to fulfil her request, taking with them a phial to hold the precious water. When they had ridden several miles, they came to a fountain in which a snow-white dove was drinking and they were amazed when the bird spoke to them, 'What are you looking for, young men?'

To this Fluvio answered, 'We seek the precious water that is said to dance.'

'Wretched youths,' said the dove, 'who sends you on such a quest as this?'

'We want it for our sister,' said Fluvio.

'Then you're looking for death, for what you seek is guarded by many fierce beasts who will devour you instantly. But if you really must have some, leave the task to me, for I will surely bring it back to you.' Taking the phial and tying it beneath her right wing, the dove flew away out of sight.

Acquirino and Fluvio awaited her return with great anxiety, and in time she came into sight bearing the phial filled with the magic water. They took it from her, thanking the bird for the great service she had rendered them, then returned to their sister and gave Serena the water, exhorting her never to impose such another task upon them because they had nearly met their deaths in attempting it.

A short time after this, the king again met the two brothers and said to them, 'Why did you not come to dine and spend the day with me after promising to do so?'

'Gracious majesty,' they answered with profound respect, 'a pressing errand called us away from home.'

'Then,' said the king, 'tomorrow I will expect to see you for dinner without fail.'

The youths having made their apology, the king returned to the palace where he met his mother and told her he had once more seen the youths with the stars on their foreheads. The queen mother was now doubly perplexed and again she gave orders to have the midwife called to whom she secretly told all she had heard, at the same time begging her to find a remedy to their danger. The old crone told her to take courage, for she would plan matters this time so that they should be seen no more. The midwife went again to see Serena, whom she found alone, and asked her whether she had got any of the dancing water.

'I have it,' the girl replied, 'but getting it nearly cost my brothers their lives.'

'I'd like for you to have an apple that sings,' said the midwife. 'You never saw fruit so fair to look upon, or listened to music so sweet.'

'But how could I get it?' said Serena, 'for my brothers will never go in search of it, seeing that their last venture put them more in peril of death than in hope of life.'

'But they won the dancing water for you,' said the woman, 'and they are still alive. They will get the singing apple for you just as harmlessly.' And having said this she went on her way.

Hardly had the midwife gone when Acquirino and Fluvio came in, and again Serena cried out to them, 'Oh, my brothers! I hear now of another wonder more beautiful by far than the dancing water. It is the singing apple, and if I cannot have it I will surely die of vexation.' When Acquirino and Fluvio heard these words they chided her soundly, affirming that for her sake they were reluctant to risk death again. But she would not cease her prayers, weeping and sobbing so sweetly that the brothers, seeing that this new desire of hers came from her innermost soul, again gave in and agreed to satisfy her at whatever risk. So they mounted their horses and rode along until they came to an inn where they demanded of the host if he could tell them where an apple might be found that could sweetly sing. He told them that he knew where it was, but warned of the dangers to anyone bold enough to attempt to pluck it. 'It grows,' he said, 'in the middle of a fair garden that is watched day and night by a poisonous beast which, with its extended wings, kills without fail anyone who goes near the garden.'

'What, then, would you advise us to do?' said the youths, 'for we are intent upon plucking the apple at all cost.'

'If you follow my orders,' said the host, 'you can pluck the apple without fear of the poisonous beast or of death. You must take this robe which, as you see, is all covered with mirrors, and one of you must put it on. So dressed, you will enter the garden, the gate of which you'll find unfastened. The other must wait outside and be careful not to let anyone see you. The beast will make for the one who enters, but seeing an exact resemblance of itself in the mirrors, it will fall to the ground dead. Then the one waiting outside can go up to the tree, delicately pluck the singing apple, and leave the garden careful not to look behind.' The young men thanked their host courteously and observed all his directions so faithfully that they acquired the apple without any harm and carried it back to Serena. Again they besought her not to compel them to run such dangers ever again.

After some days had passed, the king once again came by and met the two young men. 'And what is the reason this time that you have disobeyed my command and failed to come dine with me?'

Fluvio replied, 'We would have been there without question had weighty matters of business not intervened.'

'Then you must come tomorrow. See that you don't let me down.' Acquirino assured him that, barring matters unforeseen, the pleasure would be theirs. The king returned to his palace and there he met his mother, telling her that he had once more seen the two youths. Now he was more firmly persuaded than ever that they must be the children promised him by Chiaretta and he would feel no rest till they had dined with him at his table.

The queen mother, when she heard that they were still alive, was in dire terror, no longer doubting that her fraud had been discovered. Struck with grief and terror, she sent for the midwife and said to her, 'I thought for certain the children were dead by this time and that we should hear no more of them. But they are still alive and we stand in peril of our lives. Look to our affair, for otherwise we shall be lost.'

'Noble lady,' said the midwife, 'take heart. This time I will work their bane without fail and you will bless me hereafter, seeing that they will trouble you no longer.'

Then the old woman, raging at her failure, left the palace and went directly to Serena's house. Wishing her a good day, she enquired whether she had managed to get the singing apple and Serena told her that she had. The cunning old crone then said, 'Ah, my daughter, all you have is nothing at all unless you get one more thing, the most beautiful, and the most graceful thing in the world.'

'Good mother, what may this fair thing be?' said the girl.

The old woman replied, 'It is the beautiful green bird, my child, which talks night and day and speaks words of marvellous wisdom. If you had it in your keeping, you would be called blessed and happy.' Having said this, she went on her way.

Acquirino and Fluvio came in directly after she was gone and Serena forthwith begged them to do her one last favour. They asked her what this boon might be that she desired, and she replied, 'The beautiful green bird.' Fluvio, who had plucked the apple guarded by the venomous beast, was still haunted by the dangers of his adventure and refused to go in quest of the bird. Acquirino, though for a long time he likewise turned a deaf ear, was finally moved by the brotherly love he felt and by the hot tears of grief which Serena shed, and was determined to satisfy her wish. Once Fluvio agreed to go, they mounted their horses and rode for several days until at last they came into a flowery green meadow in the middle of which stood a fine tree, lofty and full of leafage, surrounded with sundry marble statues which mocked the living by their wondrous workmanship. Through the meadow there ran a little stream, and up in the tall tree was the beautiful green bird preening itself and hopping about from bough to bough in a lively way, all the while uttering words more divine than human. The young men dismounted from their stallions and left them free to graze in order to inspect the marble statues more closely. But upon touching them, they themselves were turned where they stood into pure stone.

Serena for several months anxiously awaited the return of her dear brothers Acquirino and Fluvio and then began to despair, fearing that she would never see them again. Overcome with grief at their unhappy fate, she resolved to try her own fortune. So she mounted a sturdy horse and set forth, riding on until she came to the fair meadow where the beautiful green bird was hopping about on the tall tree and talking sweetly on one of the branches. The first thing she saw upon entering the green meadow were her brothers' horses grazing on the turf. Casting her eyes upon the statues, she saw that two of them must be Acquirino and Fluvio, for the unhappy youths, although turned into marble, retained their features exactly as in life. Serena dismounted and, going softly up to the tree, she laid her hands on the green bird from behind.

Finding himself a prisoner, he pleaded with her to let him go, promising that at the right time and place he would show his gratitude. But Serena refused all hope of compliance unless her brothers were first returned to their former states, whereupon the bird replied, 'Look then under my right wing and there you will find a feather much greener than any of the others with certain yellow markings inside. Pluck it out and with it touch the eyes of the statues; then your brothers will return to flesh and blood.' Serena raised the wing and found the feather just as the bird had said. Then she went directly to the marble shapes and, touching them one by one, immediately the statues turned into living men. The two brothers, seeing themselves restored to their rightful states, hugged and kissed their sister most joyfully.

When this wonder was accomplished, the bird again pleaded with Serena to kindly restore his liberty, promising that if she would grant his prayer that he would come to her aid whenever she might call upon him. But Serena was not to be so easily cajoled and declared that before she would let him go free, he must help them find their father and mother, and that until he had accomplished this task, he must remain her prisoner.

There was much debate to follow among the three as to who should have the bird in keeping, but in the end they agreed that it should be left in Serena's charge, who watched over it and tended it with great care. Now that they had the precious green bird, they mounted their horses and rode home. Meanwhile, Ancilotto had often passed by their house and was astonished to find it empty. He inquired of the neighbours what had become of them, yet all he could learn was that they had not been seen for many days. But they had not been back for long before the king again went by and, catching sight of them, asked how it was that nothing had been seen of them for so long and why they had disregarded his commands so many times. Acquirino answered with deep respect that some amazing troubles and adventures had befallen them and that if they had not presented themselves at the palace before in accordance with his majesty's desires, it was through no lack of respect, and that they were anxious to amend their conduct in the future.

When the king heard they had been in tribulation, he was moved to pity and would not leave until they all accompanied him back to the palace for dinner. But before they set forth, Acquirino secretly filled a phial with the dancing water, Fluvio took the singing apple, and Serena the talking bird, and they rode back with the king. Joyously they entered the palace with him and sat down at the royal table. When the malicious queen mother and the two wicked sisters saw so lovely a maiden and such handsome youths with their eyes shining like stars, their suspicion was great and their hearts were filled with foreboding. The banquet once come to an end, Acquirino said to the king, 'Sire, we would now be pleased to show you certain things that will greatly please your majesty,' and with these words he took a silver goblet and poured the dancing water into it and set it on the table. This done, his brother put his hand into his breast pocket and drew out the singing apple, which he placed beside the water. Serena also brought out the talking bird from her lap and set it on the table. Immediately the apple launched into song most sweetly and with the sounds the water most marvellously began to dance, delighting the king and all the courtiers who laughed aloud with pleasure. But the iniquitous queen mother and the wicked sisters were overcome with ill foreboding, certain their doom was near.

At last, when the apple and the water had ceased to sing and dance, the bird opened its mouth and said, 'O sacred majesty, what doom should be dealt to those who once plotted death against two brothers and a sister?'

Then the cunning queen mother, scheming to excuse herself, cried out, 'No lighter doom than the flames,' to which all who were present agreed.

Then the singing apple and the dancing water lifted their voices and said, 'Ah, false and cruel woman, your own tongue has doomed you to this horrible death, together with those wicked and envious sisters and the miscreant midwife as well.'

At these words the king froze in silence, but the beautiful green bird continued, 'O sacred majesty, these are the three children you longed for, the children who bear the star on their foreheads. And their innocent mother is she who to this day is kept a prisoner in that foul and filthy place.'

Then the king saw clearly how he had been tricked and gave orders that the unhappy Chiaretta should be taken out of her noisome prison and robed once more in her royal garments. As soon as this had been done, she was brought into the presence of the king and of his court. And although she had for so long a time suffered such cruel imprisonment, she retained all her former loveliness. Then the talking green bird related the strange history from beginning to end and the king, understanding the entire affair, tenderly embraced Chiaretta and their three children. Therewith, the dancing water, the singing apple, and the talking bird, having been set at liberty, suddenly all disappeared.

The next day, the king had a great fire kindled in the middle of the marketplace into which he ordered his mother to be cast, along with the two sisters of Chiaretta and the midwife, to be burned to death without pity in the presence of all the people. Thereafter, Ancilotto lived many happy years with his dear wife and his beautiful children and, having chosen for Serena an honourable husband, he left his two sons to inherit his kingdom.

When Lodovica's story ended, the Signora asked her to propound her riddle, and here is what she offered:

When Sol pours down his fiercest heat,
High on Ghiraldo's lofty seat,
A man I marked, with roguish eye,
Shut fast within a closure high.
All through the day he prates and talks,
And clad in robes of emerald walks,
I've told you all except his name,
And that from your own wit I claim.

Many were the interpretations put upon this enigma, but no one came near the mark except the charming Isabella who, greatly pleased with herself, said in a merry tone, 'Lodovica's enigma can only refer to the popinjay who lives within an iron cage, which is the closure, and has plumage green as emerald, and chatters all day long.' The deft solution to the riddle pleased everybody except Lodovica, who had flattered herself that no one would be clever enough to solve it, and who for a time didn't know what to say. Then, with a face now all vermilion, she turned to Isabella and said, 'I'm feeling really envious and annoyed, not because of all your honours, but because now I'm inferior to everyone present. They had a chance to set out the solutions to their riddles when no one could guess the answers, but mine have all been guessed. Well, don't worry, because if I can come up with tit for tat, I won't be caught napping.'

'As you please, Signora Lodovica,' came Isabella's cheerful reply, 'but the early bird gets the worm.'

The Signora, seeing that words were about to multiply, imposed silence on them both, ordering Isabella to get on with telling her fable, which she began in merry spirit.

IV.3 Commentary

The various meanings of the present story are a product of its particular assembly of narrative parts, each one invested with the social values and psychological imperatives that have guaranteed their successes as story 'memes,' from the fairy-tale rise of a commoner through marriage to a king, to the wish-fulfilling incineration of the patently guilty mother-in-law. A sense of those parts arises systemically as a matter of the chunking and shedding operations of memory itself. The story just read has already, by the devious and subliminal processes of mind, been collapsed into its salient categories – the same, in theory, that are isolated for Proppian analysis, and the same, arguably, that correspond to the principal stand-alone stories that have been interlinked to make up this compound creation. These can be profiled only through paraphrase – the poorest excuse for literary criticism – because motifs are by definition little plot summaries reduced to their identifying characteristics. Inferentially, these orders of action were the same to have been trimmed and stored by the default operations of memory in the minstrel mind, thereby controlling and defining their future elaboration and recombination. It is this property of the brain that prefigures all interpretational efforts and links us on a phylogenetic basis to the operations of the makers – our brains in this regard make us equals before the 'text.' Hence, these narrative 'chunks' are the units through which the story must be investigated as an assembly of discrete parts.

For purposes of structural analysis, then, the first is the micro-romance of the three commoners overheard daydreaming by a passing king who, charmed by the prospect of offspring born with golden stars and chains, imposes a matrimonial novelty upon the royal family. The second inset story involves the animus of the king's mother, offended by this fairy-tale violation of social echelons. There follows the diabolical plot to substitute the newborns with animals and send the children to their deaths in order to discredit the young queen. This portion of the tale, with its deception mechanisms and the cruel handling of the beleaguered girl, is a moveable structure known in many other forms and contexts. The third segment moves to the story of the second generation, the recovery of the children, their childhood circumstances, their awakening with regard to their birth parents, and their quest for origins. This segment may be considered alone or in conjunction with the sequel adventures of the tripartite quest. The challenge by the midwife to find the dancing water, the singing apple, and the truth-speaking bird is a result of the stratagems employed to keep secret the crimes committed in the second part. Yet it is a questing tale of its own, a fourth and now defining episode featuring a triple pattern of adventure involving sibling loyalty and rescue and the capturing of three of the folk world's most precious talismanic objects pertaining to health, wealth, and truth. This segment, likewise, has an elaborate history of its own, alone and in conjunction with other folk-tale types. There are now three centres of energy: the king who seeks the friendship of the mysterious children; the four malefactors keen to eliminate the royal heirs; and the three children beset by the risks and dangers of their encounters with the magic kingdom. The capturing of the all-knowing bird, the culmination of the fourth narrative episode or story type, leads to the fifth and closing section, which entails reunion with the birth father (completing the third episode), and the performances of the talismanic objects (completing the fourth), leading to the recovery of their birth mother together with the apprehension and destruction of the four villainesses (completing the second episode). The design, in itself, is excellent, consisting of distinct motivic units upon which all investigations into origins and narrative coherence must be based.

These four or five parts together form a complete representation of ATU 707, 'the truth bird,' which enjoyed particular favour among the French authors of fairy tales, the first of them being Mme. d'Aulnoy in 'La princesse Belle-Étoile,' published in 1698, a story derived in all its essentials from Straparola.[60] The type consists of a double action over two generations in which the second generation brings delayed justice to the malignant parties of the preceding generation, leading to the restoration of the betrayed family. The first is a rags-to-riches tale cut short by envy and malice; the second is a tale of debasement, trial by quest and initiation, and the restoration of a birthright. The first part is also an emblematic enactment of the animosity within the extended family that threatens innocent children and leads to the psychological incarceration of the helpless young mother, robbed of the affections of her husband. The second part portrays the optimism of their three offspring who, alone in the world, engage with the realms of mystery and danger in order to equip themselves with the forces and skills for survival embodied not only in the discipline of questing but in the magic powers

60 For further classification of the type, see Paul Delarue and Marie-Louise Tenèze, 'L'oiseau de vérité,' in *Le conte populaire français: Un catalogue raisonné des versions de France et des pays de langue française et d'Outre-mer*, 3 vols. (Paris: G.-P. Maisonneuve & Larose, 1976), vol. II, pp. 633–48.

of language invested in the bird of truth. The final objective of this story is to return estranged children to their parents, but only through the preliminary redemption of their own mother from her life of lingering torment. Finally, for those who showed no humanity or bloodline solidarity, it is a tale of justice of a summary kind that fairy tales seldom avoid, whether of boilings or burnings, beheadings or quarterings, or – my favourite – of being rolled down a mountainside in a barrel driven full of nails. In sum, the story is a rich configuration of profoundly blunt but enduring motifs pertaining to family life, a tableau of envy and retributive justice, as well as of sibling loyalty and parental longings, constituting the psychological trajectory of the completed fabula. How could such a story not achieve the highest status among the archetypal creations of the race?

Latent in the inaugural episode is the question of bride selection from among commoners in tales going back to ancient India, including the Griselda group, as well as that of the clever girl (die kluge Rätsellöserin) who becomes a royal bride through the solution of riddles posed by a prince on tour in the countryside. These relate in turn to all the crux tales concerning exogamy and the elevation of brides from outside the royal circles. Their counterpart tales are those concerned with propinquity and the selection from inner circles of brides as close as daughters. Straparola has already introduced two such stories in I.4 and III.3. The second part deals with maligned, banished, or mutilated queens, our tale combining the fear of bestial births and related superstitions with the reality of household jealousies and the scheming of the old queen displaced by the arrival of the new daughter-in-law as reigning queen. It is telling that the heroine is traduced not in her capacity as consort for reasons of infidelity, but in her capacity as mother in failing to perpetuate the royal bloodline. Implicit in this assault is a deep fear and hatred of outsiders, of monstrous births, or simply of the commanding power of maternity itself, remotely associated with latent allusions to cannibalism, infanticide, and bestiality by which the slander against the queen is variously made credible.[61] Meanwhile, Chiaretta is forced to believe in

61 Margaret Schlauch, for one, in her study of Chaucer's 'Man of Law's Tale' in its broadest literary context concerning banished or incarcerated queens (a text and its tradition reviewed briefly above in relation to the story of Doralice, I.4) assumes the antiquity of the story type as an expression of anxiety over maternal infanticide and cannibalism. *Chaucer's Constance and Accused Queens* (New York: Gordian Press, 1969), originally published in 1927, pp. 12*ff.*

the science of monstrosity accounting for a litter of puppies in lieu of human infants on the authority of the midwife, in opposition to her own fantasy of triplets with stars, braids, and chains which the king embraces as a biological entitlement. This is a wonder tale.

The final section is a *Bildungs* fantasy that includes anxiety over parental identity, a rite of initiation, and the deliverance of a helpless and innocent mother through the offices of her children. It is a tale of maturation in innocence, narrow escape through perseverance and concentration, sibling loyalty and succour, and the recovery of the birth family through the delayed exposure of an essential truth. In the dancing water and the singing apple there may well be vestiges of occult healing powers, elements left over from tales of the wasteland, the water of life, and the golden bough, the sacred objects of spiritualized quests reduced to the scale of the folk tale. Readers are at liberty to make as much or as little as they choose of the meanings to be recovered through structural, seasonal, psychological, archetypal, and anthropological intimations ranging from pure allegory to the implicit cognitive categories (belief schemata) by which consciousness is invigilated to social advantage – categories that might well find expression through the elementary stories of the race. It is not the intent here to make elaborate representations of such readings, but to aver that of all the tales in the collection apt for such analysis, this one is among the most propitious. The only brakes to be set upon such procedures are those set by the hermeneute's own particular sense of the limitations of folk thinking and intentionality, or by the plausibility of analogies through which one system is imposed upon another.[62]

Straparola's version of 'The Truth-Speaking Bird' presents a particularly challenging case to the student of literary sources. It is an effective and well-integrated work composed of several narrative motifs, such as bride selection through an overheard conversation, the exposure of a queen's newborn children on the pretext that they are animals, and the quest on the part of those children for the three magic elements that will lead them back to their parents.[63] These motifs are firmly cemented

62 For a brief overview of the schools of fairy-tale interpretation, see Max Lüthi, *Once Upon a Time: On the Nature of Fairy Tales* (Bloomington: Indiana University Press, 1976), pp. 1–20.

63 Raymonde Robert's comparative structural analysis of this story in the versions by Straparola, Mme. d'Aulnoy, Eustache Le Noble, and Antoine Galland introduces roughly the same narrative divisions: I. the bride selection; II. the marriage,

together by the mid-sixteenth century, as the present tale confirms, and possibly much earlier, given the 'swan children' analogue formulated by Johannes de Alta Silva in *Dolopathos* more than three centuries earlier. But of that assembly process there is no clear record. Meanwhile, there is a closely cognate work in *The Arabian Nights*, the independent circulation of which during the Renaissance period, given the present story, must now be taken for granted, thereby becoming Straparola's self-evident source. But therein may lie a mystery, for *The Arabian Nights* as we know it was not assembled by Galland before the early eighteenth century, and not all of its parts have demonstrable former lives. The tales are so close that only two options remain: it was available to Straparola in a form proximate to his by the early sixteenth century without leaving any corroborative traces; or it was 'orientalized' from Straparola's own story. Should the latter case prove true, we are once again compelled to imagine the present story's origins among the folk raconteurs of the late Middle Ages relying on Eastern materials of much earlier provenance. The result, once again, would be that Straparola's rendition is the only pre-modern literary version of the fully assembled work. The case to be made against the early circulation of 'The Truth-Speaking Bird' featured in *The Arabian Nights*, and its source potential for Straparola, is reviewed in the following three paragraphs. Readers in haste may leap over them.

Antoine Galland, the first Western compiler of *The Arabian Nights*, collected a story closely resembling Straparola's from a Syrian raconteur and added it to the *Nights* in the early 1700s. That, in itself, does not deny its antiquity, for it may well have been in circulation in the Arabic world during the preceding centuries. On that assumption, Valentin Schmidt became the first of many to consider this tale to be Straparola's unquestionable source.[64] Something to the matter, however, is that both Galland's and Straparola's versions represent two relatively late glimpses into a far more ancient story concerning maligned queens that had spread across

childbirth, and banishment portion; and III. the royal children, their quests, and the truth pronouncements of the speaking bird. These are subdivided into eleven subsections approximating the motifs enumerated in the Thompson Motif Index of Folk Literature. *Le conte de fées littéraire en France de la fin du XVIIe à la fin du XVIIIe siècle* (Nancy: Presses universitaires, 1982), pp. 37–42.

64 'Die drei königskinder,' in *Sammlung alter Märchen: Die Märchen des Straparola* (Berlin: Duncker & Humblot, 1817), vol. I, p. 284.

the Eurasian landmass literally centuries earlier.[65] But if Schmidt is right, it becomes an academic point whether, at a time preceding Straparola, the precise folk tale upon which the present story is based travelled to the East to inspire the cognate tale collected by Galland, or the inverse, as has so often been assumed. The challenge to the latter hypothesis is that the story in more remote forms was already well known in the West and grew to its fullness through the offices of the Western folk mind. In following Schmidt and others, however, Straparola's tale would owe little to any of the individual motifs represented in antecedent European tales. There is a third option, however, that Galland attributed Straparola's tale to his mysterious Syrian raconteur while 'orientalizing' it for the *Arabian Nights* in the manner employed by Thomas-Simon Gueullette in subsequent years. The Eastern tale is a hoax, the full tale is Western, Straparola records it first, and evidence of its component parts must be sought among the writers of the late Middle Ages. Proof in this matter depends upon the appraisal of Galland's opportunism and the existence of corroborating Arabic versions confirming the story's antiquity in the East. What is revealingly clear is that it does not occur in the most complete of the fourteenth-century manuscripts of *The Arabian Nights.*[66] Nevertheless, there are related stories of Eastern provenance that were collected in the nineteenth century and included in the *Supplemental Nights to the Book of the Thousand and One Nights* dealing with a queen falsely accused of cannibalism, going all the way back to the foundations of the maligned queen tradition (see below). The fullest irony may be that the medieval core around which the Renaissance tale was elaborated is Eastern from an even earlier period, perhaps completing the circle.

---

65 Arthur Dickson had a keen interest in IV.3, 'The Truth-Speaking Bird,' because it represents 'the oldest recorded in Europe' of the folk tale which he takes as the basis for *Valentin et Orson.* Although later chronologically, it serves, nevertheless, as his oikotype for a work which originated as a romance elaboration early in the fourteenth century upon the folk tale in question concerning an exiled queen and the quest by her sons to find her. This *chanson de geste* antedates the present tale by two-and-a-half centuries, but the folk tale goes back to early Sanskrit origins. *Valentine and Orson: A Study in Late Medieval Romance* (New York: Columbia University Press, 1929), p. 23.

66 This does not eliminate entirely the chance that the tale was in independent circulation, or that it had come early to the West, but that nothing resembling Galland's tale has been located in Eastern collections is surely indicative. See *The Arabian Nights,* trans. by Husain Haddawy from the manuscript edited by Muhsin Mahdi (New York: W.W. Norton, 1990), which breaks off after the 271st night.

However the current of influence is deemed to flow, a comparative study of Straparola's 'The Truth-Speaking Bird' must begin with 'The Jealous Sisters and their Cadette' – which Galland reports to have heard in Paris in 1709 as recited by Hanna Dieb, a Maronite Christian Arab from Aleppo – for it remains the closest in its narrative pattern to Straparola, if only because it is a clever act of plagiarism or remaking (*refacimento*).[67] It is one of the few, for example, even among the many versions collected in the nineteenth century, to join in common cause the hatred of a wicked mother-in-law with the invidious envy of two elder sisters. Generally, the defamation of the young queen is managed by one or the other. In the following resume, readers will find themselves speculating upon the differences in such details and whether they are best accounted for as independent deletions and additions to a common folk source, or the kinds of choices that Galland might have made to disguise his debt – an exercise in evidential assessment. In Galland's rendition, Khusrau Shah goes walking in disguise with his Grand Vizier in a poor quarter of the city and overhears the talk of three fair sisters. Charmed by them, the Shah brings the three weddings to pass, marrying the youngest daughter himself. In the next section the promised prince is born, having virtues similar to those of Biancabella as well as the children of Ancilotto, although instead of shedding jewels from his hair he weeps pearls and laughs roses, while his gold and silver hair reflects both sun and moon. (Galland could have taken these variants from Straparola as well.) The two older sisters, seething with anger, solicit and receive from the Shah the right to serve as midwives and caregivers to the newborn. They wrap the child up and throw him into the canal, replacing him with a dead puppy. Thereafter, the Shah flies into a rage and nearly kills the queen, but the Grand Vizier intercedes and so she is given a second and a third chance. In this way she brings forth, one by one, the same two sons and a daughter as in Straparola's 'The Truth-Speaking Bird,' the last replaced in her birth-bed by a muskrat. All three are rescued by the Intendant of the Gardens, who intuits their royal pedigree, as the miller does in Straparola. The queen's third failure is determinant, for she is thereafter suspended in a wooden cage beside the mosque for all good

67 'The Jealous Sisters and Their Cadette,' in *The Great Fairy Tale Tradition*, trans. Jack Zipes (New York: W.W. Norton, 2001), pp. 270–302, from Antoine Galland, 'Histoire de deux soeurs jalouses de leur cadette,' *Les milles et une Nuit*, 12 vols. (Lyons: Briasson, 1717), Nights 678–88. See also Guy Huet, 'Le conte des sœurs jalouses,' *Revue d'Ethnographie et de Sociologie* 2 (1911): p. 200.

Muslims to spit upon in passing, upon pain of retribution. The children are raised in a country mansion where they become model pupils. Before their protector dies, he informs them of their birth and admonishes them to live in love and mutual support of each other. These admonitions are merely implicit in Straparola. While her two brothers are away, Parizad is visited by a beggar woman who tells her that she must acquire the 'Bird of a Thousand Tales,' principally as an ornament to her mansion. The bird becomes an object of insatiable curiosity and desire, setting up the first of the ensuing quests. To this, in time, are added the singing tree and the golden water which leaps up in a basin like an eternal fountain. Absent from Straparola's tale is the magic object that signals the destiny of the absent brother, in this case a knife with a colour-changing blade, although this 'life sign' motif is standard folk tale fare (see the commentary to VII.5). Trekking towards India for many days, the first brother meets an ancient sage who gives instructions and provides a ball that rolls before the hero until he reaches the magic mountain with a long path leading to the top. On both sides there are creatures who cry, moan, and hurl insults, soliciting each seeker to turn in response and so be transformed to stone. That taboo is a mere vestige in Straparola's tale in the form of the pointless command to the brother not to look back after killing the basilisk. In this fashion, both brothers in the oriental tale are turned to stone, whereas in the present tale the two are transformed merely by touching the statues. The knife blade shows gore with their transformations, inciting Parizad to disguise herself as a man (a detail suppressed in Straparola or added by Galland?) to go in search of her brothers. Undistracted by the voices, she presses on to the top, indifferent to the insults hurled after her, captures the bird, releases her brothers with the water of life, and proceeds with them back to their house, there to encounter the Shah who is invited in at last to see their newfound wonders. It is all a prelude to the *peripeteia*, the recall of the queen through the revelations of the truth-speaking bird and the execution of the wicked women, a mother and two sisters though they may be. No special pleading is required to see that this is essentially the same story as Straparola's, separated only by the substitutions typical of oral transmission or literary adaptation. Both rehearse three of the deepest crises of the human social condition: the integration of an unapproved bride, the protection of offspring from calumny and abduction, and the recovery of personal identity through the discovery of lost parents. These are among the most compelling of natural obsessions and carry innate power to drive narrative order, as they do in Straparola's tale.

Further to the comparison of the tales of 'The Truth-Speaking Bird' and the Shah Khusrau,[68] the latter has the births in succession, as in many subsequent folk versions – and it is instructive to recall that in potentially reshaping his tale, Galland had available to him the versions by Mme. d'Aulnoy and Eustche Le Noble (described below). At the same time, Straparola's tale is seen to carry vestiges of former features not present in the Galland tale, such as the birth of a son to the miller's wife who has no role to play thereafter. That feature appears to have been part of Straparola's source, for it survives in later versions in which the miller's natural child grows up to taunt the foundlings as bastards – a motif already seen in analogues to the tale of 'Fortunio' (III.4). That is a smoking gun. Less elaborated in Straparola is the ritual quest on the mountain according to the directions of a sage found dead once the talismanic objects are removed from the shrine. Whether it became a part of the tradition early or late, this ritualized trek up the mountain between menacing creatures 'feels' oriental in spirit and is featured in many of the cognate tales collected in the nineteenth century. The water of life is more clearly restorative and the bird rather more holy in the oriental tales, while the flask is sufficient to fill a fountain which shoots water far into the air in a fantasy of garden décor. These things are scaled back in Straparola, or arguably were simply absent in his 'less developed' source. In our tale, the two boys go together and complete their first two quests. Only during the third are the two boys turned to stone, compelling their sister to come to their rescue. That the sage is merely the host of an inn and that the mirror trick to defeat a guardian basilisk is represented in the place of the Arabian story's voices taunting the boys riding up the mountain means an inventive departure from the Eastern source on Straparola's part, or simply a different source. In the oriental tale, the king visits his children at their palace and is amazed by their exotic possessions, whereas in our tale the three sacred objects, on a far

68 The use of this name is a historical tease, for it may have been retrofitted upon the story at nearly any time. But it is a variant spelling of Chosroes and a possible reference to the famous and cultured Chosroes I Anushirvan (531–79 CE), the Sassanid emperor and patron of Barzoye or Burzoë, the poet who first translated the *Panchatantra* into Pahlevi. His name was spelled variously Khosru Nushirvan and Khusrau I Anosarvan. If the indication is taken literally, the story would have originated in ancient Persia in the sixth century. See the 'Introduction' to Sir Thomas North, *The Moral Philosophy of Doni, known as The Fables of Bidpai*, ed. Donald Beecher, John Butler, and Carmine Di Biase (Ottawa: Dovehouse, 2003), pp. 18*ff.*

smaller scale, are taken to the king's palace to amuse him at the table. In both stories, something of their deeper ritualistic significance may be lost; both make extraneous necessity of residual details. Only in Galland's tale is the king upbraided for his credulity in believing that women could give live birth to animals against all the laws of nature. As stated above, such variations may be late rather than early and hence reveal little about the 'Ur-text' that produced Straparola's source and much about Galland's temptations to moralize a tale in the spirit of his age that should have been made more enigmatic and spare to make it pass as Eastern. Galland's addition to the *Arabian Nights* remains the closest kin to Straparola's tale, whether as the product of a common source or as a clever plagiarism. But Straparola's departure from the model set by Galland's tale and the independent existence of all three narrative motifs in related medieval and Renaissance texts are further indicators that the present tale is a Renaissance creation from parts circulating widely in popular literary culture. Moreover, the allusion to popular tales about 'truth-speaking birds' in the contemporary letters of Andrea Calmo (1552), discussed below, offers further confirmation. In brief, the comparative evidence points to a Renaissance folk source which contributed all of the features unique to Straparola that have been suppressed in Galland's pseudo-oriental tale. Hence, the latter production becomes part of the growing Straparolan legacy, but may be discounted as a direct Eastern source.

Concerning the motif of the accused queen, there is a sense of *déjà vu* in reading the story of 'The Swans' in *Dolopathos*.[69] In effect, it is the same story as Straparola's, less the quest for the water, tree, and bird. The opening is related to 'the Mélusine' group, for the hunter marries a water nixie. But mermaid or baker's daughter, the hunter's mother hates her new daughter-in-law and so the familiar story proceeds. She gives birth not to three but to seven children, six sons and a daughter, a truly miraculous and prodigious performance. Each child has a golden necklace around its neck. The mother-in-law replaces the seven babies with seven puppies and arranges for the infants to be strangled, but they are exposed, instead, and raised in a cave by an old philosopher and for seven years nourished with deer's milk. So much is familiar, so much is strange, but the second, third, and fifth parts of Straparola's tale are

69 *Dolopathos or the King and the Seven Wise Men*, trans. Brady B. Gilleland (Binghamton, NY: MRTS, 1981), pp. 71–7.

already in congruence. The young mother, much like her queenly counterparts, is buried alive to her breasts in the courtyard, a detail redolent of the Doralice group, but she is fed on food thrown to the dogs, and courtiers are instructed to wash their hands over her head (redolent of the spitting motif in the Galland story). For seven years her health deteriorates and her flesh is eaten away. While out hunting, the father sees the children with their necklaces and feels a surge of emotion in his heart. He tells his mother of his encounter and fear grips her immediately. Now, rather than send them on dangerous missions – they are still too young – she contrives to steal their golden chains, thereby trapping them in their transformations as swans. These are children seeking their maternal heritage, after all, as the offspring of a water nymph, and in this feature the story seeks its own identity in the Lohengrin group. The swan children settle on a lake near their father's palace until the orphan sister (her necklace alone remaining), while begging bread to feed her mother, is questioned by the king. She becomes the truth-speaking bird, while the expression on the servant's face exposes his guilt. An attempt is made on the girl's life, but fails. In the end, all but one of the necklaces is restored, the mother is brought to health with baths and ointments, and the wicked mother is buried in her place. The story follows a profile similar to the present one, featuring the same principal episodes. Johannes de Alta Silva, who died in 1212, assembled his collection in the north of France from materials belonging essentially to the story tradition of *The Seven Sages*, thus materials from the Arabic and Turkish worlds that made their way to Europe at the time of the Crusades.[70] That it made a direct contribution to the sources employed by Straparola is beyond demonstration, but it appears at an early date in witness to a generic story type of mothers whose children are replaced by animals, who are victimized by cruel relatives, subjected to unspeakable torture, and who are restored through the truth preserved in the unique identities of her children. The seeker of sources is now brought to think in terms of the

70 Just how this story may have linked up with the tale that produced the version recorded late by Galland is beyond certain knowledge. Even the source of *Dolopathos* is debated, whether it comes from the Greek *Syntipas* or from the *Book of Sindebar*, the sources of which are unknown, despite the many hints of affiliations with wisdom books from India, such as the *Panchatantra*. See the 'Introduction' by Brady Gilleland to *Dolopathos* (Binghamton, NY: MRTS, 1981), pp. xiii–xix. It is perhaps revealing that 'The Swans' in particular does not occur in other versions of the Seven Sages cycle, making this telling the first in the Latin West.

wide circulation of these idiosyncratic motifs in Europe as far back as the twelfth century. As for tales of exiled queens abused by their relatives, that date can be pushed back even further.[71]

The vista, in fact, opens upon an 'ocean' of stories and, of the many examined, my candidate for the most 'primitive' version is the following in which the queen is accused not of giving birth to monsters, but of eating her children. In a Sanskrit Buddhist legend, a queen of humble origins is envied by her husband's other wives.[72] While giving birth, they cover her eyes, then remove her children and throw them into the river. At the same time, they smear her face with blood and accuse her publicly of eating the newborn twins. This motif will recur. The queen is rescued from an awful fate by a wise man who dreams the truth. The children are meanwhile adopted and raised, and eventually they are identified simply by their physical resemblances to the king. The tale has no opening bride selection plot and no quest by the royal children. It is a simple story of jealousy that entails a credulous husband ready to accept an accusation of cannibalism. It would seem to hearken back to more ancient conditions, replaced in later tales by allegations of bestiality and monster births. In both instances the representations are fraudulent, but seem to express deep-seated anxieties about paternity and legitimacy. The familiar sequence of the tale, from maligned queen and the crisis of childbirth to the recovery of foundlings through a mechanism of *anagnorisis* leading to the restoration of the nuclear family, is provided in seminal form, amenable to all the elaborations of 'the envious sisters'

71 The Anglo-Saxon 'Wife's Lament' may be one such testimonial to an exile brought on by the treachery of her brothers-in-law seeking power by dint of marriage to her sisters – a situation echoed in *King Lear.* George Philip Krapp and Elliott Van Kirk Dobbie, eds., *The Exeter Book,* Anglo-Saxon Poetic Records (New York: Columbia University Press, 1936), vol. III, pp. 210–11.

72 Raja Rajendralala Mitra, 'Avadanakalpalata,' *Sanskrit Buddhist Literature of Nepal* (Calcutta: Asiatic Society of Bengal, 1882), pp. 62–6; new ed. (Calcutta: Sanskrit Pustak Bhandar, [1971]). A similar story is that of Padmavati, falsely accused of devouring her children, maligned, and drenched in blood by the king's other wives. *Le Mahavastu,* ed. É. Senert (Paris: Imprimerie nationale, n.d.), vol. III, pp. xvii, 152. Equally 'early' in spirit is a Turkish tale telling of a childless wife replaced by a second who bears her husband twins. The jealous first wife replaces them with snakes and throws the children into the sea in boxes. They are raised as foundlings while their mother is driven into exile and cared for by shepherds. When the boy is taunted, he and his sister, still in possession of their birth clothes, set out in search of their parents. Eventually, they find their mother and the family is reunited. Ignacz Kúnos, *Türkische Volksmärchen aus Stambul* (Leiden: Brill, 1905), p. 339.

group represented in Straparola's tale without loss of narrative identity. Tales in this tradition may be the fuse to all the later tales of maligned queens. In a version translated by Richard Burton in the *Supplemental Arabian Nights*, a queen's children are stolen and she is accused of eating them after her mouth is smeared with blood. It is the jealous second wife who perpetrates these atrocities. The queen is rescued by a servant and returned to her father, while her sons are found by a fisherman and are later discovered by the king who then makes a pilgrimage to Benares to reclaim his innocent wife.[73] This has the 'feel' of a very early tale not yet close to the world of Straparola.

To be passed over lightly here are all the many stories in the Olive-Hélène-Constance-Émaré-Doralice group already explored in relation to Straparola's story of 'Doralice and her Incestuous Father, Tebaldo' (I.4).[74] Margaret Schlauch deals with the abundance of materials by

73 *Supplemental Nights to the Book of the Thousand and One Nights* (London: The Burton Club, 1887), vol. III, p. 647. For a description of many more tales in this vein, see Johannes Bolte and Jiří Polívka, *Anmerkungen zu den Kinder- und Hausmärchen der Brüder Grimm*, 5 vols. (Leipzig: Dieterich'sche Verlagsbuchhandlung, 1913–32), vol. II, p. 393.

74 The story type has not only been singled out for study by Margaret Schlauch as the folk heritage eventuating in Chaucer's 'Man of Law's Tale' in the *Canterbury Tales*, in *Accused Queens* (New York: Gordian Press [1927], 1969), but by Johannes Bolte and Jiří Polívka in their 'Anmerkungen' or annotations to the Grimms' *Märchen*, 'The Three Little Birds,' in *Anmerkungen zu der Kinder- und Hausmärchen der Brüder Grimm* (Leipzig: Dieterich, 1913), no. 96, vol. II, pp. 380*ff*; new ed. (Hildesheim: Georg Olms, 1963, 1992); and James M. Taggart, *Enchanted Maidens: Gender Relations in Spanish Folktales of Courtship and Marriage* (Princeton: Princeton University Press, 1990), pp. 41–58. Taggart studies the story type in relation to 'Cinderella' and 'Blancheflor' as narratives of marital crisis and reconciliation in the context of family conflicts and dynamics. The basic story of the accused queen and the exchange of animals for infants leading to incarceration and exposure is also at the centre of *Theseus of Cologne*, MS. Brit. Lib. Add. 16,955, *Doon de la Roche*, MS. Brit. Lib. Harleian 4404, and 'De Alixaundre, Roy de Hongrie, qui voulut espouser sa fille,' *Nouvelles françaises inédites du quinzième siècle*, ed. E. Langlois (Paris: H. Champion, 1908), pp. 61–7. This group also includes such related narratives as the story of Queen Oliva. One among the many is the *Historia della regina Oliva*, ed. Francesco Corna da Soncino and Silvia Marchi (Pisa: Istituti editoriali e poligrafici internazionali, 1998). Giuseppe Pitrè extends the bibliography of this story around the folk tale of 'La Bella Oliva' which he collected in Florence. Popular versions were known all over Italy, according to *Novelle popolari toscane, parte seconda* (Rome: Casa editrice del libro italiano, n.d.), p. 118. Another extensive examination of the story type was made by Arthur Dickson in his quest for the origins of the French *chanson de geste*, *Valentin et Orson*, in *Valentine and Orson: A Study*

listing twenty of the best known, summarizing the tale in its fullest generic terms and listing by numbers the major variants according to their sources. Common to all are the betrayal of the queen, the exposure of her children, the operations of deceitful family members, the queen's banishment or incarceration, the return of the king, the eventual rediscovery of his wife many years later through the industry of his lost children raised by strangers, and the summary execution of the treacherous family members. Many of these stories begin with a girl driven into exile by the incestuous intentions of her own father, which is markedly different from the present tale, but thereafter – in the segment concerning the betrayal of the queen – there are many common features. In the saints' lives tradition, the heroine manifests the purity and patience of a martyr and serves as an emissary of the faith, as in the Olive-Hélène group. The letter exchange whereby the king is misinformed of the true nature of his offspring and led to believe in a monstrous birth is a feature common to many. The modus of the queen's long period of absence and torment varies from live burial up to the neck, to incarceration, to exile, often in a mutilated state – the last of these typifying the Biancabella group (for which see the commentary to III.3). At this juncture the stories diverge, the 'truth-speaking bird' group concentrating on the adventures of the second generation that lead the exposed children back to their parents.[75]

---

in Late Medieval Romance (New York: Columbia University Press, 1929). He established that the version closest to the folk tale source was the Middle Low German *Von Nameloss unde Valentyn* based on a now-lost, fourteenth-century French original. A new dimension is added to the basic tale when the two 'lost' sons of the exiled queen are abducted shortly after their births, the one raised at the court of Pipin, the other by a bear in the Forest of Orleans. This replaces the sojourn of Ancilotto's children with the miller and his wife, where they remain together. The boys must first rediscover one another and bring back Orson from his wild-man state before they can undertake the many quests that lead to the snake (in later versions a brazen head) which tells the boys their history and relationship (in the manner of the truth bird) and sets them on the course for rediscovering their parents.

75 Among the literary recensions, the closest to Straparola's is perhaps the story of Dionigia (X.1) in the *Pecorone* of Ser Giovanni, written in the last quarter of the fourteenth century. The heroine, royal by birth, arrives incognito in England, yet through her beauty and innate graces she wins a royal spouse. She is destined to bear multiple children, twin sons. The queen mother refuses to attend the marriage and later claims that Dionigia bore apes and arranges to have her slain through the false-letter-exchange device. The Viceroy (now in the place of the good vizier or the compassionate servant in charge of the execution) allows her to escape with her

There is yet another from the late medieval period confirming the antiquity of this material. The *Histoire du Chevalier du Cygne* was first printed in 1499 and tells of a queen who gives birth to six sons and a daughter, each one with a golden chain.[76] This midwife reports that she has given birth to seven dogs. A squire to the queen mother is told to kill the children, but he leaves them at a hermitage instead where they are raised in stark fashion. When they are seven years old, a hunter sees them and describes them to the old queen, who once again sends out a murderer. The weight of the swan children tale from *Dolopathos* is evoked when the hunter steals six of their seven gold necklaces in a story that is otherwise directly in the folk tradition that furnished Straparola with his materials.

That Straparola acquired his story from an oral tradition is strengthened by the many folk versions of the story, collected largely in the nineteenth century, in which all three motifs are present. That heritage, to have achieved its nineteenth-century diversification, would need to reach back over several generations of storytellers, up to 800 years back when the story received literary amplification in such works as the Ur-text of *Valentin et Orson*. A source for Straparola may be hypothesized as a folk creation midway between the medieval tales and those collected in the nineteenth century in which a bride-selection opening is combined with the motif of the abused queen leading to the quest for the dancing water, the singing tree, and the speaking bird. Among the many collected in Italy are those by Imbriani, Comparetti, Pitrè, de Gubernatis, Nerucci, Visentini, and finally Calvino, whose retelling is based in the story collected by Imbriani which includes the wicked stepmother and the three now-familiar magic objects, the most prominent of which is the truth-

children, hence avoiding the separation and foundling segment of the present story. This tale concludes with the king's Psyche-like search for the missing spouse, as in the Belle-Hélène group. In this story, the psychological climax pertains to forgiving a husband (the king) believed responsible for ordering the heroine's execution. Trans. W.G. Waters, 3 vols. (London: Society of Bibliophiles, 1898), vol, II, pp. 73–90.

76 *La naissance du Chevalier au Cygne* (twelfth century), ed. Henry Todd (New York: Kraus Reprints [1889], 1960); *Le Chevalier au Cygne* (fourteenth-century revision), in *The Old French Crusade Cycle*, ed. Jan A. Nelson, 2 vols. (Tuscaloosa: University of Alabama Press, 1985). A closely affiliated work was current in Italy by 1500, bearing the title *Istoria della Regina Stella e Mattabruna*; see the following note.

speaking bird.[77] This story appears among Italo Calvino's *favole* as 'L'ucell bel-verde' (The beautiful green bird). The story is so close to Straparola's that it need not be retold. Monkeys are substituted in the place of the children. The sisters write the maligning letter to the king who replies, nevertheless, to have the queen cared for until he gets back. After three monster births, however, the queen is walled up in a cellar and fed on bread, water, and slop. The children have a palace built for them opposite

77 'L'uccellino che parla,' in Vittorio Imbriani, *La novellaja fiorentina* (Livorno: F. Vigo, 1877); new ed. (Milan: Rizzoli, 1976), no. 6, pp. 81–93. Imbriani includes in his notes (pp. 93–7) a verse version of the *Istoria della Regina Stella e Mattabruna* (the Italian equivalent of 'The Knight of the Swan') in print as early as the outset of the sixteenth century (Pesaro: Stamperia Gavelli, 1500). The first part of this story is nearly identical to the story of 'The Truth-Speaking Bird.' For the 'L'uccellino che parla,' collected by Domenico Comparetti, see his *Novelline popolari italiane* (Bologna: Forni editore, 1875), no. 30, pp. 117–24. This story is very similar to Straparola's, replicating every part from the opening conversations overheard by the king to the jealous sisters and the animal substitutes down to the quest for the three precious objects and the truth-speaking bird. The maligned young mother is immured in a narrow space while the children grow up in the household of a shepherd. They have golden hair and stars on their brows. They are lured into making the quest by a fairy disguised as an old woman. When the walls are removed the queen is found dead, but she is resuscitated by the water of life. The children wear hats to hide their hair and brows, allowing the bird to stage a dramatic discovery scene at the end. The bird then instructs the king to make three shirts of pitch for the two wicked sisters and his own mother. The story ends as the three villainesses illuminate the plaza. See also Gherardo Nerucci, *Sessanta novelle popolari montalesi*, ed. Roberto Fedi (Milan: Biblioteca universali Rizzoli, 1977), nos. 20 and 27, pp. 195–204, 238–48; and 'La fanciulla coraggiosa' (The courageous girl), in Isaia Visentini, *Fiabe mantovane* (Turin: E. Loescher, 1879), no. 46, pp. 205–8. One night three brothers are sitting around the fire when an elderly beggar woman comes asking for shelter. Upon seeing their garden the next day, she tells them of essential ornaments they must have: the water of youth, the speaking bird, and the singing branch. She gives instructions and the eldest makes the quest but fails, as do the second and third. Their sister, telling her rosary, knows of their fate, goes in quest, fetches the three wonders, rescues her brothers, and creates the most beautiful garden ever seen. The third portion of the full generic tale is here abandoned, enabling the present story to conclude as a horticultural wonder tale. The modern edition is *Le 50 fiabe mantovane* (Parma: Astrea, 1993). James Bruyn Andrews also found a version along the Ligurian coast, 'L'oiseau qui parle,' in which a prince marries a shepherdess who is hated by her mother-in-law. The childbed replacement is a pig, while a sorceress joins forces with the wicked old woman in tormenting the children, and in the end shares her fate in the fire. *Contes ligures, traditions de la rivière recueillis entre Menton et Gênes* (Paris: Ernest Leroux, 1892), no. 42.

the king's palace, perhaps inspired by the story of Aladdin in the *Arabian Nights*. The king sees the children and invites them to supper, but they are detained by quests suggested by the emissary from the old queen mother. The wonders they find, however, help to placate the spurned king. Some of the most noticeable touches of narrative tightening come at the end when the boys are turned to stone in breaking a silence taboo over concern for their mother, while the dancing water is used to heal the imprisoned queen. A final touch is the old queen's last-ditch attempt to destroy the incriminating survivors by poisoning the food at the banquet.[78] Such stories as this must have been widely current in Straparola's day, for his contemporary, Andrea Calmo, talks about them in his letters, the story of the green bird, the 'Usel bel verde,' figuring among those he was pleased to treat as 'le pi stupende panzane, stampie, e imaginative del mondo' (the most wonderful and imaginative fabrications and twaddle in the whole world). Moreover, he reveals that the several he mentions were told as part of the evening recreations of the Venetians.[79] That has to be a smoking gun. His letter invites us to think that the folk tale to which he makes allusion must have been a part of Straparola's purview as well, and very possibly a source. Yet another, published in 1575 in *Contos e histórias do proveito e exemplo* (Stories for profit and example),

78 One of the most complete retellings of this story is 'Le tre sorelle,' in Domenico Comparetti's *Novelline popolari italiane* (Bologna: Forni [1875], 1968), no. 6, pp. 23–31. The preamble of the bride selection by overhearing the fanciful chatter of the three young ladies is included. Two of them become the jealous sisters who betray the third, the birthing queen. The queen's children are exposed as the result and are raised by the rich merchant who finds them. The venture for the extraordinary objects follows, the boys are turned to stone, and their younger sister completes the exploit, returning with a fairy who speaks the truth in the place of the bird (which is now merely a singing bird). The fairy arranges the final banquet and *anagnorisis*, and the story closes with a motif from 'Pietro the Fool' in which stolen objects are placed in the pocket of the king to illustrate how the banished queen was also innocent. The two jealous sisters are tied and burned and the royal family is reunited.

79 Letter to Signora Frondosa, in Andrea Calmo (1510–71), *Lettere*, ed. Vittorio Rossi (Torino: E. Loescher, 1888), bk. IV, no. 42, pp. 346–7. The earliest letters date to 1552. Lettorio di Francia, in *Storia dei generi letterari italiani novellistica* (Milan: Francesco Vallardi, 1924), p. 713, claims that this letter was published in 1552 and hence just at the time Straparola's stories were making their appearance. Calmo does not appear to be making reference to the final sections of the Arabian story presented by Galland, but to an independent tradition of stories about dancing waters and speaking green birds, less the Oriental element of the pearls and precious stones falling from the children's hair.

merely confirms the story's Renaissance currency in forms less like the tale in the *Arabian Nights*. It too begins with the three daydreaming seamstresses who are married to members of the court circle, followed by the replacing of the newborns with serpents and the queen's banishment to a convent. The king finds his own children near the fisherman's house.[80] Only the quest for the marvellous objects is missing, reflecting an early Portuguese tradition to which the third part had not yet been added.

Giuseppe Pitrè collected a charming tale entitled 'Li figghi di lu cavuliciddaru' (The herb-gatherer's daughters) that contains all the parts of the Straparola story. The evil older sisters are placed in charge of the birth and exchange the newborns for puppies. But now the infants are rescued by a fairy and nursed by a deer (a motif seen earlier). A self-replenishing purse replaces the golden hair, and a ring that changes colours in the event of misadventure for one of the brothers is an added feature from the Galland tale (there it was the bloodied knife blade). The royal children rent a house opposite the palace and are spied by their wicked aunts who then incite the hopefully fatal desires for the water, tree, and bird. The quest, once again directed by a hermit, leads to a mountain top, as in the oriental prototype, with guardian giants and rituals for entry, as in Calvino and Imbriani. But again redolent of Galland, the water leaps in a grand basin. This story has been carefully rationalized and prepared by a pattern-conscious storyteller. Also, as in the prototype, the sister disguises herself as a page before going in search of her two brothers. It is now the bird that tells gossipy news, and responding to it leads to petrifaction, another tightening feature. The quest once completed, the king recognizes his children and is entertained by their new acquisitions, but fails to hear the bird until it arranges the final banquet at which the truth will be revealed. The young queen, on the verge of death, is restored in the nick of time. The story is from Palermo and is a version of 'The Three Golden Children,' or 'The Jealous Sisters,' or 'The Talking Bird.'[81]

80 Gonçalo Fernandes Trancoso, *Contos* (Lisbon: A. Gonçaluez, 1575–6); see Cosquin, vol. I, pp. 194–5.

81 *The Collected Sicilian Folk and Fairy Tales of Giuseppe Pitrè*, ed. and trans. Jack Zipes and Joseph Russo, 2 vols. (New York: Routledge, 2009), no. 36, vol. I, and vol. II, pp. 838–40. In the annotations, Zipes and Russo offer further examples collected in Montevago, Capaci, Casteltermini, and Noto. The story is also in *Italian Popular Tales*, ed. Thomas Frederick Crane, rev. Jack Zipes (Santa Barbara, CA: ABC Clio, 2001), pp. 16–22, abridged. Comparetti includes 'L'uccellino che parla' in *Novelline*

To illustrate the fanciful variations permitted to this story type, mention may be made of the Albanian tale of 'Les soeurs jalouses' (The jealous sisters). The king who overhears the three girls marries all three. One promises a rug; the second, a tent; and the third promises two children, a boy and a girl, with stars on their foreheads and moons on their shoulders. At the time of their births, their treacherous aunts arrange to have them replaced by a cat and a mouse, while the disgraced mother is sent where she may be spat upon. The miller who finds the children has a grotto with a magic bridle that provides them with two horses. They ride back to their hometown and open a café. There they are discovered by their father, the king, who reports this to his two remaining wives (the rug and tent makers). They, in turn, send out an old crone to lure their niece into desiring the flower possessed by 'La Belle de la Terre' (Beauty-

---

popolari italiane (Rome: E. Loescher, 1875), pp. 117–23; Laura Gonzenbach, 'Die verstossene Königin und ihre beiden ausgesetzten Kinder' (The banished queen and her two abandoned children), in *Sicilianische Märchen* (Leipzig: W. Engelmann, 1870), no. 5, pp. 19–27; and Angelo de Gubernatis, 'I cagnolini' and 'Il re di Napoli,' in *Le novelline di Santo Stefano* (Turin: A.F. Negro, 1869), nos. 15 and 16, pp. 37–40. The 'King of Naples' is very close to the present story, with the third of the daughters, Teresina, marrying the king with promises of the birth of wonder children bearing the distinguishing marks. The children are substituted by three dogs with star markings. They are found and raised humbly, but in time take their leave. They find a wonderful palace in a forest owned by a Fata or the Madonna (possibly a vestige from another version insofar as this person has no further role), and are there discovered by their father who had been inspired in a dream to go out hunting and to follow the game that leads him to the palace. He identifies them as the children promised by Teresina, yet returns home to tell his mother, leading to the quest for the dancing water, for which 100 cavaliers had already lost their lives. Adventures ensue leading to their mother's recovery and the death of the wicked old woman. Still others are mentioned in the notes to Pitrè's 'The Herb-Gatherer's Daughter,' vol. II, p. 841. A related tale is also to be found in Stanislao Prato, *Quattro novelline popolari livornesi* (Spoleto: Bassoni, 1880), pp. 92–136. See also 'La fola del trèi surèl' and 'La fola dla malediziôn di sèt fiû,' in Carolina Coronedi-Berti, *Novelle popolari bolognesi* (Bologna: A. Forni [1874], 1983), nos. 5 and 19, pp. 29–36, 121–5. (In the A. Forni reprint of her *Favole bolognesi* [1883], 1981, the page numbers are 14–18 and 19–21.) The first tells of a poor widow with three beautiful girls. The oldest would marry the king's secretary, the second the king's cook, and the third the king himself to whom she would bear children with golden markings. The king hears them at their window and brings all to pass, then leaves for the wars, placing the household in his mother's care. The traduced young queen is locked away in a tower far from the palace on a diet of bread and water, and so the familiar story flows along in the rich and challenging dialect of regional Emilia.

of-the-earth). A lamia met along the way gives instructions to the young adventurer in quest of the flower for his sister. Once there, he must feed a lion and a lamb before plucking it. His second quest is for La Belle's handkerchief and then for La Belle herself, whom he must disempower by removing a ring from her finger as she sleeps. The *contaminatio* from other popular fairy tales is evident. The princess then accompanies him home and marries him, too. She will play her part, like the truth-speaking bird, in rescuing the children from the dishes poisoned by their invidious aunts which were to have been served up at the king's banquet in their honour. To be sure, their mother is rescued from the vale of sputum and the wicked sisters (wives and aunts) are foiled again, in fact torn to pieces.[82] Clearly it is the same tale, confirmed in its signature parts, but widely departing from an imaginable medieval oikotype.

In Italy in the seventeenth century the story was given representation by Pompeo Sarnelli in his *Posilecheata*, in a tale entitled 'L'ingannatrice ingannata' (The trickster tricked). His telling includes the dancing water, the speaking bird, and the petrification of a brother, together with his rescue by a sister who brings statues back to life. Moreover, grateful animals, liberated from various distresses, come to the aid of the second-generation protagonists. A magic palace is also brought into existence where the father unexpectedly discovers his abandoned son through means of a birthmark. This section of the story is fully anticipated by intrigues surrounding the first generation and the exposure of the royal offspring through the connivances of cruel sisters who accuse their younger sibling, the queen, of giving birth to animals. The king is subsequently misinformed through a series of falsified letters and the queen's life is spared only through the compassion of her intended executioners. This compound plot is brought to a full *peripeteia* whereby the wicked sisters are brought low and the two generations of the royal family are reunited. The author of this story brings it to print some twelve decades after the publication of the *Nights*, allowing that Straparola's 'Truth-speaking Bird' provided his narrative source. That hypothesis is complicated largely by the fact that Reppone was a close student of Basile, writing likewise in Neapolitan dialect, having edited the *Lo cunto de li cunti* for reprinting in 1674. He may have had the materials for this story from a closely parallel folk source and thus, presumably like Basile, may never have known *Le piacevoli notti*. But chances are equal that he worked

82 Louis Auguste Henri Dozon, *Contes albanais* (Paris: Ernest Laroux, 1881), pp. 7–15.

with Straparola open before him, thereby extending the now-familiar tale to his Neapolitan readership as though it were a local creation. There is work here for a curious comparatist.[83]

In France, the story was taken up directly from Straparola by Eustache Le Noble and the Comtesse d'Aulnoy towards the end of the seventeenth century. No doubt their immediate source was the celebrated Louveau translation of the *Piacevoli notti*, completed only a few years after the Italian original and passing through edition after edition thereafter. In Le Noble's fanciful elaboration upon the tale, the tastes of the French salons combined with a consciousness of the language of the literary fairy tale are in clear evidence. The three sisters are now, *de rigueur*, the children of a nobleman, and the eavesdropping royal is the king of Tartelettes (little pies). The girls, in keeping, speak of turning everything to sugar or rivers of cream, while the third speaks of giving birth to children with stars on their foreheads. Offers of sugar and cream the king finds ridiculous, but the third proposal he fancies and chooses the girl on the spot. Despite mama's objections, the ceremonies are carried out with the pomp befitting the Ancien Régime. Good fairies arrive to offer aid while the king is away driving the king of l'Eau Rose (rose water) from his pie land. The newborns are reported to be cats, which are drowned, even as the children are set adrift. A miller comes to their rescue and names the girl Belle-Étoile. The Lilliput war involving King Pie and King Rose Water continues for eight years as the kids grow up. The lads get to know their dad when they are arrested as poachers; when he sees the gold stars he pardons them and they show their obeisance in return. In all this, there is no substantial deviation from Straparola's plot, yet somehow everything is changed. The three sisters are nobly born, eliminating the poverty-to-prosperity profile so objectionable to the elite set. The king himself provokes the hostility to his new queen by dismissing the elder sisters as trivial and inconsequential. The three talismanic objects are all evoked, but the quest is downscaled to a simple request to

83 Tommasino (Masillo) Reppone di Gnanopoli (Pompeo Sarnelli of Polignano, bishop of Bisceglie), *Posilecheata*, ed. Enrico Malato (Florence: Sansoni, 1962), no. 3, pp. 109–49. The work was first published in Naples by Giuseppe Roselli in 1684. See also 'La 'ngannatrice 'ngannata,' in *Posilecheata* (Naples: D. Morano, 1885), no. 3. (Carolina Coronedi-Berti calls the author Masillo Reppone and Tommaso Perrone di Polignano.) This writer, living a century after Straparola and much influenced by Basile, may nevertheless have known and been influenced by some features he found in Straparola.

their tutelary fairy, who brings these objects one by one. The king on his own figures out just who the children are and how his queen has been abused by foul play. Merely the look on the queen mum's face when seeing them all enter the palace is grounds for her conviction. The sacred objects are now delivered over to the king for his *cabinet de curiosité*, except for the liberation-seeking bird, which tells its story and then flies away. The old queen poisons herself and the young queen makes her return, having been sustained by the fairy Landirette with quails, partridges, steaks, sugar almonds, and bread. Then the king makes amends by having new garments made for her from gold. The transformation of ambience, the ethos of *préciosité*, and the pervasive role of the fairies is sufficient to justify the new category of fairy tale, while the more random and less organized appearance of the helpers in Straparola's tale merits for it the mere designation of wonder tale.[84] These are matters for discussion. Nevertheless, this tale and the following are among the most important of Straparola's direct literary legacies.

Catherine d'Aulnoy's 'Princesse Belle-Étoile et le Prince Chéri' is a more ambitious creation of many pages in which the three daughters are now the offspring of a destitute queen reduced to cooking stews and selling gold and diamonds extracted from her old throne. In this way, she too ennobles the three sisters, turning a rising tale into a restoration tale to suit the tastes of her milieu. The girls are named for their three contrasting hair colours; the youngest, to be sure, is called Blondine. This is a tale of the recovery of lost entitlements on behalf of the fallen mother through the exploits of the second and third generations. An old woman dining on the good stew pays for her fare through future protection of the children, and so with many new details, interruptions, added dialogue, and adjusted circumstances, the well-known story is recreated. Sisterly envy flares, bringing them into league with the insulted queen mother. Puppies with stars provide the scandalous monsters and Rousette, the hypocrite red-head sister, actually calls for Blondine's death upon the king's return. Meanwhile, her ally, the old queen mother, sends the three babes out to be strangled, but their intended murderess takes pity on them and bundles them into a boat, along with the equally hated Prince Chéri, son of the second sister, to meet their destiny. D'Aulnoy keeps the feature of the jewel-shedding chevelure, which enriches the

84 Raymonde Robert, *Le conte de fées littéraire en France* (Nancy: Presses universitaires, 1982), p. 39.

family of the corsair who adopts the foundling infants, and she pays particular attention to their rich and complete education. This too is new, for the corsair is in fact a gentleman of culture and a fit father for the high-born. A new story now emerges around the fourth child, Chéri, who lacks a star and chain, but who takes up with his cousin Belle-Étoile, both now adolescents, in a Daphnis and Chloe interlude. In this way a romance element saturated with sentiment imposes itself on the folk tale design. Ultimately, however, the quest for origins takes precedence over the life of innocent retreat. Many adventures follow in loose resemblance to Straparola's tale. Belle is nearly frozen and must be revived by her protective dove who instructs her in trapping the green bird through the use of a decoy. The four children must get themselves back to court not only to liberate their mother, but to block an illegitimate marriage. This is our present story expanded by a combined aesthetic of social criticism and the emerging conventions of the fairy tale insofar as Mme. d'Aulnoy advances a parallel fairy world from which creatures emerge to take charge of the critical moments of all the characters in the tale.[85]

Distinct vestiges of the story survive in a folk tale included in *Les contes populaires de la Basse-Bretagne* entitled 'Les trois filles du boulanger, ou l'eau qui danse, la pomme qui chante, et l'oiseau de vérité' (The three daughters of the baker, or the dancing water, the singing apple, and the bird of truth). When the three girls are overheard, the king grants their fantasies by marrying the two older sisters to the valet and gardener respectively, while the one promising extraordinary children he takes for himself. Jealousy, in little time, drives the senior sisters to an old fairy to find ways to get even. The midwife helps by exchanging the queen's babies with animals and sending the children down the Seine. The king's gardener rescues the infants one by one, apparently to be raised incognito by the very aunt who sought their destruction. Meanwhile, the traduced queen is enclosed in a tower, there to subsist on bread and water. When the gardener and his wife die, the king brings the children into the palace to raise them, the stars on their brows still covered with bands.

85 Eustache le Noble, 'L'oiseau de vérité,' *Le gage touché, histoires galantes* (Amsterdam, 1700), in *The Great Fairy Tale Tradition*, trans. Jack Zipes (New York: W.W. Norton, 2001), pp. 264–70; La Comtesse d'Aulnoy, 'Princesse Belle-Étoile et le Prince Chéri,' *Suite des contes nouveaux ou les fées à la mode* (Paris: Théodore Girard, 1698), in *The Great Fairy Tale Tradition*, trans. Zipes, pp. 229–63. Also, *Contes II, Contes nouveaux ou les fées à la mode*, ed. Philippe Hourcade and Jacques Barchilon (Paris: Société des Textes Français Modernes, 1998), pp. 343–406.

An itinerant witch arrives in due course to send the children in quest of the three enchanted objects. When the two brothers fail and the sister alone remains, she equips herself as a cavalier to find an old man, her future guide, whom she frees from 500 years of captivity by cutting his beard. By following his instructions to the letter, she is able to capture the bird and restore her brothers, although they do not recognize her and fret about returning home empty-handed. The king becomes so enamoured of the princess that he now wants her for his queen. Only then does the bird of truth speak up to prevent the unwitting crime. At last, the bands concealing their foreheads are removed, the rightful queen returns, not having aged at all during twenty years, while the midwife and the remaining sisters are burned.[86] 'Les deux frères et la soeur' (Two brothers and their sister) is the thirteenth tale in Luzel's *Légendes chrétiennes* wherein a scheming queen mother and a midwife exercise their destructive powers against the three children. The mother of the children, Marie, is maligned by her sisters, and after three tries is confined to a pit or ditch. The story maintains all of the subsequent episodes now familiar from Straparola's tale except that, once again, the king falls in love with his daughter and must be dissuaded by the bird, which at last tells the story of the children's birth and betrayal.[87]

This story was particularly popular in Gascony where several versions were collected in the last third of the nineteenth century by Jean-François Bladé. In 'La mer qui chante, la pomme qui danse, et l'oisillon qui dit tout' (The singing sea, the dancing apple, and the little bird that tells all), a story very similar to Straparola's unfolds in brief but complete fashion. It begins with the three sisters overheard, the third promising to give birth to twins with golden chains between the skin and muscle of their arms, down to the reunion of the family through the truth-speaking bird. The king leaves a month before the birth of the twins, a boy and a girl, and returns only a week after. But through a pair of false letters, the young queen is led to expose the royal children on the high seas in answer to the king's alleged command. Tenderly she dresses them, gives them suck for the last time, and sets them forth in a cradle. But

86 François-Marie Luzel, *Contes populaires de la Basse-Bretagne*, ed. Françoise Morvan, 3 vols. (Rennes: Presses universitaires de Rennes, 1996), vol. III, pp. 195–206.

87 F.-M. Luzel, *Légendes chrétiennes de la Basse-Bretagne*, 2 vols. (Paris: G.-P. Maisonneuve & Larose [1887], 1967), vol. II, pp. 274–92. See also 'L'arbre qui chant, l'oiseau qui parle, et l'eau d'or' (Singing tree, speaking bird, and golden water), in E. Henry Carnoy, *Contes français* (Paris: Ernest Leroux, 1885), no. 15, pp. 106–14.

upon the king's return, his mother charges her daughter-in-law with infanticide, causing the king to order her decapitation. The distraught mother, now anxious to rejoin her children in heaven, gives thanks, which provokes the angry king to commute her punishment to eating scraps under his table. The twins, for a period of seven years, are raised by a fisherman and his wife, but when they are told the truth of their status they set off at that tender age to find their parents. Their seven-day trek takes them along the seashore until they reach an apple tree with its single poppy-coloured fruit. This is picked for them by a passing man, who tells them of its unique properties; he procures for them as well the magic bird that alights in the branches and instructs them that these two will indemnify the wicked woman who had thrown them into the sea. They then march directly to the palace of their father. There they beg for food, attain an audience with the king, and explain their quest. When the king asks how they will know their parents, they describe the golden chains on their arms, and thus their father reclaims them. When the king continues to kick their mother under the table, however, the children produce the apple and the bird, the one dancing on the old queen's head, the other repeating the contents of her letters, making the entire truth known. Yet a long coda follows concerning the proper punishment for the old queen, who continually proclaims her innocence. Because no court could try a royal, and no son could condemn his own mother to death, the king sends her to a convent and then, most curiously, takes it upon himself to die in her place in an odd study of justice, jurisdiction, and obligation. Only when the executioner's blades break before a blow can be delivered does the king accept his life. The entire story of the unfortunate children, including their simple quest and the pardon of their mother, is fully represented – this group of narratives from the Gers and Agenais supporting in their way the breadth and scope of the generic tale's circulation and the certainty of its antiquity.[88]

Of interest, as well, is 'Sun, Moon, and Morning Star,' a Greek tale with charming substitutions.[89] In this rendition, the three infants are

88 Jean-François Bladé (1827–1900), *Contes populaires de la Gascogne*, ed. Michel Suffran (Bordeaux: Opales, 1996), pp. 65–79. This work was originally published in Paris by Maisonneuve, 1886.

89 'Sonne, Mond und Morgenstern' (Sun, moon and morningstar), in Johann Georg von Hahn, *Griechische und albanesische Märchen* (Leipzig: Wilhelm Engelmann, 1864), vol. II, pp. 40–8.

replaced by a puppy, a kitten, and a mouse. They are brought up by a herdsman, while the mother spends her time enclosed in a chicken coop. The stepmother sends the nurse out disguised as a beggar woman to entice the girl to initiate a search for the musical bough, the magic mirror, and the bird named Dickjeretto. The brothers fail and are turned to stone, their misfortune revealed when their shirts back home turn black. But fortunes are altered when their sister completes the quest by snagging the magic bird from behind and reviving her brothers from their petrified state with the water of life. This story contains the episode of the sausage stuffed with diamonds employed at the final banquet, redolent of the jewel-filled cucumber in Galland's analogue tale described above in *Les mille et une nuits,* neither necessitating the existence of this feature at the time of Straparola. In this scene, the bird has a dramatic role in laughing satyr-like from its perch as the hypocritical old queen whispers to the king, telling him the children are elves. The creature then mocks him, asking whether a woman can give birth to cats and dogs. And so the reversal is brought about.

In Germany, the story is most notably recorded by the Grimm Brothers as 'Die drei Vügelkens' (The three little birds), a version much reduced and damaged by the passage of time. The king meets three girls tending cows and marries the third. The two others are brought to the palace to attend the childbirth and, without provocation, they throw the newborn into the river. This motive is twice repeated, so that in sequence two boys and a girl are pulled out by a fisherman to be raised while the young queen is thrown into prison. In the quest section, the singing apple is suppressed. On the way out of the magic castle, with the bird and water in hand, the girl must strike a black dog with her wand, who is an enchanted prince now liberated from the captor animal. In rapid sequence the king meets the children during a hunting expedition, the bird provides the missing information, and all ends according to custom, except there is now a prince for the king's daughter to marry (in keeping with the new model provided by Mme. d'Aulnoy's 'Princesse Belle-Étoile'), and the wicked queen mother has disappeared altogether.[90]

---

90 *Grimm's Complete Fairy Tales* (Garden City, NY: Nelson Doubleday, n.d.), pp. 223–6; *Kinder- und Hausmärchen der Brüder Grimm* (Göttingen: Dieterich, 1856), no. 96, p. 174. The story is from Westphalia and was first published in 1819.

Heinrich Pröhle collected the story of 'Leaping Water, Speaking Bird, and Singing Tree' for his *Kinder- und Volksmärchen,* in which country sisters are overheard by the king, each one proposing to marry him, but only the third offering children marked with stars.[91] The familiar story follows. When, in later years, the king meets up with his offspring, they are more like fairy children, for they ride their horses upon the water of a moat and refuse to acknowledge his call (perhaps redolent of the swan children). Word gets back of their survival and a sorceress is sent to tempt them into questing after all three magic objects at once in order to bring their enchanted garden to perfection. Their perilous journey remains oriental in spirit with a hermit guide, a mountain, and the distracting voices that can turn intruders to stone. Despite the cotton-stuffed ears of the sirens' song tradition, however, both brothers succumb and become their own tombstones. The sister, of course, succeeds and resurrects her brothers.[92] Their garden now becomes a fantasy of music and fountains where the king finds joy until the bird begins to speak of past truths, maintaining that the false sisters should be torn apart by four horses – and so it comes to pass, together with the restoration of the queen. So faithful a rendition of the oriental tale is to be attributed either to a finer preservation of the ancient tale than Straparola knew or to the new model provided by the publication of *The Arabian Nights.*

A final few tales must complete this survey of potentially monographic magnitude. First is 'Die drei Königskinder' (The king's three children), elaborated by Johann Wilhelm Wolf in his *Deutsche Hausmärchen.* In this

---

91 'Springendes Wasser, sprechender Vogel, singender Baum' (Leaping water, speaking bird, singing tree), in Heinrich Pröhle, *Kinder- und Volksmärchen* (Hildesheim: Georg Olms, 1975), no. 3, pp. 10–16.

92 In a French tale collected by Carnoy, a queen has an incurable disease which a passing magician says will be cured only by finding the three now-familiar objects. Her two sons go on the quest and fail to fulfil the instructions, while the young princess carries through, undistracted, resurrecting many knights along with her brothers with drops of the precious water. She returns home in triumph as 'a model for good and wise little girls,' which says something about the audience to which the story was traditionally recited. 'L'arbre, que chante, l'oiseau qui parle, et l'eau d'or,' in E.H. Carnoy, *Contes françaises* (Paris: Leroux, 1885), no. 15, pp. 107–13, recorded in Provence in 1883. This story is influenced by the design and purpose of 'the three brothers' type, in which each sets out, seriatim, to find the cure for an ailing father. The third succeeds after many adventures and errors, rescuing his two brothers on the way back. See the commentary to VII.5.

version a prince goes to the country to find a simple bride.[93] There are no sisters and no promise of children with stars on their foreheads. But the mother-in-law still plays the villainess. A daughter is born, tossed into a stream, and rescued by a miller's wife. A second daughter follows, supposedly stillborn, and the royal parents are heartbroken. Fifteen years

93 (Göttingen: Dieterich'sche Buchhandlung, 1851), pp. 168–77; new ed. (Hildesheim: Georg Olms, 1972). Further examples from German-speaking regions include the story, 'Die drei Schönheiten der Welt' (The three most beautiful things in the world) in Christian Schneller's *Märchen und Sagen aus Wälschtirol* (Innsbruck: Verlag der Wagner'schen Universitäts-Buchhandlung, 1867), pp. 65–71; new ed. (Hildesheim: Olms, 1976); Ignaz Zingerle, *Sagen, Märchen und Gebräuche aus Tirol*, 2 vols. (Innsbruck: Wagner, 1859), vol. II, pp. 112*ff.*; Justus Heinrich Saal, 'Der wahrredende Vogel' (The truth-speaking bird), in *Abendstudente in lehrreichen und anmuthungen Erzählungen*, more properly *Abendzeitvertreib in verschiedenen Erzählungen* (Leipzig: Gleditsch, 1756–69). To this may be added 'The Two Sisters Jealous of the Younger' in Gustav Weil's *Tausend und eine Nacht Arabische Erzählungen*, 4 vols. (Bonn, 1897), vol. III, pp. 274–311. In this tale, the two sisters substitute for the children a dog, a cat, and a stick. The queen is imprisoned and the children are rescued by a gardener. Then an old crone tells the king he is lacking three things in his garden: a speaking bird, a singing tree, and golden water. The king's two unknown sons accept the challenge and make the quest whereupon they are turned to stone, with their sister to the rescue. The captured bird explains matters at the end in the fashion now familiar from Straparola's tale. Ignaz and Joseph Zingerle, working together, found 'Der Vogel Phönix, des Wasser des Lebens und die Wunderblume' (The phoenix, the water of life, and the magic flower), in which a knight loses his way in the forest, at nightfall finds a poor farmer's house, and there overhears the farmer's daughters, thinking him asleep, talking about what they would do if married to so handsome a man. The knight, enchanted by promises of children with golden hair, turns dreams to reality, accompanied by jealousy. The knight, absent during the parturition of his children, leaves his dear wife to her fate: the alleged birth of dogs, orders for drowning her children, their rescue by a miller, and her own death in prison. Later, the sisters lay secondary plans to have the children sent on missions that would expose them to wild animals, carrying forward the Germanic concern with endless forests and fearful imaginations. The first meets a friendly fox who becomes his guide in his search for the phoenix. The crossing of streams on the fox's back is redolent of tales in 'the grateful dead' tradition (see the commentary to XI.2). The story luxuriates in the details of fairy tale quests and evil aunts, but the entire business is conducted to happy issue by the enigmatic fox. After three rivers and many forests, the boy at last arrives with the beautiful flower – his third quest. The father in this tale is likewise attracted to his own daughter until the speaking phoenix chatters about the injustice done to his own wife. The evil sisters are now forced to confession. The tale ends with a motif from the 'puss in boots' (XI.1) and 'grateful dead' (XI.2) traditions when the boy seeks to thank the fox one last time, only to be told to strike off its head. Trapped

must pass before the mother-in-law goes to the mill, sees the children, and suspects the truth. She tells the miller outright that they are the royal children and must be slain, but he allows them to escape on a donkey. On the road they encounter a magical mist which, at their bidding, erects for them a splendid palace. Then the quests begin. The old lady makes them wish for a bough bearing golden fruit to plant in their garden. The first brother is turned to a pillar of salt for looking back, but he has the branch in his possession. His sister goes in search of the speaking bird, but after capturing the bird, finds herself rigid beside her brother. The old queen, as a beggar woman, then creates a longing in the third and last for the leaping water. It is the water of restoration which, employed, brings them all home with their booty intact. They embellish their castle until news of its wonders comes to the king. He feels the affinity of blood kinship upon his arrival and then the speaking bird tells all. There are tears of joy. The old queen, for her part, is to be boiled in oil in accordance with her own words, but the children intercede so that she might languish in a dungeon instead. What a relief! These are among the salient examples of a story type elaborated by Straparola some three centuries earlier that was itself chosen from an established storytelling tradition based on Eastern materials. Whether the three parts were assembled by folk raconteurs in the West or the Near East by the mid-sixteenth century remains a moot point – the credit could even be granted to Straparola himself. But Straparola's tale is proof that the type that found widespread diffusion throughout Europe, placing it among the most successful of all European folk tales, was known in assembled form in the Renaissance.[94]

---

all along inside the fox was a beautiful woman who suddenly appears when the beheading is done and runs to hug her liberator. It is his own mother who had silently led him through his many rites of initiation, and who now, by his efforts, is restored to her husband. It is a rich and complex tale conjoining several story types; it was collected in Obermiemingen before 1854. *Kinder- und Hausmärchen aus Süddeutschland,* intro. J.W. Wolf (Hildesheim: Georg Olms, 1975), pp. 157–73; originally published in Regensburg in 1854.

94 Further versions of this story are to be found in Mary Frere, *Old Deccan Days or Hindoo Fairy Legends Current in Southern India* (London: Murray, 1868), no. 4, pp. 55*ff*, in which 100 boys and one girl are born to the Radjah by his favourite wife. The dozen infertile wives looking on collude in their jeaolusy, accusing the innocent Guzra-Bai of being a sorceress who has converted her children into the stones which have been duly placed in all 101 cradles. The children are rescued from a garbage heap and at one point in their adventures become birds. Patrick Kennedy tells

Another version originates in Spain – one among many – entitled 'Los siete infantes' (The seven children), in which the three daughters tell the king their fantasies, the third one dreaming of children with stars on their foreheads. It is the devil himself who sends the letter to the king saying the young queen has given birth to seven dogs, at which point she is confined to a tower. The long questing story for the magic elements is not a part of this tale.[95] Another tale, closely related, derives from

---

another in *The Fireside Stories of Ireland* (Dublin: McGlashan & Gill, 1870; Norwood, PA: Norwood Editions, 1975), pp. 14–19, in which a young girl whose twelve brothers have been turned to birds by a spell is compelled to sew shirts for them all to recover them. Meanwhile, she is married to a prince and bears him two children which the wicked old queen tosses to a wolf, thereafter smearing the mother's lips with blood. After the second séance of cannibalism, she is condemned to the pyre, but as she is tied to the stake she completes the last shirt, her brothers rescue her, the babes are brought back by the good-fairy wolf, and the double plot around the abused and maligned queen and the recovered infants is brought to happy issue. See also 'The Boy who had a Moon on his Forehead and a Star on his Chin,' in Maive Stokes, *Indian Fairy Tales* (London: Ellis & White, 1880), no. 20, pp. 119–37. This is the present story in a version from India which includes even the opening chatter of the gardener's daughter about having a child with a moon and star, which is overheard by the passing king. He marries her, given that his four other wives are childless. It is these four wives, however, who become pests and temptresses, inciting the innocent new bride to make mistakes that aggravate her lord who then makes her a palace servant. The king's dog saves the child by swallowing it whole. The wives report the dog, so the child is passed to a cow, then to a horse, and each time the report is carried back. But Ketar is a magic horse and leads the boy into the adventures of Livoretto, urging him to take service at another court while it remains in the vicinity to provide gear and advice. The pattern is familiar from the 'Guerrino and the wild man' model, as well as from stories of 'the grateful dead' group in which the revenant supplies the equipment for his ward to win a princess (see the commentary to XI.2). After marrying the seventh princess and dealing with his arrogant brothers-in-law, he returns home. Then 'the truth bird' story resumes with a grand feast, followed by confessions, the quest for his mother, and an agreement to stay only if the four wicked wives are slain. This amalgam is worth the profiling to show how such elements were conjoined by imaginative folklorists. This is presumably a late tale formed under Western influence.

95 Aurelio Espinosa, *Cuentos populares españoles*, 3 vols. (Madrid: S. Aguirre, 1947), no. 119, vol. I, pp. 250–2. Wentworth Webster collected a related version in the Basque country which contains the eavesdropping king, the marriages of the three sisters, the jealousy of the elder two, the birth scandal, and the exposure of the infants. This queen spends twenty years underground before her children come of age and complete the quest for the truth-speaking bird, leading to their reunion. This seems to be an imperfect telling of a French version in which the sister cross-dresses to carry out the quest leading to the final discovery banquet. *Légendes*

Portugal and is called 'As cunhadas do rei.' This king, too, listens at doors and hears the three girls, the third promising children to the king with 'estrela de ouro na testa' (golden stars on their heads), and the Virgin later puts in an appearance to relieve the heroine in distress.[96] The role of the fairies becomes a Christian miracle.

Guillaume Spitta-Bey confirmed the modern currency of the story type in Arabic-speaking nations in the 'Histoire d'Arab-Zandyq.' It preserves the three parts, with all the 'oriental' trappings. The king goes walking with his vizier and overhears the merchant's three daughters imagining themselves as the queen. The king spends the night with each, asking them about their dreams. When the first two report that it was a harmless fantasy, he puts them to work in the royal kitchens as slaves. The third plays her part more wisely, but falls prey to the king's other wife who is successful in her treachery. A fisherman recovers the two children, but their mother is chained to a balustrade for all to spit upon in passing (echoes of Galland's tale in *Les mille et une nuits*). Years pass until the boy one day sells fish directly to the king. Connections are made that alarm the wicked other wife and her midwife accomplice. The boy is sent for the rose of Arab-Zandyq: a flower which sings and amuses, but is kept by a mistress who turns seekers to stone. Success only leads to a second mission, but in the end the boy negotiates with the dangerous girl and she not only takes him in marriage but sets the two of them up in a magic palace on the fisherman's isle. Here are new circumstances for the denouement, for the king is invited with his entire army to a

---

basques, trans. Nicolas Burguete ([Anglet]: Aubéron, 2005), pp. 240*ff*, published originally in English (London: Griffith & Farran, 1877), pp. 176*ff*. Another version was collected in Andalusia by the Spanish novelist and folklorist Cecilia Bohl de Faber (1819–89) and published in her *Cuentos de encantamiento* (1877) (Stories of enchantment) as 'El pajaro de la Verdad' (The bird of truth). In this tale it is ministers and courtiers who oppose the marriage; the replacement animals are a cat and a snake; the queen is walled up; and the children are raised by a fisherman. It is a witch who ultimately attempts and fails to thwart the children by sending them on quests. This tale also introduces some seventeen additional birds, serving as narrators and as protective fairy-like guides. The moral was that the bird of truth could never be slain because Truth itself is eternal. The story may be found in her *Obras completas* (Madrid: Ediciones Atlas, 1961), vol. V, pp. 206–11.

96 Téofilo Braga, *Contos tradicionais do povo Portugues*, 2 vols. (Lisbon: Dom Quixote, 1987), vol. I, pp. 147–50. Braga's compact bibliographical 'Nota' supplies additional references to this story type from Brazil, Poland, Hungary, Prussia, Croatia, the Basque country, Bohemia, Norway, and other regions, revealing the scope, popularity, and resilience of this story type.

forty-day bash. When the king reciprocates, Arab-Zandyq liberates the innocent mother, dresses her royally, and leads her before the king, herself serving as the 'bird' of truth.[97] A similar tale was reported by Emmanuel Cosquin. Black dogs replace the children, the queen is attached to a stairway for abuse, and the two jealous sisters throw the children into the sea in boxes. The adoptive parents are rewarded not by gems falling from the children's hair, but by bathwater that turns to gold. This tale is resolved by an encounter with their father that does not necessitate the quest, a final reminder of the distinct parts of the story and their abilities to function as autonomous units.[98]

As a final note, the story also found favour with two important playwrights, the first of whom developed the plot into a critique of Enlightenment philosophy. Carlo Gozzi found his inspiration in Pompeo Sarnelli's *Posilecheata* for his *L'augellina belverde.*[99] Raymond Roussel, by contrast, turned the story into a study of creative genius in *L'Étoile au front.*[100] With these two notices, the overview history of 'the truth-speaking bird' story type concludes – Straparola's version having played a vital part in the story tradition as the first in the European record in which the three traditional parts are combined and fully represented. Moreover, the story of the accused queen and the abandoned children in which close kin betray the fertile mother and seek to destroy dynastic continuity is a plot with Dawkinsian overtones, for it is a tale of genes, survival, and the conflicting interests which threaten their future. There was something about the tale, despite its shadowy early record, that made it one of the most successful of all the Eurasian folk tales.

The coda to follow is concerned with matters of style and one aspect of Straparola's working habits. The present story contains a minimally modified sequence of words from Boccaccio's *Corbaccio* which Straparola combines with a passage from the *Decameron* (II.9). It is the speech on the excellence of man, representing a literary interpolation into a work

97 *Contes arabes modernes* (Leiden: E.J. Brill, 1883), pp. 137–51.

98 *Contes populaires de Lorraine* (Paris: F. Vieweg, 1886), vol. I, pp. 196–7. The story is from Mardin in Mesopotamia and was first reported in the *Zeitschrift der Deutschen Morgenländischen Gesellschaft* (Leipzig: F.A. Brockhaus, 1882), p. 259. Angelo de Gubernatis in *Zoological Mythology or the Legends of Animals* (London: Trübner, 1872), vol. II, p. 174, describes a Russian story in which all three magic elements appear: the speaking bird, the singing tree, and the water of life.

99 *Five Tales for the Theatre*, ed. Albert Bermel and Ted Emery (Chicago: University of Chicago Press, 1989), pp. 239–305.

100 (Paris: J.-J. Pauvert, 1963).

undoubtedly derived from an oral source. That he might easily have paraphrased the passage makes the close wording an altogether more intriguing event. What was he doing: cutting corners, paying homage, exposing his own lack of inspiration, or simply working in the scissors-and-paste manner that was second nature to the well-garnished humanist mind brought up on gleanings and memorization from the classics? It is a substantial passage. For a sampling, Straparola writes, 'e volse che egli signoreggiasse e non fosse signoreggiato,' while in the *Corbaccio,* it is 'animale perfetto nato a signoreggiare e non ad essere signoreggiato.' Straparola picks up the 'animale perfetto' in his next sentence.[101] On the whole, Straparola remains faithful to the simpler procedures of his oral sources, yet by exceptions such as these he proves himself well read in the literature which, for the most part, he refrains from imitating.

101 From Giuseppe Rua, *Tra antiche fiabe e novelle: Le 'Piacevoli notti' di Messer Gian Francesco Straparola* (Rome: Ermanno Loescher, 1898), pp. 99–100. Boccaccio, 'Corbaccio,' in *Opere minori* (Milan: E. Sonzogno, 1879), p. 286.

IV. Fable 4
The Physician's Wife

ISABELLA

Nerino, the son of Gallese, king of Portugal, enamoured of Genobbia, wife of Messer Raimondo Brunello, a physician, has his way with her and carries her with him to Portugal, while Messer Raimondo dies of vexation.

I must tell you, noble ladies, that there are many men who, because they have spent long years in the study of letters, think they know everything, when in truth they know nothing, or next to nothing. And while men of this sort think they bear the badges of wisdom on their brows, in reality they're blind in both eyes. This happened to a certain physician who might have been most skilled in his trade but who was ignominiously duped just when he thought he was about to dupe someone else, and to his very great cost, as you'll find out from the fable I'm about to tell.

Gallese, king of Portugal, had a son whose name was Nerino. During his upbringing, the boy was so sheltered that by the time he was eighteen, he'd never even seen a woman except his mother and the nurse who suckled him. When he came of full age the king determined to send him to Padua to pursue his studies so that he might learn Latin letters and the language and manners of the Italians, a plan realized without further delay. When the young Nerino arrived in Padua, he became friends with many of the scholars. They came to pay their respects on a regular basis, and among them was a certain physician named Messer Raimondo Brunello. One day it happened that as Nerino and this friend were conversing about this thing and that, they launched into a discussion on the beauty of women, as young men will do. Nerino, despite the fact that his knowledge of women was limited to his mother and his nurse, was ready to affirm outright that no lady could be found in the entire world more beautiful, more graceful, and more exquisite than his own mother. When they brought various ladies to his notice by way of putting his declaration to the test, he insisted still that by comparison to his mother they were little better than carrion.

Now Messer Raimondo was married to a lady who was one of the fairest that nature had ever created, and when he heard Nerino's declaration, a foolish notion entered his mind which brought him to say, 'Signor Nerino, I know of a certain lady who is of such great beauty that when you have beheld her you will surely judge her to be just as beautiful as your mother.' To this Nerino answered that he couldn't believe there was a woman more lovely than his mother, but that it would give him great pleasure to see this lady and offer his opinion of her. Then Raimondo said, 'Well, if it will give you pleasure to see her, I'll offer you a demonstration.'

Nerino replied, 'Nothing could please me more; I'll be in your debt.'

'Fine, then, if you want to see her, come to the Duomo tomorrow morning and I promise, you won't be disappointed.'

So once back at his house Messer Raimondo said to his wife, 'Make certain that you rise early tomorrow and arrange your hair carefully and make yourself as pretty as you can, and put on the most sumptuous dress you have, for I've a mind that you go to the cathedral at the hour of high mass to hear the office.'

Genobbia – for that was her name – was not in the habit of going about here and there, but rather of spending all her time at home with her sewing and embroidery, so she was most surprised by these words. But seeing that her husband's request met with her own desires, she did all she was asked to do, preparing herself so carefully and decking herself so trimly that she looked more like a goddess than a mortal woman. Now when Genobbia had gone into the church in keeping with her husband's orders, Nerino, the son of the king, also arrived there, and when he had looked upon her he found she was indeed most fair. No sooner had the lady departed than Messer Raimondo arrived and approached the prince, saying, 'Now, Signor Nerino, what do you think of this lady who has just now gone out of the church, if you please? Have you anything to say against her? Tell me, is she not more beautiful than your mother?'

'Truthfully,' replied Nerino, 'she is beautiful; nature couldn't have made her fairer. So in the name of friendship, whose wife is she and where does she live, tell me?' But Messer Raimondo made no answer to this question, having no mind to humour Nerino's wish or give him any clues.

Then Nerino said, 'Well, my good Messer Raimondo, although you won't tell me who she is or where she lives, at least you can render me the good office of letting me see her once more.'

'That I'll do willingly,' answered Messer Raimondo. 'Come to church again tomorrow morning and I'll arrange it that you can see her again.'

When Messer Raimondo had gone back to his house he said to his wife, 'Genobbia, make certain to dress yourself early tomorrow, because I want you to attend mass. And if ever you've made yourself look beautiful and dressed yourself richly, make sure that you do the same tomorrow.'

Genobbia was amazed, as she was at first, but followed her husband's command and did all he required. When the next day came, now sumptuously arrayed and adorned more richly than she'd ever been before, Genobbia went off to church, and in a very short time Nerino was there as well. When he saw how ravishing she was, he was inflamed by love, more ardently than any man had ever burned for a woman before, and when Messer Raimondo arrived, he begged him to reveal this lady's name for in his eyes she was marvellously beautiful. But Messer Raimondo, making excuses that he was really pressed for time by his practice and not in the mood to tell him, went off in high spirits, leaving the young man champing at the bit. This ruffled Nerino's temper somewhat to be held in such mean account by Messer Raimondo, and he said to himself, 'You don't want me to know who she is and where she lives, then I'll find out what I want to know in spite of you.'

After he had left the church, Nerino waited outside until such time as the fair lady would emerge and then, giving her a modest bow and a grand smile, he went with her as far as her house. Now as soon as Nerino had gotten to know clearly the place where she dwelled, he began to cast amorous eyes upon her, letting no day go by without passing up and down ten times in front of her house. Then, desiring to talk to her, he began to think about what course he should follow in order to protect the lady's honour while at the same time achieving his ends. He pondered the matter and examined it from every side without hitting upon a solution that promised security. But after a great deal of reflection, he decided to make the acquaintance of the old woman who lived in the house next door to Genobbia. After sending her sundry gifts and arriving at a mutual agreement between them, he went in secret to the old woman's lodging, in which there was one window in particular overlooking the hall of Genobbia's house where he might stand and gaze at will at the lady as she went up and down about her business. At that time he had no desire to discover himself and thereby give her cause to hide from him. But after spending day after day in these amorous pursuits, Nerino found himself no longer able to resist the pricks of desire that continually pierced and consumed his heart. So he resolved to write a letter and toss it into her lodging at a time when he judged her husband would be absent. Several times he wrote such letters as he had planned and tossed them down to her. But Genobbia merely picked them up and, without reading them, cast them all into the fire, for in truth she thought little of the matter. After doing this again and again, however, it entered into her mind one day to cut one open and see what might be written inside. When she broke the seal and noticed that the author was none other than Nerino, the son of the king of Portugal, declaring fervent love to her, she was at first nearly confounded. But after a time, when she called to mind the drab times she enjoyed in her husband's house, she plucked up courage and began to look kindly on Nerino.

At last, having come to an agreement with him, she found a way to get him into the house, where the young man laid before her the story of his ardent love for her, the daily torments he endured on her account, and precisely how his passion for her had been kindled. This lady, who was as kind-hearted and compliant as she was lovely, was in no mood to reject his suit. So it came about that they were joined in mutual love and found themselves absorbed in amorous conversation, when lo and behold Messer Raimondo suddenly began knocking at the door. When Genobbia heard this, she urged Nerino to go in immediately and lie down on the bed, to let down the curtains, and to stay there until such time as her husband should once more go out. The husband came in and, taking various trifles which he needed, he went away again without noticing anything amiss or giving a further thought. A little later Nerino left as well, still without any inkling whatsoever that Messer Raimondo was the lady's husband.

On the following day, as Nerino was walking up and down the public square, Messer Raimondo by chance went that way. Nerino made a sign that he wanted to have a word with him, and when they had met, he said, 'Signor, I have some great news to tell you.'

'And what might that be?' replied Messer Raimondo.

'What would you say if I told you that I know the house where that beautiful lady lives and that I've had some delightful conversations with her? And that because her husband came home unexpectedly, she hid me in the bed and drew the curtains for fear that he would see me, but that he soon went out again?'

'Is it possible?' cried Messer Raimondo.

'Possible!' answered Nerino. 'It is more than possible; it's a fact. Never in all my life have I seen as delightful and as sweet a lady as she is. If by any chance, Signor, you should meet her, I beg you to put in a good word on my behalf and urge her to keep me in her good graces.'

Having promised to do what the youth asked, Messer Raimondo went on his way with ill will in his heart. But before taking his leave of Nerino, he said, 'And are you ever going back again?'

'What do you think?' Nerino replied.

Then Messer Raimondo went back to his house, careful not to mention a word of it in his wife's presence, but to wait for the time when she and Nerino would be together again.

When the next day had come, Nerino once more stole to a meeting with Genobbia, and while they were in the middle of their amorous delights and pleasant conversation, the husband arrived. But the lady quickly hid Nerino in a chest in front of which she piled up a heap of clothes which she had been shaking out for fear the moths would ruin them. Pretending to search about for various things, the husband turned the house upside down, looking even into the bed. But finding nothing at all of what he sought, he went about his business with his mind more at ease.

Soon after, Nerino also departed and later, happening to meet Messer Raimondo, he said to him, 'Signor Doctor, what would you say if you heard that I had paid another visit to my charming lady and that envious fortune broke in upon our pleasure, seeing that the husband again arrived and spoiled all our sport?'

'And what did you do then?' asked Messer Raimondo.

'Right away, she opened up a chest,' said Nerino, 'and placed me inside, and then piled up a heap of clothes in front of it which she had taken out to preserve them from moths. After he had turned the bed upside down more than once without finding anything, he went away.' The tortures Messer Raimondo must have suffered when he listened to these words I leave to the judgment of all who know about the humours of love.

Now Nerino had given to Genobbia a very fine and precious diamond within a setting in which was engraved his name and likeness. The very next day, when Messer Raimondo had gone out to attend to his duties, the lady once more let Nerino into the house, and while they were engaged in their pleasures and talking pleasantly together, as surely as could be, the husband suddenly returned to the house. But the crafty Genobbia no sooner noticed his arrival than straightway she opened a large wardrobe which stood in her bedroom and hid Nerino inside.

Almost immediately Messer Raimondo entered the bedroom, pretending as before to search for things he needed, turning the room upside down in the process. But finding nothing either in the bed or in the chest, like a man deranged and out of his wits, he took fire and strewed it about the four corners of the room, intending to burn the place and all that it contained.

The woodwork was already afire when Genobbia turned to her husband said, 'What on earth are you doing, husband? Surely you've gone mad. Still, if you want to burn the house down, go ahead, but I'm not letting you burn this wardrobe with all the papers in it pertaining to my dowry.' So having called up four strong porters, she told them to carry the wardrobe to the neighbouring house belonging to the old woman. Then she opened the wardrobe secretly, when no one was near, and hurried back to her own house. Messer Raimondo, like someone completely out of his mind, kept up his sharp watch to see whether someone would rush out of hiding, but he could see nothing except the smoke and the fierce flames that were consuming the house. By this time, all the neighbours had congregated to put out the fire, doing their work so courageously and well that in time it was extinguished.

The next day, as Nerino was walking towards Prato dalla Valle, he met Messer Raimondo and saluted him, saying, 'Ah, my dear man, have I got a piece of news to tell you that will please you greatly.'

'And what may that be?' said Messer Raimondo.

'I have just made my escape,' said Nerino, 'from the most frightening danger that any man ever came out of alive. I had gone to the house of my lovely mistress, and while I was spending the time with her in pleasant dalliance, her husband once more interrupted us, and after he had turned the house upside down, he set the four corners of the lady's bedroom ablaze and burned up all that was inside.'

'And you?' said Messer Raimondo, 'where were you all this time?'

Then Nerino answered, 'I was hidden in a wardrobe which she had carried out of the house.'

When Messer Raimondo heard this and knew that he was telling the very truth, he was ready to die of grief and passion. Still, he didn't dare let his secret be known because he was determined to catch him in the act. Wherefore he said to him, 'And are you bent on going there again, Signor Nerino?'

To which Nerino replied, 'Seeing that I have come safely out of the fire, what else is there for me to fear?' And without making any further remarks of this kind, Messer Raimondo begged Nerino the honour of his presence at dinner the very next day, a civility which the young man willingly accepted.

When the following day had come, Messer Raimondo invited all his own relatives and his wife's as well, and prepared for their entertainment a rich and magnificent repast. It was not in his own house, however, which had been half consumed by fire, but in another. He gave directions to his wife, moreover, that she should be present, not to sit at the table as one of the guests, but to keep herself out of sight and to look after all the preparations for the banquet. As soon as all the kinsfolk were assembled and the young Nerino as well, they were requested to take their places at the table. As the feast progressed, Messer Raimondo, using his charlatan science, tried his best to make Nerino drunk in order to get the best of him. Having several times handed to the young man a glass of malmsey wine, which he never failed to empty, Messer Raimondo said to him, 'Now Signor Nerino, why not tell these kinsfolk of mine some little jest to make them all laugh?' The luckless Nerino, who had no hint that Genobbia was Messer Raimondo's wife, began to tell the story of his adventures, keeping secret, however, the names of all concerned.

Meanwhile, as it happened, one of the servants went into the room where Genobbia was and said to her, 'Madonna, if only you were hidden in some corner of the dining room, you would hear the finest story you ever heard in your life. I suggest you go in quickly.' Having stolen into a corner, she knew that the voice of the storyteller was her lover Nerino's and that the tale he was relating to the company concerned herself as well as him.

With that, this clever and prudent lady took the diamond that Nerino had given her and dropped it into a cup filled with a very dainty drink and said to a servant, 'Take this cup, give it to Signor Nerino, and tell him to drink it all straight off, the better to tell his story.' The servant took the cup and carried it to the table, and wanting Nerino to drink it, said to him, 'Take this cup and drink it up, Signor, the better to tell your story.' Nerino grasped the cup and drank up all the wine. But seeing and recognizing the diamond lying at the bottom, he tilted the cup and slipped it between his lips. Then, pretending to rinse his mouth, he pulled the ring out and put it on his finger. Apprised now that the fair lady about whom he was telling his story must be the wife of Messer Raimondo, he had no mind to say more, and although the host and his kinsfolk pressed him to finish the tale he had begun, he replied, 'And then and there the cock crowed and the day broke, so I awoke from my sleep and lost the dream entirely.' Messer Raimondo's kinsmen, having listened to Nerino's story up to that point, believing that all he had said about the lady was true, now imagined that both their host and the young man were drunk.

Some few days afterward, it came about that Nerino met Messer Raimondo. Pretending not to know that he was the husband of Genobbia, he told him that in two or three days' time he was to leave, for his father had written to him urging him to return to his own country, and, as might be imagined, Messer Raimondo wished him good speed for his journey. But having come to a private understanding with Genobbia, Nerino took her away with him and they fled to Portugal where they lived a long and merry life together. Messer Raimondo, for his part, when he went back to his house and found that his wife was gone, was stricken with such despair that he died of grief. And this is how the poor doctor learned to his cost that a man is ill-advised to commend his wife to the attention of others.

Isabella's fable pleased all the ladies and some of the gentlemen, and they rejoiced especially that Messer Raimondo proved to be the cause of his own misfortune, and that the thing which he had courted had in fact redounded upon him. When the Signora remarked that this exchange had come to an end, she gave the sign to Isabella to complete her task in due order, whereupon she presented her enigma as follows:

In the middle of the night,
Rises one with beard bedight.
Though no astrologer he be,
He marks the hours which pass and flee;
He wears a crown, although no king,
No priest, yet he the hour doth sing,
Though spurred at heel, he is no knight,
No wife he calls his own by right,
Yet children many round him dwell.
Sharp wits you'll need this thing to tell.

Of all the company, none could find the true interpretation of Isabella's subtle riddle, except only that spiteful minx Lodovica, who, remembering the slight put upon her not long before, stood up and said, 'The enigma which our sister hath set us to guess signifies the cock, which is on the alert to crow while it is still night, which wears a beard and hath knowledge of the passage of time, although he is no astrologer. He bears a crest for a crown and is no king; he sings the hours yet is no priest. Beside this, he wears spurs on his heels but is no knight. He has no wife, and brings up the children of others, that is to say, the chicks.'

All the listeners found this interpretation to be good, especially Signor Capello, who said, 'Signora Isabella, Lodovica has given back to you a beating for your battering, seeing that a very short time ago you very cleverly declared the meaning of her enigma. Now she has mastered yours, but for this you shouldn't harbour malice one against the other.'

(Isabella) answered promptly, 'Signor Bernardo, never fear. When the time comes, I will give her back as good as I got.'

But in order to keep the conversation within bounds, the Signora imposed silence upon everyone, then turning towards Lionora, whose turn it was to tell the last story of the night, she asked her not to hesitate in telling her tale, which the damsel began with the finest grace in the world.

IV.4 Commentary

This perfectly turned *novella* invites many forms of critical attention. We are to imagine a royal youth so sheltered in his upbringing that he has seen but two women, his mother and his nurse, and that for lack of experience he is determined upon all future occasions to cite his own mother as uniquely the most beautiful woman in the world. At age eighteen, however, he is sent by his father from Portugal to the University of Padua to learn the ways of the world. If that moment is taken for a contemporary one, it correlates with discussions on the beauty of women which were then much in vogue. Agnolo Firenzuola had recently published his celebrated book *On the Beauty of Women* (*Della bellezze delle donne*, 1548), although the question of feminine beauty as a humanist *topos* reaches as far back as Boccaccio's *De claris mulieribus.*[102] When the subject comes up for discussion among Nerino's friends, however, it is not treatises and citations that come to Dr. Raimondi's mind, but a plan to wean the boy from his adolescent fixation by revealing to him the fairest women of the city, and most notably his own superlatively beautiful wife. Just how bad an idea that was is anticipated by the story's moralizing preamble: that in tricking others the trickster may find himself outmanoeuvred. In brazenly showcasing his wife's beauty in public, Raimondi

102 See the translation by Konrad Eisenbichler and Jacqueline Murray (Philadelphia: University of Pennsylvania Press, 1992).

provokes a double awakening – not only on the part of the young man who falls in love with her, but on the part of his young wife who, out of resentment and neglect, discovers she has repressed appetites of her own. Each character, in short, represents a psychological state: the husband takes an old man's delight in showing off a trophy wife; a young man transfers his affective orientation from his mother to a sexually eligible female; and a young beauty seizes upon an opportunity to escape a tedious marriage. This patterning of characters is of Straparola's own making, as a later glance at his source will reveal. Such alterations are significant, for in redefining the actors and their destinies he provides an old tale with a new set of meanings.[103]

However finely these characters may be sketched, yet it is not in their natures that the story type fixes its residual identity. Rather, the tale is typologized by the specific kind of situational irony that arises when a neophyte in love unwittingly relates all the details of his initiation to a confidant who is no other than the woman's husband, followed by that husband's complete failure to make use of his privileged information to catch the two together. Before each subsequent visit to Genobbia, Prince Nerino informs Dr. Raimondo of his plans, but the latter's attempts to apprehend him merely inspire his wife to greater protestation of her honour and more novel shifts to hide her lover, thereby bringing her husband's jealous rage to such a pitch that he seeks to smoke the youth out by setting fire to his own house. Arguably, this structure alone is the common feature among all the stories constituting this narrative group. But as a sampling of the many variants will reveal, this core plotting motif is open to a multiplicity of treatments and social interpretations.

In the present tale, a youth falls for a beauty brought twice to his attention by the offices of his friend, without realizing she is his wife. That deployment of a wife to dazzle a susceptible youth is new to Straparola and colours the entire story to follow. Nerino's reaction is that of a student seeking a caper with a citizen's wife in a fashion redolent of those so often featured in the theatre, as in Cecchi's *L'assiuolo* (The owl) in which

103 Interpretations of how much more these characters manifest archetypal positions of the psyche will depend upon the beliefs of readers about fundamental human relations. Genobbia has made a new man of Nerino by replacing his mother, and in the process the man who parcelled her out to the attention of others is destroyed by his stubborn silence and vindictive impulses. Such emblematic reciprocity carries provocative intimations, especially if Raimondo also serves as a replacement of the youth's father.

two students end up with sisters, one married to a doddering philanderer.[104] Straparola's version still maintains some of the school-of-love elements of its source in following the classic profile for picking up girls, first in attending church to see them in their finery, then speaking to them or following them home, then passing regularly in front of their houses while casting modest but longing looks, or finding a go-between if necessary to carry letters and messages, followed by words, kisses, and all the rest. It is also a study in the means for hiding lovers when husbands return unexpectedly. *Novelle* and plays of the period abound with such inventions and they nearly always succeed, to the obvious delight of readers and spectators. Stories in this tradition from Ser Giovanni's *Pecorone* to Molière's *School for Wives* furnish a full repertoire.

In all of these matters, the story is entirely theatrical. The setting is that of the *commedia erudita.* It requires no more than two or three houses, a church, and a piazza, and the action entails slipping in and out of one of these houses without being snared. There are love scenes, confessional scenes, a sequence of clever contingency measures met with rampages and threats, and a final menacing supper with its surface insouciance and undercurrents of an ensuing bloodbath. It all ends with the lovers taking flight, followed, we might imagine, by a suicidal soliloquy from the defeated Raimondo. Such is the temptation of destiny in placing a wife on show. It would have made an ideal theatre piece, but how such a play would have been classified in relation to the prolix debate among Italian academicians concerning comedy and tragedy and their hybrid forms is open to speculation. *Novelle* also invite such classifications, embracing the paradoxes of tragicomedy and comitragedy, but without a fixed point of view in this tale the lovers escape to their happiness, while the husband, erring but human and suffering, finds death in humiliation. Those who subsequently adapt Ser Giovanni's plot into actual plays will not only develop what is intrinsically dramatic in the *novella,* but adjust events to comply with the expectations of comedy.

Arguably, Straparola's story exhibits a nearly perfect narrative logic and a denouement justified by a sense of its inevitability. When it comes to rewriting the core story, however, there are many potential endings, each one holding a social vision or a corner on its own truth. The young man, upon learning at last the identity of the woman's husband, has

---

104 Trans. Konrad Eisenbichler, in *Renaissance Comedy: The Italian Masters,* ed. Donald Beecher, 2 vols. (Toronto: University of Toronto Press, 2009), vol. II, pp. 234–88.

options. He might grab the wife and run. He might sacrifice love for friendship, apologize to his mentor and confidant, plead his own innocence, and beat a retreat. Inversely, the wife's loyalty might be steadfast in giving merely false hope to the lover to purge and expel her husband's jealousy. In Shakespeare's domestic intrigue, the lover is but a pawn to be dismissed without gratification. Straparola's lover takes flight from menacing jealousy and frenzy, however, in keeping with the tale from antiquity that stands as prototype to the opening device of wife pandering. But it is associated with violence of another kind. To run away as a prince with a citizen's wife is one thing. To run as a commoner with a pandered queen is another; the king must first be slain. In a related story from antiquity, Giges, a household retainer in the retinue of King Candaules of Lydia, can think of no other way to possess the queen. The story turns upon Candaules, however; in boasting of his wife's beauty, he chooses to make demonstration of it by inviting Giges to view her secretly at her toilette. Herodotus first tells the story, but it is Plutarch in his 'Table Talk' in the *Moralia* who tries to intuit the motive. Does this indiscretion arise because lovers seek to love only that which is deemed perfectly good and beautiful in the eyes of others? Or is it because love is a boasting fool that gloats over its conquests to the point of putting the possessed object on prurient display? No doubt thanks to this author, Candaules's story became a Renaissance commonplace concerning behaviour that Jacques Ferrand defined as one of the symptoms of love as a disease.[105] Candaules epitomizes the initial impulse on Raimondo's part to enjoy a perverse pleasure in undermining a youth's illusions, only to incite the passions that spell his own doom – a kind of overreacher's tragedy in the making.

The principal source of the present tale, however, according to all of Straparola's editors and commentators, is the second novel of the first day of Ser Giovanni Fiorentino's *Pecorone*, provisionally named 'Of Bucciolo and the Schoolmaster's Wife, Giovanna.' This is a story that gained considerable favour and was imitated several times in the sixteenth

105 *Plutarch*, trans. Paul A. Clement, 'Table Talk' in the *Moralia*, 15 vols. (Cambridge, MA: Harvard University Press, 1969), bk. I, quest. 5, vol. VIII, p. 65. For the story in Herodotus, see [*History of Greece*], trans. A.C. Godley (Cambridge, MA: Harvard University Press, 1963), bk. I, sect. 8–12. See Jacques Ferrand, 'Diagnostic Signs of Love Melancholy,' in *A Treatise on Lovesickness* (1623), trans. and ed. Donald Beecher and Massimo Ciavolella (Syracuse: Syracuse University Press, 1990), chap. 14, p. 270.

century and later, ostensibly not only by Straparola, but by Shakespeare, Molière, and La Fontaine.[106] Straparola's version was but one of at least four in Italy written almost concurrently and, to all appearances, entirely independently of one another. Anton Francesco Doni's *novelle,* written in Venice over several years, do not seem to have appeared in print per se before 1606, while those of Pietro Fortini and Ser Giovanni Forteguerri remained unpublished before the nineteenth century.[107] Nevertheless, their respective handlings of the main intrigue, all based on Ser Giovanni, invite comparative consideration.

Ser Giovanni's story of 'Bucciolo' is a splendid tale. For Michel Bideaux, 'no work could manifest a greater degree of internal coherence than this little *récit.*'[108] Completing his studies early, Bucciolo requests of his schoolmaster a few lessons in the art of love to pass the time. The master complies, recommending that he start by attending church to look over the girls. Bucciolo innocently ogles them all, but at last finds one entirely to his taste – the master's wife, as it turns out. Both master and student remain in the dark until, through Bucciolo's confidences, the master realizes the truth. But instead of calling a halt by revealing identities all

106 The story was translated into French by Gabriel Chappuys. *Les facétieuses journées,* ed. Michel Bideaux (Paris: Champion, 2003), VII. 10, pp. 636–46. La Fontaine entitled the story 'Le Roi Candaule et le Maître en Droit,' *Nouveaux contes de M. de la Fontaine* (Amsterdam: C.J. Zwol, 1676), pp. 106–15.

107 Anton Francesco Doni, one of the early *polygrafici* active in Venice just before and after mid-century, published some of his letters as early as 1544, but did not come into his stride as an author before the time of the publication of the *Piacevoli notti* in 1550. The earliest publication on current record of his *Novelle* is *La filosofia morale ... & piacevoli novelle* (Venice: Giovanni Battista Bertoni, 1606). They are available in modern editions such as *Le novelle,* ed. Patrizia Pellizzari et al. (Rome: Salerno, 2002/2003), but in that multi-volume collection no version of the story identified as Novella 38 leaps from the page. In fact, he places it in a commentary on the *Rime* of Burchiello and makes up a fake source for it – typical Doni. Petraglione designates it as Novella 89 in his edition of the *Novelle* (Bergamo: Istituto italiano d'arti grafiche, 1907).

108 In the annotations to his edition of Gabriel Chappuys, *Les facétieuses journées* (Paris: Champion, 2003), p. 864. Bideaux cites Di Francia, from his *Novellistica, Storia dei generi letterari italiani novellistica* (Milan: Francesco Vallardi, 1924), vol. I, p. 210, concerning the prospects of the story's arrival from the East through the oral tradition and Ser Giovanni's loss of economy and precision that undoubtedly characterized the original. His own belief, however, is that the story copied by Ser Giovanni originated with an earlier Italian author of *novelle* in a version now lost (p. 865). Chappuys's story is VII. 10, pp. 636–46, taken from Francesco Sansovino, VII. 10.

around before more harm is done, his need for revenge against both of them, whetted by jealousy, takes precedence. There is a touch of rustic comedy in the hyperbolical manner in which the various parties arm themselves. (This is suppressed by Straparola.) Moreover, Giovanna's technique of grasping hold of her husband while Bucciolo slips from behind her back and through the door has about it more farce than *novella.* Ideas not taken by Straparola include the laundry hamper which the jealous schoolmaster runs through with his sword in a fit of anger, and which Shakespeare makes famous in *The Merry Wives of Windsor.* Moreover, Giovanna's brothers turn up and ransack the place, menacing both her and her lover with the usual family justice to be meted out upon proof of infidelity (see Straparola's 'Polissena and the Priest,' I.5, and 'Malgherita Spolatina's Death at Sea,' VII.2). The stakes are high, to be sure, but the atmosphere is altogether closer to carnival given the boy's known escape and Giovanna's own outspoken confidence and brazen avowals of innocence. (The relatives in Straparola are reduced to a passive but menacing presence at the closing banquet.) In Ser Giovanni's tale, the schoolmaster is carried back to his own classroom where he is subjected to public ridicule. He is likewise drubbed by his brothers-in-law and is recommended to confinement for the insane. (Raimondo endures nothing of this.) Once in his bed, the townsfolk come to commiserate, along with Bucciolo, who only then realizes just who's who. At that juncture, he avows to the old man the esteem of a son, says he has learned enough in Bologna, and makes a hasty retreat back to Rome. Comparatively in their generic design the two stories are one, and Ser Giovanni tells a fine, raucous tale. But Straparola varies the iterative episodes, intensifies the psychological drama, adds the motif of the beauty contest, and leaves out the peddler woman who serves as a go-between, omitting in consequence all of Giovanna's superb duplicity in short-circuiting the old woman's potentially damaging gossip by threatening to drive her out with a doorbar, while accepting the young man shortly thereafter. Feature by feature, Straparola's talents can be seen at work, including the addition of the Candaules episode and the device of the ring in the wine whereby, at the last critical moment, Nerino discovers the true identity of his lady.[109] Certain elements of Straparola's tale were carried forward

109 *The Novellino of Masuccio,* trans. W.G. Waters, 2 vols. (London: Lawrence & Bullen, 1895), pt. IV, no. 35, vol. II, pp. 171–84. A collateral challenge for comparatists is whether this story by Masuccio of Salerno is the same story as the one we have in hand or a different one. 'Same' or 'different' is to be determined by the critical

into a related version by Giovanni Sagredo, such as the ring in the cup by which the final crisis is averted.[110]

The only trace of an Eastern prototype is contained in a story under the heading 'Tales of the Brahmins, Second Traveller' in the *Bahar-Danush* of Einaiut Oollah (Shaikh Inayat Allah Kamboh, 1608–71). This collection of romantic and salty stories about the techniques of cheating wives was completed in 1651, a century after the *Piacevoli notti* appeared, but these Persian tales are associated with tradition and antiquity. When

---

degree of coincidences or departures from a signature profile, and by the point at which variations constitute a new species. Such enquiries turn out to be more vexing with regard to conscious makers building on literary sources than with stories in the oral tradition wherein, despite lapses, faults, substitutions, and inventions, there is a concerted effort to preserve traditions and maintain essential defining narrative features. Masuccio's story we may provisionally call 'Tobia and the Inn-keeper's wife, Lella.' She too is so beautiful that she takes the breath away. Her husband is jealous to a fault, but he is an inn-keeper too, and his wife is on daily display in a way that draws paying customers just for the chance to gaze at her. This is Candaules with a twist. Young Tobia heard of her reputation and booked a stay there specifically to that end, only to become a rival for her love, as her husband feared. There is the matter of curing Tonto of his jealousy, initially, but in the end the lovers, as in Straparola, lay their plans for escape. The coincidences between Masuccio and Ser Giovanni can be tallied, but straight off there is no school of love, no unwitting confidences between the husband and the lover, and no amorous encounters repeatedly interrupted by the husband's unexpected arrival. Given the arrangements at the hotel, flight is the lovers' only solution. These are significant obstacles, but the husband is made to collaborate unwittingly in helping them make their escape, as in the cognate tales associated with Straparola's 'Erminione' (IV.2). Tobia announces his departure, as Nerino does; arranges for a ship; tells his host about a sick boy he wants to take aboard with him; and offers him a tidy sum to transport the boy down to the port muffled up in his bedclothes. Needless to say, this will be Lella in disguise. Her own husband places her on horseback and makes jokes about the situation, as he imagined it to be, all the way to the port. Of a less tragic and more pragmatic frame of mind than Raimondo, the jealous Tonto grieves her loss for a time, learns a lesson, remarries, and never thinks of her again. That the publication of Masuccio's work follows Ser Giovanni's by a century (1476) sheds no light on the matter at all, for there is no evidence, in any case, that the latter is related to the former. Rather, it is the generic correspondences that tease, as though the whole of the *novella*-writing enterprise is a grand set of variations upon a vast repertory of motifs. Yet there are intimations in the reading that suggest affinities between these two stories, raising questions about the mind's own apparatuses for establishing degrees of analogy and the innuendoes upon which analogies are based that later achieve bedrock authority.

110 *L'Arcadia in Brenta*, ed. Quinto Marini (Rome: Salerno, 2004), pp. 146–9.

the husband suddenly returns home, the wife, in a panic, can think of no other solution than to hide her lover in the pond up to his chin with a gourd over his head. The husband takes note that the gourd does not move when the wind comes up and begins to cast stones at it. The boy escapes only by sinking down into the water and holding his breath until he is nearly dead. The next day he finds himself in an assembly boasting of his adventure, unaware that the lady's husband is present. The husband, needless to say, is more than intrigued and insists that the youth accompany him home to tell the same story in the presence of his wife. When the lover sees where he is, he needs no prompting, casting doubt over the entire matter by breaking off the story as though it were all a dream from which he awoke before the end. The resemblances in the overall profile and the dream mechanism in particular may be coincidental, although it is reasonable to conclude that Straparola's tale, or materials relating to it, or to the tradition that inspired Johann Agricola and Hans Sachs (their stories profiled below), originated in the East.[111] That prospect calls for further investigation, for it may prove that a variation upon the story in the *Bahar-Danush* made its way to the West and provided the model for the entire tradition.

Even though related stories by Fortini and Forteguerri are neither sources for nor indebted to Straparola, they are treatments contemporary with his of Ser Giovanni's 'Bucciolo' in full novelistic mode, each offering a subtle and inventive reinterpretation of the story. Fortini situates his drawn-out rendition in Siena with a considerable degree of detail about the places and customs of the city, extending his setting from the university to the duomo.[112] An aging professor of medicine takes a particular interest in one of his students, the introverted and self-disciplined Imenio. After drawn-out explanations taken from Galen, Avicenna, and Hippocrates, mixed with laudatory appraisals of women out of Boccaccio and Petrarch, he induces his student to get out a bit more, go to Mass, and choose the woman he likes most for a lover. Imenio undergoes a conversion, follows the professor's young wife home, and the familiar plot is set in motion. The employment of an old woman to carry his

111 *Bahar-Danush, or Garden of Knowledge*, trans. Jonathan Scott, 3 vols. (Shrewsbury: J. & W. Eddowes, 1799), vol. III, pp. 291–4 (Orig. *Bahār-i-Dānish*).

112 Pietro Fortini was active at much the same time as Straparola; he worked in Siena and died in 1562. His fiction was completed towards 1560 and also remained in manuscript until the nineteenth century. *Le giornate delle novelle dei novizi* (Bologna: Forni, 1967; reprint, Rome: Salerno, 1989; ed. Adriana Mauriello), no. 6.

messages is filled out by a full sociological analysis of her function and avocation, and the subtlety with which she manages her mission is stunning. The professor is not excessively jealous, but when he begins to understand the situation his suffering verges on pathos, for during the innocent interviews when the neophyte in love reveals his experiences, the husband must feign encouragement even as he covers his tears. His mounting pain is described in distracting detail as he doubts himself, laments his age, and grows delirious. A full-scale domestic drama ensues as husband confronts wife, baffled by his inability to demonstrate the boy's presence after seeing him enter the house. We no longer have the justification for jilting the old one proffered by Ser Giovanni and Straparola. When Imenio slips out the door as the old man enters, as in *The Pecorone*, the stage is set for a safe rampage against geriopsychosis on the part of a witheringly self-righteous wife; Fortini winds up the scene to a breaking point. At last, the teacher tells the student that his challenge was an error and that his wife was the lady in question, warning him away, offering pardon, and asking merely for secrecy. The student, on his side, as in the source, promises that nothing serious had taken place and offers his apologies. But a new cynicism, in the era of Machiavelli's *Mandragola*, has now set in, so that Imenio simply stops confiding in the professor, yet continues the affair for a long time thereafter.

Ser Giovanni Forteguerri, active in Pistoia, was born in 1520 and was chancellor of the commune. There was little chance that either author could have known the work of the other, and particularly in the direction of Straparola, given that Forteguerri's work remained in a mid-sixteenth-century manuscript until its publication in the nineteenth century. The tale in question is 'Quanto uno è più geloso, più facilamente venta becco' (The more one is jealous the easier it is to make him a cuckold).[113] The story follows the conventional profile. A Bolognese businessman, Timido Agghiadati, meets Pollone, a young student from Siena, who 'voleva imparare a vagheggire alla Bolognese' (wants to learn how to make love to women in the Bolognese way). Pollone follows instructions, finds a lover, and confides in Timido, without realizing it is his wife. The latter, meanwhile, seeks in vain to catch them in the act. The wife's name is Sagace, 'shrewd,' and she lives up to it in every way in cheating on her

113 *Novelle edite e inedite*, ed. Vittoria Lami (Bologna: Commissione per i testi di lingua, 1968), no. 6, pp. 137–57, from the edition by Gaetano Romagnoli (Bologna: Forni, 1882).

unhandsome and abusive old husband, a man to whom her family had married her for money. It is, of course, Sagace who teaches Pollone the arts of love, or rather the arts of tricking jealous husbands. Amazed by her husband's repeatedly inconvenient arrivals, she begins to suspect that Pollone is boasting about his exploits in her husband's shop. After several futile house searches, Timido, the merchant, goes berserk, but his jealousy is cured when Pollone, hidden near the chimney, on cue, pours a pot of liquid on him which he is induced to comprehend as a miracle. This charming version includes a chaperone mother-in-law who inadvertently leaves the lovers alone at a merry-go-round while she attends vespers, allowing for a great deal of punning on doing the merry-go-round several times. The young wife is ultimately pushed to the limits of her rhetoric, however, and in the manner of the probative test employed in 'Erminione and Hippolito' (IV.2 above) she must take a live coal in her hand to prove her innocence. In this way she regains verbal dominance over her husband, insisting upon her innocence even as the liaisons continue. Such parallel versions confirm the popularity of the tale insofar as three authors made independent use of the story type to fill out their collections in the years approaching mid-century. This is one of the few instances in which Straparola writes as one of the *novellieri*, taking his materials from a literary source, or so it would appear in this case. It is equally revealing, perhaps, that a version of the story appears in a German collection in 1558, clearly in the tradition at hand, but owing less to Ser Giovanni and presumably nothing at all to any of his Italian contemporaries.

Michael Lindener sets up the narrative events in rather different terms. A goldsmith, married to a wife who for her beauty receives the attentions of many men, out of jealousy determines to prove her infidelity, yet he cannot hit upon the right means. When a poor student comes to town and asks him for money, he decides to employ the youth as bait, setting him up to call upon his wife under what he assumed to be controlled and secret conditions. He begins by instructing the boy in how he might enjoy the attentions of a certain woman without telling him that it was to be in his own house. The youth follows the lead, but when it comes to catching them in flagrant delight, the youth is so well hidden and the wife so vociferous about her innocence that the poor goldsmith can prove nothing. In each instance, however, the young man returns to boast of his exploits and hiding places. The husband grows increasingly frantic, but never more crafty or lucky. 'Mit dem imm hawss umbher lieff, alle winckel auffs hinderst durchsuchet, die bett ab dem betladen warf, and suchet, ab er ine irgendt finden möcht.' In short, he runs about the house searching, turning bed and stead upside down, but never finds anything. Even when the young man has had enough, having been hidden on nail-boards and stuffed in cupboards, of which he complains to his mentor, the goldsmith insists he return. When the husband enters for the final time, the youth is stuffed into a clothes hamper in the pantry, which the wife prevails upon her husband to remove before he sets fire to the house. With this final failure, the goldsmith is compelled to reveal all to the boy and swear him to silence for his honour's sake, which is incentive enough for the student to leave town in haste.[114] If such a variant does not come from Ser Giovanni, then the old dilemma emerges that the common story could only have been derived in these several places from a *novella*-like tale in wide oral circulation. I have been partial to this interpretation in many instances where the evidence seemed to require it, but here remain uncommitted.

The plot in Shakespeare's *Merry Wives of Windsor* (entered in the Stationer's Register in January 1602) involving Falstaff and Mr. Ford is, arguably, indebted only to the *Pecorone*. Just how Shakespeare managed to absorb the signature features of the plot is an intriguing question, but

114 'Of the Poor Student and the Goldsmith,' in *Rastbüchlein und Katzipori*, ed. Franz Lichtenstein (Tübingen: Litterarischen Verein, Stuttgart, 1883), no. 3, pp. 8–13. This story is preceded in Germany by a tradition of tales that passes through the *Fabeln* of Hans Sachs in which a young man is employed by a merchant who discovers by degrees that his employee is sleeping with his own wife while seeking his advice on how to handle the affair. The boy tells him everything but does not make the connection until the master invites him home to a social gathering to tell his adventures to his guests in the presence of his wife. When the boy arrives at the unique house with the red door and the green columns he puts two and two together. To save face, he must tell his story, but ingeniously makes it out to be but a dream from which he awakes. This satisfies everyone, so that the next day the boy is given a sum of money and sent on his way. 'Der Pueller mit der rotten thüer und den zway grüenen seülen' (The lover, the red door, and the two green columns) in *Sämtliche Fabeln und Schwänke*, ed. Edmund Goetze (Halle: Max Niemeyer, 1913), vol. I, pp. 278–80. This story, written just after mid-century, was taken from Johann Agricola, *Sybenhundert und fünfftzig teutscher Sprichwörter verneüwert und gebessert* (Hagenau [Braubach], 1534), no. 624; new ed. (Hildesheim: Georg Olms, 1970). It holds no prospect of cross-fertilization with Straparola in either direction, but reveals the widespread circulation of the story type at the time Straparola was writing, always with Ser Giovanni in the background, and the tradition from which he derived his story. It contains the confession turned to a dream motif that appears in the *Bahar-Danush* mentioned above. This motif clearly enjoyed wide currency.

one no more difficult to explain in the case of the *Wives* than in the case of *The Merchant of Venice*, which he took from the same collection. There is the prospect, however, that Shakespeare drew upon an English translation for the *Wives* plot. However he accessed the story, he made use of it in a way that brought Italianate features to the English stage. That much can be answered to the question regarding the Italian influence upon the English theatre that has preoccupied scholars for decades. Paradoxically, however, the story that brings seductive intrigue, Italianate stage business and situational irony, urbane cynicism, spicy repartee, and symmetrical episodes to the English stage produces a quintessentially English play in which the women of small-town England are celebrated for their honesty, high moral values, and playful spirits. The clothes hamper in which Falstaff is concealed, Shakespeare adapts directly from his source, and Ford's incrementally bad humour and incipient madness is likewise redolent of the original. More importantly, the rhythm of events, the disposition of episodes, the wife's clever ruses, and the husband's futile attempts to find the culprit in ransacking the premises are in the *novella*'s debt. Mistress Quickly undoubtedly owes her existence to the old peddler woman in Ser Giovanni, who has no counterpart in Straparola. Ford's associate, Page, says that if Falstaff were after his wife he would turn her loose, entirely confident of her fidelity. But Shakespeare employs the old plot to his own chauvinistic ends. The seducer is a fat, aging knight in whom Mistress Ford has no amorous interests whatsoever. The Italian women are mendacious and adulterous in intent and deed, in the spirit of Italian vice. The wife of Windsor, by contrast, has been imposed upon and plays pranks as a payback, in the process whipping up her husband's jealousy to teach him to know her better, in the spirit of English folly. Shakespeare continues to acknowledge his source in the proposition that Ford should be 'pinioned' for his insane behaviour. But in all this action, Shakespeare avoids adultery, cures Ford of his jealousy, and celebrates the loyalty and cunning of English wives, while pursuing the lecherous knight with communally conducted petty chastisements in a *tutti* finale using English fairies in an English forest. As Giorgio Melchiori encapsulates the metamorphosis, 'Shakespeare translated the plot of Ser Giovanni Fiorentino's novella out of Italian into honesty.'[115]

---

115 William Shakespeare, *The Merry Wives of Windsor* (Walton-on-Thames: Thomas Nelson and Sons, 2000), p. 15. The standard work on the sources of Shakespeare's plays is Geoffrey Bullough, *Narrative and Dramatic Sources of Shakespeare* (London: Routledge, 1958), *Merry Wives*, vol. II, pp. 3–58.

The hitch in the pursuit of Shakespeare's sources is raised by the anonymous work published in 1590 entitled *Tarletons Newes out of Purgatorie*, which contains 'The Tale of the Two Lovers of Pisa, and why they were whipt in Purgatory with Nettles.'[116] That story is a remarkable conflation of Straparola and Ser Giovanni, in its very creation a critical recognition of the relationship between the two. The *Pecorone* is featured in the friendship between the old law master, Mutio, and the young man, Lionello, but the final episodes in particular are pure Straparola: the burning of the country house and the lover's escape in a cabinet full of the old man's professional papers; a supper party at the mother-in-law's house to which Lionello is invited to recount his amorous adventures before all the family present; and the moment of recognition when the clever wife slips her lover a ring in a drink. In a sense, Shakespeare had as much as he needed to write the *Wives* out of an English source, except that he makes no use of the many features peculiar to the story of the Pisan lovers that would firm up the borrowing – and there are many such particularities. It would appear that little of *Tarletons Newes* and hence less of Straparola passed through Shakespeare's imagination.

That question can be left aside, however, to look briefly at the fine interpretation of the story's materials in this anonymous work, which is one of the few instances in which our author received overt treatment in an English text before the late nineteenth century. The Candaules motif is replaced with an account of the young wife's enforced marriage to an old, white-haired, impotent lawyer who is jealous to a fault. It is a stock opening, to be sure, but one that generates sympathy for the young. From the outset, Mutio knows that it is his wife in question, but imparts precise information to the boy about his movements the better to catch them together. The author remains faithful to Ser Giovanni in the fury with which Mutio pursues his ransacking of the premises in search of the lover, Lionello. His wife Margaret's personality, meanwhile, is altogether closer to Straparola's Genobbia. This author, in the hiding devices, follows neither source. The first is a dry vat of feathers, the second is a space between the ceiling and the roof, while the last is Mutio's own chest of papers which he arranges to have removed from the burning house, adding another touch of irony by furthering his unwitting collaboration. At the same time, the story is potentially crueller, for the old lawyer fully

116 *The Cobler of Caunterburie and Tarletons Newes Out of Purgatorie*, intro. and ed. by Geoffrey Creigh and Jane Bellfield (Leiden: E.J. Brill, 1987), pp. 177–185.

intends to kill Lionello in the conflagration. But the finest twist of all is that the young man, in retelling his adventures at the supper party, rather than breaking off as though waking from a dream, as in Straparola, breaks off to say that he has never even met Margaret, that he has fabricated the entire series of events to cure the old geezer of his jealousy. Thus, in the end, Mutio dies not of melancholy grief, but of shame, and so frees the lovers. Only much later in purgatory is he allowed to whip them with nettles for their many deceptions. Ultimately, Straparola's is the darker and more searching rendition, well-designed in its tripartite proportions and nuanced in its intimations of interiority and motivation, but the anonymous English tale carries the trickery and deceptions to even greater lengths, makes good use of the invented country house episode with its *fabliau* overtones, and provides a reversal that concentrates on the cure of jealousy in a way that might have been of interest to Shakespeare. Moreover, the language is fresh and imaginative – worthy of the best of Robert Greene or Thomas Lodge, while lacking the stylistic excesses of Thomas Nashe or even of Shakespeare, for that matter. The collection was made in the name of the famous comic actor Richard Tarleton, who had died two years earlier in 1588. The conceit of seeking out the recently deceased, hovering in limbo, purgatory, or the Elysian fields, to have them tell their tales came to a height of exploitation in the years following the death of Robert Greene in 1592, issuing from the pens of Henry Chettle, Thomas Nashe, and John Dickenson, who published his *Greene in Conceit, New Raised from his Grave to Write the Tragic History of Fair Valeria of London* as late as 1598.[117]

Brief mention must be made here of Molière's *The School for Wives* (*L'école des femmes*) which appeared in 1662.[118] The author's adaptation of the signature plot design of having the young lover confide in an old man who encourages him the better to trap him has now become so generalized in its deployment as to make the assignment of precise sources difficult. Nevertheless, Ser Giovanni enjoys founder's status, even though Louveau's Straparola may have provided the outline. In Molière's version, Agnes's old guardian raises his ward in a convent in order to keep her innocent and naïve, thinking to marry her himself when she comes of age. The trysts and rendezvous between Agnes and her beau,

117 John Dickenson, *Greene in Conceit*, ed. Donald Beecher and David Margolies (Toronto: CRRS Publications, 2008).

118 In *The Misanthrope, Tartuffe, and Other Plays*, trans. Maya Slater (Oxford: Oxford World's Classics, 2001).

Horace, which the old man tries to intercept, are now the schemes of the young to deceive a man who is *in loco parentis* rather than a husband. Horace is forced to hide in a cupboard; then he is knocked off a ladder. When Arnolphe, the old guardian, orders Agnes to throw a stone at her lover, she ties a note to it setting their next rendezvous. The Ser Giovanni/ Straparola legacy is entirely broken off when the girl's father appears to approve of the wedding between the youngsters, leaving the old man to deal with his misplaced desires and fixations about everything from the education of youth to the confinement of young girls to self-serving ends, and the excesses of possessive jealousy. In this play, the design of the Italianate intrigue has been structurally maintained, but its 'world' has been utterly transformed.

Jean de la Fontaine included among his verse fables 'King Candaules and the Doctor of Laws,' in which he made formal acknowledgment of the resonances that brought Herodotus and Ser Giovanni into a common sphere.[119] His story, like Straparola's, illustrates the ills that arise with one's own imprudence. In the first part, La Fontaine elaborates upon the ancient story in which Giges is invited to see the queen naked, with the proviso that he is never to tell a soul and never to have any silly ideas about getting closer. But when the husband afterward explains the joke to the queen, she is not amused. Suspecting desire on the part of the voyeur, she chooses him as her means to pay back her foolish husband. Thus it comes about that Candaules is poisoned by the lovers. The second tale is presented in close juxtaposition with the first, inviting readers to work through the interconnections. A visiting French student asks his law professor for a few lessons on how to meet and court women in Rome and is taught the precise tactics recommended by Ser Giovanni's schoolmaster. Not realizing the full extent of who he is dealing with, the student reports everything and laughs at husbands in the process. La Fontaine asks us to imagine the professor's pain. Thereafter, he considers his options, including assuming the student's place – in effect, creating his own bed trick. But in the process his wife recognizes him, despite the

119 'La Roi Candaule et le Maître en Droi,' *Contes et nouvelles en vers* (Hamburg, 1731), vol. II, pp. 187*ff*; *Tales and Novels in Verse by J. de la Fontaine*, 2 vols. (London: For the Society of English Bibliophylists, n.d.), vol. II, pp. 121–32. For a later tale based on the signature plot design, see 'Sur le moine Amador, qui fut un glorieux abbé de Turpenay' (About Brother Amador, the glorious abbot of Turpenay), in Honoré de Balzac, *Contes drolatiques*, in *Oeuvres completes* (Paris: Calmann-Lévy, 1879), vol. 19, pp. 365–83.

old lady's efforts to introduce him adequately disguised. She accuses him of being mad and then abandons both husband and lover to retire to a convent. This is a darker turn than one finds in *Il pecorone* and a different one than is found in Straparola. La Fontaine kept the central situational irony, but his directions are his own in superimposing elements from alien traditions, displacing the lover entirely and turning back to the Church when all secular options fail.

These examples display the fortunes of the plot type which supplies the narrative core of 'The Physician's Wife,' although Straparola's tale is not the prototype behind the variations. It is but one among the several that owe their origins to the *Pecorone* or to its source tradition. Straparola, in that regard, creates his *novella* according to the humanist practice of *imitatio.* The cognate tales based on this common source provide contexts for comparative evaluation. The proportion, sobriety, irony, and melancholy, and the teetering between comedy and tragedy of Straparola's reworking of the materials all bear witness to his talents as a maker, provided that he made all the choices that distinguish his work from Ser Giovanni's. The story bears all the markers of the essential Italian *novella* in its design, contemporary setting, and social concerns. It appears to carry few of the markers of the popular tradition. Straparola, in this tale, would no longer seem to be collecting in the field, but adapting in the study from written sources. Yet we can never be sure. Doubts of this nature would hardly come to mind in the case of his fellow *novellieri.* But Straparola's heretofore persistent commitment to the popular tradition now blurs, as never before, that fine line that separates the literary from the oral and the formal from the popular. Moreover, a folk tale may have given rise to Ser Giovanni's *novella,* not to mention the early German variants, and thus such a tale may have been in Straprola's vicinity as well. His production reopens the debate regarding the facility with which written tales went back to the folk, or returned from the folk to the written page. That no nineteenth-century folk versions of this tale have come to light is no certain proof that Ser Giovanni's tale was never of the folk, or that such a tale did not exist in the popular tradition both before *Il pecorone* and after. But if there was such a tale, there is some significance in the fact that it did not prevail in the oral tradition.

IV. Fable 5
Flamminio in Seeking Death Discovers Life

LIONORA

Flamminio Veraldo sets out from Ostia in search of Death, but not finding it, meets Life instead. This latter lets him see Fear and make trial of Death.

There are many men who go searching for things with care and diligence. But some things, once they're found, they wish they had never set eyes on, fleeing from them as fast as the Devil from holy water. This was the case for Flamminio, who when he went in search of Death found Life, but only after encountering Fear and making trial of Death. You will find all of this clearly set forth in my fable.

In Ostia, an ancient city situated not far from Rome, there lived in former days, as is commonly told, a young man somewhat wanting in wit and more eccentric than steady and prudent; his name was Flamminio Veraldo. Over and over he had heard it said that in the entire world there was nothing more hideous, terrible, and frightful than Death, seeing that he showed pity to none and respected no man however rich or poor he might be. Filled with wonder by what he heard, Flamminio made up his mind, come what may, to hunt out and examine with his own eyes what manner of thing this might be which men called Death. So, attiring himself in coarse garments and taking in hand a staff of strong service wood tipped with iron, he set out from Ostia. When he had travelled over many miles of road, Flamminio came one day to a certain street in the middle of which he spied a cobbler sitting in his stall making shoes. And although there were a goodly number of finished shoes lying about, this cobbler kept on steadily at his task of making more.

Flamminio, going up to the cobbler, said to him, 'God be with you, my master!'

To this the cobbler replied, 'You're right welcome my son.'

Then Flamminio said, 'What is this task you labour at?'

'I toil hard,' said the cobbler, 'and work that I may not want, for as you see, I labour over my shoes.'

'Why do you do this, seeing that you have so many pairs already made?' said Flamminio. 'What is the good of making more?'

'I make them,' said the cobbler, 'to wear myself, to sell for my own sustenance, and for the sustenance of my little household, so that when I've grown old I may be able to live on the money I've made by my handicraft.'

'And what will you do after that?' asked Flamminio.

'After that,' said the cobbler, 'I must die.'

'You will die?' Flamminio replied.

'Yes, of course,' said the cobbler.

Then he cried, 'O, my good master, can you tell me perhaps what this thing is they call Death?'

The cobbler answered, 'Truthfully, I can't.'

'What, have you never seen him?' said Flamminio.

To this the cobbler answered, 'I have never seen him, nor have I any wish to see him now, or to taste of his nature, for in fact they say that he's the strangest and most terrible monster the world holds.'

Then Flamminio said, 'At least in your wisdom you'll be able to teach me where he resides, because day and night I wander over mountains and through valleys, by pools and rivers, seeking him, but without ever hearing news about where he can be found.'

The cobbler answered, 'No, no, I know nothing about where Death may dwell, nor where he's to be found, or of what he's made. But if you carry onwards with your journey, by chance you'll find him.'

This conversation ended, Flamminio took his leave from the cobbler and travelled on to a place where he entered into a dense and shadowy forest. In a certain place he saw a peasant who, although he had already cut a huge pile of wood for burning, yet he went on cutting more. When they had exchanged greetings, Flamminio said to him, 'My brother, what are you going to do with so much wood, I ask you?'

To this the peasant made answer, 'I'm preparing it to kindle fire in the coming winter when there will be snow, ice, and frosts, so I'll be able to keep myself and my children warm, and to sell whatever is left over, and to buy bread, wine, and clothing with the profits, and all other things needed for our daily sustenance, thus passing our lives until Death comes to fetch us.'

'Now by your courtesy,' said Flamminio, 'could you tell me where this same Death is to be found?'

'Why no,' the peasant replied, 'seeing that I've never once seen him myself, nor do I know where he dwells. I'm here in this wood all day long busy with my own affairs. Very few wayfarers come into these parts and I know hardly any of them who pass by.'

'What then should I do to find him?' demanded Flamminio.

To this the peasant answered, 'You're asking me? I wouldn't have a clue what to tell you, nor how to direct you. I can only urge you to keep on travelling further afield and by chance you may meet up with him.'

Having taken leave of the peasant, Flamminio walked and walked until he came to a certain place where a tailor lived who had a great number of clothes upon pegs and a shop full of all kinds of the finest garments. Flamminio said to him, 'God be with you, my master.'

The tailor replied, 'And the same good wish to you.'

'What are you going to do with such rich and beautiful clothes and all these noble garments? Do they all belong to you?'

Then the master tailor answered, 'Certain of them are mine, some belong to the merchants, some to the gentry, and some to various other folk.'

'But what use can they find for so many?' asked Flamminio.

'They wear them in different seasons of the year,' the tailor answered, and showing them all to Flamminio, he went on, 'These they wear in the summer, and these in the winter, and these others in the seasons that come between, clothing themselves sometimes in one fashion and sometimes in another.'

'And in the end what do they do?' asked Flamminio.

The tailor answered, 'They go on in this manner until the day of their death.'

Flamminio, hearing the tailor speak of Death, said, 'O, my master! My dear master! Could you tell me where I can find this Death you speak of?'

The tailor, almost angry, replied in a passionate tone, 'My son! My dear son! You go about asking mighty strange questions. I surely cannot tell you where he might live, nor direct you there, for I never let myself even think about him, and it is a cause of real offence to me when anyone starts talking about him. So I ask you either to talk of some other matter or be on your way, for I hate all this kind of discussion.' So Flamminio, taking his leave of the tailor, departed on his journey.

Now it came about that Flamminio, after crossing many lands, came at last to a deserted and solitary place where he found a hermit with his beard all matted with dirt and his body worn away by the passage of the years, and by fasting and devoting his mind entirely to contemplation. Certain that he had at last found Death, Flamminio spoke to him, 'In truth, holy father, I'm very glad to meet up with you.'

'The sight of you is welcome to me, my son,' the hermit replied.

'My good father,' said Flamminio, 'what are you doing here in this rough and inhospitable spot, cut off from all pleasures and all human society?'

'I pass my time in prayers, fasting, and contemplation,' answered the hermit.

'What for?' Flamminio enquired.

'Why, my son,' exclaimed the hermit, 'I do all this to serve God, to mortify my flesh, to do penance for all the offences I have committed in the sight of the eternal and immortal God, and of the true son of Mary, and in the end to gain salvation for my sinful soul, so that when the hour of my death arrives I may render it up pure of all stain, and in the awful day of judgement, by the grace of my Redeemer and by no merit of my own, I may make myself worthy of that happy and glorious home where I may taste the joys of eternal life, to which blessedness may God lead us all!'

Then Flamminio said, 'Oh, my dear father, offer me just a few more words, if it is no offence to you, telling what manner of thing this Death is, and in what fashion he is made?'

The holy father answered, 'No, my son, don't trouble yourself to gain knowledge of this thing you're seeking, for Death is a most terrible and fearful being, and is called by wise men the last end of all our sufferings, a misery to the happy, a happiness to the miserable, the end and limit of all worldly things. It divides friend from friend. It parts father from son and son from father, mother from daughter and daughter from mother. It cuts the bond of marriage. And finally it separates the soul from the body, causing the body to lose all its powers and to grow so putrid and evil that all men flee it and abandon it as an abominable thing.'

'And have you never set eyes on him, my father?' asked Flamminio.

'Heavens no,' answered the hermit.

'So what can I do to see him?' asked Flamminio.

'Ah, my son,' said the hermit, 'if you're so dead set on finding him, you've only to keep on going farther and farther, because the longer the road taken through this world, the closer a man is to Death.' The young man, having thanked the holy father and received his benediction, went on his way.

Then Flamminio journeyed through deep valleys, craggy mountains, and forlorn forests, strange places all, seeing along the way all sorts of fearsome beasts, asking of each whether it was that thing called Death, but always being told 'no.' At last, after passing through many lands and seeing many exotic things, he came to a mountain of some height, and after climbing over it he descended into a deep and gloomy valley surrounded on all sides by caverns. Here he saw a fearful and hideous beast which made all the valley echo with its roaring. 'Who are you?' said Flamminio. 'Is it possible that you may be Death?'

To which the beast made answer, 'I am not Death, but continue along here and very soon you will find him.'

When he had heard the answer he had so long desired to hear, Flamminio felt his heart grow lighter. Worn out by fatigue from the long and weary labour, this miserable youth had almost drowned in despair. But now he found himself on the edge of a wide and spacious plain. Climbing to the summit of a pleasant little hill all covered with flowers, he looked about him in all directions and saw the lofty walls of a fair and noble city not far distant. Then he began to walk with more nimble and lively steps, and when the shadows of evening were gathering he came to one of the city gates, which was adorned with the finest white marble. When he had entered by permission of the gatekeeper, the first person he met was a very old woman full of years with a face like a corpse and a body so meagre and thin that through her skin it would have been possible to count each bone in her body. Her forehead was heavily marked with wrinkles, her eyes were squinting, watery, and scarlet red, her cheeks all puckered, her lips sucked in, her hands rough and callous, her head and limbs shaking and trembling with palsy. She was bent almost double in her gait and was dressed in coarse and dusty clothes. In addition to all this, she carried by her left side a sharp-edged sword, and in her right hand a weighty cudgel, at the end of which was a point of iron in the shape of a triangle, and upon this staff she would now and again lean as if to rest herself. On her shoulders she carried a large wallet in which she kept a great quantity of phials, glasses, and bottles all filled with divers sorts of liquors, unguents, and plasters for remedying all manner of human ailments and wounds. As soon as Flamminio laid eyes upon this toothless and ugly old crone, he was taken by the thought that perhaps she might prove to be that Death which he had wandered the world to find.

So approaching her, he said, 'Ah, my good mother, may God save and keep you.'

'And may God keep and preserve you, my son,' the old woman answered in a robust voice.

'Tell me, my mother,' Flamminio continued, 'whether perchance you may be that thing men call Death?'

'No, not at all. Rather, I am Life. Know too that I carry with me here in this wallet on my back such liquors and unguents that, by their special operations, I am able with ease to purify and cure the mortal body of all the heavy diseases which afflict it and in a short time to relieve it from all the tortures of pain.'

Then said Flamminio, 'Ah, my good mother, can you not inform me where Death is to be found?'

'And who might you be,' asked the old woman, 'to make this demand of me with such persistence?'

Flamminio answered, 'I am a youth who has already spent many a long day wandering about in search of Death and I've never yet been able to find someone who knows anything about him in all the lands I've crossed. So if you know of these things, by your courtesy tell me, because I'm possessed of a most ardent desire to look upon him and see what he's like, so that I can be certain whether he really is the hideous and dreadful thing that all men describe him to be.'

When the old woman heard this young man's foolish request, she said to him, 'My son, when would you like me to show you Death, to judge how hideous he is when you experience his terrors?'

Flamminio replied, 'Don't keep me in suspense any longer, I urge you, but let me see him right now, at this very moment.'

Thereupon, to satisfy his desire, the old woman made him strip himself completely naked, and while he was taking off his clothes she mixed together certain of her drugs used for the curing of various diseases. When the concoction was ready, she said to him, 'Lean down here, my son.' He obeyed her instructions and bent down. 'Now hold your head and close your eyes,' and Flamminio did as she asked. Hardly had the old woman finished her speech than she took the sharp blade worn at her side and with one blow struck off his head from his shoulders. Then she quickly took up the head, and having refitted it upon the torso she smeared it well with the plaster which she had prepared and thereby the wound was quickly healed. Just how this thing came about I cannot say, whether it resulted from the old hag's speed in replacing the head on the shoulders, or whether she herself brought it to pass through her medical skills. But the head, when it was set upon the body, was placed on backwards. So when Flamminio looked down upon his shoulders, his loins, and his large protruding buttocks – all of which he had never seen before – he fell into a fit of dismay and terror. Unable to think of a place where he might hide himself, he cried out to the old woman in a trembling and pitiful voice, 'Alas, alas, good mother, bring me back once more to my old shape. Bring me back, for the love of God, for by my faith I've never seen anything more frightful and more hideous than this. Deliver me from the miserable condition in which I now find myself. My God, my God, don't delay your help my sweet, good mother. Aid me, for I know you can help me if you so desire.'

The cunning old woman kept her silence, feigning all the while to understand nothing of the misfortune that had been created, letting the wretched fellow work himself into an agony and fry in his own juices. But at last, after keeping him in this plight for the space of two hours, she agreed to perform the cure he sought. So, making him bend down as before, she put her hand to her sharp-cutting sword and struck off his head from his shoulders. Then she took the head in her hands, and having placed it upon the trunk and smeared it well with her ointment, she brought Flamminio back to his former condition.

When he perceived that he was once again his old self, the young man put on his clothes. Now that he had seen with his own eyes what a terrible thing Death was, how ugly and hideous, as his own experiences proved, and without saying a word of farewell to the old woman he returned to Ostia by the shortest and quickest route he knew, now preoccupied for the future with reaching after Life and flying from Death, devoting himself more diligently to the pursuit of a better existence than he had sought before.

It only remained now for Lionora to propose her enigma, which she did as follows:

About a meadow fair and wide,
Gay decked with flowers on every side,
Three nymphs on a task of divine intent,
Pass to and fro, all firmly bent
To hasten their work, nor night nor day
Take pause, nor rest upon their way.
One in her left hand the distaff plies,
Between another's feet swift flies
The spindle, and the last one stands
With keen-edged weapon in her hand,
To cut in twain the fragile strand.

This enigma was very easily understood by all the company, because it was clear that the fine and spacious meadow must be this world in which all men dwell. The three nymphs are the three sisters, Clotho, Lachesis, and Atropos, who are thought by the poets to represent the beginning, the middle, and the end of our lives. Clotho, who holds the distaff, shows forth our birth; Lachesis, who spins, tells the seasons of our existence; while Atropos, who severs the thread just spun by Lachesis, is inevitable Death.

Already the watchful cock, bird sacred to Mercury, by his crowing, had given the signal of the approaching dawn when the Signora brought to an end the storytelling for the night. All the guests departed to their own homes, pledging, however, to return on the following evening under whatever penalty the Signora might deem fitting to inflict.

The End of the Fourth Night

IV.5 Commentary

The tale of Flamminio Veraldo appears in the *Piacevoli notti* looking for all the world like one of Straparola's own creations. It offers its own unique profile of the dim-witted boy who sets off in the world looking for an abstraction in personified form and, in the process, undergoes a rite of passage that in some fundamental way provides an experience that alters his life priorities. Viewed more closely, however, it is seen to be a conflation of two distinct story types: 'the boy without fear' and 'the search for Death,' the former a folk tale that retained its popularity down to the nineteenth century, the latter a medieval allegorical fable best known through Chaucer's 'The Pardoner's Tale' from *The Canterbury Tales.* Just how these types were drawn into a single narrative in Straparola's own time is beyond demonstration, but there are really only two options: either Straparola collected his story much as he presents it in the form of a folk tale, which seems probable given its rather mixed and imperfect narrative logic; or he generated his own version, in the manner of Chaucer, from narrative 'ideas' then current in moral allegories and sermon exempla.

The narrative begins with the witless boy who sets off in search of Death merely to see that which men have described as horrible and terrifying. It is related to all the stories associated with ATU 326, 'The youth who wanted to learn what fear is.' But it belongs simultaneously to a darker mode of meeting Death as the result of a misguided quest. Unlike Chaucer's revellers, however, Flamminio is not out to settle a score because Death has slain one of his mates. Yet the protagonists in both stories ask of the pious and aged they meet along the way whether they are Death, only to be pointed further down the road where Death in some form awaits Everyman. Flamminio, likewise, crosses a landscape that becomes increasingly allegorical. His penultimate encounter is with a hermit who preaches to him all the characteristics of death: the loss of family and loved ones, along with life itself, leaving only the body to putrefaction and decay. This is weighty matter. Undaunted, the doltish protagonist struggles forward to the point of despair in seeking that which is ironically his own terror and destruction. These features are squarely in the medieval fool and morality traditions. But in the final meeting, Straparola's story returns to folklore, for the hideous old hag with her sword and club is not only 'Life' and a life force with her unguents and medications, but a remote ancestor to the princess who carries the waters of life and death – she who can slay both princes and kings and resuscitate only those whom she desires. Thus, Straparola's powerful sermon exemplum on the horrors of death comes down to a bit of strategic therapy on the part of this old woman who can show Death to the hero by cutting off his head, but who can make him experience and acknowledge its horrors only by placing the head on backwards.[120] His new perception of himself through the disorientation pertaining to his own anatomy is not a powerful revelation, but suffices to make the protagonist return to Ostia now anxious to embrace life and shun death, as though he had experienced a profound spiritual awakening. Such a conclusion is incongruous, however, in light of the diminished intellect upon which his entire peregrination is based.

This strange commingling of morality and folk tale elements accounts for the story's remarkable depth, yet leaves it somehow less than satisfactory. Viewed from the folk perspective, Straparola replicates the many

---

120 Fantasies of severed and replaced heads go back to antiquity, whether to chilling or comic effect. A story in *The Katha sarit sagara or Ocean of the Streams of Story*, trans. C.H. Tawney (1889; reprint, Calcutta: Munshiram Manoharlal, 1992), vol. II, pp. 261–4, in the section of bk. XII that constitutes *The Twenty-five Tales of a Vampire* (Vetala), the sixth story, tells of a woman who has lost both brother and husband to beheadings. She hears a voice telling her to replace their heads and that through the power of the goddess of the temple where the men had sacrificed themselves they would be brought back to life. In her haste, however, she places them on the wrong bodies, raising the problem of just who, then, was her husband. It almost reads like a mind experiment in a modern study of the brain, the body, and the self. In the ten-volume edition published in Delhi by Motilal Banarsidass (1923), the story is in vol. VI, pp. 203–8.

popular tales of knuckleheads who lack the brains to be frightened and thus bully their way through every terror they meet in near-trickster fashion. There is a rich legacy of such stories about German *Buben* who sleep in churches, play at ninepins with devils, and make light of every imaginable Hallowe'en situation, coming to their rewards in the end through an unimaginable indifference to things that go thud in the night. In their 'heroic' insouciance to fear, such heroes become instruments not of existential discoveries concerning the deepest anxieties, but for trivializing the world of noises, hobgoblins, creeping corpses, and menacing supernaturals in the childish imagination. At the same time, Straparola recreates the sombre and ironic quest for Death that can only be resolved in death itself for the protagonist, or in some ritual form of death whereby he is brought to a state of fear and understanding. The fear factor associated with death becomes the common feature that draws these two story types together. The double purposes of teaching fear to a fool through his search for Death and of confirming Life through a near-death experience are thereby advanced in parallel, but never arrive at a perfect aesthetic and thematic harmony.

There are reasons, nevertheless, why the story is also satisfactory. It is a deft illustration of the way in which humans have attributed intentional stances to the mysterious and powerful elements of their life environment, granting to them the properties of being that allow us to see them, talk to them, and, in that way, perhaps gain some control over them. There is a form of animism in Flamminio's laughably simplistic assumption that Death, in order to have agency in the world, must have not only beliefs and desires, but a physical being that can be met in the material world. It is a profoundly human way of thinking, a form of personification run wild as a prelude to cognitive computations about the nature of things. Flamminio simply could not imagine Death as a condition of the body from which life has been extracted. His quest for Death is conducted as a protagonist who is both computationally limited and at the same time fearless – a personality configuration that provides him with his unique view of the material and spiritual world. This missing instinct leaves him an idiot savant of sorts whose destiny it is to progress through a semi-allegorical landscape of hermits, monsters, and hags, not to mention dark and cavernous vales and mystical cities, in search of that which will startle his emotional brain. Always the test is equivocal, insofar as the mastery of fear is a marker of heroism while at the same time its possession is the beginning of wisdom. There is real force in the vision. Fear, especially of death, gives birth to theism and all that such systems can offer by way of future security, often at the cost of rendering service and sacrifice to deities. The absence of fear would seem to liberate the hero, to grant to him automatically the power to 'be,' even without courage. But a second truth interposes itself: that the discovery of 'life' arrives only after the knowledge that comes with the felt quality of fear. Straparola's story of fearless Flamminio leaps over the trivial encounters with ghosts in the night and trickster sextons who affix skeletons on bell ropes in order to progress directly towards a meeting with that which most terrifies the instinctual self: the loss of its own being. This is the quest of a Sir Gawain who has played beheading games at court with a Green Knight on the condition that he must subject his own neck to a similar blow a year hence. That story too is based on fear – not that which Gawain could not feel, but that which he must master in order to complete his entente. He too must venture to meet death and in the process find a form of self-understanding that so shocks his sensibilities that he never regains spiritual composure or complacency. Gawain's head is not severed, but nicked in ritual fashion. Such a near-death encounter may not be as remote in its significance from Straparola's tale as it would at first appear.

It is in relation to these two states, life and death, that the self orients its own most basic desires and drives. Those who counselled Flamminio sought to dissuade him from seeking death in his naïve way because it was tantamount to a wish, a desire for extinction. The story projects this category confusion upon a landscape, another fundamental construct of the mind that envisions the passage of biological time as the traversing of emblematic spaces. The hermit speaks of redeeming his time in prayer and mortification of the flesh in relation to the time after time, which is easily superimposed upon the mountains and forests to be crossed before Death is met. That the hero should be horrified by the existential contemplation of his own protuberant buttocks is difficult to evaluate as a closural strategy. The boy without fear, unimpressed even by the monster he meets along the way, takes fright at his own anatomy through a redeployment of the old folk motif of the double beheading. Humour and irony prevail around the questioning of the simpleton. Nevertheless, in the descriptive portraits of the cobbler, hermit, and old crone, the tale achieves a remarkable homiletic power. They are archetypal figures of work, prayer, and healing who perform in this relatively slight narrative of questing, fear, ritual death, and resurrection. There is something starkly true in asking the old palsy-stricken creature if she is Death, thereby drawing readers into the profoundly significant 'misrepresentations' of the allegorical mode in which abstractions, by definition, walk as persons.

By the time the story reaches Straparola, it has passed through many constructional phases of which mere traces remain, making his all the more precious as one of the few Renaissance survivors of this medieval legacy. As stated above, it would appear to be a pastiche of folk and allegorical elements in an unstable alignment, now struggling to retain its power as a meditation on death in the tradition of the medieval sermon and the *timor mortis* aroused by the Black Death. That tradition, handed over to the folk narrator, posed real challenges in meeting such heavy demands. When the folk tale hero, characterized by his fearlessness, undertakes the quest of the spiritual pilgrim en route to his final destiny, the two teleologies create an inevitable dissonance. Flamminio is destined to meet both death and fear in a folklorish way, yet never to experience a dark night of the soul or to embrace in his own person some version of the deep Romantic life force.[121]

Chaucer's moving relation of the story of the revellers and the old man that constitutes 'The Pardoner's Tale' is not entirely free of the same

121 Of necessity banished to a footnote are further musings about the absence of the neurobiological competence in this protagonist to manifest fear responses in the presence of 'emotionally competent stimuli' (ECS), to use the terminology of Antonio Damasio, *Looking for Spinoza: Joy, Sorrow, and the Feeling Brain* (Orlando, FL: Harcourt, 2003), p. 53. But the story is, ultimately, a thought experiment in that regard and not a case study, for the fear response is primal and predates the development of the cerebral cortex and all rational faculties in its preparation of the organism to deal with menacing contingencies in its environment; hence it is rarely lacking even in the dumbest among us. Fear may be partially conditioned, but its fundamental salience as a mid-brain response mechanism is architecturally basic and a sine qua non of survival. Nevertheless, as an identifiable emotion, the imaginative writer (or reciters in the oral tradition) could attempt a narrative such as this one, in which an engagement with the social world is depicted in the absence of fear. Because the avoidance of death is fear's ultimate purpose, moreover, there is an apt sense in which a fear response becomes synonymous with the initial death quest, thereby making sense of a narrative in which absolute fear replaces an encounter with the finality of death; the transfer allows for the protagonist's survival. With the completion of the experience, something like the homeostasis of full humanity is restored. But it is an odd literary inquest into the constitution of the subliminal regulatory systems of the body, a fantasy in which a severe emotional handicap is equated with deficient intelligence. Yet the story, as a modern allegory, is a reminder that primal emotions remain a part of our full complement of neurobiological wisdom in relation to relevant stimuli in the environment.

dilemma. His *récit* is set in motion when three revellers, desensitized by drink and devil-may-care attitudes, go in search of Death. They are moved by the imminent reality of sudden death when one of their buddies suddenly expires; in the stupor of their category confusion they too go in search of a personified cause. They engage with an elder, tapping on Mother Earth to gain entry, whom they take for Death until he persuades them otherwise, as in each of Flamminio's encounters with the aged and withered. This much the two stories clearly have in common. Chaucer, too, in sending barroom brawlers to ironic deaths, follows the order of the constitutionally fearless who, in their searches, experience the transition from things figurative to actual fact. However, at the moment Chaucer's old man points the three revellers towards Death by indicating a pile of gold under an old oak at the end of a crooked path, the two stories take their divergent ways. Chaucer here invokes a well-known story originating in the *Jataka* of the robbers who divide themselves into groups to raise their percentage of the spoils by plotting death to each other, causing all to perish in the process.[122] Straparola, by contrast, in the meeting with the old lady with club, sword, and medications, draws upon an entirely separate story tradition. She re-enacts the tale of the twice-severed head and double restoration through her magic potions, causing the protagonist to experience 'monstrification,' to coin a term, followed by restoration to his normal state. That tale has been traced throughout Europe by the nineteenth-century folklorists. But by

122 For Chaucer's 'The Pardoner's Tale' I have turned to the edition by Albert C. Baugh, *Chaucer's Major Poetry* (New York: Appleton-Century-Crofts, 1963), pp. 490–500. It is, of course, widely available in several editions. Baugh points out that the exact version employed by Chaucer has not been found, but that it relates to tales – undoubtedly of Eastern origin with regard to the killing and poisoning of the revellers – that have cognate versions in the *novelle* and sermon exempla of the period (p. 490). For these, see W.F. Bryan and Germaine Dempster, eds., *Sources and Analogues of Chaucer's Canterbury Tales* (Chicago: University of Chicago Press, 1940). Morlini tells the tale in his *Novelle* (Naples, 1520), in which a wizard learns that a treasure lies beneath the Tiber. When the party goes to fetch it, however, the members divide up, some going to the city, the others remaining to guard the treasure. These two groups then conspire against each other, the one party killing the members of the other by force before eating the poisoned food brought to them. Of other stories in this tradition (not connected to our present tale), see a series of articles in *Notes and Queries*, series VII, vol. I (March 6, 1886), pp. 182*ff* by W.A. Clouston entitled 'Oriental Sources of Some of Chaucer's Tales.' For the earliest version in the *Vedabbha Jataka*, see the translation by C.H. Tawney in *Journal of Philosophy*, II (1883), pp. 203–8.

dint of Straparola's use of it, the story must also have been current as a folk tale in the sixteenth century.

Before turning to those popular tales of severed heads and fearless Hans, there is reason to linger over the question of Chaucer's sources, because the version the closest to his tale, entitled 'The Hermit, Death, and the Robbers,' appears in the Giunti edition of the *Novelle Antiche*, Florence, 1572, where it replaces the older version of No. 82 (or 83).[123] A hermit lies down in a cave, whereupon he sees a pile of money. He then takes to flight and when robbers see him running they ask him what he fears. He says he is being pursued by Death. They then demand to see Death, which the hermit has personified in his moral zeal, creating allegory out of his primordial terror. He, like Chaucer's pious old man, points them in the direction of the money. There the robbers laugh at his ignorance and simplicity, but of course fall prey to their own double-crossing greed and thereby make truth of the hermit's fearful intimations. The publication of this tale in Straparola's own time and geographical vicinity does not imply a direct relationship, but it signals the currency of a story type involving a quest for Death that goes back to the fourteenth century. None reveals the overlay of the folklore motifs evident in Straparola pertaining to fearless boys or severed heads. That amalgamation can only be engineered in reverse from Straparola's own story.

An early trace of a life-restoring herb such as that employed to resuscitate Flamminio appears in the 'Lai of Eliduc' among the *Lais* of Marie

123 The Giunti version is much older, however, for it appears in the third section of the MS. Panciatichiano 32, dating to 1330–40, included in the supplementary section of the *Novellino e conti del duecento*, ed. Sebastiano Lo Nigro (Turin: Unione Tipografico-editrice, 1968), pp. 392–4. Lo Nigro cites fifteenth-century versions (p. 392, note), one of which is in *Exempla aus Handschriften des Mittelalters*, ed. Joseph Klapper (Heidelberg: C. Winter, 1911), no. 98. This is one of the undoubtedly many representations of the story among the sermon exempla of the age which inspired Chaucer's opening motif of the quest for Death. The original version in the *Novellino*, ed. Lo Nigro, pp. 189–90, is a Christianized rendition of the ancient Eastern tale in which Christ, out walking with his disciples, sees a great treasure. The disciples seek the treasure, naturally, and Christ warns them away from that which deprives the Kingdom of so many souls. He promises future confirmation. The gold is later found by two companions who, for their greed, murder each other in the now-familiar way. Christ then returns with his disciples to show them how greed leads to death. It is very much in the sermon exemplum tradition, given the manner in which 'the Enemy' works in the thoughts of the two companions. See *The Novellino*, trans. Roberta L. Payne (New York: Peter Lang, 1995), p. 120.

de France. It is a tale of illicit love that produces the most delicate of reticences and sympathies. The married knight, Eliduc, has a beloved who is discovered by his own wife lying on the altar of a hermitage in a deathlike swoon. Meanwhile, a weasel appearing from beneath the altar is slain by a servant. A second weasel then appears, goes in search of a healing herb, returns, and places it in the dead creature's mouth, whereupon it returns to life. When the herb is appropriated, it proves to have the same virtues for the lady, who is thereby restored to life.[124] Closer to Straparola's tale is yet another from the MS. Panciatichiano 32, dating to the first half of the fourteenth century, which tells of a rich man, comfortable in all the ways of the world, who lacked only an encounter with the 'ire of God.'[125] Thus begins his curious quest in which he meets two serpents, one of which bites off the head of the other, which is then restored through the miraculous powers of an herb, as in the *lai* of Marie. What they had witnessed in the serpent beheading, opines the servant, is the result of God's wrath. They then go in search of the herb and make tests of its powers. In the final episode, the protagonist has his own head severed, but grows menacing and angry when he discovers the erroneous positioning of its replacement. His servant admits that it came out all wrong, which weighs upon him greatly, and offers as a remedy to remove it a second time and replace it as it was at first. With this, the master declares that he has never felt such sorrow, which could be no less than God's wrath. And so he returns to his house wiser from his evil venture. In this tale, we may have as much as the record retains of medieval tales of ultimate quests into the secrets of God's nature, predicated on illogical assumptions that lead directly to a beheading ritual and the reversed replacement of the head. This tale has no extended allegorical landscape, no personifications of ire, or encounters with supernatural beings. It progresses from the motif of the healing animals to self-inflicted dangers which become, in the protagonist's mind, tantamount to an encounter with God's wrath, just as Flamminio's faulty restoration was his equivalent to a meeting with Death. Much separates this austere fourteenth-century morality, complete with closing proverb, from Straparola's more elaborate

124 *The Lais of Marie de France*, trans. Glyn S. Burgess and Keith Busby (Harmondsworth: Penguin, 1986), pp. 111–26. Weasels in medieval lore were associated with the herb of life.

125 From the MS. Panciatichiano 32, the final section, transcribed by Sebastiano Lo Nigro in his edition of the *Novellino* [*sic*] *e conti del duecento* (Turin: Unione Tipografico-editrice, 1968), no. CXLV, pp. 378–80.

tale, but given its narrative design there may be no closer literary source. Straparola's had to have been drawn from this narrative tradition.

Stith Thompson speaks briefly of the type of tale already familiar from the Livoretto group in which a princess in possession of the water of life will behead the hero to make him more handsome, thereby inciting an old king to attempt the same, only to be deprived of the healing powers of the water. These may be juxtaposed with quests for death that lead to beheading as an initiation rite or a spring ritual of death and resurrection. Such stories tie in with those already alluded to in the Arthurian Cycle pertaining to green knights and the obligation to receive blow for blow in contexts surrounded by mystery and fear. These in turn join in with 'The youth who wanted to learn what fear is,' creating a cupboard full of interrelated motifs.[126] Thompson describes more fully those in which the fearless hero inhabits haunted houses, plays at bowls with giants, and re-kills dead men attempting to escape from coffins. In some versions, the hero overcomes the most terrifying of situations only to be frightened to death by his own shadow, an eel put down his back, or a bird issuing from a loaf of bread, much as Flamminio fears the sight of his own buttocks. A few of the many may be summarized to profile the type, although Thompson concludes that 'in exactly this form the story does not have any early literary treatments.' Much as we are looking forward from the sixteenth century, he looks back to Straparola's 'Flamminio' as the type's earliest predecessor, citing at the same time an Icelandic saga in which the protagonist makes a similar journey to find out what anger is (completing the circle with the 'ire of God' tales).[127] He is confident of the European provenance of this story, which is unknown in either Asia or Africa.

Vestiges of this generic tale are evident in the dimwittedness of Straparola's hero, his lowly origins, the naïveté with which he poses his questions, the indifference with which he meets imposing or frightening persons, the categorical stupidity of his quest, and the final response to

126 Stith Thompson, *The Folktale* (1946; reprint, Berkeley: University of California Press, 1977), p. 105. Among the more recent tales gathered in India by Maive Stokes is that of 'Loving Laití' which concludes with the restoration of the prince's severed head by his wife using her own blood as a healing elixir. *Indian Fairy Tales* (London: Ellis & White, 1880), no. 14, pp. 73–84.

127 Thomson's reference for this is Bolte-Polívka, I, 32, and 37, by which he means Johannes Bolte and Jiří Polívka, *Anmerkungen zu den Kinder- und Hausmärchen der Brüder Grimm* (Hildesheim: G. Olm [1913], 1963), vol. I, pp. 32, 37.

his beheading adventure in merely being frightened of his own posterior. If they existed in his prototype, Straparola has suppressed any episodes involving sextons, corpses, sassing devils, reckless wagers, and haunted buildings, although these may all have been invented later. These are the features of folk tales seeking to outdo one another in instilling fright.

Laura Gonzenbach collected one such tale, entitled 'The Fearless Young Man,' in which the young trickster hero is sent to his brother-in-law the priest to be frightened. The priest arranges for a friend to be carried into the church as though dead, commanding his nephew to keep watch. In the middle of the night, the dead man lifts an arm – whereupon the hero tells him to be quiet – and then a leg. In danger of a beating from the boy, the impersonator of death flees the church. In a subsequent episode there are skulls with candles and skeletons attached to the bell cord that the boy is ordered to pull, and in another he strikes the old man who was destined to frighten him in the dark. The uncle gives up and a second segment begins as the hero sets off in the night to travel the world. He meets robbers and manages to frighten them and so capture their booty, then beats them when they return.[128] This boy learns nothing because he remains impervious to fear to the very end. The fear instinct is simply missing and thus becomes the decisive feature that determines the protagonist's relationship to the world.

A closely related tale was collected by Giuseppe Pitrè in *Novelle popolari toscane*. This protagonist is more foolish than most, for in every instance in which he is requested to act, he responds with such questions as, 'What are lights? What is a church? Whatever you say I'll do, I fear nothing.'[129]

---

128 *Beautiful Angiola: The Great Treasury of Sicilian Folk and Fairy Tales Collected by Laura Gonzenbach*, trans. Jack Zipes (New York: Routledge, 2004), pp. 81–4. It also appears in the original collection of Laura Gonzenbach, *Sicilianische Märchen aus dem Volksmund gesammelt* (Leipzig: Wilhelm Engelmann, 1870), no. 57, vol. II, pp. 1–4.

129 'Giovannino senza paura' (Fearless Little John), in *Novelle popolari toscane* (Rome: Società editrice de libro italiano, [1941]), no. 39, pp. 257–9. Also (Florence: A. Forni, 1981). The versions in Italo Calvino's *Italian Folktales* are worth mentioning, but are less specific than usual, for in the case of no. 1, 'Dauntless Little John,' Calvino confesses to taking bits and pieces from several versions – although his principal inspiration seems to be from the Florentine story collected by Pitrè, cited above. Typically, the story ends when Little John is given an unguent for reattaching heads, allows his own to be severed, and then dies of fright in seeing his own posterior. Not pleased with this ending, Calvino takes over the one from the Sienese version collected by Angelo De Gubernatis, 'Giovannino senza paura,' in *Novelline di Santo Stefano* (Turin: Negro, 1869), no. 22, p. 46, in which the

This tale for a moment has overtones of Straparola's 'Cassandrino the Master Thief' (I.2) when the sacristan lowers a basket while asking who wants to see the kingdom of heaven. The boy climbs in but then cuts the rope. It ends, tellingly, with an instrument that will cut off heads in an instant and an unguent that will heal them. When the hero undergoes the adventure, his head is replaced 'davanti di dietro,' which so frightens him that he runs into the streets shouting 'I am dead, I am dead.' He then reports to his uncle that he has known true fear and therefore death as well. Then his uncle restores his head to its proper position. Of all the modern folk tales, none will come closer to Straparola's in its generic ethos of the fearless boy who at last meets both fear and death in a double head-severing ritual. Whether this story owes its origins to Straparola or the folk tradition which inspired him is a moot point, but it has shed much of the sober medieval fear, the sermonizing hermit, and the allegorical landscape.[130]

---

protagonist is frightened by his own shadow. This is a light story of terrifying encounters with spirits and wraiths. When it is Giovannino's turn, however, the boy jokes, plays, and sits down to dinner with them without a moment of fear until the enchantment is broken and he inherits the castle and all its wealth. It is then that he marries, lacks for nothing, yet one day dies of fright from seeing his own shadow. The Calvino reference is to the edition translated by George Martin and published in New York by Pantheon Books (1980), pp. 3–4. A second story in the group is no. 80, 'Fearless Simpleton,' pp. 294–5. It does not get beyond bashing the reanimated corpse with a blunt object to keep him as dead as the simpleton thinks he should be. Another such was collected by Carolina Coronedi-Berti, 'La fola d' Zanòn sèinza poura,' in *Favole bolognesi* (Bologna: Arnaldo Forni, 1981), no. 33, pp. 132–4. This little hero, too, after many intrepid adventures in spooky palaces, upon seeing his head cut off and installed backwards, dies of fear.

130 This story has its consonances with the story from the *Novellino e conti del duecento* concerning the wrath of God, and with the variant collected by Nerucci, 'Giovannino insenza paura,' in *Sessanta novelle montalesi*, ed. Roberto Fedi (Milan: Rizzoli [1891], 1977), no. 44, pp. 363–6. This is another in the tradition of the boy who recoils at nothing, even in strange places in the middle of the night. When the others come singing the misereri, thinking to find him dead, they find the contrary and chant 'Bravo Giovannino.' In a second sequence, he allows his head to be cut off, but when it is set on backwards and he contemplates his rear end, he becomes so frightened that he drops down dead and so his adventures come to a close. See Sebastiano Lo Nigro, *Racconti popolari siciliani: classificazione e bibliografia* (Florence: L.S. Olschi, [1958]), p. 42; and Reinhold Köhler's annotations to Gonzenbach's *Sicilianische Märchen* (Leipzig: W. Engelmann, 1870), vol. II, pp. 237–8.

Much of this lore clearly passed through France, as well, for there is a longer version of the tale, 'Yann the Fearless' (Yann heb aon), that is a virtual medley of these motifs. It was collected as late as 1953 on the Côtes du Nord. This little hero is also an orphan who is assigned to the keeping of a priest who locks him up for punishment in a spooky church; here he blusters about unfazed, even upon hearing the confession of a dead priest. He keeps a stole that will make him entirely fearless, although the trait already appears to be innate. In the next episode he is in an ancient, ruined castle for the night, where he offers to sleep in the room from which no one returns. The boy negotiates with the restless wraith and locates the money he has stolen. Yann then goes on his way without taking a reward. Subsequently, he experiences the body parts falling down the chimney with which, unperturbed, he plays at skittles. When the parts come back to life as the Devil, he sasses him and eventually compels him to sign a non-aggression pact by nearly strangling him with the magic stole. The story progresses in the direction of romance with girls offered to him in marriage in gratitude for his exploits, but Yann is in search of something else: true fear. More episodes follow in which he rescues the king's daughter from the Devil, splashing his adversary all the while with holy water. He then forces the Devil to make him handsome. Finally, the princess, eager for marriage, takes matters into her own hands and places a blackbird in the middle of a loaf of bread which she hands to Yann to eat. When the bird flies out, the boy is truly frightened for the first time and thus, knowing at last what real fear is, he is ready for marriage and a most cautious life ever after, because fear has become a part of his emotional registry. The many motifs corresponding to stories from the past place this creation in a direct line of descent from the ancient tradition of folk tales about the boy who knew no fear, sometimes to the end, and sometimes only until a trivial fright stuns or kills him. The editor, Geneviève Massignon, posits that the first European version was given by Grimm at the beginning of the nineteenth century, yet goes on to cite the *Mémoires* of Roger de Rabutin, written in the years just before his death in 1693, who tells of the old tales about frightening dinners served up by strangers, and of body parts falling down the chimney to form people who disappear after drinking or revealing a secret.[131] The hero 'sans peur' tales clearly enjoyed a substantial European

131 *Les mémoires de messier Roger de Rabutin, Conte de Bussy*, 2 vols. (Amsterdam: Henry de Lourme, 1699), vol. I, pp. 76–7.

tradition going back not only to the seventeenth century, but to the Middle Ages.[132]

The best of the folk tradition concerning fearless fools and their trickster exploits is to be found in Germany, from whence only a few samples must suffice for the many. In *Deutsche Hausmärchen,* assembled by J.W. Wolf in the mid-nineteenth century, are to be found two of the most representative: 'Hans ohne Fürst' and 'Fürchten lernen' (Fearless Hans, and Fear to be learned).[133] Elements in both are already familiar. In the first, a fearless cobbler's son is sent to the priest, who turns him over to the sacristan to frighten him. Now there are black men who appear in the church at midnight and toss down skulls, but the boy merely joins in the sport. More of the same Hallowe'en fare takes place in the bell tower on the following night. On the third night there are nine black men who throw down spheres. The hero plays at ninepins with them, sasses them about, and refuses to send the money he owes. Ultimately, he comes to a great quantity of gold which he divides between the priest, the sacristan, and himself before taking to the road. There follows a long sequence involving his exploits in the army and a romance closure in which Hans may keep his princess bride by liberating a haunted mill just outside the city, intended as a suicide mission as in the Livoretto and Costanza stories. Of course, he prevails over the devil with the long nose, treating him as insignificant and disempowering him by his brash bargaining and indomitable nature. Hans does not encounter Death, but banishes Fear on behalf of all who are intimidated by sprites, devils, and goblins. 'Fürchten lernen' deals more directly with the need

132 *Folktales of France,* ed. Geneviève Massignon, trans. Jacqueline Hyland (London: Routledge & Kegan Paul, 1968), pp. 3–8, 247. The edition mentions additional versions in Corsica, elsewhere in France, and in the New World.

133 *Deutsche Hausmärchen* (Göttingen: Dieterich'sche Buchhandlung, 1851), pp. 328–9, 408–16. The story was known as far away as Iceland where it was collected by Jón Arnason. The boy is taken to the parish priest, but his night in the church has no effect. During subsequent wandering he encounters many other ghoulish adventures. He deals casually with the giant that falls into the kitchen and with a goblin that breaks in half and recedes into the ground; he sleeps in dangerous beds and witnesses the resuscitation of slain warriors with the contents of a phial. His response to this final adventure is to kill the healer and the men who had returned to life. In the final episode he participates in a beheading game in which he finds his own replaced backwards, which consumes him with fear until the error is rectified. His story runs true to form. 'The Boy Who Did Not Know What Fear Was,' in *Icelandic Legends,* trans. George E.J. Powell and Eiríkur Magnússon (Felinfach: Llanerch Publishers [1864], 1995), pp. 161–70.

to learn fear, which the foolish farmer's son is never taught by his schoolmaster. Peter, too, is locked in churches overnight, there to deal with demons and the dead who come back to life. More black men appear from behind the altar and Peter treats them as friends. Then the sinister bowling resumes, but the hero looks upon his adversaries as minor nuisances, reporting back to the schoolmaster that he never felt a moment's fear. He too is sent into the wider world where he meets a swineherd. They end up in a castle kitchen and are taken as intruders by the Devil himself. He offers to join in their repast, but they send him out to get his own food. When he fails to catch anything, it is attributed to the length of his claws, which Peter offers to trim. Contests are proposed, the castle is explored, three black ladies are reconverted to princesses, more tricks are played on the Devil, and Peter ends up with wealth, castle, and all, never having learned what fear is. In ethos and design, they are remote from Straparola's tale, yet participate in the folk tradition that supplied Flamminio with his generic nature.

Two others may be mentioned in passing: 'Der Fürchten zu lernen,' entitled in English 'The King's Son who Feared Nothing,' from the Grimm Brothers' *Kinder- und Hausmärchen* (1857); and 'For Three Shillings' from *Danish Fairy Tales.*[134] In the first, the king's son meddles with the giants' bowling game and brazens it out with his boasting, so they send him on a death mission to fetch the apple from the tree of life in a magical and protected garden. He too encounters a grand and potentially allegorical landscape before entering the garden by stepping over beasts, thrusting his arm through a menacing ring and grasping the fruit. The ring gives him such powers, however, that he can now get out by tearing the gate off its hinges. The lion follows him home as a pet. The giant takes the apple for his bride but cannot present the ring, fixed on the hero's arm. There is brawling and subterfuge to get it away before the giant blinds the boy. But the trusty lion comes to his rescue until he is healed by the waters of a magic brook. He then turns a black princess white by taking the abuse given him by the imps of the sleepover castle. Fearlessly, he succeeds in this initiation rite and is healed with the water of life in the princess's possession. But this is all now a fairy tale far removed from Straparola. In the Danish tale a fearless soldier gives all

134 *Grimm's Complete Fairy Tales* (Garden City, NY: Nelson Doubleday, n.d.), pp. 441–5; and Sven Grundtvig, *Danish Fairy Tales* (London: G.G. Harrap & Co., 1914), pp. 137–47.

his money to an old crone, down to the last shilling, and for that earns three wishes, the last of which is the ability to fill and empty his knapsack by mere thought-power. He too agrees to sleep in a room in an inn from which no one has ever come out alive. There he plays cards with devils and in the end wills them all into his knapsack, which is in turn taken to the forge for pulverizing. And so the story proceeds to the end with rewards aplenty, but no sense of fear ever felt.

Further stories in this vein, of which there are many, would add little more to our purpose, for they bear witness only after the fact to an ancient hero 'senza paura' tradition from which Straparola derived the characterization of his protagonist – if he did not find his entire story already made and circulating among the folk. The equivocal nature of 'Flamminio' as a story is that it is either a medieval moral exemplum in the process of losing its chilling force through the contamination of popular culture, or the budding folk tale of fearless Hans shedding its late medieval encumbrances. As it comes to us in the *Piacevoli notti*, however, the tale proposes that the double beheading and the quest for Death motifs share in a common thematic cause, with the morality ethos dominating the lighter folk tale of careless adventure in the spirit of Poggio or Hans Sachs. Once again, Straparola provides us with the earliest version in the literary record of a story type at an early stage in its transmigration from a medieval exemplum to a popular folk tale, with certain of the heterodox traits still in apposition. It is a curious feature that after so many shocking adventures, something banal and familiar – a strange corruption of the body or a surprise from nature – suffices to reorient an entire limbic system, as though restoring a missing circuit, thereby reducing the undaunted trickster hero to the conventional proportions of humanity. The young protagonist would seem to benefit from the absence of incapacitating emotions imposed by the processes of evolutionary selection upon phylogenetic humankind, yet these limitations are precisely the object of the boy's quest. Just which phase in the integration of the human psyche this Jungian tale illustrates remains open to speculation, but in spirit it is very old indeed, as though going back to the earliest phases of reflexive, emotionally invigilated consciousness.

The Fifth Night

The sun – the glory of the shining firmament, the measurer of fleeting time, and the true eye of the universe from which the horned moon and all the stars receive their radiance – had now hidden his ruddy and resplendent rays beneath the briny waters of the sea, and the chaste daughter of Latona, environed round by bright and beaming stars, was already lighting up the dim shadows of dusky night. The shepherds, leaving the wide and open fields, the fresh herbage, and the cool and limpid streams, had returned with their flocks to their folds and, worn out and weary as they were, had sunk into deep slumber on their beds of fair, fresh rushes, when the gallant and noble company hurried back to their meeting place. Once it had been made known to the Signora that everyone had arrived and that it was time to recommence the storytelling, she smiled and went along joyfully to the salon with a soft and measured step, most courteously and reverently escorted by the other ladies. Then, having graciously greeted the company of friends with a gladsome face, she asked them to bring out the vase of gold. Into this were placed the names of five ladies, and of these the first lot fell to Eritrea, the second to Alteria, the third to Lauretta, the fourth to Arianna, and the last to Cateruzza. This done, in slow measure they all began to dance in a circle to the music of the delightful flutes, conversing the while in pleasant and charitable words. With the Signora's permission, when the dance ended, three damsels began the following canzona.

Madonna, when the springs of passion rise,
And through thy fair sweet bosom surge and swell;
In those most lucent sacred eyes,
Is the power to raise my life or quell;
From those genial looks and kind,
A gracious hope my longings find.
Now calm, and now spurred on by rage,
With hope and fear a fight I wage.
In time my hope the vantage gains,
And I am rid of all my pains,
And know no stroke of fate can lure,
Or drive me from my course secure.

Wherefore I bless the passing days;
Great nature, and the stars I praise,
That thy fair self my passion fired,
Thy service sweet my song inspired.

As soon as the three damsels had brought to an end their amorous canzonet, which seemed to break up the air around into sighs of passion, Eritrea, designated the first to speak on that evening, received from the Signora a sign that she should begin her tale. Having no grounds to excuse herself, and mindful not to break the established order, the maiden put aside all signs of reluctance and so began.

V. Fable 1
Guerrino and the Wild Man of the Woods

ERITREA

Guerrino, the only son of Filippo Maria, king of Sicily, sets free a wild man of the woods from his father's prison. His mother, through fear of the king, sends her son into exile, and the wild man, now humanized, delivers the boy from many pressing ills.

I have heard by report, and also gathered from my own experiences, most gracious ladies, that a kindly service done to another – even when the identity of the benefactor is unknown – more often than not will return multiple benefits to the giver. This happened to the son of a king who, having liberated from one of his father's prisons a wild man of the woods, was more than once rescued from a violent death by the captive he had freed. This will be made clear by the present tale. And because I care for you all, I exhort you never to be slow in aiding others, because, even though you may not be repaid by those you have helped, God Himself, who rewards all things, will never allow a good deed to go unrewarded, but will make you partakers with Him of His divine grace.

My dear ladies, as you all must know, Sicily is in itself a most fertile and self-sufficient island and surpasses all other islands of antiquity, with its towns and villages adding an even greater beauty. In past times, the lord of this island was a king named Filippo Maria, a man wise, amiable, and of rare virtue, who was married to a courteous, winsome, and lovely lady, the mother of his only son, Guerrino. The king took greater delight in the hunt than any other man in the country and for that reason he was strong and robust, for this recreation was well suited to him.

Now it happened one day as he was returning from the hunt in the company of various barons and sportsmen that he saw a wild man coming out of a thick wood so tall, deformed, and ugly that they all stared at him with amazement. For strength, he didn't seem a bit inferior to any of them, wherefore the king, preparing himself to do battle, boldly attacked him, together with two of the most valiant of his barons. After a long and vigorous struggle they overcame him and took him prisoner. Having bound him, they then conveyed him back to the palace, where they kept him guarded and in close confinement under lock and key according to the king's commandment. And because the king prized his captive so greatly, he ordered that the keys to the prison be held in charge by the queen, thereafter never letting a day pass without going to visit the wild man by way of pastime.

Before many days had gone by, the king once more prepared himself for the chase. When all the provisions were in readiness, he set out with a gallant company of courtiers, entrusting to the queen's care the keys to his prisons. During his absence, Guerrino, who was then still a young lad, felt a great desire to see this wild man of the woods. So all alone, with his bow in hand in which he took great delight, he went to the prison grating behind which the monster dwelt. When he saw the wild man, he began to converse with him in a familiar way. As they were talking along, the creature, cajoling and flattering the boy, most dexterously snatched the richly ornamented arrow from his hand. Then the lad began to cry and protest, asking for his arrow back. But the wild man said to him, 'If you will open the door and let me go free from this prison, I will give you back your arrow, but if you refuse, I will not let you have it.'

The boy answered, 'How would you expect me to open the door and set you free, seeing that I haven't the means?'

The wild man continued, 'If you were truly willing to release me and let me out of this narrow cell, I would very soon teach you how it might be done.'

'Then how?' replied Guerrino. 'Tell me the way.'

To which the wild man answered, 'Go to the bedroom of your mother, the queen, and when you see her taking her midday nap, put your hand gently under her pillow and take the keys of the prison, but carefully so she won't notice the theft, and bring them here to open my prison door. When you've done this, I'll give the arrow right back to you and by chance at some time in the future I may be able to reward you even further for your kindness.'

Since he was just a boy, he wanted his arrow back more than anything. So without delay, he ran to his mother and found her asleep. Slowly he reached under her pillow and pulled out the keys, then rushed back to the prison where he said to the wild man: 'Look, here are the keys, but if I let you out of this place, you must go so far from here that no scent of you may be traced, for if my father, who is a great huntsman, should find and capture you again, he's sure to kill you outright.'

'Don't let that bother you, my boy,' said the captive, 'for as soon as you open the prison and set me free, I'll give you back your arrow and get myself into such distant parts that neither your father nor any other man will ever find me.'

Guerrino, who was a very strong lad for his age, laboured at the door and finally managed to throw it open, whereupon the wild man, having returned his arrow, thanked him heartily and went his way.

Formerly this wild man had been a most handsome youth. But because he was unable to win the lady he loved beyond all measure, he abandoned his amorous ways and civilized pursuits and went to live among the beasts of the forest, dwelling ever in the gloomy woods and bosky thickets, eating grass and drinking water in the manner of the animals. On this account, the wretched man had become covered with a great mat of hair, his skin had grown hard, his beard thick, long, and tangled, and all of him green from his diet of herbs and grass – a monstrous sight to behold.

As soon as the queen awoke from her slumbers, she thrust her hand under her pillow to seek the keys, but to no avail. After turning the bed upside down and still not finding them, she was suddenly terrified and ran straight to the prison as though out of her wits. As she feared, she found it standing open. When her search for the wild man proved equally vain, she was so stricken with grief that she thought she would die. Once more at the palace, she searched diligently in every corner, all the while interrogating first one courtier and then another to find out who had been so brazen and presumptuous as to lay hands on the keys to the prison without her knowledge. But one and all declared they knew nothing of the matter. Meeting his mother and seeing her vexed and beside herself, Guerrino said to her, 'Mother, don't blame any of these for opening the prison door, because if some punishment is in order, it must come to me, for I, and I alone, unlocked it.'

When the queen heard these words, she was plunged into deeper sorrow than ever, fearing lest the king, when he came back from the hunt, might kill his son in anger, seeing that he had given the keys into her charge to guard them as preciously as her life. So out of her desire to escape the consequences of a small mistake, the queen now committed a far weightier one. Without more delay, she summoned her son and two of her most trusted servants, provided them with gold, silver, and good horses, and sent the boy out to seek his fortune, while begging the servants most earnestly to take the greatest care of Guerrino.

Hardly had they started on their way before the king came home from the hunt, and dismounting, made straight for the prison to visit the wild man. When he found the door wide and the captive gone, he was inflamed with such violent anger that he vowed to slay whoever it was who had done such a flagrant misdeed. Then he sought out the queen who was sitting in her chamber and commanded her to tell him the name of the impudent, rash, and presumptuous knave who had opened the prison door and let the wild man of the woods escape.

The queen answered him in a trembling voice, 'O, sire, don't be distressed over this thing, because Guerrino our son, according to his own confession to me, is to blame for this.' Then she told the king everything that Guerrino had said to her, and when he had heard the story out, he was incensed with rage. Next she told him that fearing he might slay his own son, she sent the boy away into a far country, accompanied by two of their most faithful servants, bearing with them a store of jewels and money sufficient for their needs. Hearing all this, the king felt one sorrow heaped upon another, at one point nearly falling to the ground, at another nearly losing his wits. Had the courtiers not grabbed and restrained him, most assuredly he would have slain the queen on the spot.

When in time the poor king had recovered a measure of his composure and calmed his rage, he said to the queen, 'Alas, my wife, what fancy took you to send our son, the fruit of our mutual love, away into some foreign land? Is it possible that you imagined I would hold this wild man of greater value than my own flesh and blood?' Without waiting for a reply to these words, he ordered up a great troop of soldiers to mount their horses immediately, to divide themselves into four companies, and to make a close search in an effort to find the prince. But their entire inquest was in vain, for Guerrino and his attendants had journeyed in secret so that no one might know who they were.

Having ridden great distances over mountains and through valleys, staying first one place and then another, Guerrino at last attained his sixteenth year. By this time, he was so fair a youth that he was like nothing if not a fresh morning rose. Yet in the course of time, the servants who accompanied him were seized with the devilish idea of killing him for the cache of jewels and money, intending to share it between themselves. This wicked plot came to nothing only because by God's will they weren't able to come to a mutual agreement. Then by good fortune, a very fair and graceful young man rode by, mounted upon a fine steed with rich accoutrements. This youth bowed and courteously saluted Guerrino, 'Most gracious sir, if it would not displease you, I'd like to ride along with you.'

Guerrino replied, 'With so much politeness in your request, I couldn't possibly refuse the pleasure of your company. Please, then, join us on the road. We're strangers in this country and know little about the highways. Perhaps in this you may be able to direct us. Moreover, as we ride along, we can discuss our adventures and so make the journey less irksome.'

Now this young man was no other than the wild man whom Guerrino had set free from the prison of King Filippo Maria, his father. He had been wandering through various countries and strange lands, and one day by chance had met a beautiful fairy, albeit she was in a sorry state of health. When she looked upon him and saw how misshapen and hideous he was, she laughed so violently at the sight of his ugliness that she burst an abscess that had formed in the vicinity of her heart – a disorder that might well have suffocated her to death. But at that very moment she was delivered from all the pain and suffering from this infirmity and was restored to health, as though her affliction had never existed. In reward for so great a blessing, the good fairy, not wishing to appear ungrateful, said to him, 'Oh you poor creature, so deformed and ugly, because you have restored me to the health I so much desired, you too shall go your way and be transformed from what you are now into the fairest, wisest, and most graceful youth to be found anywhere. More than this, I will share with you all the power and authority conferred upon me by nature, so that you can do anything you might desire.' Then she presented him with a noble fairy horse and gave him leave to go wherever he wished.

Guerrino travelled along with the young man, not knowing who he was, although Guerrino was well known to him. At last they came to a mighty city called Irlanda, at that time ruled over by King Zifroi. This king was the father of two daughters, both very beautiful, modest, and surpassing Venus herself in beauty, the one named Potentiana, the other Eleuteria. The king, their father, held them both so dear that he could in no wise live without them. As soon as Guerrino entered the city of Irlanda with the unknown youth and his train of servants, he took lodging with a certain householder, the wittiest fellow in the entire city, who treated his guests with the best of cheer. On the following day, the unknown youth feigned to have business in another country. Before his departure, he went to thank Guerrino for the benefit of his company and kind treatment. But Guerrino, who felt the strongest love and friendship for him, refused to let him go, showing him such strong evidence of his attachment that, in the end, the young man agreed to stay.

In the countryside around Irlanda, there were two most fearful and savage animals, one of which was a wild stallion and the other a mare of like nature, so ferocious and cruel that they not only ravaged and devastated all the fair cultivated fields, but they also killed domestic animals and the villagers, both men and women. The countryside was in such lamentable condition from the ruin created by these beasts that no one was willing to stay there. The peasants abandoned their farms and houses so dear to them and sought new dwellings in other lands. Nowhere was there a man strong and bold enough to face these marauders, much less to fight and slay them. The king, therefore, seeing that the whole country was increasingly desolate of food, cattle, and humans, and not knowing how to correct this devastation, fell into dolorous lamentations and cursed the evil fortune that had befallen him.

Guerrino's two servants, formerly frustrated in their evil designs by their disagreements, and then by the arrival of the unknown young man, now resumed their scheming over how they might bring about Guerrino's death while holding on to his money and jewels. One said to the other, 'We should confer together on the easiest way to take our master's life.' But they still couldn't hit upon a suitable means without putting their own lives in peril of the law. Finally they decided to speak in secret to the innkeeper, reporting that Guerrino was a young man of great prowess and valour and that often he had boasted in their presence that he could slay the wild stallion without any danger to himself. Thus they reasoned between themselves that, with luck, these thoughts might be passed along to the ears of the king, who was so keen on destroying these two animals and protecting the welfare of his country that he would straightway order Guerrino into his presence to ask of him just how he intended to accomplish this feat. Then Guerrino, not knowing what to say or do, would be put to death by the king and they would remain the sole masters of his jewels and money. Such was the plan they then set into motion.

When the host heard this news, he was delighted – the happiest man in the world – and without losing a minute, he ran as swiftly as he could to the palace, knelt before the king, made his reverence, and said to him privately, 'Sire, I have come to tell you that there is a fair and gallant knight errant presently staying in my hostel named Guerrino. In talking to his servants I found out, among other things, that their master is a man of great prowess and skilled in the use of arms. In times like ours one might search in vain to find another to compare with him. Moreover, on many occasions they heard him boast that with his strength and valour he could easily overcome and slay the wild horse that plays such havoc with your kingdom.'

When King Zifroi heard these words, he commanded that Guerrino be brought to him immediately. The innkeeper, obedient to the king's command, returned at once to his inn and said to Guerrino that he was summoned to appear that instant and alone before the king, who greatly desired to speak to him. Upon hearing this, Guerrino went directly to the palace and presented himself to the king. After saluting him with becoming reverence, he begged to know the reason that he had been honoured by this royal command. King Zifroi replied, 'Guerrino, I have been moved to send for you because I have heard you are a knight of great valour, excelling all other knights now living in the world. They tell me, too, that you have many times declared that you can tame the wild horse that is now laying waste to my kingdom without any risk of injury to yourself or others. If you will undertake this enterprise, I promise to bestow upon you such a gift that you will be happy for the rest of your days.'

Guerrino, upon hearing the king's lofty proposition, was amazed beyond measure, denying at once that he had ever spoken such words as had been attributed to him. Disconcerted at this reply, the king addressed him, 'Guerrino, it is my will that you undertake this task without delay, assuring yourself that if you refuse to comply with my wishes, I will take away your life.' Guerrino returned to his inn overwhelmed with sorrow, which he dared not disclose to anyone. When the unknown youth noticed that Guerrino was plunged into melancholy, he asked the reason why he was so sad and full of grief. By reason of the brotherly love between them, Guerrino found himself unable to refuse so kind and just a request, telling him word for word all that had happened to him.

The unknown youth then said, 'Rouse your spirits and fear for nothing, because I will show you a way to save your life, prevail in your enterprise, and fulfil the king's desire. Go back to the king and beg him to grant you the services of a good blacksmith. Then order this smith to make you four horseshoes thicker and broader by the breadth of two fingers than the ordinary size of horseshoes, to be fitted on the hind hooves with two spikes of a finger's length. Shoe my horse with these, which is enchanted, and then there is nothing more to fear.'

Guerrino returned to the king and told him everything, just as the young man had directed him. The king, summoning a well-skilled marshal smith, gave orders that he should carry out whatever work Guerrino might require of him. When they had gone to the smith's forge, Guerrino instructed him how to make the four horseshoes according to his friend's instructions. But when the smith understood the manner in which he was to make them, he mocked Guerrino and treated him like a madman, for this way of making shoes was entirely foreign to him. When Guerrino saw that the marshal smith was inclined to make fun of him and was unwilling to serve him according to his orders, he returned to the king and complained that the smith would not carry out his instructions. Wherefore, the king asked to have the marshal brought before him, there giving him express command that, under pain of his highest displeasure, he should at once carry out the duties imposed upon him or, failing that, he must himself carry out the perilous task that had been assigned to Guerrino. Hard pressed by the orders of the king, the smith made the horseshoes to Guerrino's specification and therewith shod the horse.

When the shoeing was done and the young stranger's horse was fitted out with everything needed for the adventure, he said to Guerrino, 'Now quickly mount my steed and go in peace. As soon as you hear the neighing of the wild horse, dismount, take off the animal's saddle and bridle, and let him range at will. You yourself should climb into a high tree and there wait for the end of the battle.' Having been instructed by his cherished friend in all that he had to do, Guerrino took his leave and set out with a light heart.

Already the glorious news had spread throughout Irlanda how a valiant and handsome young knight had undertaken to tame and capture the wild horse and present him to the king. For this reason, everyone in the city, men and women alike, flew to their windows to see him pass by on his perilous errand. When they saw how handsome, young, and gallant he was, their hearts were moved to pity on his account, and they said to one another, 'Ah, the poor fellow, going to his death with such a willing spirit. Surely it's a pitiful thing that so valiant a youth should die so miserable a death.' Such compassion they felt that they couldn't hold back their tears.

But Guerrino, full of manly boldness, went blithely on his way, and when he had arrived at the place where the wild horse was most often found, he heard the sound of neighing. Then he dismounted his horse, removed the bridle and saddle and let him go free, himself climbing into the branches of a great oak, there to await the fierce and bloody contest.

No sooner had Guerrino climbed up into the tree than the wild horse appeared and right away attacked the fairy steed, and the ferocity of their fight was beyond imagining. They rushed at one another like two unchained lions, their mouths foaming like those of wild boars pursued by savage hounds. After a long combat, fought with the greatest fury, the fairy charger dealt the feral stallion two kicks full on the jaw, putting it far out of joint. Thus disabled, the wild beast could no longer fight or defend itself. When Guerrino saw this, his joy was complete. Coming down out of the oak, he took a halter brought for the purpose, attached it to the wild horse and, by his broken jaw, led him back to the city. There, amid great rejoicing, the young hero was welcomed by all the people. According to his promise, he bestowed the horse upon the king, who kept high festival with the entire city in celebration of this gallant deed.

Grief and confusion overtook the servants of Guerrino, whose evil designs had completely miscarried. Now more angry and full of hatred than ever, they again brought false word to King Zifroi's ear of Guerrino's boasting – how he would capture or kill the wild mare without the slightest danger. When the king heard this, he placed the very same commands upon Guerrino as he had done regarding the stallion, and when the young man refused to undertake so impossible a task, the king threatened to have him hanged by one foot as a rebel against his crown.

When Guerrino returned to his inn, he told everything to his unknown companion, who broke into a smile, 'My good brother, don't fret yourself over this, but go and find the marshal smith and command him to make four more horseshoes for you as large as the last and see that they are duly equipped with good sharp spikes. Then you must follow exactly the same course as you took with the wild horse and you'll return with greater honour than ever.' So Guerrino ordered the spiked horseshoes to be made and attached to the hooves of the enchanted steed, and then he set out on his gallant mission.

When he arrived at the place where the wild mare might be grazing and heard her neighing, he did exactly as he had done before. When he had set the fairy horse free, the mare advanced and attacked it with such fierce and terrible biting that it could barely defend itself. Bravely it bore the assault and at last succeeded in planting so sharp and dexterous a kick on the mare that she was lamed in her right leg, whereupon Guerrino came down from the high tree, caught her, and bound her tightly. Then he mounted his own horse and rode back to the palace where he presented the savage creature to the king amid the cries and acclamations of all the people. Moved by wonder and curiosity, everyone ran to see this beast, which, on account of the grave injuries received in the fight, died soon after. By these means the country was liberated from this great plague that had vexed it for so long.

Overcome by fatigue, Guerrino returned to his hostel to seek some repose, but he couldn't get to sleep because there was a strange noise somewhere in the room. Rising from his bed, he noticed that there was something, he couldn't tell what, buzzing about inside a pot of honey unable to get out. So Guerrino opened the container and there he found a large hornet struggling to free its wings. Moved to pity, he took hold of the insect and let it go free.

King Zifroi, meanwhile, remembered his promise to reward Guerrino for these two valiant deeds, knowing that disgrace would follow should he break his word. So he had the boy called into his presence and addressed him, 'Guerrino, thanks to your noble deeds the entire kingdom is now free from a terrible scourge. Thus, I intend to reward you for the great benefits you have wrought in our behalf. For this, I can think of no other gift worthy and sufficient for your merits than to give to you one of my two daughters in marriage. The first is called Potentiana, with hair so marvellously braided that it shines like fine gold. The second is called Eleuteria, whose tresses gleam brightly like the finest silver. Once I have them closely veiled, if you can guess which one has the golden tresses, I will give her to you as your wife together with a generous dowry, but if you fail in this I will have your head struck from your shoulders.'

When Guerrino heard the king's cruel proposal, he remonstrated with him saying, 'Your Sacred Majesty! Is this an appropriate reward for all the perils and weariness I've endured? Is this just payment for the strength I've spent on your behalf? Is this the gratitude you give for delivering your country from the scourge that of late made all so desolate? Alas, I've done nothing to deserve such treatment. Truly, this is not a deed worthy of a noble-hearted monarch. But if this is your pleasure, I'm helpless in your hands and you must do with me as you please.'

'Then leave,' said Zifroi, 'and don't linger in my presence. I'll give you until tomorrow to come to your decision.'

After Guerrino left the king's presence, in his sadness he sought his dear companion and told him everything the king had said. The unknown youth hardly seemed troubled by all this, saying, 'Don't be downtrodden, Guerrino, don't despair, for I will deliver you from this great danger. Remember how, a few days ago, you set free the hornet that you found with its wings entangled in the honey? That same hornet will now be the means to save you, for tomorrow after the dinner at the palace when you are put to the test, it will fly three times, buzzing and humming around the head of the girl with the golden hair, which she will drive away with her white hands. When you see her do this three times, you will know for certain that this is the one who will be your wife.'

'Glory be,' cried Guerrino to his companion, 'when will the time come that I'll ever be able to repay you for all the generous things you've done for me? Were I to live for a thousand years, I'll never have it in my power to repay you for the smallest portion of it. But He who redeems us all will surely compensate for my shortfall.'

To this speech, the other replied, 'No, my brother, in truth there is no need for you to trouble yourself about making any return to me for the services I've done you, for the time has come for me to reveal to you just who I am. In the same fashion that you delivered me from death, I, for my part, have desired to render to you the recompense that you so well deserve. Know then, that I am the wild man of the woods whom you, with such loving compassion, set free from the king your father's prison-house, and that I am called Rubinetto.' Then he went on to tell Guerrino the means by which the fairy had brought him back to his former state as a handsome young man. When he heard these words, Guerrino stood like someone in a trance and out of the great tenderness and pity he had in his heart he embraced Rubinetto, weeping the while, kissing him, and claiming him as his own brother.

Forasmuch as the time was now approaching for Guerrino to solve the question set for him by King Zifroi, the two went to the palace. The king then ordered that his two daughters, Potentiana and Eleuteria, should be brought into the presence of Guerrino covered from head to foot with white veils, which was done without delay. When the two daughters appeared looking so much alike that it was impossible to tell the one from the other, the king said, 'Now which of these two, Guerrino, do you wish to have for your wife?'

Guerrino stood still in a state of doubt and hesitation, saying nothing. But the king, eager to bring matters to their conclusion, urged him to speak up, that time was flying, and that it was in his interests to give his answer at once. To this Guerrino replied, 'Sire, time, in truth, may be flying, but the end of the day is still far off, which is the limit you have given to me for my decision.' In this, all who were standing by affirmed that Guerrino was in his rights.

After the king, Guerrino, and all the others had stood for a long time in expectation, behold a hornet suddenly appeared, which at once began to fly and buzz around the head and fair face of Potentiana with the golden hair. As if she were afraid of the creature, she raised her hand to drive it away, and when she had done this three times, the hornet flew away out of sight. Even after this sign, Guerrino remained for a short while uncertain, although he had complete faith in the words of Rubinetto, his well-beloved companion.

Then said the king, 'How now, Guerrino, what do you say? The time has come for you to make up your mind.'

Guerrino, looking closely first at one and then the other of the maidens, put his hand on the head of Potentiana, indicated to him by the hornet, and said, 'Sire, this one is your daughter with the golden tresses.' The maiden then raised her veil and revealed clearly that it was she indeed, to the great joy of all present and to the satisfaction of the people of the city. Zifroi the king gave her to Guerrino for his wife, and they did not depart until Rubinetto had wedded the other sister. After this, Guerrino declared himself to be the son of Filippo Maria, king of Sicily, which fact pleased Zifroi greatly and brought him to celebrate the marriages with the greatest pomp and magnificence.

The news was sent to Guerrino's father and mother, which gave them immense joy and contentment, since by that time they had given up their son for lost. When he returned to Sicily with his dear wife and his well-loved brother and sister-in-law, they all received a gracious and loving welcome from the king and queen. Many years of peace and happiness followed thereafter, and Guerrino left behind him fair children to inherit his kingdom.

This touching story won the highest praise of all the auditors. When they all fell silent, Eritrea proposed her enigma in the following words:

A cruel beast of nature dread
From out a tiny germ is bred.
In hate all beings else it holds,
And each one trembles who beholds
Its form of fear. Death all around
It spreads, and oft itself is found
The victim of its fatal rage,
And war on all the world will wage.
Beneath its breath the trees decay,
The living plants will fade away.
A beast more cruel, fierce, and fell,
Ne'er rose from out the pit of hell.

When the enigma set forth by the damsel had been considered and highly praised by everyone, some found one solution for it and some another, but not one of them gave the one which best explained its meaning. Wherefore, seeing that her riddle had not been understood, Eritrea said, 'The cruel beast is nothing other than the basilisk, which hates all other living creatures and slays them with its sharp and piercing glances.

But if, by chance, it should happen to see its own form mirrored anywhere, it immediately dies.' When Eritrea had come to the end of the interpretation of her enigma, Signor Evangelista, sitting by her side, said to her with a smile, 'If truth be known, you're this basilisk yourself, young lady, for with your beautiful eyes you bring soft death to all who gaze upon you.' But Eritrea, her cheeks suffused with the lovely tint of nature, didn't utter a word in reply. Alteria was sitting nearby, and when she perceived that the enigma was now completed, she remembered that her turn was next to tell a story, according to the Signora's pleasure. Her most pleasant fable began in the following manner.

V.1 Commentary

Wonder tales are nearly always concerned with thought-provoking gestures of reciprocity and alliance, as in the present tale, between a young prince who loses a toy and gains a lifelong friend and a creature of the wilds who, in exchange for that toy, gains his freedom. Because the king has vowed death to anyone responsible for letting the wild man go free, the prince, for his deed, is in jeopardy of his life. For the loss of his family, however, he gains a protector and benefactor with magic powers, a one-time wild man, whose relationship to the boy is variously that of a martial commissariat, counsellor, mentor, friend, *ersatz* brother, alter ego, or shadow of the self. These are symbolically significant exchanges and realignments. How they are interpreted depends on the degree to which a tale of spare archetypal proportions is granted emblematic force – upon the cultural and psychological resonances the reader sees in such bonds – for the wild man is a savage creature of nature rather than of civilization, an angry and trapped sub-human prisoner, dangerous and feral, who, nevertheless, is docile, speaks the language of the land and keeps promises, has insight into the future, knows hidden intentions, gives flawless counsel and unfailing aid, and commands preternaturally intelligent animals. What the wild man is to the story depends upon the cultural values assigned to this composite, even paradoxical, set of characteristics. This creatural enigma is partially resolved by Straparola in treating the wild man as a self-degraded human who is subject to escape from savagery through the 'disenchanting' powers of a fairy. Nevertheless, during that enchantment he performs all the acts and assumes all the traits of the traditional, typologized, woodland, animal-man of ancient and medieval lore. 'Deep readings' of this tale will inevitably come back, not to 'the little warrior' Guerrino, who is a conventional fairy-tale prince in exile on his way to capturing the hand of a princess by proving himself a courageous and determined boy in foreign parts, but to the 'Murlu,' the 'Iron Man,' the mysterious outsider, who oversees and supports the progress of the hero.[1]

Valentin Schmidt, in his commentary on the story, senses these deep resonances, for he sees in the wild man (as in the satyr of 'Costanza,' IV.1) a creature of contemplation and wisdom who assists in the active life, using reason and insight to overcome all dangers and hindrances; his approach paradoxically assigns the best of human thought to the 'natural' man of the woodlands. He becomes a creature of freedom and for that reason attains to the rewards associated with questing and striving in the pursuit of power and self-actualization. Schmidt does not, in this German romantic mode, pass judgment on the tale of Guerrino as a frivolous precursor to such writers as von Arnim or Vulpius, but protests the trivialized representation of the wild man in related tales in the *Cabinet des fées* as falling far short of their *Sturm und Drang* potential.[2] This interpretation of the wild man as spirit guide is remote, indeed, from the medieval 'wodewose' or savage man of the forest, bearing in his name the link between 'woodlands' and 'madness.'

The progression of this character in Straparola's story, however, is a clear illustration of the plasticity of meanings whereby, through set transformations, not only the human but the superhuman is recovered from the self-alienated recluse of the wilderness. All scholars of the wild man must, in related terms, account for his equivocal nature. Nancy Canepa begins by placing him ambiguously between the hairy, uncivilized, half

1 The American poet Robert Bly was particularly attracted to this tale and its long tradition in relation to his own concerns with the confusion of the modern American male due to the breakdown of the mentoring relationships that were once in place whereby young men found positive role models in their male elders. Bly's book entitled *Iron John*, from the Grimms' version of the 'Guerrino' type recounted below, briefly reviews the collective narrative tradition as a myth of mentoring by which the wild man becomes the source of the young hero's dynamic energy, direction, and renewed courage in times of despair. This, he would argue, is the particular dimension that made the story useful to its auditors throughout the history of its dissemination. Bly reads and interprets this story in relation to his group clinics intended to help restore the dignity and emotional life of the American male. *Iron John* (Reading, MA: Addison-Wesley, 1990).

2 *Die Märchen des Straparola*, in *Sammlung alter Märchen* (Berlin: Duncker & Humblot, 1817), vol. I, p. 302.

infernal beast and the woodland fertility god Silvanus.[3] In both 'Costanza' and 'Guerrino' the protagonists are sent to the forests or wild spaces to do battle with figures menacing civilization as ravagers of the land. Even Orson, of the celebrated French *chanson de geste, Valentin et Orson,* although born a prince, not only tears knights apart with his bare hands, but terrorizes the local peasantry and drives them from their dwellings in fear. These creatures, thus, whether as satyrs, dragons, or wild men may, in the first instance, be associated with anarchy, realms of death, disease, displacers of rural populations, as well as with interior savagery, untamed emotions, and psychological barriers to the normal expressions of the affective life; they are inner and outer demons (as in the pre-remedial phases of the hero of *Robert le Diable*) and hence serve as 'open' signifiers regarding the savage and the civilized. In 'Costanza' it is a young woman who tames a masculine animal force, whereas in 'Guerrino' it is a young man against wild horses aided by a mentor released from the wild man he once was. They are different but related stories, coinciding in their quests into wild places to overcome beasts as a precondition to their own achievement of pairing, love, and domestic stability in the next generation. In sum, the story of 'Guerrino' appears late in a long history of taming wild men within the context of romance. In one capacity, the man of savage strength, through training and loyalty, is made fit to participate in the adventures of chivalry as a mighty warrior. In another, he becomes the guiding force behind a sympathetic adolescent to whom he owes his freedom. Those themes emerged as raconteurs and romance writers, step by step, realized the potential in the relationship between a disaffected mighty man and his child liberator.

New potential emerges when the wild man is taken into captivity, for he becomes not only the treasured possession and *objet de curiosité* of kings, but a creature subject to negotiation and taming.[4] Although

---

3 *From Court to Forest: Giambattista Basile's 'Lo cunto de li cunti' and the Birth of the Literary Fairy Tale* (Detroit: Wayne State University Press, 1999), p. 178.

4 The entire medieval-Renaissance debate concerning the wild man pertained to his nature, whether he was 'bare unaccommodated man' following self-reduction through melancholy (related to lycanthropy), a hybrid offspring of human and animal parents, hence a form of monstrosity, or an intermediary species between man and animal. Because he fell outside discussions of the soul and related theological matters, he became a perfect laboratory for examining heterodox social and psychological states. The question was whether he was a beast trained up to human capacities through obedience and language acquisition, or a man reduced to animal depravity by melancholy and madness and thus in need of enforced

ferocious, yet he bears intimations of the human in his physique, his potential for speech, and his predilection for naked women, who, in some wild man stories, are used as 'bait' to trap them.[5] (Swift reverses this test to compelling effect in making Gulliver the object of the sexual attentions of a young female Yahoo.) Once again the paradoxical emerges, for even in his repudiation of order and civility, this creature is capable not only of a high level of defiance, but of moral integrity in honouring the terms of his release. The 'meaning' of the wild man is also framed by cultural periods, as alluded to above. He achieved prominent stature in the medieval imagination, but gained new significance in the Renaissance when the medieval wild man found himself juxtaposed with the 'ethnographic' savages encountered in the New World, each type demonized and idealized in relation to the ideological missions of their observers. In Straparola's era, the figure reached a liminal point between an object of terror and an object of wonder and respect, or in the words of Hayden White, between 'loathing and fear' and 'envy and admiration.'[6] He serves to frighten civilization by its own fragility, whether as a reversion to the savage life, or the indulgence of the animal side of human nature, while at the same time he calls mankind to the life of freedom in natural reason. Choosing between those options has preoccupied thinkers over the past several centuries. The wild man in 'Guerrino' rescues the little warrior from courtly hypocrisy and corruption, but also qualifies him to be reintegrated into that same courtly life through marriage, whereupon (almost uniquely to Straparola, as it turns out) the unknown young man (the metamorphosed wild man) joins the community of lovers himself. Thus, the wild man of European fable vacillates

---

treatment, therapy, and regimen. This lapse into savagery, as Richard Bernheimer points out, was often reflected in the names of knights, such as 'Sir Dodinel le Sauvage.' *Wild Men in the Middle Ages: A Study in Art, Sentiment, and Demonology* (Cambridge, MA: Harvard University Press, 1952), p. 8. This study contains important chapters on the complex mythology associated with the wild man and related topics, pp. 21–48.

5 According to John of Trevisa, fauns and satyrs are declared bestial because of their uncontrollable lust for women. Thus, the satyr in the story of 'Costanza' is not essentially such a creature, for he knew that she was a young woman all along, but made no effort to assault her. *On the Properties of Things*, 3 vols. (Oxford: Oxford University Press, 1975–88), vol. II, pp. 1199–1200.

6 'The Forms of Wildness: Archeology of an Idea,' in *The Wild Man Within: An Image in Western Thought from the Renaissance to Romanticism*, ed. Edward Dudley and Maximilian Novak (Pittsburgh: University of Pittsburgh Press, 1972), p. 22.

between Merlin the soothsayer, the hairy Nordic creature of the wilds, the green man of fertility rites, the lecherous Pan, the noble savage, and the natural man.

The making of the wild man in Straparola, from the tales of the wodewose to romance, is not yet complete, for there are two further stories overwritten upon his character. Defeated in love, the youth who became the wild man took to the wilderness to escape or embody his melancholy transformation, for in the medical treatises, lycanthropy is but a slight remove from the mechanisms of *amor hereos*, or *ilischi*, the condition of lovesickness. Haly Abbas called it 'melancholy canina' and Rhazes likewise associated erotic melancholy with *qutrub* or lycanthropy, a condition in which the imagination turns upon itself and, through its alterative forces, degrades the body and abandons the mind to raving and craving compulsions. 'At the height of the disease, the lover is seen wandering by night through cemeteries howling like a wolf. For this advanced state there is no other remedy but death.'[7] In 'Guerrino,' the wild man has replaced the werewolf as unrequited lover; his transformation is now expressed by his solitary and aggressively antisocial behaviour, his life among the animals eating grass, his green colour and hirsute appearance. These are precisely the 'classic' traits of his type in the later Middle Ages.[8] Arthur Dickson concurs: 'frequently it is reported that [the wild

---

7 Jacques Ferrand, *A Treatise on Lovesickness*, ed. Donald Beecher and Massimo Ciavolella (Syracuse: Syracuse University Press, 1990), p. 62. This discussion arises from Ferrand's inclusion of lycanthropy in his study of the madness of unrequited lovers. In his words, 'Avicenna teaches that if this disease becomes habitual it is incurable and renders the victim hectical, sottish, dull, and sometimes so savage that he turns lycanthropic or takes his own life, as I demonstrated earlier with several examples,' p. 307. An account of this phenomenon also appears in Robert Burton's *Anatomy of Melancholy*, ed. A.R. Shilletto (London: Bell, 1912), pt. I, sect. 1, memb. 1, subsect. 4, vol. I, pp. 160–4.

8 Malcolm Jones, 'Wild Man,' in *Medieval Folklore*, ed. Carl Lindahl, John McNamara, and John Lindow (Oxford: Oxford University Press, 2002), p. 433. Jones elaborates on this portrait and provides many iconographical sources. In the Medieval Latin *Historia Alexandri Magni de Preliis*, Alexander is met by a huge hairy man with a voice like a boar's and an outsized phallus. Alexander orders a naked maiden to be put in front of him to see his reaction. When he attacks her with an excess of male aggression it is determined that he is not a man out of control but a true beast and thus subject to slaughter, although in related tales it is the female who becomes responsible for rendering the male civilized, as in Chaucer's 'Wife of Bath's Tale' in which the old lady takes a rapist for her husband after giving him a lesson on 'gentillesse.' These themes are central to the wild man in literature, but do not

man] has been disappointed in love,' as when Yvain, in a state of erotomania, is so designated, but that when the lover is captured, shaved, and cared for he returns to his senses.[9] When it comes to cures in the present tale, however, the logic of the fairy tale takes over from the logic of pathology, for Rubinetto recovers his full human status by the time he rediscovers Guerrino on the road, the gift of a fairy who had been cured of her illness simply by looking at him in all his former ugliness. In that moment he is reconstituted not only as a man but as a seer and wonder worker whose sole new purpose in life is to succour the boy who has granted him his freedom. Variously he imposes obedience as he proffers aid and implicitly looks for gratitude as he has shown gratitude. The terms of the tale shift steadily before our eyes, offering perhaps more hermeneutic innuendoes than hard inflections. But in sum, Straparola's wild man is defeated in love and returns to nature. He is presented as the traditional green and hairy man with savage traits who finds himself disinclined to tell his human tale when he is taken captive and placed on display. He is, however, willing to speak to the young boy to negotiate his freedom. Later in the story, the wild man, reconverted by fairy power, becomes a friend and alter ego to the hero, his wild man status eliminated, yet strangely perpetuated in his outsider status, his powers of prescience, and his unfailing adherence to a principle of devotion and loyalty. Straparola's fairy transformation of Rubinetto from savage to companion places the narrative at a challenging crossroad between medieval folklore and the 'early modern' fairy tale. In this, the story is a harbinger of a transformational phase in the development of the European storytelling imagination.

The relationship between romance and the folk-cum-fairy tale under investigation here is unavoidable, because the story follows a generic profile, that of the adolescent male who becomes separated by choice or crisis from his family, develops as a person while wandering through foreign and often supernatural landscapes, aids animals in distress, even hornets, encounters dangerous persons and tames beasts, and ultimately meets all the requisite conditions for marrying a princess. The story can

---

pertain to the story under investigation here. See *The Prose Life of Alexander*, ed. J.S. Westlake, for the Early English Text Society (London: K. Paul, Trench, Trübner & Co., 1913), pp. 89–90. Further to the erotomania of the wild man, see Richard Bernheimer, pp. 121*ff.*

9 '*Valentine and Orson*,' *A Study in Late Medieval Romance* (New York: Columbia University Press, 1929), p. 116.

contain as many or as few episodes as the raconteur wishes to include, but Straparola's *récit* has been defined by four well-integrated folk motifs: the wild man's capture and release, the subsequent meeting and bonding of liberator and liberated (the latter serving the former in the manner of the ghostly helper in the tales of the grateful dead, as in XI.2), the betrayal of the hero by his own men and the ensuing exploits in capturing wild horses, and the final rather illogical bride selection plot through the help of a grateful hornet. These are four distinct motifs with mix-and-match potential, assembled at an unspecified time before Straparola found the story.[10] The formula has already achieved a degree of proportion, logical consequence, and economy in confining the open-ended plotting of the initiation tale to a few episodes constituting a micro-romance. The readiest formula for combining the adventures in the wilderness and the business of mating in the context of a court is to attach the hero to a royal family through service and then send him out on dangerous missions through a combination of palace treachery and royal whim enforced by despotic powers. It is the very same pattern already seen in 'Livoretto' (III.2) and 'Costanza' (IV.1). Straparola's story assumes the profile of the emerging fairy tale, not only in the fairy's cameo appearance to heal and release the noble youth captured within the wild man and equip him with her powers, but in the restoration of the exiled prince to a royal destiny through initiation and marriage under the guidance of his mentor and benefactor. This story remains a wonder tale rather than a fairy tale only because it is the enchanted wild man rather than the fairy herself who masterminds it all.

The potential autonomy of the parts herein assembled into a story tradition entails a pre-history, a requisite period of time for framing the narrative formula available to Straparola by the mid-sixteenth century. Yet once again, Straparola is the first to bring that story into history, for 'Guerrino' is, by current knowledge, the oldest recorded version of the

10 The final episode is illogical simply because the king offers one of his two daughters to the hero, then says that if, by blind chance, he chooses the silver-haired Eleuteria he would lose his life. To be sure, it is in keeping with the ancient tradition of high risk bride selection games of the type featured in Shakespeare's *Merchant of Venice*. Nevertheless, Eleuteria was a perfectly acceptable bride for Rubinetto and was hence not a poison maiden. An animal helper was a conventional means for resolving the dilemma. What we might otherwise have expected is a plot in which the hero had to identify his beloved disguised and placed among unacceptable choices.

story type it represents (ATU No. 502). Subsequently, it gave rise to an instance of direct borrowing by a French writer in the late seventeenth century, but the necessary folk tale upon which it is based left a far richer legacy for collectors in the nineteenth century. These materials, passing through Straparola's hands, do not constitute part of a linear history with a beginning and an end, but a community of motifs in recombinant evolution around an oikotype or 'home' tale. Stith Thompson identifies the type as the *Goldener Märchen* (ATU No. 314), 'the boy with the golden hair' in conjunction with 'the wild man' group, because in many such tales of the boy with a wild-man guide, the hero's hair (or other parts of his body) is turned to gold, forcing him to wear disguises. This story type of undoubted antiquity, in one of its many manifestations, provided Straparola's source tradition with basic materials, while in its more generic form it gave rise to the many later tales with which 'Guerrino' has affinities.

Most of these tales begin with a pact with the Devil, according to which the newborn child is to be turned over to him on its twenty-first birthday (a relationship that finds later parallels in the mentor-pupil relationship of the wild man and the young prince in exile). It is in his service that the young man enters a forbidden place and has his hair turned to gold. When the Devil tells him to abuse a horse containing an enchanted prince, the boy is urged by the talking animal to flee on its back, thus gaining a counsellor who guides him through all his following adventures (the horse becomes a guide, as in the Livoretto group). Hiding his golden hair is a challenge. At one point it is seen by a princess, who begins to tease the hero as the gardener's boy (several instances of which will follow). When the lad is taunted by the king's brothers, he goes to his horse for help and, in the end, performs valiant feats of war or dragon slaying, each time avoiding a triumphal return until his identity is discovered thanks to the golden hair.

Thus far, there is not a great deal that looks familiar. Thompson, however, describes a less well known version in which an iron man living at the bottom of a lake is captured and then negotiates for his release when the prince's ball rolls into his cage. Immediately, we recognize our story. The wild man carries the child away on his shoulders and promises to care for him if he is obedient, but the boy fails the test by approaching an enchanted well, thereby turning his hair and fingers to gold (we see the stories coming together). There is no horse in this tale until the iron man furnishes one upon request, thereby enabling his ward to perform several 'impossible' feats (in the manner of Guerrino). Thompson states that 'while this story of the wild man is by no means as popular as the other, it is spread over almost exactly the same territory in Europe, but it hardly goes outside that continent. It has been carried to Siam, to Missouri, and to Brazil.' (An Armenian version is also known.)[11] Clearly such a tale was known to Straparola, but with differences in its details: the boy is not carried away on the iron man's shoulders but meets the wild man later, nor does he have golden hair.[12] Straparola's source also involves an additional helper, the hornet, to identify the princess, rather than to have the boy identified by his golden locks. The present story comes from a separate folk tradition, that of disguised brides and fatal consequences. The template of the generic tale has been reconstructed by abstracting from the Germanic versions of the eighteenth and nineteenth centuries, but Straparola's variant is a text to be reckoned with as a much earlier representation of the type, indicating that by the mid-sixteenth century, a version was in circulation which had already integrated the golden-haired boy tradition (without the golden hair) with the wild man's release and grateful mentorship, leading to the restoration of the little warrior – a composite folk creation already moving away from the '*Goldener*' oikotype. It would have a legacy of its own, the early appearance of which is certified by the present story. The '*Goldener*' influence remains apparent, but equally prominent are the Nordic elements that had worked their way south to provide the necessary materials for the wild man stories known throughout Europe.

Clearly the second of the '*Goldener*' types, with which we are concerned here, relies upon the wild man, such as he was represented in one of the best known *chansons de geste* of the late Middle Ages, *Valentin et Orson*, together with its sources and derivatives.[13] This work cannot be consid-

11 Stith Thompson, *The Folktale* (Berkeley: University of California Press, [1946], 1977), pp. 60–1.

12 Another feature almost universal to the story type abandoned by Straparola is the 'obstacle flight' in which the horse advises the boy to drop his talismanic objects behind him at critical moments in his flight to stop his pursuers. These include a comb that turns to a forest, and other magic objects that turn to lakes and other natural barriers.

13 The reader is directed to the 'Introduction' in the critical edition of the English text of *Valentine and Orson*, ed. Arthur Dickson, trans. Henry Watson (London: Oxford, 1937; reprint, New York: Kraus Reprints, 1971). One of the most thorough investigations of the sources of this work is to be found in Arthur Dickson's *Valentine and Orson: A Study in Late Medieval Romance* (New York: Columbia University Press, 1929). Versions in languages other than French predate the earliest surviving

ered a narrative progenitor to the present story, and yet it extends a generic folk tale (the same that gave rise to 'The Truth-speaking Bird,' IV.3) into a chivalric romance by incorporating the lore of the wild man in a way that is fully comparable to Straparola's *novella*-scale treatment of a folk tale as the micro-romance of 'Guerrino.' The work is of French provenance dating to the first half of the fourteenth century and became one of the most popular cycles of the Middle Ages. It tells of the two sons of the emperor of Greece (or Constantinople) who were first separated from their parents in infancy and then from each other. Valentin was raised at the court of Pepin while Orson was abducted and raised by a bear as a wild man in the forests around Orléans. Valentin is destined to become the only man of sufficient prowess to capture and tame this wild creature and draw him back to civility through an imposition of complete obedience. In this way, Orson becomes the servant and comrade of his own brother through a number of adventures until a brazen head reveals the conditions of their birth and then self-destructs.

Orson's story is clearly built up from the folk tale tradition of the wild man with his shaggy hair, animal traits, savage temperament, but human potential. The tale of twin brothers becomes, in effect, a new frame for the close alliance between civilized and natural man as doubles of each

---

French version, but internal evidence, such as the setting in the Charlemagne Cycle, nevertheless indicates French origins in the early fourteenth century. Because the Middle Low German version *Von Nameloss unde Valentyn* (MS. 102 c of the Staats- und Universitätsbibliothek, Hamburg) is altogether closer in ethos and design to the folk tale upon which the entire tradition is based, it is to be presumed that the French original resembled it rather more than it did the later *Valentin et Orson* from which all the English versions are derived. It reveals how the work emerged from the 'envious sisters' type that informed 'The Truth-speaking Bird' (IV.3), otherwise referred to as 'the traduced or banished queen' type. The basic story, it is to be recalled, involves a queen who, at the time of the birth of her children, is betrayed by her sisters, or a wicked stepmother, after which her children are exposed, she is blamed for their disappearance, and she too is banished or locked up. The onus is placed upon the children to recover their birthright and rescue their mother. Imagine now that the children are two boys, that after their exposure they are separated, that one is raised in the wilds by a wolf or bear while the other is raised at a neighbouring court, and that the civilized brother must capture, train, befriend, and gain the loyalty of the savage brother before they can embark on the adventures that lead to the liberation or rediscovery of their beleaguered mother. In that version, the wild man is superimposed upon the brother raised in the forest (Orson from *ours*, bear). 'Guerrino' issues from a different folk tale, that of the child who liberates, is succoured by, disobeys, yet has recourse to the special powers of a wild man. The two stories stood side by side in the late medieval imagination.

other. The wild man must meet his liberator and bond with him as Orson does with his brother through the additional attraction of blood affinity. Nevertheless, deprived of speech, the bear brother must resort to the sign language of fawning animals to show his submissive frame of mind, as in the stories of men imprisoned inside wolves who must employ the language of gestures to communicate their plight and set up the circumstances for the recovery of their human nature. Marie de France tells just such a story in 'The Lay of the Were-Wolf.'[14] It studies the relationship between wilderness and court and the bonding that leads to the recovery of brotherhood, as in the tale of 'Guerrino.' One of the brothers' tasks was to rescue their repudiated mother, Bellisant, from the giant Ferragus. There were Italian versions of the story taken from the lost French source.[15] The wild man is the oldest element of the story of the two brothers, and the date at which he was superimposed upon the story of the children of the calumniated queen is difficult to set, just as it is difficult to specify when the quest for the wonderful objects, the bird, the singing tree, and the speaking bird were added to the ancient tale of the queen accused of cannibalizing her own children. Both represent critical moments in the development of their respective story traditions. In these combinatory ways, then, the story of Guerrino and the wild man are drawn into the circle of the separated brothers, inviting us to superimpose the stories.

14 *French Medieval Romances from the Lays of Marie de France*, trans. Eugene Mason (New York: E.P. Dutton [1911], 1924), pp. 83–90. Sir Orfeo, during the quest for his wife Heurodis, also takes on the properties of the wild man, growing long black hair, again linking the sufferings of love to the reversion to nature and depravation as well as to the pathology of melancholy. *Middle English Romances*, ed. A.C. Gibbs (Evanston, IL: Northwestern University Press, 1966), ll. 247–52; 'Sir Orfeo,' in *Middle English Verse Romances*, ed. Donald Sands (New York: Holt, Rinehart & Winston, 1966), ll. 240–3, p. 192.

15 *Valentin et Orson* survives in a prose version published in Lyons by Jacques Maillet in 1489. There followed the translation by Henry Watson published by Wynkyn de Worde, ca. 1510, and again as *The Historye of the two Valyaunte Brethren: Valentyne and Orson*, published by William Copland in 1548, 1555, 1565; ed. Arthur Dickson for the Early English Text Society (Oxford: H. Milford, Oxford University Press, 1937). Richard Hathwaye and Anthony Munday also reworked the material for publication in 1598. The tale has many sequels including that which appears in *Tabart's Collection of Popular Stories*, 3 vols. (London: Tabart & Co., 1809), vol. III, pp. 127–63. It comes under close scrutiny by Dorothy Yamamoto in *The Boundaries of the Human in Medieval English Literature* (Oxford: Oxford University Press, 2000), *passim*.

The name 'Guerrino' is an invitation to investigate whether the Straparola story, in employing the name, is in some sense a crafted diminution of the greatest of all the works of that era bearing the name, *Il Guerrin meschino*, written in Italian around 1410 by the Tuscan minstrel Andrea da Barberino.[16] Beyond the name, however, the similarities may be more generic than real, insofar as all the chivalric romances of the era proffer quests, trials of friendship, separation from family, treks through barren places, and earned marriages to princesses. The story of Guerrin the Wretched offers all of these things. His father is dethroned on the day of his birth and the boy is rescued by a Greek slave and sold in Constantinople where he befriends the Emperor's son Alessandro and falls in love with his sister Elisena. Many of the features are replayed centuries later in 'Das treue Füllchen' in Wolf's *Hausmärchen*, while other features are redolent of those in *Valentin et Orson* – particularly the foundling's loyalty to and sacrifices for his royal friend. When the Turks take Alessandro prisoner, Guerrin stops at nothing to bring about his liberation. He also demands military equipment from the barons and rides incognito into war to save the city from the besieging Astiladoro. In the second part he leaves his adopted city to find his parents, freeing Christians from giants along the way. The entire work is in eight substantial parts featuring travels, battles, encounters, and searches of many kinds, throughout which the boys remain together as a model of friendship. Readers must abide all the way to chapter 16 of Part VI to experience the boy's recovery of his father, with many adventures still to come. To the extent that popular storytellers borrowed names and parallel motifs from the 'high' literature of their age, *Guerrin meschino* may have made a contribution, but it does not replicate the order or the characters of the *Goldener Märchen* type in any transparent way.

Among the folk tales collected in the late nineteenth century, 'Le Tartaro reconnaissant et le Herensuge' (The grateful wild man and the Basque dragon) is one of the closest to Straparola. A king brings home from the hunt the unique satyr-like creature, the 'Tartaro' of Basque legend, which he was keen to place on display. But his two sons, playing at pelote, lose the pelote in the stables and must free the creature to get it back. The Tartaro tells them where their mother keeps the key and how to trick her, but does not leave without first promising aid in the

16 *Il Guerrin meschino*, ed. Mauro Cursietti (Rome: Antenore, 2005).

future. Their father swears to eat the heart of the liberator half cooked, yet when the boys begin to argue, tattling ensues. The mother, alarmed, sends Yorge away with money, and when the young protagonist finds himself without resources, he calls the Tartaro for help, who thereafter becomes his guide and purveyor. The boy is sent ahead to a royal city where he becomes a gardener (in 'the golden-haired boy' tradition). Many episodes ensue, borrowing from several parallel story motifs, but principally 'the grateful dead' (see the commentary to XI.2) and 'the dragon slayer' (see the commentary to X.3). He takes flowers to the youngest of the three princesses and she takes him lunch with love. But the girl is destined to be eaten by a dragon. The Tartaro provides the hero with a horse, sword, and clothes for the task ahead. That the horse severs one of the dragon's seven heads is redolent of the active role it plays in the story of Guerrino. As in the tale of Cesarino (X.3), girl and boy go their separate ways after the dragon is slain and the tongues are set aside as future evidence. Yorge returns to his gardening, while the king calls in vain for the conqueror to come forward until a coal porter with the seven heads claims the princess. When the princess resists the claim, a tournament is called for. Yorge assumes a new disguise and comes away victorious, but this time wounded. When the king sees the mark of his own lance, the princess is promised to him alone. Nevertheless, much unsettled business remains: the tongues must be produced to expose the impostor, and the boy's father – he who threatened to eat the culprit's heart – is called to witness the wedding, where he is served a sheep's heart in reference to his vengeful vow. The Tartaro is likewise thanked for his faithful stewardship which will be extended into the future. The creature's transformation from wild animal to ghost, satyr, wild man, or even gentleman is not described, although he is clearly of a complex nature, for he was once too wild to keep in captivity, yet rational, prescient, articulate, and loyal.[17]

Jack Zipes states that 'the goldener' type (the folk tale core of 'Guerrino') was formed during the Middle Ages and that the work having the greatest influence upon its formation was a twelfth-century romance entitled

17 Wentworth Webster, *Légendes basques*, trans. Nicolas Burguete ([Anglet]: Aubéron, 2005), pp. 55–67; published originally in English as *Basque Legends* (London: Griffith & Farran, 1877), p. 176.

Robert der Teufel or *Robert le Diable.*[18] This proves truer for those tales in which the boy is consigned to the devil and runs madly renegade than it does for the concurrent tale of the golden-haired boy who acquires his golden features through insouciant disobedience to the wild man he has liberated and who remains his lifelong friend. In *Robert the Devil,* the boy's mother, in a reckless moment, desperate for a child, makes an oath to the devil which results in the birth of a child who is inclined to every vice. He is formidable and deadly in tournaments, killing knights indiscriminately. He goes raping and pillaging across the countryside in ways roughly analogous, perhaps, to those of a wild man. He puts out the eyes of those who seek to apprehend him, and as a child, when he is sent to school, kills his own master. After building a house in the woods, he hires criminals to make up his entourage, and their sport is in killing holy hermits. His conversion follows, making a bipartite design similar to those works featuring the before and after phases in the career of the captured and redeemed savage man. Upon hearing his mother's confession concerning his birth, he seeks to convert his murderous friends to save their souls. Failing in this, he kills them all with a sledgehammer in accordance with what they deserved. He then goes to Rome after dividing his massive ill-gotten possessions between his father and the poor. The pope sends him to places about the city to do penance. In due course, an angel tells him he must cease to speak and to eat only the food rejected by dogs until God's time in the matter is fulfilled. When the emperor stops to laugh at him, however, he becomes a kind of trickster in presenting canine posteriors for kissing, tripping queens, and putting cats in the stew. Trickster cycle elements invade the saint's life. Then God sends a white horse and arms to Robert to make war against the Saracens incognito until he is wounded on the thigh; in this he gains a place in the chivalric world order. These precise traits are replicated in the folk tale, or inversely they are taken from the tale, thereby confirming its early existence. The wicked Seneschal, rejected in love, then impersonates the hero to win the princess by sleuth whom he could not abduct through war; it is a version of the usurping nephew who attempts to steal the

18 *Robert le Diable,* ed. Élisabeth Gaucher (Paris: Champion, 2006). This may have been predated by the German version, but served as the source for the early translations into English as Anon., *The lyfe of Roberte the Devyll* (Cambridge: Chadwyck-Healey, 1992). See Élisabeth Gauchet, *Robert le Diable: Histoire d'une légende* (Paris: Champion, 2003). Anon, *La terrible et merveilleuse vie de Robert le diable* ([Paris]: Claude Blihart, n.d.).

hero's rewards seen in many of the cognates in the Livoretto (III.2) and Cesarino (X.3) traditions. At last God pronounces the end of Robert's penance, the princess reveals her devotion, the wound speaks of the hero's prowess, the court celebrates his bravery, a hermit restores his speech, Robert marries, and at long last he returns to his home in Rouen. Many of the *Goldener* features are here, to be sure, but only a scant few are represented in Straparola. The devil's child turned saint, the excruciating penitence, and the periods of madness and degradation pertain to an order of their own. Moreover, the ethos and causes characterizing the protagonist of *Robert le Diable* are remote from those of the wild man as seer, helper, and loyal friend. In the conventional way that links stories within a narrative tradition, particularly in relation to the lesser version of 'the golden-haired youth' embedded in 'Guerrino,' Robert is at best a cousin twice removed.

Only the briefest sampling of more recent analogues can be discussed, given their abundance and geographical distribution. The German storytellers had a penchant for the *Goldener Märchen*, with features still lingering from the *Robert der Teufel* tradition. J.W. Wolf in 'Das treue Füllchen' provides an inventory, as it were, of episodes relating to the story.[19] Hans begins as a sassy and impervious little trickster who can dance with millstones around his neck and drive his sheep onto the

19 *Hausmärchen* (Göttingen: Dietrisch'sche Buchhandlung, 1851), pp. 269–85. In this same group is 'Der eiserne Mann, Der Lohn des Gehorsams' (The iron man or the reward of obedience) by Christian August Vulpius in his *Ammenmärchen* (Weimar: 1791), pp. 173–240. This work is an extensive meditation on love, duty, obedience, and the doublings in relationships that pleased the Romantic imagination. At the same time, the work is a complete representation of the betrayal of the good-hearted iron man living far away in the forest who, in helping the king, loses his territory, is captured, and presented to the queen as an amusement in despite of his good will. The young prince Salker is his liberator and for that deed narrowly escapes death. The soldiers slay a wild pig in his place and return the heart while leaving the boy at the edge of the forest. There he meets with the iron man, but with two critical pages missing (186–7) the terms of his earliest apprenticeship with him are missing. What follows is the story of obedience step by step in winning the princess by tempting her with beautiful balls, while fighting incognito in the king's wars. With each ball the prince asks to sleep nearer and nearer the princess, until, with the third, he gains access to her bed. But the king takes his daughter's place and in examining the mysterious boy he finds the battle wound that identifies the unidentified warrior. There is no rival, no golden hair, no departures on a crippled horse, no episodes in the garden, but the story is in direct line with the later tales of Wolf and von Arnim. More than either, however, it is a meditation on fate and

heaths of an ogre, thereafter provoking and killing him. His adventures lead him on three different horses up to the kingdom on the mountain, taking him through a town where in his shabbiness the citizens laugh at him, while higher up his magic horses shake themselves three times and turn him into a golden knight, who, episode after episode, rides away from his conquests without being identified until the king traps him. At one point the pony becomes a gold producing animal by shaking itself, and further along, the princess sees the beautiful rider in the palace garden and asks for him in marriage, accepting a new life as a gardener's wife. Then comes the inevitable war in which the gardener's boy heads off on his broken horse with a wooden sword, transforms himself into a splendid knight along the way, only to return to laughter in his humble gear boasting of exploits which no one believes. The wound on his leg becomes the proof of his deeds. It is a tale of transformations around the golden boy motif, as well as a tale of magic speaking horses. To all of these tales, 'Guerrino' bears a likeness, given their origins in a common folk tale, but their differences through time and distance are equally marked.

The story of 'Der Eise Hans' of Friedmund von Arnim narrows the affiliations somewhat, for it begins with a wild man living at the bottom of a pond who makes off with every hunting party wandering into the region until he is captured by draining off the water.[20] He is taken to a royal court and kept in a cage. When the prince's golden ball is held for ransom, the boy supplicates three times until the wild man tells him how to get the key that will liberate him. His freedom earns from him a promise that if ever in the future the boy should find himself in distress, he only had to call for Iron Hans at the edge of the forest. For such a misdeed, the king orders his own child to be slain, but the huntsman commissioned with the task takes off his finger which, along with some hog's entrails, is presented as proof of the deed. Iron Hans comes to the

---

domestic happiness, reconciliation and gratitude, with the final twenty pages devoted to a quest in fairyland through enchanted castles that goes far beyond the outlines of the traditional tale. It is a full scale work of the Romantic imagination.

20 'Der Eise Hans,' in *Hundert neue Märchen in Gebirge gesammelt* (Charlottenburg: E. Bauer, 1844), in *The Great Fairy Tale Tradition*, ed. Jack Zipes (New York: W.W. Norton, 2001), pp. 326–9. The story also occurs in the most southerly German-speaking regions as 'Goldener' in Ignaz and Josef Zingherle, *Tirols Volksdichtungen und Volksgebräuche*, 2 vols. (Innsbruck: Verlag der Wagner'schen Buchhandlung, 1852–4), vol. I, pp. 192–9.

boy's rescue and sets him to watch over a sacred spring, but Hans touches the water and ends up with a gold star on his brow, for which reason he is dismissed. In alignment with the second part of Wolf's tale, the boy becomes a gardener's helper, attracts the notice of the princess, fights in the king's tourneys, and issues victorious with the help of equipment granted by Iron Hans, much as the wild man lends a magic horse to Guerrino. He has three golden balls for prizes which entitle him to the hand of the princess, but he hides his identity until he is wounded by pursuing knights. When all is revealed and the marriage is to transpire, the boy's father is invited to attend, and also to pronounce a fitting punishment for filicide, which of course is inflicted upon him, before happiness overwhelms everyone else. Such analogues call for a very carefully qualified statement of affiliation, for while the generic story type can be variously visited upon each new telling from Straparola to the Grimm brothers' 'Iron John' (still to be profiled), the filiations demonstrating direct lines of influence are not so easily drawn.

In effect, the Grimms' story would appear to predate both Wolf and von Arnim, yet hold very close correspondences with von Arnim, in fact retelling the same story, while nevertheless possessing more details in common with 'Guerrino.'[21] The wild man is a Grendel-like figure whose arm extends from the lake to grab hunters and their dogs. He is tied up and placed in an iron cage, never to be opened upon pain of death. This wild man knew that the key was not in the king's pocket but under the queen's pillow. Again, the boy asks for his ball three times, an oral feature scaled back in Straparola. After the good deed, the boy is carried away on Iron John's shoulders. He is told to be obedient in all things, particularly concerning the sacred well. Again, the boy attempts to hide his infractions but his deeds are known by definition, in keeping with the *Goldener* model. He must go and learn about poverty in the wide world; the protection of innocence is over. He becomes the cook's helper at court, but refuses to take off his hat in the presence of the king. Then the princess sees his golden hair and a teasing relationship begins. When

21 'Iron Hans,' in *Kinder- und Hausmärchen Gesammelt durch die Brüder Grimm* (Berlin: Realschulbuchhandlung, 1812), in *The Great Fairy Tale Tradition*, ed. Jack Zipes, pp. 323–5; *Grimm's Complete Fairy Tales* (Garden City, NY: Nelson Doubleday, n.d.), pp. 435–40. Zipes also includes 'The Wild Man' (De wilde Man), from the same work, 1815, no. 50 in the original collection, although it was omitted from the edition of 1843 because of its close resemblance to 'Iron Hans.' *The Great Fairy Tale Tradition*, pp. 323–5.

he asks for knight's gear he gets a lame horse until Iron John supplies his needs, including a battalion of men. The king stages a tournament in which he appears incognito on different horses, each time winning the golden apple tossed by the princess, but is wounded. The wound, his golden hair, and the golden apples all serve to confirm his identity. He then asks for the princess and meets with his parents, while the reappearance of Iron John, who again offers gratitude for his freedom, caps the entire story.

This tale was also widely known in France, as in Henry Carnoy's 'L'Homme de fer' in which the boy's mark is not his golden hair but a golden star on his forehead.[22] The iron giant plagues the kingdom until he is captured and caged. The prince frees him, is carried away by the giant, now as his teacher and taskmaster, in this curious reversal of roles. Once banished, he too seeks to excel in a tournament and does so with the giant's help. This giant dies, however, before the boy realizes the customary rewards of the fairy tale. Even closer to Straparola's tale is a version from Lower Brittany in which the story itself is set in Keranrais, Plouaret.[23] In this tale, a rival appears at the end attempting to steal the rewards of the hero by presenting himself as the dragon slayer, much as Robert the Devil must expose the impostor Seneschal, and as many of the heroes in the Livoretto group must expose the false nephew. This story begins with the story of 'Costanza' when the youngest of three daughters rides off to court to fight for the king, finds herself blamed for the pregnancy of a maid of honour, and must reveal her true gender to the king. She becomes the mother of the prince whose compassion allows the 'Murlu' to escape, but not without first revealing how it was trapped, which was essentially how Costanza trapped the satyr with food. At that time, the creature would only grind its teeth and screech horribly. With the boy, however, it makes a deal in rational terms and directs him to the key in the king's pocket. The young hero then exiles himself on the Murlu's back, who carries him directly to the palace of the king of

22 *Contes français*, vol. 8 of *Collection de contes et de chansons populaires*, ed. Henry Carnoy (Paris: Ernest Leroux, 1885), vol. VII, pp. 43–50. There are also features pertaining to wild men and to episodes from the *Goldener Märchen* tradition in the *Cabinets des fées* (Geneva: Barde and Manget, 1785–9), vol. V, 80–101, and in Count Hamilton's 'Les quatre facardins,' vol. XX, pp. 472*ff.*

23 F.M. Luzel, 'Le Murlu ou l'homme sauvage,' *Contes populaires de Basse-Bretagne* (Paris: Maisonneuve & Leclerc, 1887), vol. II, pp. 296–313.

Naples where he takes service. With the elimination of the golden well episode and the transformed hair, one may ask if the tale (as with Straparola's) can still belong to the 'Goldener' group. In this story he is set to work to increase the numbers of sheep, swine, and cows in the king's herds, and does so admirably with the help of the Murlu. Thereafter, he kills the ogre and possesses himself of all the creature's treasures. In a subsequent episode, he sees the princess being taken as a sacrifice to the beast with seven heads. He defeats this creature in a fight lasting two days with further help from his friend. A coal digger sees the seven heads and appropriates them in order to claim the reward, but the hero has retained the severed tongues (as in all the stories of the 'dragon slayer' group, X.3). In the end France is united to Naples and the Murlu reappears as the queen who had attempted to seduce the page at the French court, who in turn became the young prince's mother! In effect, then, she had been a wild woman, and it had been her role to protect the son of the queen whom she had once loved as a page in disguise. This contrasting tale is yet another example of the plasticity of the materials and the creative forces of the oral tradition whereby a matrix of identifying features is submitted to endless transformation.

Other stories with corresponding details include 'Granadoro,' collected in Pisa by Domenico Comparetti. This adventure tale converges at telling moments with the tale of 'Guerrino,' but is essentially closer to the Livoretto group (III.2) and its many analogues.[24] The prince of Portugal leaves home to meet his uncle and is displaced by an impersonator. He is compelled to become a stable boy. At the same time, he becomes the victim of false reports that he is a champion horse breaker. The horse in question takes pity on the boy and allows itself to be tamed. Only then does the story develop the motif of the wild horse, Belverde, who is ravaging the countryside, and which the prince is also compelled, though the lies of the false nephew, to subdue. Once again the tamed horse serves as counsellor, suggesting how the wild horse can be decapitated with a sabre. Further slander causes his departure on a grand quest to persuade the king's estranged queen to return. This is accomplished with the aid of the fish, swallow, and butterfly helpers. Only the third is of interest because the queen must be chosen from among three identical sisters, which can only be accomplished by the butterfly which, like the hornet

---

24 *Novelline popolari italiane* (Bologna: Forni editore, 1875), no. 5, pp. 18–22.

in the present story, makes the right choice. This is a talking wonder horse story that includes the swallow that brings the water of life needed to revive the slain hero and the butterfly that resolves the identity riddle, but there is no bride choice at the end. The story of Queen Granadoro and the tasks she sets for the young hero may never have belonged to the type in question, but rather to have borrowed select features. The tale collected by Giuseppe Pitrè called 'The Symphonic Eagle' is part of the 'Fortunio and the King's Daughter' group (III.4) in which a golden eagle that is both a music machine and a container large enough to hold the young adventurer is carried, Trojan horse fashion, to the girl's secret underground chamber. By degrees the prince answers all the riddles as required to liberate a sequestered princess. One corresponding motif is the selection of the girl from among twenty-four look-alike candidates, which is easy enough. By prearrangement, the true princess wears a different coloured bow on her head.[25] This is the feature that corresponds most closely with the story of 'Guerrino.' Equally remote is the story of 'Corvetto' (III.7) in Basile's *Pentamerone.*[26] It coincides insofar as the protagonist in service at a foreign court becomes the victim of jealous courtiers and falls prey to their false reports concerning his prowess, all of which he is powerless to deny. Basile speculates at modest length on the luck that produces favourites and the malignity and deceit that is exercised to bring them down. The setting is Scotland and the king's enemy is a ghoul, a savage and brutal creature living in a desert place destined for extermination. The king desired not the ghoul but his horse, which Corvetto is sent out to capture and on whose back he escapes bears, wolves, lions, and monkeys in hot pursuit. Once the ogre is slain and the keys of his abode are delivered to the king, the hero takes a royal wife and lives to spite his enemies. And there his tale is done. All of these are, in a sense, disappointingly remote, but serve to illustrate how coinciding motifs may wander from one narrative type to another over time. The problem is that Straparola's own tale may not represent the oikotype current in its own day, but a departure or condensation, for his is closer in nature to the boy with the golden hair under the protection of a wild man released by his own hand than any other type, yet Straparola's does not contain the critical defining motif. Similar stories lacking the wild

25 *The Collected Sicilian Folk and Fairy Tales of Giuseppe Pitrè*, ed. and trans. Jack Zipes and Joseph Russo, 2 vols. (London: Routledge, 2009), vol. I, pp. 411–16.

26 *Il Pentamerone*, trans. Richard Burton (New York: Boni & Liveright, 1927), pp. 247–52.

man figure – and there are many – may be said to belong to other groups, but it is telling how many have features or generic plot designs in common with the 'Guerrino' type. Thus it comes about that Straparola's story is everywhere, yet not quite anywhere in its entirety.

This story bears a relationship to those concerning the grateful dead (XI.2), for in certain of the tales a young adventurer exposes himself to exile or penury in arranging for the proper burial of a dead body (as in liberating a wild man) and thereby gains a secret friend and spirit guide, usually in the person of a revenant chevalier or knight. The young hero, alone in the world for the favour he had wrought, is able to thrive and prosper through his counsel. In the present story the wild man helps the hero in his pursuit of a princess, but in a story entitled 'Die hälfte von allem' (Half of everything) the merchant guide, buried at the boy's cost, offers his help if the boy will share all he gains at the end of seven years.[27] This includes a beautiful princess whom he has won in marriage. When the time is fulfilled, they meet, the goods are divided, but still the merchant is dissatisfied until the boy offers half interest in his bride, at which point the wraith retires, stating that he was now satisfied, for he had found a true friend. There are overtones of just such an obligation to the wild man, an obligation conveniently met through the availability of Potentiana's sister.

Consider a final example from as far as Armenia in which a king banishes his son for letting a beast escape in exchange for his arrow. In his exile, he meets up with the creature who in turn supplies his needs and helps him marry a princess. He lives as a swineherd, having been displaced by a chamberlain, for which reason he engages in compulsory exploits similar to those in the Livoretto group.[28] It is one last example

---

27 Joseph Haltrich, *Deutsche Volksmärchen aus dem Sachsenlande in Siebenbürgen* (Munich: Jubiläumsausgabe, [1856], 1956), pp. 28–30.

28 'The Swineherd,' in *Apples of Immortality, Folktales of Armenia*, ed. Leon Surmelian (Berkeley: University of California Press, 1966), no. 2, pp. 53–64. The story of the wild man liberated by a young boy was also combined with other familiar fairy tale motifs as in 'The Princess on the Glass Mountain.' That story was collected by Benjamin Thorpe and published in his *Yule-Tide Stories: A Collection of Scandinavian and North German Popular Tales and Traditions* (London: Henry Bohn, 1853), pp. 86–97. The opening is so like Straparola's tale that it requires no summarization. The boy in exile, before meeting up with the liberated wild man, seeks employment at a foreign court where an eligible princess demands of the one who is to win her that he ride to the top of a glass mountain. The prince has taken up cattle herding for the king and rediscovers his wild man, who then supplies him

of the fortunes of these favoured motifs and their aptitude for being grafted one upon the other, while in far looser terms preserving the signature parts of the Guerrino group.

Finally, there is the story of 'Prince Guerini' by Jean de Mailly, which is a direct elaboration upon Straparola's tale.[29] The story is faithful to its original in all the particulars of the plot, but supplies a commentary of its own on the themes implicit in the tale. The king was curious about the customs of the savage race, yet was intent upon holding the creature 'in irons until he saw some signs that the wild man had been tamed and showed that he was disposed to submit to the laws and customs of civilized men.'[30] The boy, not only keen to retrieve his precious arrow snatched by the prisoner, but also moved to compassion, thinks it well to liberate the creature, given that he had committed no crime. This queen also tries to assume all the blame for the boy's act. Jean de Mailly understood the clumsiness in having the iron man restored by a fairy who had been cured by seeing his ugliness. This fairy simply touched him with her wand as he slept. Conventionalized fairy tale gesturality is already in place. Now 'instead of thirsting for blood and carnage, he only thought of leading a gentle life and was ashamed of his natural ferocity,' and now too 'he sensed an indescribable joy' in his new condition.[31] It is the fairy, in fact, who commissions the new knight to seek out Guerini to thank him. This is how the young prince is rewarded for his compassion 'for those less fortunate than he'; the good fairy was behind it all. By degrees, the fairy tale motifs transform the myth of the wild man into a moralizing tale for the little gentlemen of the salons. The irresistibly handsome Guerini the Lombard must go to France, there to conduct himself with charm at the court of the king of Arles – a little joke in itself. The one-time wild man is now the knight Alcée, who accompanies his little friend in person throughout all his adventures. Now the two knights set out to subdue the ravaging giants, and it is no longer the young prince counting on the help of his protector, but Alcée himself counting on the aid of the fairy. The story comes full circle in the giants they encounter who carry tree-sized clubs, live in caves, relish

---

with a steed and several splendid suits of armour that serve as disguises. When the princess identifies the mysterious knight as the herd-boy in the crowd, a fairy tale ending ensues and the wild man simply disappears.

29 *Les illustres fées, contes galans* (Paris: M-M. Brunet, 1698); in *The Great Fairy Tale Tradition*, ed. Jack Zipes (New York: W.W. Norton, 2001), pp. 316–25.

30 *The Great Fairy Tale Tradition*, ed. Jack Zipes, p. 316.

31 *The Great Fairy Tale Tradition*, ed. Jack Zipes, p. 318.

drawing blood, and wear the skins of their prey. The hero is particularly genteel and deferential in claiming the princess as his wife and arranges for the marriage of his friend to her younger sister. The story has considerable charm, but its mythological nucleus has been exposed to the plain light of common day.

Despite the impression that both the folk tale and the novella do not readily participate in the 'other speaking' of allegory, there remain, nevertheless, the names of the two princesses, for the little warrior wins the hand of Potentiana, and the wild man that of Eleutheria: 'Power' and 'Liberty,' or 'Force' and 'Freedom.' If these qualities are rewards through the conventional allegorical application of marriage, then martial (Guerrino) is to force what the wild man is to freedom; each bride is the perfect counterpart to her mate. But they are not the favoured reconciliation of opposites usually employed, making the allegorical reading more circumstantial than real. The story itself is a conflation of early folk tales, the wild man (ATU 502) and the golden youth (ATU 314). It is the earliest surviving representation of this configuration in a format that remains close to the original folk material, paralleling similar amalgamations in the medieval *chansons de geste.* Arguably, it is a reliable depiction of the story at that historical moment, one in which the wild man is explained in terms of love melancholy but remains attached to the province of the fairies; it shows some of the plot rationalization of the novella, yet maintains the episodic logic of the folk tale.

Determining just what Straparola's story is in relationship to this sprawling sampling of related motifs, prequels, and sequels is a challenging exercise, for in his 'Guerrino' major features of the 'Goldener' type are missing while other motifs are only partially developed or are in the process of being forgotten. The wicked servants who accompany the boy during his years of wandering continually plot his death, yet fail to settle upon a means until they frame him to be sent on suicide missions, after which they are forgotten either as enemies or subjects of final punishment. Likewise, the ruler who promises death to the liberator of the wild man, including his own son, is tempered at the outset by grief and is not called back at the ending for a final reckoning. Guerrino does not take up preliminary employment at King Zifroi's court and flirt as a menial with his future bride. But we are hard pressed to say whether, in relation to these many roads not taken, Straparola's unique sixteenth-century snapshot is fully representative of its story tradition, or a deviation from an established 'international form' through the accidents of the local oral culture. There is work here for the geniuses of narratological inference from reconstructed contexts.

V. Fable 2
Adamantina's Astonishing Doll

ALTERIA

Adamantina, daughter of Bagolana of Savona, by the acts of a doll becomes the wife of Drusiano, king of Bohemia.

Man's wit is so clever, strong, and subtle that there can be little doubt it surpasses every other human force in the world. Not without cause it is said that the wise man is above the stars. This brings a fable to memory that, in the telling, will make clear to you, I hope, just how a young girl of mean and poor estate by the help of fortune became the wife of a mighty king. Although my fable is short, still you'll find it no less pleasing and amusing. So lend me your closest attention and listen carefully as you have listened formerly to my most honourable associates, who have earned your thanks.

In the land of Bohemia, dear ladies, there lived not long ago a poor old woman of Savona named Bagolana. She was miserably destitute in her way of life and the mother of two daughters, one of them called Cassandra and the other Adamantina. Now this woman, although she had hardly a thing to call her own, was anxious to set her affairs in order so that she might die in peace. Seeing that the sum of her disposable wealth consisted of a small coffer filled with tow, she left it to her two daughters, at the same time begging them to live peacefully together after her death.

These two sisters, impoverished as they were in the endowments of fortune, were by no means wanting in mental gifts, so that in matters of virtue and upright behaviour they weren't in the slightest inferior to other women. With their mother now dead and placed in her sepulchre, Cassandra, the elder sister of the two, took a pound of the tow, sat down, and with great care began to spin, making thread which, when it was finished, she gave to Adamantina, her younger sister, to take out into the marketplace to sell in order to buy bread and so keep themselves alive. Adamantina took the thread, placed it under her arm, and went on her way to the marketplace to sell her wares according to her sister's bidding. But as chance would have it, things went entirely counter to her wishes and those of her sister, for as she was walking in the square, she fell in with an old woman who had on her lap the most beautiful and most perfectly made doll that was ever seen. Adamantina's fancy was so taken by the poppet that, after she had feasted her eyes upon it, her thoughts became more absorbed with how she might obtain it than how she might dispose of her yarn. Her thoughts led her on, but finding no other words or means to acquire the doll, bartering seemed the only way. She approached the old woman saying, 'Good mother, if you are in agreement, I'll give you this thread of mine in exchange for your doll.'

The old woman, seeing such a fine and handsome girl, so eager to have the doll for her own, could not disappoint her, so taking the thread, she handed the doll over to Adamantina, who took it with the greatest delight and wrapped it in her apron.

Full of happiness and gaiety, she went back to her house. But presently her sister Cassandra asked her whether she had sold the yarn, to which Adamantina replied that she had. 'Well then,' Cassandra inquired, 'where is the bread that you bought with the money?'

Then Adamantina opened her fresh-laundered apron which she always wore in front and showed her sister the doll which she had gotten by bartering her wares. But the starving Cassandra, when she saw the doll, was filled with such violent anger and indignation that she seized Adamantina by the hair and belaboured her so grievously with cuffs and blows that the wretched girl could hardly move. Yet she took the pummelling with patience and, without attempting to defend herself, took her doll and hid in another room.

When evening came, Adamantina cradled her doll in her arms, as children might do, and sitting down by the fireside, took some oil out of the lamp and anointed the doll's stomach and legs. Then she wrapped it carefully in bits of tattered cloth and placed it in her own bed. A short time later, she herself went to bed, lying down beside the doll. Hardly had she fallen into her first sleep when Adamantina heard the doll cry out, 'Mamma, mamma, I have to go potty.'

Wakening from her sleep, she said, 'What's the matter, my little child?' And the doll repeated, 'Mamma, I have to poop.'

'Wait a moment, little one,' and she got right up, took the apron she had worn the day before, placed it under her and said, 'Now, my child.' Then to her amazement, the doll filled her apron with a heap of coins.

As soon as Adamantina saw what had happened, right away she woke up her sister Cassandra and showed her the money excreted by her doll. When Cassandra realized how much money there was in front of her, she was wonder-struck and rendered hearty thanks to God for sending them such welcome help in their time of need. Turning to Adamantina, she asked pardon for the mean and unwarranted drubbing she had given her. Then she took the doll and caressed it tenderly, kissing it and holding it closely in her arms. When the next day arrived, the two sisters used some of the money to buy bread, wine, oil, wood, and all manner of other provisions needful to a well-equipped house, taking care every evening to anoint the doll's stomach and loins with oil, wrap it in a piece of the finest linen, and ask it often if it felt an urge coming on, to which the doll replied 'yes' and then dumped a heap of coins.

On a certain day, by chance one of their neighbours, after visiting the house of the two sisters, noticed that their place was well furnished with all the necessities of life, and in such abundance, that she began to wonder how they could have grown rich in so short a time, remembering how miserably poor they had been formerly, and knowing full well that they were honest and upright in all their ways. Having given the matter full consideration, the neighbour resolved to find out the source of their ostentation. Going over a second time to their house, she asked them, 'My daughters, you really must tell me just how you manage to furnish your house so plentifully, seeing how you were in such want but a few days ago.'

Cassandra, the elder sister, offered a reply, 'Good neighbour, we have done all this by means of a single pound of flaxen yarn, which we gave in exchange for a doll, and this doll gives us money in abundance for everything we need.'

Upon hearing these words, their neighbour was filled with envy at their good fortune and made her resolve to steal the doll. As soon as she got back home, she told her husband how the two sisters had a certain poupée that supplied them every night with a great store of gold and silver, and how she had made up her mind to steal the doll from them at any cost.

It didn't matter that at first her husband made light of her words, for she went on with her story with such a show of reason that she convinced him in the end that it was the very truth. Then he said to his wife, 'So how then do you mean to steal it?'

To that the good woman answered, 'One of these evenings you must pretend to be drunk. Then you take up your sword and run after me threatening to kill me, but you only strike the wall. Then I feign to be in great terror of you and run out of the house into the street. The two girls, who have good, passionate natures, will assuredly open their door to me and take me in for protection. I'll stay there for the night and do my best to carry out my plan.'

On the following evening, the good dame's husband took a rusty old sword of his, and swinging it about, striking now the wall, now something else, ran after his wife who fled out of the house screaming and crying in a loud voice. When the two sisters heard this hullabaloo, they ran to look out into the street to see what might be the matter and recognized the screaming voice of their neighbour. At once they rushed from the window down to the door leading out to the street, opened it and pulled her into the house. Asked why her husband was pursuing and assaulting her in such anger, the good woman replied, 'This evening he came home so besotted with wine that he doesn't know what he's doing. And when I chided him for his binging, he grabbed his sword and ran after me threatening to kill me. Well, I was only too ready to get out of his way to keep him from causing more scandal. Being more nimble and swift-footed than he is, I rushed over here for protection.'

The sisters said with one voice, 'You did well, good mother. You'll stay with us tonight, no question about that, so you don't imperil your life with some new danger, while your husband's drunken fit works itself off.' Then they prepared the supper, to which all of them sat down together.

Going to bed, Adamantina took her doll with her, and when the time came for it to go potty, it called out, 'Mamma, I have to go.' Adamantina put a fresh cloth under it, in her usual way, and the doll pooped coins to the great astonishment of everyone. The good woman who had sought refuge with the sisters saw the whole thing and was most suspicious. Every hour now seemed a thousand years until she could steal the doll and cause it to perform this miracle for her own benefit.

When the morning came, the good woman secretly arose from her bed, left the two sisters still sleeping, and stole the doll from Adamantina's side without her detecting the theft. Then arousing the girls, she begged her leave of them to return to her own house, affirming that by this time her husband would no doubt have gotten over his drunken fury. No sooner in the door, she reported to him with a joyful countenance, 'Husband of mine, we've found our fortune at last. Just look here at the doll I told you about, which can do such amazing things.' It seemed like the night time would never come when it would make them rich. But when the darkness finally arrived, she took the doll, kindled a good fire in her bedroom, anointed the doll's stomach and loins with oil, and wrapped it carefully in swaddling clothes. Then undressing, she got into bed and placed it by her side.

After the first sleep of the night was over, the doll woke up and, not knowing who this woman was, cried out, 'Lady, I have to crap.'

The good woman, anxiously awaiting the result to follow, arose from her bed and took a very white linen cloth and put it under her and said, 'Now, my little one!' The doll, bearing down hard, now, instead of coins, filled the cloth with such foul-smelling feces that it was nearly impossible to go near.

'For god's sake,' said her husband, 'now look what a fool you are, and what a pretty trick this dolly has played on you. I'm just as big a fool for lending my ear to such stupidities.' At this the wife grew furious with her husband, affirming and swearing oaths that she had seen with her two eyes the heap of money the thing had made by shitting. Seeing just how determined she was to try it all over again on the following night, the husband, who was in no mood to face the same stench a second time, began to abuse her roundly with the most vindictive language a man ever levelled at a woman. Not satisfied with this, he also seized the doll in his hand and, opening the window, he hurled it out into the street, where it fell upon a heap of sweepings in front of the house. Not long after, by chance, a group of peasants who tilled land outside the city loaded this heap of refuse on their cart, intending to use it when the season came for fertilizer.

Not many days after this, Drusiano the king happened to go out into the country to find recreation in the hunt. Seized with a sharp pain in his intestines, he straightaway sought relief according to nature's course. Then finding nothing to wipe himself with, he called out to one of his servants to go in search of something that might serve his purposes. So the servant made his way towards the manure heap collected and deposited there by the peasants to see what he might locate suitable to such ends. By chance his eye fell upon the doll, which he took in hand and carried to the king. Without a moment's fear or hesitation, the king applied it directly to his butt to clean his excuse me, followed by the biggest scream you've ever heard. The doll had fastened its teeth into the king's rump and clamped down with such a grip that he bellowed out in agony at the top of his lungs. When those in his entourage heard his frightful yelling, they all ran at once to offer their aid. By then he was writhing on the ground more dead than alive. Great was their astonishment to find that his pain was caused by a doll fastened on to him, which they attempted at once to disengage from his posterior. Yet their efforts were all in vain, for the more they tugged to pull the thing away, the more torment it inflicted on the poor king. No one could break its hold, much less make it let go. Now and again, the doll would grab hold of his jungle bells and squeeze them so hard that he saw all the stars of the firmament even though it was the middle of the day.

So the miserable king returned to his palace with the doll still clutching his ass, unable to find any means of getting rid of his plague. A proclamation was then published to the sound of the trumpet declaring that any man, no matter what his condition, who had the wit and courage to remove the doll would be rewarded by a gift of one-third of the king's dominions. If a maiden, by chance, might be found to perform this work, he would make her his dearly-beloved wife, swearing by his own head to observe every letter of the aforesaid proclamation. No sooner was the king's decree made public than a vast crowd of people headed towards the palace in the hope of winning the promised reward, but not one of them was granted the fortune of being able to rid the king of his trouble. On the contrary, as soon as someone came near the king, the doll tormented him more grievously than ever. Thus cruelly vexed and tortured, the wretched Drusiano, unable to light upon a remedy for his strange and incomprehensible affliction, lay there like a man almost dead.

Cassandra and Adamantina, who, in the meanwhile had shed many tears over the loss of their doll, as soon as they heard the terms of the proclamation, went directly to the palace and presented themselves before the king. Cassandra, the elder of the two, began at once to fondle and caress the doll with signs of the greatest affection. But the poppet merely bit down harder and tightened its grip, torturing the king worse than before. Then Adamantina, standing apart from the others, now came forward and said, 'Your Sacred Majesty, please let me try my luck,' and accosting the doll, she began to speak, 'Ah, my child! Leave my lord the king now in peace and torment him no more.' With these words, she took hold of it by its clothes and began to fondle and caress it. The doll, as soon as it recognized its own mamma who had tended and cared for it, suddenly turned loose of the king's butt, to his majesty's great relief, and leaped into Adamantina's arms. When Drusiano saw this, he was utterly astonished and amazed and forthwith lay down to get some repose, for during many days and nights he hadn't been able to find either rest or peace from his sharp agony.

When in time Drusiano was healed of his wounds, in order not to break the promise he had made, he had Adamantina called into his presence, and when he saw that she was a graceful and pretty young girl, he married her in the presence of all his people. Shortly after that, he bestowed her older sister, Cassandra, in an honourable marriage amid sumptuous feasts and triumphs. Thereafter, they all lived together for a long time in great peace and happiness.

When the doll saw that both of the sisters were honourably and richly married and that all had come to a happy end, it suddenly disappeared; no one ever knew what became of it or where it went. But in my opinion it merely disappeared in the usual way of phantoms.

Alteria's fable, which was now at an end, gave great pleasure to everyone. They all laughed out loud and for a long time when they recalled the pretty way the doll went to stool, and how it hung on savagely by tooth and nail to the poor king's bum. When the laughter ended, the Signora asked Alteria to follow the customary rule and propose her enigma. Here are the damsel's words:

Just a span in length is he,
And plump in form in due degree,
Full of eagerness and pride,
And ready aye with men to bide.
Very fair his seeming shows;
Capote red he wears and hose,
And also bells. A thing of pleasure
To those who love him in due measure.

By the time Alteria's challenging riddle had come to an end, the Signora was no longer in a good mood, but casting angry looks upon the girl and saying that it was most impolite to speak such immodest words to the ears of honest women in her presence, and that in the future she must take care not to trespass like this again. But Alteria, blushing somewhat, turned towards the Signora and said, 'Signora, the enigma which I have just proposed is not immodest as you think, and this I will make quite clear to you by offering the real interpretation, which I'll reveal immediately to you and the rest of my gracious audience. You should all understand that my riddle signifies nothing other than the falcon, which is a bird at once tractable and bold, and cometh readily to the falconer's call. It wears jesses and bells on its feet, and it gives pleasure and diversion to anyone who takes it out to hunt birds.' When the real interpretation to this crafty riddle had been given and the Signora's perverse reading put aside, all the auditors gave it their hearty praise. The Signora, having by now abandoned her suspicions against Alteria and her enigma, turned her countenance towards Lauretta and made a sign for her to approach, to which the damsel complied at once. And because it was Lauretta's turn to offer the next fable, the Signora said to her, 'It is my wish that you put off telling us your story for a time, and that you hear first what the others may say. It is not because I hold you in light esteem that I say this to you, or that I rate your abilities less than those of your companions, but only so that we may be entertained this evening in a way that exceeds our expectations.'

Lauretta replied, 'Signora, any word of yours is my command,' and so, making her a deep courtesy, she went back to her place.

Then the Signora let her eyes fall upon Molino, to whom she made a sign with her hand for him to approach, whereupon he got up quickly from his seat and most respectfully went towards her. Then she said to him, 'Signor Antonio, this last evening of the week is a special time for us, a season of privilege for anyone to say whatever he may wish. So for my own pleasure and for the pleasure of this honourable company, I want you to give us one of your best and most joyous tales – nothing less. If you will grant us this favour, as I hope you will, we will all owe to you our lasting obligation.'

Molino, when he rightly understood the Signora's speech, at first appeared baffled and confounded, but when he saw there was no escape, he said, 'Signora, it is for you to command and for us to obey, but I would warn you not to expect anything from me that will give you any great pleasure, seeing that the illustrious damsels all around me have brought the art of storytelling to such a pitch of excellence that there is no possibility of surpassing them. Nevertheless, such as I am, I will do my best to give you satisfaction – perhaps not as much as you would wish, or as I could hope to give, but according to the measure of my humble powers.' Having so spoken, Molina returned to his seat and began his story in the following words.

V.2 Commentary

The story of Adamantina is a singular and grotesque variation on the rags to riches romance, for this child of poverty comes to her marriage with a king by relieving him of a fistula, or some related disease, if the doll represents anything other than an enchanted child's toy who plants her teeth into a royal posterior for no apparent reason except to spite him for attempting to use her for a bum wipe (or to win for her ward, in the way of a fairy, the benefits of a royal marriage). That the story offers no help at all in decoding just what went wrong with his majesty's rump, and just how Admantina's uniquely efficient ministrations relieved his ailment through and beyond a story of an antagonized doll, will dissuade no one, given the innate will to believe in real social, medical, magical, or psychological realities embedded in such representations. The story has to be an allegory of something, of healing and redemption, for otherwise in dwelling on sphincters, doo-doo, and gripping pains, it can only be about the psychological counterpart to the excrementally human, a deep story in relation to the repressed consciousness of the race concerning poop, pleasure, perversity, and disgust. The doll, moreover, has claws with an unspecified reach which are constantly active in tormenting the king each time someone attempts to help him. Are those hands the counterpart to mental phobias or fixations? Is this doll the enactment of a castration complex? Is the promised marriage to the helpless and impoverished girl, so tenderly maternal with her doll, yet suddenly old enough to marry, the cure for his highness's residual suffering, thereby connecting the excremental to the marital? Joël Gayraud thought so, according to his annotations of the story.[32] Such readings intrigue, as though early folk formulators understood the need to symbolize such deep (and recently formulated) anxieties through their fables. But there is little denying that the story generates compelling images involving feces and money, dolls and posterior pains, and hyperbolical deliveries of excrement with the attendant odours. Thus, we may begin with the purely Rabelaisian, recalling the chapter in Book I in which the young Gargantua explains to his uncle his preferences regarding the materials and techniques for post defecatory cleansing.[33] More compelling than the view of the doll making her fecal mess on the delicate white cloth of

32 Giovan Francesco Straparola, *Les nuits facétieuses*, trans. Joël Gayraud ([Paris]: José Corti, 1999), p. 624. 'On y trouve la fixation à l'enfance, avec la poupée, qui joue ici le rôle du symptôme, et la pulsion sadique avec menace de castration, dans l'épisode où la poupée mord les fesses du roi et lui pincer cruellement les testicules.' In his analysis, the doll's biting and squeezing is symptomatic of the king's childhood fixations, sadistic impulses or fears, and a castration complex (all of which Adamantina resolves, perhaps, through marriage?).

33 *Five Books of the Lives, Heroic Deeds and Sayings of Gargantua and His Son Pantagruel*, intro. Anatole de Montaiglon, trans. Thomas Urquhart and Peter Antony Motteux, 2 vols. (London: Lawrence & Bullen, 1892), vol. I, pp. 43–7. The finest of these was 'the neck of a goose, that is well downed, if you hold her head betwixt your legs,' etc.

the acquisitive neighbours, more compelling than the picture of a king writhing in pain as a poppet clamps down on his arse, more compelling than the scene of crowds pouring into the palace to attempt to win a prize for dislodging the tenacious doll, is the image of Cassandra, the elder sister, stroking and caressing the *poupée* while it is still attached to his royal fundament – a propinquity that taunts the imagination. Does the mind make pictures of such things, and if so, are we invited to think of the doll's condition as it leaps willingly into the arms of its loving 'mother' when she tells it to desist? The reader may well question the nature of the ideal response. The tale is a tale and thus 'other speaking' in its way, yet as with all such creations, it foregrounds its own concrete phenomenology. Before it 'means,' it requires mental representation.

Conventions pertaining to dolls, inanimate by definition, yet evincing human intentional states and acts of volition, are endorsed and processed without a second thought. They are accepted as readily as any child's willingness to believe in talking bunnies or envious lions. Living dolls are metaphors in action whereby categorical imperatives are playfully dissolved; here such a creature is programmed to excrete money as an act of charity and feces as an act of retribution and justice. The 'truth' is in those actions, not the agent. Moreover, the doll is selectively endowed with a tick's ability to cling, a child's inclination to recognize and trust only a mother's ministrations – two primal instincts perhaps – and powers of language sufficient to announce an imminent bowel movement. But does the doll have a real social agenda? What are its intended ends as a volitional creature? The question must be misleading, because while readers have difficulty enough in attributing to the representations of persons in fiction all that pertains to personhood, they will have even more in attributing all the perquisites of consciousness to this pretty toy, whose reality arises strictly within the conditions of a literary mode. So how does the fable mean? Because the doll disappears as a phantom when it is no longer needed, as fairies are inclined to do once their services are rendered, it may be nothing more than an agent of the fairyland 'intentionality' of seeing a pauper wedded to a king, just because that's what fairies do.

If it is in the order of such tales not to dwell on psyches except as agents in the shaping of emblematic narratives, then characters merely think what they have to think to shape the story. The *récit* is about a doll purchased by a little girl for whom it opts to generate wealth in the tradition of the golden-egg-producing goose and the coin-excreting donkeys of medieval folklore – pure innocent wish fulfilment or patent fraud. It is, moreover, a story about rudimentary justice, as when the doll refuses to reward those who have stolen it, or when the king follows through in marriage to a commoner who knows how to control her kid. Inversely, it is the agent doll that enables its graceful and pretty owner to enjoy a fairy tale life ever after by compelling the king to make a lavish and reckless offer of marriage. Adamantina thus follows in the wake of all the little obscure heroines who answer riddles and marry kings, or the poor doctor's daughter who goes off to court to cure the king's intractable disease and thereby win the groom of her choice. With regard to the symbolism of the narrative, 'Adamantina' and Shakespeare's 'All's Well that Ends Well' share a common order. Of phobias and complexes, of the anal and genital, of gender and sex, the story is a *potpourri* of wild signifiers as binding as the reader's inventive fantasies and intellectual predilections demand. Nevertheless, of the filth associated with money, the story bids reflection, as it does concerning the touchstone bond between mothers and their offspring and the obedience attached to instinct. At the same time, it is a parodic re-enactment of the romance rise from abjection to the pinnacle, a fairy tale without fairies, yet employing an old crone who sells the doll for a wad of yarn, and the recycling of a story type with a confirmed popular approbation even in antiquity. If the king's posterior is a wasteland, the story is a ritual proceeding to romance, but in such miniature proportions as to suggest parody. And perhaps the story really is a brilliant deconstruction of the frivolous dream of kings and weddings, for Adamantina makes herself ready for the matrimonial transition by expending her prattling care upon a creature defined by its bodily effusions seen variously as treasure and ordure, while the doll as the prelude to royal progeny literally holds the parent hostage to fortune, if not to the king's own fantasies about the pains of childbirth. Or perhaps it is just a story about one of the fundamental factors of the human animal attached to a squeamish mind chosen out for delivery to the elegant members of a literary salon, members (in Straparola's framing tale) who found the greatest delight in the most objectionable scenes. As with all good oral tales, it has a calculated design on its audience, this one to bring limbic approbation out of amusing incongruity. In that it surely succeeds.

'Adamantina' does not begin as a romance, but rather as a variation on the story of the gold-emitting animal – a snake, goose, or dragon – and the attempt on the part of someone associated with the animal's benefactor and beneficiary to kill it out of greed, thinking to come into possession of all its wealth at once. It is a tale of simple benefice and wish-fulfillment followed by the losses associated with greed and ignorance. Behind it, to be sure, is a complex belief system concerning the will of the world's hidden forces to reward the meritorious, coupled with an animism that invests in lower creatures specific quotients of wisdom, magic powers, and agency. Oddly, in the *Mahåbårata*, it is the king's son who excretes gold, making a child the source of his father's financial well-being. This bounty is brought to an end by the robbers who slay him to get at once all the gold presumed to be inside his body.[34] They were deceived like the neighbours in the tale of Adamantina. All of these stories depend upon the self-evident wisdom that things that excrete do not contain at any one time all that they are capable of excreting over time. It is the fallacy committed by all who slay geese that lay golden eggs (in contradistinction to those who believe that geese can indeed lay golden eggs as a precondition for manifesting their virtue in waiting for them one by one). A parallel version appears in the *Panchatantra* concerning a tutelary serpent which is worshipped by a Brahmin. In exchange for the gift of daily milk the Brahmin receives a gold coin; the gods are grateful and generous. When his son is commissioned to feed the creature during the Brahmin's absence, however, he attempts to kill it and retrieve all the gold from the mound (anthill) it protects. The snake, however, detects the betrayal, bites the son and kills him.[35] In this regard, the gold producers of Western fables and fairy tales are remotely related to the serpents and dragons that protect treasure mounds and barrows.

Aspects of this story type turn up among the fables of the Middle Ages. Marie de France, in 'Le villain et le dragon' (The peasant and the dragon), joins the golden egg with the egg of the man-without-a-soul, as in the stories of the mighty ogres who become vulnerable only when the hero engages upon a long quest for the object that contains his soul. (With regard to these precious eggs and their destruction, see the commentary to 'Fortunato,' III.4). In Marie's version, a dragon planning a trip asks a friend to keep an egg that contains all of his potency and might. The peasant who accepts the care of the egg begins, in time, to think of his advantage and hence breaks it open. When the dragon

34 *Metrical Translations from Sanskrit Writers*, trans. John Muir (London: Trübner, 1879; reprint, London: Routledge, 2000), p. 27. See also *The Mahabarata*, trans. R.K. Narayan (London: Mandarin, 1991).

35 *Panchatantra*, trans. Chandra Rajan (London: Penguin, 1993), bk. III, no. 6, pp. 305–6; 'Le Brahmane et le serpent,' in the *Panchatantra*, trans. Édouard Lancereau (Paris: Gallimard, 1965), pp. 241–2.

returns, he realizes the man's intent and moralizes on his untrustworthiness, in essence explaining the enmity between man and dragons ever after. Just what the egg did or did not contain goes unspecified, along with any nefarious results for the dragon, apart from his deception. The tale seems to have lost its own soul, but carries the outlines of the golden egg fable.[36]

The 141st story of the *Gesta romanorum* provides a misogynist twist, because it is a greedy wife who attempts to slay the magic provider.[37] A serpent, pitying the indigence of a knight, supplies him with gold in exchange for sweet milk. (The Eastern influence is in full view.) There followed much good fortune and the birth of a beautiful son. The wife was convinced that the serpent was hiding even greater treasure and advised her husband to kill it. The knight made the attempt, missed, and immediately his ruin was in the making, including the death of his son. The wife, the cause of yet another paradise lost (but also in collaboration with her husband), tells her husband to beg for pardon in search of 'grace' by shedding tears. The serpent tells him he is a fool, that the attempted blow can never be forgotten, that no peace can ever follow between them, and that he must beware in the future, for the nature of the serpent is subtle and venomous. As in Marie de France's *Fables*, the story has been redesigned to homiletic ends, but the basic type prevails. Avianus offers his version of the simple tale of 'The Goose that Laid Golden Eggs,' to mock naïve ambition and to reconcile men to slow and steady increase.[38]

---

36 *Fables*, ed. Harriet Spiegel (Toronto: University of Toronto Press, 1994), no. 52, pp. 155–6.

37 *Gesta romanorum*, trans. Charles Swan and Wynnard Hooper (New York: Dover [1876], 1959), pp. 246–7.

38 *The Fables of Avianus*, trans. David R. Slavitt (Baltimore: Johns Hopkins University Press, 1993), pp. 43–4. The gold-excreting donkey and all his many literary relatives need only be mentioned briefly here because they were merely natural donkeys made to appear magical by their dishonest owners. The donkey of the *Historia di Campriano contadino* will serve in illustration of the generic trick of shoving coins into the anus so that the donkey may appear to be excreting them to the eyes of naïve beholders willing to pay a very high price for such an animal. Typically, this donkey fails to perform after purchase, in a way roughly parallel to Adamantina's doll in the hands of the neighbours, which brings the purchasers back to the shrewd peasant, who always puts them off with a clever reply: that it is all their fault in not following instructions or not treating the animal properly as he professes to have explained. This story is closely related to the tricks in the 'Scarpacifico' group (I.3). The story is suitably old, at one time attributed to Giovanni Pietro Polendrini

The most important transformation to have overcome this story tradition before reaching Straparola is the conversion of the beast fable, exemplum, or rustic anecdote into a micro-romance by appending the story of the gold-shitting doll to the story of the ass-bitten prince. The idea may have arisen merely through the bathroom humour fixed in both stories, that of the magical gift stolen by a neighbour who is punished for the theft by an effusion of dung, and that of the king out hunting who, while relieving himself, encounters something unusual, such as the conversation of animals nearby who tell where a treasure is hidden. Straparola's tale is the first to record the amalgamation in print in which the story of a defecating king is made the continuation of the story of a defecating doll cast out on the garbage heap. But the credit may not be his for the amalgamation, simply because the story in that compound form was collected widely among the folk reciters of the nineteenth century. Of course, Straparola's tale may have gone back into circulation – an eternal ambiguity in the history of folklore.

In the world of the Italian social vignette, jest, and proto-novella, Girolamo Morlini tells the story of the priest who shitted gold and was killed by a Basque who took him for an instant repository of limitless wealth. He sought to make demonstration of the priest's potential in the presence of the king by compelling him to imbibe a fatal dose of myrobalan nuts, cassia, and prunes. Hence the priest found death and the foolish Basque soldier exile. Given, however, that the priest had

(or Palantrini). It was first published in 1518 as well as in 1550 and 1579. The coin trick is preserved in Italo Calvino's 'The Story of Campriano,' in *Italian Folktales*, trans. George Martin (New York: Pantheon, 1980), no. 82, pp. 298–301; it is a late folk version of an established and widely circulating medieval tale. See Jan M. Ziolkowski, *Fairy Tales from Before Fairy Tales: The Medieval Latin Past of Wonderful Lies* (Ann Arbor: University of Michigan Press, 2007), pp. 157–60. W.A. Clouston, in *Popular Tales and Fictions*, ed. Christine Goldberg (Santa Barbara, CA: ABC Clio, 2002), pp. 31–6, has a small chapter on 'Gold-Producing Animals,' in which he mentions further examples linked to the Eastern tale of the benefactor animal slain to capture all its wealth, as in 'Le lion aux sequins d'or,' in *Contes albanais*, trans. Louis Auguste Henri Dozon (Paris: Leroux, 1881), pp. 139–46, that features a poor man with a wife and son, and a lion that drops coins from its lips. Somehow the boy's family fortunes, and the fact that he is jeered by the neighbourhood boys for being a booby, causes him to take it out on the lion which he assumes to be the cause of it all. The mother foolishly gives him the key to the cage, where, for nicking the lion's tail with his saber, he is torn to pieces. The lion continues to give gold to the penitent father, but renounces all future friendship with humankind.

swallowed his gold to keep it secure, the story falls between tales of donkeys with inserted coins and tales of wonder creatures slain for their singular talent.[39]

It would appear that the only literary version of the story in the form presented by Straparola published within a century of his is 'La papara,' the first diversion of the fifth day of Basile's *Pentamerone*.[40] Unusual is that this version coincides so closely with Straparola's when so many other cognate tales by Basile differ substantially. Lolla buys a goose at the market and discovers that it drops gold coins, a godsend for two sisters living in abject poverty. To be sure, a goose is not a doll, but the girls had sold thread to buy it, and they keep it with them in their own bed at nights. The goose no doubt belongs to the 'primitive' tale, but the doll is an altogether more likely bed partner, because geese don't bother to ask. When a show of prosperity from the proceeds attracts the attention of the neighbour, it is deemed that the girls had found a hoard or had sold their honours. That latter option is alluded to by Straparola only in the vaguest of terms. The truth is discovered by boring a hole in the wall to watch their activities, including the spreading of sheets and the gathering of coins. Less dramatically than in Straparola, the neighbour appears merely to borrow the goose. For the great quantity and stench which the goose then produces, it gets its neck wrung and is cast into the street for dead. Shortly thereafter, the king's son passes the house, is overcome by colic, and opts for an alleyway. Near to hand was the goose, destined to serve the king in the most ignominious fashion. Surpassing its counterpart, employed as Gargantua's 'torcheculative' (asswipe) this one springs to life and follows the script, leading to untold pain, proclamations, and the appearances of many to attempt a cure. When Lolla arrives, however, the goose, hearing its mistress's voice, relinquishes its hold to seek her caresses. Before the prince makes the girl his 'queen,' he has the thieving neighbours whipped and exiled, and so the tale concludes. The variations are evident, perhaps due to the regional differences in the story's telling. They are important, however, in confirming

39 *Novelle e favole*, ed. Giovanni Villani (Rome: Salerno, [1983]), no. 41, pp. 198–201; *Les nouvelles de Girolamo Morlini* (Paris: E. Sansot, 1904), pp. 102–3. Andrea Calmo (1509–1570) testifies to the wide circulation of 'tante fanfalughe' (such folderol) in his day, mentioning the story of the 'Aseno che andete remito.' *Le lettere*, ed. Vittorio Rossi (Turin: E. Loescher, 1888), p. 346.

40 Giovanni Battista Basile, 'The Goose,' in *Il Pentamerone*, trans. Sir Richard Burton (New York: Boni & Liveright, 1927), pp. 393–6.

the unlikelihood that Basile worked out of the *Piacevoli notti*, but rather that both built independently upon a fable then widely current and varied, yet already fixed in its pervasive form – purchase, gold production, theft, deception, disposal, the royal party, ironic and ignominious rediscovery, and the romance-formula ending.

That general formula is reconfirmed in the many examples of the tale recovered in the nineteenth century. Of these, one must suffice to illustrate its endurance and confirm its popularity. Again it must be said that in terms of narrative fitness, this configuration carries in its 'memes,' for better or for worse, the staying power of a true survivor. The version collected by Giuseppe Pitrè is so similar to Straparola's that only the differences require mention.[41] The doll is purchased with the only bit of money the widow could earn from the sale of her thread to buy bread. The child, Ninetta, is captivated by the doll. She is not only roundly beaten by her mother and two sisters, but locked out of doors to suffer cold and poverty. Only then does the doll ask to 'make doo-doo!' and so produces the coins. The girl is now welcomed back and the mother becomes extravagant in her purchases, which include a house and carriage. The neighbours create the domestic spat as a pretext for the wife to spend the night as a houseguest. Following the theft, the doll raises both ire and disgust by her evacuations and is spurned in consequence, ending up as rural detritus. The doll's white apron attracts the king's attention, and for his attempt, this poppet goes right up his fundament and lodges

41 'The Biting Doll' (La pupidda), in *The Collected Sicilian Folk and Fairy Tales of Giuseppe Pitrè*, ed. and trans. Jack Zipes and Joseph Russo, 2 vols. (New York: Routledge, 2009), no. 288, vol. II, pp. 785–9. A further example is 'Il Ciuchino caca-zecchini' (The coin-shitting doll), in Gherardo Nerucci, *Le sessanta novelle popolari montalesi*, ed. Roberto Fedi and Eugenio Montale (Milan: Rizzoli, 1997), no. 43, pp. 359–63. This story shares in common merely the coin-excreting animal given to the son of a poor widow by his uncle with advice not to share his secret. From that point onward, it is the story of the boy who loses each gift given to him by his benefactor to a shrewd inn-keeper, including the banquet-furnishing tablecloth, until he arrives with the beating stick, which so clobbers the host that he is brought to return all three gifts to the boy. The story is taken over in truncated form by Ludwig Bechstein in his *Neues deutsches Märchenbuch*, in which the second part is discarded dealing with a king, his malady, and the sudden rise of the doll's owner from pauper to queen. It tells of the little girl whose special doll makes golden eggs only for her and smelly eggs for everyone else. 'Dukaten-Angele,' in *Neues deutsches Märchenbuch* (Leipzig: Hartleben, 1856), no. 50, and also in Bechstein's *Sämtliche Märchen* (Munich: Winkler Verlag, 1971), pp. 692–9.

itself in his rectum, placing all Freudian hermeneutes back on deck, now that the doll is in the hole. Then all the king's men tug and tug, but can't get dollie out again. The doctors fail, too, and the proclamation goes out with the same happy issue. The malady *in ano* has been ousted, 'all's well when the end's well,' Ninetta is declared seventeen, and a month of celebrations follows.

V. Fable 3
The Three Hunchbacks

ANTONIO MOLINO

in Bergamese dialect

Bertoldo of Valsabbia had three sons, all of them hunchbacks and much alike in appearance. One of them, called Zambò, goes out into the world to seek his fortune and comes to Rome where he is killed and thrown into the Tiber, together with his two brothers.

It is really difficult, most pleasing ladies and gracious madonnas, I mean really difficult 'to kick against the pricks' (durum est contra stimulum calcitrare), for the kick of an ass is a cruel thing, but that of a horse is worse. So seeing that fortune wills me to tell a tale, well, patience, for obedience trumps sanctimoniousness; obstinacy is wickedness and he who is such will surely go to the devil's house. But then, if I tell you something that is not to your tastes, don't place the blame on me, but on the Signora over there who has put me up to it.

How often it happens that a man goes looking for what he had best leave alone, because many times he lights upon things he never expected to find, and in the end is left with his hands full of flies. This is exactly what happened some time ago to Zambò, the son of Bertoldo of Valsabbia, who tried to snare two of his brothers, but who was himself snared by them. Thus in the end they all three died miserably, as you'll hear if you lend me your ears and listen with open minds and understandings to the story I'm about to relate.

I must tell you that Bertoldo of Valsabbia, in the territory of Bergamo, had three sons, all of them hunchbacks, and all resembling each other so closely that it was impossible to tell one from the other. In fact, they might be likened to three shrivelled pumpkins. One of them was called Zambò, another Bertaz, and the third Santí. The eldest was Zambò, who was not yet sixteen. One day it came to Zambò's ears that his father,

Bertoldo, intended to sell the small parcel of land that was his patrimony for the family's sake, because there was a great famine in the surrounding areas and throughout the rest of the land. But because there was practically no one to be found in that country who didn't have some property of their own, Zambò addressed himself to his younger brothers, Bertaz and Santí, saying, 'It would surely be a wiser plan, my dear brothers, that our father retain the little bit of property that we happen to have so that, after his death, we have something by which to gain our sustenance. You two should go out into the world and try to earn something that will help us maintain our house, while in the meantime, I remain at home to take care of the old man. That way we won't waste our substance and that should get us through this time of scarcity.'

Bertaz and Santí, the younger brothers, who weren't a whit less crafty and cunning than Zambò, answered him at once, 'Dear brother Zambò, this has all come up rather suddenly and you pose to us questions we hardly know how to answer. Give us one night to think it through. We'll consider the matter and tomorrow we'll let you have our reply.'

These two brothers, Bertaz and Santí, had been born together and between them there was a greater sympathy than there was between either of them and Zambò. And if Zambò had an ounce of roguery in his nature, these two had a good couple of pounds of it, for often it comes about that where cultivation is lacking, ingenuity and malice make up the loss. When the following morning arrived, Bertaz, by agreement with Santí his brother, went to find Zambò to pursue their conversation, beginning thus, 'My dear brother Zambò, we have carefully considered and thought about our situation, and seeing that you're our elder brother, we think it more appropriate for you to go out into the world first and that because we're the smaller ones we should stay here to look after our father. In the meantime, if you come across any good fortune for you and us, you write to us so we can go right out to join you.'

Zambò, who had hoped to snare both Bertaz and Santí, was most disconcerted by this answer and muttered to himself, 'These two scamps are more cunning and malicious than ever I thought.' He had hoped to be rid of his two brothers and to be left the master of all their property, trusting that both of them might die of hunger by reason of the famine in the land. Moreover, their father was not long for this world and already had one foot in the grave. But the outcome of this affair turned out vastly different from anything Zambò had expected.

So when Zambò heard the answer given by Bertaz and Santí, he made a small bundle of the few rags he possessed, filled a pouch with some bread and cheese and a small flask of wine, put his feet in a pair of broken pigskin shoes, and set out towards Brescia. Finding nothing to suit him there, he went on to Verona where he met a master hosier who asked him if he knew the trade, and to whom he answered 'no.' Seeing that there was nothing for him to do there, he left Verona, and, after passing through Vicenza he came to Padua, where certain doctors saw him and asked him whether he knew how to care for mules, to which he once more answered 'no,' saying only that he could till land and tend vines. Because he came to no agreement with them, he went on his way to Venice.

Zambò wandered about the city for a long time without landing upon any employment to his taste, and seeing that he now had neither money nor food about him, he realized the bad way he was in. After walking back and forth, by God's will he ended up at Fusina, but because he was penniless no one would assist him. Not knowing which way to turn, the poor chap, noting that the ragged wastrels who turned the winches that drew the boats ashore earned a few pence by their trade, he took it up himself. But Fortune, who always persecutes the poor and unfortunate, one day willed, when he was working one of these machines, that the leather strap should break. In untwining, it caught a spar which hit him full in the chest and knocked him to the ground, where for a time he lay as though dead. Had it not been for the quick aid given to him by a few charitable chaps who hauled him into their boat and rowed him back to Venice, I believe most certainly that he would have died.

As soon as Zambò had recovered from the ill effects of this accident he went in search of further employment, and as he passed by a grocer's shop, the master, who was pounding almonds to make into marzipan, asked him whether he was of a mind to work in the shop and Zambò replied that he was. Once engaged, the grocer set him to work sorting sweetmeats, instructing him how to separate the black from the white. He worked alongside another shop boy (may he get a cancer!), the two of them carrying out the task by stripping off the rind and outer covering, eating the sweet parts, and leaving only the hard bits behind. When the grocer saw what was going on, he took a stick in hand and gave each of them a sound beating, saying, 'If you're intent on plunder, you thievish knaves, I prefer that you pilfer your own stores and not mine.' Then he gave them a further taste of the stick and told them both to be damned.

Smarting from the grocer's blows, Zambò went to San Marco, and passing by the place where herbs and vegetables are sold, by good fortune he met a market gardener from Chioggia named Vivia Vianel, who demanded of him whether he would be willing to work for him, promising him good food and fair treatment as well. Zambò by this time looked like the famished wolf on the arms of Siena and was longing for a good meal, so he said 'yes.' When Vianel finally sold his last few bunches of herbs, they took a boat and returned to Chioggia where Zambò was immediately set to work in the garden tending the vines.

Now, after he had gone all around in Chioggia for some time, Zambò became acquainted with several of his master's friends, and when the season for the first ripe figs had come, Vivia took three of the finest he could pluck from his garden, placed them on a platter, and sent them as a gift to his friend Peder in Chioggia. He called Zambò, gave him the three figs, and said to him, 'Zambò, take these three figs, carry them to my friend Ser Peder, and ask him to accept them for love of me.'

In obedience to his command he replied, 'With pleasure, my master,' and taking the figs he went merrily on his way. But then his ill luck caught up to him, for as he was going along the street his appetite took possession of him. He looked at the figs again and again and said to his gullet, 'What shall I do? Shall I eat them or shall I refrain?'

His gullet replied, 'A starving man observes no law, so eat.' Gourmand by nature and very hungry – that was the reason Zambò listened to the ill counsel of his food pipe. Laying hands on one of the figs, he began to tear the skin from the neck. Then he took a bite here and a bite there, all the while saying 'It is good. It is not good.' And so he went on tasting until he had eaten the whole thing, leaving only the skin.

Once eaten, he began to wonder whether he might have done the wrong thing, but with his gullet still urging him on, he wasn't long in his indecision. He took the second fig in his hand and treated it as he had treated the first. After the greedy fellow had made an end of the second, he was again assailed by fears and, on account of his fault, he hardly knew whether he should go on or turn back. But after short deliberation, he took courage and decided to proceed. As soon as he had come to Ser Peder's door, he knocked and the door was instantly opened to him, because he was well known by the householders. He entered and went in search of Ser Peder, whom he found walking about. The good man asked him, 'So what has Zambò come to tell me? What's your good news?'

'Good morrow, good morrow,' answered Zambò. 'My master gave me three figs to bring to you, but of these three I have eaten two.'

'But how could you do such a thing as that?' said Ser Peder.

'Oh, I did it like this,' replied Zambò, and with these words he took the last fig and ate it deliberately, and so it happened that all three of the figs ended up in Zambò's belly. When Ser Peder saw this saucy jest, he said to him, 'My son, tell your master that I thank him, but that in the future he needn't trouble himself to send me more presents like this.'

Zambò answered, 'No, no, Messer Peder, don't say that, for I'll never grow weary of such errands,' and having said this he turned about and headed for home.

When the report of Zambò's trick came to Vivia's ears, and when he learned moreover that he was both lazy and a glutton, guzzling when he was hungry until he was ready to burst, and how he would never work except when he was driven to it, the good man chased the hunchback out of his house. Zambò, poor devil, finding himself again without employment, didn't know where to turn, so after a little delay he decided to go to Rome in hope that he might find better fortune there than he had found so far, until what he thought about doing was what he did.

When he arrived in Rome, Zambò went about everywhere looking for a master, and at last he met a certain merchant named Messer Ambros dal Mul, who kept a great shop full of cloth. Zambò took service with him and was put to work minding the store. Seeing that he had suffered so much in the past, he made up his mind to learn the trade and to live a decent life in future. Although he was deformed and ugly, still he was very shrewd, and in a short time he made himself so useful in the shop that his master saw no further need to do the buying and selling, but trusted everything to him and employed him in many services. It came about that one day Messer Ambros had occasion to go to the fair of Recanati with a stock of cloth, but seeing that Zambò had become so competent in the business and had proved himself trustworthy, he decided to send Zambò to the fair and to remain at home to mind the establishment himself.

After Zambò's departure, there was more ill fortune, for Messer Ambros was seized with so grave a disease, worse than a terrible dysentery, that after the lapse of a few days he died. When his wife, who was called Madonna Felicetta, found herself a widow, she nearly died of grief over the loss of her husband and from the anxiety that she might lose her clientele. As soon as Zambò heard the sad news of his master's death, he returned immediately and set about, by God's grace, to manage the affairs of the business. Madonna Felicetta, as time went on, remarked that Zambò behaved himself well and honestly and was diligent in managing affairs. She was mindful too that a year had now rolled by since the death of her husband, Messer Ambros. Because she feared one day to lose Zambò, along with many of her customers, she sought advice from some of her closest friends whether she should remarry and whether it might not be best for her to take Zambò for her husband – the factor of her business who had been in the service of her first husband for such a long time and who had gathered a great deal of experience in the management of her affairs. These worthy confidants deemed her proposition a wise one and advised her to marry Zambò. Little time passed between the word and the deed, for the nuptials were celebrated soon thereafter. Madonna Felicetta became the wife of Ser Zambò, and Ser Zambò the husband of Madonna Felicetta.

Now when Ser Zambò found himself raised to this high estate, what with a wife of his own and a fine shop well stocked with all manner of cloth goods, he wrote to his father, telling him he was now in Rome, and of the great stroke of luck that had come to him. His father, who had heard no news of his son since the day of his departure, having never received a written word from him, suddenly gave up the ghost from sheer joy. Bertaz and Santí meanwhile found their own consolation in such affairs.

One day it came about that Madonna Felicetta needed a new pair of stockings, because the ones she wore were all rent and torn. She said to Ser Zambò, her husband, that he must have another pair made for her. To this Zambò replied that he had other business to do and that if her stockings were torn she had better go mend them, patch them, and put on new heels. Madonna Felicetta, who had been greatly pampered by her late husband, replied that it had never been her manner to wear mended and reheeled stockings, and that she must have a new pair. Ser Zambò shot back that where he came from customs were different and that she simply must do without. Thus the bout of wrangling began, and from one angry word to another, it came about in the end that Ser Zambò lifted his hand and cuffed her so heavily over the head that she fell to the ground. Madonna Felicetta was little disposed to come to terms with him or to seek out any conditions of peace, but planned how she could return him blow for blow, and with that she began to swear at him. But feeling his honour impugned, Ser Zambò worked her over so soundly with his fists that the poor woman was compelled to shut her mouth.

When the summer had passed and the cold weather set in, Madonna Felicetta asked Ser Zambò to let her have a silken lining to repair her fur coat, which was in very bad condition, and which she set out to prove to him by bringing it in for him to inspect. But Ser Zambò didn't bother even to look at it. He simply said that she had to mend it and wear it as it was, for in his country people were not used to such pomp. Madonna Felicetta was greatly angered at his words and declared that she'd have what she asked for at any cost. Ser Zambò replied that she had to be quiet and not arouse his wrath, or else things would go far worse for her. Still Madonna Felicetta pursued the matter, insisting upon her needs, till the two of them, one after the other, worked themselves up into such a fury that they were nearly blinded with rage. Ser Zambò, in his customary way, started thumping her with a stick, covering her with as many blows as she could stand until she lay on the floor half dead.

When Madonna Felicetta saw how radically his humour had changed towards her, she began to blaspheme and curse the day and hour when she had first spoken to him, remembering as well those who had advised her to take such a husband in the first place. 'Is this the way you treat me,' she yelled, 'you craven rogue, jerk, useless bastard that you are? Is this my reward for all the benefits you've received? From the base hireling you were before, haven't I made you the master not only of my wealth but of my person? And still you treat me in such a way? Well never fear, you treacherous thug, because I'm going to make you regret every bit of this.'

When Ser Zambò heard how his wife grew even angrier and poured out her abuse on him more copiously than before, he continued to ply his cudgel upon her back to give her the finishing touch, which reduced Madonna Felicetta to such a state of fear that whenever she heard the sound of Zambò's voice or footsteps she trembled like a leaf in the wind and wetted her linen with terror.

When the winter had passed, it chanced that Ser Zambò had to go to Bologna on business to collect certain sums of money due to him. Because the journey would take a few days, he said to Madonna Felicetta, 'Wife, I want you to know that I have two brothers, both of them hunchbacks like I am; in fact, they resemble me so much that were you to see the three of us together, you wouldn't know which was which. Now I'm asking you to keep a close watch in case they come here and try to lodge with us. Make sure that you don't let them come over the threshold on any account, for they are wicked, deceitful, and crafty knaves, and would assuredly play you some evil trick, only to scamper away and leave you with your hands full of flies. Let me find out that you have ever harboured them in this house and I'll make you the most wretched woman in the world.' With these words he left.

Within a week of his departure, the brothers Bertaz and Santí arrived and went about asking for Ser Zambò's shop, which was pointed out to them. When these two scoundrels saw the fine boutique richly furnished with all kinds of cloth goods, they were astonished and wondered out loud how he could have amassed so much wealth in so short a time. Lost in wonderment, they went to the shop door and asked to talk to Ser Zambò. They were told that he was neither in the house nor even in the city, but that if they needed anything they could ask for it. At that, Bertaz repeated that they'd willingly speak to him, but that if he wasn't at home they'd speak to his wife, asking the servant to call Madonna Felicetta. As soon as she came into the store, she knew right away that these men were her brothers-in-law. Bertaz, when he saw her, asked right out, 'Madonna, are you the wife of Zambò?'

And she answered, 'Most certainly, yes.'

Bertaz replied, 'Madonna, shake hands, for we are the brothers of your husband, and thus your brothers-in-law.'

Remembering the words of Ser Zambò and the beating he had given her, Madonna Felicetta refused to touch their hands, but they went on plying her with so many affectionate words and gestures that in the end she shook hands with them. As soon as she had thus greeted them, Bertaz cried out, 'Oh, my dear sister-in-law, give us something to eat, because we are half starved.' Well, this she wouldn't do. But these rascals knew the arts of flattery so well, and begged so persistently, that Madonna Felicetta was moved to pity, took them into the house, gave them plenty of food and drink, and likewise a room to sleep in.

Hardly three days had passed since Bertaz and Santí had arrived at Madonna Felicetta's house before Ser Zambò returned. Seeing who it was, his wife was beside herself with fear and hardly knew what to do to keep the brothers out of Ser Zambò's sight. Hitting upon no better plan, she made them go into the kitchen where there was a trough used to scald pigs, telling them to hide themselves underneath.

When Ser Zambò entered the house and remarked upon his wife's dishevelled and worried appearance, he grew suspicious and said, 'Why do you look so frightened? What's the matter with you? I suppose there's your lover hidden away somewhere in the house?'

She replied in a faint voice that there was nothing the matter with her. But Ser Zambò, who was all the while looking at her sharply, said, 'For certain, there's something the matter with you. Are those brothers of mine in the house by any chance?'

She answered boldly that they weren't, whereupon he began to give her a taste of the stick, according to his custom. Bertaz and Santí, underneath the pig trough, could hear all the hurly-burly, which so terrified them that they crapped their britches and dared not so much as move or cough. When at last he put down his stick, Ser Zambò began to search the house in every corner to see whether he could find anyone hidden, but discovering nothing he calmed down and went about his affairs. He was preoccupied in this manner for such a time that Bertaz and Santí, the luckless brothers, forced to keep their hiding place for so long, what with the fright, the heat, and the terrible stench of the trough, in sheer distress as they lay there soon gave up the ghost.

When the customary hour came for Ser Zambò to go to the market-place to meet with merchants and conduct his trade, he left the house. No sooner had he gone out than Madonna Felicetta went to the pig trough to figure out some scheme for getting rid of her brothers-in-law so that Ser Zambò might never suspect her of giving them shelter. But when she uncovered the trough, she found them lying there both stark dead and looking exactly like two pigs. Seeing the mess she was in, the poor woman fell into a fit of grief and despair. But to keep her husband in ignorance of what had transpired, she set her mind directly to work to figure out how to get them out of the house so that the mishap might be hidden from everyone.

I have heard people say that in Rome there is a custom that should the dead bodies of strangers or pilgrims be found in the public streets or in any man's house, they are given immediately to certain undertakers, deputized for the task, to carry outside the walls of the city to be cast into the Tiber, so that nothing thereafter is ever heard or seen of them. Going to the window to see if by chance any of her friends might be passing who could lend a hand in getting rid of the two dead bodies, by good fortune Madonna Felicetta spotted one of these corpse-bearers. She called to him to come in, telling him that she had a body in the house and that she wanted him to take it away at once and cast it into the Tiber according to the custom of the city. Already Madonna Felicetta had pulled one of the bodies out from under the cover of the trough and left it lying on the floor nearby. So when the corpse-bearer had come upstairs, she helped him to load the dead man on his shoulders, urging him to come back to the house after he had thrown him into the river, when she would pay him for his services. With that, the porter of the dead went outside the city wall and threw the body into the Tiber and, having done his work, he returned to Madonna Felicetta to ask for his customary fee of a florin. But while the corpse-bearer was engaged in carrying off the first body, Madonna Felicetta, crafty dame that she was, drew out the other body and placed it at the foot of the trough in exactly the same place where the first had lain, and when the corpse-bearer came back for his payment, she said to him, 'Did you really carry the corpse I gave you to the Tiber?'

To this the fellow replied, 'I did, Madonna.'

'Did you throw it into the river?' asked the dame.

And he answered, 'Did I throw it in? Certainly I did, and in my best manner too.'

At this speech Madonna Felicetta said, 'How could you have thrown it when it's still lying right here?'

When the corpse-bearer saw the second dead body, he really thought it must be the one he had carried away and was covered with dismay and confusion. Cursing and swearing the while, he hoisted it upon his shoulders, carried it off, cast it into the Tiber, and then stood there for a long while to watch as it floated down the stream. While he was once more returning to Madonna Felicetta's house to receive his payment, it happened that he met Ser Zambò on his way home, and when the corpse-bearer saw a man so much resembling the other two hunchbacks he had carried to the Tiber, he flew into such a violent fit of rage that it was as though he spat forth fire and flames on all sides giving free rein to his passion. In truth, he thought the fellow in front of him was no other than the one he had twice before tossed into the river, and that he must be some evil spirit that kept coming back again and again. So he crept around behind Zambò and dealt him a deadly blow on the head with the crowbar he carried in his hand, saying, 'So there, you wretched villain, do you think I want to spend all day long hauling you to the river?' Railing at him with such words and handling him so violently, poor Zambò, what with the thwacking he had received, was soon a dead man and gone to speak with Pontius Pilate.

Then the fellow hoisted the third corpse on his shoulders, bore him away, and threw him into the Tiber after the two others. Thus Zambò, Bertaz, and Santí miserably ended their lives. Madonna Felicetta, when she heard the news, was delighted beyond measure and felt no small contentment in knowing that she was free from all her hardships and might once again enjoy her former liberty.

Molino's fable here came to an end. It pleased the ladies so much that they couldn't stop laughing and talking about it. And although the Signora requested their silence several times over, she found it no easy matter to put an end to their merriment. Finally, when the noise died down, she asked Molino to set them an enigma to guess at, which he delivered to them as follows:

Out of their prison grave so dark
Arise the bones of dead men stark,

And 'twixt the hours of tierce and sext,
By signs will tell to mortals vext
What chance's smiles or frowns of fate
May bless or ban till time grows late.
Savage and deep the miser's curse,
Marking the signs of chance averse.
But he, untouched by lust of gold,
Unmoved, will fortune's freaks behold.
Next, one with beard of flesh upsprings,
And beak of bone, and warning sings
To bid the watchers bury deep
Their bodies in a downy sleep,
And lie, poor fools by care unstirred,
On welcome boon of foolish bird.

Although Molino's fable had greatly pleased the entire company, this ingenious and somewhat gruesome enigma diverted them even more. But insofar as no one had gathered an inkling of its meaning, the ladies with one voice begged him to reveal the answer. When he saw that the company was of one accord in the matter, in order not to appear stingy with his gifts, he solved the enigma in the following terms: 'My riddle, dear ladies, signifies the game of hazard. The bones of the dead which quit their graves are the dice which fall out of the dice box. When they mark tray, deuce, and ace, these are the points that show good luck. Now won't just such points as these put spirit into the play and money into the purse of the man who often wins such throws? Does the loser ever like to go away a loser, and does not all this come by the change and variations of fortune? The avaricious player who always seeks to win will now and again curse and swear so fiercely that I can't think why the earth does not open up and swallow him. Then, after they have sat at play late into the night, the cock, which has a beard of flesh and a beak of bone, will get up and crow, thus letting the gamesters know that it is past midnight and that they should repair to their beds of goose down. When they lie in these, is it not like sinking into a deep grave? What do you all think of my explanation?'

The unriddling of this subtle enigma was received by the whole company with great laughter – laughter so hearty, in fact, that they could barely keep themselves from rolling about on their chairs. Then after the Signora had asked everyone for silence, she turned towards Molina and said, 'Signor Antonio, as the fair orb of Diana outshines all other stars, so the fable you just told, no less than your enigma, bears off the palm from all others we have heard so far.'

Molino answered, 'The praise you give me, Signora, is by no means due to my skill, but rather comes from the great courtesy that always abides in you. And if the Trevisan here would tell you a story in the dialect of his country, I'm sure you would listen to his with even greater pleasure.'

The Signora, who much desired to hear a story told in this fashion, said, 'Signor Benedetto, do you hear what our Molina has said? There is no question but that you would be doing him a great wrong were you to make his words false. So put your hand in your pouch and draw out a pleasant story to bring us merriment.' The Trevisan thought it improper on his part to take Arianna's place, whose turn it was next, and at first excused himself, but seeing that he couldn't weather this point, he began his fable in the following words.

V.3 Commentary

This tale is not among Straparola's best, yet its final episode is constituted of one of the most enduring of the medieval farcical tales, that of the look-alike hunchbacks, monks, or minstrels who, as unwonted cadavers, are toted one after the other for disposal, usually in a river, by a comic porter who thinks, upon seeing a second dead victim, that it is the first which has somehow returned to the house. Frustrated by the repeated task, he is brought to kill a still living look-alike he encounters on the way back for his pay – in our story the hunchback husband returning home. The cruelty is paramount in many redactions, some of them dealing in cold-blooded murder; it is a feature of the story that can only be mitigated by the idiocy of the porter, the shrewdness of the lady in a fix who commissions him, and the stupidity and cruelty of the victims themselves, which allows for a measure of comic justice.[42] Always better are the versions in which a jealous husband is killed by the exasperated porter, rather than a look-alike innocent bystander. To this stand-alone little farce, Straparola, or possibly a Bergamasque predecessor telling the tale in dialect, adds an episodic prelude in which the hunchback

42 On the suspense and excitement generated by the iterative forms and the ironic readings of reality in these *fabliaux*, see Thomas D. Cooke, *Old French and Chaucerian Fabliaux: A Study of Their Comic Climax* (Columbia: University of Missouri Press, 1978), pp. 47, 125.

protagonist sets out in the world to seek his fortune, in the manner of many a fairy tale in which brothers of impoverished circumstances embark on parallel life journeys before their reunion. Straparola may have had his own story of 'The Three Brothers' (VII.5) in mind, in which two of the three learn professions while the third masters the ostensibly useless talent of understanding the language of animals (which of course will serve to brilliant and prosperous ends). It is a fairy tale in the making in which the little hunchback, in marrying the boss's wife, parodies a wonder tale-rising tale from rags to riches. But in the present rendition, all that promise is thrown away in a monstrous parody. This is a harsh social vignette in a familiar geographical landscape in which two shrewd and treacherous brothers scheme against the eldest, sending him out into the world alone to make his way, with the understanding that should he come to prosperity, he is to write home and let them know. Zambò the adventurer fulfils his promise after he marries the prosperous widow of his employer, but fulfils it most incongruously, insofar as the entire final episode turns upon the warning to his wife never to entertain his brothers or let them into the house should they show up on the doorstep. Linking the two parts together necessitated this clumsy slippage in narrative logic.

The first part consists of three rather uneven episodes in the life of a *picaro* who is first the pathetic victim of a workplace accident in the Arsenal of Venice that nearly costs him his life, then a doltish employee of a grocer who gets himself beaten for eating and ruining the food he was to prepare, and third, a smart alec who, in literal response to a question about how he had eaten two figs intended as a gift, eats the third in demonstration. This is reminiscent of one of Tyl Eulenspiegel's less creative pranks, although Straparola derived it from some such source as the *Farce nouvelle tres bonne et fort joyeuse de Guillerme qui mangea les figues du cure* (The joyous new farce of Guillermo who ate the priest's figs).[43]

---

43 *L'Ancien théâtre françois*, ed. Viollet Le Duc (Paris: Bibliothèque Elzeverienne; reprint, Paris: P. Jannet, 1854), vol. I, pp. 328–50. In this little play, an impatient *curé* has an exasperating, literal-minded, headstrong, talkative theology student. In one episode he is sent to invite the priest's *commère* to supper – in effect a neighbour's wife with whom he is having an affair – bearing two figs as a gift. He too stops on the way, examines them, thinks about eating them, eats one, recites his comic rationale, and thanks God the other has escaped a similar fate. When the *curé* asks what happened to the first, Guillerme confesses, and in response to the question 'How did you do that?' he shows him by eating the other one, which leads to threats and near dismissal. Antoine le Métel, Sieur d'Ouville, 'D'une servante qui mangea

This section might have become a picaresque view of the world had Ser Zambò become a witty narrator, and something of his personality might have emerged had there been more developmental coherence to the episodes. Of the managing classes, we learn only that they are fell in their punishment, humourless, and decisive in their dismissals.

Perhaps the most interesting feature of the protagonist's life on the road, beyond his privations and suffering, is the trajectory itself, for he begins in a village near Bergamo called Valsabbia (forty kilometres north-east of Brescia), or generally from the valley itself, from whence he makes his way to Brescia looking for work, then on to Verona, passing through Vicenza on his way to Padua where he declined a job offer involving the care of mules, only to end up in Venice doing odd jobs around the city and in Chioggia at the end of the lagoon.[44] This is the itinerary that Ruth Bottigheimer maps provisionally upon Straparola's own career, in that he came from Caravaggio, made the setting of the *Piacevoli notti* the island of Murano, and published his two books in Venice. The biographical value of such indices is circumstantial, at best, but holds an intriguing prospect. Moreover, this is one of the few stories in the collection that is told in a local dialect – that of Bergamo, the home of the *commedia dell'arte*'s Harlequin and Brighella, who would carry their linguistic idiosyncrasies to the world. It is told by the comic poet, Antonio da Molino, no doubt known to Straparola for his talent in the local patois, a long poem which he would publish in 1561. This, however, is in the dialect from the region where Straparola himself grew up; he was showing off, while making Molino his buffoon by playing to the Murano elite for laughs.[45] This is, of course, the patois of Zambò and his

deux perdrix' (Of the servant who ate two partridges), in *Élite des Contes*, ed. P. Ristelhuber (Paris: Alphonse Lemerre, [1643], 1876), no. 23, pp. 40–2, develops the same motif. The maid tells the invited guest who had taken liberties with her that the master intended to cut off his ears, hence his mysterious departure. When her master arrives, having eaten both birds, she may now report that she had sent both birds home with the departed guest. Similar tales can be found among the *fabliaux* and in the *Nouveaux contes à rire* (Amsterdam: George Gallet, 1699), p. 266. See Giuseppe Rua, *Tra antiche fiabe e novelle* (Rome: E. Loescher, 1898), p. 110, which brings us back to Straparola's story.

44 *Fairy Godfather: Straparola, Venice, and the Fairy Tale Tradition* (Philadelphia: University of Pennsylvania Press, 2002), pp. 54–8.

45 See Marie-Françoise Piejus, 'Le couple citadin-paysan dans les "Piacevoli notti" de Straparola,' *Ville et campagne dans la littérature italienne de la renaissance*, ed. Anna Fontes-Baratto et al. (Paris: Université de la Sorbonne Nouvelle, 1976), p. 168.

brothers, hailing from a region already noteworthy for its blowhard but stalwart labour force who descended from the mountains in search of work (see the commentary to IX.5).

At the centre of the tale is a comic porter as the carrier-out of corpses, a character with a highly principled work ethic, but unconcerned with any other form of morality in relation to his work. Hence, in the *Estormi* of Hugues Piaucèle, a thirteenth-century *fabliau*, the entire tale is named after this dogged labourer, the name itself signifying 'fight' or 'tumult,' while at the same time evoking the verb *estourbir*, 'to kill.'[46] Others in this role, in cognate tales, are household servants or village idiots, foreigners, drunks, or the most literal-minded of menial labourers. In humdrum fashion he is called in to haul away a dead priest in a sack and toss him into the river. He asks no questions in light of the generous pay. When he returns for his money, however, a second priest has been brought out of hiding, which, in Estormi's befuddlement, he likewise hauls to the river, thinking it the same cadaver. Upon encountering the third, he begins to curse amidst talk of miracles and revenants. His mood is not wonderment, but exasperation. How will he get his pay if the bodies keep coming back? The final humorous incongruity is that in returning the third time, he meets a live priest having nothing to do with the affair, takes him for one of the dead, and kills him for good measure with a blow over the head that spatters brains and blood in all directions, uttering all the while lines such as the following:

Comment, sire boçus, tornez?	What, Mr. Hunchback, back again?
Or me semble ce enresdie.	You're darned stubborn it seems to me.
Mès, par le cors sainte marie	But, by the body of St Mary,
Mar retornastes ceste part.	This time you'll regret coming back,
Vous me tenez bien por musart.	Taking me for an idiot like that.

This particular brand of humour, a mainstay of the farce, alone reconciles us to the brutal events. *Estormi* is a particularly anti-clerical variation on the stock tale in which a wife hides three minstrels or hunchbacks from her husband, finds them accidentally dead, and then must get rid of the bodies, only to lose her husband (another hunchback) into the bargain,

46 This *fabliau* has often been reproduced. It occurs in the *Recueil général et complet des fabliaux des XIIIe et XIVe siècles*, ed. Anatole de Montaiglon and Gaston Raynaud, 6 vols. (Paris, 1872; reprint, New York: Burt Franklin, 1964), no. 19, vol. I, pp. 198–219.

taken for a resuscitated corpse – a loss seldom to her regret. In *Estormi*, a loyal wife, Dame Yfame, finding herself solicited by three priests for sexual favours and promised great sums of money, is told by her husband to invite them in, whereupon he kills them himself with a sledgehammer as they enter, or later in bed, in order to steal their belongings together with the money intended to pay for favours. Estormi is then called upon to dispose of the bodies, on his return killing a fourth in his exasperation. (To approve of this story, one must really hate priests.) He then receives his pay for a job well done. This story's narrative kinship with Straparola's *favola* is patently clear, but there are no self-evident conclusions to be drawn in terms of transmission and borrowing.

Of potential sources and analogues there are many, ranging from the thirteenth to the nineteenth centuries. A noteworthy study of the story type at the end of the nineteenth century by Joseph Bédier makes the present commentary from the perspective of Straparola both easier and more difficult.[47] He works with fourteen texts, beginning with those versions in the *Historia septem Sapientum* and the Hebrew version of the *Seven Sages*, the *Mishle Sendebar*. The important factor is that both works are putatively derived from Arabic, Indian, Turkish, or Hebrew sources, although the final answer on the origin of that textual tradition is not yet in. With regard to this tale, Bédier is prepared to cede the point that it originated in the East upon demonstration, although the general bias of his entire study is to disprove, with some rhetorical expostulation, the penchant then current for tracking all Western folklore to Eastern sources. His strong predilection is to attribute this story to medieval European writers, despite its appearance in two collections traditionally

47 *Les Fabliaux: Études de littérature populaire et d'histoire littéraire du moyen âge* (Paris: Édouard Champion [1894], 1925), pp. 236–50. The story of the three chevaliers who all seek to seduce the same married woman, their fates at the hand of the husband, and the ignominious disposal of their bodies in the manner of the three hunchbacks appears among select, perhaps late, versions of the *Roman des sept sages de Rome*, one of them published in Geneva in 1482. The porter, the woman's brother, takes a live knight for the corpse making its return, captures him, and burns both horse and rider. The husband and wife then begin to fight in public and in the cross accusations, the wife reveals the crime, making this a further lesson in the treachery of women in accordance with the framing tale of the *Seven Sages*. According to A. Loiseleur Deslongchamps, the story is taken from a manuscript in the Bibliothèque de l'Arsenal, no. 1309; the text is reproduced in the Appendices to the *Roman des Sept Sages* in his *Essai sur les fables indiennes et sur leur introduction en Europe* (Paris: Techener, 1838), pp. 103–10.

associated with the East, given that these same collections in the *Seven Sages* tradition were elaborated in the West, not before the thirteenth or fourteenth century, around a limited number of core stories to which were added many others, some arguably of Western provenance, in essence 'orientalized,' much as Galland may have done in filling out the *Arabian Nights.* Two points are in his favour concerning this particular story: that no correlative versions have come to attention from works of unquestioned early Eastern provenance; and that the story features the kind of slapstick redolent of the medieval *sottie.* In brief, the story has an ethos of its own arguably not characteristic of Eastern tales. Moreover, Bédier remarked that of the fourteen texts he examined, six told of lovers who were hidden from the husband and died in the process, whether identical-appearing chevaliers or monks, while eight told of hunchbacks, whether brothers or minstrels, who were invited into the house behind the husband's back for reasons of pity or for the wife's amusement. He deemed the hunchback versions to be closest to the generic tale, largely because the lovers and anti-clerical versions have weaker narrative logic and less humour. Why, for example, if the husband is involved in the murders, must he hire a porter at all? Why, if the lovers are called in one by one, are the bodies accumulated? Concerning those hunchback tales, he could not tell whether they were literary or folk in origin, nor could he decide whether the 'minstrels' or the 'brothers' version should be given precedence. That, in brief, is a summary of his complex argumentation, from which we may deduce that Straparola's 'The Three Hunchbacks' is a descendant of the hunchback brothers group. Of these, his story is the first literary survivor (there are prior minstrel versions). Moreover, in relation to Bédier's analysis, Straparola's tale is closest to the oikotype which, three centuries earlier, had produced several versions even then showing signs of degradation. They were early literary breakaways from the generic tale central to the story tradition.

According to that scenario, the folk tale of the 'hunchback brothers' existed, not only before Straparola, but even before the much earlier *fabliaux* in which the victims are minstrels. That is my intuition. The alternative scenario is to assign the birth of the tale to one of the early *fabliaux* writers, such as Durand, from whose single and clever invention the entire story phenomenon derives, spreading to the folk reciters, collector-editors in the *Seven Sages* tradition, subsequent talent-challenged *fabliaux* writers, and *novellieri.* That too seems possible but perhaps less plausible. In the latter case, the present tale must be seen to follow in the well-trodden path of the *novellieri* who, formerly, had written *fabliaux* into *novelle* – Straparola taking his story directly or, far more likely, from a current version of the tale taken over by the popular tradition.[48] It may be reasoned further that, whether as folk tale or *fabliau*, there had to have been a 'good' version before the mangled rendition in the *Mishle Sendebar*, one having far more in common with the 'better' folk versions collected during the nineteenth century. To follow are the resumes of the tales, early and late, upon which all this inferential analysis has been based, forming a story trajectory in which Straparola's contribution is among the most significant.

Whatever their origins, the stories in the *Historia septem Sapientium* and the *Mishle Sendebar* are remote from Straparola's tale, despite John Colin Dunlop's view that 'the immediate original is one which occurs in some versions of the Seven Wise Masters.'[49] To have constructed the present tale as he did from such a source, given the later analogues, would be miraculous. Arguably, his source resembled closely what he wrote. Nevertheless, the earliest traces of that story's tradition begin with the *Seven Sages*, in which the sage's sixth story tells of a husband and wife who set about to trap passers-by as prospective lovers to the lady.[50] She sings in public and makes assignations in close sequence with three cavaliers to whom she has made eyes. The husband kills them as they enter and the bodies are dealt with in the now familiar way. Then, however, the wife quarrels with her husband, denounces him, and both are arrested and dragged behind horses to the place of hanging. It is a tale of outright fraud and punishment involving three look-alike victims and the disposal of three bodies. The Hebrew redaction of the *Seven*

---

48 On the spread of French literary culture in Italy from the early thirteenth century and the influence of the *fabliaux* writers on the early *novellieri*, see John Colin Dunlop, *History of Prose Fiction*, ed. Henry Wilson, 4 vols. (1896; reprint, New York: Burt Franklin, 1970), vol. II, p. 43.

49 John Colin Dunlop, *History of Prose Fiction*, ed. Henry Wilson, 4 vols. (1896; reprint, New York: Burt Franklin, 1970), vol. II, p. 42.

50 *Historia septem sapientum*, ed. Detlef Roth (Tübingen: Niemeyer, 2004); or ed. Goerg Buchner, after the Innsbruck manuscript (Amsterdam: Rodopi, 1970). This story is not to be found in Johannes de Alta Silva's *Dolopathos* nor in any of the French and English versions of the collection. The *récit* of the sixth sage can also be found in *Deux redactions en prose du roman des Sept Sages*, published by Gaston Paris, according to *Bédier*, p. 237, although it is not found generally in the work called *Le roman des Sept Sages de Rome*. In essence, it is found only in the Latin and Armenian versions of this textual tradition, thus raising questions about its oriental provenance and its relationship to the two very different versions of the story in the *Historia* and the *Mishle*.

Sages 'est étrangement défiguré et si sottement conté qu'il ne serait pas intelligible' (is so strangely disfigured and so stupidly told that it would hardly make any sense) if we did not know it from other versions.[51] The January–May situation is introduced, involving the old man married to the pretty young girl, who, because of her husband's jealousy, is made to live a sequestered life. Bored, she one day sends a servant out to find some entertainment for her and he comes back with a hunchback minstrel, who then brings in his two fellow hunchbacks. The husband doesn't even have to return home to set up the cadaver crisis. The three companions drink themselves into a stupor and are shoved into a neighbouring room where they kill each other. Then she calls for an Ethiopian (the setting is quite inexplicit) to carry the bodies away in a sack one after the other. The porter is then paid. The humour of the porter is largely absent and there is no fourth victim taken for one of the returning hunchbacks, nor is there any indication that the wife's husband was one of their kind. Because the story is so badly told, it could not have been the source for the subsequent versions involving hunchbacks, but must, itself, be a degraded literary version of the farce or folk tale.

The work of greatest interest in relation to Straparola, and predating him by at least two centuries, is the French *fabliau*, 'Les trios bossus ménestrels.'[52] It is the clearest testimony in existence of an early story tradition dealing with hunchbacks who come to atrocious ends and are unceremoniously disposed of by a 'niais' porter. Durand or Durandus (twelfth to thirteenth century) tells the story of a beautiful girl who is married to a singularly ugly, vile, jealous, and rich hunchback. When Christmas arrives, three hunchback minstrels come to the house asking to spend the holiday with one of their own. The rules of hospitality prevail and they are well-feted and provided with gifts, but upon parting,

---

51 *Les Fabliaux*, p. 244. *Tales of Sendebar*, trans. Morris Epstein (Philadelphia: Jewish Publications Society of America, 1967), the sixth tale of the wise man; Bédier speaks of an edition by Heinrich Sengelmann in 1842, by which he must mean *Das Buch von dem sieben weisen Meistern* (Halle: J.F. Lippert, 1842). Also the edition of the *Historia septem sapientum* (Der sieben weisen meister) by Alfons Hilka is actually the *Mishle Sendebar* (Heidelberg: C. Winter, 1912).

52 Durand, 'Des trios boçus,' *Recueil général et complet des fabliaux des XIIIe et XIVe siècles*, ed. Anatole de Montaiglon and Gaston Raynaud, 6 vols. (Paris, 1872; reprint, New York: Burt Franklin, 1964), vol. I, pp. 13–23; *Fabliaux ou contes du XIIe et du XIIIe siècle*, ed. P.J.B. Le Grand d'Aussy (Paris, 1781; reprint, Geneva: Slatkine Reprints, 1971), vol. IV, pp. 241–9. See also *Fabliaux Fair and Foul*, ed. Raymond Eichmann, trans. John DuVal (Binghamton, NY: MRTS, 1992), pp. 140–7.

they are warned never to return. Prevailing upon the pity of the pretty wife in the husband's absence, however, they are called back to sing and perform. When the husband arrives, they are hidden in a coffer where all three expire. The alarmed wife calls in a porter, urging him never to speak of these things in exchange for a substantial amount of money. Then she presents him with three corpses one after the other, as though the first had twice returned or had never been taken in the first place. The porter's growing consternation is evident. The third time there is no laughter but grim imprecations and a stoic mission. After the third, he keeps looking about himself on the way back and sees the master coming home, who is dispatched as though he were a revenant. First he rounds with him for making a fool of him, then clobbers him with a pestle and puts him in a sack. The wife is cognizant of the fourth death only by innuendo, but is pleased by her loss and pays out the money. The story is remarkably close to Straparola in spirit and design, in the wife's compassion for the three hunchbacks, in their accidental deaths in a confined space, and in the death of the husband at the hands of an exasperated porter, thereby accomplishing her wishes without involving the lady in malfeasance. That Durand invented or borrowed, or that Straparola elaborated upon the *fabliaux* tradition directly or indirectly, or took his story wholesale from a folk elaboration remains a moot point. Forced to a choice, I would say either that Durand worked from a popular tale of Western origins, to which Straparola added the picaresque preliminary material and the Bergamasque dialect to a literary tradition in debt to the French *fabliaux* or, more plausibly, that he transcribed it from local folklore.

Closer to Straparola in time and place is Giovanni Sercambi's *novella*, 'De vitio luxurie in prelato di Ranieri pellaio in Pisa' (De visio lusurie in prelatis). But the work belongs squarely to the *Estormi* group and thus has little bearing on the present story.[53] It is a witness, nevertheless, to the success of the story type in its alternate version. Three monks from St. Nicholas Church in Pisa impose their affections upon Nece, harassing her in eroto-suggestive ways at various points in the church; no doubt their hypocrisy partly reconciles us to their fates. Nece asks her husband – a tanning merchant – what to do. According to the confidence game he devises, he will be absent, she will invite them to supper, allow

53 *Novelle*, ed. Giovanni Sinicropi, 2 vols. (Bari: Laterza & Sons, 1972), no. 11, vol. I, pp. 61–7.

them their *ultima cena*, and lure them into the bath, all in anticipation of his return. When he arrives, they are hidden in a huge vat into which the husband pours lime and boiling water. The routine of the porter ensues, a foreigner this time, who agrees to get rid of the body of a monk who had died in the house. When they went looking for Andrea the priest on the following day, they found only his prayer book, a candle, and a trail of blood. Only then do they realize that their trick, placed in the hands of a foreign porter, had also cost an innocent clergyman his life.

There remain several versions of the story type roughly contemporary with Straparola, of interest for their comparative elements, but unlikely to have had any connection to him. There are still others which may be directly in Straparola's debt, and still others collected as folk tales in the nineteenth century, some with uncanny resemblances to the present story. In 'Ain lied von einer vischerin' (The fishwife's lament), the tale has been adapted to the wandering scholars tradition of the late Middle Ages and is set in Vienna. It is the same basic story told by Sercambi, except that the fishwife has been on a lark with her visitors. When her husband returns with a fine catch of carp, he insists on putting them in the very basin where the 'clerks' are hidden, which must first be filled with water. They drown. Then one by one they are disposed of by an oafish porter by being pitched into the Danube. Upon his return, he too meets with a priest, takes him for one of the scholars, and sends him towards Budapest.[54] It is a simple variation on the *Estormi* type. Another work from that same late medieval period, 'The Three Monks of Colmar,' bears further witness to the popularity of the tale epitomized by Sercambi.[55] The three lovers in hiding are so terrified by the frightening noises made by the menacing husband that they spontaneously throw themselves into a cauldron of boiling water.

54 *Erzählungen aus altdeutschen Handschriften*, ed. Adelbert von Keller (Stuttgart: Literarischer Verein, 1855), pp. 347*ff.*

55 'Die drî münche von Kolmaere' (The three monks from Colmar), in *Gesammtabenteuer: Hundert altdeutsche Erzählungen: Ritter- und Pfaffen-Mären, Stadt- und Dorfgeschichten, Schwänke, Wundersagen und Legenden*, ed. Friedrich Heinrich von der Hagen, 4 vols. (Stuttgart: Cotta, 1850; reprint, Darmstadt: Wissenschaftliche Buchgesellschaft, 1961), no. 62, vol. III, pp. 163–85. Each one of the monks is invited to the house, bashed senseless with a mace, and stashed in a butter tub. One is dragged to the front door and a porter is hired to dump the corpse in the Rhine. Each new one is taken for the first and is more ruthlessly handled until a fourth and still living monk is also killed as one of the preceding victims deemed to have returned to life. This story is rough and heavy fare.

Of greater interest is a farce on the topic of the three hunchbacks mounted as one of the *théâtre de la foire* productions – popular outdoor spectacles held in conjunction with the annual fair of Saint-Germain or Saint-Laurent. (Their heyday was the late seventeenth and eighteenth centuries until their suppression in 1789.) *Les rencontres, fantaisies et coqs à l'asne facetieux du baron Gratelard, tenant sa classe ordinaire au bout du Pont Neuf* contains a theatrical version of the story of the three hunchbacks in seven scenes so similar to the tale of 'The Three Hunchbacks' that the farce may rightfully be considered another of Straparola's progeny.[56] There is Trostole, the ugly old hunchback, married to a young and pretty wife. Horace, who seeks her love, employs the fool, Gratelard, to carry his letters. The plot we are familiar with is taken up in the play when Trostole tells his wife never to open the door to his three hunchback brothers. Then he leaves on business. The brothers arrive, cajole, crave shelter, and are taken in by pity. They are soused by the time Trostole unexpectedly returns and they expire inside coffers from the effects of their inebriation. Gratelard does his work with all four. 'All four?' asks the wife and realizes her good fortune, for now she can marry Horace. In the final scene, Trostole and his three brothers really do come back and start a huge *melée*, a concession to the ways of the popular theatre. Straparola would seem the only logical source for a work so proximate in design. Joseph Bédier mentions a version in the *Contes nouveaux et plaisants, par une société*, which may be passed over briefly.[57] The story is transported to Asia, no doubt to disguise its direct debt to Straparola. According to Bédier, (quite significantly) it contains the preliminary adventures before the unwonted visit of the two brothers. The hunchbacks in hiding die of a surfeit of alcohol as in the farce. Then, quite unexpectedly, the Caliph of Baghdad, Harun al-Rashid (historically, 763–809), puts in an appearance, having had a dream about the river with its nets. Upon inspection, the three hunchbacks are found alive,

56 (Troyes: Chez Pierre Garnier, 1736). The work is also contained in Jean Salomon Tabarin (Antoine Girard dit Tabarin), *Oeuvres complètes de Tabarin,* [*avec les rencontres, fantaisies et coc-à-l'âne facétieux du baron de Gratelard*], ed. Gustav Aventin, 2 vols. (Paris: Jannet, 1868), vol. II, pp. 193*ff. Una covata di gobbi, ovvero I tre gobbi della Gorgona con Stenterello, facchino ubriaco* (Florence: Salani, 1872) is an Italian farce on the same topic in which Stenterello (The starved), a drunk porter from the piazza, drowns the three humpback brothers one at a time. This farcical play, too, may have had direct debts to Straparola. See Giuseppe Rua, in *Intorno alle 'Piacevoli notti' dello Straparola* (Turin: Loescher, 1890), p. 69.

57 *Contes nouveaux et plaisants, par une société* (Amsterdam, 1770), pp. 44*ff.*

whereupon the Caliph admonishes the married hunchback for his inhospitality towards his two brothers. The story reflects the orientalizing of Western stories that had become popular in France.

Another of this kind, equally indebted to Straparola, is the 'Tale of the Three Crump Twin-Brothers of Damascus' of Thomas-Simon Gueullette.[58] But Gueullette did not complete his retelling without fully incorporating the preceding version from the *Contes nouveaux* and then adding several other now familiar folk tale motifs too long to summarize. The story begins and ends with instances in which a crime committed by one triplet can never be punished unless it can be determined which of the three is the real culprit. As long as all confess or none confesses, the guilty one is safe. One had wounded a merchant's son at the opening, but in standing together, the guilty one goes free, although all three are exiled. Thus begins their life on the road. Each learns a trade, but only Barbakan prospers in marrying the widow when his master dies. The two brothers at last visit him in Baghdad, but Barbakan wants to avoid the ridicule that would follow from being seen together. His wife, nevertheless, lets them in, then hides them behind a brandy vat where they are ostensibly asphyxiated. The porter now dumps them in the Tigris and then throws Barbakan into the river as well under the usual mistaken assumption. When the porter and the wife get into a spat, this vigorous chap decides to drown the wife as well, but meets a fisherman carrying one of the three bodies back. The porter then confesses everything and ends up before the Caliph telling how the little crump came back to life and had to be carried a second time. A triplicate resurrection follows – all the brothers are back – and now the identity stunt is repeated in which the wife must correctly choose her husband from the three of them as each makes the claim for himself. This idea too may have derived from Straparola's 'The Three Brothers' (VII.5) in which it is to be decided which of the three merited marriage to the princess in whose rescue all three had played crucial parts. Matters are settled only when the wise Caliph declares that the real Barbakan would be bastinadoed, at which point the other two sell him out. With this story, we may have come to the limits of Straparola's direct influence upon the tradition of the three

58 *The Thousand and One Quarters of an Hour or Tartarian Tales*, ed. Leonard Smithers (London: H.S. Nichols, 1898), pp. 81–98.

hunchbacks, but the story type by other channels enjoyed widespread circulation in both oral and written form.[59]

One oral version was collected by Giuseppe Pitrè in Sicily.[60] The hunchback now has a pretty daughter, and while he is away, he tells his wife to give her anything she wants. She asks for her father, so the mother brings

59 A parallel group of texts often cited by Straparola's commentators may be epitomized by the story of 'Jean le Pauvre and Jean le Riche' collected by Emmanuel Cosquin in *Contes populaires de Lorraine*, 2 vols. (Paris: F. Vieweg, 1887), vol. II, pp. 333–7, a group which may otherwise be passed over as belonging to a quite separate narrative category. They bear superficial resemblances because there are brothers, even hunchbacks, and there is a cadaver that is made to reappear as though refusing to die. But the story follows a fundamentally different order of logic. In particular, there is only one corpse and its exploitation is part of the porter's scheme to dupe others. In Cosquin's tale, a poor brother seeks revenge against the rich one for hoarding all the family wealth. He begins by digging up his recently deceased mother and dumping her at his brother's door. Frightened, the rich one merely pays the poor one to rebury her. The money for removing the body begins to flow. In other versions, her return is attributed to an insufficiently lavish funeral. The old girl wants to be buried with greater pomp and expense. Jean le Pauvre continues to work the unwanted cadaver trick by depositing her first in a baron's orchard. He too becomes desperate to have her borne away in secret to avoid trouble. The priest behaves likewise and Jean is always there to profit as the willing porter. His last trick is to place her on a mule's back and send her through the market where merchants throw stones at her to drive her away. Fearing they have killed her, they too open their purses. The shock of it all is Poor Jean's indifference to his mother's remains, but perhaps no more so than those who harvest organs from the dead. Cognate tales in this group are numerous and allegedly derive from 'The Little Hunchback' in the *Arabian Nights*, in which the body of the crump is taken from place to place by different persons, each one fearing to be taken for the murderer. See 'The Tale of the Hunchback with the Tailor, the Christian Broker, the Steward, and the Jewish Doctor,' *The Book of the Thousand Nights and One Night*, ed. J.C. Mardrus and E.P. Mathers, 5 vols. (London: Routledge, 1964), vol. I, pp. 174–80, 268–71. A hunchback taken in by a couple chokes on a fishbone. They deposit the body on the doorstep of the Jewish doctor and then a whole series of receivers think they have killed him by their abuse and so pass the corpse along from party to party. In the end, when a Christian is accused of the murder, the Muslim and the Jew rush in to claim responsibility. The body is then resuscitated by a barber who removes the fishbone. As a source for our story, this tale may be discounted altogether, as well as the many others inventoried by Cosquin, vol. II, pp. 336–7. Stories in this tradition from the early *fabliaux* include 'La long nuit,' and 'Le sacristan de Cluny,' both to be found in the major collections.

60 *The Collected Sicilian Folk and Fairy Tales of Giuseppe Pitrè*, ed. and trans. Jack Zipes and Joseph Russo, 2 vols. (New York: Routledge, 2009), vol. I, pp. 599–601. Collected in Palermo.

in first one minstrel hunchback, then a second and a third to play the part, each one charming and amusing the little girl until alarm sends them into hiding. The order of the narrative is replayed with bare precision, having been pared down to an efficient formula. Imbriani collects two versions in his *Novellaja milanese.*[61] Pitrè found another in Tuscany, in which the wife goes to the well where the monks pester her.[62] These are lured to the house by a promise of supper and sex. One is hidden in the chimney and there burned by the husband. Another ends up in a wardrobe; his throat is cut. The third dies in a grain bin. A man comes, puts them in sacks and throws them into a whirlpool. This porter, too, swears and complains. It is all pretty murderous and matter-of-fact business. He too is paid for a job well done. Finamore found another version in the Abruzzi.[63] Salvatore Bongi includes 'Gobbi' (hunchbacks) in his *Lettere.*[64] And this has merely scratched the surface.[65]

---

61 Vittorio Imbriani, *Le novellaja milanese* (Bologna: Fava & Garagnani, 1872): 'Voglio-ffà, Aggio-ffatto e Vene-mm'annetta' and 'Il convento delle monache delle fotticchiate.' These may also be consulted in *Il propugnatore,* (Bologna: Gaetano Romagnoli, 1871), vol. IV, pt. 1, pp. 279–81 and *Il propugnatore* (Bologna: Gaetano Romagnoli, 1872), vol. V, pt. 1, pp. 146–53.

62 'I frati,' in *Novelle popolari toscane,* intro. Laura Regina Bruno, 2 vols., Centro Internazionale di Etnostorie (Palermo: Documenta edizioni, 2005), no. 58, vol. I, pp. 321*ff.*

63 Gennero Finamore, *Tradizioni popolari abruzzasi* (Lanciano, 1882; Turin: Carlo Clausen, 1894), no. 9.

64 *Lettere di Luigi Pulci a Lorenzo il Magnifico et ad altri,* ed. Salvatore Bongi (Lucca: Tipografia Giusti, 1868).

65 For those determined to locate the many more versions of this popular tale, the following works are recommended: Gabriel Chappuys, *Les facétieuses journées,* ed. Michel Bideaux (Paris: Champion, 2003). This work was first published in 1584, and made frequent use of Francesco Sansovino's *Cento novella scelte* (Venice, 1561), in which twenty-two of Straparola's stories were initially included, although 'The Three Hunchbacks' was not among them. See also Christian Maximilian Habicht, *Tausend und eine Nacht,* from a Tunisian manuscript (Breslau: Max, 1825), vol. 14, Night 496; Celio Malespini, *Ducento novelle* (Venice: Al segno dell'Italia, 1609), pt. I, no. 80, pt. II, no. 95; Nicolas de Troyes, *Le grand parangon des nouvelles nouvelles,* ed. Émile Mabille (Paris: E. Gouin, 1866; and F. Vieweg in 1869), no. 13, pp. 58–65; new ed. (Bassac: Plein Chant, 1993), no. 13; *Les cent nouvelles nouvelles,* ed. Roger Dubois (Paris: Champion, 2005), no. 14 (but not in the edition of *The Hundred Tales,* trans. Rossell Hope Robbins [New York: Crown, 1960], for some bizarre reason); Pierre-Honoré Robbé de Beauveset, *Oeuvres badines* (London, 1801; and Brussels: J.J. Gay, 1883), no. 56; Cailhava de l'Estendoux, *Le Soupé des petits maîtres* (Brussels: J.H. Briard, 1870), vol. II, chap. 26; D'Auberville, *Contes en Vers* (Brussels: Demanet, 1818), vol. II, p. 43; and Michele Angeloni, 'Il miracolo,' in *Novelle* (Lugano: 1863).

The most compelling evidence for the wide geographical spread of this tale is a story, remarkable in its affinities, from faraway Vietnam. Four bonzes (Buddhist priests) are killed in a hostel and the elderly owner, to avoid accusations, is eager to dispose of the bodies in secret. Three of the bodies she hides, and the fourth, whom she calls her nephew, a passing monk is hired to bury. By the time he returns for his pay, she has produced another body, saying that her nephew is so attached to her that he doesn't want to leave; he must be buried deeper in the ground. After all four are disposed of, the porter-monk is so obsessed with the 'returning' nephew that when he sees another monk on a bridge, he draws conclusions and kicks him into the river. This time five bodies are buried for the price of one and the story has been stripped back to its central conceit. But it is the same anecdote and clearly a member of the unit, having traveled afar in the brains of sequential raconteurs, all of them 'infected' with the story schema. The Annamites to whom it belongs originated in Tibet and migrated into the peninsula through China, centuries back, carving out a state for themselves between the north (Tonkin) and the south (Cochinchina) by warring with the Khmer.[66] For how long has it been one of their stories? Is it a Western tale, carried stepwise so far away? When did it make its breakaway from the tradition that inspired Straparola, for the stories are kissing cousins, or little islands once part of a main in the great ocean of stories?

The tale in *Le grand parangon des nouvelles nouvelles* is that of an orphan girl and her three beaux. None was sincere and she knew she had to protect her interests. She asks one of them to accompany her to the cemetery to pass the night in an attempt to calm the ghost of her tormented mother. He is to wrap himself in a sheet, and if he remained for three or four hours in prayer for the mother's soul, he could have his way with her. She tells the second to appear well armed with sticks, and that she was his if he stayed the appointed time. The third agrees to go there dressed as a devil under similar terms. When the ghost sees the armed man, he hides under the raised slab of the tomb. When the devil arrives with fire and chains, the armed one likewise hides under the stone. Then the spirit makes a run for it, which the devil takes for the mother's ghost. Thus, all of them take to their heels in terror and the girl is freed of all obligations.

66 A. Landes, *Contes et legends annamites*, in *Cochinchine française; Excursions et Reconnaissances*, 5 pts. (Saigon, Nov., 1884–Jan., 1886), no. 80.

V. Fable 4
Tia Rabboso, or the Ruses of an Adulterous Wife

BENEDETTO OF TREVISO

in Trevisan dialect

Marsilio Verzelese, being enamoured of Tia, wife of Cecato Rabboso, enters her house during her husband's absence. When her spouse returns unexpectedly, Tia deceives him by pretending to work a spell during which Marsilio secretly makes his escape.

In very truth, my lady mistress and fair damsels, what more would you have? Hasn't Messer Antonio acquitted himself well? Has he not told you an excellent story? Well, by dog's blood, I'll make an effort to do something for my own honour.

We village folks have always heard tell that among the gentlemen of the world, this man will manage his affairs in one way and that man in another. But me, well, I'm me, an ignorant yokel who knows nothing of learning except what I've always heard from our elders, which is that he who dances badly raises the loudest laugh. So be patient while I do my best to amuse you. But don't think I'm saying these things because I'm trying to escape the trouble of telling you a tale, for I'm afraid of nothing on that score. Quite the contrary, the tale Messer Antonio has told you with so much clever doing, and to which nothing could be added, has given me so much encouragement that waiting to get mine started seems like a thousand years. Maybe mine will be no less pleasing and make you laugh as much as Messer Antonio's, particularly because I intend to tell you of the ingenuity of a peasant woman who played a trick upon her fool of a husband. So if you'll listen to me and give me your kind attention, I'll tell it to you in the best way I know how.

As you all know, lying below Piove di Sacco in the back-country of Padua is the sector of land called Salmazza where, a long time ago, there lived and laboured a poor farmer named Cecato Rabboso. He was a solid and loyal type, but he was as thick-headed as they come. This Cecato Rabboso had for his wife the daughter of Gagiardi, a farmer from the village of Campolongo. Her name was Tia, and she was as wily, crafty, and mischievous a young thing as you could ever find. Besides being shrewd, she was a stoutly-built wench with a handsome face, and commonly it was said that there wasn't another peasant woman her equal for miles around. Because she was so sprightly and nimble at country dances, the young gallants who saw her would often lose their hearts to her in no time at all. As it happened, a certain young dandy from Padua named Marsilio Verzelese – a handsome enough fellow and from a good house too – became enamoured of this Tia. He was so ardently consumed by the flame of his love that whenever she went to a village dance, this fellow would be sure to follow her there and, to tell it without error, he danced with her most of the time. Yet even though this gallant was fiercely in love, he kept it as much a secret as he could so as not to let it be known to anybody, and to avoid becoming the common gossip of all the neighbours round about.

Now this Marsilio knew well enough that Tia's husband Cecato was a poor man who supported his household by the work of his hands, labouring hard from early morning till late at night for one person or another. He began to prowl around Tia's house and, by making eyes at her, he hoped to enter into familiarity and conversation, for he had made up his mind to disclose to her the feelings he had for her. Still Marsilio worried that she might get angry and refuse to see him again should he blurt his passions right out, for it didn't seem to him that she looked as kindly upon him as he deserved, given all the love he felt for her. Besides this, he was afraid of being discovered by someone who would warn Cecato her husband, which could fall out badly for him and lead to injuries – for although Cecato was a numskull, he had wits enough to be jealous.

Marsilio spent his days turning around Tia's house, gazing at her so long and intently that at last she could no longer fail to take notice of his devotion. Still, for reasons known only to her, she gave him no favourable look, refusing to show that she was in the least inclined to return his passion. For even though in the depths of her mind she knew that she was willing to meet his wishes, she pretended to indifference by turning her back on him.

One day it happened that Tia was sitting all alone on a log outside the door of her house with a distaff in hand winding some flax and busying herself with some work for her lady. Taking heart, Marsilio walked up and said to her, 'God be with you, my friend Tia.'

'Welcome, young gentleman,' she replied.

'How can you not know that I'm consumed by my love for you and am like to die if you don't take any account of me and give a care for my cruel sufferings?'

Tia responded, 'How should I know whether you love me or not?'

Marsilio then said, 'Although you may never have known it before, I'm telling you now that I'm consumed by all the grief and passion that a man can feel.'

Tia answered, 'Well, now you've told me.'

'And you?' asked Marsilio. 'By your faith, come on, tell me the truth. Don't you love me too?'

With a smile, she answered, 'O, maybe a little.'

'Heaven help you,' Marsilio continued, 'tell me how much.'

'Enough,' she replied.

Then Marsilio cried, 'Alas, Tia! If you want me as much as you say, you'd show it to me by some sign, but you won't give me a drop.'

Tia answered, 'Well, and what sign would you have me give you?'

'Oh Tia,' said Marsilio, 'you know very well what's on my mind without my having to tell you.'

'No, I can't possibly know it unless you say it,' said Tia.

Marsilio then replied, 'I'll say it if you promise to listen and not get mad.'

Tia replied, 'Say on, sir, for I promise you on my soul that if it's a fair and honourable thing and not against my honour, I'll not be angry with you.'

'Then, when can I enjoy your most desirable body?'

'Now that's clear enough,' said Tia, 'but you're only deceiving and mocking me. How can I be suitable for you, a gentleman and citizen of Padua, while I'm a peasant from the village? You're rich and I'm poor. You're a somebody and I'm a working woman. You can have fine ladies to your liking, while I'm of low condition. You walk gaily in your embroidered overcoat and your bright-coloured stockings all worked with wool and silk, while I, as you see, have nothing but an old petticoat all torn and mended. I've nothing better when I go to dances than this old frock you see on me now. You eat wheaten loaves while I eat millet and beans, and even then I'm often left feeling half famished. I've no furred garments for the cold winter, poor wretch that I am. Nor would I know which way to turn to get one, for I've neither money nor goods to sell that would enable me to buy the few necessities I need. We lack corn to eat to keep us alive till Easter, and who knows what we'll do during the great dearth.

Besides all this, there are the taxes we must pay daily to Padua. Ah, poor peasants that we are. What pleasure do we have in life? We toil hard to till the earth and sow our wheat, which you fine folk consume, while we poor people have to make do with rye bread. We tend the vines and make the wine of which you drink the best while we satisfy ourselves with the lees or plain water.'

Marsilio replied to Tia's speech, 'Don't bother yourself about all these things. If you'll grant me the favour I'm after, I'll see that you lack for nothing that will bring you happiness.'

Tia replied, 'Ah, that's what you cavaliers always say until we've done your pleasure. Then you go away and we never see more of you. We're left in the lurch, deceived, duped, and shamed in the world's esteem. Meanwhile, you go your ways, bragging of your good fortune, washing out your mouths, treating us as though we were carrion and fit only to be cast on the dunghill. You worthy citizens of Padua, I know full well the tricks you can play.'

'The message is clear,' replied Marsilio, 'but let's have done with words once and for all. I'm asking you again whether you'll grant me the favour I seek?'

'For the love of God, please go away, I'm asking you,' cried Tia, 'before my husband comes back, for nightfall is drawing nigh and he'll be here for certain in a few minutes. Come back sometime tomorrow and we'll talk as long as you wish. Yes, I want you well enough.' Marsilio, passionately enamoured of her as he was, regretted to cut short this pleasant conversation and remained by her side. So once more she urged, 'You must leave immediately, I beg you, and don't stay here any longer.'

Seeing how moved she had become, Marsilio uttered, 'God be with you, Tia, my sweet soul. I commend my heart to you, for it is surely in your keeping.'

'May God go with you, dearest hope of my life!' said Tia. 'I commend you to His care.'

'By His good help,' said Marsilio, 'we'll meet again tomorrow.'

'Very well, let it be so,' said Tia, and with these words Marsilio finally left.

When the next day came, Marsilio – who thought the time a thousand years before he could once more go to Tia's house – made his way there and found her busy in the garden digging around some vines. As soon as they saw one another, they exchanged greetings and began to talk lovingly together. When this conversation had gone on for some time,

Tia said to Marsilio, 'Dear heart of mine, tomorrow morning early my husband Cecato has to go to the mill and he won't return here till the next day. So if it's what you want, you can come here late in the evening. I'll be on the lookout for you. Just be sure to come without fail and not deceive me.' When Marsilio heard this good news, there was nobody in the world as happy as he was. Jumping and dancing about for glee, he told Tia goodbye, half out of his wits for joy.

No sooner had Cecato come home than the crafty Tia went up to him and said, 'Cecato, my good man, you must go to the mill right away, for we have nothing left in the house to eat.'

'Very well, very well, I'll look into it,' answered Cecato.

'I tell you that you have to go tomorrow, whatever happens,' said Tia.

'Tomorrow it is,' replied Cecato. 'I'll head out before daybreak to borrow a cart and a pair of oxen from the people I work for. Then I'll come back to load up and leave at once for the mill.'

'Perfect,' said Tia, and went to prepare the corn and put it into sacks, so that the next morning he'd have no more bother than to load it in the cart and head off singing.

The following morning, Cecato took the corn which his wife had put into sacks the night before, loaded it on the cart, and went on his way to the mill. Seeing that it was now the season of short days and long nights, that the roads were broken up and in bad condition, and that the weather was foul with rain, ice, and intense cold, poor Cecato found himself obliged to remain that night at the mill. Nothing could have fallen out more perfectly for the plan that Tia and Marsilio had put together for their own satisfaction.

When night came, according to the agreement he'd made with Tia, Marsilio took a pair of fine, well-cooked capons and some white bread and wine, undiluted by a single drop of water, all of which he had carefully prepared before leaving home, and secretly stole across the fields to Tia's house. Having opened the door, he found her sitting by the fireside winding thread. After greeting one another, they spread the table and both sat down to eat, and when they had enjoyed the excellent cheer Marsilio brought over, they headed straight for the bed. So while the poor fool Cecato was having his corn ground at the mill, in his bed at home Marsilio was sifting flour.

As the sunrise approached and the day was beginning to break, the two lovers awoke and rose out of bed, afraid that Cecato might return and find them there together. And sure enough, while they were still in amorous chatter, Cecato came into the yard whistling aloud all the while and calling upon Tia, saying 'Oh my Tia! Make up a good fire, I'm asking you, because I'm more than half dead from the cold.'

Clever and artful minx that she was, Tia was nevertheless in consternation at hearing her husband's voice, terrified that some ill would happen to Marsilio and that shame and reproach would land straight on her. Well, she managed to get Marsilio hidden behind the door before she threw it open. Then with a merry face, she ran to meet her husband to make a big show of hugging him. Cecato was still in the courtyard, crying out to her, 'Make a fire at once, good Tia, for I'm very nearly frozen stiff. By the blood of St. Quintin, I was almost starved to death by the cold up at that mill last night. It was so nippy that I could hardly sleep a wink.' At that, Tia went in haste to the woodhouse, took a good armful of kindling, and lit a fire so Cecato could warm himself, keeping him always near the hearth for fear that he'd see the other fellow.

Keeping up a line of chatter about this and that, Tia said, 'Ah, Cecato, my good man, I've a fine bit of news to give you.'

'What's happened?' Cecato enquired.

'While you were away at the mill, a poor old man came to the house begging alms of me, for the love of God, and in return for some bread I gave him to eat and a small cup of wine, he taught me an incantation for casting a spell over the kite, which I learned from him by heart.'

'Is it possible, what you're telling me?' asked Cecato.

'Honestly, it's the truth,' replied Tia, 'and I tell you I value it highly.'

'So tell me about it. How's it done? Don't keep me in suspense.'

Whereupon Tia said to her husband, 'You must lie down flat on the ground stretched out to your full length as though you were dead – may God forbid it – and then you have to turn your head and your shoulders towards the door and your knees and feet towards the stove, and then I have to spread a white cloth over your face and put our corn measure over your head.'

'It won't go in,' said Cecato.

'Yes it will, yes it will,' Tia replied. 'Just look here.' And with these words, she took the measure, which happened to be close at hand, and put it over his head, saying, 'There's nothing in God's whole world that could fit you better than this. Now you've got to keep yourself really quiet without moving a limb or saying a word or else we're wasting our time. Then I'll take the sieve in my hand and start to jump and dance around you, and while I'm dancing, I'll speak the incantation which the old man taught me. That's the way the spell can be made to work really well. But I repeat that you can't stir a finger on any account until I've repeated the incantation three times, for it must be repeated above you three times over before it will take effect. After this, we'll see whether the kite will give us any more trouble or come to steal our chickens.'

To this Cecato replied, 'Well, God grant what you say to be true so we can have some rest and a little breathing space. You know how hard it's been to bring up a few chickens what with that fiend of a kite devouring every darned one we hatch. We've just never been able to rear enough chickens to sell. But now with the money we'll gain we can pay our landlord and the tax-gatherer, buy oil and salt, and all the other provisions we need for keeping house.'

'Let's get started, then,' said Tia, 'because with this we can do ourselves a good turn, so lie down quickly, Cecato.' Immediately he stretched himself out as far as he could. 'That's right,' said Tia. Then she took a cloth of thick white linen and shrouded his face. Next she took the corn measure and rammed it down on his head, and then caught up the sieve and began to dance and skip around him and to repeat in the following manner the incantation which she claimed had been taught to her by the old beggar:

Thievish bird, I charge you well,
Hearken to my mystic spell.
While I dance and wave my sieve,
All my tender chicks shall live.
Not a bird from all my hatch,
Thievish rascal, shall you snatch.
Wolf nor rat his prey shall seek,
Nor bird with sharp and crooked beak.
Thieves who stand behind the door,
Hearken, fly, and come no more.
If my speech you still can't read,
Well, you're just a fool indeed.

When Tia had come to the end of her mummery, she went on dancing around Cecato, all along keeping her eyes fixed upon the outer door, making signs to Marsilio, who was still hidden there, that he'd better skedaddle right now. But Marsilio, who wasn't all that quick in his head or nimble enough to catch her meaning, couldn't make out what all her gesturing meant, or what her purpose was in going through these rites of exorcism. So he kept still in his hiding place and didn't budge an inch. Meantime, the half-stifled Cecato, getting tired of lying stretched out on the floor and anxious to get up, muttered to Tia, 'Well, is it over now?'

But Tia, who had not been able to induce Marsilio to move from his place behind the door, answered Cecato, 'Stay where you are, for heaven's sake, and don't move at your peril. Didn't I tell you I'd have to repeat the incantation three times? I hope you haven't wrecked everything as it is by starting to get up.'

'No, no, surely not,' said Cecato. So Tia made him lie down stretched out as he was before and began to chant her incantation anew.

By this time, Marsilio had at last come to understand how matters really stood, and what Tia's mummery was all about, so he grabbed his chance to slip out from his hiding place and run away as fast as his legs would carry him. When she saw that Marsilio had taken to his heels and cleared the courtyard, she finished her exorcism against the kite, and having brought it to an end, she allowed her cuckold of a husband to get up from the floor. Then with Tia's help he began right away to unload the flour which he'd brought back from the mill. Once outside in the courtyard, she saw Marsilio in the distance hurrying away at full speed, whereupon she began shouting after him in a lusty voice, 'Ah, ha, what a wicked bird. Ah, ha, get out of here and be gone, for by God I'll send you packing with your tail between your legs if ever you show yourself around here again. Away, I tell you! Isn't he a greedy wretch? You can see just how intent that wicked beast was on coming back, may heaven give him a wretched year.'

So it came about that every time the hawk swooped down into the courtyard to carry away a chick or two, he would first have a bout with the hen herself, who would set to work with her conjuration as before. Then he would take to flight with his tail down, so that ever after Cecato and Tia's fowls were no longer hurt by his harassment.

The ladies found this fable, presented by the Trevisan, to be so mirthful and amusing that they almost split their sides with laughter. He imitated the rustic speech so well that there was no one in the group who wouldn't have taken him for a peasant. When the merriment had abated, the Signora turned her face towards the Trevisan and said to him, 'Truthfully, Signor Benedetto, you have diverted us this evening in such featly wise that we all agree in declaring your fable as deserving as Molino's. But to fill up the measure of our pleasure, both mine and this honourable company's, I entreat you, if you're not opposed, to set forth an enigma just as graceful in form and as amusing in matter.' The Trevisan, noting the Signora's inclination, was unwilling to disappoint her. So standing up, he began his riddle in the following words.

Sir Yoke goes up and down the field
To every tug is forced to yield.
One on the left, one on the right,
Plods on, and next there comes a wight,
A cunning rascal who with power
Beats one who goes on carriers four.
Now if an answer you can give,
Good friends, we shall for ever live.

When the Trevisan, with the true manner and bearing of a peasant, had finished his enigma, which was understood by no one in the company, he gave out his interpretation in peasant dialect to underscore its meaning to them all. 'I must not keep this gentle company waiting any longer. Tell me, do you understand the meaning of my riddle? If you don't, then I'll help you. Sir Yoke goes to and fro, that is to say the yoke to which the oxen are attached, going up and down the fields and roads, which they drag here and there. Those that are on the one side and the other are the oxen. He that beats one which stands on four is the ploughman who walks behind lashing the bull, which has four legs, with his whip. And to end my explanation, I'll tell you once more that the answer to my riddle is the yoke, which I hope you all now understand.'

Everyone was greatly interested in this riddle dealing with country life, which they both praised highly and laughed at heartily. But the Trevisan, remembering that only one more story remained to be told that night, that of the charming Cateruzza, turned with a smiling face towards the Signora and said, 'Signora, it is not that I want to disturb the settled order of our entertainment or dictate to your Highness, my mistress and sovereign lady, but only to satisfy the desire of this devoted company that I beg your Ladyship, with your customary grace, to make us sharers, for our delight and recreation, in some charming and fanciful story of your own. If I have by chance been more presumptuous than is becoming in making this request – may God forbid – I beg you to forgive me, seeing that the love I bear toward this gracious assembly has been the chief cause why I have been led to prefer it.'

The Signora, upon hearing the Trevisan's courteously worded request, at first cast her eyes down to the ground, not for any fear or shame that she felt, but because she deemed, for various reasons, that it was more appropriate for her to listen than to discourse. But after a time, with a gracious and smiling look, she turned her face towards the Trevisan and said, 'Signor Benedetto, what though your request is a pleasant and decorous one, it appears to me that you insist too much in your supplication, insofar as the duty of storytelling pertains to these young damsels round about than to me. Thus, you must hold me excused if I decline to acquiesce at once to your demand. I here bid Cateruzza, duly chosen by lot, to tell the fifth story of this evening and thus favour you with her recitation.'

The merry listeners, keen and eager to hear the Signora tell her story, at once rose to their feet and seconded the Trevisan's request, humbly begging her not to stand too severely upon the exalted dignity of her position, because the present time and place permitted anyone, however high in rank, to freely speak anything that might be pleasing. The Signora, when she heard the gentle loving terms of this petition, so that she would not seem ungracious in her bearing, replied with a smile, 'Since this is the wish of you all, and it is your pleasure that I conclude this evening with some little story of my own, I'll gladly grant your wish.' So without further demur, she blithely began to tell her fable.

V.4 Commentary

The story of Marsilio, Tia, and Cecato develops one of the most common themes of the Renaissance *novella*, the act of infidelity hidden from a spouse through improvisatory subterfuge. The added charm of this account, indeed the substance of its social complexity, is the particularity of its setting in a village outside Padua and the pointed social profiling of the participants. Piove di Sacco is, in fact, just eighteen kilometres to the south-east of Padua, a brisk three-hour walk. Marsilio is a materially comfortable townsman who goes off to the local countryside to play courtier to Tia, a clever but impoverished peasant woman. How cynical his intentions were in the first place we might well wonder, skulking around her house and stealing glances, and in a sense looking for a vulnerable catch. Tia's meagre fare, the daily taxes, the improbability of having enough to get them through Easter, and her life of endless labour is contrasted not only with Marsilio's urban means and status, not to mention his fine clothes, but his inclination to exploit and abandon her without a moment's consideration, for Tia states before the fact that he will leave her like 'carrion' in the end.[67] There are no romantic illusions here. Tia makes these observations as part of her negotiation; she too pretends to liking, 'enough' at least, but the underlying bargaining over benefits in exchange for sex can hardly be suppressed. Her husband is a bit of a lump, perhaps dull and no match for her *ingegno* or wit, but he is hard-working and by no means insensitive to her, and she knows this. Yet she makes her calculations for reasons left entirely to innuendo, ranging from an evening's holiday, a moment of respite from the malady of the quotidian, to hopes for tangible tokens of remuneration. In the end, she settles for a good meal in return for the duties of the bed, for her pleasure in the affair is not described.[68] Equally poignant is her firm dismissal of her gallant, making clear to Marsilio through her extended malediction upon the kite in the presence of her husband that he had better not set foot there again. Her determination to secure her interests by rejecting all future stands is part of her peasant pragmatism, her realistic social expectations, and an admission that their two worlds could never be one.

This is the social world of Ruzante, the famous Paduan playwright, who in that same era had celebrated the bittersweet, rustic drive and endurance of the Paduan peasantry. The present story merits consideration beside his *Moschetta* and *Fiorina* (1552) in terms of their depictions of the harsh realism of country life in a time of wars, displacement,

---

67 This passage contains some of the most pointed social commentary in the whole of the *Piacevoli notti*, perfectly integrated into a confrontation between rural helplessness and urban privilege. Her perspective is entirely in keeping with complaint literature of the period, such as the anonymous *Alfabeto dei villani* (1525), in *Antichi testi di letteratura pavana*, ed. Emilio Lovarini (Bologna: Romagnoli, 1894), p. 84. See also E. Menegazzo, 'Stato economico-sociale del Padovano all' epoca del Ruzante,' in *La poesia rusticana nel rinascimento* (Rome: Accademia Nazionale dei Lincei, 1969), p. 161.

68 An argument has been made for her 'joie de vivre,' her stereotypical rural freshness and robustness, her impish delight in tricking her dull *contadino*, and her pragmatic indifference to the language of fashionable love talk, all of which seems incontestable, even though her motives for consent as a kind of rural acceptance of sexuality as a fact of life as fatalistic as the barnyard itself, or her natural desire to be seduced, remains open to interpretation. See Marie-Françoise Piejus, 'Le couple citadin-paysan dans les "Piacevoli notti" de Straparola,' in *Ville et campagne dans la littérature italienne de la renaissance*, ed. Anna Fontes-Baratto et al. (Paris: Université de la Sorbonne Nouvelle, 1976), pp. 153, 155–6. This article also profiles the military, economic, and political circumstances in the region that brought about such adverse conditions for the rural population.

and privation.[69] The latter play may have been specifically indebted to Straparola, insofar as Tia's speech protesting her poverty in contrast to Marsilio's wealth, and her low expectations of generosity, offers touches of diction dealing with her tattered clothes that reappear in the prologue of Ruzante's play, according to Domenico Pirovano.[70] More pervasively, the Trevisan, or Straparola on his behalf, draws upon the common regional dialect found generally throughout Angelo Beolco's (Ruzante's) plays, as in Straparola's 'ma mi mo ch' a' son mi e ch' a' no so ninte de lettra' (but me, which is me, who doesn't have any book learning' and Ruzante's 'mo mi, che a' son mi mo, e che a' sè quelo che se pò saere' (but me, which is me, who knows everything).[71] This is but one of the many speech affectations characterizing the local lingo. Everyone in the framing tale congratulates Benedetto for imitating it so well.

In contrast with the contemporary immediacy that connects the *novella* to a social time and place, as though the vignette were a bit of reporting on real events in a local dialect, is the simultaneous awareness that this tale is a formulaic *beffa*, a tried and true trick put upon an unsuspecting husband to get a lover out of the house. Such shifts have already come to attention in the story of 'Simplicio, or The Lover in the Sack' (II.5) in which the lover is exposed, and 'The Physician's Wife' (IV.4) in which the lover is spirited out of the house again and again, even while sharing all his confidences with the husband. Clearly the topic fascinated, delighted, and alarmed readers, depending on their perspectives in the matter, for such stories have to do with unequal marriages, jealousy, sexual dissatisfaction, sexual desire and adventure, calculated risks, the imperatives felt by those surprised by love, marriage vows, social duties,

69 Kenneth Bartlett and Antonio Franceschetti, in their 'Introduction' to Angelo Beolco's *La Moschetta* (Ottawa: Dovehouse Editions, 1993), p. 15, describe Ruzante's (Beolco's) world in similar terms: 'The name of Ruzante remained associated mostly with the life of the country folk and lowest social classes ... In a variety of situations [he] depicts such characters and their frustrations and distresses, such as famine, the depredations of invading armies ... and the exploitation of rich and powerful landlords. They are people who must often fight just for survival ... Love, honour, friendship, loyalty and all other traditional virtues that dignify man find only a casual place in this world. Love becomes a simple outlet for sexual urges ...'

70 *Le piacevoli notti* (Rome: Salerno, 2000), vol. I, p. 392.

71 Ruzante, *L'Aconitana* (The woman from Ancona), trans. Nancy Dersofi (Berkeley: University of California Press, 1994), p. 38. The date of this play is entirely uncertain, so that, with regard to these lines, the direction of influence can be but speculative.

and the stability of the Renaissance family. The plots of the erudite plays, popular throughout the sixteenth century, could hardly do without the ruses connected to such drives. These plots, on the one hand, are concerned with marital exclusivity and the investment of resources in raising one's own genetic progeny, and on the other, with the ingenuity of the human spirit, the inventiveness provoked by fear, the false value of honour and reputation, and the clever management of contingency. No matter of trust and betrayal has been more central to the consciousness of the race. The more such deceptions play upon the unwitting complicity of the dull or deserving spouse, the better, as in the present instance. Among the best ruses are those in which the intruding husband is lovingly welcomed and made to participate in an improvisatory scenario that temporary obscures his vision while the lover gets away. One variation involves two lovers, one inside the house and another seeking to get in just as the husband arrives. The husband is deceived when the wife makes them out to be enemies, creating a little *coup de théâtre* in which the *amorosi* must improvise their parts. She explains one man's presence inside the house as a potential victim of violence whom she has hidden and whom the husband must then escort safely back to his own house. The ingenuity of these pranks is limited only by material circumstances, the subtlety of human wits, and the gullibility of the trusting or even intensely jealous husbands. Tia's invention has a local, rustic, and innovative particularity all its own, the invention of a folk raconteur, but as a trick type involving the temporary blinding of a husband and a double entendre recitation, it is not without a long and distinct history.

The theatrical performance of the concocted incantation against kites and falcons preying upon their chickens (a fact of farm life that keeps the story firmly tied to its setting) caps the entire tale. It is a kind of exorcism (*scongiuro*) based on the magic power in incantatory words known to have been used in the country to frighten away nuisance animals.[72] When Tia's slow-witted lover, frozen behind the door, refuses to move and the husband grows restless in his ludicrous position sprawled on the floor with his head covered, she must resort to a prolonged performance while making violent gestures to Marsilio to take to his heels, incorporating double semantics into her chant. There are similar moments in literature in which a wife gives instruction to her lover in words designed to be interpreted otherwise by her husband. In a notoriously scatological

72 Giuseppe Cocchiara, *Le origini della poesia popolare* (Turin: p. Boringhieri, 1966), pt. III.

tale by Morlini, the wife talks horses in the presence of both, in the process giving covert instruction to her lover on how to mount her properly the next time by finding the right aperture and causing her less physical pain. The present *fabliau*-like creation comes to nothing so graphic in dwelling on a mode of *tromperie* that leaves the entire assembly laughing in innocent and harmless approbation over a vignette in comic dialect they take for no more than a mere 'riding tale.'

Insofar as no folk material from the sixteenth century bearing this configuration of events has come down to us besides Straparola's tale, we are once again invited to assume that his source was collected locally, this one from a Paduan or Trevisan storyteller, and that Straparola was, himself, sufficiently familiar with the dialect that he could replicate it for a laugh before his imagined Venetian assembly. As a story type, however, it has many cousins, for it involves first hiding the lover, then temporarily blinding the husband, followed by an incantation or spell performed to dupe him while signalling to the lover to scram. To the 'hiding,' 'blinding,' and 'reciting' motifs may be added a fourth, 'feuding,' as in the generic profile given above. A history of these practices in the stock cuckold plot, going as far back as the *Hitopadesa* and up to the boudoir comedies of the eighteenth century, is more than a monograph's worth of hunting and gathering and would not bring us a lot closer to the inspiration behind Straparola's source. But a selective micro-history of those featuring the 'blinding' and 'reciting' motifs may reveal something of the course by which they came to rest in the present tale.

Cuckolds and clever wives are by no means absent in the 'Eastern' stories that made their way to Europe from the time of the Crusades onwards, and a few of them are so particular in nature as to merit fountainhead status for many a Western replay. The *Hitopadesa* provides the matrix for the 'feuding' tale involving two lovers pitted against each other as the husband arrives. One is told to draw his sword and rush past the husband in a state of rage, setting her up to explain the presence of a hidden lover as his intended victim. She is, in fact, the cowherd's wife who is sleeping with the magistrate and his son, and has every reason not only to keep her husband in the dark, but the identities of her lovers from each other.[73]

73 Narayana, *The Hitopadesa*, ed. M.R. Kale (Delhi: Motilal Banarsidass, [1896], 1967), pp. 59–60. See also the *Hitopadésa, ou l'instruction utile*, trans. Edouard Lancereau (Paris: P. Jannet, 1855), pp. 102–3.

One of the most important links between East and West is the *Disciplina clericalis* of Petrus Alfonsi, a Sephardic Jew who converted to Christianity in 1106 at the age of forty-four.[74] This widely circulating collection contained three formative texts, No. 9, 'The Parable of the Grape Farmer,' No. 10, 'The Parable of the Linen Sheet,' and No. 11, 'The Parable of the Sword.' The first is of particular interest, because the husband, while working in the vineyard, injures one of his eyes. Returning home as the result of his accident, he interrupts his wife with her lover. She quickly invents a ruse by convincing him that he should avail himself of medications and a magic charm to protect his good eye. In offering such ministrations she effectively cuts off his sight while her lover makes his escape. Then she puts him to bed. In this tale, the lover is hidden, the husband is temporarily 'blinded,' and she makes use of a trumped up ceremony involving magic to allow the getaway. This is Straparola's story in ovo. In the second, the mother and daughter in complicity prevail upon the returning husband to examine their handicraft by showing him a large sheet behind which the lover makes his escape. In the third, the wife quickly constructs the enmity between the two lovers by having one draw a sword and exit past the husband without speaking, while the other cowers in her bedroom. All are of Eastern origin, making the *Disciplina clericalis* a potential bridge whereby the Straparola type made its way into Europe.[75]

---

74 Petrus Alfonsi, *The Scholar's Guide: A Translation of the Twelfth-Century* Disciplina clericalis *of Pedro Alfonso*, ed. Joseph Ramon Jones and John Esten Keller (Toronto: The Pontifical Institute of Mediaeval Studies, 1969), p. 13. The story of the vintner and his wife's prayer for his good eye while her lover makes his escape is recycled in Jean Gobi's *La scala coeli*, ed. Marie-Anne Polo de Beaulieu (Paris: Centre Nationale de Recherche Scientifique, 1991), no. 509, p. 374.

75 *The Scholar's Guide*, pp. 56–60. For an excellent introduction to this text, including sections on the circulation of these stories, what they bear of Eastern wisdom, and how they relate to the emergence of the *novella*, see the introduction by Eberhard Hermes, *The Disciplina Clericalis of Petrus Alfonsi* (London: Routledge & Kegan Paul, 1977), pp. 8–35, and 120–2 for the three stories. An alternative entry point for the story of 'The Sword' is 'Of the Officer and the Merchant's Wife' in *The Book of Sindibad or The Seven Vazirs*, in which a slave is on visit as a lover when a second arrives, namely the officer. The wife tells the soldier to draw his sword, pretend to great anger, and leave the house as her husband arrives. The slave is then 'discovered' as his intended victim, both men playing out their parts to deceive the husband. Ed. W.A. Clouston ([Glasgow]: Privately Printed (for Subscribers), 1884), pp. 35–7, with a variant version, pp. 148–50. This work is mentioned in Arabic sources as early as 880, and was translated into Greek as *Syntipas* around 1100 or a

Of all the strategies for expelling lovers, the two of greatest interest are those in which the husband is 'blinded,' and those in which he is duped by an incantation or a similarly distracting ceremony. The tale of the *Disciplina clericalis* is replicated in the *Gesta romanorum,* through which this seminal tale receives extended circulation. A knight picking grapes injures his eye and returns home. His wife prevents him from lying down by insisting upon caring for his eye with a large plaster in a way that will temporarily impair his sight so that her lover can sneak away. The story of the mother and daughter holding a sheet up for inspection before making the bed is also included.[76]

A century before *Le piacevoli notti,* there appeared the collection entitled *Les cent nouvelles nouvelles* containing 'Le borne aveugle' (The one-eyed man blinded).[77] The husband is now a rich knight who had been away to the wars as far as Prussia in the service of God, in which service he had lost an eye. Meanwhile, his beautiful lady had given herself

---

decade earlier. All three of Peter Alfonso's stories are contained in *Le castoiement ou instruction du père à son fils,* a work originating in the thirteenth century, which is, in fact, the French *Disciplina clericalis.* It was published in Lausanne by Chaubert and Paris by Claude Herrisant in 1760, pp. 47–53. There are subtle differences; the wife has her husband sit, whereupon she places her mouth over his good eye, telling him not to open it until she said to.

76 These are stories no. 122, 'Of Ecclesiastical Blindness,' and no. 123, 'Of Absence of Parental Restraint,' so named because of the morals drawn from them at the end of each. *Gesta romanorum,* trans. Charles Swan and Wynnard Hooper (London: Bohn Library, 1876; reprint, New York: Dover Publications, 1959), pp. 222–3.

77 English readers may find this tale in *The Hundred Tales* (the collection is often attributed to Antoine de la Sale), trans. Rossell Hope Robbins (New York: Crown Publishers, 1960), pp. 61–5. This is based on an established anecdote, at least as old as the thirteenth century, for the returning knight blind in one eye appears in 'Qualiter uxor medicata est oculum mariti' in Thomas Wright, *A Selection of Latin Stories from Manuscripts of the Thirteenth and Fourteenth Centuries* (London: Percy Society, 1842), no. 102, p. 91, based on British Library MS. Harleian no. 2851. A later variant on the motif is to be found in Antoine le Métel, Sieur d'Ouville, 'D'une femme qui subtilement trompa son mari qui étoit borgne' (Of a wife who subtly cheated her one-eyed husband), in *L'Élite des contes,* ed. P. Ristelhuber (Paris: Alphonse Lemerre [1643], 1876), no. 21, pp. 37–8. Being married to a one-eyed man, this young wife wondered what she might be missing, so she found a full-sighted lover, but they were trapped by the husband coming up the stairs. She catches him coming in the door, tells her dream about his eye being healed and wants to test it. He indulges her, making light of the whole matter, while the lover sneaks away. Also, 'D'une femme qui subtillement trompa son mary qui estoit borgne,' in *L'Élite des contes,* ed. G. Brunet, 2 vols. (Paris: Librairie des bibliophiles, 1883), vol. I, pp. 1761–72.

to a squire. Longing for her after so lengthy a sojourn abroad, the knight hastens for home arriving early in the morning, as Cecato does in our story, also in search of warmth and comfort after a freezing night at the mill. The wife stalls for time by refusing to acknowledge his knocking, a standard feature of the story. As the lover is pushed behind the door, she greets her husband with a shifty fib about a dream in which his sight had returned, a revelation she insists on verifying by blindfolding his good eye to test the other with a candle. The examination is a failure, of course, but permits the squire to make off, at which point the good wife welcomes her husband home with other consolations.

Three further examples may be mentioned in passing in demonstration of the widespread popularity of this particular formula of the astute wife who deceives her husband by temporarily limiting his sight. One close to Straparola in its design from the fifteenth century is entitled 'Ich schätz nein' or 'Die Beschwörung' (The exorcism) in which a rustic working his fields finds himself feeling ill with a weakness in his head, for which reason he goes home early. Predictably, a lover is sequestered in a closet before the husband enters and the wife must then think of a ruse to get him out of the house. Feigning solicitude, she takes the poor man's aching head in her arms, wraps it in a cover, and pronounces her magic spell: 'Ich setz dir uff einem nüwen kübel / Gott vertrib dir din uvel! – Prutz ussen!' (I place you on a new tub / May God drive out this evil thing! – Now get the hell out!) Under the guise of speaking to an evil spirit she indicates to her lover to get a move on, fast. This clever appeal to a double audience is a part of the story tradition kept by Straparola. When her husband grows suspicious, the wife replies in a German phrase that buckles up the story in several Latin versions collected by Alfred Stern and Reinhold Köhler, 'Ich schetz neyn,' the middle word meaning literally to esteem, assess, reckon, allowing for nuanced translations such as 'I don't know what you're talking about' or 'I have nothing to hide,' before turning the accusations against her husband.[78] A related version by Jakob Ayrer, 'Ein schön singets Spil der Förster im Schmaltzkübel' (A fine play about the woodsman in the lard bucket), is of particular interest because the lover is now a priest and the husband's head is placed inside a bucket while the spell is pronounced.[79] An even earlier version is 'Le

78 'Ein Novellenstrauss des XV Jahrhunderts,' *Zeitschrift für deutsche Philologie*, 4 (1873), pp. 304–13.

79 'Ein schön singets Spil der Förster im Schmaltzkübel,' *Ayrer's Dramen*, ed. Adelbert von Keller in *Bibliothek des Literarischen Vereins in Stuttgart* 80 (1865), pp. 3063*ff.*

dit dou pliçon,' a fourteenth-century *fabliau* in which a bourgeois wife takes a squire for a lover and is surprised by her husband in the middle of the night. Recovering quickly from her shock, she begins to talk down his suspicions. While distracting her husband, she sees her lover all naked with a knife in his hand and bursts out laughing at the absurdity of it all. Her husband then hits his head on the bed and begins to wonder if he is losing his senses. Then he tells her he didn't return to frighten her and she begins to laugh again and to comfort him by holding his head in her arms while her lover makes his final exit.[80]

Others in this vein, now from Straparola's own century, include Matteo Bandello's story in Part I, No. 23, 'Astuzia d'una fanciulla innamorata per salvar l'amante ed inganner la nutrice' (Of the cleverness of a young girl in love in rescuing her lover by tricking her nurse).[81] In this tale, it is the nurse who is blind in one eye, and she is playfully clasped by the neck in order to cover the good one long enough for the lover to escape. The point is moot which story was written first, but its divergence from Straparola's suggests an even greater distancing of their respective sources, even though they belong to a common type.

Hans Wilhelm Kirchhof, whose *Wendunmuth* was published in 1563, also tells the now familiar story of the one-eyed knight who cut short his Turkish campaign to hurry home to his beloved spouse. His surprise arrival leads to the now familiar ruse of the dream concerning his restored vision and the strategic test. This wife likewise vigorously signals

80 *Recueil général et complet des fabliaux des XIIIe et XIVe siècles*, ed. Anatole de Montaiglon and Gaston Raynaud, 6 vols. in 3 (1872–90; reprint, Geneva: Slatkine Reprints, 1973), vol. 6, appendix II, pp. 260–3.

81 *Tutte le opera*, ed. Francesco Flora, 2 vols. ([Milan]: Arnoldo Mondadori [1934], 1952), pt. I, no. 23, pp. 294–302. It is known in German as 'Die einäugige Amme.' *Italiänischer Novellenschatz*, trans. Adelbert Keller (Leipzig: F.A. Brockhaus, 1851), no. 77, pp. 172–82. Others in this tradition include Giovanni Sabadino degli Arienti, 'Marcasino and Pippa,' in *Novelle porretane* [*sic*], ed. Pasquale Stoppelli (L'Aquila: L.U. Japadre editore [1483], 1975), pp. 11–16. (Named after the baths at Porretta.) This merchant's pretty wife, Pippa, is pursued by Aghinolfo, nephew of the king of France, who had come to Bologna to study. The lover followed the couple into the mountains during a retreat from the plague and there the men became friends. The story is full of touching speeches and social embellishments. When the husband leaves on business, opportunity presents itself, but affairs in the silk industry in Imola go so well that the merchant makes an early return. The lover is told to dress quickly, for Pippa already had a plan. It was to tell her husband of her dream about his blind eye, which she insisted on testing – just a silly notion which demanded his indulgence. Thus the lover makes his escape.

to her lover with her head to take to his heels.[82] One final example is found in *L'Héptameron* of Marguerite de Navarre, which may be entitled provisionally, 'The subtlety of a woman who allowed her lover to escape when her husband, blind in one eye, thought to take them by surprise.'[83] This husband is a one-eyed valet-de-chambre, much older than his wife, who is kept for long periods away from home by his patron, the Duke d'Alençon. He gets wind of foul play and proposes his absence in order to double back to catch them. When he hammers at the door, the lover collapses into cowardly curses and regrets. The wife bluffs with the man outside, 'If my husband were here, he would put an end to this knocking,' and so she gains for time. She too pretends to have had a dream in which her husband had recovered his sight, showing him a good deal of affection while covering his good eye to test the veracity of her impressions. This time, however, the husband recognizes the trick and swears that bad women can never be made good, telling her that if she wouldn't behave well when she was well treated, that he would now treat her as she deserved. The discussion among the guests in the framing-tale audience touch upon the very concerns that give these stories such vitality and urgency – the wiles of the two sexes in satisfying their sexual cravings outside of marriage, the varieties of marital inequality, and the cunning of the human spirit in its own right. None of these tales may be cited as Straparola's source and yet by dint of the circulation of signature motifs, they are all part of a generic type predicated upon this elementary narrative idea.[84]

---

82 'Einen einäugigen ritter betreugt seine listige haussfraw' (A one-eyed knight tricked by his lecherous wife), in *Wendunmuth*, ed. Hermann Oesterley, 5 vols. (Tübingen: Litterarischen Verein in Stuttgart, 1869), bk. III, no. 242, vol. II, pp. 529–32.

83 Ed. Gisèle Mathieu-Castellani (Paris: Librairie générale, 1999), Day I, no. 6, pp. 133–7; *The Heptameron*, trans. P.A. Chilton (London: Penguin, 1984). This story is taken over by Henri Estienne for his 'Des larrecins de nostre temps,' in *Apologie pour Hérodote: Satire de la société au XVIe siècle*, ed. P. Ristelhuber (Geneva: Slatkine Reprints, 1969), chap. 15, pp. 207–90.

84 Other tales employing the motif of the visually impaired husband include Francesco Sansovino's, *Cento novelle scelte* (Venice: Francesco Rampazetto [1561], 1563, and many subsequent printings), bk. VII, no. 10; La Motte-Roullant, 'Of the trick played by a certain dame on her husband to let her lover escape, who was hidden in her chamber,' in *Les facetieux de Viz de cent et six nouvelles nouvelles* (Paris: Longis, 1550), no. 24; Celio Malespini's *Novelle scelte*, ed. Ettore Allodoli (Lanciano: Carabba Editore, 1915), pt. I, no. 44 (first published in Venice: Al segno d'Italia in 1609, as *Ducento novelle*); and Giovanni Sagredo's *L'Arcadia in Brenta* (1687), ed. Quinto Marini (Rome: Salerno, 2004), Day III, pp. 140–4. In this tale a lascivious

Boccaccio's little story of Gianni Lotteringhi (VII.1) is a good example of those in which the wife concocts a magic chant that speaks one message to her husband and another to her lover now banging on the door to be let in.[85] The positions have been reversed, but the effect of the ruse is much the same. Tessa's affair with Federigo has been going on for some time and they have worked out an elaborate technique using the head of an ass on a post in the garden to indicate her husband's presence or absence. When the head is accidentally turned in the propitious direction, the lover comes knocking with confidence. But with her husband present, Tessa must find a means to send her lover away. Gianni Lotteringhi is fortunately a bit dense. We are told of his interest in the chants, lauds, and prayers he had picked up from the monks of Santa Maria Novella, which in turn gives Tessa her inspiration. She attributes the knocking at the door to the devil and therefore improvises an exorcism in which she involves her husband in the ritual spitting, while at the same time telling Federigo that there is food in the garden, but otherwise

---

wife has two lovers who appear at various moments of the night and between whom the wife plays favourites and arouses jealousy. Her husband had a defective eye and was so fearful of the loss of his remaining sight that he made a pilgrimage to Loreto. Upon his return he surprises her during her nocturnal activities. She too resorts to the ruse of testing his good eye while her lover hides behind the door and afterwards makes his escape. See also Johann Gast's *Convivalium sermonum utilibus ac iucundis historiis et sententiis* ... (Basel: Brylinger, Johann Georgii a Werdenstein, 1554), vol. I, p. 27; and Gabriel Chappuys, *Les facétieuses journées*, ed. Michel Bideaux (Paris: Champion [1558], 2003), VII, no. 10, pp. 636–46. To these may be added the version by Pietro Fortini in which the lady receives her suspicious husband, tricks him, and then proceeds to tell the trick to him in detail in the form of a story about a lady in Padua just as beautiful as she is who had her scholar lover in the room, but tricked her husband by wrapping up his head in this particular way. By getting her husband to participate in the story, she also manages to have him participate in the reality described by the story, for at that same moment her real lover makes his escape. *Le piacevoli e amorose notti dei novizi*, ed. Adriana Mauriello, 2 vols. (Rome: Salerno, 1995), III.25, vol. II, pp. 1264–8. Gast's version is anticipated by that in Ottomaro Luscinio (Othmar Nachtgal), *Joci ac sales mire festivi* (Augustae Vindelicorum (Augsburg), 1524). The two lovers staged as men in a feud for the returning husband also figure in subsequent French creations, such as in *Les ruses d'amour pour render ses favoris contens* (Amsterdam: Joli Le Franc, 1681), no. 26, and *La farce du poulier, à quatre personage* (namely, the master, his wife, her lover, and the neighbour) (Paris: Techener, 1837).

85 *The Decameron*, trans. Edward Hutton (New York: The Heritage Press [1620], 1940), pp. 317–20. Pietro Fortini, in the ninth of his *Novelle* (1562), imitates Boccaccio VII.3.

to retreat. Of all the cuckold tales in Day VII, this one holds the greatest comparative interest to the present tale.[86]

English literature abounds with tales of cuckoldry and clever wives, as well as of husbands who are jealous old fools, but the closest to the folk tradition under investigation here is really only a neighbour. In *Women Pleased*, a play by Francis Beaumont and John Fletcher, there are three related scenes. Isabella taunts her jealous husband Lopez because he treats her so badly, taking Claudio for her lover.[87] Meanwhile, an older married man, Bartello, takes a fancy to her and persists with his unwanted flirtations. When both Claudio and Bartello are on hand – Claudio in hiding – her husband returns and once more the old ruse of having Bartello unsheathe his sword and feign anger is offered up as a fresh new invention. Later, the playwrights take up a second Boccaccian plot when the husband mutilates the maid who assumes Isabella's place in bed while

86 This Day of the *Decameron* is taken up with the many ruses unfaithful women employ to rescue their reputations, in a sense providing a larger context for the present story. In the second *novella*, Peronella hides her lover in a barrel. When her husband arrives, she concocts a story about selling the barrel, a purchaser for which is already inside inspecting it. Both wife and lover are then permitted to look on amused as the husband struggles to carry the tun to the purchaser's house. In the third, the wife improvises an explanation for the presence of the priest, who is also the godfather to their child. She pretends to have called him in to diagnose the child's sudden malaise and to employ a charm to kill off worms around its heart. The credulous husband then finds the priest holding the child, barely back into his robe, and they all join together for supper. In the fifth, a jealous husband, disguised as a priest, hears his wife's confession concerning her love affairs, but is never able to catch the two of them together. In the sixth, Isabella, having two lovers, deceives her husband by inventing the now familiar pursuit with a weapon motif, similar to the tale told later by Poggio on the formula going back to the *Hitopadesa*. The seventh is another successful betrayal of a husband who, to catch his wife, assumes her person by donning her clothes to await the lover in the garden – a lover who meanwhile enjoys the lady inside and then descends to the garden to thrash him. The eighth *novella* is a variation on the *Kalila wa Dimna* model of the husband who cuts off the nose of his wife's maid, here reduced to a beating and the lopping off of her hair. Such abuse of the wrong party allows the wife to call in her brothers to discipline her husband. In the ninth, the wife enjoys her lover expressly by following her husband's commands, duping him in the process. All such tales form part of a huge repertory concerning wives and their wiles in cuckolding their husbands without apprehension or recrimination. All have comparative value in contextualizing Straparola's story of 'Marcilio Verzelese'; yet while some are close kin, none are direct sources or sequels.

87 *Works*, 10 vols. (Cambridge: Cambridge University Press, 1909; reprint, New York: Octagon, 1969), vol. VII, pp. 237–310.

she is off with her lover. The Eastern origins of both have been confirmed above. The entire arrangement is explained to her husband as an attempt to trap the unwanted but persistent Bartello. In a third encounter, Bartello, once more invited into the house, is now made to hide up the chimney and listen to Lopez court his wife before chimney sweeps arrive to expose him like an old Falstaff in her presence. This motif is familiar from the commentary on 'The Physician's Wife' (IV.4). Clearly, these playwrights had been gathering up familiar stories with long histories going back through *novella*, *fabliaux*, and sermon exempla to fill out the dramatic action of their plays, illustrating once again the persistent and wide circulation of these narrative 'memes.'

To bring the matter full circle, consider as a parting example the replay of the one-eyed husband motif in *The English Rogue* in which Mistress Dorothy hides her lawyer-lover behind the door. She deceives her husband by telling him of a dream in which she was led to believe that he had regained his sight. Despite his bemused scepticism, he allows her to make trial of the matter while her lover slips away to safety.[88] These and related tales, in greater numbers than can be told, incorporate Straparola's creation into a virtual treasury of the tales of witty women who improvise distractions in order to facilitate the escapes of their *beaux*. Concerning an immediate source, the current tale tells as much as we can imagine through inference, for none of the surviving written versions antedating it have any of its local particularity. Of all of Straparola's tales, this one suggests a folklorist's recovery of a local production, perhaps much as it was heard. The story type is old, indeed, and was in wide circulation throughout the Middle Ages, but presumably achieved its present form only in the folk imagination of the sixteenth century, adapted to the Paduan setting by local raconteurs, or by Straparola himself.

88 Richard Head and Francis Kirkman, *The English Rogue, Described in the Life of Meriton Latroon* (London: George Routledge, 1928), pt. III, chap. 16, pp. 588–91.

V. Fable 5
Madonna Modesta's Shoes

S. LUCREZIA

Madonna Modesta, wife of Messer Tristano Zanchetto, in her young days gathers together a great number of shoes offered by her various lovers. Grown old, she gives them all away to members of the serving class and other folk of mean estate.

Commonly it happens that ill-gotten wealth and riches are dispersed after a short time or perish altogether, for it is the divine will that their return should follow the same path by which they arrived. This was indeed the case with a certain woman of Pistoia, for had she been as honest and wise as she was dissolute and foolish, the occasion leading to the story I'm about to tell you would never have come about. This fable of mine may scarcely be suitable for your ears, because it ends up with a picture of shame and dishonour which obscures and tarnishes the fame of those women whose lives are upright and honest. Nevertheless, I'll not hesitate to relate it to you, for it may serve as an incentive to pursue the ways of righteousness and to eschew all wicked courses.

I'll begin by telling this worshipful company that in our own time there lived in that ancient Tuscan city of Pistoia a young woman named Madonna Modesta, although the name hardly suited her on account of her evil life. In her person she was truly lovely and graceful, but her condition was of the meanest. She had a husband called Tristano Zanchetto – a name that contrasted with her own because it fitted him perfectly, buffoon that he was. He was a good-tempered fellow who enjoyed merry company and thought of little else besides his business of buying and selling, whereby he gained a good living for himself. Madonna Modesta was lecherous by nature and engaged continuously in the pleasures of love. When she saw that her husband had devoted himself heart and soul to commerce and was preoccupied strictly with matters of business, it came into her head that she too might embark in merchandising by setting up a new trade about which her husband, Messer Tristano, would never find out a thing.

Every day she placed herself in plain view at her window or on the balcony, amusing herself by throwing glances at any gallant who might be passing in the street. When her eye fell upon a young man whose appearance pleased her, she would employ every nod and wink she knew in an attempt to excite and lure him in. As time moved along, it proved that Madonna Modesta had no ordinary skill in the art of traffic, for she was so diligent in the display of her merchandise, and so attentive to the needs of her customers, that in all the city there was no one, rich or poor, noble or plebeian, who was not eager to sample and enjoy her goods. Once Madonna Modesta had attained a position of great notoriety in her calling and had gathered thereby a great deal of wealth, she decided to exact only a very small reward from all who came to claim her favours. In brief, it became her custom to demand of her lovers no greater price than a pair of shoes, stipulating, however, that each one should give shoes of a kind that he might wear himself in an ordinary way. Thus, if her lover should happen to be a nobleman, she expected of him a pair of velvet shoes, if a burgher, she would ask for a pair of shoes made of fine cloth, if a mechanic, a pair made of leather. So great a concourse of clients flocked to this good woman's place of business that it was continuously occupied. Because she was young, beautiful, and shapely, and because the price of her favours was so modest, all the men of Pistoia went readily to her house and took their pleasures, gathering the ultimate fruits of love.

Now over time, Madonna Modesta filled a very large storehouse with shoes, the accumulated wealth of her tender calling. So vast was the tally of footwear that if a man here in Venice were to search every shop in the city, he wouldn't find a third as many as Madonna Modesta had piled up in her stockroom.

Now it came about that one day Messer Tristano needed this same storage place for stowing away certain merchandise consigned to him from several parts of the world. So he called his beloved wife to ask her for the keys to the warehouse. She, crafty wench that she was, presented them to him without any explanation whatsoever. When the husband opened the storehouse, which he expected to find empty, and saw that it was quite full of shoes of various sorts and qualities, as I've already explained, he was astounded and could hardly guess where so huge a cache of footwear had come from. Calling his wife, he questioned her as to the meaning of all those wares in his storehouse, to which the astute lady made him this reply: 'What do you think, good husband Tristano? That you are to write yourself down as the only merchant in this city? In believing that, you'd be hugely mistaken, for you should know that we women also know a thing or two about the art of traffic. So while you've been a great merchant, used to numerous and weighty ventures, I've contented myself with commerce on a smaller scale. That's why I store my merchandise in this warehouse under lock and key to keep it safe. I'm only suggesting that you take care and keep a watch over your own goods and I'll do the same for mine.' Messer Tristano, who knew nothing more than what his wife told him and asked no further questions, felt most gratified by the ingenuity and foresight of his clever Modesta, and urged her to pursue her enterprise with even greater diligence. So the good Madonna carried on in secret with her amorous trade, in which she so excelled and prospered that she gathered together so vast a store of shoes that she could easily have supplied not only the needs of Pistoia, but of any great city in the world.

While Madonna Modesta remained young, full of grace and beauty, her trade showed no signs of abatement. But alas, with the passing years, cruel Time – the master of the sublunary world, who fixes the beginning, middle, and end of all things – found her out. Once fresh, plump, and the picture of loveliness, her face and form were now altered. Wrinkles furrowed her brow and her countenance sagged, though her love of the game was as hot as ever. Still her eyes filled with rheum and her breasts dried up like shrivelled bladders. Whenever she smiled, the skin of her cheeks puckered in creases, bringing those who saw her to laughter. Madonna Modesta had grown old and grey-haired, and lovers no longer paid her court as formerly they had done. There were no more shoes to add to her store, and for that she lamented bitterly in her heart.

From the earliest years of her youth down to the present hour she had given herself entirely to dispensing her favours with all the material gains. She had grown accustomed to her dainty ways and the luxuriousness of her life, more than any other woman in the world, so that withdrawing herself from lechery exceeded all her means or powers. Even though in her body the vital fluids were on the wane, which make all plants and living things take root and grow, yet the yearning to satisfy her forbidden but insatiable appetites was as violent as ever. Seeing that she was bereft of her youthful beauty and was no longer flattered and caressed by handsome young gallants as she had been in former days, Madonna Modesta reordered her mode of life. Once more she displayed herself on the high balcony of her house ogling and casting her snares, but now towards the serving men, porters, chimney sweepers, and come-hither wastrels below. Those whose eye she caught she would entice into her house to serve her ends, taking such pleasure with them as she had been accustomed to take before. But whereas in times past she had demanded from each of her lovers a pair of shoes of a quality in keeping with the donor's condition as the price of her favours, she now found herself obliged to give a pair of shoes from her stock to all those she had beckoned in. Madonna Modesta had now sunk into such a shameful state that all the meanest ruffians of Pistoia frequented her dwelling, some to satisfy their itch, others to mock and tease, and still others to collect the shameful reward she was now accustomed to give. So it came to pass that the storehouse, once crammed full of shoes, was nearly emptied out.

Messer Tristano one day, having a mind to go in secret to see how his wife's commerce was prospering, and whether her store of merchandise was increasing, took the key to the depot without his wife's knowledge and opened the door, only to discover upon looking in that nearly all the shoes were gone. This amazed him beyond measure, for he couldn't understand how his wife could have disposed of the great trove of shoes he had seen there earlier. Then he began to imagine that she must be made of gold by now through her wheelering traffic, consoling himself with the thought that from then on he might take advantage of the profits.

Losing no time, he called her to him and said, 'Modesta, I've always rated you as a wise and prudent woman, but today I happened to open your storehouse to see how your commerce was thriving, thinking that by this time your stock of shoes must have increased by leaps and bounds, but instead I found that your wares have nearly all disappeared. At first I was amazed by it, but afterwards I understood that you must have traded them for a great sum of money. Thus I reassured myself. Now if this notion of mine proves true, I'm led to think that your profits have been substantial indeed.'

When her husband completed his speech, Madonna Modesta heaved a deep sigh and answered him, 'Messer Tristano, my husband, don't be amazed at what you've just witnessed, for I must explain that all those shoes you saw some time ago in my warehouse have all walked away in the same fashion they came to me. Over and above this, let me add as a rule that things ill-gotten ill-go within a little space of time. So once more I ask you not to be surprised or to wonder at what you have seen.' Messer Tristano, without in the least understanding the meaning of his wife's words, fell into a state of fear and confusion, terrified that a similar misfortune might befall his own goods and merchandise. With that, he ceased to discuss the matter with her further, but took anxious measures to prevent his own merchandise from vanishing as his wife's had done.

Madonna Modesta, now finding herself slighted by men of all walks and conditions, and entirely beggared of all the shoes she had gained in the course of her lecherous youth, fell into a grave sickness through grief and passion and in a very brief space of time died from her declining condition. So it happened that Madonna Modesta, in life so mindless of the future, made a shameful and miserable end. Of all the possessions she had gathered together, she left nothing behind her to serve as an example to the rest of the world except a disgraceful memory.

When the Signora had ended her short fable, all the company began to laugh out loud, heaping abundant blame upon Madonna Modesta, whose life was modest in all things except her lecherous cravings. Nor could they stop laughing when they recalled the part about the shoes which were acquired with no less sweetness than with which they were lost. But because it was on Cateruzza's account that the Trevisan had urged the Signora to tell this fable, the lady now began to spur the damsel on with words that carried a sting, even though they were gently spoken. As a penalty for having failed to tell her story, she commanded Cateruzza expressly to propose an enigma that was relevant to the subject of the fable they had just heard.

When she heard the Signora's command, Cateruzza rose from her seat and, turning towards her, said, 'Dear Signora, I'm not in the least displeased by your taunts. On the contrary, I accept them gladly for myself with my entire heart. But the task of making my enigma agree in some measure with the fable you have just told us is no easy one, seeing that I'm entirely unprepared. But since it is your pleasure to punish my fault, as an obedient girl and your most compliant handmaiden, I'll begin at once.'

My lady seats her in a chair,
And raises then her skirt with care;
And as I know she waits for me,
I bring her what she fain would see.
Then soft I lift her dainty leg,
Whereon she cries, 'Hold, hold, I beg!
It is too strait, and eke too small;
Be gentle, or you'll ruin all.'

And so to give her smallest pain,
I try once more, and then again.

Cataruzza's enigma provoked as much laughter as the Signora's ingenious fable. But because certain of the listeners imposed upon it a lewd interpretation, she set about at once to make clear to them the honesty of her intent, in terms as civil as she could find: 'Noble ladies, the real subject of my riddle is neither more nor less than a tight shoe, for when the lady is seated, the shoemaker, with the shoe in his hand, raises her foot, whereupon she tells him to put the shoe on gently because it is too tight and gives her pain. Then he takes it off and then puts it on again and again until it fits her well and she is pleased with it.'

When the explanation of Cateruzza's enigma had come to an end and reaped the praise of the entire company, the Signora, seeing that the hour was now late, gave order that under pain of her displeasure no one should leave the place. Then bidding them summon the trusty steward of the household, she asked him to set out the tables in the great hall. While the feast was in course of preparation, she proposed that the ladies and gentlemen should divert themselves with dancing. Then, after the measures were finished, they sang two songs, whereupon the Signora rose to her feet and went into the dining hall with Signor the Ambassador on one hand and Messer Pietro Bembo on the other, with the rest of the company following in their due order. When they had all washed their hands, each one sat down according to his rank at the table, which was richly spread with rare and delicate dishes and clear, exquisite wines. When this merry feast had come to an end amid the loving discourse of the guests, everyone now in a happier mood than ever, they rose from the table and once more began to dance. But insofar as the rosy light of dawn was then beginning to appear, the Signora bade the servants to light the torches and attend Signor the Ambassador as far as the steps, begging him and all the others to return to the meeting place at the appointed hour.

The End of the Fifth Night

V. 5 Commentary

A pregnant detail is seen in the final sentence in which the revellers are reminded to return for further stories after this, the final night of the first volume. It signals that at the time of publication, Straparola had stories in mind for successive gatherings, although they would not appear for another three years. Meanwhile, the order of narrators is broken so that the Signora, herself, might provide the finale to the collection. Straparola does not appear to have given much thought to the matching of tales with their narrators. The young ladies are too much alike to have made it possible. But the present tale may be an exception, for the noble, dignified, and upright Signora has been prevailed upon to supply a story of her own, and for her contribution, she has been assigned the tale of Madonna Modesta – a married woman who is all but in name a prostitute. In keeping with Lucrezia's own posture of moral rectitude, the story is sandwiched between a sermonizing prologue and a categorical epilogue of the most cautionary and straight-laced kind. For Lucrezia, it would seem that Modesta's curriculum is that of a nymphomaniac who died in misery after a life of abject debauchery. On her part, there are no signs of the empathy that might be felt for a creature imprisoned by her libidinous constitution, whose drives are expressed as erotic charity reduced to the taking and eventual giving of shoes. Yet what she relates as an exemplum of depravity doubles as a heartrending glimpse into the crisis of passing beauty and an aging woman's inability to relinquish the mating game. For despite the didactic stance, the story presents a profile of complex personhood – that of a sinner in God's eye because she is a woman of emphatic appetites in excessive measure, yet a creature of personable instincts and compulsive temperament, whose humour it is to calibrate the trajectory of her life in terms of sexual conquest and gratification. This is the economy of her life, as it is for Chaucer's Dame Alyce, the celebrated and controversial Wife of Bath, who, like Modesta, despite her advancing age, has no personal identity outside her involvement in the battle of the sexes. The sanctimonious Signora may cast the first stone at a harlot born, yet of this fallen soul she lets slip that 'in her person she was truly lovely and graceful.' Straparola is up to something.

The story's extraordinary 'idea' is that Madonna Modesta receives her remuneration in the form of shoes, each lover contributing a pair in keeping with his class and station in life. A warehouse full of these tokens becomes the objective correlative of her prodigious appetite, while the variety of shoes from velvet to leather and all grades between bespeak the catholicity of her tastes and democratic liberality in her choice of partners. Overtones remain of the sinner who becomes an all-embracing saint. At the same time, the shoes represent the comic codification of her favours, which dimension alone could have brought the assembly to such hollow laughter at the end of the story. In imitation of her husband, she too becomes a successful merchant, trading her own endlessly renewable commodity for footwear. How ironic, then, that with the passage of time she continues to service her sexual cravings only by disposing of her favours to men of the downtrodden classes by enticing them with the offer of free shoes – those she had formerly collected from lovers and admirers. And how poignant it is that when her warehouse is at last empty, her life is culminated shortly thereafter in sickness and death. Modesta is ambiguously a nymphomaniac with the heart of a vital woman whose sexual cravings are a costly addiction. Paul Meyer, for that reason, may have gotten it partially wrong, 'that the story is more moral in its substance than in its form, in which the sense is that goods badly acquired profit nothing.'[89] All is vanity, to be sure, but some enactments elicit more pathos than others.

A less rigorous view of the human condition suggests that instincts and appetites, mediated through personal predilections and habits, are tantamount to destiny. The story invites a smile at the commoditisation of the sexual drives and the scope of her prodigality. But it is also a story about the ripening and withering that comes with time, a transformation that alienates Modesta from her former self, yet does not free her from her youthful appetites. This perspective is furthered by the little meditation on the contrasting ages of life which forms the apex of the narrative – a reflection upon withered skin and sagging breasts, evoking a sense of nostalgia and loss that can only be met with resolve or self-deception. As will be seen, the story had been an illustration of this complex mood of regret and persistence throughout a history going back more than three centuries.

Two documents came to the attention of Paul Meyer, cited in the article mentioned above, pertaining to the origins of this tale. Both involve knives rather than shoes, often decorated with pearls and precious stones, given to a beautiful woman in exchange for sexual favours in her youth, which she then, in her later years, trades away to lovers just to bring them to her bed. One is in Italian, dates to the fifteenth century, and explains the origin of the proverb, 'Ta farai come colei che renderai i coltellini' (you're just like the woman who gave back the little knives), suggesting that at one time the story was well enough known to generate

---

89 'Le conte des petits couteaux,' *Roumania* 13 (1884), ed. Paul Meyer and Gaston Paris (Paris: F. Vieweg, 1884), pp. 595–7.

a lasting dictum.[90] The other is in a French treatise on the four ages of man by Philippe de Navarre, demonstrating that as early as the first half of the thirteenth century the story was in circulation as an exemplum and cautionary tale about squandering the resources of youth and resisting the wisdom that should come with age. Both tell of the passage of time and the loss of lovers to younger women, and how the once great supply of precious knives becomes the protagonist's only resource for drawing in partners in her advancing years.[91] Philippe de Navarre currently holds the credit for launching the vignette, which he undoubtedly found among the exempla gracing sermons or among the tales of the folk, but a rival literary version exists in the Panciatichiano-Palatino MS. of the *Novelle antiche* dating to the 1260s.[92] Moreover, Francisco Delicado redeployed the same idea in his *Portrait of Lozana*, confirming the story's early circulation. Just how the object given and received changed from knives to shoes, and precisely where Straparola found his story are matters, for the moment, of pure speculation, whether he transcribed the work from a written record or collected it from an oral source. It is not a story that appears to have survived among the folk during nineteenth century; that fact may tip the scales in favour of a written source.

Overlooked, however, is an important intermediary version associated with the *Sermones vulgares* tradition of Jacques de Vitry. It does not occur in the edition of *The Exempla or Illustrative Stories* edited by Thomas Frederick Crane because Jacques de Vitry probably did not make his own

90 A variant on this proverb is 'Non ti vuol veder persona se non rendi coltellini.'

91 Giovanni Papanti, in his *Catalogo dei novellieri italiani in prosa* (Livorno, 1871), vol. II, p. 45, lists the little story among those on the 'Origine del proverbio.'

92 Paul Meyer cites the two following sources. The Italian MS. is cited as Laurentienne, Plut. XC super. no. 89, first edited by Zambrini in his *Catalogo della scelta di curiosità letterarie inedite o rare, pubblicata a spese del libraio-editore G. Romagnoli* from the year 1861 (Bologna: Romagnoli, 1867). He cites Philippe de Novare from a MS. in the Bibliothèque Nationale Fr. 12581, fol. 401 b. Philippe de Novare, 1195–1265, *Les quatre âges de l'homme*, ed. Marcel de Fréville (Paris: Firman-Didot, 1888; reprint, New York: Johnson Reprints, 1968). Philippe de Novare's place is challenged, however, by 'La femina dei coltellini' overlooked by Meyer, in Sebastiano Lo Nigro, ed., *Novellino e conti del duecento*, 'Libro di novelle e di bel parlare gentile' (Le novelle antiche dei codici Panchiatichiano-Palatino 138) (Turin: Unione Tipografico-editrice, 1968), no. 2, among the 'Fragments,' pp. 237–8. This collection, first published in Bologna in 1525, goes back to the end of the thirteenth century; it includes the tale of the sinful woman who took in pretty knives in exchange for sex but who, in her later years, was obliged to give them all away to maintain the flow of lovers once her youthful charms had faded.

collection of the exempla. Rather, once the tradition was begun in his name, manuscripts appeared which included many other exempla not included in the original sermons, among them Brit. Lib. MS. Harl. 463. It tells of the woman who stored up knives and who later gave them away to lovers in her old age to keep up her carnal life. She too had to lure them from members of the inferior classes with the promise of gifts, the exemplum touching upon the ages of life. The manuscript collection is not attributed to Jacques de Vitry because the opening pages are lost, but the coincidence of materials almost assures that association. This version may predate that which occurs in the Panciatichiana-Palatino MS.[93] In sum, the story of Madonna Modesta is a literary variation upon a well-established story dealing with the ironies of aging and the indomitable drives of human nature, but a variation for which no immediate sources survive. Those changes may hence be credited to Straparola, to the makers of the folk tradition, or to a lost intermediary source – a now familiar dilemma. It may, again, come down to predilections concerning the scope, variety, and vitality of the oral tradition from which Straparola was inclined to furnish himself versus impressions of Straparola's own talents and inclinations for invention.

Regarding 'the ages of man' as a thematic perspective, Modesta's story is not without literary counterparts – and particularly those concerning old wives or aging prostitutes who, speaking in moments of candour, longing, or stoic resignation, reflect upon the loss of the beauty and enchantment that once empowered them. Leading examples are Chaucer's Dame Alyce and Francesco Delicado's Lozana and her associates. In the Prologue to her tale, the Wife of Bath famously reminisces over her life, attributing to her composite constellation her 'venerian' compulsions and her manly drives.[94] 'I koude noght withdrawe / My chamber of Venus from a goode felawe,' she confessed, as long as he liked and appreciated her, no matter what his size, shape, or colour (ll. 622–5), in Madonna Modesta's same spirit of catholicity. In this she followed her appetite. She was simply born lecherous, having 'a coltes tooth,' making it a terrible pity that casual sex was also deemed a sin. Dame Alyce had also advanced in age and had lost much of her younger charms, bereft of her beauty and 'pith,' which elicited from her one of the most plangent

93 Brit. Lib. MS. Harl. 463, no. 168, fol. 20, col. 2.

94 *Chaucer's Major Poetry*, ed. Albert C. Baugh (New York: Appleton-Century-Crofts, 1963), pp. 390, 392.

moments in all of literature when she says she will let it go, the devil take it. Now that the flour was all sold, she would market the bran to the best of her remaining ability (ll. 474–80). She too, in spite of the passage of time, could not give up the game, for her sexual desires were her life force and the centre of her being. That existential core expressed in libidinous desires is the same as in Straparola's tale.

Equally apt for comparison is the heroine of Francesco Delicado's work, the title of which translates as the *Portrait of Lozana the Lusty Andalusian Woman.*[95] Lozana is a wonderfully worldly-wise, aging courtesan whose perspective on the times, conditioned by years in the sex industry, is witty, frank, deeply sardonic, stoic, and compassionate all at once. She meditates upon the men who sought to enjoy favours without paying, making allusion to Saint Nafissa, canonized for liberal and indiscriminate acts of sexual charity for the needy. Having been recently deceived by a fool who 'wanted to ejaculate his load ... without paying the bridge-toll,' she confesses, nevertheless, to her enjoyment of the encounter while vowing never to let it happen to her again. Her associate, Madam Divicia, is described as having a grand collection of knives gained free of charge which she will in turn give out gratis. Sagueso, a customer, comes along teasing them as old whores, while Divicia contemplates the inadmissibility of returning to her own village where her sullied reputation would follow her in retirement. There is nothing left but to brave it out with aging customers, pretending the best is still to come. Here too, as with the Wife of Bath and Modesta, is the language of merchandising, forming a metaphor of life as sexual brokering, a giving and receiving that can somehow never be replaced. The women engage in mutual banter over their advancing age and the decay of their bodies. Divicia boasts, in a moment of nostalgia, of how in her youth she had been the best there was, if only she had protected what she had earned. Later, in her room with her lover who seduces her while she is asleep, she tells him that if he wants to repeat it while she is awake, she would give him a pair of the most beautiful knives ever to be seen. Such gifts were incentives to retain a few indulgent lovers, as with Madonna Modesta, fearful that her life was otherwise at an end. These narratives recommend themselves to the attention as bittersweet, humorous representations of the crisis of aging epitomized by diminishing sexual desirability. We may be amused

95 Trans. Bruno M. Damiani (Potomac, MD: Scripta Humanistica, 1987), esp. pp. 215–32, the quotation to follow is from p. 215.

or scandalized by the raw drives of the human animal, advancing and retreating with the passage of biological time, here emblematized as a warehouse of waxing and waning quantities of shoes. There is something fetishistic about payment in shoes in the first place, and something pathetic on the part of a woman past her prime in soliciting sex from riff-raff in need of footwear. But the sex drive is a life force, the passage of time is inexorable, habits and cravings run deep, and the rituals of the game are all that remain. Or in the words of Alexander Pope, 'Think not, when Woman's transient Breath is fled, / That all her Vanities at once are dead; / Succeeding Vanities she still regards, / And tho' she plays no more, o'erlooks the Cards.'[96] Desire for the game even survives the grave.

96 'The Rape of the Lock,' in *The Poems of Alexander Pope,* ed. John Butt (London: Methuen, 1965), I. 51–4, p. 220.

www.ingramcontent.com/pod-product-compliance
Lightning Source LLC
LaVergne TN
LVHW040154080826
844660LV00014B/960/J

* 9 7 8 1 4 4 2 6 4 4 2 6 7 *